North Africa

North Africa is undergoing major transformations; it is an area where business is booming and where vibrant civil societies are emerging. This region, which lies alongside the Mediterranean, has acquired strategic significance not only for North Africans themselves, but also for Europe, a close neighbor, and the United States, the world hegemonic power. However, despite the substantial, positive changes taking place, the region remains dominated by despotic regimes unwilling to allow genuine democratic transitions. This book addresses salient aspects of contemporary developments in the Maghreb region (Algeria, Libya, Mauritania, Morocco, and Tunisia, as well as developments concerning the Western Sahara conflict). The contributors, all leading scholars in their respective fields, provide thorough understanding of the evolution of those countries and the problems, such as terrorism, Islamism, migration, political oppression, and the socioeconomic imbalances, which have delayed the development of each nation.

With profiles of individual countries and regional issues, such as migration, gender, integration, economics, and war in Western Sahara, as well as a section dealing with international relations and the Maghreb, including US and EU foreign policy and security issues, *North Africa: Politics, Region, and the Limits of Transformation* is a major resource for all students of Middle Eastern Studies and North African Politics.

Yahia H. Zoubir is Professor of International Relations and International Management and Director of Research in Geopolitics at EUROMED MARSEILLE, École de Management.

Haizam Amirah-Fernández is Senior Analyst of the Mediterranean and Arab World Program at the Elcano Royal Institute for International and Strategic Studies in Madrid, and Associate Professor of Arab Studies at the Autonomous University of Madrid.

North Africa

Politics, Region, and the Limits of
Transformation

**Edited by
Yahia H. Zoubir and
Haizam Amirah-Fernández**

Foreword by
William B. Quandt

Routledge
Taylor & Francis Group

LONDON AND NEW YORK

First published 2008
by Routledge
2 Park Square, Milton Park, Abingdon, Oxon, OX14 4RN

Simultaneously published in the USA and Canada
by Routledge
270 Madison Ave, New York NY 10016

Routledge is an imprint of the Taylor & Francis Group, an informa business

Transferred to Digital Printing 2008

© 2008 Yahia H. Zoubir & Haizam Amirah-Fernández

Typeset in Times New Roman by Taylor & Francis Books

British Library Cataloguing in Publication Data
A catalogue record for this book is available from the British Library

Library of Congress Cataloging-in-Publication Data
    North Africa: politics, region, and the limits of transformation / [edited
by] Yahia H. Zoubir & Haizam Amirah-Fernández.
        p. cm.
    Includes bibliographical references and index. [etc.]
    1. Africa, North – Politics and government – 21st century. 2. Africa,
North – Economic conditions – 21st century. 3. Africa, North – Foreign
relations. I. Zoubir, Yahia H. II. Amirah Fernández, Haizam, 1974–
    JQ3198.A58N67 2007
    320.961 – dc22
                              2007020403

ISBN 978-0-415-42920-7 (hbk)
ISBN 978-0-415-42921-4 (pbk)
ISBN 978-0-203-71559-8 (ebk)

To the Memory of my mother (1933–78)
Y. H. Z.

To my grandparents, Asclepiades and Isabel,
for their love, support, and example
H. A.-F.

Contents

List of illustrations

Contributors

Ahmed Aghrout is Research Fellow at the European Studies Research Institute, University of Salford, United Kingdom. He specializes in the politics and economics of North Africa and Euro-Maghreb relations. He is the author of *From Preferential Status to Partnership: The Euro-Maghreb Relationship* (2000) and principal editor of and main contributor to *Algeria in Transition: Reforms and Development Prospects* (2004). He has also published many articles and book chapters. His most recent article "Embracing Free Trade: The EU's Economic Partnership with Algeria" has appeared in *Intereconomics – Review of European Economic Policy.*

Haizam Amirah-Fernández is Senior Analyst of the Mediterranean and Arab World Program at the Elcano Royal Institute for International and Strategic Studies in Madrid, and Associate Professor of Arab Studies at the Autonomous University of Madrid. He is co-editor with Richard Youngs of *The Euro-Mediterranean Partnership: Assessing the First Decade* (2005). He specializes in international relations, political Islam, and transitions to democracy in the Arab world. He has worked for the United Nations in New York and has lectured at Saint Louis University (Madrid campus) and the University of Barcelona.

Michael Collyer is Lecturer in Human Geography at the University of Sussex. He has worked closely with migrants and refugees around the Mediterranean for the past ten years, including recent visiting fellowships at Abdelmalek Essaadi University in Tetouan, Morocco, and the American University in Cairo. His work is published in a variety of journals including recent articles in *Political Geography, Antipode, Mediterranean Politics, Journal of Refugee Studies,* and *Ethnic and Racial Studies.* He is currently completing a research monograph on links between Moroccan emigrants and friends and family in Morocco, entitled *Locating Transnational Space in the Moroccan Diaspora.*

Jean-François Daguzan is Senior Research Fellow at the Fondation pour la recherche stratégique (FRS) in Paris, and Editor-in-Chief of two scholarly journals, *Géoéconomie* and *Maghreb-Machrek.* He is specialist in

Mediterranean Strategy Studies, Proliferation Issues, Non Conventional Terrorism, and Technology Policy and Globalization. He was formerly Senior Analyst at the Secretariat général de la Défense nationale, of the French Prime Minister's Office, and fellow at the Centre de recherches et d'études sur les stratégies et les technologies de l'École polytechnique. He is also Associate Professor in Economics at the University of Paris II (Panthéon-Assas). His latest book is *Terrorisme(s): Abrégé d'une violence qui dure* (2006).

Cherif Dris is Senior Lecturer in International Conflict at the Ben Youcef Ben Kheda University's School of Political Science and Information in Algiers, and is completing a doctoral thesis, entitled *Decentralized Cooperation between Algeria and France.* He is also Research Associate at various research centers in Algeria and has published many articles on Maghrebi and Mediterranean politics.

Louisa Dris-Aït-Hamadouche is Senior Lecturer at the Institute of Political Science and International Relations of the University of Algiers. She is currently completing her PhD with a dissertation entitled *The Strategic Functions of Islamism in American Foreign Policy.* She is associated with the National Institute of Security Studies (ISESN) and serves as consultant for the National Institute of Global Security Studies (INESG). She has been a contributor to the Algerian daily newspaper *La Tribune* since 1998.

John P. Entelis is Professor of Political Science and Director of the Middle East Program at Fordham University (Bronx, New York). He is also the US Editor of *The Journal of North African Studies* and Secretary of the American Institute for Maghrib Studies (AIMS). He is author/editor of *Islam, Democracy, and the State in North Africa* (1997). He has written dozens of articles and book reviews which have appeared in leading scholarly journals in the fields of political science, international relations, Middle Eastern affairs, and North African studies. His latest was a chapter on Tunisia in the fifth edition of *The Government and Politics of the Middle East and North Africa* (2007).

Gonzalo Escribano is Professor of Applied Economics at the Spanish Open University (UNED), Madrid. His recent publications include, "Promoting EU–Israel Trade Integration: The Bilateral and Regional Dimensions," in Roby Nathanson and Stephan Stetter; *The Monitor of the EU–Israel Action Plan* (2006); "An International Political Economy View of EU–GCC Partnership," *Journal of Development and Economic Policies* (2005); "The Ups and Downs of Europeanization in External Relations: Insights from the Spanish Experience," *Perceptions* (2005); and "Euro-Mediterranean versus Arab Integration: Are They Compatible?" in Belkacem Laabas, *Arab Development Challenges of the New Millennium* (2002). He has also contributed to the FEMISE reports on Morocco (2004) and Euro-Mediterranean agricultural liberalization (2003).

Clement M. Henry is Professor of Government and Middle East Studies at the University of Texas at Austin. He specializes in comparative politics and the political economy of the Middle East and North Africa. His latest book, co-edited with Rodney Wilson, is *The Politics of Islamic Finance* (2004). He has also co-authored, with Robert Springborg, *Globalization and the Politics of Development in the Middle East* (2001). Earlier writings include *The Mediterranean Debt Crescent* (1996); *Politics in North Africa* (1970); *Tunisia since Independence: the Dynamics of One-Party Rule* (1965); and, with Samuel P. Huntington as co-editor, *Authoritarian Politics in Modern Society* (1970). He has been Director of the Business School of the American University of Beirut, and is currently a consultant for the United Nations Development Programme on Governance in the Arab Region.

Miguel Hernando de Larramendi is Professor of History of the Contemporary Arab World at the Castilla-La Mancha University in Toledo, Spain. He is associate researcher at the Mediterranean International Studies Workshop at the Autonomous University of Madrid, where he is Supervisor in the PhD program. He specializes in Maghreb politics and in Spanish foreign policy towards the Arab World and the Mediterranean. He has published several books: *La política exterior de Marruecos* (1997, translated into Arabic in 2005), *La política exterior y de cooperación de España hacia el Magreb (1982–1995)* (1996), and *Los sistemas políticos magrebíes* (1996).

George Joffé specializes in Mediterranean and North African affairs. He was formerly Deputy Director at the Royal Institute of International Affairs (Chatham House) in London and is now affiliated with the Centre of International Studies in the University of Cambridge and a visiting fellow at the Centre of Islamic Studies at the University of Oxford. He is also a visiting professor at King's College London. Joffé has published dozens of articles on the Middle East and North Africa that appeared in leading scholarly journals.

Alejandro V. Lorca holds the Jean Monet Chair in the Department of Economics at the Autonomous University of Madrid, where he is director of the Doctorate in Economics and International Relations (DERI), as well as of the European and Mediterranean Study Group (GREEM). Professor Lorca has taught in many universities in Spain and abroad. He holds memberships in several international fora and organizations, such as the Club of Rome, TEPSA, and EuroMeSCo, among others. He has published hundreds of articles. Some of his most recent books are: *Tres Poderes, Tres Mares, Dos Ríos* (1996); *Las Economías del Magreb*, with Gonzalo Escribano (1998); and *La Seguridad en el Mediterráneo: Amenazas y Percepciones*, with Martin Jerch (forthcoming).

Mohameden Ould-Mey is Associate Professor of Geography in the Department of Geography, Geology, and Anthropology at Indiana State

University. His publications include "Geopolitical Genesis and Prospect of Zionism," *International Journal of the Humanities* (2006); "Currency Devaluation and Resource Transfer from the South to the North," *Annals of the Association of American Geographers* (2003); "The Non-Jewish Origin of Zionism," *The Arab World Geographer* (2002); "The New Global Command Economy," *Environment and Planning D: Society and Space* (1999); and a book, *Global Restructuring and Peripheral States: The Carrot and the Stick in Mauritania* (1996).

William B. Quandt holds the Edward R. Stettinius chair in the Department of Politics at the University of Virginia. He teaches courses on the Middle East and American Foreign Policy. Prior to this appointment, he was Senior Fellow in the Foreign Policy Studies Program at the Brookings Institution. Dr. Quandt also served as a staff member on the National Security Council (1972–74, 1977–79). He was actively involved in the negotiations that led to the Camp David Accords and the Egyptian–Israeli Peace Treaty. His books include: *Peace Process: American Diplomacy and the Arab–Israeli Conflict Since 1967* (2005, 3rd edition); *Between Ballots and Bullets: Algeria's Transition from Authoritarianism* (1998); and *Revolution and Political Leadership: Algeria, 1954–1968* (1969).

Larbi Sadiki is Senior Lecturer in the Politics Department, University of Exeter. He teaches courses on democracy and democratic transitions in the Arab Middle East. He is currently on a Leverhulme fellowship, completing a manuscript on Arab democratization. He is also completing two additional projects on Islamist democracy. His book *The Search for Arab Democracy: Discourses and Counter-Discourses* was published by Columbia University Press in 2004. Other publications have appeared in the *International Journal of Middle East Studies* and *Political Studies*, among others.

Ronald Bruce St John served on the International Advisory Board of *The Journal of Libyan Studies* and The Atlantic Council Working Group on Libya. His publications include the *Historical Dictionary of Libya* (2006, 1998, and 1991); *Libya and the United States: Two Centuries of Strife* (2002); and *Qadhafi's World Design: Libyan Foreign Policy, 1969–1987* (1987). He also authored essays on Libya in the *Encyclopedia of the Modern Middle East and North Africa* (2004), *Africa Contemporary Record* (2004, 2006), *Encyclopedia of Religious Practices* (2005), *Governments of the World* (2005), and *Biographical Encyclopedia of the Modern Middle East* (2007). A general history, *Libya: From Colony to Jamahiriya*, is scheduled for publication in 2008.

Gregory W. White is Associate Professor of Government at Smith College, Northampton, Massachusetts, and a member of the graduate faculty at the University of Massachusetts–Amherst. He has also taught at Mount Holyoke and Amherst Colleges. He is the author of *On the Outside of*

Europe Looking In: A Comparative Political Economy of Tunisia and Morocco (2001) and is currently working on a new book on *Migration, Borders, and Sovereignty: Moroccan Labor Migration and Spanish–Moroccan Relations.* His work has appeared in *The Middle East Journal, The Journal of Developing Areas, Review of African Political Economy, Third World Quarterly,* and *Policy Studies Journal.* Professor White is also the North Africa editor for the *Africa Contemporary Record.*

Michael J. Willis is Mohammed VI Fellow in Moroccan and Mediterranean Studies at St Antony's College, Oxford University. He specializes in the politics, modern history, and international relations of the Maghreb. He is the author of *The Islamist Challenge in Algeria: A Political History* (1996) and has published articles in *The Review of International Affairs, Mediterranean Politics,* and *The Journal of North African Studies.* He is currently writing a book on the comparative politics of Algeria, Tunisia, and Morocco.

Yahia H. Zoubir is Professor of International Relations and International Management, and Director of the Research Center for Euro-Mediterranean Geopolitics at EUROMED MARSEILLE, École de Management. He is the co-author of *Doing Business in Emerging Europe* (2003); editor and main contributor of *North Africa in Transition: State, Society, and Economic Transformation in the 1990s* (1999); co-editor of *L'Islamisme Politique dans les Rapports entre l'Europe et le Maghreb* (1996); and co-editor and main contributor of *International Dimensions of the Western Sahara Conflict* (1993). His publications have appeared in major US, Canadian, European, and North African scholarly journals, and as chapters in edited volumes, and he has contributed to various encyclopedias. He is presently preparing a book on US Policy in North Africa.

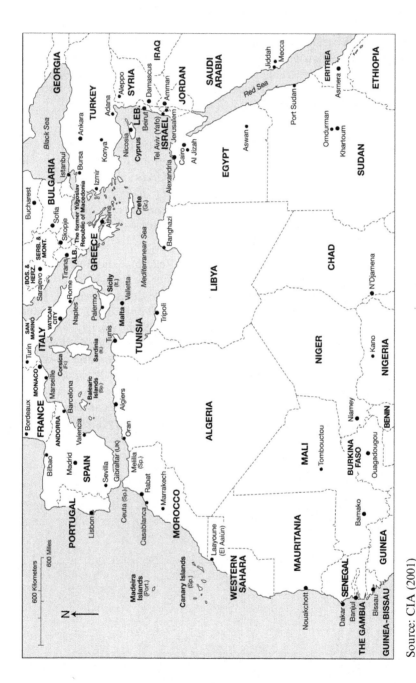

Source: CIA (2001)

Foreword

William B. Quandt

At a time when Middle East crises—Iraq, Iran, Palestine, and Lebanon—are front-page news every day, many may be surprised to learn, as this volume makes clear, that one significant part of the Arab world, the Maghreb, is engaged in the mundane tasks of development without exceptional turmoil or violence. With a population of around 85 million, this region provides relief from the horrific events of the eastern Arab world, while nonetheless reminding us of how challenging the processes of economic and political reform can be. This is a region where slow strides forward are being made, but there are no dramatic success stories as in Southeast Asia. But then again, no disasters seem to be looming on the horizon either. And, with the holding of democratic elections in Mauritania in spring 2007, one might even say that the least developed of the Maghreb countries is well ahead of many others in the Arab-Islamic world.

A snapshot taken in early 2007 would show that the three key Maghreb states of Morocco, Algeria, and Tunisia are engaged in long-running efforts to deal with a host of political, economic, and social problems. My own take on these three cases—I will not comment very much on Libya or Mauritania, since I know less about them—is that Morocco has probably done the best in recent years to overcome some of its historical deficits. But, according to the UNDP, it is clearly Tunisia that has outdistanced the others in terms of overall human development. According to the 2006 Human Development Report, Tunisia ranked 87th in the world, followed by Algeria at 102 and Morocco at 123. (The index is a composite of measures of per capita income, education, literacy, and longevity. Mauritania ranks near the bottom, at 153; Libya, largely due to oil wealth, is listed at 64).

Under the late King Hassan II, Morocco enjoyed stability, but we now know that the cost in terms of human rights was high. The current monarch, King Mohammed VI, widely considered something of a lightweight at his accession, has won considerable support among Moroccan citizens by opening the doors of prisons, by shining a light on abuses of the past, and by introducing fairly progressive legislation concerning the status of women. In addition, he travels around the country meeting with people and distributing some of the regime's largesse. On balance, the economy has been growing at a fairly good rate in recent years, which also enhances the regime's popularity. The monarch's devotion to water sports has earned him the title Sa MaJetSki, and Moroccans today do not seem to be afraid of poking a bit of fun at their rulers.

Despite these positive developments, Morocco still faces a huge gap between rural and urban areas, between rich and poor, between educated and illiterate. But the country seems to be on the move. As Gregory White correctly notes in his chapter on Morocco, the upcoming parliamentary elections in September 2007 will be a real test for the liberalizing tendencies within the regime. The PJD (Parti de la Justice et du Développement) stands poised to do well in the elections, and many believe the regime will think twice before allowing an Islamist party—even a supposedly moderate one—to win a free election. Of course, even if the PJD does win, there is a precedent for the King to retain control of key security ministries, so there might be an outcome that preserves a large measure of power in the hands of the monarch. Stay tuned. I, for one, am fairly hopeful that Morocco will move steadily along a promising path.

Algeria is a harder case to summarize than Morocco, in part because of the "black" and "red" decades of the 1980s and 1990s, respectively. If one were to have looked at Algeria from the perspective of the mid-1990s, the picture would have been very grim indeed. After a period of gradual liberalization in the 1980s, that had done little to address the underlying socio-economic problems, there had been countrywide demonstrations in October 1988 calling for a change of policies and of regime. The response was surprising. In 1989, Algeria revised its constitution, allowed new political parties to form, as well as civil society groups and a relatively free press. For the next two years Algeria seemed to be the pace setter for democratic reforms in the Middle East and North Africa. But this all came to an end with the legislative elections of December 1991–January 1992. With the first round of the elections showing that the Front Islamique du Salut (FIS) was well ahead of the historic nationalist party, the Front de Libération Nationale (FLN), the military stepped in to depose the president, to cancel the elections and to ban the FIS. Before long, radical Islamists had begun to take up arms, and by the mid-1990s Algerians were dying in political violence between the regime and the Islamists at the rate of at least a 1,000 per month. Some observers placed most of the blame on the FIS and its offshoots, others on the regime. From either perspective, the reality was shocking, especially in a country that had already paid such a high price for achieving its independence.

If we now jump forward to early 2007, the picture looks considerably better, although not without troubling signs. First, the level of violence has dropped dramatically. One still reads about the occasional incident, usually in remote parts of the country, but on the whole life has returned to normal. The end of the insurgency came in several stages. First, toward the end of the 1990s, the military reached a truce with one of the largest Islamist factions, the Islamic Salvation Army (AIS). Most of the fighters laid down their arms in return for amnesty. Over the next several years, the amnesty was extended to other groups, and the military intensified its operations against militant holdouts. The remaining insurgents of the Salafi Group for Predication and Combat (GSPC), now calling themselves al-Qaeda of the Islamic Maghreb, are thought to number a few hundred at most.

From the time of independence in 1962, the Algerian military had always played a central role in the nation's politics. The crisis of the 1990s seemed to deepen the power of the military and security services. When Abdelaziz Bouteflika was elected president in 1999, he was clearly the candidate of the military. In fact, on the eve of the day of balloting, all other candidates withdrew, charging fraud. This was hardly an auspicious sign for those who hoped to see Algeria move in a democratic direction. But Bouteflika, who had earlier served as Algeria's foreign minister (1963–79), was determined not to be just a figurehead. He set about trying to establish his own legitimacy by ending the conflict that had been tearing the country apart. His major initiative in his first years in power was a somewhat controversial offer of near-blanket amnesty. Algerians voted overwhelmingly for the idea in a referendum held in September 2005.

With a measure of domestic security restored, Bouteflika set about reinforcing his own power base. This involved regaining control over the FLN, which had become an opposition party, and then gradually freeing himself of the influence of key military figures—many of whom were forced to retire. As of 2007, he had made considerable progress along these lines, although close observers could still argue that key military and security officials played an excessively powerful role in the political and economic life of the country. When he ran for re-election in 2004, Bouteflika actually won a contested election by a large margin without overt support from his former military patrons.

Also on the plus side of the ledger is the relative openness of the Algerian press, one of the most impressive gains from the liberalization of the early 1990s. In recent years, the Internet and mobile phones have made rapid inroads in Algeria, all of which gives ordinary Algerians much more access to information than they have ever had before. This same phenomenon can also be seen in Morocco.

A mixed blessing for Algeria has been its rentier economy, marked by an extremely high dependence on earnings from oil and gas exports (more than 90 percent). In recent years, when the world price of energy soared, this meant that Algeria's revenues skyrocketed, so that by early 2007 the country had surplus reserves of over $80 billion, and much of its foreign debt had been repaid, totaling currently less than $5 billion, down from nearly $30 billion. Algeria was now able to contemplate major infrastructure investments that had long been deferred.

But great wealth for the government does not always translate into improved living standards for ordinary Algerians. Instead, many complain that they see little in their daily lives to reflect the windfall profits that have come to Algeria. This leads to suspicions that those with power are misusing the country's wealth and the charge of corruption in high places is readily heard. The availability of surplus revenues also reduces the pressure on the government to carry out reforms that might eventually strengthen the productive sectors of the economy. And, great wealth in the hands of the government has the effect of undermining opposition political parties and civil society, a setback for real hopes of democratization.

Algeria entered 2007 with a number of question marks about the future. Some wonder about Bouteflika and a possible third mandate. According to the constitution, he is only allowed to finish his current second term. But there has been talk of amending the constitution to allow him to run again. At the same time, there have been rumors that his health is not so good, and that may make a third term less likely. One also has reason to wonder about which other political forces might come to the fore in the near future. The Islamist current seems to have lost momentum, but it is not at all clear who might step in if a political vacuum were to open up. One also must wonder what would happen if oil prices declined, as they did in the mid-1980s. The underlying socioeconomic fabric of the country is still not so robust that it could easily stand major shocks.

Over the next several years, most of the so-called "revolutionary generation" that has dominated Algeria's political life will pass from the scene. We simply do not know what the new generation will be like. Many seem to share the modernist/nationalist views of their elders, but not all do. The educational system has a very mixed record. It has provided some degree of education for the masses, including hundreds of thousands of students now crowded into universities. But the quality of the education provided is open to question, and Algeria risks falling behind unless it can do something soon to improve the quality of instruction given to its students. So, Algeria still faces many challenges, but the path ahead is much brighter today than it was just ten years ago.

Tunisia is the country of the Maghreb that seemed to be on its way to setting the standard for being a progressive social democracy. Indeed, many authors from an earlier era were confident that Tunisia, with its relatively small, homogeneous, and educated population, with its moderate early nationalist leadership, and with its progressive social and educational policies would indeed be a model of sorts. And, to a certain extent, that has been true. Many look at the social policies, the status of women, the level of literacy, the rate of economic growth, and the relatively egalitarian social structure and they conclude that Tunisia is doing well. What, then, is missing from the picture?

Pick up a newspaper in Tunisia and you will be struck by how much less free it is than comparable publications in Morocco and Algeria. In fact, the political system as a whole remains quite closed to competition. While not quite a one-party state, Tunisia certainly fits the mold of an authoritarian, dominant-party state. Part of the rationale for the limitation on political freedom is the fear that radical Islamists will take advantage of any political opening, as occurred in neighboring Algeria. Tunisia presents itself as the counter to the Algerian case, one of gradual movement on the political front, combined with serious efforts to advance in the social and economic arenas. Some talk of following the Chinese model, and there are some parallels, although China's economic performance has far outstripped that of Tunisia.

While there is much to admire in the Tunisian case, many observers also feel that it is time for the regime to open up, to allow more genuine contestation, and to prepare for an eventual transition to a fairly elected government. President Zine al-Abidine Ben Ali has been in power for 20 years. As Larbi Sadiki argues in this book, Ben Ali has favored national unity over democracy, but in the Tunisian case one feels that more of the latter would pose little risk for the former.

There is, of course, much more to say about the contemporary Maghreb. In its diversity, it presents us with a variety of models of development. Compared to the eastern Arab world, where the Arab–Israeli conflict and now Iraq have troubled the surrounding countries, the Maghreb seems less adversely affected by external influences. Read this fine collection of essays and learn more. I continue to believe that many of the trends in the region are positive and they may eventually result in relatively well-developed societies, in both the political and economic sense.

William B. Quandt
University of Virginia

Preface

The rationale for producing this edited volume emerged during a discussion that Yahia H. Zoubir and Haizam Amirah-Fernández held in San Francisco in November 2004, while attending the Middle East Studies Association annual meeting there. The two of us felt that books on the Maghreb were lacking and that no major publication on the region had appeared in English since Zoubir's edited volume, *North Africa in Transition: State, Society, and Economic Transformation in the 1990s* (University Press of Florida, 1999). We concluded that a sequel to that book was necessary; we thought that people interested in the Maghreb would be keen on learning about the major changes that have taken place in the region since the close of the 1990s. We shared our idea with Michael J. Willis, a contributor to this book, who enthusiastically supported it. During a meeting in Madrid in spring 2005, Michael provided some input as to the themes that we should include in the volume. Subsequently, we invited what we believe are some of the best specialists in Maghrebi studies. Our objective was to bring together scholars from the Maghreb region itself, Europe, and the United States. Despite our persistent attempts, we, unfortunately, did not succeed in getting a native Moroccan scholar either in Morocco or living abroad, to contribute a chapter. Nevertheless, we were pleased to secure the contribution of Gregory White, a leading Morocco scholar. We were also not fortunate to have more women contributors, despite several attempts; most of them already had other commitments and thus could not join us.

Obtaining the commitment of leading scholars to contribute to an edited volume is not an easy task, especially when the chapters have to be original or have not been part of conference proceedings. We are truly privileged to have brought together 16 Maghreb experts for this volume. They have worked with us since summer 2005 and always abided by the deadlines that we set for them. They have revised their respective chapters, always taking into account the recent changes and our comments. They also followed our guidelines as well as the questions that we asked them to address. They made sure to consider the suggestions and criticisms the blind reviewers made.

Three chapters in this volume are revised articles that have been published elsewhere. John P. Entelis' chapter is a thoroughly revised and updated version of his, "The Democratic Imperative vs. the Authoritarian Impulse: The Maghrib State Between Transition and Terrorism," published in *The Middle East Journal*, vol. 59, no. 4, fall 2005, pp. 537–58. We would like to thank *The Middle East Journal* for granting Dr. Entelis permission to republish the article, albeit in a different version. Larbi Sadiki's chapter is a revised version of his article "The Search for Citizenship in Bin Ali's Tunisia: Democracy versus Unity," published in *Political Studies*, vol. 50, no. 3, 2002, pp. 497–513. We thank *Political Studies* for granting Dr. Sadiki permission to republish the article as a chapter in this volume. We felt that some of the other chapters (e.g., Entelis, Henry) contained sufficient information regarding developments in various areas in Tunisia that we did not require Dr. Sadiki to follow the same guidelines as the other authors in Part I. We also thank Elcano Royal Institute for granting permission to republish a revised version of the working paper by Gonzalo Escribano and Alejandro V. Lorca, titled "Economic Reform in the Maghreb: From Stabilization to Modernization."

We cannot stress enough the fantastic collaboration that we have obtained from the contributors. We sincerely thank them for their promptness in making the changes we asked from them and in returning the revised versions to us in a timely fashion. We would also like to thank the blind reviewers whose comments have been extremely helpful in improving the quality of the manuscripts. Our thanks go as well to the President, Director, and Deputy Directors of the Elcano Royal Institute in Madrid for having supported this project from the beginning and for the Institute's financial support.

We extend our sincere thanks to James "Joe" Whiting, Acquisitions Editor at Routledge, for his support and encouragements and to Natalja Mortensen for her patience and guidance. Stephen J. Thompson provided outstanding help during the production process. We are also thankful to Judith Oppenheimer for her skilful copy-editing of the manuscript, to Lindsey Williams for her meticulous proofreading, to Susan Boobies for doing the index, and to Imogen Crowle for diligent work on the bibliography. Jessica A. Eise provided valuable research and editorial support and Marisa Figueroa efficient administrative assistance.

Producing an edited volume is always arduous, and without the moral support of a number of people it would be an impossible task. Zoubir would like to thank his wife, Cynthia, for her incessant moral support and encouragement. This acknowledgment is no compensation for the missed weekends together but is a modest recognition of deep gratitude to her. He also wishes to thank his children, Nadia, Jamel, and Malek, who give him many reasons to be proud of them. Their unconditional support has been invaluable. Special thanks go also to his friend and co-editor for enduring the nagging but also for making him discover the wonderful Spanish cuisine during breaks from work in Madrid! Amirah-Fernández would like to dedicate this volume to Hisham, Isabel, Nadia, and Dina for their love and for being there always. A special thanks to Velina for being such a supportive and consistent person and to Jesús M. de Miguel for his constant encouragement and friendship. Many thanks go to Lucía for her inspiration and to those friends at Café Comercial who cheer up his mornings! Last, but by no means least, Amirah-Fernández would like to acknowledge that this book would not have been possible without the experience and patience of his co-editor and, above all, friend.

Introduction

Yahia H. Zoubir and
Haizam Amirah-Fernández

The Maghreb countries Algeria, Libya, Mauritania, Morocco, and Tunisia have experienced important events and transformations since the 1980s. The five countries founded in 1989 the Arab Maghreb Union (AMU), which aimed at regional integration. This union was triggered by domestic and international events. The most noteworthy domestic events have had important consequences for subsequent developments within each of these countries: popular uprising in Algeria in October 1988; liberalization process in Algeria and Morocco; rise of radical Islamism in Algeria, Tunisia, Libya, and more recently in Morocco; and, socioeconomic difficulties in Morocco and Mauritania. External events, too, played a critical role in compelling the countries in the region to seek some sort of union to resolve and confront collectively their domestic problems: the lack of resolution of the Western Sahara conflict; the collapse of the Soviet bloc; the wave of democratization in Central and Eastern Europe; the rise of the United States to sole superpower status; Libya's confrontation with the United States and the United Nations and US-imposed sanctions on Libya; and the European Union's focus on the emerging markets in Eastern Europe rather than on the southern Mediterranean countries also played a critical role in influencing the Maghreb countries to seek unity in order to face the new challenges. However, due to their numerous differences (e.g., Algeria and Morocco's disagreement over the conflict in Western Sahara, among other issues) this resulted in paralysis of the AMU.

In the 1990s, the Algerian state was on the brink of collapse due to the armed conflict between security forces and radical Islamists, which ended only recently—though some terrorist groups still commit atrocities, albeit on a very small scale. While it has succeeded in stamping out the Islamist threat so far, the Tunisian regime has resorted to the most repressive measures to maintain one of the fiercest dictatorships in the Arab world. Libya suffered unbearable costs due to the sanctions (1992–2004), which led to discontent throughout the country and to a potential alliance between Islamists and the disgruntled military to weaken the authoritarian regime. Morocco has not been spared from such gloomy developments; the passing away of King Hassan II in July 1999 did not bring about the hoped-for reforms under the rule of his son, Mohammed VI. For its part, Mauritania witnessed a coup on 3 August 2005. Clearly, the Maghreb is undergoing major changes. Positive or negative, such changes have had their limits. Furthermore, the regimes in place have yet to genuinely open up the political space and allow authentic democratization to take place. Even if the Algerian and Moroccan regimes have allowed some degree of democratization, they have not relinquished their tight grip on power. Thus, democratization moves at a much slower pace than what occurred in the former Communist bloc in Central and Eastern Europe.

This volume deals with various salient aspects of contemporary developments in the Maghreb region. In order to cover the most significant issues, the book, which brings together some of the leading experts in their respective fields, is divided into three sections: 1) The Maghreb states: the limits of transformation, 2) Regional issues in the contemporary Maghreb, and 3) Strategic and security relations of the Maghreb.

In general, the authors in the first section have reviewed the major developments that have taken place within each of the five Maghrebi countries and analyzed the ways through which the regimes have sought to resolve the challenges they have faced. The contributors have also addressed a number of issues and concentrated on the major transformations that occurred in the last decade. They have also analyzed political (elections, human rights, democratization, authoritarianism, Islamism) and economic (debt, integration into the WTO, negotiations with the US, Free Trade Zones with the EU and/or the United States, energy) developments and other salient issues, such as the role of the armed forces in politics, and freedom of the press.

The first section starts with an assessment of the dynamics that affect democratization and authoritarianism in the Central Maghreb. John P. Entelis points out that demands for democracy, political pluralism, and improvements in living standards continue to make themselves felt both within and outside society in the region. However, he argues that there is no reason to believe that the Maghreb's robust authoritarianism will dissolve anytime soon. According to Entelis, continued state intransigence in the Maghreb makes it unlikely that necessary conditions currently exist for a democratic transition in which independent political parties can emerge.

Ahmed Aghrout provides an overview of the major developments that Algeria has witnessed since the end of the 1980s and how they have influenced the political, economic, and social life of the country. He shows that there are signs of a gradual return to normality after the decade-long civil conflict, such as renewed institutional legitimacy, reduced levels of violence, and improved stability and security. However, the lack of progress in the socioeconomic and political reforms, despite the healthy financial position boosted by rising oil prices, is causing large segments of Algerian society to become disillusioned. Aghrout believes that it remains to be seen how the Algerian regime will press ahead with this process of change while taking in hand the deteriorating living standards in order to test its commitment to the democratic process.

Over the past few years, Libya has re-established diplomatic and commercial relations with the rest of the world after having been an international outcast for more than a decade. Ronald Bruce St John analyzes Libya's rehabilitation and the current reform process. He argues that the Libyan regime is interested in attracting new foreign investments, particularly in the hydrocarbons sector, and that the reform policy can be expected to follow a dual path, with reform proceeding much faster in the hydrocarbons sector than in other areas of the economy. St John does not expect economic reform to be accompanied by political liberalization.

Mohameden Ould-Mey examines recent developments in Mauritania, a country that has not received much attention in the academic literature. He assesses Mauritania's process of democratization in light of the fluctuation between contested elections and military coups d'état in the context of the country's delicate geopolitical positioning. He points out the serious challenges that Mauritania faces in balancing geopolitics, improving political stability, strengthening social cohesion, and reducing poverty.

Gregory W. White explores the developments that have taken place in Morocco since the accession to the throne of King Mohammed VI in July 1999. Despite important steps taken to pursue economic and political reforms in the early years of the new king's reign, White argues that Morocco's measured opening began to recede by 2002 and that crucial elements of the current reign have sustained the rudimental components of the Moroccan political system. He also argues that the discontent about the slow pace of change in Morocco's society and the persistence of social problems continue to draw the appeal of radical Islamist groups and politicians.

The last chapter in the first section provides a critical assessment of Tunisia's "democratic" gains and reverses nearly 20 years after Ben Ali's bloodless coup d'état of 7 November 1987. Larbi Sadiki considers that the regime has power but still lacks the required flexibility to create a genuine democratic breakthrough. He places Tunisia in the Maghrebi context to conclude that stability has come at the expense of political pluralism and that ethnic homogeneity and national unity are not sufficient conditions for genuine democratization.

The section on regional issues is divided into five major themes. The first theme focuses on the economies of the Maghreb. Gonzalo Escribano and Alejandro V. Lorca concentrate on the Maghrebi economies. Of particular interest is their handling of such issues as micro- and macroeconomic reforms, privatization, state control, parallel economies, Free Trade Zones, unemployment, external trade, deficits, foreign debt, and intra-Maghrebi trade.

Michael Collyer examines migration and the Maghrebi immigrant communities in Europe. Inevitably, the focal point is on the economics of migration, the policies on both sides of the Mediterranean, the effects of the brain drain, the consequences for the home states, and state relations with the immigrant communities. This is certainly an important topic, especially since it was mostly Maghrebi immigrants who committed the bombings in Madrid on 11 March 2004 that left almost 200 people dead and hundreds wounded.

Miguel Hernando de Larramendi deals with intra-Maghrebi relations, particularly the status of the AMU, trade relations, and security affairs. He has also evaluated the cost of no-Maghreb (i.e., of the absence of regional integration) in an era when regionalization plays a key role in alleviating some of the negative impact of globalization. Hernando de Larramendi argues that the Maghrebi integration project does not constitute a priority in the diplomatic agenda of states in the region and analyzes the responses of the actors to the blockage of the integration project, as well as the strategies of accommodation of the regional actors to the new international context.

Louisa Dris-Aït-Hamadouche's chapter deals with women in Maghrebi societies. She looks at the legal reforms, the formal representation of women, high-profile women, as well as the role of feminist NGOs. She also points out the limits of women's representation in the Maghrebi political systems, demonstrating that these limits are linked to both cultural and political reasons. She identifies some prejudices found in Islamist discrimination against women, indicating that though all the political parties (liberal and conservative, government and opposition) speak about promotion of women's role in the society, they do not abide by those promises.

Michael J. Willis tackles the sensitive Berber question, which has attracted a great deal of attention in recent years. He scrutinizes the World Berber Congress, the Kabylie events in Algeria and their spillover, the Royal Commission in Morocco, the dialogue between organized Berber groups and the states, Berber movements and parties and their relations with other parties be they secular or Islamist.

The third part of the book deals with the strategic and security relations of the Maghrebi states; it, too, has been divided into a number of themes. In the first chapter in this section, Cherif Dris deals with security issues: NATO and its relations with the Maghrebi states, intra-Maghrebi security, external menace, and intra-regional threats. He also tackles the debates on multilateralism in the security domain and how this applies to the region. He shows the structural and circumstantial obstacles, stressing the role of history, states' perception of threats and national interest, and external factors. He demonstrates that the regional environment is not only encouraging Maghrebi cooperation but also in which way it is imposing it upon them. Furthermore, Dris focuses on increasing European and American concerns about illegal immigration, drug trafficking, and terrorism and examines the similarities and differences between the "South" and the "North" in eradicating these threats.

Yahia H. Zoubir analyzes US relations with the Maghreb in the pre- and post-9/11 periods. He focuses on the political, economic, and security relations as well as on the way the US has sought to balance its relationships with the two rivals in the region, Algeria and Morocco. The chapter also examines the US push for democratization in the Arab region and the question of Islamism in the Maghreb and how these are thwarted by security considerations, which seems more important in US eyes than promotion of democracy.

Clement M. Henry's chapter examines how the regimes of Algeria, Morocco, and Tunisia took advantage of new opportunities offered by the Bush Administration's "Global War on Terror" (GWOT) while minimizing the risks. He argues that increased US assistance and military cooperation bolster the regimes' coercive capabilities but distance those regimes further from their respective population. Henry also discusses how the GWOT has redefined the region's "strategic rents" and indicates how the US government might reassess them if advancing democracy were really at the heart of the strategy of the GWOT.

George Joffé concentrates on the EU's relation with the Maghreb. His primary focus is on the Euro–Mediterranean Partnership (EMP), European Neighbourhood Policy (ENP), trade, and policymaking process toward the Maghreb. The European initiatives in the Mediterranean have created a new dynamic in the EU's relationship with the southern Mediterranean states, made up mostly of the Maghreb region. Joffé looks at how these dynamics and initiatives have affected transatlantic ties.

Jean-François Daguzan deals with France's multifaceted relationship with the Maghreb. He shows how France seeks to develop a constantly renewed approach to its political relations with each country in order to preserve the special ties as well as trying to push the Maghrebi governments toward modernization at the economic and political levels. Daguzan also describes how France attempts to circumvent the European Union to avoid tackling certain "hot topics," such as democracy, that could lead to direct confrontation with its European allies. He believes that the weight of colonization is strong and remains a sensitive issue and thus has an impact on France's policy formulation toward the region.

Haizam Amirah-Fernández focuses on Spain's role in the region and analyzes how Spain has sought to balance its relations in the Maghreb, where it has considerable interests. He compares policies under different Spanish governments and their influence on Spain's relations with its southern neighbors. Amirah-Fernández concentrates on economic interests, migration/immigration issues, territorial disputes (Western Sahara, the Parsley Islet crisis, and Ceuta and Melilla), and drug trafficking, as well as recent developments in Spanish–Moroccan relations on the one hand and Spanish–Algerian relations on the other.

Clearly, this book deals with the various facets of the Maghreb and practically all the challenges that Maghrebi states and societies are facing. It is a sequel to the book that Yahia H. Zoubir edited in 1999, titled, *North Africa in Transition: State, Society, and Economic Transformation in the*

1990s (Gainesville, FL: University Press of Florida, 1999). The stakes in the Maghreb for Europe and the United States, and for the local populations themselves, are tremendous, especially since the Algerian tragedy in the 1990s, the events of 9/11 in New York and Washington, and more recently the bombings in Casablanca in May 2003, Madrid in March 2004, and London in July 2005. This explains our decision to produce such a book.

The editors take pride in having succeeded in bringing together scholars from Europe, the United States, and the Maghreb who endeavor to provide in-depth knowledge of the region. We gave authors a choice either to cover the Central Maghreb (Algeria, Morocco, and Tunisia) or to expand their analysis to the five countries that make up the AMU, that is, the Central Maghreb plus Libya and Mauritania. The chapter on Tunisia is more theoretical in scope; however, given its pertinence and the fact that numerous contributors discussed current events in Tunisia, we thought that we should include the chapter as it is.

Marseille and Madrid
September 2007

Part I

The Maghreb States

The Limits of Transformation

1 Democratic Desires and the Authoritarian Temptation in the Central Maghreb[1]

John P. Entelis

Algeria, Morocco, and Tunisia (as well as Libya and Mauritania, the two other members of the Arab Maghreb Union) stand at a crucial crossroads in their political evolution as they face simultaneous challenges from domestic, regional, and global forces. Despite all surface appearances to the contrary, all three central Maghrebi states are governed autocratically. As such, they will be unable to meet the upcoming threats to their political stability, social cohesion, cultural integrity, and economic viability. One result will be increased domestic, regional, and global tensions as militant forces seep through these sociopolitical fault lines, finding support from and identification with similarly discontented co-religionists living in Europe. Terrorism is the most extreme manifestation of this diffused discontent made "legitimate" through an Islamic idiom of martyrdom.

The demands for political pluralism, democracy, and transparency continue to make themselves felt both within and outside society.[2] The Broader Middle East and North Africa Initiative[3] is but one important and highly visible such effort originating from Washington, but similar appeals derive from diverse sources including international human rights organizations, NGOs, domestic political opponents both secular and Islamist, multilateral lending institutions, and regional groupings like the Arab League, which has produced three scathing reports, co-published with the United Nations Development Programme (UNDP), on the absence of political freedoms in all of the Arab world.[4]

Economically and socially as well, the demands for visible improvements in living standards and the quality of life cut across diverse social classes and occupational groupings. Despite repeated promises by ruling elites of significant improvements in macro- and microeconomic performance through accelerated structural adjustments, expanded privatization efforts, increased foreign direct investment, implementing transparency and the rule of law, rooting out corruption and nepotism, and creating an overall environment conducive to productive human effort, the full potential of all three Maghrebi economies remains unrealized.

These combined failures in the political and socioeconomic spheres have impacted negatively on migration flows and levels of foreign remittances.

Such disruptions in critical financial life-lines have disoriented co-religionists on both sides of the Mediterranean as Maghrebis surviving precariously in ghetto-like suburbs outside large, prosperous European cities mirror the situation of many of their Arab brothers and sisters living in the "homelands."[5]

Such conditions of political oppression, social marginalization, economic deprivation, and cultural alienation, whether perceived or real, have created a wide-ranging landscape of disaffected young people ever ready to engage in militant activity often catalyzed by religious invocation and Islamist appeal, inspiring, among the most fanatical of them, a sense of martyrdom justifying the use of terror, including suicide bombing.[6]

Thus, there now exists a complex and intricate web of interrelated forces connecting autocratic political orders with anemic levels of socioeconomic development impacting most directly on a broad swathe of alienated and angry youth at home and abroad who find salvation in the cathartic appeals of a puritanical Islam communicated in the militant language of the urban mosque and the charismatic imam.[7]

To the extent that the West in general and the United States in particular are perceived as deeply implicated in the maintenance of this "unjust" system based on "oppression" and "exploitation," they will be the natural targets for terrorists and terrorism. If this cycle of violence rooted in a complex interdependency is to be broken, it must begin with political change in the Maghreb itself.

This chapter's principal finding sees no fundamental political change taking place in any of the three North African countries in the near or intermediate future.[8] Indeed, rather than "transitions to democracy" occurring, as many have suggested and even more have hoped, a "robust authoritarianism" has been maintained. At the same time, however, a vibrant civil society is also emerging which potentially can serve as the natural challenge to the autocratic state and thereby facilitate the evolution of a political society within which democracy can be nurtured, liberal or otherwise.[9] Yet, to date, the state has succeeded in manipulating, co-opting, or coercing civil society's most politically potent organizations—mass-based political parties both secular and Islamist.[10]

Despite the current preoccupation among academics and analysts with "democratic transition" in the Middle East and North Africa (MENA), no such transition has taken place anywhere in the region, if only because the necessary precondition—the collapse of authoritarianism—has yet to take place.[11] Save for the fully democratic election of non-state actor Mahmoud Abbas as president of the Palestinian Authority on 9 January 2005, and the relatively democratic election of Abdelaziz Bouteflika in 2004,[12] no Arab leader has ever arrived to national-level power democratically. It is thus premature to assess the conditions for either democracy's emergence or its eventual consolidation when political power remains firmly in the hands of the authoritarian state best represented by the tripartite pillars of control and coercion—the military, the business technocracy, and the executive, whether presidential or monarchical.

To be sure, the system's harshest features have been softened through the establishment of so-called "liberal autocracies," "illiberal democracies,"[13] or "quasi-democracies" involving "guided pluralism, controlled elections, and selective repression"[14] as currently in evidence, for example, in Jordan, Morocco, Yemen, Kuwait, Algeria, and Egypt. Yet, in the final analysis, and despite a multitude of separate and overlapping domestic pressures and external incentives for substantive democratic change, power remains as it always has—in the hands of the unaccountable few governing over the unrepresented many.

The Authoritarian Impulse

Michael Hudson's prescient observation about Arab politics made 30 years ago is still fully applicable: "The central problem of government in the Arab world today is political legitimacy. The shortage of this indispensable political resource largely accounts for the volatile nature of Arab politics and the autocratic ... character of all present governments."[15]

Numerous scholars have sought to explain this legitimacy deficit and the concurrent durability of authoritarianism in the Arab world by identifying a number of overlapping causal and contributing factors. These conditions revolve around several broad categories of interpretation—economic explanations,[16] cultural causes,[17] political determinants,[18] patterns of societal-state formation,[19] the role of religion,[20] and gender-based factors.[21] Despite the current appeal of culturally based explanations for the authoritarian impulse, most analysts privilege more complex dynamics "involving economic growth and stagnation, social-structural transformation, state formation and institutional inertia, and ideological transformation."[22]

The strength, coherence, and effectiveness of the state's coercive apparatus serve to highlight the "robustness" of authoritarianism. It is this robustness that provides the most useful framework of analysis in attempting to explain North Africa's enduring authoritarianism. What are the broader comparative and theoretical assumptions about state capabilities, and will they help explain the sustainability of the security establishment (*mukhabarat*) in the face of internal challenges and external pressures?

Focusing on the enabling capabilities of the national security state, Eva Bellin identifies the following determinative conditions: the status of a country's fiscal health, including access to rentier income in the form of oil and gas resources, geostrategic utility, and control of crucial transit facilities; the level and kind of international support networks; the degree of institutionalization of the military and whether it operates according to legal–rational criteria or patrimonial ones; the existence of popular political mobilization; and the use of perceived or real threats to state security.[23]

These do not encompass the full universe of possible reasons why North African authoritarianism remains so robust but they do identify critical structural factors that transcend issues of culture, history, personality, or religion that have often been invoked by analysts trying to explain MENA's non-democratic "exceptionalism."[24] One researcher has usefully summarized this overall pattern by stating that

> a set of interdependent institutional, economic, ideological, social, and geostrategic factors has created an adaptable ecology of repression, control, and partial openness. The web-like quality of this political ecosystem both helps partial autocracies to survive and makes their rulers unwilling to give up final control over any strand of the whole.[25]

Each of the variables identified above applies to the Maghreb.

Fiscal Health

It has been shown from experiences in Africa and elsewhere that there is a direct link between the state's coercive capabilities and the maintenance of fiscal health. The *mukhabarat* cannot long endure if it lacks the financial resources to pay its soldiers, purchase arms, upgrade equipment, maintain supplies, and acquire externally gathered intelligence data. When presumed-to-be-strong states began to collapse in Africa, for example, as Bellin reminds us, it was because prolonged fiscal crisis had "hollowed out" the coercive apparatus of the state.[26]

In North Africa, while economies underperform and human and material resources are underutilized, the overall fiscal health of Algeria, Morocco, and Tunisia is sufficiently robust to sustain more than adequate expenditures on security apparatuses. In fact, the Maghreb ranks noticeably above average in the proportion of gross national product (GNP) spent on security, approaching 5 percent in 2000 as compared to the global average of 3.8 percent.

Rentier income derived from such critical resources as oil and gas enables strong states to sustain elaborate coercive structures even if a country's overall economic health is poor, as the case of Algeria so clearly demonstrates. While Morocco and Tunisia may lack these valuable resources in large enough quantities to make a financial difference, other strategic rents such as foreign aid, tourism revenues, remittances from abroad, and so forth serve the same function of insuring that the state will pay itself first, including covering the costs of maintaining bloated military and security forces.[27]

It should be noted that "strong" states are being defined in a narrow coercive sense not as possessing enduring political legitimacy. Indeed, Ayubi's distinction between a "strong" state and a "fierce" state applies directly to the North African situation. As with the rest of the Arab world, the Maghreb state "is not a natural growth of its own socio-economic history or its own cultural and intellectual tradition."[28] Instead, the North

African state can better be understood as "fierce" since, in order to preserve itself, it resorts to the use of raw power as its default function. It is not "strong," because the Maghreb state "lacks the infrastructural power that enables [it] to penetrate society effectively through mechanisms such as taxation. [It also] lacks ideological hegemony (in a Gramscian sense) that would enable it to forge a historic social bloc that accepts the legitimacy of the ruling stratum."[29]

The state's "fierce" attributes are reinforced by its rentier status that enables the country's fiscal health to remain disconnected from society's productive economic forces, yet directly tied to the international political economy with its critical hydrocarbon lifeline. The connection between abundant oil rents and the aggrandizement of the authoritarian state, at the expense of an autonomous civil society, cannot be overemphasized. Sadiki summarizes this relationship accurately when he writes:

> [T]he huge returns from external oil rent have contributed primarily to aggrandizement of the state ... This aggrandizement applies to both oil producers and non-producers. The former directly accrue billions of petrodollars from external oil rent. The latter ... profit from the Arab oil boom. ... This latter group has become partly rentier economies. They rent labor, skills, and expertise to the scarcely populated Arab oil-producing states and thereby earn billions of dollars in remittances. Transfers of millions of Arab petrodollars either in the form of aid or investment are another factor in the equation. Petrodollars have endowed the Arab state with an independent resource to cement and reproduce itself.[30]

The current situation in Algeria best supports the observation Sadiki makes in the passage cited above. The huge hydrocarbon revenues in recent years have strengthened the authoritarian regime's repressive capabilities. They have also helped the regime elicit the international support that it had lacked throughout the 1990s.

International Support

More than any other world region, the MENA's sustained authoritarianism has been shaped by the successful maintenance of international support networks. While the Middle East portion of MENA has exploited these networks more extensively than the Maghreb, the latter has become a critical staging area in the fight against Islamic terrorism. Representative examples of terrorist activities occurring in or originating from the region include the prolonged bloodletting taking place in Algeria since 1992,[31] the terrorist bombing in Djerba in April 2002, the Casablanca suicide attacks in May 2003, the deadly explosions in Madrid in March 2004, and the murder of controversial Dutch film-maker Theo van Gogh in November 2004 in

Amsterdam by a Moroccan militant with ties to al-Qaeda. The war against global terrorism has significantly raised the Maghreb's geopolitical profile, especially in American eyes. In so doing, fighting terrorism has joined access to reliable oil and gas supplies as two key concerns justifying intense foreign involvement with existing army-backed regimes in Algeria, Morocco,[32] and Tunisia.

Among the unintended consequences of increased US and other international military, political, and economic assistance to all three Maghrebi countries has been a clamp-down on press freedoms, increased violations of human rights through random arrests of hundreds if not thousands of so-called Islamic terrorists in Morocco, and a general deterioration of political and civil rights.[33] It is within such a degraded political environment that terrorism finds its most willing recruits.

As Bellin has pointed out, in Eastern Europe, Latin America, and parts of Africa, the withdrawal of international backing for authoritarian states "triggered both an existential and financial crisis for the regimes that often devastated both their will and capacity to carry on."[34] Not only are such international withdrawals highly unlikely in the Maghreb but, as reported above, the region enjoys a unique position in the international arena that, given the importance of access to hydrocarbons and meeting the continuing challenge of Islamic terrorism, seems destined to be maintained into the indefinite future.

Patrimonialism

The Maghreb security apparatuses are shot through with patrimonial influences seriously compromising their rational–legal, professional, and institutionalized pretensions.[35] While Algeria, Morocco, and Tunisia possess "professional" security forces, they are organized along patrimonial lines in which staffing decisions are often ruled by cronyism, the distinction between public and private mission is blurred, leading to flagrant corruption and abuse of power, and discipline is maintained through exploitation of primordial cleavage.

The terrorist challenge confronting the region has worked to enhance state security resources through increased domestic expenditures for the military and expanded foreign arms assistance. Rather than forcing a further professionalization or institutionalization of the security apparatus, however, such increases have deepened patrimonial privileges to the advantage of state authority and at the expense of civil society.

In all three Maghrebi countries the *mukhabarat* constitute the state's most advantaged institution, serving as the bastion of elite privilege and guardian of regime interests. Even Tunisia's security apparatus, once modest by Arab world standards, has ballooned under President Ben Ali, himself a military man.[36] The decade-long civil war in Algeria and Morocco's 30-year struggle in Western Sahara have further empowered the armed forces of both states.

It seems unlikely that the authoritarian state will soon wither away or voluntarily relinquish power as long as the security apparatus, the linchpin of state survival, is permeated with patrimonial influence in which personalism pervades staffing decisions, political reliability supersedes merit in promotions, intercorp and intracorp discipline is maintained by relying on balanced rivalry between primordial groups, the distinction between public and private is not scrupulously observed, and the military continues to serve as a major path to personal enrichment.[37]

Popular Mobilization

In other situations and in different world regions, the authoritarian state's ability to maintain itself in power has been shaped by the degree to which it faces a high level of popular mobilization. Violently repressing or killing thousands of people in order to maintain authority carries huge political costs for the regime and is thus not used lightly or regularly. What is astonishing, but common, in the Maghreb is how infrequently and limitedly such popular mobilization has taken place in the modern period. Either society remains eerily passive, as in present-day Tunisia, or it erupts into civil war, as in Algeria.

This is not to suggest that North Africa has not experienced or does not continue to experience sporadic social unrest, labor strikes, student demonstrations, or even anarchic outbursts as in the Berber uprising of 1980 and the October riots of 1988 in Algeria. Yet such public expressions of social discontent are rarely rooted in organized political movements reflecting ideological coherence and political purpose that would serve serious notice to state incumbents that the people's wants and demands are to be taken seriously.[38] Nowhere in North Africa, and indeed throughout the Arab world, for example, "do mammoth, cross-class coalitions mobilize on the streets to push for reform," thus making the costs of repression relatively low for the regime.[39]

Only among Islamists have popular forces been capable of being mobilized in large numbers sufficient to force incumbent regimes to think seriously about political reform, including the possibility of legitimizing a democratic transition.[40] Yet, in every instance where political Islam has posed such a challenge in the Arab world, as in the cases of Jordan, Yemen, Algeria, Egypt, Tunisia, Syria, and Morocco for example, the state has ultimately decided either to violently suppress such movements (Algeria, Egypt, Syria) or apply a combination of harsh legal constraints and political co-optation to delimit the movement's influence, as in Jordan and Yemen (Tunisia has utilized both force and legal constraints). Where coercive measures have been applied, all three countries of North Africa have found external support, either directly or indirectly, for their actions. France and the US, for example, were virtually silent when the army staged a *coup d'état* against an impending Islamist parliamentary victory in Algeria in January 1992.[41]

As long as civil societies exhibit a variety of socioeconomic and cultural cleavages and remain seriously divided along religious–secular, urban–rural, male–female, modern–traditional, literate–illiterate, and indigenous–global lines, it will be difficult for high levels of popular mobilization to develop, thus facilitating the state's ability to repress political reform and choose coercion over compromise when such challenges do emerge. It seems highly unlikely, for example, that what successfully transpired in Iran under the Islamic revolution will be duplicated anytime soon in the Maghreb. Indeed, the Iranian experience has served as an object lesson of what incumbent regimes need to do to insure that neither revolution nor democracy erupts in the Arab world.

The Question of Palestine

Probably no single issue has so mobilized state and society in the Arab world as the question of Palestine. The conflict between Israel and Palestine touches virtually every emotional and political chord among Arabs, serving as the touchstone of Arab identity, integrity, and importance. To be sure, the military threat posed by Israel can serve as additional fodder for regimes seeking to further empower the security apparatus. Yet, as one researcher has accurately observed, "the arc of authoritarianism in the [MENA] region far exceeds the fly-zone of the Israeli air force; that is, countries far removed from the epicenter of the [Palestinian–Israeli] conflict still share the region's propensity for robust coercive apparatuses."[42]

Thus, the Palestinian issue in the Maghreb is less about enhancing security to protect against "Zionist aggression" than it is about further advantaging the state in its ability to stand up to the ideological, political, global as well as military challenge that Israel represents to the Arab world. The continuous suffering taking place in Palestine, as communicated daily on national and satellite television, serves to antagonize and anger vast majorities of Maghrebi peoples. Yet, rather than being transformed into an effective agent of popular mobilization against authoritarian rule, such anger is co-opted by incumbent regimes to further justify robust state power.

Like Islamism, the question of Palestine has been effectively integrated into the political language of the state as a way to disarm and delegitimize potential opponents. This tactic of ideological co-optation of key symbols of popular mobilization such as Islamism and Palestine has undercut the ability of autonomous groups to develop a truly democratic if not liberal Islam while making compromise on the Palestinian issue more difficult to achieve. As one observer has correctly pointed out, "the greatest obstacle to democracy is posed not by Islam but by military and intelligence organizations unaccountable to democratic authority."[43] The result is a robust authoritarian state secure in the knowledge that neither domestic, regional, nor international forces can fundamentally alter its autocratic practices which, in any case, have increasingly been repackaged as experiments in "democracy," "liberalism," and "reform."

State–Society Dynamics

Algeria, Morocco, and Tunisia confront serious political, security, and socioeconomic challenges that only political reform and institutionalized democracy can help solve. Yet, in all three cases, robust authoritarianism rather than effective reform dominates regime policies. As reported above, several interrelated variables help explain this condition of enhanced state authority in the face of challenges from an increasingly animated civil society. Yet one wonders how long such inherently conflictive conditions can be maintained without causing further problems, some leading to the kind of extremist politics currently evident both within and outside the region.

This chapter has argued that terrorism is one outcome of the failure to fundamentally reform and restructure Maghrebi political orders. It is no accident that despite widely varied socioeconomic conditions all three countries remain politically autocratic. Tunisia, for example, represents an exceptional case of a very successful albeit incomplete economic and social transformation.

Tunisia

Over the past years, significant progress has been made in the country's overall development. Tunisia today is a fully modern country with impressive quantitative and qualitative indicators supporting such a conclusion. It is common for a visitor to be particularly impressed by the level of political awareness and consciousness among society's educated classes and their ability and willingness to talk openly about sensitive political issues albeit in private gatherings, yet in public places.

Given this high level of socioeconomic development, cultural consciousness, and political sophistication it is that much more striking to observe the continued maintenance of a security state with all the trappings of police surveillance and intimidation.[44] The widening gap between society's material prosperity—nearly 75 percent of Tunisians own their own home—and its political primitiveness is reaching crisis proportions. Despite its draconian security measures, for example, the regime was unable either to stop terrorists from attacking a Jerba synagogue in April 2002 or to prevent scores, maybe even hundreds, of Tunisian nationals living in Europe and elsewhere from participating in terrorist activities, including involvement in the train bombings in Spain in March 2004.[45]

The pattern of state-led oppression has been maintained through a fused system of social liberalization on the one hand and political subjugation on the other. Yet this framework of control and coercion is operationalized through a democratic façade intended to convey a sense that democracy is alive and well in Tunisia. One such exercise in political manipulation took place with the October 2004 presidential and legislative elections, further reinforced by the May 2005 municipal election results in which the ruling Constitutional Democratic Rally (RCD—*Rassemblement Constitutionnel Démocratique*) party gained 4,098 seats out of the 4,366 being contested in the 269 communal electoral districts.

To the surprise of no one, on 24 October 2004 Tunisians turned out in record numbers—91.5 percent of the country's 4.6 million eligible voters—to re-elect President Zine al-Abidine Ben Ali to a fourth consecutive five-year term. Voters also gave his ruling party, the RCD, an overwhelming victory in parliamentary elections held on the same day.

The election results were never in doubt once Ben Ali had pushed through a constitutional amendment, approved in a landslide referendum in May 2002, which eliminated the three-term limit for presidents. Intentionally or not, Ben Ali seems to be following in the footsteps of his predecessor, Habib Bourguiba, whom he overthrew in a "constitutional coup" on 7 November 1987, partially in response to Bourguiba's self-designation as "president for life."

The early optimism that the post-Bourguiba era would see the arrival of political pluralism if not democracy has been all but extinguished in the last 15 years as the president and his ruling party have come to dominate the political scene while eradicating all sources of opposition, secular or religious. To be sure, the regime has been enormously successful in pursuing progressive social policies as regards women's rights and in advancing economic development—the country's GNP per capita tops $3,500. But this success has simply added to the discontinuity that defines the Tunisian paradox in which enhanced material well-being coexists alongside a robust political authoritarianism.

In part to offset a negative political profile among actual and potential foreign allies and investors, the regime has contrived a carefully crafted but thoroughly transparent pseudo-democracy predicated on a tightly controlled political pluralism and predetermined electoral outcomes. The October 2004 elections were one manifestation of this political ploy.

Determined to solidify his "democratic" credentials among his own people and his supporters in Europe and the United States, Ben Ali permitted three non-threatening candidates to contest his re-election, as compared to two competitors in 1999 and none in 1994 and 1989. Of these challengers, only Mohamed Ali Halouani, head of the *Ettajdid* Party (ex-Communist) and representing a bloc of independent politicians under the "Democratic Initiative" label, publicly decried the results after obtaining just 0.95 percent of the vote. Mohamed Bouchiha, secretary-general of the Popular Unity Party (PUP—*Parti de l'Unité Populaire*), who also happens to be related to Ben Ali's wife, received 3.78 percent,while Mounir Béji of the Liberal Social Party (PSL—*Parti Social Libéral*) obtained 0.79 percent.

None of these government-approved candidates has a significant political following nor does any challenge the President's personality or policies. In the view of regime supporters, Ben Ali's "modest" 94.48 percent victory, down from his previous highs of 99.7 percent, 99.6 percent, and 99.4 percent in 1989, 1994, and 1999 respectively, highlights the "contested" nature of the presidential election.

The outcome of the parliamentary election paralleled that of the presidency. While not constitutionally mandated, four-fifths of the legislature's seats are effectively reserved for the ruling party while the remaining 20 percent are contested by the country's seven officially sanctioned opposition parties. Thus, of the total 189 seats in the unicameral parliament, the RCD won 152, and the remaining 37 seats were distributed among the Social Democratic Movement (MDS—*Mouvement des Démocrates Socialistes*), the PUP, the Union of Democratic Unionist (UDU—*Union Démocratique Unioniste*), *Ettajdid*, and PSL.

The ruling party is especially proud of its commitment to make at least 25 percent of its candidates women. RCD women won 39 seats, compared to 20 in the previous parliament. Overall, 43 of the 189 newly elected deputies are women, one of the highest levels in the world. Unfortunately, for both men and women legislators, the Chamber of Deputies plays a marginal political role and its influence over national policy is virtually nil.

None of the opposition parties represented in parliament challenge the regime's hegemony or the absolute power of the presidency. The "real" opposition is banned, imprisoned, or harassed. It includes the still-popular Islamist party, An Nahda, headed by Rachid Ghannouchi, who lives in self-imposed exile in London. Modernist and secular figures representing a broad spectrum of political tendencies from liberal democrats (Moncef Marzouki) to communists (Hamma Hammami) to progressive socialists (Nejib Chebbi) have all decried the blatantly manipulative character of the political process. Outspoken journalists, human rights activists, academics, lawyers, and other public personalities have joined them in condemning the oppressive nature of political life where the media are tightly controlled, the Internet is monitored, and freedom of political expression is all but banned. Marzouki's description of Ben Ali's three-pronged policy accurately reflects the way this leader is perceived by these and other democratically inclined groups: "To remain indefinitely in power, to remain indefinitely in power, to remain indefinitely in power."[46]

Morocco

Morocco faces greater and potentially more lethal challenges as its socio-economic performance remains modest at best and its political opening tepid and uneven. The Casablanca attacks of 16 May 2003 exposed the country's vulnerabilities and the degree to which Moroccan nationals have been deeply implicated in a global network of loosely interrelated terrorist groups.[47] Interviews conducted in Spain with European and Moroccan respondents, for example, revealed the intensity of commitment to "militant Islam" as compared to the monarchy's attempt to project a "moderate Islam."

Much of Morocco's militancy has been self-induced. A radical interpretation of Islamic belief has become increasingly appealing to those frustrated by the failure of secular policies to deal with poverty, inequality, and corruption. In addition, Wahhabism has been propagated by preachers from Saudi Arabia and has won adherents, particularly among the marginalized classes of the urban areas. Wahhabi clerics were allowed to carry on their work because Saudi Arabia has been an important source of investment and financial aid for Morocco, and the Moroccan and Saudi royal families have long had close ties.

Prior to the Casablanca suicide bombings, the authorities had arrested members of radical Islamist groups active in the poorer neighborhoods of major Moroccan cities that had used violence to enforce their vision of Islam. They also began to shut down unauthorized mosques, and ban bookshops and itinerant booksellers peddling radical and inflammatory Islamist texts and prerecorded tapes. However, these measures did not prevent the 2003 suicide attacks, and, indeed, may even have helped to provoke them.

The current wave of Islamic militancy in Morocco has spread across the globe, with evidence that Moroccan radicals, some with military training in Afghanistan, are deeply involved in terrorist activities. Moroccans have been implicated in terrorist networks involved in the 11 September 2001 attacks in the US, the attacks in Jeddah, Saudi Arabia in May 2003, and the suicide bombings in Madrid, Spain in March 2004. According to intelligence reports, the Madrid bombers belonged to the Moroccan Islamic Combatant Group (GICM, *Groupe islamiste combattant marocain*), formed in Afghanistan with links to *Salafia Jihadia* (Salafiyya Jihadiyya, or Jihad for Pure Islam), a Moroccan extremist Islamist movement accused by Rabat of carrying out the Casablanca suicide bombings. One of those arrested in Spain is Jamal Zougam, who is reported to have links with both Mohamed Fizazi, the founder of *Salafia Jihadia* currently in jail serving a 30-year sentence, and Amer Azizi, a Moroccan charged in 2003 with belonging to an al-Qaeda cell that helped to plan the September 11 attacks.[48]

Evidence provided by investigatory journalists, intelligence services, and government officials in Morocco and Spain provides a chilling portrait of how frustrated, discontented, and deeply angry Moroccan youth living in poor quarters of big cities, especially in the north, have been recruited to militant activities, with some receiving training in Afghanistan, and then transformed into human explosives prepared to commit suicide in the name of some primordial interpretation of Islam that guarantees instant salvation through martyrdom. Many of these Islamists returning from Afghanistan have also found recruits among wealthier Moroccans who span two worlds but, frustrated by their secondary status in Europe, discovered a purpose in political Islam.

"My brothers were not like this when they left Morocco," said Jamal Benyaich, scion of a rich Tangier family whose eldest brother, Abdelaziz, has emerged as a central figure in the Moroccan militant network. Jamal's other brothers, Salaheddin and Abdullah, both became Islamic fighters, too. "They became Islamists in Europe," he said. "All of them lived a very European life in Morocco but came back with a new personality."[49]

This is not to suggest that the European experience has been determinative in transforming *beurs* into jihadists.[50] But one insider's account of his Algerian "assassin brothers" does present a complex interaction of diverse experiences involving the workings of a jihadist cell, the radicalizing effects of exile from the Algerian civil war, and the challenges for a Western democracy (France) of assimilating Muslim immigrants.[51] Although focusing specifically on Algerian militants in France, the making of a jihadist terrorist described by Sifaoui applies broadly across the Maghreb.

The depth of terrorist activity involving Moroccans both in Europe and in Morocco itself was highlighted in a 25 July 2004 article in *El País*, Spain's largest and most widely read newspaper, which reported the results of a government investigation into the Madrid bombings. According to Spanish investigators, Moroccan authorities had informed Madrid that it had lost track of 400 of the 600 Moroccans known to have trained in terrorist camps run by al-Qaeda in Afghanistan. The article also reported that Morocco had told Spanish officials that it had more than 2,000 Islamic militants within its borders. Of the roughly 60 men suspected to be connected to the 11 March 2004 train bombings in Madrid, 40 are from Morocco, the article said. According to the Spanish judge heading the investigation into al-Qaeda's presence in Spain, "the most serious problem that Europe has right now with this type of terrorism is in Morocco."[52]

In a separate but related terrorist investigation, Spanish authorities in October 2004 charged and jailed 33 Moroccans and Algerians involved in an alleged plot to slam a truck carrying 1,100 pounds of explosives into Madrid's National Court, which is overseeing Spain's anti-terror investigation related to the Madrid bombings of March 2004.[53]

The ideological and operational fusion of in-country and overseas Moroccan militants has raised the stakes for the government, whose survivalist strategy has led it to further limit rather than expand political and civil rights. Since the passage of a tough new anti-terrorism law that was rushed through the parliament in 2003 following the Casablanca bombings, thousands of terrorism suspects have been arrested. Numerous trials of arrested Islamic radicals have taken place, with severe sentences meted out to many. The result has been a return to some of the regime's worst authoritarian excesses as practiced under Hassan II, including flagrant abuses of human rights, like arbitrary arrest, torture, and unfair trials.[54]

The monarch's July 2004 decision to build 20 new mosques throughout the country to operate under tight government supervision as a means by which to counter the plethora of unofficial mosques in which self-appointed imams preach radical Islamic precepts reflects the regime's basic incomprehension of the nature of the challenge it faces, which remains, at bottom, fundamentally political. In October 2006, Morocco canceled compulsory military service out of fear of radical activities within the barracks, but also the fear of providing martial training to potential terrorists. This came shortly after the dismantling of the Ansar Al Mahdi' cell, led by an officer in the Moroccan Royal Armed Forces.[55]

Algeria

In Algeria, political liberalization in the form of relatively free, albeit controlled, presidential elections seems to be taking hold without necessarily, however, compromising the state's ultimate command and control of polity and economy.[56] President Bouteflika's resounding electoral victory on 8 April 2004, when he secured 85 percent of the registered vote, provides the Algerian leader with another five years to try to overcome the country's dismal socioeconomic conditions.[57] As discussed earlier, a country's fiscal health works to enhance the position and power of the security apparatus. With oil prices above the $60 per barrel range in 2006, Algeria's macroeconomic profile has improved. This has done little, however, to ameliorate the country's microeconomic condition, which still finds ordinary Algerians struggling with the basic necessities of life.

In the absence of a thorough and unambiguous democratic transformation of political life, and not withstanding the resignation in July 2004 of General Mohammed Lamari, the army's most influential figure,[58] most Algerians still believe that Bouteflika's election serves merely to consolidate the power of the shadowy military elite that has held sway in one form or another since independence in 1962. In the Algerian press, robust and independent-minded by Arab standards,[59] commentators have drawn parallels between Bouteflika and Ben Ali of Tunisia, accusing him of seeking to emulate the centralization of power achieved by his autocratic neighbor who, as discussed above, successfully amended the constitution so that he could run for a fourth term in October 2004 following his 99+ percent victories in 1989, 1994, and 1999.[60] However, Bouteflika did not carry out his project in 2006; the planned referendum on the constitution was postponed, but has been put back on the agenda of the government following the legislative elections held in May 2007.

While daily violence has declined and terrorist attacks are reduced, including the killing and capture of leading GSPC figures,[61] the Algerian government's human rights record as reported by numerous human rights monitoring organizations remains poor to very bad. Arbitrary arrests, prolonged incommunicado detentions, excessive use of force, extrajudicial

killings, reported cases of torture, and official impunity have all been identified as routine practices of the regime. Similarly, deprivations of basic
human and civil rights have taken place in the areas of speech, assembly,
and political activity. Even *Al-Jazeera*'s Algiers bureau was forced to close
following critical reports of the country's security laws that have led to
increases in short-term disappearances of prisoners deemed "threats to
national security."

To be sure, until the armed insurgency and its expanding links to al-
Qaeda's jihad are completely squelched, the Algerian "crisis" will continue.
Yet more decisive will be the need to resolve the system's fundamental
constitutional questions—"the armed forces' political role, presidential prerogatives, judicial independence, and, more generally, the problem of establishing law-bound government."[62]

The Democratic Imperative

North Africa's authoritarian impulse has sabotaged, at great human cost,
all efforts to advance the region's developmental goals. Rentier-based
economies have empowered "the *mukhabarat* state with its military and
police apparatuses. It continues to be able to reproduce itself and perfect its
coercive capacity."[63] Only a successful transition to a democratic system of
rule involving, at minimum, application of Dahl's dual polyarchical
requirements of public contestation and the right to participate[64] can overcome the current condition of political stasis, economic stagnation, social
atrophy, and cultural discontinuity.

Yet the one social class capable of animating civil society in its challenge
to the authoritarian state remains remarkably indifferent, if not hostile, to
pluralistic politics. Moore's dictum of "no bourgeoisie, no democracy"[65]
seems not to have taken hold in the Maghreb, where the professional middle
class functions, at best, as "contingent democrats"[66] or "reluctant democrats."[67] The potentially powerful and influential business communities in
each of the three countries seem to want "money even more than they want
political participation. If they can find non-democratic ways to protect
economic interests, they can live with that. [In the final analysis,] business-
men, interested primarily in profit, are more concerned with a regime's
effectiveness than with its openness: they want a state weak enough to loot
but strong enough to be worth looting."[68]

The only social movements in Maghrebi countries insistent on democratic
change, government accountability, the rule of law, transparency, and civilian authority are non-violent Islamist political parties. Rooted in civil
society and representing mass-based interests, Islamists challenge state
power directly, at the levels of both rhetoric and action. Since government
accountability and the rule of law are central to the democratic project,
Islamists are best positioned to promote substantive change. Yet no Arab
regime in North Africa or the Middle East has ever permitted an Islamist

movement to come to power through peaceful, democratic means save for a brief moment at the municipal level in Algeria from 1990 to early 1992 (the second round of the legislative election held in December 1991 was canceled in January 1992).

The democratic imperative in North Africa needs no Islamic qualifier but Islamists are the most committed to the democratic project. As long as all actors play according to the democratic rules of the game, then none should be excluded from participation.[69] How else can political differences be resolved peacefully? Stepan makes this point clear.

> Democracy is a system of conflict regulation that allows open competition over the values and goals that citizens want to advance ... As long as groups do not use violence, do not violate the rights of other citizens, and stay within the rules of the democratic game, *all* groups [including Islamists] are granted the right to advance their interests, both in civil society and in political society. This is the minimal institutional statement of what democratic politics does and does not entail.[70]

An institutional or procedural approach to democracy implies "that no group in civil society—including religious groups—can *a priori* be prohibited from forming a political party. Constraints on political parties may only be imposed *after* a party, by its actions, violates democratic principles."[71] The "twin tolerations"—freedom for democratically elected governments and freedom for religious organizations in civil and political society—serve as the minimal definition of democracy.[72]

Radical politics seem the inevitable alternative both domestically and internationally when these "twin tolerations" are absent or systematically compromised by autocratic ruling elites. While theories of economic deprivation and psychological alienation play a role in explaining the radicalization of Islamic politics in North Africa and beyond, in its essence Muslims rebel in response to political oppression. This thesis is most forcefully and convincingly presented by Hafez when he writes:

> Muslims become violently militant when they encounter exclusionary states that deny them meaningful access to political institutions and employ indiscriminate repressive policies against their citizens during periods of mass mobilization. Political exclusion and state repression unleash a dynamic of radicalization characterized by exclusive rebel organizations that isolate Islamists from their broader society and foster antisystem ideologies that frame the potentially healthy competition between secularism and Islamism as a mortal struggle between faith and impiety.[73]

Given the determinate role of the United States as a critical outside actor, can it provide support for the "twin tolerations" as a way of promoting institutionalized democracy and thereby reduce the impact of global terrorism?

Conclusion

In the face of continued state intransigence in the Maghreb, it seems unlikely that civil society, however animated and robust, can produce the necessary conditions for the establishment of a political society within which independent political parties can emerge serving as the institutional spearhead of a democratic transition. The international support variable has demonstrated the importance of external actors in shaping the style and direction of state behavior. In this regard, current US objectives to bring democracy to the Arab world through the Broader Middle East and North Africa Initiative are laudatory and logical. The Initiative's underlying assumptions regarding the need to break the link between political authoritarianism, socioeconomic deprivation, cultural alienation, and terrorism by creating a democratic alternative are compelling and convincing.

Unfortunately, the situations in Iraq, Israel–Palestine, Lebanon, and Saudi Arabia, among others, have seriously undermined the credibility of such efforts in the minds of many Arabs.[74] More harmful has been the way in which North African leaders, with Ben Ali serving as prime example, have usurped the symbolism, rhetoric, and outward manifestations of democratic practices to serve authoritarian ends. As one analyst has correctly observed: "Insofar as survival strategies have increased the perceived costs of democratization while not providing for effective economic development, [even liberal autocrats] have shown themselves unwilling or unable to cross anxious hard-liners in the military, the security forces, and the business community."[75]

For its part, the US simply cannot stand by and allow its democratic efforts to fail, if only because terrorism is so deeply embedded into the authoritarian impulse that can only be overcome through the democratic imperative. Given the region's paucity of will and robust authoritarianism, there are not likely to be any substantive political changes in the Maghreb until the US presses leaders like Ben Ali, Bouteflika, and Mohamed VI, all of whom have close personal and political ties to the current administration, "to transcend an involuted gradualism whose small steps trace the sad contours of an unvirtuous circle [of conflict, stalemate, reform, and conflict] rather than the hopeful lineaments of a real path forward."[76]

As Brumberg has correctly pointed out, if a policy of substantive democratic change is to succeed, the US must insist on the creation of effective and independent political parties, the institutionalization of truly representative legislative bodies, and the firm application of the rule of law. All this must also "be accompanied by vigorous international support for effective monitoring of local and national elections."[77]

In the absence of such efforts there is no reason to believe that the Maghreb's robust authoritarianism will dissolve anytime soon. Sadly, therefore, the conclusion of someone who is otherwise a severe critic of America's efforts to promote democracy in North Africa and the Middle East will continue to be true. "The entire Arab world is blighted by a group of remarkably similar regimes that share several characteristics in common, notably their stagnant political systems and the ubiquitous, brutal efficiency of the means of repression that keep their respective oligarchies safely in power to siphon off and profit from their societies' surplus."[78]

Notes

1 This chapter focuses on the central Maghreb states (Algeria, Morocco, and Tunisia); it does not deal with Libya and Mauritania, although these two states are part of the inactive Arab Maghreb Union. For treatment of Libya and Mauritania, see Chapters 3 and 4 of this book.

2 A compelling case for democracy's primacy in both politics and economics is made by Joseph T. Siegle, Michael W. Weinstein, and Morton H. Halperin, "Why Democracies Excel," *Foreign Affairs*, vol. 83, no. 5 (September/October 2004), pp. 57–71.

3 For a partisan argument supporting the Initiative see Danielle Pletka, "Arabs on the Verge of Democracy," *The New York Times*, 9 August 2004. Another more credible, albeit unexpected, source of support for President George W. Bush's democratic initiative comes from Neil Hicks of the Lawyers Committee for Human Rights. See Neil Hicks, "Bush Fires Up Mideast Reform," *The Los Angeles Times*, 8 August 2004. Yet, despite these initial optimistic appraisals, the first meeting of Arab and Western leaders dedicated ostensibly to advancing political change in the Middle East under the rubric of "Forum for the Future" turned into a rehash of ongoing grievances against American support for Israel and a noticeable downplaying of any Washington-inspired political initiative to encourage democratic change in the Arab world. See Joel Brinkley, "U.S. Slows Bid to Advance Democracy in the Arab World," *The New York Times*, 5 December 2004. See also Amr Hamzawy and Radwan Masmoudi, "Support Freedom in the Arab World," *Washington Post*, 11 October 2006. Available at: http://www.carnegieendowment.org/publications/index.cfm?fa=view&id=18779&prog=zgp&proj=zdrl,zme.

4 See United Nations Development Programme/Arab Fund for Economic and Social Development, *Arab Human Development Report 2002: Creating Opportunities for Future Generations* (New York: UNDP, 2002), United Nations Development Programme/Arab Fund for Economic and Social Development, *Arab Human Development Report 2003: Building a Knowledge Society* (New York: UNDP, 2003), and United Nations Development Programme/Arab Fund for Economic and Social Development, *Arab Human Development Report 2004: Towards Freedom in the Arab World* (New York: UNDP, 2005). The most recent UNDP report, *Arab Human Development Report 2005: Toward the rise of women in the Arab world*, was published in December 2006.

5 An incisive comparative analysis of the relationship between Muslims and the state in major European countries is found in Joel S. Fetzer and J. Christopher Soper, *Muslims and the State in Britain, France, and Germany* (New York: Cambridge University Press, 2005).

6 On the "making" of religiously-inspired terrorists see Jessica Stern, *Terror in the Name of God: Why Religious Militants Kill* (New York: HarperCollins, 2003).

7 Detailed profiles of Muslim militants being radicalized within a European milieu can be found in Susan Sachs, "North Africans in Europe Said to Preach War, Enlisting Young Immigrants: How a Tunisian was Recruited—A Case Study," *The New York Times*, 11 December 2001; Elaine Sciolino, "Portrait of the Arab as a Young Radical," *The New York Times*, 22 September 2002, p. 14; Craig S. Smith, "A Long Fuse Links Tangier to Bombings in Madrid," *The New York Times*, 28 March 2004, p. 20; Craig S. Smith, "Europe Fears Islamic Converts May Give Cover for Extremism," *The New York Times*, 19 July 2004; Craig S. Smith, "Web of Jihad Draws in an Immigrant Family in France," *The New York Times*, 31 July 2004; Lawrence Wright, "The Terror Web: Were the Madrid Bombings Part of a New, Far-Reaching Jihad Being Plotted on the Internet?" *The New Yorker*, 2 August 2004; and Sylvie Kauffmann and Piotr Smolar, "Le Djihadiste Français est plus fruste, plus jeune, plus radicalise," *Le Monde* (Paris), 24 May 2005.

8 For an equally pessimistic projection extended to the whole of the Arab world, see Lisa Anderson, "Arab Democracy: Dismal Prospects," *World Policy Journal* (fall 2001), pp. 53–60.

9 See, Yahia H. Zoubir, "The Rise of Civil Society in Arab States," in David Lesch (ed.), *History in Dispute: The Middle East since 1945*, (St-James Press/Manly Publishers 2003, pp. 81–5). The functional role of civil society as a prelude to democracy's emergence in the Middle East and North Africa is presented by Augustus Richard Norton (ed.), *Civil Society in the Middle East*. Volumes 1 and 2 (Leiden, Netherlands: E. J. Brill, 1995 and 1996). The idea of "in-house" reform emerging within official institutions as a prelude to democratization is provided in the example of judges in Egypt who have begun to exhibit greater independence from the government than ever before. See Hassan M. Fattah, "Egyptian Judges Are Entering Growing Reform Movement," *The New York Times*, 21 May 2005.

10 A survey of state–society relations in the Maghreb is provided by John P. Entelis (ed.), *Islam, Democracy, and the State in North Africa* (Bloomington, IN: Indiana University Press, 1997).

11 A representative example of incipient "democratic transition" taking place in the Arab world is found in Rex Brynen, Bahgat Korany, and Paul Noble (eds), *Political Liberalization and Democratization in the Arab World* (Boulder, CO: Lynne Rienner, 1995).

12 It should be noted, however, that although the re-election of Bouteflika was fair, the president has consolidated his rule through authoritarian means.

13 Its most forceful expression is found in Fareed Zakaria, "The Rise of Illiberal Democracy," *Foreign Affairs* (November/December 1997), pp. 22–43.

14 Daniel Brumberg, "Democratization in the Arab World? The Trap of Liberalized Autocracy," *Journal of Democracy*, vol. 13, no. 4 (October 2002), p. 56.

15 Michael C. Hudson, *Arab Politics: The Search for Legitimacy* (New Haven, CT: Yale University Press, 1977), p. 2.

16 See Jill Crystal, "Authoritarianism and its Adversaries in the Arab World," *World Politics*, vol. 46, no. 2 (January 1994), pp. 262–89.

17 See Elie Kedourie, *Democracy and Arab Political Culture* (Washington DC: Washington Institute for Near East Policy, 1992) and Hisham Sharabi, *Neopatriarchy: A Theory of Distorted Change in Arab Society* (New York: Oxford University Press, 1988).

18 See Mohammed M. Hafez, *Why Muslims Rebel: Repression and Resistance in the Islamic World* (Boulder, CO: Lynne Rienner, 2003).

19 See Nazih N. Ayubi, *Over-Stating the Arab State: Politics and Society in the Middle East* (London: I. B. Tauris, 1995) and Sami Zubaida, *Islam, the People*

and the State: Political Ideas and Movements in the Middle East* (London: I. B. Tauris, 1993).

20 See Samuel P. Huntington, *The Clash of Civilizations and the Remaking of World Order* (New York: Touchstone, 1996) and Bernard Lewis, *The Crisis of Islam: Holy War and Unholy Terror* (New York: The Modern Library, 2003).

21 See M. Steven Fish, "Islam and Authoritarianism," *World Politics*, vol. 55, no. 1 (October 2002), pp. 4–37.

22 Crystal, "Authoritarianism," p. 263.

23 Eva Bellin, "The Robustness of Authoritarianism in the Middle East: Exceptionalism in Comparative Perspective," *Comparative Politics*, vol. 36, no. 2 (January 2004), pp. 144–6. See also Marsha Pripstein Posusney and Michele Penner Angrist (eds), *Authoritarianism in the Middle East: Regimes and Resistance* (Boulder, CO: Lynne Rienner, 2005).

24 As Muslim-majority countries become more fully democratic, as in Turkey, Indonesia, and Bangladesh, "Muslim" exceptionalism is now being refocused on the Arab world,which remains uniformly nondemocratic. See Alfred Stepan and Graeme B. Robertson, "Arab, Not Muslim, Exceptionalism," *Journal of Democracy*, vol. 15, no. 4 (October 2004), pp. 140–6. See also Alfred Stepan, "Religion, Democracy, and the 'Twin Tolerations,'" *Journal of Democracy*, vol. 11, no. 4 (October 2000), pp. 37–57.

25 Brumberg, "Democratization," p. 57.

26 Bellin, "Robustness," p. 144.

27 *Ibid.*, p. 148.

28 Ayubi, *Overstating*, p. 3.

29 *Ibid.*

30 Larbi Sadiki, "Popular Uprisings and Arab Democratization," *International Journal of Middle East Studies*, vol. 32, no. 1 (February 2000), p. 87.

31 Algeria's decade-old civil war has produced a sizable journalistic and scholarly literature. One of the most recent, that incorporates and synthesizes the relevant findings of many earlier studies argued within a global perspective, is that of Lounis Aggoun and Jean-Baptiste Rivoire, *Françalgérie: Crimes et Mensonges d'Etats* (Paris: La Découverte, 2004). See also Hugh Roberts, *The Battlefield Algeria 1988–2002: Studies in a Broken Polity* (London: Verson, 2003) and Youcef Bedjaoui, Abbas Aroua, and Meziane Ait-Larbi (eds), *An Inquiry into the Algerian Massacres* (Geneva: Hoggar, 1999).

32 A recent book has detailed France's unconditional, astounding support for Morocco; see, Jean-Pierre Tuquoi. *"Majesté, je dois beaucoup à votre père..." France–Maroc, une affaire de famille* (Paris: Albino Michel, 2006).

33 See Eric Goldstein, "Morocco's New Truth Commission: Turning the Page on Human Rights Abuses?" Carnegie Endowment for International Peace, *Arab Reform Bulletin* (2004) (http://www.ceip.org). See also Jean-Pierre Tuquoi, "Le Maroc s'efforce de tourner la page des 'années de plomb,'" *Le Monde*, 15 December 2004.

34 Bellin, "Robustness," p. 144.

35 The most developed argument of Arab patrimonialism is found in Sharabi, *Neopatriarchy*.

36 Widely contrasting assessments of Ben Ali's rule are presented by Emma C. Murphy, *Economic and Political Change in Tunisia: From Bourguiba to Ben Ali* (New York: St. Martin's Press, 1999) and Nicolas Beau and Jean-Pierre Tuquoi, *Notre Ami Ben Ali: l'envers du 'miracle tunisien.'* (Paris: La Découverte, 1999), who critique, at times brutally, his authoritarianism, and Andrew Borowiec, *Modern Tunisia: A Democratic Apprenticeship* (Westport, CT: Praeger 1998) and Georgie Anne Geyer, *Tunisia: A Journey Through a Country that Works* (London: Interlink, 2004), who compliment effusively the Tunisian leader's

democratic achievements. Other critical assessments can be found in Neil Mac-Farquhar, "Tunisia's Tangled Web is Sticking Point for Reform," *The New York Times* (25 June 2004) and Michael Slackman, "Tunisia's Two Faces of Progress," *Los Angeles Times* (10 June 2002).

37 See Bellin, "Robustness," p. 149.

38 Sadiki, "Popular Uprisings," provides a contrasting interpretation, arguing that "popular uprisings" do in fact result in regime reforms paving the way for "Arab democratization." He develops this argument more fully in Larbi Sadiki, *The Search for Arab Democracy: Discourses and Counter-Discourses* (New York: Columbia University Press, 2004).

39 Bellin, "Robustness," p. 150.

40 François Burgat, *Face to Face with Political Islam* (New York: I. B. Tauris, 2003), provides the most partisan argument regarding the contestatory role of Islamists. For more nuanced interpretations see Quintan Wiktorowicz, "Conceptualizing Islamic Activism," *ISIM Newsletter*, no. 14 (June 2004), pp. 34–5, Quintan Wiktorowicz (ed.), *Islamic Activism: A Social Movement Theory Approach* (Bloomington, IN: Indiana University Press, 2004), and Vickie Langohr, "Of Islamists and Ballot Boxes: Rethinking the Relationship Between Islamisms and Electoral Politics," *International Journal of Middle East Studies*, vol. 33 (2001), pp. 591–610.

41 Florence Beaugé, "Paris et Alger rétablissent leur coopération militaire et vont signer un accord de défense," *Le Monde* (20 July 2004), elaborates on the deepening military and security relationship between Paris and Algiers.

42 Bellin, "Robustness," p. 151.

43 Stepan, "Twin Tolerations," p. 52. For his part, Fish, "Islam and Authoritarianism," locates Islam's attitude towards women as the source of its authoritarianism.

44 A scholarly yet highly critical interpretation of Tunisia's "authoritarian syndrome" is presented by Michel Camau and Vincent Geisser, *Le Syndrome Autoritaire: Politique en Tunisie de Bourguiba à Ben Ali* (Paris: Presses des Sciences Po, 2003). For its part, Human Rights Watch has published two scathing assessments of Tunisia's human rights situation. See Human Rights Watch, "Tunisia: Long-Term Solitary Confinement of Political Prisoners," *A Human Rights Watch Report*, vol. 16, no 3(e) (July 2004) and "Tunisia: Crushing the Person, Crushing a Movement: The Solitary Confinement of Political Prisoners," *A Human Rights Watch Report*, vol. 17, no. 4(e)(April 2005).

45 See José María Irujo, "The Series of Events that Led up to March 11," *El País* (Madrid) (13 May 2004) (English edition).

46 John P. Entelis, "The Sad State of Political Reform in Tunisia," *Arab Reform Bulletin*, vol. 2, issue 10 (November 2004) (www.ceip.org).

47 See, Fiona Govan, "Town that Breeds Suicide Bombers," *The Daily Telegraph*, 25 November 2006. On why Moroccans seem so over-represented among Islamic terrorists, see Thomas Omestad, "The Casablanca Connection: Why Morocco is Producing some of the World's Most Feared Terrorists," *U.S. News and World Report*, 9 May 2005, pp. 20–33.

48 See Frédéric Chambon, "La double vie de Jamal Zougam," *Le Monde*, 19 April 2004.

49 Smith, "A Long Fuse," p. 20. A similar profile of Islamic radicalization applies to Mohammed Bouyeri, the 26-year old Dutch-Moroccan accused of assassinating Theo van Gogh in Amsterdam in November 2004 on the pretext that the controversial Dutch movie director was making anti-Islamic films. See Andrew Higgins, "Rude Awakening: A Brutal Killing Opens Dutch Eyes to Threat of Terror," *The Wall Street Journal*, 22 November 2004, A1 and A11.

50 See Fetzer and Soper, *Muslims and the State*.

51 See Mohamed Sifaoui, *Mes Frères Assassins* (Paris: Le Cherche Midi, 2003).

52 *El País* (Madrid), 25 July 2004.

53 See *The New York Times*, 14 December 2004 and *Le Monde*, 20 October 2004.
54 See Goldstein, "Morocco's New Truth Commission" and Tuquoi, "Le Maroc." For a compelling and deeply insightful assessment of the political, social, and cultural implications of Morocco's efforts to come to terms with its past human rights violations while still imprisoning and torturing a new generation of Moroccan dissidents, see Susan Slyomovics, *The Performance of Human Rights in Morocco*. (Philadelphia, PA: University of Pennsylvania Press, 2005).
55 See http://www.moroccotimes.com/paper/article.asp?idr=2&id=16849.
56 See John P. Entelis, "Civil Society and the Authoritarian Temptation in Algerian Politics: Islamic Democracy vs. the Centralized State," in A. R. Norton (ed.), *Civil Society in the Middle East* (Leiden, Netherlands: E. J. Brill, 1996), pp. 45–86
57 See Steven A. Cook, "Algeria's Elections: No Democratic Turning Point," Carnegie Endowment for International Peace, *Arab reform Bulletin*, vol. 2, issue 4 (April 2004).
58 *Le Monde*, 20 July 2004, p. 4.
59 See John F. Burns, "Algeria: Remember that Name," *The New York Times*, 2 January 2000, p. 4 and Craig S. Smith, "Islam and Democracy: Algerians Try to Blaze a Trail," *The New York Times*, 14 April 2004.
60 See Murphy, *Economic and Political Change in Tunisia*.
61 See Forestier, "Le Ben Laden du Sahel."
62 International Crisis Group, "Islamism, Violence and Reform in Algeria," 30 July 2004.
63 Sadiki, "Popular Uprisings," p. 87. See also Burhan Ghalioun, "The Persistence of Arab Authoritarianism," *Journal of Democracy*, vol. 15, no. 4 (October 2004), pp. 126–32.
64 Robert A. Dahl, *Polyarchy: Participation and Opposition* (New Haven, CT: Yale University Press, 1971).
65 Barrington Moore, *The Social Origins of Dictatorship and Democracy* (New York: Penguin, 1966).
66 Eva Bellin, "Contingent Democrats: Industrialists, Labor, and Democratization in Late-Developing Countries," *World Politics*, vol. 52, no. 1 (January 2000), pp. 175–205. See also Eva Bellin, *Stalled democracy: Capital, Labor, and the Paradox of State-Sponsored Development* (Ithaca, NY: Cornell University Press, 2002).
67 Crystal, "Authoritarianism," p. 271.
68 *Ibid.*
69 This point is made emphatically clear by someone who is well positioned to understand its personal and political meanings. See Saad Eddin Ibrahim, "Islam Can Vote, if We Let It," *The New York Times*, 21 May 2005.
70 Stepan, "Twin Tolerations," p. 39.
71 *Ibid.*, p. 40.
72 *Ibid.*
73 Hafez, *Why Muslims Rebel*, p. xv.
74 This point was made abundantly clear by Arab leaders at the Forum for the Future conference in Rabat on 11–12 December 2004.
75 Brumberg, "Democratization in the Arab World," p. 64.
76 *Ibid.*, p. 66.
77 *Ibid.*, p. 67.
78 Rashid Khalidi, *Resurrecting Empire: Western Footprints and America's Perilous Path in the Middle East* (New York: Beacon Press, 2004), p. 69.

2 Policy Reforms in Algeria

Genuine Change or Adjustments?

Ahmed Aghrout

Algeria has experienced remarkable transformations since the end of the 1980s. This process of transition, with all its societal consequences, has gone through changing sequences. The process has witnessed periods of great success, while other periods were marked by blatant failures. Reforming the political system and introducing multiparty elections were important developments in the country's post-independence history. Yet the annulment in January 1992 of the second round of parliamentary elections held in December 1991 and the decreeing of a state of emergency in March 1992 were indicative of the entrenched resistance to change. With the country having plunged into a chasm of instability—as a result of the brutal conflict and violence that followed the cancellation of the electoral process—it was obvious that the reforms engaged could not be sustained with the same degree of commitment.

The assumption of power by Abdelaziz Bouteflika in 1999 was expected to give impetus to the slow-moving pace of political and economic reforms. Nonetheless, the ending of violence and the rehabilitation of Algeria's image abroad dominated most of the president's first term (1999–2004). In view of that, the country has made significant headway against its international isolation on account of an extensive and vigorous diplomatic effort.[1] The signs of a steady return to normality are discernible in the reduced level of violence, improved stability and security, and some institutional legitimacy. Restoring the country's stability and international standing are indisputably positive steps in the right direction; however, large segments of the Algerian population have become disillusioned with the lack of progress in the reforms that the authorities have promised.[2] The re-election of Bouteflika in April 2004, deemed as a "mandate for reforms," is another opportunity for the government to speed up the reform drive and deal with popular grievances. With a healthy financial position boosted by rising oil prices, it remains to be seen how Algeria will press ahead with this process of change while taking in hand the significant decline in living standards. Over this period of transition, mobilization of popular support is definitely fundamental and contingent upon how effective public demands are addressed.

It is timely, after more than a decade, to explore some of the changes that have taken place and explore their real and potential outcomes for Algeria. This chapter attempts to bring to light the complex nature of this critical phase in Algeria's development and examines both the achievements made and what lies ahead in terms of structural reforms and their social implications.

From Impasse to Renewed Momentum

Algeria, like many other developing countries, was also affected by the 1980s unparalleled movement toward democratic rule in the developing world. Indeed, the move towards political pluralism came after the riots of October 1988, marking a decisive period in the country's political development. The single-party regime had come in for criticism as a corollary of a mixture of mounting economic, social, and cultural problems.[3] What followed such events was described as "ground-breaking" political changes that involved, amongst other things, liberalizing the political system and widening political participation.

In this regard, the Chadli Benjedid regime, in its attempt to respond to the crisis, introduced a number of changes formalized in a revised version of the constitution. These constitutional modifications, approved by referendum in February 1989, constituted a rupture with the then prevailing ideological and political conditions. Not only was the reference to the country's "revolutionary socialist option" abandoned, but also the identification of the state with the single party, the National Liberation Front (FLN), was ended. This separation prompted the opening of the political system with freedom of expression, association, and organization no longer restricted.[4] As the right to form "associations of a political nature" was legally recognized, this signaled the end of the FLN's 27 years of unchallenged political rule. Opening the door to multiparty politics led to scores of political parties springing up—about 60 parties were officially registered prior to the municipal and provincial elections of June 1990.[5]

These transformations, by prompting significant changes in the country's political life, were seen as a milestone on the road to democratic rule. Yet it turned out to be just a short-lived experience of political liberalization. Multiparty municipal and provincial elections took place without any major incident in June 1990. That was not the case with regard to the legislative elections of December 1991. Once it had become obvious that the Islamic Salvation Front (FIS) was heading toward a sweeping victory after the first round of balloting, these elections were cancelled. Under pressure, President Benjedid resigned and a collegial presidency, the High Council of State, was established to run state affairs temporarily during a transitional period (January 1992–January 1994). The FIS was dissolved and a state of emergency declared. Whatever the justification given for halting the electoral process, the fact is that the political stalemate that resulted was to herald an era of instability and violence. The escalation of violence that followed caused considerable damage to numerous socioeconomic infrastructures and resulted in the death of thousands of people.[6] Yahia Zoubir argued that, in the aftermath of the annulment of elections, "the Algerian regime lacked any strategy to overcome the ensuing political crisis. The weakness of the regime led to an intensification of violence that almost destroyed the state in 1993–95."[7]

Early initiatives taken by both sides of the political establishment—the regime and the opposition—to put the political process back on track and end the cycle of violence proved to be vain attempts. The "Platform for a Political and Peaceful Solution to the Algerian Crisis," endorsed by a number of opposition parties in their Sant'Egidio (Rome) meeting in January 1995, was an illustrative example.[8] The regime rebuffed the platform from the start "as interference in Algeria's internal affairs; as a plot of international forces, including the Vatican; and as an attempt to manipulate the Algerian political debate."[9] In the same way, hardly anything developed from the regime's sponsored 1994 Conférence Nationale du Consensus, as the main opposition political parties stayed away from it.[10]

As the prospects for reconciling the divergent positions looked remote, if not impossible at that point in time, the regime pressed ahead with its own "normalization" process. An initial step was the holding of the presidential election in November 1995; the first ever multi-candidate presidential election to take place in the country. Liamine Zeroual—who was already serving as head of state since his appointment in January 1994—was elected with 61 percent of the votes cast.[11] Irrespective of their reservations about this election, a number of observers were rather optimistic as to its political implications, contending that "many Algerians had cast their votes for Zeroual in the hope that he would use his new legitimacy to find a way out of the crisis,"[12] and that "after the relatively peaceful election, hope arose that Algeria finally was on its way toward authentic re-democratization."[13] Having acquired legitimate authority, Zeroual used his mandate to revive dialogue with political forces, introduce in 1996 new amendments to the 1989 Constitution, and organize the general and local elections of 1997.[14] The restoration of the institutional process subsequent to these elections has provided a degree of an incipient multiparty political system.

In September 1998, less than three years after his election, Zeroual announced his resignation. The decision to stand down from office was, in all likelihood, motivated by the constraining environment—including press allegations of corruption aimed at some of his close advisers and political allies—that made it difficult for him to carry on with his policy of institutional consolidation.[15] Of the seven candidates in the final race, Bouteflika won nearly 74 percent of the votes cast in the presidential election held in April 1999, according to official figures. Even though six of the candidates decided to withdraw on the eve of polling day, claiming proof of electoral fraud to favor the "national consensus" candidate (referring to Bouteflika), there was no formal appeal by them for a boycott and voting papers for all candidates were provided at the polls.[16]

Regardless of the controversy that surrounded this presidential election, the new leadership was faced with the pressing and challenging task of restoring political stability to the country. Surely this was not an easy business in an environment marked by an armed insurgency, factional conflict within the ruling establishment, and declining socioeconomic conditions. How Bouteflika assumed his new responsibilities in this "perilous political terrain," argues a close observer, "was to depend essentially upon his own political skills and his ability to exploit the potential for legitimacy inherent in the presidential office."[17]

The Path to Stability

It is quite possible to assert that the late 1990s have given way to hope rather than despair. Interesting developments have been taking place that, while they have not put an end to the crisis in every respect, can be seen as building blocks towards this goal. A fundamental issue of critical importance to the country's institutional stability has been the organization of elections on a regular basis since 1995. Indeed, after the 1992 aborted legislative elections, the authorities endeavored to rebuild the state's institutional framework and give it a measure of constitutional legitimacy. Presidential, legislative, and local elections have been held to set up institutions that would play a role in resolving or, at least, easing the political crisis and, in due course, providing the context "for a properly working pluralistic democracy."[18] On a number of occasions, there were allegations that some of the elections were marred by fraud, but it appears that this has been less and less the case, as demonstrated by the latest elections.[19] The 2002 legislative election gave rise to no major controversy, whether about its conduct or its results.[20] International monitors and observers considered the 2004 presidential election as "peaceful and generally free."[21] Even the military institution, a central force in Algerian politics, openly declared its neutrality by respecting the election's outcome.[22] Having obtained almost 85 percent of the vote, Bouteflika was re-elected for a second term (2004–9).

By and large, the reinstatement of representative and consultative institutions has certainly contributed to a "formal return to civilian rule." Whether this will move Algeria a step further in its arduous effort to promote democratic rule remains to be seen. At this juncture, one can only be tempted to state that there are signs of change in the country's power structure, which might portend a gradual reinforcement of the civilian power. There were claims of power struggle and strained relationship with the army command at particular phases of Bouteflika's first term in office, something that fueled a great deal of speculation over his eventual re-election. By securing a second mandate, this has "entailed a dramatic strengthening of the presidency and has accelerated the army's retreat from the political stage."[23] The resignation of the chief of staff, Lt-General Mohamed Lamari in August 2004, and Bouteflika's ensuing changes in the army hierarchy a few months after his re-election could lend credence to this ascendant power of a civilian presidency.[24] This process may well provide the potential for further change that, if positively exploited by the political forces involved, could smooth Algeria's transition to an environment conducive to democratic development. A state of affairs that also partly hinges on how successful is the range of initiatives taken by the regime so far to end the cycle of violence.

In this context, one should mention that until the election of Bouteflika to the presidency in 1999, there was a predominant tendency within the Algerian regime that favored the military option to deal with the armed groups. Whilst the pursuit of this hard-line policy produced some results, it did limit the scope for conciliatory and peaceful attempts to settle the crisis—the rejection of the Rome peace plan of early 1995 was a case in point. Also the military campaign was the subject of criticism, emanating mainly from some local and international human rights groups. Bouteflika pledged, after his inauguration, to make the restoration of the country's security and stability his agenda's top priority. The truce observed by the Islamic Salvation Army (AIS), FIS armed wing, since 1997 was to pave the way for the president's initiative, the "Civil Concord Law," which was widely approved in a referendum held in September 1999.[25] In a nutshell, this initiative offered an official amnesty for militants who laid down their arms and those who had not taken part in "blood crimes." As for those militants who had been involved in serious crimes, reduced sentences were offered to them provided that they surrendered to the authorities within six months. Although some armed groups had rejected the president's offer, it is believed that a significant number of militants took advantage of it.[26]

The "Civil Concord" was meant as the start of a process of political reconciliation while, at the same time, the army would continue its fight against recalcitrant armed groups. It was clear that this amnesty plan would be objected to or denounced by various parties, including families of victims and certain human rights groups. In spite of that, the fact remains that this plan has had the effect of contributing to the reduction in the level of violence and the improvement in the security situation.

Yet the prospects for promoting peace and stability seemed at some point compromised. The eruption of violence in the Kabylie region in April 2001, initially triggered by the death of a 19-year-old student while in police custody, was to become a broader form of protest soon after. Besides the socioeconomic hardship, evidently common to many parts of the country too, cultural and linguistic matters of particular concern to this region also came to the fore. A 15-point platform, adopted in June 2001 by the local movement (*Coordination des Archs, Dairas et Communes*—CADC) was to serve as a basis for dialogue with the authorities. Notwithstanding the division within the movement between two groups, "*dialoguistes*" and "*non-dialoguistes*," a series of talks with the former group was held and, as a consequence, their demands have been met in a number of cases.[27] Amongst these were the recognition of Tamazight (Berber) as a national language in March 2002 and the holding of partial new local elections in November 2005. It is plausible that these concessions have relatively helped appease the tensions in the region. At this stage, the expectation that further negotiations will take place raises at least two main concerns. With the recent election of legitimate representatives, this brings into question the status and mission of the CADC delegates. Put differently, it is not clear whether they will continue negotiating on behalf of the region's population. On the other hand, there are still issues of contention, not least the official status of the language.[28] In the final analysis, the way these concerns are dealt with, as well as the outcome of forthcoming negotiations, could, to some extent, play a part in the degree of success of the government flagship policy of "national reconciliation" to restore lasting peace and stability in the country.

The "Charter for Peace and National Reconciliation" is actually a key constituent of this policy. Endorsed overwhelmingly in a referendum held in September 2005, this peace charter, as maintained by the government, "will serve as a roadmap to settle definitely the consequences of the crisis that the country had gone through."[29] In other words, this paved the way to more appropriate policy measures to deal with the various facets of the crisis. In the main, with the exception of those individuals who perpetrated massacres, rapes, and attacks in public places, this plan offers a broad amnesty, together with the proviso for assistance for families whose relatives joined the insurgency or disappeared.[30]

The authorities are obviously placing high hopes on this amnesty plan to end the cycle of violence that gripped Algeria for more than a decade, and enable the country to move forward. Like the "Civil Concord" initiative before, this charter has also caused a number of politicians, political parties, associations of victims of terrorism, and human and civic rights groups to object to the measures it consists of.[31] Whilst there is a consensus on the principle of peace, their criticisms have ranged from denouncing this charter as a breach of the right of victims' families to truth and justice, to presenting it as a way for Bouteflika to consolidate his grip on power.[32] No matter what one makes of these allegations, the fact remains that, on the whole, "most Algerians certainly will welcome any gesture which seems to move towards peace and reconciliation."[33] Any efforts to bring in peace cannot be dismissed outright; to the same degree, doing justice to the victims' families cannot be ignored entirely.

The question of the "disappeared" or those missing as result of the brutal conflict—the bulk of which is believed to have occurred between 1994 and 1996—has ultimately been acknowledged by the authorities. The seriousness of this issue persuaded the government to give it due consideration. Surely, Bouteflika can be credited for recognizing the scale of the problem in the early months of his first mandate, but it was not until September 2003 that the establishment of an "ad-hoc commission" to deal with thousands of cases of missing persons was announced.[34] The task entrusted to this entity, headed by Farouk Ksentini, was merely of liaising with the families of victims to verify the "disappearances" and to advise on compensatory provisions. The way the issue has been handled seems to have fallen short of these families' expectations, especially the commission's incapacity to investigate and expose the perpetrators behind the disappearances and to hold them legally accountable; something also shared by some human rights groups. On his part, Nourredine Yazid Zerhouni, Minister of the Interior, stated during a press conference that 70 percent of these families are favorable to the commission's proposal for compensation; as for the remaining families (30 percent) who are against, they can take legal action.[35]

It is clear that the commission's final report on the "disappearances," submitted to the President in March 2005, was an important ingredient in the drafting of the "Charter for Peace and National Reconciliation." Compensatory measures are, for the moment, the preferred means by which the government is trying to settle this highly serious and sensitive issue, but only time will tell how effective such policy action is.[36] Started in September 2006, these compensatory measures have thus far targeted about 42,000 families, according to Djamel Ould-Abbes, Minister in charge of National Solidarity and Employment.[37] It should be borne in mind that needy families whose relatives died while part of the insurgency are also concerned about state assistance.[38]

A final issue of no lesser importance and also worth referring to is the way the regime has dealt with the Islamist movement. Even during the worst years of violence and the regime's hard-line stance towards armed groups, some Islamist organizations were not banned, nor prevented from participating in mainstream politics, once the political process resumed through the holding of elections. Furthermore, the initiation of successive reconciliatory measures—already touched on before—to end the cycle of violence has paid dividends. It is therefore not surprising that one of the most obvious features of this is the appeasement of militant Islamism. At this point it is quite safe to assert that the Algerian regime has now restored much greater control over the political sphere at a time when radical Islamism seems to have lost most of its fervor and more and more militants are less reluctant to work within the system. With security and stability having considerably improved, it remains to be seen how these changes will impinge on Algeria's future political development, and particularly its transition to democratic governance. Certainly, the progress made towards a more stable political environment would normally enable Algeria to focus on much-needed economic reforms.

Facets of Economic Liberalization

In the economic sphere, some reforms were introduced during the early years of the 1980s. These reforms were neither sufficiently substantive nor wide ranging by market economy standards. In spite of that, they denoted the beginning of a reversal or, more accurately, a change of direction as regards economic policy. As the public sector started to face growing problems and levels of public investment could no longer be sustained, it became clear for the decision makers that a different vision of the conduct of the country's economic affairs needed to be considered. The new leadership, after the death of Houari Boumedienne, having spelled out the shortcomings of the previous strategy of economic and social development, embarked on a restructuring process which targeted public enterprises and the state agricultural sector in particular. This amounted to reducing these companies' size to small, functional enterprises and enhancing their autonomy and financial responsibility. The ultimate aim was to remedy these enterprises' poor performance—particularly their accumulated losses—by enabling them to operate on different norms and to improve their efficiency as a result. The state farming sector, made up of self-managed farms and agrarian reform production cooperatives, was also reorganized into large units.[39]

However, this initial phase of economic restructuring seemed to have had no major impact on the performance and direction of the country's economy, as demonstrated by the mid-1980s slump in oil prices.[40] This made plain not only the heavy dependence of the Algerian economy on hydrocarbon exports, but also its vulnerability to fluctuating oil prices. As the country's socioeconomic situation deteriorated subsequently—for instance, GDP per capita declined from $2,752 in 1987 to $1,607 in 1991—the authorities, coinciding with the premiership of Mouloud Hamrouche, had no alternative but to initiate a series of "self-imposed" reform measures in the late 1980s.[41] This led an observer to remark that "Economic policy set in motion a radical change of the society ... Algeria could have made an unprecedented achievement; it would have been the first emergent country to undertake a policy of adjustment without the assistance of the IMF."[42] Although these measures marked the first genuine attempt at liberalizing the economy, their implementation was to be delayed, if not hampered, by the political crisis, which emerged in the early years of the 1990s.

Governmental instability during these years had not favored the formulation and adoption of a clear plan of economic reforms. As a matter of fact, the rapid change of governments, along with the different visions held by these governments as to the conduct of the country's economic policy, made any reform program rather unsustainable. Prime Minister Sid Ahmed Ghozali's market-oriented "recovery program" of February 1992 was called into question after Belaid Abdessalem was appointed to the premiership in July of the same year. Belaid's opposition to free market reforms and debt rescheduling did not make things better, as the economy continued to deteriorate. He was dismissed in August 1993. His successor, Rédha Malek, advocated economic liberalization, and it was under his government that Algeria applied for debt relief to the International Monetary Fund (IMF). The depression of oil prices put the country's economy into the grip of a severe financial crisis. Debt-servicing reached more than $9bn—representing about three-fourths of the value of exported goods and services in 1993. By rescheduling its external debt, Algeria committed itself to undertaking comprehensive economic reforms, this time under the auspices of the IMF. A stand-by agreement was concluded with this organization in April 1994. Other arrangements with the Paris and London Clubs enabled Algeria to reschedule a significant part of its commercially held foreign debt. The IMF, under its extended fund facility, agreed to a $1.8bn structural reform credit for a three-year period (1995–98).[43]

Consisting of a combination of macro-economic stabilization and medium-term structural adjustment measures introduced from 1994, the program of reforms sought to achieve the following aims: restore sustainable economic growth and reduce unemployment, bring inflation down to reasonable levels, improve the balance of payments situation, and attenuate the impact of the reforms on the most vulnerable sections of the society.[44]

In its early assessment of the four-year phase (1994–98) of stabilization and structural adjustment, the IMF considered that "despite the fact that the reform program was launched ... in a difficult social and political environment, it has been remarkably successful in restoring financial stability and establishing the building blocks for a market economy."[45] During a visit to Algeria in March 2005, the IMF Managing Director, Rodrigo de Rato, remarked that "Algeria has made progress over the past decade in moving from a state-controlled to an open, market-based economy. Remarkable success has been achieved in restoring macroeconomic stability, and progress has been made in liberalizing foreign trade and increasing economic growth."[46]

The reform agenda that Algeria embarked upon has undeniably enabled the country to accomplish some progress in its move towards a market economy (see some indicators in Table 2.1). At the same time, this transitional phase is revealing a number of challenges, either still not seriously addressed or prompted by the reform process itself. The economy has shown signs of an improved response of inflation to monetary policy. Estimated at 39 percent in 1994, inflation fell to around 3.1 percent in 2005, suggesting that it is now under control.[47]

To facilitate their transition to a market-based environment, public enterprises have been the target of a number of restructuring measures. This resulted in the liquidation of many loss-making and non-viable local public enterprises, including state-owned large importing and distribution agencies, while some of these companies simply had their assets transferred to employees. On the other hand, the privatization of the largest publicly owned enterprises, a key element in the reform agenda, has not been a success story.[48] Only a handful of more or less important transactions have hitherto taken place.[49] The revamping of the legal and institutional framework in 2001 has had no decisive impact on moving the privatization plan ahead both steadily and quickly. Not only fluctuating government policy

Table 2.1 Selected Economic Indicators

	1994	1998	2000	2002	2004	2005
GDP ($bn)	42.4	48.2	54.4	56.9	84.8	102.8
GDP growth rate (%)	−0.7	5.1	2.4	4.1	5.2	5.3
GDP per head ($)	1,542	1,633	1,790	1,816	2,621	3,109
Imports ($bn)	9.15	8.63	9.35	12.01	17.95	19.50
Exports ($bn)	8.89	10.14	21.65	18.71	32.22	46.38
of which						
Hydrocarbons	8.61	9.77	21.06	18.11	31.55	45.59
Foreign debt ($bn)	29.5	30.5	25.3	22.7	21.8	17.19
Debt service/exports (%)	47.1	47.5	19.8	21.7	12.6	8.0

Sources: Ministère des Finances (Algeria), *Principaux indicateurs de l'économie algérienne*, available at: http://www.finances-algeria.org/dgep/a5.htm; Banque d'Algérie, *Evolution de la dette extérieure de l'Algérie*, available at: http://www.bank-of-algeria.dz/docs2.htm; Banque d'Algérie, *Statistiques monétaires 1965–2005 et statistiques de la balance des paiements 1962–2005*, available at: http://www.bank-of-algeria.dz/statistiquesmonetaires.pdf; IMF, Algeria — Staff Report for the 2005 Article IV Consultation, available at: http://www.imf.org/external/pubs/ft/scr/2006/cr0693.pdf.

priorities, but also resistance on the part of some stakeholders—particularly the bureaucracy and the trade unions—are to blame for the lack of effective impetus behind the process. In spite of that, the government has repeatedly stated its determination to privatize practically all public enterprises. Abdelhamid Temmar, minister in charge of participation and promotion of investments (minister of privatization for others), remarked that "privatization is the best formula for some 1,230 enterprises."[50] Moving privatization beyond the point of stated intentions calls for a coherent policy that takes on board both the particulars of the process and its overall aims and implications within the broader economic reform agenda. For instance, making privatization conditional on maintaining employment and activity in the public enterprises may well act as a disincentive to would-be investors/bidders. The IMF, for its part, suggested the introduction of a safety net as an alternative to cushion against possible job losses.[51]

As for the banking sector, the 1990 law on money and credit for the first time allowed for the establishment of private banks.[52] Even by permitting the setting up of new private banks and the gradual entry of foreign banks into the domestic market, the sector has remained dominated by publicly owned banks, which still account for almost 93 percent of the Algerian financial system's assets.[53] Because of their accumulated sizable losses, stemming primarily from the provision of massive non-performing loans to the unprofitable public enterprises, various operations of *assainissement* (stabilization) have been undertaken. Consequently, the banks saw a large influx of liquidity as the government implemented recapitalization and debt takeover measures at a cost of $30bn.[54]

It was expected that the presence of private banks would help boost competition and so improve the public banks' financial performance.

Nevertheless, the collapse in 2003 of two private banks—Khalifa Bank and Banque Commerciale et Industrielle d'Algérie—has seriously damaged the public image of and confidence in the private-sector banks.[55] While it will take some time for this sector to regain credibility, new legislation was introduced in 2003 to ensure strict bank licensing and rigorous supervision of their activities by the Bank of Algeria.[56] Yet one should mention that, in actual fact, this mission of control is far from being properly carried out, as demonstrated by some of the latest financial scandals in the public-sector banks.[57]

The government is now in the process of opening up the capital of three publicly owned banks—Banque Nationale d'Algérie, Banque de Développement Local, and Crédit Populaire d'Algérie—to private-sector participation.[58] If it does materialize, this gradual approach could pave the way for a greater role for this sector in the banking system.[59] For the time being, it seems that the authorities are more intent on pursuing the IMF analysts' recommendation to quickly sell one healthy public bank to a reputable foreign one.[60] In the same way, the modernization of the banking sector is equally a high priority on the government's agenda.[61] This sector's role and capacity in financing investment and growth will depend on the improvement of its operational capacity, of which privatization is certainly a key ingredient. Promoting this industry and its fair distribution of credit is vital if one considers the excess of liquidity—about $10bn in 2005—in public banks.[62]

In relation to the external financial position, improvement in the country's stock of foreign exchange reserves and foreign debt is clearly perceptible. In 2003, these reserves stood at $32.9bn, and reached an unparalleled level of about $80bn at the end of December 2006.[63] This is mainly due to the favorable international market prices for oil since 2005. Also Algeria seems to have managed its debt burden efficiently. In 1994, the total external debt was around $29.5bn, corresponding to just about 70 percent of the country's GDP.[64] Surely, the rescheduling of the debt under the stabilization and adjustment programs did provide some breathing space, but more importantly, it was the contribution of other factors—such as the availability of foreign exchange reserves and the recent government decision to anticipate the repayment of some of the outstanding debt—that made it possible to reduce the debt levels, leading to the reclassification of Algeria from severely indebted to less indebted.[65] As a corollary, the debt service or ratio, which was more than 47 percent at the end of 1994, dropped to less than 10 percent in 2005.[66] The latest official figures for 2006 show that the total foreign debt has decreased from $15.5bn to about $4.7bn, indicating the country's enhanced debt-management control.[67]

Besides dealing with the domestic economic and social issues, Algeria's program of reforms is also faced with the challenge of managing opening up to the global economy. Substantial progress has so far been made in reforming the country's external trade regime, with a commitment to press ahead with regional and multilateral trade liberalization. Within the framework of the Euro-Mediterranean Partnership, launched in Barcelona in 1995, Algeria concluded an association agreement with the EU in April 2002. Entered into effect in September 2005, the agreement has, as its core component, the gradual phasing in of a free trade area between the two parties over a 12-year period.[68] This new phase in the relationship would amount to Algeria unilaterally liberalizing its trade *vis-à-vis* the EU by progressively removing all tariff and non-tariff barriers to goods imported from Europe. At the multilateral level, negotiations to join the World Trade Organization (WTO) are believed to be, at the present time, at an advanced stage.[69] Nevertheless, the most recent round in October 2005 was, in a way, a missed opportunity since nothing of substance was achieved. According to *Le Quotidien d'Oran*, influential members of the organization—especially the EU and the US—still seem not entirely satisfied with the efforts Algeria has made at opening its market and bringing its legislation in line with the WTO rules.[70] The tenth round has yet to take place, having been postponed on a number of occasions during 2006.

The external trade liberalization, to be triggered by the association arrangement with the EU and membership of the WTO, is indeed a major step towards integration into the world economy. It is, however, the case that the potential impact of this opening up on the Algerian economy has still not been rigorously investigated. A range of studies conducted on individual and/or groups of developing countries has come up with different conclusions as to the potential benefits and costs stemming from trade liberalization. To the extent that Algeria is concerned, it is inevitable that this liberalization will cause disruption to its economy, at least in the near future. The sectors likely to be affected the most are in industry. At an early stage, this will be felt in terms of labor force displacement. About 50,000 jobs will be lost as a result of the implementation of the association agreement with the EU, as confirmed by El-Hachemi Djaaboub, Minister of Commerce.[71] But the minister remains positive as to the numerous jobs that will be generated by this agreement as a result of new investments, especially from the European partners.[72]

By and large, more than a decade after the introduction of the World Bank and IMF-sponsored reforms, the case is still not one of a strong and prolonged economic recovery. The record of these reforms on growth has been mixed. Economic growth, measured in real GDP increase, shows that the average annual growth rate had not exceeded 2.7 percent over the period 1994–98, and even remained within the region of 2.6 percent during the succeeding three years of the post-adjustment era (1999–2001).[73] From 2002, nevertheless, Algeria started to experience improved rates of growth: 4.1 percent (2002), 6.8 percent (2003), 5.2 percent (2004), and 5.3 percent (2005).[74] Yet it remains to be seen whether these good years of recorded growth can be sustained, given the prevailing structural nature of the economy. Even though the agricultural, construction, and services sectors registered some good performance during the years in question, the contribution of the hydrocarbon sector was—and will certainly be for some time to come—preponderant in the country's economy.

This sector has witnessed a phase of increasing liberalization, which started since the mid-1980s. However, the liberalization trend has, to some extent, been reversed following a recent revision of the 2005 legislation.[75] The amendments endorsed give Sonatrach, the state-owned oil company, at least a 51 percent stake in future oil and gas ventures concluded with foreign companies.[76] There is also a case for imposing a windfall tax, ranging from 5 to 50 percent, on these companies' profits when the monthly average of Brent crude prices exceeds $30 a barrel, something that could earn Algeria $500m to $600m in 2006 and about $1bn in 2007.[77] At this juncture, it seems less likely that these amendments could cause too much concern amongst foreign oil firms operating in Algeria and thus prove detrimental to Algeria's hydrocarbon sector. For instance, recent reports about Anadarko's plans to divest its operations in Algeria have been denied; and the company has confirmed its intention to continue doing business in the country.[78] Also the foreign firms are cognizant of the need to adjust to these changes as they echo the growing trend of resource nationalism among producer countries.[79]

On the whole, it is important to note that the recorded growth performance mentioned above coincided with the 2001–4 economic recovery plan (PSRE), which the government embarked on in the second half of 2001.[80] This $7bn plan of public investment was intended to provide a stimulus for economic growth.[81] From the authorities' perspective, the PSRE's ultimate goal was "to attenuate the negative effects of a deep crisis and create the conditions propitious for a genuine long-lasting development strategy."[82] That being so, a more ambitious follow-up five-year program (PCSRE), with an initial allocation of $55bn, was launched in 2005 to give a stronger boost to the economy and alleviate more of the current social problems.[83] For instance, more than about 45 percent of this financial package is aimed at improving the living conditions of the population in areas such as housing, health, education and vocational training, and water.

The Welfare Impact

It is evident that the structural reforms Algeria has gone through within the context of the stabilization and structural adjustment programs have and may still continue to have social costs, particularly affecting the lower-income population groups. The economic restructuring, notably its main process of privatization–liquidation of public-sector enterprises, has resulted in considerable numbers of layoffs. For instance, between 1995 and 1997 more than 400,000 workers lost their jobs and 400 firms were liquidated.[84] With the public sector's low capacity for generating jobs becoming a reality, this has contributed to the contraction of the domestic labor market, with its upshot of a rise in the proportion of unemployed population. In addition, first-time job seekers entering the labor market have been on the increase, something that has, to a large extent, played a part in the aggravation of the unemployment problem. Over the period 1990–2003, the average annual growth rate of the labor force was almost 4 percent.[85]

As indicated by a government official, the unemployment rate was in the region of 30 percent in 1999.[86] A figure of this scale is to blame for the deterioration in living conditions, with poverty becoming a salient feature in society, mainly in rural areas—the rural population represented 41 percent of the total population in 2003.[87] Furthermore, one should not lose sight of the fact that the abolition of subsidies, the devaluation of the local currency, and the state's deficit in the provision of public services have also been amongst the causes that severely affected the purchasing power of large sections of the population, including the middle class (today, there are many in Algeria who would argue that the middle class is in decline and, in many cases, is not doing better than poor families).[88] This partly explains the migration in the period 1992–96 of close to 0.5 million highly educated Algerians to Europe and North America.[89] A recent report by the Algerian-based National Centre for Study and Analysis of Population and Development (CENEAP) claims that the proportion of the population living on $1 a day fell from 12.1 percent in 2000 to 5.7 percent in 2005.[90] However, this downward tendency in the ratio of poor population "remains transitory because of the fragile social and economic conditions and the vulnerability of certain households," the report reveals.

It is quite apparent that the implementation of the PRSE has led to some progress in social conditions. As well as helping fuel the fairly solid economic growth recorded over the last years, this plan of public expenditure also induced an upturn in terms of job generation. The latest estimates of the Office National des Statistiques put the unemployment rate at 12.3 percent in 2006, against 15.3 percent in 2005 and 17.7 percent in 2004.[91] The authorities consider that, because of increased social transfers and boosted incomes, the living conditions of the population have improved on the whole. Moreover, some 45.5 percent of the PCSRE financial package is to be devoted to raising living standards (health, education, water, housing, and so forth) in the period 2005–9. For the moment, social tensions remain a feature of Algerian life, and their persistence reflects the limited effect of government policy actions so far, including its economic recovery plan (PSRE). In their debate of the 2006 financial bill, deputies in the national assembly warned against possible social explosion, which they impute to "the blatant imbalance in the distribution of the country's wealth and in the marginalization of the society's less well-off groups who cannot manage to provide for the basic needs."[92]

The second phase in the government public investment program (PCSRE) is, therefore, faced with the great challenge of delivering public services together with promoting the conditions that underpin a real and sustained economic take-off. There is no doubt that tackling and lessening the many and varied problems experienced by large segments of the populace are of crucial importance to the country's social stability and cohesion.

Conclusion

Algeria is emerging from the chaotic situation that it endured over the last decade. At the present time there is a new sense of stability in the country and a considerable relief within society that security has, in the main, been restored. Even though criticized by some human rights groups in particular, it is evident that the successive amnesty measures taken—Clemency (*Rahma*) Law, Civil Concord Law, and the Charter for Peace and National Reconciliation—have had an impact on reducing the level of a decade-long violence that left the country in deep crisis. The resumption of the electoral process has enabled the country to publicly reinstate legitimate institutions of government, albeit allegations of vote-rigging were made at an early stage.

However important the above issues may be for a smooth political transition, there are yet major challenges lying ahead. Reforming the state's institutions and strengthening their independence and prerogatives, and increasing the freedom of association and expression are all key ingredients for future democratic development.[93] Clearly, democracy is an evolutionary process that "is fundamentally shaped by the historical and cultural context out of which it emerges."[94] And it is these domestic factors which contribute to explaining how smooth or difficult a transition is. It remains to be seen whether the imminent constitutional reform, hailed "as an advanced and complementary stage in the process of reform and modernization of the state's structures,"[95] together with the holding of municipal and parliamentary elections in 2007, will represent a step further towards promoting institutions and practices of a democratic nature. To be sure, these coming political developments are likely to be significant in the sense that they will give an indication of the level of commitment to the democratic process as well as the direction the reform path is taking.

A related and parallel development in the country's return to stability is the undertaking being made to transform the country's economy. Certain progress has, indeed, been made in terms of market-based economic reforms, and present economic performance is quite encouraging. Obviously, this performance is very much the result of the energy sector and the favorable oil market conditions—for instance, this sector earned a total of almost $54bn in 2006.[96] Yet some measures of relatively good economic performance are projected to peter out. Not only may oil prices dip below their 2006 level, but there may be some slowing down in GDP growth rate as well—an expected slowdown in the economy to 3 percent in 2006 according to the latest World Bank estimate.[97] Hence, further commitment to speeding up the pace of market reforms remains necessary, including the privatization program and modernization of the financial sector, to raise economic growth and generate much-needed job opportunities for the unemployed, especially for the young people who are the most affected by this problem.[98] It is imperative that the current program of public investment (PCSRE) is soundly managed to allow the country to move away from a hydrocarbon-based economy. The oil windfall should be managed in a manner that is conducive to the development of the non-hydrocarbon sector, particularly by improving business conditions and giving a boost to private-sector-led growth. In this respect, there is a pressing need to tackle prevailing bureaucracy and corruption practices that are amongst the chief apprehensions of existing and prospective investors.[99] The year 2007 has witnessed a number of important trials for corruption and fraud, one of which is Algeria's biggest financial scandal ever, involving the former Khalifa Group.

In short, it is in Algeria's interest to make up for the lost time as it is attempting to move further down the path of political and economic reforms. The process of sustaining and deepening these reforms entails a credible policy to which the government must pledge itself. Meanwhile, the availability of financial resources would make it easier to address some of the challenging social problems and, in so doing, could secure broader social adherence to and support for the reform policies.

Notes

1 For a more recent account on this issue see Yahia H. Zoubir, "The Dialectics of Algeria's Foreign Policy, 1992 to the Present," in Ahmed Aghrout and R. M. Bougherira (eds), *Algeria in Transition: Reforms and Development Prospects*, London and New York: RoutledgeCurzon, 2004, pp. 151–82; "The resurgence of Algeria's foreign policy in the twenty-first century," *The Journal of North African Studies*, vol. 9, no. 2, summer 2004, pp. 169–83.

2 A good assessment of Bouteflika's first presidential term in office is provided by Robert Mortimer, "Bouteflika and the Challenge of Political Stability," in Aghrout (ed.), *Algeria in Transition*, pp. 183–98.

3 For further details on these problems, see Keith Sutton, Ahmed Aghrout, and Salah Zaimeche, "Political Changes in Algeria: An Emerging Electoral Geography," *The Maghreb Review*, vol. 17, no. 1–2, 1992, p. 5.

4 A law passed on 5 July 1989 laid down the rules by which these political organizations or parties could be officially legalized.

5 Sutton, Aghrout, and Zaimeche, "Political Changes," p. 7.

6 The most recent official figures estimate the loss of life to be 150,000.

7 Zoubir, "State and Civil Society in Algeria," in Yahia H. Zoubir (ed.), *North Africa in Transition: State, Society, and Economic Transformation in the 1990s*, Gainesville, FL: University Press of Florida, 1998, p. 39.

8 Amongst the proposals made in this platform was the call for the respect of a multiparty system, the resumption of the political process through free and pluralist elections, and the rehabilitation of the banned FIS; for further details about this platform, see Robert Mortimer, "Islamists, Soldiers, and Democrats: The Second Algerian War," *Middle East Journal*, vol. 50, no. 1, winter 1996, pp. 35–8.

9 Marco Impagliazzo, *The St Egidio Platform for a Peaceful Solution of the Algerian Crisis.* Available at: http://www.usip.org/pubs/peaceworks/smock20/chap3_20.html.
10 Françoise Germain-Robin, "Pas de consensus à Alger." Available at: http://www.humanite.presse.fr/journal/1994-01-27/1994-01-27-693103.
11 The other candidates were the late Mahfoud Nahnah (25 percent), Said Saadi (10 percent), and Noureddine Boukrouh (3 percent).
12 William B. Quandt, "Algeria: How Pivotal Is It? And Why?" Available at: http://www.people.virginia.edu/~wbq8f/pivotal.html.
13 Phillip C. Naylor, *France and Algeria – A History of Decolonization and Transformation*, Gainesville, FL: University Press of Florida, 2000, p. 230.
14 The constitutional changes were mainly concerned with the institution of a bicameral legislature, provision for the revision of the legislation on political parties and elections, and redefinition and strengthening of presidential powers; see Robert Mortimer "Algeria: The Dialectic of Elections and Violence," *Current History*, vol. 96, no. 610, May 1997, p. 233.
15 General Mohamed Betchine, president's adviser, and Mohamed Adami, minister of justice, resigned following a media campaign against them.
16 Lucy Dean (ed.), *The Middle East and North Africa 2006 – Regional surveys of the world*, 52nd edn, London: Europa, 2005, p. 175.
17 Mortimer, "Bouteflika," p. 184.
18 Youcef Bouandel, "The presidential election in Algeria, April 1999," *Electoral Studies*, vol. 20, no. 1, 2001, p. 158.
19 At the presidential election in April 1999, Bouteflika's six rivals pulled out on the eve of polling day amid charges of widespread electoral fraud. Similarly, the 1997 legislative elections were also marred by fraud allegations.
20 Ahmed Aghrout, "The 2002 Algerian Parliamentary Elections: Results and Significance," in Ahmed Aghrout (ed.), *Algeria in Transition*, pp. 199–211.
21 Bruce George, representing a group of observers from the Organization for Security and Cooperation in Europe, was reported to have said "It was not a perfect election but by the standards of the region it was excellent," cited in *Keesing's Record of World Events*, vol. 50, no. 4, April 2004, p. 45983.
22 Some have claimed that this "neutrality" was meant to signal "implicit acquiescence for Bouteflika's re-election," see Azzedine Layachi, "Algeria's presidential election: a post mortem." Available at: http://www.dailystar.com.lb/article.asp?edition_id=10&categ_id=5&article_id=2108.
23 Hugh Roberts, "Political Issues and Developments in Algeria," written evidence submitted to the UK Parliament Select Committee on Foreign Affairs, 25 January 2005. Available at: http://www.parliament.the-stationery-office.co.uk/pa/cm200405/cmselect/cmfaff/36/5020105.htm.
24 Major-General Salah Ahmed Gaid was appointed as army chief of staff, replacing Lt-General Mohamed Lamari who, according to some commentators, "retired for political reasons and noted recent differences with Abdelaziz Bouteflika," *Keesing's Record of World Events*, vol. 50, no. 7–8, July 2004, pp. 46181–2.
25 Law 99-08 of July 1999. This was followed by a presidential decree in January 2000, called *grâce aministiante*, which exempted militants of two armed groups from prosecution following their agreement to lay down their arms and disband.
26 About 5,500 militants were believed to have taken advantage of the "Civil Concord Law," according to official authorities cited by Human Rights Watch. Available at: http://hrw.org/backgrounder/mena/algeria0905/2.htm#_ftnref11. For details, see, Yahia H. Zoubir and Louisa Aït-Hamadouche, "Between Democratization and Counter-Terrorism: Penal Reform in Algeria," in Chris Ferguson and Jeffrey O. Isima (eds), *Providing Security for People: Enhancing*

Security through Police, Justice, and Intelligence Reform in Africa, Swindon, UK: Global Facilitation Network for Security Sector Reform, 2004, pp. 75–84.

27 Service du Chef du Gouvernement (Algeria), *Accord pour la mise en œuvre de la plateforme d'El-Kseur*, 15 January 2005. Available at: http://www.cg.gov.dz/ actualites.htm.

28 President Bouteflika was reported to have opposed this demand, arguing that "There is no country where two official languages exist. Arabic is the official national language. This does not prevent us from learning the Amazigh language with its dialects: Kabyle, Targui, Mozabite and Oranian," see *El-Watan* (Algerian daily), 24 September 2005. Bouteflika overlooked the fact that Switzerland has four official languages and Belgium two.

29 *La Tribune* (Algerian daily), 3 October 2005.

30 See *Projet de la Charte pour la Paix et la Réconciliation Nationale* for a more detailed explanation of the measures and their underlying principle.

31 Fayçal Oukaci, "Le référendum sur la Charte pour la Paix et la Réconciliation Nationale – Les opposants, qui sont-ils? Que veulent-ils?" *L'Expression* (Algerian daily), 29 September 2005, p. 2.

32 Hocine Aït Ahmed, the leader of the *Front des Forces Socialistes*, was reported to have branded this charter as "new aggression against the Algerian society and whose aim is nothing than to pave the way for a constitutional revision to allow Abdelaziz Bouteflika a third mandate," quoted in *Liberté* (Algerian daily), 22 September 2005.

33 *The Estimate*, Political and Security Intelligence Analysis of the Islamic World and its Neighbors, vol. 11, no. 14, 2 July 1999.

34 The commission was a temporary body operating within the existing institutional framework, that is the Commission Nationale Consultative de Promotion et de Protection des Droits de l'Homme set up in March 2001.

35 Reported by *Le Quotidien d'Oran* (Algerian daily), 26 September 2005.

36 Presidential Decree no. 06-93 (28 February 2006) relating to compensation of victims of the national tragedy.

37 Cited in *L'Expression*, 23 September 2006.

38 Presidential Decree no. 06-94 (28 February 2006) concerning state aid to needy families affected by the involvement of their relatives in terrorism.

39 These units were called *Domaines Agricoles Socialistes*.

40 Michael Hodd, "Algeria: Economic Structure, Performance and Policy, 1950–2001," in Ahmed Aghrout (ed.), *Algeria in Transition*, pp. 35–57.

41 The series of legislative measures adopted were concerned with, amongst other things, the ending of state monopoly over external trade, liberalization of prices, granting autonomy to public enterprises, and subjecting them to market-place discipline, establishing the independence of the central bank and opening the financial sector to private investment.

42 Omar Akala, "L'économie algérienne, de l'ère des réformes (1989–1991) à celle de l'adjustement structurel (1994–1998)," in Ahmed Mahiou and Jean-Robert Henry (eds), *Où va l'Algérie*, Paris: Editions Karthala, 2001, p. 166.

43 IMF, "IMF Approves Credit under Extended Fund Facility for Algeria," *Press Release*, 95/31, 22 May 1995.

44 For more details on the policy measures adopted to achieve the reform program targets, see for instance Abdelouahab Keramane, "Algeria: Present Economic Situation and Prospects," *Euro-Mediterranean Partnership*, no. 2, 1997, p. 27; Karim Nashashibi, Patricia Alonso-Gamo, Stefania Bazzoni, Alain Feler, Nicole Laframboise, and Sebastian Paris Horvitz, "Algeria: Stabilization and Transition to the Market," IMF Occasional Paper no. 165, IMF, Washington DC, 6 August 1998; and Brahim Guendouzi and Khelifa Kadri, "Les retombées de l'adjustement

structurel sur le développement local en Algérie," *Les Cahiers du Cread*, no. 46–7, 1998, pp. 135–52.

45 Martha Bonilla, "Algeria's Reform Program Promotes Economic Growth and Transition to the Market," *IMF Survey*, vol. 27, no. 17, 31 August 1998, p. 277.

46 Statement quoted in *Press Release*, 05/49, 2 March 2005.

47 Banque d'Algérie, *Tendances monétaires et financières au premier semester 2005*. Available at: http://www.bank-of-algeria.dz/notes2.htm; see also IMF, "Statement by IMF Mission in Algeria," *Press Release*, 05/233, 19 October 2005.

48 A review of the privatization process can be found in Ahmed Aghrout, Mohamed Bouhezza and Khaled Sadaoui, "Restructuring and Privatization in Algeria," in Ahmed Aghrout (ed.), *Algeria in Transition*, pp. 120–35.

49 These transactions included, amongst other things, the opening up of the capital of three public sector enterprises (Eriad in the agro-food, Saidal in the pharmaceuticals, and the El-Aurassi Hotel) on the Algiers Stock Exchange and the establishment of joint ventures with foreign companies in the areas of the steel industry, chemicals, and telecommunications.

50 Cited in *El-Moudjahid* (Algerian daily), 11 October 2005.

51 IMF, Algeria: Staff Report for the 2004 Article IV Consultation, *IMF Country Report*, 05/50, February 2005, p. 21.

52 See Law 90-10 of 14 April 1990 on Money and Credit.

53 Speech by Mohamed Laksaci, governor of the Bank of Algeria, delivered to the *Assemblée Populaire Nationale* (parliament) on 24 October 2004. Available at: http://www.bank-of-algeria.dz/communicat.htm.

54 Figure given by the governor of the Bank of Algeria; cited in *Liberté*, 19 October 2005.

55 The banks were accused of fraud and money laundering and the authorities decided to withdraw their licenses to operate and put them into administrative receivership. For instance, the collapse of Khalifa Bank is believed to have caused the Algerian government a loss of $1.5bn; see Farid Alilat, "Où sont passés les milliards?" Available at: http://www.jeuneafrique.com/jeune_afrique/article_jeune_afrique.asp?art_cle=LIN04125osontsdrail0.

56 Ordinance 03-11 of 26 August 2003.

57 Salima Tlemçani, "La BNA au centre d'un grand scandale: Un préjudice estimé à 15 milliards de DA," *El-Watan*, 29 October 2005; "Etablissements bancaires: La tirelire des scandales à répétition," *El-Watan*, 7 November 2005; "Procès du détournement des 12 milliards de dinars de la BADR," *El-Watan*, 23 September 2006; Farid Alilat, "Où sont passés les milliards?" *El-Watan*, 23 September 2006; Ahcene Aribi, the Islah deputy, was reported to have said that $12bn have illegally been transferred, see *La Nouvelle République* (Algerian daily), 15 November 2005.

58 *El-Khabar Weekly* (Algerian newspaper), 12–18 February 2005; *El-Watan*, 5 September 2005; *Liberté*, 7 November 2005.

59 BNP Paribas, Société Générale, Natexis Banque, Crédit Lyonnais, Crédit Agricole Indosuez, Crédit Industriel et commercial, and HSBC are believed to be interested in the Crédit Populaire d'Algérie, *La Tribune*, 23 October 2006; "L'overture du capital du CPA est fixée pour le premier semestre 2007," *Le Soir d'Algérie* (Algerian daily), 6 November 2006.

60 For the IMF analyst, this "would be important for its demonstration effect, including by transferring know-how to the sector, and would help contain the cost of restructuring other public banks"; see Jules J. De Vrijer, "New Roles for Banks in Algeria." Available at: http://www.imf.org/external/np/speeches/2005/020305.htm.

61 The President himself was reported to have said that "I expect the banks' managers to speed up banking reforms in order to provide our economy with a

framework that is favorable to growth and investment ... For this reason, the delay in the banking reforms is not tolerated any more." See Presidency website (Algeria) at: http://www.elmouradia.dz/francais/president/activites/PresidentActi.htm.

62 President Abdelaziz Bouteflika mentioned this figure in his speech delivered on 7 April 2005; see *El-Watan*, 9 April 2005.

63 The recent figure was quoted in *Liberté*, 25 January 2007.

64 Banque d'Algérie, *Evolution de la dette extérieure de l'Algérie 1994–2004*. Available at: http://www.bank-of-algeria.dz/docs2.htm.

65 World Bank, *World Development Indicators 2005*, Washington DC: World Bank, 2005.

66 *Liberté*, 28 October 2005.

67 *La Tribune*, 28 December 2006.

68 The agreement covers political and security; economic and financial; and social, cultural, and human dimensions. Yet it is the economic and the financial dimension that is central to the whole association agreement; see Ahmed Aghrout, *From Preferential Status to Partnership – The Euro-Maghreb Relationship*, Aldershot: Ashgate Publishing Limited, 2000; "The EU–Algeria Partnership Agreement: A Preliminary Assessment," *ESRI Working Paper*, University of Salford (UK), 31 July 2005.

69 Algeria applied to join the WTO on 3 June 1987 and a working party entrusted with the negotiations was set up two weeks later. Its first meeting took place in April 1998.

70 *Le Quotidien d'Oran*, 26 October 2005.

71 Quoted in *El-Watan*, 11 October 2005.

72 On the issue of foreign investment, see Ahmed Aghrout and Michael Hodd, "FDI in North Africa: A Comparative Perspective," in Sima Motamen-Samadian (ed.), *Capital Flows and Foreign Direct Investments in Emerging Markets*, London: Palgrave Macmillan, 2005, pp. 115–32.

73 Ministère des Finances, *Principaux indicateurs de l'économie algérienne*. Available at: http://www.finances-algeria.org/dgep/a31.htm; World Bank, *Algeria Data Profile*. Available at: http://devdata.worldbank.org/external/CPProfile.asp?PTYPE= CP&CCODE=DZA.

74 *Ibid.*

75 See the Hydrocarbons Law no. 05-07 of 28 April 2005. Amongst its aims are: establishing competition in a free market; establishing transparency in contract awards; improving environmental standards; providing a clear, simple and competitive fiscal regime and contractual conditions; separating the government's regulatory role in order to enable Sonatrach to focus on its commercial role; liberalizing price controls. Its scope covers all upstream and downstream activities (except natural gas distribution, being governed by different legislation), becoming open to all investors, private or public, and national or international. This law was published in the *Journal Officiel de la République Algérienne* (*JORA*), no. 50, 19 July 2005. For more details about the amendments made to it, see the Presidential Ordinance no. 06-10 of 29 July 2006, published in the *JORA*, no. 48, 30 July 2006.

76 The above-mentioned law proposes an optional right of 20 to 30 percent only.

77 Figures cited by Chakib Khelil, energy and mines minister, in a statement given in a meeting with foreign oil companies representatives; see "Les amendements à la loi sur les hydrocarbures expliqués aux partenaires de Sonatrach," *El-Moudjahid*, 23 November 2006; "Chakib Khelil rencontre les compagnies pétrolières – La taxe sur les superprofits n'est pas une injustice," *El-Watan*, 23 November 2006.

78 "We won't sell our assets in Algeria. We stay here and we hope for a good future in your country," David Holmes, vice president for international operations of

Anadarko, was reported to have said; see *United Press International* at: http://www.upi.com/Energy/view.php?StoryID=20061122-071026-6202r; "Anadarko ne quittera pas l'Algérie," *La Tribune*, 23 November 2006.

79 This resource nationalism gathered pace in Latin America (Bolivia and Venezuela), and now includes Russia, Algeria, and Chad.

80 The *Programme de Soutien à la Relance Economique* (PSRE) was aimed at favoring spending on modernizing infrastructure and services, restructuring of public enterprises, developing human capital, and improving living conditions.

81 For a detailed account on the impact of this program, see *Bilan du Programme de Soutien de la Relance Économique*. Available at: http://www.cg.gov.dz/psre/bilan-psre.htm.

82 *El-Watan*, 11 April 2005.

83 The current financial package earmarked for the *Programme Complémentaire de Soutien à la Croissance Economique* is estimated to be around $114bn according to the World Bank.

84 The Permanent Mission of Algeria to the United Nations, *Mémorandum sur les Réformes en Algérie*. Available at: http://www.algeria-un.org/reformf.asp.

85 World Bank, *World Development Indicators 2005*. Available at: http://www.worldbank.org/data/wdi2005/wditext/Section2.htm.

86 See statement made by Djamel Ould-Abbes, minister in charge of national solidarity and employment, during the first meeting of the National Observatory for Employment and Fight against Poverty on 28 February 2005; cited in *Le Soir d'Algérie*, 1 March 2005.

87 World Bank, "New Business Plan for Algeria to Focus on Fighting Poverty, Supporting Reform Program," *News Release*, no. 2003/417/MENA, 12 June 2003; "World Bank Loan to Fight Poverty in Rural Algeria With Job Creation," *News Release*, no. 2003/314/MENA, 29 April 2003; *World Development Indicators 2005*. Available at: http://www.worldbank.org/data/wdi2005/wditext/Section3.htm.

88 Some studies have focused on the link between poverty and displacement effects of the violence, see Meredeth Turshen, "Armed Violence and Poverty in Algeria," Centre for International Cooperation and Security, University of Bradford (UK), November 2004. Available at: http://www.brad.ac.uk/acad/cics/projects/avpi_Algeria.pdf.

89 See, Mourad Saouli, "Algérie: Fuite des cerveaux," *Arabies*, October 2003.

90 This report was produced with the support of the United Nations Development Programme; see the survey entitled "Niveau de vie et mesure de la pauvreté en Algérie." Available at: http://www.ceneap.com.dz/HPage3.htm.

91 Figures quoted in *Liberté*, 24 January 2007. The government claims that the PSRE generated 728,666 new jobs between September 2001 and December 2003; see *Bilan du Programme de Soutien de la Relance Économique.*

92 "Les députés mettent en garde contre une explosion sociale," *Le Jeune Indépendant* (Algerian daily), 10 November 2005; see also *Horizons* (Algerian daily), 10 November 2005.

93 For an early discussion about the prospects for democratic transition in Algeria, see Ahmed Aghrout, "The 2002 Algerian Parliamentary Elections ... ," in Aghrout (ed.), *Algeria in Transition*, pp. 207–9.

94 Rex Brynen, Bahgat Korany, and Paul Noble (eds), *Political Liberalization and Democratization in the Arab World: Theoretical Perspectives*, Boulder, CO: Lynne Rienner Publishers, 1995, p. 4.

95 *Le Quotidien d'Oran*, 28 December 2006.

96 Figure given by Chakib Khelil; quoted in *Gulf Times* (Qatar). Available at: http://www.gulf-times.com/site/topics/article.asp?cu_no=2&item_no=128823&version=1&template_id=48&parent_id=28.

97 World Bank, *Global Economic Prospects 2007: Managing the Next Wave of Globalization*, Washington DC: World Bank, 2007, p. 175.

98 About 70.1 percent of the unemployed were aged less than 30 years in 2006, according to the *Office National des Statistiques* (Algeria); quoted in *Liberté*, 24 January 2007.

99 For an account about the issue of corruption In Algeria, see Transparency International, *Global Corruption Report 2006*. Available at: http://www.transparency.org/publications/gcr/download_gcr#download.

3 Libya

Reforming the Economy, not the Polity

Ronald Bruce St John

The government of the Great Socialist People's Libyan Arab Jamahiriya, commonly known as Libya, underwent a remarkable transformation over the past decade. Once an international outcast, Libya re-established commercial and diplomatic relations with most nations of the world, including the United States. Domestically, it began to evolve from a socialist command economy to a Western-style free market system in which its citizens were increasingly expected to fend for themselves. Only the domestic political arena escaped meaningful change.

African Initiatives

In August 1998, a decade after the bombing of Pan Am flight 103 over Lockerbie, Scotland, the Libyan government accepted a joint American–British proposal to try two Libyan suspects in the case, Abdel Basset Ali Mohammed al-Megrahi and Al-Amin Khalifa Fhimah, in the Netherlands under Scottish law. Once the two suspects were remanded into UN custody in April 1999, the UN Security Council suspended the multilateral sanctions, in place since 1992. The United States government pursued a separate course of easing, but not suspending, the bilateral sanctions that had been in place since the late 1970s. In a minor concession, Washington permitted the sale of food and medical supplies to Libya, policies long advocated by farm-state lawmakers. The UN Security Council later reaffirmed in July 1999 that the multilateral sanctions would be lifted permanently only after Libya had complied with all outstanding Security Council demands.[1]

Responding immediately to the suspension of multilateral sanctions, Mu'ammar al-Qaddafi launched a series of fresh initiatives in Africa, designed to end Libya's economic and political isolation. At the July 1999 Organization of African Unity (OAU) summit in Algiers, he was feted as a long-lost brother by fellow African heads of state. In response, Qaddafi resurrected his vision for African unity, calling for the creation of a Pan-African Congress to boost political unity, together with an Integration Bank to accelerate implementation of a treaty for the Economic Community of Africa. He also invited African leaders to attend an extraordinary

OAU summit in Tripoli, timed to coincide with the thirtieth anniversary of his One September Revolution, to discuss a restructuring of the OAU charter to strengthen relations among member states.[2]

Prior to the Tripoli summit, Qaddafi called for the creation of a United States of Africa, pressing the idea in a meeting of OAU foreign ministers. While African heads of state later refused to endorse his call for a United States of Africa, they did issue a declaration at the end of the summit which called for a stronger OAU, together with the creation of a Pan-African parliament, African Monetary Union, and African Court of Justice. In conjunction with these regional initiatives, Libya also expanded bilateral ties with a number of African states and launched a series of diplomatic efforts to resolve disputes in the Congo, the Horn of Africa, Sierra Leone, and Sudan. This round of diplomatic initiatives, which yielded few practical results, signaled Qaddafi's intention to play a wider role in regional issues.[3]

In July 2002, the African Union (AU), a regional organization modeled after the European Union (EU), replaced the 35-year-old OAU. At the opening ceremonies, Qaddafi rejected preconditions on foreign aid, contradicting AU chairman and South African president Thabo Mbeki, who called for donor nations to steer aid and investment to countries demonstrating good governance. He later conceded to Mbeki's endorsement of the New Partnership for Africa's Development (NEPAD), a plan to promote democracy and good government in Africa in exchange for increased aid and investment from the developed world. President Mbeki disregarded Qaddafi's idea for a standing, continental army. Instead, the AU endorsed the presence of a standby force consisting of civilian and military contingents based in countries of origin. The African Union later deployed an observer mission to the troubled Darfur region of Sudan in mid-2004, and the Pan-African parliament met for the first time in September 2004. Qaddafi later criticized UN Secretary General Kofi Annan's call in February 2005 for the European Union and NATO to help end the humanitarian crisis in the Darfur region, arguing that the AU should increase its involvement to meet the challenge.[4]

Celebrating the third anniversary of the AU's formation, Qaddafi in July 2005 hosted the fifth ordinary session of the AU assembly. In a long opening address, he again stressed the importance of greater African unity, citing specific needs like a common defense system and a single monetary zone. Amid global calls to combat poverty in Africa, Qaddafi also counseled African nations to stop complaining, and called for the G8 nations to drop existing debts. AU leaders later asked their members to present a united front in their dealings with the developed world, exhorting the richer nations of the world to make good on promises to help Africa climb out of poverty. With banners at the summit proclaiming "The United States of Africa is the hope," Qaddafi also called for creation of a single African passport to facilitate movement on the continent.[5]

Qaddafi took the lead in establishing the Community of Sahel–Saharan States (COMESSA), linking poor African states with oil-rich Libya. The COMESSA project included the creation of the Eastern and Southern African Trade and Development Bank with 75 percent Libyan capital, as well as regional development initiatives like the upgrading of the Trans-Saharan Highway. The governments of Burkina-Faso, Chad, Libya, Mali, Niger, and Sudan were founding members, with the Central African Republic and Eritrea joining in 1999. COMESSA's membership later expanded to 20 states, representing more than half of the continent's population. Libya later joined the Common Market for Eastern and Southern Africa (COMESA) in mid-2005.[6]

Looking East and West

Qaddafi's renewed interest in Africa came at the expense of his long-standing focus on the Middle East, especially the Palestinian question. According to Libyan diplomats, the shift in focus was rooted in the failure of Arab states, including the Maghrebi neighbors, to support Libya in its clash with the United Kingdom and the United States over the Lockerbie issue. At the opening session of the OAU summit in Lusaka in July 2001, for example, Qaddafi concentrated on African issues, generally ignoring the Palestinian question and the *intifada* (uprising) in particular. Elsewhere, the Libyan leader occasionally referred to the Palestinian issue; however, his comments often blended ideology and indifference as he distanced himself from an issue that had dominated Libyan foreign policy for much of the previous three decades. At the fifth ordinary session of the AU assembly in May 2005, Qaddafi mocked the very concept of a Middle East:

> Colonialism divided Asia into the Middle East, Far East, and Near East, which have nothing to do with Africa. From now on, I hope no one will try to link North Africa to the Middle East, because this [is] a colonialist racist tag. Please excuse my language, but we normally refer to the Middle East as the "Dirty East."[7]

In North Africa, Qaddafi moved to revitalize the moribund Arab Maghreb Union (AMU), founded by Algeria, Libya, Mauritania, Morocco, and Tunisia in February 1989 to promote regional peace and prosperity. With the Lockerbie issue moving toward resolution, violence in Algeria diminishing, and a resolution of the Western Sahara question in the offering, the stage seemed set to reinvigorate the AMU, hamstrung by regional disputes since 1994. In May 1999, representatives from the five AMU member states agreed to hold the first AMU summit in five years before the end of the year. The Libyan representative also expressed interest in increasing the scope of the AMU, possibly integrating the newly formed COMESSA grouping.[8]

In mid-2000, Libyan leader Qaddafi and Tunisian President Zine Al-Abidine Ben Ali called for the North African summit, which did not meet in 1999, to be held as soon as possible. However, a variety of issues, including the conflict over Western Sahara and the domestic political situation in Algeria, combined to block meaningful progress. The AMU foreign ministers met in Algiers in January 2002, but once more failed to agree on a venue for the pending AMU summit. Informed observers at the time agreed progress on the issue was unlikely until Algeria and Morocco resolved the Western Sahara dispute. The AMU summit was again postponed in May 2005, when Morocco rejected an Algerian proposal to include the Western Sahara issue on the agenda.[9]

The Qaddafi regime also moved to expand Libyan ties with Asia. Chinese foreign minister Tang Jiaxuan paid an official visit to Libya in January 2001, concluding agreements on cultural and information cooperation; and Chinese president Jiang Zemin visited Libya in April 2002, the first visit to Libya by a Chinese head of state. In the course of his visit, the two states agreed to open Libya's oil sector to Chinese firms, as well as the signing of a $40m deal for a Chinese company to extend Libya's rail network. A high-level North Korean delegation also visited Libya in mid-2002, signing agreements covering scientific and technical cooperation, as well as investment promotion. Observers generally dismissed rumors that the visit included discussions related to missile sales, which was an issue that took on new meaning in the wake of Libya's December 2003 decision to renounce unconventional weapons, a decision North Korea later denounced.[10]

Return to Europe

In conjunction with its diplomatic overtures to Africa and Asia, the Qaddafi regime moved quickly to expand already extensive relations with several European states. Throughout the 1990s, the European Union attracted 85 percent of Libyan exports and generated 75 percent of Libyan imports. Germany, Italy, and Spain alone absorbed 80 percent of Libya's exports. Libyan imports were dominated by Germany and Italy, but the United Kingdom was also a significant exporter to Libya.[11]

Encouraged by Libyan initiatives, the EU in 1999 reassessed Libyan participation in the Euro-Mediterranean Partnership (EMP), a regional process inaugurated by the 1995 Barcelona Declaration. Libya was a first-time observer in April 1999 at the Euro-Med Conference, which aims to create a Euro-Med free trade area by 2010. However, the Qaddafi regime later proved reluctant to become overly active in the regional process, in part due to its desire to play the role of intermediary between Africa and Europe. EU officials in June 2005 announced they would work with Libya to stop the flow of illegal migrants transiting Libya on their way to Europe, again expressing the hope Libya might fully engage in the EMP. One month later, the European Commission gave €1m to support Libya in its fight against

HIV/AIDS. Libya currently enjoys the status of an observer country in the EMP but has delayed application for full membership. While Libya and the EU share common interests in areas like trade, immigration, health, and transport, to name only a few, Libya knows it can achieve much of what it wants from Europe without a total commitment to the Barcelona Process.[12]

With extensive trade and investment at stake, Italy was an early champion of Libyan rehabilitation. The Italian foreign minister met with Qaddafi just one day after the two Lockerbie suspects landed in the Netherlands; and the Italian prime minister completed a two-day visit to Libya at the end of the year. Since then, Italian relations with Libya have been a mix of old and new. Libya provides some 25 percent of Italy's total energy imports; and with activation of the "Green Stream" gas pipeline, its share will increase to 30 percent. The end to multilateral sanctions also invigorated bilateral economic ties that slowed but never ceased during the embargo years. Libya also continues to press Italy for the restitution for damages from the colonial era, as part of a broader Libyan policy of encouraging all African states to press for damages from their former colonial rulers. Most recently, the Qaddafi regime has pressed Italy to build a coastal road from Tunisia to Egypt in token reparation for its colonial past. Italy has agreed to fund the feasibility study for the project, but not construction of the road. The tide of illegal immigrants now flooding southern Europe, especially Italy, from Libya remains a subject of discussion.[13]

Like the Italians, the British government moved quickly to re-establish commercial and diplomatic relations with Libya. Once Libya had surrendered the two Lockerbie suspects, Britain agreed to restore full diplomatic relations as soon as Libya assumed responsibility for the 1984 murder of Yvonne Fletcher, a London policewoman. The Qaddafi regime soon responded, and the British ambassador to Libya took up his post in December 1999. British officials later opened a commercial fair in Tripoli in May 2000, the largest of its kind since the suspension of sanctions. The British also served as the key intermediary in the tripartite negotiations leading to Libya's renunciation of unconventional weapons in December 2003, and Prime Minister Tony Blair later visited Libya in March 2004.[14]

Diplomatic relations between France and Libya improved in the early 1990s, but France later supported the UN embargo in conjunction with its investigation into the 1989 bombing of UTA flight 772. A Paris court in March 1999 condemned *in absentia* six Libyans to life imprisonment for the attack, but did not raise the question of Qaddafi's personal responsibility. Hamstrung by legal proceedings, French interests initially struggled to exploit the global rehabilitation of Libya. The normalization of Franco-Libyan relations proceeded slowly after 2001, receiving a boost in early 2004 when Libya agreed to compensate the families of the victims of the UTA bombing. President Jacques Chirac visited Libya at the end of the year. Two months later, the French defense minister signed a letter of intent covering military cooperation and procurement with Libya.[15]

Libyan relations with Germany suffered initially from legal proceedings regarding the 1986 bomb attack on the La Belle discothèque in West Berlin. After a four-year trial, a German court in mid-November 2001 found four people guilty of planting the bomb that killed three people and injured 229 others. The judge said the court was convinced that Libya was largely responsible for the attack, but also stated that neither Qaddafi's role nor his responsibility in the attack had been proven. Libya long denied involvement in the attack, but in September 2004 it agreed to pay compensation to the victims. Already Libya's second largest trading partner after Italy, Germany's commercial interests in Libya increased with the end of the La Belle affair. In October 2004, Chancellor Gerhard Schroeder traveled to Libya, where he met with Qaddafi and visited a site operated by Wintershall, the oil arm of the chemical giant BASF. Active in Libya since 1958, Wintershall at the time accounted for some 10 percent of Libyan oil production, making it the country's third-largest oil producer. Chancellor Schroeder in May 2005 renewed an invitation for Qaddafi to visit Germany, but the visit was still pending when Angela Merkel replaced Schroeder in November 2005.[16]

The United States and the "War on Terror"

Once Libya had remanded the two suspects in the Lockerbie bombing, the United States revised its policy toward Libya. Ambassador Ronald E. Neumann, Deputy Assistant Secretary for Near East and South Asian Affairs, signaled the change in a November 1999 address in which he acknowledged the "positive steps" taken by the Qaddafi regime.[17] Indicative of the change, the White House in February 2000 elected not to challenge Libyan participation in a UN mission to the Democratic Republic of the Congo, the first Libyan participation in an international peacekeeping operation in a decade. Concurrent with its evolving public diplomacy, the Clinton administration opened secret talks with Libya in mid-1999, aimed at ensuring Libyan compliance with all relevant UN resolutions. These bilateral negotiations were suspended in the run-up to the 2000 US presidential elections out of concern that they might become public and cause a scandal.[18]

Responding immediately to the 11 September 2001 terrorist attacks on the United States, Qaddafi was an enthusiastic recruit to the "war on terror," condemning the attacks and expressing sympathy for the victims. In the following months, American and British officials conducted lengthy information-sharing sessions with their Libyan counterparts. Saif al-Islam al-Qaddafi, Qaddafi's eldest son by his second wife, and his apparent heir, emphasized in January 2003 that Libya was doing its part to support the United States in the "war on terror," "exchanging intelligence about the al-Qaeda network." Libyan leader Qaddafi reiterated this point in a March 2004 *Newsweek* interview.[19]

Libyan cooperation in the "war on terror" was motivated largely by the fact that the Islamist organizations targeted by the White House had also threatened the Qaddafi regime.[20] At the first session of the secret talks opened by the Clinton administration in May 1999, the Libyan representative recognized a common threat from Islamist fundamentalism and agreed to cooperate actively with the United States in fighting al-Qaeda. Having long been a target of Islamist radicals, Qaddafi, post 11 September, freely shared intelligence information on alleged allies of Osama bin Laden, such as the Libyan Islamic Fighting Force. Libya also launched a website in January 2002, offering a $1m reward for information about regime opponents with ties to Islamist movements.[21]

In August 2003, Libya accepted responsibility for the actions of Libyan officials in the Pan Am flight 103 bombing and agreed to pay $2.7bn in compensation to the 270 families of the victims of the attack. After some delay due to French efforts to increase a prior Libyan payout to the families of the victims of the UTA flight 772 bombing, the UN Security Council lifted its multilateral sanctions on 12 September 2003. The United States welcomed the change, but again followed a different course, announcing that US sanctions would remain in place until Libya fully addressed a number of concerns underlying those measures. The concerns articulated by US officials included Libya's alleged poor human rights record, lack of democratic institutions, destructive role in African regional conflicts, and pursuit of weapons of mass destruction. Of the concerns cited by the Bush administration in the fall of 2003, observers noted that only the pursuit of unconventional weapons had figured in the original US rationale for imposing bilateral sanctions on Libya.[22]

In March 2003, Libyan representatives approached the British government, initiating talks with the United Kingdom and the United States aimed at dismantling Libya's unconventional weapons programs. Over the next nine months, three-party talks took place in London under the sponsorship of the British government. Similar to the Lockerbie negotiations, these talks were structured around an explicit *quid pro quo*. In return for a verifiable dismantlement of Libyan weapons programs, the US government was prepared to lift its bilateral sanctions. The London talks were conducted in the utmost secrecy. However, indications of progress soon surfaced. For example, Saif al-Islam al-Qaddafi, in an interview with the author in late October 2003, spoke persuasively of Libya's desire to rejoin the international community, suggesting that Libya would soon be making an important announcement in this regard. Eventually, on 19 December 2003, the Libyan foreign minister announced that Libya had decided of its own "free will" to be completely free of internationally banned weapons and associated delivery systems and to do so in a transparent manner under the observation of international inspectors.[23]

In response to Libya's renunciation of unconventional weapons and related delivery systems, the US government began to lift its bilateral sanctions, expanding commercial and diplomatic ties with Libya. Washington lifted the travel ban on 26 February 2004 and announced an easing of economic sanctions two months later. On 21 September 2004, President Bush ended the national emergency with Libya, effectively lifting most of the remaining travel and trade sanctions. At that point, the only sanctions still in place were certain export restrictions related to Libya's retention on the US State Department's list of State Sponsors of Terrorism. These export controls made it difficult to ship certain types of essential oil-field equipment to Libya because of dual-use restrictions.[24]

In mid-November 2004, the Bush administration asked Congress to lift the US ban on Export–Import Bank loans to Libya, arguing that action was necessary to facilitate US investment. In late January 2005, the Libyan government, in the first of a series of new tenders for Exploration and Production Sharing Agreements (EPSA), awarded 11 of 15 new EPSAs to American oil companies, operating alone or in partnership with other companies. The other bid winners, Petrobras of Brazil, Indian Oil and Oil India of India, Medco Energy International of Indonesia, Oil Search of Australia, Verenex Energy of Canada, and Sonatrach of Algeria, reflected global interest in Libyan hydrocarbon deposits. In February 2005, the United States lifted travel restrictions on Libyan diplomats, allowing them to move freely about the country. As relations expanded, Washington in the summer of 2005 announced a plan to establish military relations with Tripoli; and later in the year, Qaddafi invited President Bush to visit Libya. Libya was eventually removed from the US terrorism list in May 2006, signaling the end to US commercial and diplomatic sanctions. In the interim, the United States continued to express interest in adding Libya to the Trans-Sahara Counter-Terrorism Partnership (TSCTP), an organization linking the United States to nine other North and West African states working to deny al-Qaeda a sanctuary in the region.[25]

Domestic Economic Reforms

Throughout the 1970s, the Qaddafi regime pursued a radical socioeconomic policy that included housing redistribution and currency exchange, and led to the state takeover of all import, export, and distribution functions. In March 1987, after almost two decades of this type of socialism, the Libyan leader announced the first in a series of new measures, dubbed "green *perestroika*" by some observers, rescinding in part earlier socialist directives. Qaddafi envisioned an expanded role for the private sector, accompanied by limited political reforms. This early attempt to promote economic liberalization, a harbinger of things to come, failed to generate widespread popular support. At the General People's Congress in March 1990, delegates rejected regime efforts to reduce public expenditures, calling instead for lower taxes, free health care, cheaper housing loans, and increased spending on state-owned industries.[26]

Libyan oil production flagged throughout the 1990s for a variety of reasons, including the imposition of economic sanctions,[27] falling demand, and aging oil fields. With the level of domestic dissatisfaction tied closely to economic issues, the Qaddafi regime recognized the need to revitalize the ailing economy; however, it was understandably reluctant to initiate broad economic reforms as long as the country was subject to sanctions. At the end of the decade, the Libyan economy responded positively to the relaxation of economic sanctions, increased demand for petroleum products, and stronger global oil prices. Oil-based revenues increased sharply, contributing some 50 percent of GDP, 97 percent of exports, and 75 percent of government revenues in 1999–2003. Heavily dependent on the oil sector, the Libyan economy also remained largely state controlled, with an International Monetary Fund (IMF) report issued in March 2005 estimating that 75 percent of employment continued in the public sector while private investment remained low at approximately 2 percent of GDP. In addition, Libya faced a mounting unemployment problem, compounded by a high rate of population growth and a low rate of job creation.[28]

Stating that the public sector had failed and should be abolished, Libyan leader Qaddafi, as early as June 2003, called for the privatization of the oil industry, together with other sectors of the economy. Pledging to bring Libya into the World Trade Organization (WTO), he replaced Prime Minister Mubarak Abdullah al-Shamikh, with the former minister of economy and foreign trade, Shoukri Ghanem, a proponent of liberalization and privatization. In response, Prime Minister Ghanem in October 2003 announced a list of some 360 public-sector firms targeted for privatization or liquidation. Libya also unified its multi-tiered exchange rate, in effect devaluating the Libyan dinar. This much-needed currency devaluation increased the competitiveness of Libyan companies and attracted foreign investment to Libya. Foreign direct investment in Libya totaled some $4bn in 2004, up six-fold from the previous year.[29]

Even as Libya reiterated its commitment to economic liberalization, focused on diversification, privatization, and structural modernization, real progress in the non-hydrocarbon sectors of the economy remained tentative, subject to considerable uncertainty and periodic reverses. An articulate spokesman for privatization, Prime Minister Ghanem emphasized the gradual nature of proposed reforms, and stressed that an increased role for the private sector did not mean the role of the public sector would abruptly end; nevertheless, his much-trumpeted privatization program gained little traction after 2003. The IMF in 2006, for example, reported that only 66 of the 360 state enterprises targeted for privatization or liquidation some three years earlier had actually been sold. The IMF blamed the lack of progress on the Libyan approach. "Progress in developing a market economy has been slow and discontinuous ... and the government has yet to clearly break from past shortcomings in policy formulation and implementation."[30]

Public criticism of liberalization policies escalated after May 2005, after the government imposed a 30 percent hike in fuel prices and doubled the price of electricity for consumers of more than 500 kilowatts a month. A related decision in July 2005 to lift custom duties on more than 3,500 imported commodities raised job security concerns in Libyan factories ill-equipped to face competition. Adding to public concern, the reform process was often implemented in an *ad hoc*, unclear manner, with its pace and effectiveness frequently compromised by human capacity constraints. In response to mounting criticism of economic liberalization and privatization policies, a major cabinet reshuffle in early March 2006 replaced Prime Minister Ghanem with his more malleable deputy, Ali Baghdadi al-Mahmudi. As part of the shake-up, Ghanem was named chairman of the National Oil Company (NOC), giving him effective control over oil policy. The cabinet reshuffle was widely viewed as a victory for conservative hardliners.[31]

The reform process in the oil and gas sector, when compared to the uncoordinated, piecemeal approach that characterized other sectors of the economy, was more efficient and effective. In support of an investment target of $30bn by 2010, NOC launched several rounds of Exploration and Production Sharing Agreements, intended to provide enhanced incentives for both oil and gas development. Widely hailed as generally transparent, the EPSA process adopted by the government to award contracts marked a significant shift in the way Libya conducted business, validating government claims to be committed to opening the business environment and streamlining approval procedures. In addition to the EPSAs, Libya also negotiated bilateral agreements with companies like Occidental Petroleum and Royal Dutch/Shell in an effort to stimulate foreign investment and accelerate development. It also experimented with Development Production Sharing Agreements (DPSA), in which foreign companies revive and expand output at oil fields that are losing production after decades of use. The development of known reserves is attractive to oil companies, especially smaller ones, because it eliminates the risk associated with drilling in new areas.[32]

Political Organization, Opposition, and Human Rights

Qaddafi in the mid-1990s suppressed dissent within military and tribal groups; thereafter, internal opposition has come largely from Islamist fundamentalist groups. Dismissing Islamist radicals as "mad dogs" or terrorists, Qaddafi checked their influence through a three-part policy, undermining the religious authority of the *ulama*, refuting Islamist ideas, and harshly repressing Islamist opposition. To enhance his political legitimacy and establish his undisputed authority, Qaddafi called for a stricter application of Islamic law. The General People's Congress responded in February 1994, extending the application of Islamic law and granting new powers to religious leaders, including the right to issue religious decrees. At the same time, the regime sought to refute Islamist authority through an anti-Islamist campaign. Steering a middle path between hard-line religious opponents and the general population, which is largely opposed to militant Islam, Qaddafi used the security forces to deal severely with radical Islamists. The General People's Congress in 1997 passed a series of measures authorizing collective punishment for tribes or individuals harboring Islamists.[33] In April 2000, Libya executed three of eight Islamist militants extradited from Jordan. Benghazi was a center of opposition activity in the 1990s; and anti-regime activities, including the assassination of two senior security officers, were again reported in mid-August 2000.[34]

For a time, it appeared Qaddafi had largely contained the radical Islamist threat; however, riots in Benghazi in February 2006, which later spread to Darnah and Tobruk, suggested otherwise. Sparked by an Italian politician who boasted on television that he was wearing a T-shirt emblazoned with caricatures of the Prophet Muhammad, violent demonstrations outside the Italian consulate in Benghazi left at least 10 Libyans dead and several dozen injured. The furor at the time over cartoons of the Prophet Muhammad resulted in riots throughout the Islamic world, but witness accounts said the Benghazi demonstrations were the work of Islamist extremists who joined forces with anti-government forces.[35]

A plethora of opposition groups operate outside Libya, but they have never coalesced into an effective, united front. Six of these groups, the Libyan Change and Reform Movement, Libyan Constitutional Grouping, Libyan Islamic Group, Libyan National Organization, Libyan National Democratic Rally, and National Front for the Salvation of Libya, met in August 2000 to discuss joint strategy. The vagueness of the joint statement issued at the end of the meeting revealed that ideological differences and factional disputes continued to bedevil attempts to work together. Before the meeting, the Qaddafi regime made the first of several attempts to entice exiles to return home, eventually calling on the General People's Congress to establish a committee to resolve the cases of exiled opponents willing to return to Libya.[36]

A fresh attempt to coalesce groups opposed to the Qaddafi regime took place in London in June 2005, when the National Libyan Opposition Conference held its first meeting. Emphasizing a return to constitutional legitimacy, the conference brought together a number of mostly moderate, mainstream opposition groups, but it was not for everyone. Among others, the Muslim Brotherhood Movement, which rejected the narrow agenda insisted upon by the organizers, did not attend. The "Declaration for National Consensus" issued at the end of the conference called for a return to constitutional legitimacy, creation of a transitional government, and the prosecution of all members of the Qaddafi regime who had committed crimes against humanity. Calling for Qaddafi to resign, the conference rejected armed action, saying the United Nations was responsible for restoring Libya's constitution. In a statement before the conference opened,

the organizers had stressed that political change in Libya should be undertaken without foreign interference, criticizing the United States for normalizing ties and practicing a double standard when it came to human rights
violations in Libya.[37]

Organizations like Amnesty International and Human Rights Watch, as
well as the US Department of State, have long catalogued the human rights
violations of the Qaddafi regime. The legacy includes disappearances, arbitrary arrest, detention without trial, unfair trials, and torture. The case of
five Bulgarian nurses and a Palestinian doctor charged with deliberately
infecting more than 400 children in a Benghazi hospital with HIV/AIDS
became a *cause célèbre*. The European Union and the United States, together with numerous human rights groups and others, rejected a guilty verdict, urging Libya to free the detainees. In December 2006, Libya reiterated
the accusations against the nurses and the doctor despite the report in
Nature Magazine asserting that new evidence proved the innocence of the
six medical workers accused of causing the HIV pandemic in the Benghazi
hospital. Examining blood samples from 44 of the HIV-infected children,
scientists determined that the virus was present in the hospital and the surrounding area long before the six began their work at the hospital. After
prolonged negotiations, the EU finally secured the release of the six medical
workers in late July 2007.[38] Amnesty International, following its first visit to
Libya in 15 years, issued a scathing report in April 2004, calling on the
Qaddafi regime to address the grave human rights concerns detailed in
its report. The Department of State, in its annual report on human rights
practices, issued in March 2006, described the Qaddafi regime as an
authoritarian government with a poor human rights record. In a long
report released in January 2006, Human Rights Watch recognized that
Libya had taken important first steps to improve its human rights record,
but concluded that serious problems remained, including the use of violence
against detainees, restrictions on freedom of expression and association,
and the incarceration of political prisoners.[39]

In March 2000, Qaddafi abolished a number of central government
executive functions, devolving responsibility to the 26 municipal councils
making up the General People's Congress. While a number of government
ministries were eliminated, central control was retained in the areas of
defense, education, health, infrastructure, social security, and trade. With
the elimination of the energy ministry, responsibility for hydrocarbons
policy passed to the National Oil Company (NOC). In October 2000, the
public security minister was replaced, the information ministry liquidated,
and the finance minister removed. Qaddafi again reshuffled ministerial
positions in January 2003, appointing Shoukri Ghanem head of the General
People's Committee (prime minister). Ghanem was replaced in March 2006
by his deputy, Ali Baghdadi al-Mahmudi, and appointed NOC chairman.[40]

The National Oil Company has long exerted strong influence over
hydrocarbon policies; however, its role changed in September 2006 when the

General People's Committee announced the creation of a Council for Oil and Gas Affairs to oversee related policy, including production levels, pricing, and foreign contracts. Headed by Prime Minister Mahmudi, the new council included several cabinet ministers as well as the central bank governor and NOC chairman. Shoukri Ghanem moved immediately to reassure investors that the new body would not change oil and gas policy; nevertheless, its creation represented a dilution of powers long enjoyed by NOC, suggesting Libyan authorities were dissatisfied with the management of oil and gas policy. On the other hand, it should be recognized that the council was not a unique step, as it mirrored similar arrangements in Saudi Arabia and the Gulf, where senior political figures oversee hydrocarbon policy.[41]

Frequent ministerial changes, long characteristic of the Qaddafi regime, have been a favored way to prevent potential political competitors from building a power base and have seldom heralded a substantive shift in the domestic political environment. On the contrary, they serve to underscore the relative stability of the power balance in Libya and the dominant power position of Qaddafi. A report by the National Democratic Institute for Foreign Affairs, based on a visit to Libya in April 2006, highlighted several governance issues, including the lack of transparency in Libya's direct democracy.

> Qaddafi has created a system with a highly opaque decision making process, in which it is difficult if not impossible to identify how and by whom a decision is taken. In this way, Qaddafi is able to control the country from behind the scenes while blurring the lines on issues of authority and accountability.[42]

In spite of occasional signs of public discontent over issues like official corruption or the uneven distribution of resources, the vast majority of Libyans remain either generally supportive of Qaddafi or politically apathetic. Popular dissent remains a regime concern, but less so now than in previous years, as Qaddafi has effectively employed his enhanced international status to co-opt the opposition. As a result, there appears to be little prospect for an effective anti-Qaddafi opposition to arise in the foreseeable future.

Facing no obvious rival and not old for a head of state, Qaddafi, for over four decades, has demonstrated the political skills necessary to remain in power. No clear rules exist for his succession; and while Saif al-Islam al-Qaddafi is most often mentioned as a possible successor, he has repeatedly denied interest in the job. Nevertheless, Qaddafi appears intent on being replaced by a family member, and Saif al-Islam al-Qaddafi remains the current front-runner. Outside the family, there is no obvious successor in bureaucratic, government, or military ranks; but in the right circumstances one could suddenly emerge, much as Qaddafi did in 1969. In any case, Qaddafi's unique role as leader of the revolution will almost certainly disappear with his passing. As for the institutions created by Qaddafi, which offer elements of participation and representation, as well as fulfilling important distributive and security functions, they could prove valuable to his eventual successor and might well be maintained for some time without major overhaul.[43]

Conclusion

After 1998, Libyan leader Qaddafi introduced major changes to the direction, tone, and content of Libyan foreign policy. Moving to end Libya's commercial and diplomatic isolation, he focused initially on the African continent, largely ignoring the Palestinian question and often chiding former allies in the Middle East. He also expanded existing relationships with the European Union and key European states, and developed new ties in Asia. However, the critical Libyan initiative, following resolution of the Lockerbie question and the lifting of UN sanctions, was the decision to renounce unconventional weapons and related delivery systems. In so doing, Qaddafi paved the way for full commercial and diplomatic relations with the United States, a foreign policy objective dating back to the 1970s. With Libya's removal from the US list of state sponsors of terrorism, its international rehabilitation is now virtually complete.

Since the discovery of petroleum deposits in commercial quantities in 1959, Libya has relied heavily on its hydrocarbons sector; and with petroleum reserves estimated to be 39 billion barrels and natural gas reserves to be 1.49 trillion cubic meters, it will continue to do so in the foreseeable future. In this sense, Libya remains the classic example of a rentier economy, a state relying upon externally generated monies or rents for income, instead of extracting income from domestic production. Tentative attempts at economic reform in the late 1980s were frustrated by a rentier-state pattern deeply rooted in distributive mechanisms originated by the monarchy and extended by the revolutionary government to attract regime support. Those same attitudes are again constraining more recent efforts to move from a socialist command economy to a free market system.

The current reform process is geared toward strengthening global economic ties and attracting new foreign investment, particularly in the hydrocarbons sector. Progress to date in other areas of the economy has been slow, hindered by policy inconsistency, structural problems, and bureaucratic bottlenecks, with entrenched interests constraining the pace of policy implementation. Consequently, a future reform policy can be expected to follow a dual path, with reform in the hydrocarbons sector proceeding much faster than reform in other areas of the economy.

Whatever the speed and scope of economic reform, it is not expected to be accompanied by political liberalization. The Qaddafi regime is approaching four decades in power, and well over half the Libyan population has known no other political leader or system in their lifetime. Moreover, a significant percentage of the population, in an innately conservative society, has a vested interest in the status quo, with many Libyans accepting an implicit trade-off between limited social and political freedom and a relatively high standard of living. In lieu of political reforms that might compromise his hold on power, Qaddafi is more likely to introduce changes designed to consolidate his pre-eminent position in the political system he created. In the process, he can be expected to continue reshuffling the country's leadership to balance competing power structures and to prevent any individual from developing a personal power base. With no formal mechanism in place to ensure a smooth transition of power, the post-Qaddafi era can be expected to be a time of tension and uncertainty, with numerous socioeconomic and political groups vying for power.

Notes

1 Ronald Bruce St John, *Libya and the United States: Two Centuries of Strife*, Philadelphia, PA: University of Pennsylvania Press, 2002, pp. 175–84.

2 Asteris Huliaras, "Qadhafi's Comeback: Libya and Sub-Saharan Africa in the 1990s," *African Affairs*, vol. 100, no. 398, January 2001, pp. 5–25; Ronald Bruce St John, "Libya Coming in from the Cold: Ties Re-established in Europe and Africa," *Africa Contemporary Record*, vol. 27, Colin Legum (ed.), New York, Africana Publishing Company, 2004, p. B630.

3 Ronald Bruce St John, "Libya in Africa: Looking Back, Moving Forward," *The Journal of Libyan Studies*, vol. 1, no. 1, summer 2000, pp. 27–9.

4 "Ministers Urged to Object to Libya Role," *BBC News*, 21 August 2002. Available at: http://news.bbc.co.uk; "Gaddafi Attacks Annan's Proposals for Darfur," *Reuters*, 15 February 2005. Available at: http://news.reuters.com.

5 Muammar al-Qaddafi, "Statement by Brother Leader of the Revolution," on the Occasion of the Opening of the Fifth Ordinary Session of the Assembly of the African Union, Sirte, Libya, 4 July 2005. Available at: http://www.africa-union.org; "Decisions, Declarations and Resolutions, Fifth Ordinary Session of the Assembly," Sirte, Libya, 4–5 July 2005. Available at: http://www.africa-union.org.

6 Saïd Haddad, "La politique africaine de la Libye: de la tentation impériale à la stratégie unitaire," *Maghreb-Machrek*, no. 170, October–December 2000, p. 35; Ronald Bruce St John, "Libyan Foreign Policy: Newfound Flexibility," *Orbis*, vol. 47, no. 3, summer 2003, p. 466; James Munyaneza, "Libya Now 20th to Join COMESA," *All Africa*, 3 June 2005. Available at: http://allafrica.com.

7 M. Qaddafi, op. cit., p. 10; "Libyan Leader Ignores Intifadah," *Al-Quds al-Arabi*, London, 14 July 2001, United States Government, Foreign Broadcast Information Service, Near East and South Asia (FBIS-NES)-2001-0714; St John, "Libya in Africa," op. cit., p. 28.

8 Andrew Borowiec, "Maghreb Union a 'Paper Camel'," *The Washington Times*, 15 November 2000. Available at: http://www.washtimes.com; Mohamed Krichene, "Internal Concern Killed Maghreb Dream," *Al-Quds al-Arabi*, London, 21 February 2001, FBIS-NES-2001-0221.

9 Munayyah al-Wazzani, "Libyan Foreign Minister Says POLISARIO Issue Hinders Joint Maghreb Action," *Al-Majallah*, London, 20 May 2001, FBIS-NES-2001-0524; Yahia H. Zoubir and Karima Ben Abdallah-Gambier, "Western Saharan Deadlock," *Middle East Report*, no. 227, vol. 33, no. 2, summer 2003, pp. 8–11; Morad Aziz, "The Arab Maghreb Union: Back to the drawing board," *Morocco Times*, 25 May 2005. Available at: http://moroccotimes.com.

10 "China and Libya Issue a Press Communique," *Beijing Xinhua Domestic Service*, Beijing, 14 April 2002, FBIS-CHI-2002-0414; "Agreements, Plan Signed between DPRK and Libya," *KCNA*, Pyongyang, 16 July 2002, FBIS-NES-2002-0716; David E. Sanger and William J. Broad, "Uranium Testing Said To Indicate Libya–Korea Link," *The New York Times*, 2 February 2005.

11 George Joffé, "Libya and Europe," *The Journal of North African Studies*, vol. 6, no. 4, winter 2001, pp. 75–92, particularly pp. 77–80.

12 "Europe Cooperates with Libya to Limit Illegal Migration," *Arabic News*, 4 June 2005. Available at: http://www.arabicnews.com; "Commission Releases Funds to Fight AIDS in Libya," 12 July 2005. Available at: http://europa.eu.int; Haizam Amirah-Fernández, "Libya's Return: Between Change and Continuity," Elcano Royal Institute for International and Strategic Studies, 1 June 2006, pp. 4–6. Available at: http://www.realinstitutoelcano.org/analisis/986.asp.

13 The Atlantic Council of the United States, *U.S.–Libyan Relations: Toward Cautious Reengagement*, Atlantic Council Policy Paper, April 2003, pp. 4–6; "Italy–Libya ties continue to deteriorate over coastal highway," *BBC News*, 3 June 2005. Available at: http://news.bbc.co.uk; Sara Hamood, "African Transit Migration through Libya to Europe: The Human Cost," American University in Cairo Forced Migration and Refugee Studies, January 2006; Human Rights Watch, "Stemming the Flow: Abuses against Migrants, Asylum Seekers and Refugees," vol. 18, no. 5, September 2006. Available at: http://www.hrw.org.

14 Warren Hoge, "New Libyan Cooperation Leads to Renewed Ties with Britain," *The New York Times*, 8 July 2002; George Joffé, "Libya: Who Blinked, and Why," *Current History*, May 2004, pp. 221–5; Michael Binyon, "British must move fast to profit on trade front," *The Times*, 18 January 2005. Available at: http://business.timesonline.co.uk.

15 Sayyed Rashid Husain, "French President Jacques Chirac Was in Libya Last Week," *Middle East North Africa Financial Network*, 12 February 2004. Available at: http://www.menafn.com; Katrin Bennhold, "France looks for deals with Libya's military," *International Herald Tribune*, 7 February 2005.

16 Isabelle Werenfels, "How to Deal with the 'New Qaddafi?'" *SWP (Stiftung Wissenschaft und Politik) Comments*, vol. 29, October 2004, pp. 1–2; "Schroeder invites Gadhafi to visit Germany," *The Washington Times*, 11 May 2005. Available at: http://www.washtimes.com.

17 Ronald E. Neumann, "Libya: A U.S. Policy Perspective," *Middle East Policy*, vol. 7, no. 2, February 2000, pp. 142–5, quote 143; Yahia H. Zoubir, "Libya in US foreign policy: from rogue state to good fellow?" *Third World Quarterly*, vol. 23, no. 1, 2002, pp. 42–6.

18 "Secret Libyan–US Meetings in Rome Paves Way for Turning New Page," *Al-Sharq al-Awsat*, London, 5 May 1999, FBIS-NES-1999-0505; Martin S. Indyk, "Iraq did not force Gadaffi's hand," *Washington Post*, 9 March 2004.

19 Amir Taheri, "Libya's Future: Talking to Muammar Kaddafi's Son," *National Review Online*, 2 January 2003. Available at: http://www.nationalreview.com; "Libya gives US tips on al-Qaeda," *BBC News*, 12 January 2003. Available at: http://news.bbc.co.uk; "Kaddafi Reformed?" *Newsweek*, 15 March 2004.

20 See Yahia H. Zoubir, "Libye: Islamisme radical et lutte antiterroriste," *Maghreb-Machrek* (Paris), no. 184, summer 2005, pp. 53–66.

21 John Barger, "From Qaddafi to Qadadfa: Kinship, Political Continuity, and the Libyan Succession," *The Journal of Libyan Studies*, vol. 2, no. 1, summer 2001, pp. 34–5; St John, "Libyan Foreign Policy," p. 474.

22 United States Department of State, "Libya – Pan Am 103," 15 August 2003. Available at: http://www.state.gov/secretary/rm/2003; Irwin Arieff, "U.N. Security Council Lifts Sanctions on Libya," *Washington Post*, 12 September 2003.

23 Saif al-Islam al-Qaddafi, interview with author, London, 24 October 2003; Flynt Leverett, "Why Libya Gave Up on the Bomb," *The New York Times*, 23 January 2004; Ronald Bruce St John, "'Libya Is Not Iraq': Preemptive Strikes, WMD and Diplomacy," *The Middle East Journal*, vol. 58, no. 3, summer 2004, pp. 386–402.

24 "Bush Scraps Most U.S. Sanctions on Libya," *The New York Times*, 20 September 2004; Caroline Drees, "As ties warm, U.S. pushes Libya on terror financing," *Reuters*, 13 July 2005. Available at: http://news.reuters.com; Yahia H. Zoubir, "The United States and Libya: From Confrontation to Normalization," *Middle East Policy*, vol. 13, no. 2, summer 2006, pp. 63-5.

25 "Col Gaddafi Invites Bush to Libya," *BBC News*, 21 August 2005. Available at: http://news.bbc.co.uk; Kevin Morrison and Doug Cameron, "US oil groups win Libyan permits," *Financial Times*, 31 January 2005; Ronald Bruce St John, "Libya and the United States: The Next Steps," Atlantic Council Issue Brief, March 2006, pp. 4–5; Mark Trevelyan, "US courts Libya for Africa security network," *Middle East Online*, 16 October 2006. Available at: http://www.middle-east-online.com/english.

26 Dirk Vandewalle, "Qadhafi's *'Perestroika'*: Economic and Political Liberalization in Libya," *The Middle East Journal*, vol. 45, no. 2, spring 1991, pp. 216–31; Dirk Vandewalle, "The Failure of Liberalization in the Jamahiriya," in *Qadhafi's Libya, 1969 to 1994*, Dirk Vandewalle (ed.), New York, St. Martin's, 1995, pp. 203–22.

27 On the impact of the UN and US sanctions on Libya, see, Tim Niblock, *Pariah States and Sanctions in the Middle East: Iraq, Libya, Sudan*, Boulder, CO: Lynne Rienner 2001, pp. 60–92.

28 Mustafa Bakar Mahmud and Alex Russell, "An Analysis of Libya's Revenue Per Barrel from Crude Oil Upstream Activities, 1961–93," *OPEC Review*, vol. 23, no. 3, September 1999, pp. 213–49; International Monetary Fund, "Socialist People's Libyan Arab Jamahiriya 2004 Article IV Consultation – Staff Report; Staff Statement; and Public Information Notice on the Executive Board Discussion," IMF Country Report no. 05/83, March 2005, pp. 5–6. Available at: http://www.imf.org; Ronald Bruce St John, "Libya: Lockerbie Trial Ends, Sparking New Libyan Initiatives," *Africa Contemporary Record*, vol. 28, New York, Africana Publishing Company, 2006, pp. B643–B645.

29 "Libya now top African nation for Investment – UN," *Reuters*, 12 January 2005. Available at: http://news.reuters.com; Kevin Morrison and Doug Cameron, "US oil groups win Libyan permits," *Financial Times*, 31 January 2005.

30 Kevin Morrison, "Libyan PM woos big oil companies," *Financial Times*, 1 February 2005; International Monetary Fund, "The Socialist People's Libyan Arab Jamahiriya: Staff Report for the 2005 Article IV Consultation," IMF Country Report No. 06/136 (April 2006), p. 9, 22, quote p. 22. Available at: http://www.imf.org; Eman Wehbe, "Libya is reforming, but Libyans don't feel any better off," *The Daily Star*, 11 June 2005. Available at: http://www.dailystar.com.

31 William Wallis, "Libya's reformist PM is ousted," *Financial Times*, 6 March 2006.

32 Maher Chmaytelli, "Libya may let foreigners own oil," *Houston Chronicle*, 5 October 2005. Available at: http://www.chron.com; Roula Khalaf and Thomas Catan, "BP and Libya in talks over gas project," *Financial Times*, 6 January 2006; Shokri Ghanem, "These Are Our Priorities for the Upcoming Phase," First Interview on the NOC website, 18 September 2006. Available at: http://www.en.noclibya.com.ly.

33 Zoubir, "Libye: Islamisme radical et lutte antiterroriste," op. cit.

34 Ray Takeyh, "Qadhafi's Libya and the Prospect of Islamic Succession," *Middle East Policy*, vol. 7, no. 2, February 2000, pp. 154–64; Yehudit Ronen, "Qadhafi

and Militant Islamism: Unprecedented Conflict," *Middle Eastern Studies*, vol. 38, no. 4, October 2002, pp. 1–16.

35 Daniel Williams, "At Least 9 Killed in Libya In Clashes Over Cartoons," *Washington Post*, 18 February 2006; Steven R. Hurst, "Witnesses: Anti-Gadhafi Forces in Protest," *Daily Democrat*, 21 February 2006. According to some Libyans interviewed by Yahia H. Zoubir the day after the riots, the demonstrations were organized by the regime; however, they went out of control due to the unexpectedly high turnout and the small number of security forces. The latter fired at the crowds when they were overwhelmed by the demonstrators who sought to enter the Italian Consulate.

36 Ronald Bruce St John, "Round Up the Usual Suspects: Prospects for Regime Change in Libya," *The Journal of Libyan Studies*, vol. 4, no. 1, summer 2003, pp. 8–10; "Gadhafi wants political exiles home," *The Washington Times*, 12 January 2005. Available at: http://washtimes.com.

37 "Libya Opposition Seeks Gadhafi's Ouster," *The New York Times*, 25 June 2005; The Oversight Committee, "Declaration for National Consensus," 26 June 2005. Available at: http://www.libya-nfsl.org; May Youseff, "Anti-Gaddafists Rally in London," *Al-Ahram Weekly On-Line*, no. 749, 30 June–6 July 2005. Online. Available at: http://weekly.ahram.org.

38 "Libya Denies Newest Evidence for Bulgarian Nurses' Innocence," 8 December 2006. Available at: http://www.novinite.com/view_news.php?id=73785. "A press conference to reveal the details of the secret negotiations in the case of the Libyan children, the victims injected with the AIDS virus," *Jamahiriya News Agency*, 29 July 2007. Available at: http://www.jananews.com.

39 Amnesty International, "Libya: Time to Make Human Rights a Reality," 27 April 2004. Online. Available at: http://www.amnesty.org; U.S. Department of State, "Libya: Country Reports on Human Rights Practices – 2005," 8 March 2006. Available at: http://www.state.gov; Human Rights Watch, "Words to Deeds: The Urgent Need for Human Rights Reform," vol. 18, no. 1, January 2006. Available at: http://www.hrw.org; Declan Butler, "'A shocking lack of evidence'," *Nature*, vol. 443, 26 October 2006, pp. 888–9.

40 Economist Intelligence Unit, *Country Report: Libya*, January 2003, pp. 12–13; "PM goes in Libya reshuffle," *BBC News*, 14 June 2003. Available at: http://news.bbc.co.uk; William Wallis, "Libya's reformist PM is ousted," *Financial Times*, 6 March 2006.

41 "Libya sets up oil and gas council to oversee energy policy," *Platts Commodity News*, 5 September 2005. Available at: http://www.platts.com.

42 National Democratic Institute for International Affairs, "The Libyan Political System and Prospects for Reform: A Report from NDI's 2006 Delegation (17–25 April 2006)," p. 5. Available at: http://www.ndi.org.

43 St John, "Round Up the Usual Suspects," op. cit., pp. 10–12; George Joffé, "Frustration and Stagnation in Libya," *Middle East International*, 23 September 2004. Available at: http://meionline.com; David Mack, "Libya and the United States at a Turning Point," *Middle East Institute,* 24 March 2005, p. 3.

4 Mauritania

Between the Hammer of Economic Globalization and the Anvil of Multiparty Factionalism

Mohameden Ould-Mey

Mauritania's military coups and attempted coups made headlines in 1978, 1979, 1981, 1982, 1984, 1987, 2003, 2004, and 2005. After 1991, contested multiparty elections added more to the overall image and reality of Mauritania's political instability, erratic geopolitics, and widespread poverty. In the wake of the December 1984 military coup, the Mauritanian government embarked on an International Monetary Fund (IMF) and World Bank-backed structural adjustment program. The program was part of a broader development strategy conceived by the G7 countries in response to the economic crisis of the 1970s, which developed out of a fundamental contradiction between nationalist policies (adopted by most developing countries at the time) and the G7-supported neo-liberal economic policies. In 1991, the Mauritanian government also embarked on a French-backed democratization process. This process was initiated after the end of the first US-led Gulf War and on the eve of the official dissolution of the Soviet Union and the end of the Cold War. These policies contributed to what has been conceptualized and analyzed as the denationalization of the Mauritanian state, the devaluation of its economy, and the fragmentation of its sociopolitical system.[1]

Drawing upon the above analytical perspective, this chapter summarizes and critiques selected geopolitical economy developments in Mauritania in the areas of state sovereignty, economic liberalization, political democratization, and geopolitical positioning. The concept of geopolitical economy refers to an eclectic synthesis of the national political economy and international geopolitics and argues that inter-state struggle has often been more significant in world history than intra-state struggle.[2] First, the chapter briefly explains the concept of denationalization and gives examples illustrating the shift from a national to a multilateral state in Mauritania. Second, it examines the impact of currency devaluation on the US dollar value of Mauritania's national production. Third, it assesses Mauritania's process of democratization in light of the fluctuation between contested elections and military coups amid increased multiparty factionalism. Fourth, it attempts to pinpoint the delicate geopolitical positioning of Mauritania in the context of the Arab Maghreb Union (AMU), the Western

Sahara conflict, the controversial relations with Israel, and the active collaboration in the US-led "war on terror." It concludes by suggesting that any
serious tackling of the challenges facing the country may require going
beyond "representative democracy" to a form of "direct democracy" involving direct popular participation in the complex processes of defining policies, enacting laws, and allocating resources.

Denationalization and the Shift from a National to a Multilateral State

The denationalization of the state has been conceptualized and articulated
as a shift from a national state, which strives to adapt its external relations
to the imperatives of its internal structures, to a multilateral state, which
attempts to adapt its internal structures to the imperatives of its external
relations.[3] In other words,

> some state capacities are transferred to a growing number of panregio-
> nal, plurinational, or international bodies with a widening range of
> powers; others are devolved to restructured local or regional levels of
> governance in the national state; and yet others are being usurped by
> emerging horizontal networks of power—local and regional—that by-
> pass central states and connect localities or regions in several nations.[4]

This strategy appears to provide a solution to the tension between the
increasingly global nature of the economy and the persistently local and
national character of politics. A denationalized state has less control over
the formulation of its development strategies, the choices of its foreign
policies, and the tenets of its national sovereignty. In this context, the *UN
Human Development Report 2002* (subtitled *Deepening Democracy in a
Fragmented World*) observed that, even in countries with well-established
democratic institutions, citizens and their governments often feel powerless
to influence national policies because of international forces beyond their
control. US State Department Director for Policy Planning, Stephen Krasner, went even further to suggest that powerful states should "share" sovereignty with "failed, failing, and post-conflict countries."[5]

   The following two examples illustrate how the denationalization of the
Mauritanian state started at the nerve-center of economic planning and
foreign policy. First, the Mauritanian state began to lose sovereignty over
the diagnosis of development problems, the formulation of development
policies, and the assessment of policy output as early as January 1979, when
the United States Agency for International Development (USAID) prepared a Country Development Strategy Statement (CDSS) for Mauritania
and launched the Rural Assessment and Manpower Surveys (RAMS) project,
which criticized Mauritania's nationalist policies and advocated economic
liberalization. The 44 RAMS reports provided Mauritanian policy makers

and academicians with a *prêt-à-porter* neo-liberal analysis of the economy combined with an American functionalist approach to society, emphasizing descriptive ethnography over other social theories (see the carefully selected titles of the two major RAMS studies of sociological profiles: *Les Maures* and *La Mauritanie Négro-Africaine*).[6] Since then Mauritania's national plans of economic development were progressively superseded by World Bank and IMF Policy Framework Papers (PFPs), which commit the government to implement development strategies focused on managing demand and strengthening supply via a matrix of policy measures.[7] Today, this policy continues unabated. According to the IMF Staff Report for the 2006 Article IV Consultation, the Mauritanian authorities have by now "implemented an impressive policy shift toward transparency and good governance and have resolved the data issues."[8]

Second, the Mauritanian state realigned itself with the State of Israel despite popular opposition. This realignment began in the aftermath of the 1991 Gulf War, when Mauritania broke relations with Iraq and established ties with Israel in order to improve relations with the US government. In November 1995, the foreign ministers of Israel, Mauritania, and Spain met in Barcelona and decided that Spain would represent Israeli interests in Mauritania through its embassy in Nouakchott and Mauritanian interests in Israel through its embassy in Tel Aviv. In May 1996, Mauritania opened a diplomatic mission in Tel Aviv. By the same token and under the banner of combating terrorism and normalizing relations with Israel, Mauritania and Jordan (both countries with no access to the Mediterranean) joined NATO's Mediterranean Dialogue, which includes Algeria, Egypt, Israel, Jordan, Mauritania, Morocco, and Tunisia, whereas other Mediterranean countries, such as Lebanon, Libya, and Syria, were excluded.

In its relations with Israel, Mauritania has been and continues to be influenced by a long list of Arab and Muslim governments' normalizations with Israel and "Zionism."[9] The list includes: the signing of the Egyptian–Israeli peace agreement in 1979; the upgrading of Turkish–Israeli relations in 1991; the signing of the Palestinian–Israeli Declaration of Principles in 1993; the signing of the Jordanian–Israeli peace treaty in 1994; the opening of an Israeli liaison office in Morocco in 1994; the opening of Israeli trade representation or interest offices in Oman, Qatar, and Tunisia in 1996; the meetings of Pakistani–Israeli foreign ministers as well as Indonesian–Israeli foreign ministers in 2005; the beginning of Saudi–Israeli trade relations via the US and the World Trade Organization (WTO); and the forerunner decision by Bahrain to end the boycott of Israeli goods because that is one condition of a free trade agreement with the United States.[10] However, Mauritania had no declared domestic or regional interest when its foreign minister was dispatched to the US State Department's ballroom in Washington DC in October 1999 to sign an agreement establishing full diplomatic relations with Israel and to become the third Arab country (after Egypt and Jordan) to do so, despite strong opposition at home and criticism abroad. Since then, Mauritanian–Israeli relations have moved on a fast track because Mauritanian policy makers believed that normalization with Israel was a *sine qua non* condition for normalization with the United States.[11]

In April 2000, shortly after the first shipment of fish from Mauritania reportedly arrived in Israel, a delegation of the Israeli Knesset visited Mauritania, and an Israeli–Mauritanian Friendship Society was reportedly established. Israeli Knesset member Naomi Chazan (Meretz), who was accompanied by Maxim Levy (One Israel), Gideon Ezra (Likud), and Hashem Mahameed (United Arab List), called the visit "historic for Israel and the Arab world."[12] After the outbreak of the Palestinian Al-Aqsa Intifada in September 2000, Morocco and Tunisia closed their representations in Israel, and Oman closed Israel's trade representation office. Mauritania, however, did not sever ties with Israel and sent foreign affairs minister Dah Ould Abdi on a visit to Israel in May 2001, and the Mauritanian ambassador in Tel Aviv attended Israel's celebration of its May 2002 Independence Day, which the Egyptian and Jordanian ambassadors boycotted.

Israeli Deputy Prime Minister and foreign minister Shimon Peres visited Mauritania in October 2002 in the aftermath of the bloody Israeli attacks on the Palestinian cities of Jenin and Nablus in April. In May 2005, Tunisian-born Israeli foreign minister Silvan Shalom visited Mauritania and called the visit "the road map for relations between the Arab world and Israel," while Mauritanian President Maaouiya Ould Taya asked for "Israel's assistance in getting a little attention for his country in Washington."[13] Since the coup on 3 August 2005, Mauritanian officials have reiterated that Mauritania will keep its relations with Israel. In an interview on Al-Jazeera TV Channel (13 October 2006), the new Mauritanian leader, Colonel Ely Ould Mohamed Vall, declared that he would have established relations with Israel as his predecessor Ould Taya did because, he argued, the Palestinians, the Egyptians, and the Jordanians accepted a peaceful settlement with Israel.[14] But a closer look indicates that the US did use its bilateral assistance programs, leverage over loans from international financial institutions, and annual country reports on human rights to engage or pressure Mauritania to recognize Israel.[15] This policy may or may not continue under President Sidi Mohamed Ould Cheikh Abdallahi. *Voice of America*'s West African Bureau in Dakar noted that "Of almost 20 candidates in the recent presidential election, Mr. Abdallahi was the most moderate in his views on Israel."[16] However, Ould Abdallahi declared that Mauritania's relationship with Israel will be determined in consultation with the Parliament, civil society, and various state institutions. In light of such consultations, he added, we will make our decision of "freezing, severing, or continuing" relations with the State of Israel.[17] The situation seems so serious that he had even hinted at holding a popular referendum on Mauritania's relations with Israel.[18] What makes this a catch-22 situation is the fact that Mauritania normalized with Israel in order to normalize with the United

States and the United States normalized with Mauritania because Mauritania normalized with Israel.[19]

Currency Devaluation or the Devaluation of National Production

The pillars of the Mauritanian economy consist of the agro-pastoral sector and the export sectors of iron ore, fish, and, recently, oil. The agro-pastoral sector supplies the country with meat, while exporting an unknown quantity of its livestock to neighboring countries. This sector is vulnerable to recurrent drought and locust plagues, which, according to the July 2005 report of the UN Office for the Coordination of Humanitarian Affairs, affected 26 percent of the population in 2004. Some limited attempts to export agro-pastoral products have demonstrated that Northern countries' markets are less accessible to Southern countries' exports than the other way around. This is exemplified by the case of Nancy Abeid Arahmane, who reportedly campaigned for over a decade without success in exporting pasteurized camel cheese from her Tivisky dairy in Mauritania to the European Union, due to EU trade regulations.[20] The huge popping of NGOs in every country, the emergence of more than 200 regional trade agreements over the past two decades, and the calls for "regional regroupings" have further exposed the limits of the denationalized state in the age of globalization.[21] In the meantime, Mauritania is not a member of any of the 26 most frequently cited Regional Trading Agreements in 2005.[22] The map of the world today is increasingly dominated not by nation-states but by geopolitical and economic organizations like the European Union, the African Union, the Association of Southeast Asian Nations, the Commonwealth of Independent States, the South Asian Association for Regional Cooperation, the Shanghai Cooperation Organization, the South American Community of Nations, and the North American Free Trade Agreement.

Mauritania has extensive deposits of iron ore which were initially exploited by *Mines de Fer de Mauritanie* (MIFERMA), a French-led multinational mining company, whose infrastructure included a 650 km railroad, the longest trains in the world, a mining town (Zouerat) and its exporting port (Nouadhibou). MIFERMA was nationalized in 1974, renamed *Société Nationale Minière de Mauritanie* (SNIM), and later denationalized and opened to international capital through a mining project (Guelb Project) which aimed at replacing the depleted site of high-grade ores (64 percent Fe) in the Kedia site (near Zouerat) with the larger but lower-grade ores (38 percent Fe) of the Guelbs site 30 km north of Zouerat.

In addition to iron ore, which has been exported at around 11 million tons per year, the Atlantic coast of Mauritania is adjacent to some of the richest fishing grounds in the world. In 2002, benefiting from a fishing protocol with the EU that provides some 86m euros per year, the fishing sector, whose potential output was estimated at 630,000 tons, generated 45 percent of foreign currency earnings, 25 percent of the government budget and 12 percent of GDP, and created 36 percent of the jobs in the modern sector.[23] The UN Environmental Program, however, has warned about the devastation of over-fishing by foreign fleets, saying that catches of Mauritania's octopus have been reduced by half in four years, sawfish has completely disappeared, and the number of traditional octopus fishermen has fallen from about 5,000 in 1996 to about 1,800 in 2002.[24]

In 2001, oil was discovered 90 km off the shore of Mauritania, southwest of Nouakchott, by the Australian company Woodside Petroleum, whose production from the Chinguetti oil field (in 800m of water) began in February 2006, with a projected peak production of 75,000 barrels a day. Based on expected production rates and current prices, Woodside has predicted that average revenue flowing to the Mauritanian Government over the first five years of production from the Chingetti oil field will be around USD 300m a year.[25] There are other promising offshore oil and gas fields, such as the Tiof and Banda fields. Mauritania has also awarded onshore Taoudenni blocks in the northeast deserts of the country to several oil companies.[26] According to the World Bank's Country Brief, proven and probable oil reserves in Mauritania amount to around 310 million barrels.[27] The discovery of offshore oil and the completion of the highway between the capital city of Nouakchott and the northern port city of Nouadhibou are raising expectations and are likely to have a significant impact on European tourism and African worker migration.[28] While some have argued that oil "impedes" democracy due to the effect of "rent,"[29] it remains to be seen whether or not this will apply to Mauritania since the "trickle-down" of oil revenues has just begun. But resource endowment is not a sufficient enough condition for economic prosperity, because politics often determine economics and resource control is often more important than resource quantity or location. In addition, the value of Mauritania's export earnings has been systematically eroded by the impact of currency depreciation and devaluation under the IMF and World Bank-backed adjustment programs.

The IMF and the World Bank have loaned large sums of money to Mauritania. The World Bank boasts that, as of January 2005, it approved 69 credits and grants for Mauritania reaching a total of USD 1.02bn.[30] Between April 1985 and July 2002, the Paris Club arranged eight debt reschedulings and treated over USD 1bn of Mauritania's debt, of which USD 518m were fully repaid during the first six reschedulings. In exchange for loans, policy measures and implementation deadlines are detailed in a series of PFPs. A typical PFP can include over 100 policy measures aimed generally at reducing total demand through an austerity program involving an exchange rate policy that almost always depreciates or devalues the national currency, the ouguiya (UM). For example, to implement one policy measure ("further liberalize the exchange rate system to promote external competitiveness") out of 124 required under the PFP for the 1999–2002 period, the Mauritanian government had to implement 13 detailed measures including the adoption of a new method for the calculation of the weekly official exchange rate.[31] Between 1980 (USD 1 = UM 45.91) and 2004 (USD 1 = UM 272) the ouguiya has depreciated by 592 percent. The depreciation of the ouguiya *vis-à-vis* the US dollar means that more units (i.e., more units of iron ore, or fish, or more recently oil) of the ouguiya are needed in a given year to import the equivalent of the previous year's imports. Since increasing exports is not always an option, reducing imports and/or contracting more foreign debts would be the logical consequence of currency devaluation.[32]

When both population growth and inflation are taken into consideration, Mauritania's GDP per capita (measured according to the World Bank Atlas method) has declined from USD 497 in 1980 to USD 174 (USD 400 market prices) in 2004, while external debt per capita in 2000 reached nearly USD 1,000. The World Bank's updated Mauritania Brief of March 2007 estimates that current oil reserves could bring Mauritania's GNI (gross national income) per capita from USD 420 in 2004 to around USD 1,000 in 2010. According to Mohamed Ould El-Abed, minister of economic affairs and development, the rate of economic growth for 2006 reached 11.7 percent. But despite this apparent economic growth, a couple of examples might illustrate the overall devaluation of Mauritania's purchasing power in the global market. In 1990, a lecturer at the University of Nouakchott received a net monthly remuneration of UM 40,000 (USD 500 at the 1990 exchange rate: USD 1 = UM 80). In 2000 (after a 50 percent salary raise), the same lecturer received a net monthly earning of about UM 60,000 (USD 240 at the 2000 exchange rate: USD 1 = UM 250). Due to currency devaluation and despite the 50 percent salary raise, the purchasing power of the lecturer (as measured in US dollars) has actually declined by 52 percent. With expected improvement of the economic situation following debt cancellation and new revenues from oil production, the government has recently proposed 50 percent increase in public and private employees' salaries and 20 percent increase in retirement pensions beginning in January 2006.[33] But it should be noted that the above salary increase may not necessarily translate into a real increase in purchasing power, given the continuous devaluation and depreciation of the national currency, as indicated by the April 2007 exchange rate of the ouguiya: USD 1 = UM 281. In this regard, the IMF has announced Mauritania's commitment to more of the same monetary policies: "The transition government has achieved important progress in structural reform. Key steps included the passing of an ordinance that will increase central bank autonomy in the conduct of monetary policy, and the successful launching of the foreign exchange market in January 2007."[34]

Also between 1987 and 2001, consumer price indexes for foodstuffs and lodging in Nouakchott reached 288 percent and 271 percent respectively. Such increases in consumer price indexes were never fully offset by commensurate salary and wage raises. The resulting resource transfer to the global North and severe poverty in the global South were implicitly recognized by the IMF and the World Bank, when the "Policy Framework

Paper" was renamed "Poverty Reduction Strategy Paper" (PRSP).[35] They were also acknowledged by the G8 when they agreed, in July 2005, to cancel most debts of the 18 heavily indebted countries, including Mauritania. They could be seen in the short life expectancy at birth in Mauritania, estimated by the 2006 UN Human Development Report at 53.1 years. The 2005 UN Report on the World Social Situation (subtitled "The Inequality Predicament") and the debates at the 2005 World Summit have acknowledged that poverty widens the gap between the "haves" and the "have nots," threatens developing democracies, and breeds violence and terror. While the IMF Country Report No. 07/40 sounds optimistic and considers that poverty in Mauritania fell from 56.6 percent in 1990 to 54.3 percent in 1996, 51 percent in 2000, and 46.7 percent in 2004, it also provides a less optimistic assessment of the first poverty action plan for 2001–4:

> It must be observed that implementation of the first phase of the PRSP was not very satisfactory inasmuch as more than one third of the actions called for were not carried out and many actions were taken that did not contribute directly to meeting PRSP objectives. In this context, the growth rates recorded were below forecast levels (4.6 percent on average for the period, as compared to the anticipated 6 percent) and inflation exceeded forecasts, largely owing to the poor fiscal and monetary policies pursued on the basis of imprecise data. The economic policies followed resulted in an extremely high fiscal deficit (9.9 percent of GDP over the period), the collapse of official reserves (ranging from 0.4 to 1.3 months of non-oil imports), and an unprecedented increase in the money supply.[36]

Political Democratization or Multiparty Factionalism

The 2002 *UN Human Development Report* focused on the global progress of democracy. During the prior two decades, 140 of the world's nearly 200 countries held multiparty elections, and 33 military regimes were replaced by civilian governments. However, the Report noted that despite the hope and enthusiasm about democratization worldwide, there is a sense that democracy has not kept its promises and that it is actually being undermined. In most African countries, multiparty democracy came after a decade of structural adjustment programs and after the collapse of single-party rule in the Soviet Union in 1991.[37] While African opposition parties welcomed multiparty democracy, there were genuine concerns about its imposition from the outside and its potential centrifugal implications on national unity and social cohesion in the most politically fragmented and culturally diverse region of the world (the African Union includes over 50 nation-states, and Africa south of the Sahara has over 1,000 mostly non-written languages). In a sense, the coming of the military coup of August 2005 after 15 years of multiparty democracy in Mauritania confirms the

2002 UN Human Development Report's concern and disappointment about the democratization process.

Effective pressure for "democratization" in Mauritania came mainly from the international community of lenders and donors, especially France and the United States. In the US Congress, Thomas Lantos (Democrat from California) and John E. Porter (Republican from Illinois) managed to pass a Congressional motion on human rights violations in Mauritania, which was published in the 1991 Congressional report entitled *Human Rights in the Maghreb and Mauritania* (the title even questions Mauritania's membership in the Maghreb).[38] Though they expressed some concerns about the ethnic clashes during the 1989 border crisis between Mauritania and Senegal, they were in reality concerned mostly about Mauritania's verbal opposition to Israel and to the 1991 US-led war against Iraq. US pressure, however, stopped, and the two Congressmen kept quiet about human rights abuses under the Ould Taya government as soon as Mauritania began establishing ties with Israel. It was also in 1991 that Thomas Lantos (dubbed "the only" Jewish Holocaust survivor in the US Congress) used his Congressional Human Rights Caucus to foster the infamous "Nurse Nayirah hoax" (a completely fabricated story like the Iraqi "weapons of mass destruction hoax"), which consolidated public and congressional approval for the 1991 Gulf War against Iraq.[39]

By the same token, Thomas Lantos led the introduction of the Palestinian Anti-Terrorism Act of 2006 to Congress following the democratic victory of Hamas (Arabic acronym of *Harakat al-Muqawama al-Islamiyya*, or Islamic Resistance Movement) in the January 2006 Palestinian legislative elections.[40] The Act stipulates that it shall be the policy of the United States "to urge members of the international community to avoid contact with and refrain from supporting the terrorist organization Hamas until it agrees to recognize Israel, renounce violence, disarm, and accept prior agreements, including the Roadmap." The American-Arab Anti-Discrimination Committee has warned about the aim of this Act, which stipulates that failure to meet some "congressionally defined democracy qualifiers" would end US assistance to the Palestinians, prohibit Palestinian diplomats entry to the United States, designate Palestinian territories as a terrorist sanctuary, and reduce US-based contributions to money spent on UN Palestinian bodies. This Act caused and continues to cause a great deal of human suffering in the Palestinian territories. These examples demonstrate that Thomas Lantos was concerned with Israel's security and Arab normalization with Israel, not with human rights or democracy in Mauritania or Kuwait.

The French were more efficient in bringing about multiparty democracy through quiet diplomacy. They dispatched foreign minister Roland Dumas to Nouakchott in April 1991, and he apparently persuaded the president of the Military Committee for National Salvation, Colonel Ould Taya, that he had nothing to fear and perhaps a lot to gain from the multiparty system. Ten days after Dumas' visit, Ould Taya announced his intention to hold a constitutional referendum, open the political system, legalize political parties, and give freedom to the press. The process began with the July 1991 constitution, which proclaimed "attachment to Islam and to the principles of democracy." However, the constitution accorded near despotic powers to the President of the Republic (Articles 28 to 43). The democratization process culminated in April 1992 with highly contested elections involving four presidential candidates. Colonel Ould Taya reportedly obtained 62.7 percent of the votes, Ahmed Ould Daddah (former minister of finance and half-brother of the first Mauritanian president, Mokhtar Ould Daddah) obtained 32.8 percent, and the remaining 4.5 percent was shared by Moustapha Ould Mohamed Salek (a retired army colonel and former president of the Military Committee of National Salvation that staged the coup against President Mokhtar Ould Daddah in 1978) and Mohamed Mahmoud Ould Mah (a Nouakchott University professor of economics and former mayor of Nouakchott).[41]

While the elections made Mauritania more credible in the eyes of its international financial benefactors, they also drove a wedge between the government and the opposition parties. Political factionalism along party, ethnic, Islamic, and tribal identities intensified to the extent that no unified or coordinated national policy or strategy could be identified and agreed upon. The number of recognized political parties increased from one in 1978, to 18 in 1993, and to 24 in 2005, about 30 when counting the banned parties. Marianne Marty argues that democratization in Mauritania was further undermined by the neopatrimonial nature of the political regime and its manipulation of ethnic and tribal divisions through control of state resources.[42] In the face of the factionalism and impotence of political parties, serious and organized opposition within the military establishment became increasingly visible in June 2003 with an attempted coup. Its leader, former army Major Saleh Ould Hanenna, and his companions from the *fursan et-teghyir* (Knights of Change) organization admitted in court that they had wanted to end the Ould Taya regime. Overall, the constitution of 1991 and its multiparty democracy raised expectations before opening the door wide to political disappointment. People witnessed purges against various political factions (Islamist, Arab Nationalist, Negro-African, or Liberal), while Article 13 of the constitution reads: "All forms of moral or physical violence shall be proscribed." People witnessed the erosion of sovereignty over economic and foreign policies, while Article 2 of the constitution reads "The people shall be the source of all power," and "No partial or total surrender of sovereignty may be decided without the consent of the people." Under these critical circumstances of legitimacy and security crises, people began to lose faith in words and look for deeds at a time when the state was largely reduced to its repressive and relatively oversized security apparatus.

The political impasse must have encouraged the 20-year Director of the National Security, Colonel Ely Ould Mohamed Vall, and the Commander of the Presidential Guard, Mohamed Ould Abdel Aziz, and other military officers to mobilize on 3 August 2005 and overthrow President Ould Taya, who was out of the country attending the funeral of Saudi Arabia's King Fahd. They announced the establishment of the Military Council for Justice and Democracy (MCDJ) to put an end to "the despotic practices" of the regime and create favorable circumstances for an "open and transparent" democracy. In his first public address, a month after the bloodless coup, the President of the MCDJ, Colonel Ely Ould Mohamed Vall, declared a welcomed amnesty to "all Mauritanians found guilty of political crimes or offences." However, the amnesty did not include all the detained Islamists, since it excludes the so-called Salafists, who continue to be jailed without trial as of April 2007.[43] The MCDJ also decreed that all its members and those of the new cabinet are barred from running for the legislative and presidential elections. Whatever the real motives and intentions of the MCDJ, one can argue that the recurrent coup attempts[44] by the military and the repeatedly disputing of elections by opposition parties indicate that the process of multiparty democracy has failed, not just Ould Taya or his party. But this failure does not seem to be acknowledged by Mauritania's Eurocentric political elites. It does not seem to encourage any serious critical thinking "outside the box" of representative democracy and its multiparty divisive technique. This seems to leave the door open for the vicious cycle of cliquish military committees (who often lack the required political theory and vision) and factious political parties (who often lack the necessary unity and strength) to start again from square one.

The transition from military to civilian rule began soon after the military coup and the dissolution of the national assembly in August 2005. It progressed through the national referendum on constitutional amendments in June 2006, the election of *el-majlis el-watani* (the 95-member National Assembly) in November and December 2006, the election of *majlis esh-shuyukh* (the 56-member Senate) in January and February 2007, and the presidential election in March 2007. It was complete with the inauguration on 19 April 2007 of President Sidi Mohamed Ould Cheikh Abdallahi. He defeated ex-opposition leader Ahmed Ould Daddah by a narrow 52.85 to 47.15 percent (24.79 to 20.68 percent in the first round) margin in a run-off from the 11 March presidential elections, in which 19 candidates vied for the presidency. Ould Cheikh Abdallahi, who was elected for a five-year term (with eligibility for a second consecutive term), collected 373,519 out of 706,703 votes cast by 1,132,176 registered voters.[45] He had a lead over his rival in 10 of the 13 provinces and obtained more than 70 percent of the votes cast in two provinces: Adrar (home of deposed President Ould Taya) and El-Hodh Es-Sharqi (home of Ould Taya's appointed Prime Minister Ould M'Barek). Ould Daddah obtained 333,184 votes and had a lead in his native Trarza (67.01 percent) as well as in the capital city Nouakchott (58.20 percent) and the province of Inchiri (52.18 percent). Though the political map emerging from the legislative and presidential elections seems reminiscent of the pre-coup balance of power, nothing is certain because of the endless making and unmaking of political parties, factions, coalitions, and alliances. The highly fragmented political elites and the widely distributed votes between nineteen presidential candidates and dozens of political parties and independent candidates confirm that no single party or candidate represents or can claim to "represent" the Mauritanian people.

One should not be naive regarding Mauritania's domestic politics, as they often reflect the country's geopolitics. Moreover, democratic relations at the local or national level will remain insufficient amid undemocratic geopolitical relations at the international level, as embodied in the undemocratic veto power within the UN Security Council and voting power within the IMF and the World Bank. It is worth mentioning in this context that while Mauritania's Military Council for Democracy has shown a great deal of determination to revisit many domestic policies (including amending the constitution and holding new elections), it has equally shown little determination to change any of Ould Taya's controversial geopolitical alliances, such as normalization with Israel and partnership in the "war on terror." The dominance of geopolitics over domestic politics was clear when the Military Council for Democracy and Justice dissolved the Mauritanian National Assembly but preserved Mauritania's commitment to all the international treaties and agreements which it has signed. It was also clear during the "historic" televised debate between presidential candidates Sidi Mohamed Ould Cheikh Abdallahi and Ahmed Ould Daddah. The candidates focused mostly on domestic issues and deliberately avoided important foreign affairs issues. The six topics debated were: (1) strengthening national unity,[46] (2) good governance and the rule of law, (3) struggle against poverty and for the well-being of citizens, (4) education, (5) economy and land management, and (6) external relations. Some of the "sensitive" domestic issues raised included the sequels of slavery, the question of Mauritanians deported to Senegal following the 1989 ethnic clashes, human rights abuses committed under the Ould Taya government, and administrative and financial corruption. However, the well-prepared debate did not include any questions on Mauritania's relations with Israel or Mauritania's position on the conflict over Western Sahara.

Historical Geopolitics of Mauritania

Unlike Mediterranean Algeria, Libya, Morocco, and Tunisia, Mauritania falls mostly within the Sahara and straddles West Africa and the Maghreb. This significant position merits a brief presentation of the country's historical geopolitics before discussing the delicate geopolitical positioning of Mauritania in the context of the AMU, the Western Sahara conflict, the controversial relations with Israel, and the active collaboration in the US-led "war on terror." The Islamic Republic of Mauritania occupies a vast land area (1,030,700 km^2) of the Sahara and Sahel regions along a lengthy northwest African coastline (754 km) stretching northward from the delta of the Senegal River to the Nouadhibou Peninsula. The estimated population in 2006 was three million, with probably one-fourth living in the capital city of Nouakchott on the Atlantic coast. According to the 2006 UN Human Development Report, Mauritania's Human Development Index ranked 153 (Libya ranked 64, Tunisia 87, Algeria 102, and Morocco 123) among those of 177 countries listed.

Historically the country represents a strong link between the Maghreb and West Africa. The *murabitun* movement unified the Berber Zenega tribal confederations of central Mauritania in the eleventh century, conquered Morocco and founded Marrakech in 1056 AD, captured Ghana's capital, Koumbi Saleh in 1076, and intervened in al-Andalus in 1086, thus founding a short-lived (1053–1147) but vast Islamic trading empire linking West Africa, the Sahara, the Maghreb, and al-Andalus. Most Mauritanians refer to the *murabitun* as the founding fathers who completed the Islamization and began the country's Arabization. The process of ethno-linguistic Arabization accelerated after the thirteenth and fourteenth centuries when several Arab tribal confederations, mostly known as Banu Maqil, were pushed south to Western Sahara by the Zenata Merinid dynasty in Morocco. By the end of the seventeenth century, several clans from the Hassan branch of Banu Maqil had penetrated and gradually overwhelmed the Zenega tribal confederations, after whom the Portuguese explorers of the fifteenth century had named the Senegal River (Zenega River).

This profound process of Islamization and Arabization constitutes the core of the dominant Arabic Moorish culture (with its distinct *Mahadhra* system, a sort of nomad universities focused on higher education in Quran and Arabic). For centuries, the Arabic culture interacted and lived in symbiosis with the Muslim communities of the Halpular, Soninke, Wolof, Bambara, and other black ethnic groups in and around the Senegal River basin and the great curve of the Niger River. The name *Mauritanie*, which was coined by the French at the turn of the twentieth century, was based on the names of ancient Roman colonies in North Africa (*Mauretania Caesariensis* in northwestern Algeria and *Mauretania Tangitana* in northern Morocco). It is derived from the Latin or Latinized word *Maurus* (a term which still lives in the names *Mor*occo and *Maur*itania) from which came the French word *Maures* (Moors), which designates the dominant Arabic-speaking ethno-linguistic group in the country.

After the Treaty of Paris in 1814 and the Congress of Vienna in 1815, French colonial intentions north and south of the Sahara began with the reoccupation of Saint Louis (lost earlier to the British) at the mouth of the Senegal River in 1815 and the conquest of Algiers in 1830. In the aftermath of the 1885 Berlin Conference, the French concluded a draft agreement with Spain on the delimitation of Franco-Spanish possessions in the Peninsula of Nouadhibou in 1891 and conquered Timbuktu at the great curve of the Niger River in 1893. These geopolitical developments carved out what would become Mauritania and made it part of colonial and post-colonial French geopolitics. The French viewed Mauritania as *le grand vide* (the great emptiness) or the *trait d'union* (hyphen) between their Algerian and Senegalese colonies or between the Arab Maghreb and West Africa. The vast geographical barrier of the Sahara, the French conquest and administration of Mauritania from Saint Louis in Senegal as part of French West Africa, and Morocco's (and consequently the Arab League's, excluding Tunisia) strong opposition to Mauritania's independence on 28 November 1960 alienated the country from the Arab world until the early 1970s. It was pushed deeper into West African regional politics and was highlighted as a geographical and cultural transition zone. This geopolitical position was also accentuated by lengthy northern and eastern boundaries which divided Moorish tribes in neighboring Western Sahara, Algeria, and Mali, similar to the southern boundaries dividing the Halpular, Soninke, Wolof, and other ethnic communities around the Senegal River basin. It is this complex historical geography that made Mauritania a geopolitical state par excellence.

Perhaps the most serious conflict affecting Mauritania's geopolitics today is the conflict over the former Spanish Sahara, which shares a long history and a porous border with Mauritania. The territory is sparsely populated, phosphate-rich, adjacent to some of the richest fishing waters in the world, and believed to have offshore oil deposits. Initially the conflict opposed the Algeria-backed Popular Front for the Liberation of the Saguia al-Hamra and Río de Oro (POLISARIO Front) and Morocco, with the support of Mauritania. In 1979, Mauritania signed a peace treaty with the POLISARIO Front and gave up all claims over Western Sahara. The widely expected solution to the conflict is a free and fair referendum of self-determination, according to pertinent UN resolutions. Morocco continues to oppose such a referendum, the POLISARIO continues to insist on it, and the UN does not seem to be willing to impose it. The referendum is probably the only peaceful and face-saving exit for all parties involved in the 30-year fratricidal conflict, which continues to paralyze the Arab Maghreb Union. UN Security Council Resolution 1754 of 30 April 2007 once again extended the mandate of the United Nations Mission for the Referendum in Western Sahara (MINURSO) until 31 October 2007 and has once again reaffirmed the Security Council's "commitment to assist the parties to achieve a just, lasting and mutually acceptable political solution, which will provide for the self-determination of the people of Western Sahara in the context of arrangements consistent with the principles and purposes of the Charter of the United Nations." Mauritania has learned a tough lesson from its involvement in the Western Saharan war from 1975 to 1979. Since then, successive Mauritanian governments have come to the conclusion that neutrality in the conflict is the best policy. In light of the spring 2007 Moroccan plan to give greater autonomy to Western Sahara, the Mauritanian position was again reiterated by the President of the MCJD, Colonel Ely Ould Mohamed Vall, when he stressed that Mauritania "is not a party to this conflict" but will support any solution agreed upon by all parties.[47] The same position was paraphrased by the newly elected President, Sidi Mohamed Ould Cheikh Abdallahi, when he said that Mauritania must have good relations with all its neighbors, particularly "Morocco, Algeria, and our Sahrawi brothers."[48]

The other serious conflict affecting Mauritania's geopolitics today is the so-called "war on terror." Between 1995 and 1999, Mauritania broke ties with Iraq, established relations with Israel, and joined NATO's Mediterranean Dialogue countries. After 11 September 2001, the US and NATO became even more interested in Mauritania as a base for antiterrorist operations in the Sahara and North Africa. Former US ambassador to Mauritania Joseph LeBaron once portrayed the geopolitical basis of US–Mauritania relations in these terms: "we are deepening and expanding our relationship with this important country that is situated so strategically between Europe and sub-Saharan Africa, with hundreds of miles of Atlantic Ocean coastline."[49] The US European Command came up with a USD 6m program, the Pan Sahel Initiative, to train and equip light infantry companies from Chad, Mali, Mauritania, and Niger. In 2005, the initiative was renamed the Trans-Sahara Counterterrorism Initiative, and its funding was increased to USD 100m a year to train battalions from the following nine countries: Algeria, Chad, Mali, Mauritania, Morocco, Niger, Nigeria, Senegal, and Tunisia. Under the initiative, some 1,000 US troops, including 700 Special Operations Forces, will train 3,000 soldiers and provide them with vehicles, radios, uniforms, global-positioning devices, and fuel trailers. Perhaps in line with Stephen Krasner's idea of "shared" sovereignty, the initiative calls for assigning more military officers to US embassies in these countries, linking their militaries with secure satellites, and expanding military cooperation to other arenas. The US Justice Department would train local police, the Treasury Department would help develop financial controls, the Customs Department would assist with border security, and the Agency for International Development would construct local schools.[50] In this context, an armed group, believed to be the Algerian Salafist Group for Preaching and Combat (GSPC), led a surprise attack against an isolated Mauritanian Army outpost (Lemghayti, near the border of Algeria) that killed 15 Mauritanians in June 2005. This attack further exposed Mauritania's collaboration in the "war on terror." *The Wall Street Journal* of 1 March 2006 quoted Mauritania's ambassador in Washington both before and after the coup, Tijani Ould Mohamed El Kerim, as saying "Terrorists are not happy with the fact that Mauritania is among the three Arab countries to have diplomatic relations with Israel," and "They are not happy Mauritania is active in joining the war against terror."

There are some indications that Mauritania's collaboration in the "war on terrorism" is likely to continue under the presidency of Sidi Mohamed Ould Cheikh Abdallahi. When he was asked about his position on US intention to establish a military base in Mauritania, he noted that terrorism came to Mauritania from "the outside" and "our" fight against terrorism "will prompt us to cooperate and coordinate with the United States."[51] It should be noted that the US military are planning to have a fully operational US Africa Command (AFRICOM) to oversee military operations throughout the entire African continent (excluding Egypt, which will remain within the area of responsibility of the US Central Command) by 1 October 2007.[52] President Bush called President-elect Sidi Mohamed Ould Cheikh Abdallahi to congratulate him, while he sent Deputy Secretary of State John Negroponte the first-ever Director of National Intelligence, to represent him at Ould Cheikh Abdallahi's inauguration on 19 April 2007.[53] Negroponte, who was leading a 32-strong delegation, including the deputy commander of US European Command, indicated that the United States will strengthen bilateral relations with Mauritania in the areas of food security, health, education, security, democracy, and terrorism.[54] The inauguration was attended by representatives from a number of countries and regional and international organizations, including the presidents of seven African countries (Burkina Faso, Cape Verde, Guinea-Bissau, Mali, Niger, Senegal, and Togo), the prime minister of Morocco, the president of Algeria's Council of the Nation, the Special Adviser to the Tunisian President, the Chief of Staff of the Libyan leader, and the French minister of defense.[55] It is quite remarkable to notice that while Arab media and political elites seem to have been widely thrilled by Mauritania's transition and elections, no Arab head of state attended the inauguration of President Ould Cheikh Abdallahi.

Conclusion

Mauritania continues to face serious challenges in balancing geopolitics, improving political stability, strengthening social cohesion, and reducing poverty. The sensitive geographic location of the country requires even more sensitive geopolitics. For example, it is now clear that Mauritania's full participation in the war in Western Sahara broke its geopolitical balance and ultimately brought down the Ould Daddah government in 1978, despite sustained military and political support from both France and Morocco. Similarly, the high-speed normalization with Israel and the full collaboration in the US-led "war on terror" again broke Mauritania's geopolitical balance and led to the collapse of the Ould Taya government in 2005, despite strong support from Israel and the United States. The government elected in 2007 has a lot to learn from these unnecessary geopolitical ordeals, in order to pinpoint Mauritania's optimal geopolitical position within Maghrebi, Arab, African, Islamic, and international geopolitics, without overrunning signals as did the governments of Ould Daddah and Ould Taya.

However, Mauritania's political instability has been fueled not just by its geopolitics, but also by its failed political models and their lack of popular and direct participation in the complex processes of defining policies, enacting laws, allocating resources, and waging war. First, Mauritania experienced the single-party rule of *hizb ash-shaab al-muritani* (Mauritanian People's Party) from 1963 to 1978. The party, however, failed to represent the people when important decisions, such as intervening in the war in Western Sahara, were made by the politburo of the party without popular consultation and participation. Second, Mauritania was under the dictatorship of the Military Committee for National Recovery/Salvation from 1978 to 1992. The military came to power to stop a war they could not win and to put an end to the single-party rule that launched it. Somehow they succeeded in achieving these goals but could not move forward because of the lack of an appropriate political model and vision. Perhaps the most salient episode of the military dictatorship was Ould Haidalla's *heyakil tehdhib al-jemahir* (Structures for Educating the Masses), which could be viewed as a sincere but theoretically uninformed political model of administration. Third, Mauritania experienced the despotism of *al-hizb al-jumhuri ad-dimuqrati al-ijtimai* (Democratic and Social Republican Party) and its "multiparty" ideology from 1992 to 2005. This ruling party also failed to represent the will of the people when it established/diplomatic relations with Israel, joined the US-led "war on terror," and shifted Mauritania's weekend from Friday (the Muslim holy day) and Saturday to Saturday and Sunday without popular consent.

There is little doubt that the issue is still democracy. But the question is what kind of democracy, for whom, and by whom? The remaining contemporary political models of government that have not been implemented in Mauritania are: first, the single-family rule model in the eight Arab monarchies; second, the *wilayet al-faqih* rule model in Iran; third, the *Taliban* rule model in pre-11 September Afghanistan; fourth, the failed-state model in Yugoslavia or Somalia; and fifth, the *jamahiriyya* model in Libya. Given that Mauritania is an Islamic Republic, any preferred political model should be inspired by Islamic teachings, especially the kind of political participation implied in the principle of conducting public policy by mutual consultation,[56] the type of redistribution of wealth and income implied in the idea of spending that which is beyond one's need,[57] and the code of morality and social cohesion implied in the ideals of tolerance and forgiveness.[58] It seems that unless the wide-ranging debate over "the government of national unity" is qualitatively transformed into another carefully and peacefully planned transition from representative to direct democracy, there is little evidence that the rule of the winning party (Ould Cheikh Abdallahi's supporters are reportedly in the process of establishing a new political party) will be qualitatively different from the rule of *hizb ash-shaab al-muritani* or *al-hizb al-jumhuri ad-dimuqrati al-ijtimai* when it comes to the bottom line of a fair and genuine sharing of power, wealth, and weapons within an orderly society. The interesting question is: when will Mauritania's political elites be *emotionally* confident, *intellectually* able, and *organizationally* prepared to question traditional representative democracy and contemplate the prospect of a more direct form of democracy? The great North African thinker Ibn Khaldun observed 600 years ago that the followers of the Maliki School of Islamic Jurisprudence were more inclined toward "tradition" (*el-athar*) than toward "contemplation" (*en-nadhar*). Is not it time to prove him wrong?

Notes

1 Ould-Mey, 1994; 1995; 1996; 1998a; 1998b; 1999; 2003.
2 Ould-Mey, 1996.
3 George, 1992; Amin, 1990; Ould-Mey, 1996; Jessop, 1999; Sassen, 2003.
4 Jessop, 1999.
5 Krasner, 2005.
6 It could be argued that the *epistemological* and *political* ramifications of these sociological studies had impacted ethnic consciousness in Mauritania and could still impact national unity.
7 Ould-Mey, 1996, Table 6: p. 110.
8 IMF, 2006.
9 Ould-Mey, 2005.
10 Al-Jazeera.net English, 2005.
11 Ould-Mey, 2007 (forthcoming).
12 Cooper, 2000; *IslamOnline*, 2002; Israel Ministry of Foreign Affairs, 2005.
13 *Ya'ari*, 2005.
14 *Al-Jazeera*, 16 October 2006.
15 Ould-Mey, 2007.
16 *Voice of America*, 11 April 2007.
17 *Al-Ahram*, 27 March 2007.
18 *Al-Akhbar*, 2007.
19 Ould-Mey, 2007.
20 Bianchi, 2005.
21 Osava, 2005; Lawrence, 2003; World Bank, 2005a; Amin, 2003.
22 World Bank, 2005a.
23 Kumar, 2005.
24 Brown, 2002.
25 Woodside, 2006.
26 *Oil & Gas Journal*, 2004; *Energy Economist*, 2005.
27 World Bank, 2007.
28 Vesely, 2004; Ford, 2003. Thousands of African migrants trying to escape poverty have drowned in recent years while attempting to reach European shores. In 2006 the European Commission adopted a package of measures to help Mauritania contain the flow of African illegal migrants to the Canary Islands. In April 2007 Spanish authorities announced that, for the first time, when their patrol boats tried to detain African migrants off the coat of Mauritania, the migrants threw Molotov cocktails at the patrol boats. Europa Press Release, 2006.
29 Ross, 2001.
30 World Bank, 2005b.
31 Ould-Mey, 2003: Table 4, p. 475.
32 Ould-Mey, 2003: p. 477; *Economist Intelligence Unit*, 2005; US Bureau of Labor Statistics, 2005.
33 Al-Jazeera.net, 2005, 28 December 2005.
34 IMF, 2007b, 27 February 2007.
35 Ould-Mey, 2003.

36 IMF, 2007a, January 2007.
37 Ould-Mey, 1995; 1996, see Table 36, p. 217.
38 Ould-Mey, 1996.
39 It turned out later that the 15-year-old "nurse" (Nayirah al-Sabah) was actually the daughter of the Kuwaiti ambassador to the US and a member of the Kuwaiti royal family. Claiming she was a refugee volunteering in a hospital in Kuwait City, Nayirah tearfully testified before the US Congress in October 1990 about how the Iraqis threw 312 babies out of their incubators when they took over the hospital and shipped the incubators back to Baghdad. Eno, 2003; Beresford, 2003; Editorial Desk, 1992; Regan, 2002.
40 Nir, 2006.
41 Ould-Mey, 1996.
42 Marty, 2002.
43 *Al-Akhbar*, 9 April 2007.
44 In an interview with Al-Majalla (25 March 2007) reported by *Al-Akhbar* (6 April 2007) and *Eelaf* (2007), Colonel Ely Ould Mohamed Vall cited the fear of "repeated coup attempts" as a main reason that motivated the coup of 3 August 2005.
45 *Chaab*, 27 March 2007.
46 This is a Mauritanian approach to other social and political reconciliation models such as the Algerian Charter for Peace and National Reconciliation (2005), the Moroccan Equity and Reconciliation Commission (2004), and the South African Truth and Reconciliation Commission (1995).
47 Al-Jazeera.net, 2006.
48 *Al-Ahram*, 27 March 2007.
49 US Embassy, 21 April 2007.
50 Schmitt, 2005; Tyson, 2005.
51 *Al-Ahram*, 27 March 2007.
52 There seems to be some connection and concomitance between the establishment of AFRICOM and the announcement of the name change of the Salafist Group for Preaching and Combat to "the al-Qaeda organization in the Islamic Maghreb," whose members claimed responsibility for the deadly bomb attacks in Algiers on "4/11" (11 April 2007). French counterterrorism magistrate Jean-Louis Bruguière believes that the organization wants "to become a regional force, not solely an Algerian one." Smith, 2007.
53 *Sahara Media*, 2007.
54 *Agence Mauritanienne d'Information*, 19 April 2007.
55 *Al-Wikala Al-Muritaniya lilanba*, 19 April 2007.
56 Quran, 3:159; Quran, 42:38.
57 Quran, 2:219.
58 Quran, 7:199.

5 The "End of the Era of Leniency" in Morocco

Gregory W. White

On 23 July 1999 King Hassan II of Morocco died. His eldest son, Mohammed VI, immediately acceded to the throne. Although the transition to 36-year-old Mohammed's rule was uneventful, the challenges confronting the new monarch were enormous. Mohammed VI had inherited a gradual process of top-down liberalization from his father. In the late 1990s, after a series of constitutional reforms, Hassan II had initiated Morocco's first experiment with a *gouvernement d'alternance* that, in theory, would alternate between centrist coalitions of the left and right.[1] In March 1998, after national elections, Hassan appointed Abderrahman Youssoufi as prime minister and charged him with the formation of a cabinet. Youssoufi, the longtime leader-in-exile of the center-left Socialist Union of Popular Forces (USFP) and a strong critic of the Palace, appointed a cabinet of 40 ministers from seven political parties. Notably, however, Youssoufi was not charged with appointing four dominant "sovereign" ministers: Interior, Justice, Islamic Affairs, and Foreign Affairs. Since the *Makhzen* (the powerful, central government surrounding the King and the Royal Palace) selects sovereign ministers, it was justifiable to wonder how a government of *alternance* could be held accountable when its powers were so carefully limited.

In 1999, Mohammed inherited a system that was changing. His appointment, in some respects, breathed life into the *alternance* experiment.[2] By the summer of 1999, criticisms of Youssoufi's government and its performance had been mounting, even if it did not have the full range of policy instruments at its disposal, and frustrations with Hassan's close control of the political process were evident. Mohammed's accession shifted attention away from the Parliament back to the Palace and introduced energy and optimism to the political scene. Although a honeymoon period may typically follow a new monarch's accession, Mohammed VI displayed a new style that was very different from that of his father. He appeared to be a ruler who was truly close to the people. Even after the blow delivered to the international community with the terror attacks in New York and Washington DC, on 11 September 2001, Morocco continued important reforms, such as holding parliamentary elections in September 2002 and opening human rights dossiers from the years of Hassan's rule.

Despite these important developments, Morocco's measured opening began to recede by 2002. The early steps were not followed by more substantive political and economic reforms. In particular, the Palace continued to circumscribe the power of the executive branch, and major reforms regarding the labor code, health care, and the national budget were not achieved. Many claimed that at the heart of the slowing of the *glasnost* (liberalization/opening) was the government's clampdown on political Islam—a response to the popularity of the Justice and Development Party (PJD) and the banned Islamist movement *Al-'Adl wa-'l-Ihsan*, as well as pressure from Washington and European capitals in the aftermath of 11 September. The attacks in Casablanca on 16 May 2003, in which 45 people were killed, intensified the tightening of the political system. In a royal discourse on 29 May 2003, the King declared:

> The moment of truth has come, heralding the end of the era of leniency in dealing with people who take advantage of democracy to undermine the authority of the state, those who spread ideas which create fertile ground to sow the seeds of ostracism, fanaticism, and discord, and also those who are bent on preventing the public and judicial authorities from displaying the firmness required by the law, in their effort to protect the integrity and security of people and property.[3]

The King's announcement of "the end of the era of leniency" marked a significant turning point in Morocco's political evolution in the post-Hassan period.[4]

The declaration, however, solicits an important question: Was the promise of the early years of Mohammed's reign truly squandered, or was the promise over-inflated? A skeptical interpretation might even challenge whether a few years of gradual opening constitute an "era." Seen in this light, expectations for a new era in Morocco in the aftermath of Hassan's death should not have been so high. Indeed, crucial elements of Mohammed's reign have sustained the rudimental components of the Moroccan political system and its position on an international scale. Exploring the dimensions of this argument requires a careful appraisal of the legacy of Hassan's regime, the ongoing challenges of governing Morocco in the new era, and dramatic changes in the international context.

Hassan's Legacy

Hassan II had been present in the Moroccan political and social landscape for 38 years. The Alawite monarchy can trace its lineage back to the Prophet Mohammed, and the dynasty is linked to the Idrisids who founded Fes in the ninth century.[5] As the *Amir al-Mu'minin* (the Commander of the Faithful) and leader of the *dar al-mulk* (Royal Administration), the King claims supreme religious authority.[6] Many accounts of Morocco, particularly in journalistic descriptions, stress the degree to which the monarchy's stability is derived from religious legitimacy. The symbolic power of the monarchy is undeniable and provides the Moroccan state with a set of powers far greater than its Maghrebi counterparts, and comparable perhaps to Jordan's Hashemite monarchy.[7] The constitution also asserts the King's authority. Article 19 of the Constitution, adopted on 13 September 1998, stipulates that the King is the "Supreme Representative of the Nation and the Symbol of the unity thereof ... The King shall be the guarantor of the independence of the Nation and the territorial integrity of the Kingdom within its rightful boundaries."[8] Despite the symbolic legitimacy and constitutional authority, Morocco's stability is also fundamentally derived from the *Mahkzen*'s willingness to suppress internal dissent, manipulate and co-opt political opposition, nurture alliances with rural elites, and adroitly navigate the international arena.[9]

In the latter years of Hassan's rule, the government continued to confront acute economic and social problems. Despite a decrease in population growth, the population size continued to surpass the economy's ability to provide jobs, especially for its youth. Young people under the age of 20 represent 47 percent of Morocco's 29 million people, with urban areas boasting ample numbers of *hittistes*, literally "those who lean against the wall."[10] Official unemployment averaged 20 percent, reaching 21.5 percent in 2000.[11] Actual unemployment levels are significantly higher, exacerbating social pressures and discontent, especially in volatile urban areas. Morocco's labor market suffers from deep segmentation between the high-pay formal sector and the low-pay, unregulated informal sector.

Morocco's rank on the Human Development Index (HDI) of the United Nations Development Programme remained low throughout the 1990s. At the time of Hassan's death at the end of the decade, Morocco's ranking stood at 126.[12] Adult literacy stood at 46 percent, and nearly two-thirds of women were illiterate; life expectancy at birth stood at 67 years, and only 35 percent of the population had access to safe water. Chronic drought plagued the country, with crucial water resources devoted to the tourist sector's hydrological demand for swimming pools, hotels, and golf courses. Finally, according to the IMF, Morocco's urbanization rate surged in the 1980s and 1990s, increasing from 41.1 percent in 1980 to 55.9 percent in 2001.[13]

During the 1990s, the *Makhzen*'s ability to govern authoritatively began to show signs of strain. The government's move to pursue gradual reforms was prompted in part by international changes wrought by the end of the Cold War—including enhanced pressure from Western allies for electoral, economic, and human rights reform—as well as the proliferation of satellite television and cellular technology exposing the populace to external influences. At the same time, it was a crafty step on Hassan's part to maintain the Palace's role as the supreme arbiter of political life.[14] The challenge was to manage the change.

Being of poor health for several years, Hassan anticipated his son's accession. He had increasingly given his son a more important decision-making role. Hassan took similar steps with his younger son, Rachid, but it was Crown Prince Sidi Mohammed who throughout the 1990s played increasingly visible roles in domestic and foreign affairs. Given that his 1992 doctoral dissertation at France's Université Sophia Antipolis de Nice was on Euro-Maghrebi relations,[15] it seemed appropriate that many of his tasks involved high-profile encounters with European leaders. He was also a general in the Royal Armed Forces (FAR), giving him visibility and stature within the "military *Makhzen*." At the same time, whether intentionally or otherwise, Mohammed remained relatively isolated from Hassan's closest advisers. After Hassan's death, this enabled Mohammed to avoid appearing beholden to his father's advisers and associated with the negative aspects of Hassan's legacy.

At the constitutional level, Hassan also anticipated the coming succession. The constitutional revision of September 1996, which split the previously unicameral Parliament into a Chamber of Representatives directly elected by universal suffrage, and a Chamber of Advisers chosen by an electoral college, was a significant event for Morocco and the region. The direct election of a parliamentary chamber was an important development, as it responded to longtime claims by the opposition that elections under the unicameral system were undemocratic and too easily manipulated by the Palace. Moreover, the reform provided the juridical context for the November 1997 election, which resulted in a relatively equal split between three main political coalitions: the pro-Palace *Wifaq*, the opposition *Koutla*, and the center right.

In the aftermath of the election, in February 1998, Hassan appointed Youssoufi, head of the USFP and a member of the *Koutla* coalition, as prime minister and directed him to form a government. While Youssoufi's power, and the power of the Parliament, was still sharply circumscribed, the gradual liberalization in the late 1990s went far to satisfy external observers and to shift criticism of the government's handling of economic and social affairs away from the Palace and towards the Parliament. Thus, the accession of Mohammed VI bought time for the struggling *alternance* government, and also allowed the new King to be less criticized by popular frustration than if the reins of power had been fully in the hands of the Palace.

In addition to Morocco's troubled political economy and electoral reforms, in the 1990s Hassan continued to grapple with the challenges posed by political Islam, Berber activism, and the Western Sahara conflict. The Moroccan monarch's status as a descendant of the Prophet Mohammed and as *Amir al-Mu'minin* has resulted in a complex relationship with societal groups espousing political Islam. In the view of some analysts, the religious legitimacy of the Moroccan monarchy has attenuated the force of Islamism evident in other North African countries.[16] On the other hand, one might argue that the monarchy's status has proven to be a source of frustration and criticism for Islamists who do not recognize the monarchy's legitimacy or who criticize the Palace for its failure to adhere properly to Islamist interpretations of theology and political philosophy.[17] The correct interpretation is likely to be somewhere in between, with the Palace working closely with official, moderate Islamic groups and cracking down on Islamists who are hostile to the regime.

In the 1997 elections, the moderate Islamist group *Al-Islah wa-l-Tajdid* (Reform and Renewal) ran for election under the banner of the Constitutional Movement for Popular Democracy (MPCD) and won nine seats. While it did not receive a cabinet post in the 1998 or 2000 governments, the MPCD, renamed the Justice and Development Party (*Parti de la justice et du développement* – PJD) in 1998, emerged as a powerful force in Moroccan politics, as demonstrated in the 2002 elections.[18]

The PJD is quite different from the Islamist movement *Al-'Adl wa-'l-Ihsan* (Justice and Charity) and its leader, Abd al-Salam Yassin. In contrast to the PJD, *Al-'Adl wa-'l-Ihsan* is unwilling to acknowledge the legitimacy of the monarchy. The movement effectively began in 1974, when Yassin wrote an open letter to Hassan II questioning the legitimacy of the monarchy. Yassin addressed Hassan as "My Brother," rather than "Your Majesty."[19] In addition, Yassin espouses the establishment of an Islamic government to eradicate the state of *jahiliya* into which Hassan had led the country; in Islamic thought, a *jahili* society is a pre-Islamic and/or non-Islamic society, in which people exist in a spiritual and moral ignorance. Some analysts expect "Justice and Charity" will seek legal status after Sheikh Yassin's death, but, as discussed further below, such developments would come about only after elaborate negotiations.

Paradoxically, perhaps, Moroccans on the left and right, who are not supporters of political Islam, may be more anxious about the PJD than about Yassin's *Al-'Adl wa-'l-Ihsan*. Although Yassin commands respect and support from a significant portion of Moroccan society, the PJD's willingness to play the electoral game has led to its growth in credibility and popular strength. However, although the PJD accepts the legitimacy of the monarchy, its social programs and views on important issues, such as the status of women, are seen as potentially more extreme than those of *Al-'Adl wa-'l-Ihsan* or, at least, more likely to influence a Palace concerned about social tensions.

Regarding the challenges of Berber activism in the 1990s, the significant weight of Amazigh culture and identity has remained an important part of Moroccan society. It is important to note, however, that the four tribal groups stretching from north to south—Rif, Braber, Shulh, and Soussi—comprise at least 40 percent of Morocco's 29 million inhabitants. The increasing salience of Berber identity throws into question the facile characterization of Morocco as part of the "Arab world."[20]

In the 1990s Hassan's control of Amazigh expression began to weaken, and greater cultural activism reflected the gradual *aperture* of the period.

Amazigh activists protested against educational and cultural margin-alization. Children from rural Amazigh households would learn Arabic in school and return home unable to communicate with their parents regarding their educational experience. Nonetheless, little progress was made in the 1990s; the ferment and activism generally met with challenges from the *Makhzen.*

The challenges posed by the status of Western Sahara are a lasting legacy of Hassan's rule. Known as the "southern provinces" in Morocco, the phosphate-rich region remained the subject of a UN-supervised ceasefire and one of the UN's longest-running disputed areas. Morocco laid full claim to the territory after Franco's death in 1975 and Spain's withdrawal in early 1976.[21] In 1976, Morocco formally annexed the territory. The Algerian-backed POLISARIO Front, founded in 1973, began armed struggle for the independence of the Sahrawi Arab Democratic Republic (SADR). More than 70 countries have recognized the SADR, as well as the Organization of African Unity (renamed African Union in 2000), with the UN General Assembly according the POLISARIO Front observer status. For its part, Morocco withdrew from the OAU in 1984 and remains the only African country that is not a member of the African Union. Morocco has persisted in urging many countries to retract their recognition of the POLISARIO and the SADR; in 2006 Togo withdrew its recognition of SADR, but South Africa recognized the SADR a year earlier. Morocco has also spent a great deal of money, as well as lives, to consolidate its military grip on the territory, building a defensive sand wall and developing local infrastructure. Two general elections have been held in the territory. The centrality of Western Sahara to Moroccan politics should not be underestimated. Actors across the political spectrum accept the region as indisputably Moroccan; those who disagree are ostracized by the state's security apparatus or are quickly marginalized.

Since the early 1980s, both Morocco and the POLISARIO have accepted a UN-sponsored self-determination referendum, and a ceasefire has been in place since 1991. However, due to differences regarding the voting rolls for the referendum, the dispute has continued. The POLISARIO wants the electoral rolls limited to a 1974 Spanish census and accepted the 1995 criteria established by the UN Security Council, but Morocco insists that individuals of Saharan parentage living in the territory or in Morocco should be eligible to vote. In addition, Morocco transferred Moroccans into the territory in order to shift the results of the referendum in a favorable direction.

Prior to Hassan's death, the former US Secretary of State, James A. Baker III, brokered the 1997 Houston Accords.[22] Given that the accords gave some ground to Morocco in allowing more voters to be included in the planned referendum, Rabat was generally satisfied. However, the Moroccan government could not be assured that the referendum's outcome would work in its favor and continued its attempts to postpone it. Since both sides expected to win the referendum, it was uncertain whether the losing side would accept the outcome.[23] The UN Mission for the Referendum in Western Sahara (MINURSO) postponed elections in November 1999. On an international scale, Morocco continued to receive criticism from various quarters, most notably the human rights community, activists in different countries, and international bodies, such as the European Parliament. Strong backing from the US, France, Spain, and the European Commission, however, enabled the country to withstand the disapproval.

On the eve of Mohammed VI's rise to the throne, Morocco was a country wracked by profound problems: economic, political, social, and diplomatic. Frustrations with the government remained high, with the Parliament and the Palace receiving sharp criticisms from many sectors. The paradox associated with Hassan's death was the outpouring of grief at his funeral. As Maghraoui instructs, despite Hassan's fundamental lack of popularity, the popular flood of emotions should be viewed not so much as lamentation for Hassan's passing, but as "a demonstration aimed at recovering a degree of popular control over political validation that the modern nationalist movement and the political parties to which it gave rise have never been able to achieve."[24] Thus, Mohammed VI had to approach the throne with the recognition that circumstances had changed and that expectations of him were high, possibly too high.

Challenges for the New Monarch

Observers noted Mohammed's early intimations of his admiration for the Spanish monarchical model, one in which King Juan Carlos played a quiet, stabilizing force in Spain's transition to democracy after Franco's death in 1975. Yet, this role did not become manifest for the new monarch. Mohammed did not move behind the scenes like Juan Carlos; nor did he provide Youssoufi with the kind of powers and prerogatives that Spain's Prime Minister, Adolfo Suárez, enjoyed in the early years of the post-Franco era (1977–81). The Palace even suppressed such speculation, releasing a statement that: "Morocco's unique history and cultural specificity preclude imported models."[25] And, in a September 2001 interview with the French newspaper *Le Figaro*, Mohammed VI championed the notion of a "democratic executive monarchy," which, as more than one observer has pointed out, has a somewhat oxymoronic character.

Nonetheless, Mohammed took important steps to indicate a break with the past. For example, he broke political taboos by openly speaking of those who had disappeared and of arbitrary arrests in the past. This process included the gradual and controlled opening of dossiers on the so-called "years of lead" (*les années de plomb*), the years of repression of political dissidents within Morocco. The headiness of such an opening cannot be overstated. Mohammed took the extraordinary step of touring a prison in December 2001. In January 2004, the King took another significant step in forming an Equity and Reconciliation Commission (IER) to investigate the "years of lead" and, in his words, to "reconcile Morocco with its past." The IER's final report was released in late 2005.[26] The return of longtime dissident Abraham Serfaty from exile in France in September 2000 and the dismissal of the immovable Moroccan minister of interior and information, Driss Basri, in November 1999 were also important events. Serfaty had been arrested in 1974, tortured, imprisoned for 17 years, and exiled in 1991.[27] Basri had been Hassan's right-hand man, controlling a powerful ministry responsible for a wide array of police, security, surveillance, and paramilitary functions. Finally, the new king strengthened the Consultative Council for Human Rights (CCDH) and amended the penal code to abolish torture.[28]

Despite these positive steps, celebrated as part of Mohammed's early years, the fundamental components of the political system remained in place: namely weakened parties and a powerful *Makhzen*. In the aftermath of the 1998 elections, the government was controlled by seven parties: the USFP, the Istiqlal Party (*Parti Istiqlal* – PI), the National Assembly of Independents (*Rassemblement national des indépendants* – RNI), the National Popular Movement (MNP), the Party for Progress and Socialism (PPS), the Social Democratic Party (PSD), and the Democratic Forces Front (FFD).

The September 2002 election was the first election since 1997. It effectively consolidated the electoral reforms made by Hassan.[29] Prior to the 2002 elections, some striking developments were seen in Morocco. The government invested a significant amount of energy in voter education campaigns, with pamphlets, billboards, and radio and television commercials celebrating the electoral process. Many of the public-service announcements were geared towards a population with high rates of illiteracy. They patiently explained, for example, how to put check marks next to the symbols of the voter's preferred party—a rose for the USFP, a balance for the Istiqlal Party, a dove for the RNI, and a lantern for the PJD. The stakes were high, and the international community and domestic analysts closely observed the election. One of the most-watched aspects of the election was the potential outcome for the PJD. After having won nine seats in the 1997 elections, a number that increased to 14 after by-elections and changes in party affiliations, the PJD was in a position to do very well. Significantly, the PJD chose to limit its campaign to 56 out of 91 precincts, in order to concentrate its energy in potentially successful areas and economize its resources. This limitation was also a reflection of an agreement made with the Ministry of Interior.[30]

In the end, the election results broke down as follows. Out of a population of nearly 30 million, 13.9 million Moroccans were registered to vote. The total number of votes cast stood at 7.2 million, giving a turnout of 51.8 percent. Of the 7.2 million votes cast, 5.9 million (82 percent) were valid. The remaining 1.3 million votes were invalidated due to improper or protest markings. In December 2002, Mohammed announced plans to lower the voting age from 20 to 18, in an attempt to engage the largely alienated youth.

Table 5.1 Results of the 28 September 2002 Election to the *Majlis al-Nuwwab*[31] (Moroccan Parliament)

Political Party	Seats	Percentage of valid votes
Socialist Union of Popular Forces (USFP) [Abderrahman Al-Youssoufi]	50	15.38
Istiqlal Party (Independence Party) [Abbas Al-Fassi]	48	14.77
Justice and Development Party (PJD) [Abdelkrim Al-Khatib]	42	12.92
National Assembly of Independents (RNI) [Ahmed Osman]	41	12.62
Popular Movement (MP) [Mohamed Laenser]	27	8.31
National Popular Movement (MNP) [Mahjoubi Aherdane]	18	5.54
Constitutional Union (UC) [Mohamed Abied]	16	4.92
Democratic Forces Front (FFD) [Thami El Khyari]	12	3.69
National Democratic Party (PND) [Abdallah Kadiri]	12	3.69
Party of Progress and Socialism (PPS) [Ismail Alaoui]	11	3.38
Democratic Union (UD) [Bouazza Ikken]	10	3.08
Democratic and Social Movement (MDS) [Mahmoud Archane]	7	2.15
Democratic Socialist Party (PSD) [Aissa Ouardighi]	6	1.85
Parti Al-Ahd [Najib El Ouazzani]	5	
Alliance of Liberties (ADL) [Ali Belhaj]	4	
Party of the Unified Socialist Left (GSU) [Mohamed Ben Said Ait Idder]	3	
Moroccan Liberal Party (PML) [Mohamed Ziane]	3	
Reform and Development Party (PRD) [Abderrahmane Al-Kouhen]	3	
Citizen Forces (FC) [Abderrahman Lahjouji]	2	
Democratic and Independence Party (PDI) [Abdelwahed Maach]	2	
Environment and Development Party (PED) [Ahmed Al-Alami]	2	
National Ittihadi Congress Party (CNI) [Abdelmajid Bouzoubaa]	1	

The PJD tripled its parliamentary representation and emerged as the third-largest force in the Parliament, after the USFP and the Istiqlal Party. Its performance received close attention from analysts, as it was noted as marking the Islamists' emergence as an official political force. Given the aforementioned exclusion of *Al-'Adl wa-'l-Ihsan*, the support for Islamist forces in the country is likely much higher than the elections indicate.

After weeks of negotiations, Mohammed appointed the government in November 2002. Formed by Prime Minister Driss Jettou, the government included 22 newcomers, with 16 remaining from the previous government. Six parties made up the government: the USFP (8), Istiqlal Party (8), RNI (6), MP (3), PPS (2), and MNP (2). The PJD did not join the government. Jettou himself was appointed by the King, a striking development as Jettou had no formal party affiliation. Jettou replaced the USFP's Youssoufi.

Critics of the elections were not so much critical of the government's conduct of the elections as they were of the focus on the electoral process without genuine constitutional revision that would facilitate control of the powerful sovereign ministries.[32] More disconcerting is that, while the elections were initially deemed free and fair, allegations have surfaced in recent years that the polls were "managed" by the major parties. Evidence for these allegations, however, remains unclear. An additional development was the first-ever use of a "national list" of women candidates. In the election for the Parliament, which has 325 seats, 295 seats were part of a "local list," with 30 seats reserved on a "national list" for women.

Two additional developments with respect to women in the post-Hassan era were Mohammed's promulgation of a reformed *Mudawwana* (personal status code) in February 2004 and his marriage to Salma Bennani in March 2002. In the 1990s, Hassan had recoiled from profound changes that would challenge the power of the *ulama* (religious scholars) and conservatives. Yet, Hassan demurred from capitulating to the Islamists in order to avoid raising the specter of Algeria or Iran.[33] Mohammed VI, by contrast, braved criticisms and pushed for the *Mudawwana*'s passing. Under the new law, passed with sharp opposition by Islamists, including the "moderate" PJD, both spouses were to have equal authority within the family, with the wife receiving property rights. In addition, the marriage age was raised from 15 to 18, with divorce made easier for women. Finally, polygamy was made more difficult, although not illegal; it is required for a man to get consent from his existing wife (or wives) before marrying another.[34] Problems of implementation remain, however, with judges not well trained in the new code and a lack of information among women about their rights.[35] Moreover, activists have pointed out that there is little significance in giving a woman the right to divorce if she is illiterate or lacks means of supporting herself.[36]

Mohammed's marriage to Salma Bennani in March 2002 represented a striking break with the past in several ways. Benanni, a 24-year-old computer engineer, is the daughter of a professor from Tangiers. This marked a contrast to Mohammed's father, Hassan, and his grandfather, Mohammed V, who not only took several wives, but also never publicly married. Mohammed VI's mother, Latifa, never even appeared in public. While she is known as the "mother of the princes," not a queen, the Palace has presented Bennani as a figure who would play a high-profile role with regard to women's issues and the role of women in public life.

With respect to the economy, Mohammed's early years benefited from improved rainfall. After stagnant years at the end of the 1990s and in 2000, Morocco enjoyed a significant improvement in its per capita annual economic growth rate in 2001 and 2002: 4.8 percent and 2.9 percent, respectively. The primary reason for the solid figure in 2001 was an annual growth rate of 23 percent in the agricultural sector. In a country with nearly 50 percent of its population devoted to agricultural production, the solid growth was a function of good rainfall and an abundant crop. From 1992 to 2002, the agricultural sector's average annual growth rate was 1.7 percent. Despite the years of respectable growth in the early portion of Mohammed's reign, the World Bank reported that GDP per capita growth for the entire economy for 2004 and 2005 was 0.7 and 0.4.[37] The Economist Intelligence Unit also pointed to a slowdown in Morocco's economic growth, especially after poor winter rains in 2005, with real GDP growth for that year reported at a meager 1.5 percent.[38]

In 2006, the IMF's Article IV consultations claimed the country to be on a good track, praising the macroeconomic stability of the previous decade.[39] The IMF commended the government's policies on maintaining a low inflation rate and a solid reserve position, and it praised the banking reforms taken since 2003. It also praised the value of the dirham, which has been pegged since 2001 to a basket of currencies dominated by the euro. Criticism in the report, however, focused on the poor results achieved in raising living standards, noting that poverty remains very high, especially in rural areas.

Despite the positive assessment, after reasonably successful years in 2003 and 2004, with annual growth rates in real GDP at 5.5 and 4.2 percent respectively, 2005 saw a drop to 1.7 percent in annual GDP growth, largely due to poor performance in the agricultural sector. The current-account balance, for its part, dropped in 2004 and 2005 to 1.7 and 1.5 percent of GDP respectively, a fall-off from the 3.4 percent in 2003.[40]

Mohammed had been hailed by the media as the "King of the Poor" due to his frequent encounters with the citizens in Moroccan cities and towns. He traveled so often throughout the country in his first years in power that he was known informally as *al-Jawal*, Moroccan Arabic for portable telephone.[41] In addition, he made repeated references to poverty and drought, and personally visited poor communities. This appeared to come from genuine concern on behalf of the monarch. It also lessened the power of arguments that criticized the regime for its neglect of the poor. At the same time, Mohammed remains exceedingly wealthy. He is the pre-eminent figure in the private holding company, Omnium Nord Africain (ONA), which continues to acquire key holdings in a wide array of business sectors, including mining, agro-alimentary, shipping and distribution, and financial services.[42]

Despite the rhetoric with respect to eradicating poverty, Morocco remains ranked 123, a slight improvement from the ranking of 126 in the 1990s noted earlier.[43] Moreover, its Human Poverty Index (HPI-1), a ranking for developing countries, places Morocco 59th among 102 developing countries. The HPI-1 measures severe deprivation in health by the proportion of the population not expected to survive age 40.[44]

Upon his accession to the throne, Mohammed promised greater consideration for Amazigh demands. In October 2001, he set up the Royal Institute for Amazigh culture, a step that, as suggested above, would have been inconceivable for his father. It is important to note, however, that authorities banned a January 2002 conference in al-Hoceima, which was organized by the Association for the Defense of Victims of the Rif War in order to examine the use of poisonous gas by Spanish troops against Rifian troops and civilians, including Berbers, during the revolt in the 1920s. No explanation was given for its banning.[45]

Al-Hoceima is also the site of a key event in the post-Hassan era: the devastating earthquake of February 2004: nearly 600 people died in the rumble that struck rural areas around al-Hoceima. After several days of delay and angry protests due to postponements in relief efforts, Mohammed visited the region and, according to press reports, met with adoring crowds. Yet, charges have been made that local authorities slowed the relief efforts in part to make way for the passing of the royal motorcade.[46] Regardless of the merit of such charges, the earthquake exposed deep problems within the political economy as well as the unclear prerogatives/responsibilities of local and national-level officials: substandard housing construction, ineffective responses to natural disasters, and regional dynamics tied into Amazigh politics in the Rif.

Finally, with respect to the Equity and Reconciliation Commission (IER), while its mandate is laudable, and its existence is relatively unique in the Middle East, North Africa, and throughout the world, its operation has been the subject of criticism, as victims testifying before the commission are not allowed to give names. There was poor coordination with the main human rights organizations within the country.[47] Moreover, the focus on the past may well ignore the present issues associated with human rights, especially pertaining to the wide security sweeps conducted after the bombings that took place in Casablanca in May 2003.

International Context

The world has changed dramatically since 1999, and evaluations of Mohammed's reign and the Moroccan government have to be considered within a fraught international context. Prior to 11 September 2001, Western governments formed closer ties with governments that had been criticized by international human rights observers. There had been a diminution of emphasis on key human rights standards, at least at the level of official practice.[48] North Africa, and in particular Egypt, Tunisia, Morocco, and Algeria became subject to less criticism from European and North American capitals, especially as the governments confronted the domestic opposition of political Islam.[49]

These trends have only deepened in this decade, especially as the semiotic field and policy positions associated with the "war on terror" emanating from the US prompted a willingness to look the other way. Increasingly, Western governments, particularly the US, have collaborated directly with interior ministries and *Mukhabarat* (intelligence agencies) in the region. For example, in 2002, Tunisia's Ben Ali received clearance from his ruling party to run for two additional presidential terms, likely stretching his tenure from 7 November 1987 until 2014. Ben Ali was subsequently "re-elected" in October 2004 with 94.48 percent of the vote. US Secretary of State Colin Powell visited the region in December 2003 and offered minimal criticism of Tunisia's human rights record and its poor electoral reform.[50] In an interview with Fox News on 14 March 2004, Powell even praised Tunisia for its progress in democratic reforms.[51] European capitals also softened their disapproval of North African governments' human rights records.

Perhaps the most notable development with respect to the economy has been the signing of a Free Trade Agreement (FTA) with the United States in 2004. From Morocco's perspective, it is an attempt to diversify after a longstanding dependence on the European market.[52] The Association Agreements put in place with Europe in 2000 stipulated a 12-year process of lowering tariffs between the EU and Morocco. Despite the initial optimism regarding the agreement's benefits for Morocco, there have been increasing frustrations, as some observers characterized it as "an economic mirage."[53] Problems include disappointment with European tourism, non-tariff protectionism by individual EU countries, the growing agro-alimentary dependence on Europe, and the stagnant levels of trade. Although the transition toward the EU–Moroccan Association is still under way and may ultimately prove successful, the early indications are not promising. Europe and Morocco remain at a standstill with respect to the pivotal agricultural trade.

In addition to its desire to diversify trading partners, the Moroccan government envisions the FTA with the US as fulfilling several additional goals, such as stimulating economic growth, increasing employment, encouraging direct foreign investment, and providing impetus for domestic reforms.

The US has oriented its efforts, since the attacks on the World Trade Center and the Pentagon, to deepen trade and diplomatic relationships with allied countries in the region. In 2002, the Bush administration first put forward a modest Middle East Partnership Initiative (MEPI), which was then followed by the more ambitious Broader Middle East and North Africa Initiative (BMENA), promulgated at the G8 meeting at Sea Island,

Georgia, in June 2004. Bush announced his goals of creating a greater Middle East free trade region in May 2004 in stating:

> The combined GDP of all Arab countries is smaller than that of Spain. Their peoples have less access to the Internet than the people of Sub-Sahara Africa. The Arab world has a great cultural tradition, but is largely missing out on the economic progress of our time.[54]

The BMENA goals included supporting political, economic, and social reforms in the region through, for example, programs supporting civil society groups, electoral reforms, microfinance initiatives, and literacy programs. It addressed universal problems within the region and development deficits identified in a series of prominent *Arab Human Development Reports*, prepared by Arab scholars for the United Nations Development Programme (UNDP).[55] The final version of the BMENAI, however, was met with skepticism and frustration, and its prospects remain uncertain.[56]

Equally pivotal in the US–Moroccan relationship is the naming of Morocco as a major non-NATO ally in June 2004. This status is only enjoyed by close allies. In recognition of the country's strategic importance to the US, Morocco joined Israel, Egypt, Jordan, and Bahrain, along with several Asian countries (Pakistan, Japan, the Philippines, South Korea, and Thailand), Australia, New Zealand, and Argentina. Such a distinction makes Morocco eligible for priority delivery of defense material, participation in defense research and development programs, and a beneficiary of US government loan guarantee programs for the purchase of military material. Finally, Morocco is the only country in the MENA region to receive funding from the Millennium Challenge Account. Pressure from within the Moroccan political system towards slow progress is therefore supported by an international climate that does not place a high premium on thoroughgoing reforms, but rather on gradual and controlled changes.

Morocco's position across the Straits of Gibraltar, and its complicated historical relationship with Spain, also merits attention. The stability of Morocco's political system is of pre-eminent importance for Spanish policy makers. After the unsteadiness of José María Aznar's government and the Popular Party (PP), the new Socialist government of José Luis Rodríguez Zapatero, elected in March 2004, has diminished tensions that existed between the two countries. Nonetheless, profound issues have not been resolved, most importantly the security and economic dimensions of undocumented labor migration. The clashes and subsequent tragic deaths of migrants trying to storm the Spanish enclaves of Ceuta and Melilla in 2005 and 2006 brought these issues once again into the spotlight, as had the dispute over ownership of Parsley islet (Perejil in Spanish; Leila to the Moroccans) in the summer of 2002, and the influx of migrants to the Canary Islands in 2006. The Moroccan government has displayed a characteristic public position of willingness to work on resolving the issues, even though its ability to affect policy reform and assist European officials is hampered by the sheer complexity of the migration dynamic, within Morocco as well as within the African continent.

Therefore, it is impossible to divorce "the end of the era of leniency" from the crucial international context in which Morocco is situated. In October 2005, the US officially designated the Moroccan Islamic Combatant Group (GICM)—implicated in both the Casablanca and Madrid bombings—as a foreign terrorist organization; and Morocco is now clearly a battleground in the global "war on terror." It is difficult to ascertain whether this is accidental and reluctant on the part of Rabat, or whether it is sought actively by the Palace and the Parliament as a strategic consideration to further domestic political calculations.

Conclusion

Important changes have taken place in Morocco since Hassan's death in 1999. For example, it would have been inconceivable during the 1990s to imagine a Minister of Communication publicly stating that Amazigh should be incorporated into public media broadcasts or that national television stations 2M and TVM would broadcast news in Amazigh, as was announced in March 2005. Similarly, reform of the *Mudawwana* was unanticipated, as well as the efforts of the IER to investigate human rights abuses.

Nonetheless, one could not argue that everything has changed. In deep and profound ways, the *Makhzen* and its constituent components—i.e., the military *Makhzen* and the economic *Makhzen*—remain central to Moroccan political life. In turn, the fundamental structures of Moroccan society remain firmly entrenched. Even Mohammed VI has worked assiduously not to overestimate his role as a transforming agent. For example, in a 2004 interview with *Paris Match*, he argued: "Protocol is and remains protocol. A rumor abounded that I have tried to turn things upside down. That's false. The style is different but ... I am seeking to preserve the rigor of each and every existing protocol."[57] Although Mohammed VI does not appear to be pursuing a strategy of political dualism—a skillful combination of blending political pluralism with royal arbitration—to the same degree as his father, he is hardly moving toward a dramatic *perestroika*.[58]

The greatest challenges for the government remain the ongoing strength of political Islam and the economy. Some suggest that the PJD will be brought into the cabinet within the coming years, with the PJD agreeing to attenuate further the hard edges of its political platform. Similarity, *Al-'Adl wa-'l-Ihsan*'s leader, Abd al-Salam Yassin, is in failing health, and after his death, the role of the movement is likely to change, perhaps under the leadership of his energetic daughter, Nadia. In September 2005, she faced a jail sentence for criticizing Mohammed VI.[59] Criticism from Western actors, especially from the US, kept her from jail. If the economy fails to improve measurably or if more effective social policies are not implemented, the strength of political Islam is likely to intensify as Islamist leaders campaign on anti-corruption and justice platforms.[60]

John Waterbury, in his 1970 path-breaking book, *The Commander of the Faithful*, argued that Hassan had succeeded in crafting inertia in the political system and, thereby, control. In a provocative comparison with the Shah's Iran, Waterbury wrote:

> The essential dilemma of such a monarch is to promote economic development without upsetting the delicate political stalemate that he has helped maintain. The recent development of Iran would indicate that, under highly favorable economic circumstances, a monarch can encourage, at least on a short-term basis, economic development while maintaining the political status quo. Unlike Iran, however, Morocco receives no massive revenues from the sale of its natural resources, and King Hassan has no financial cushion with which to meet the country's economic crisis.[61]

Despite oil rents, the Shah fell in 1979; Hassan remained in power for nearly 30 more years. Yet, Waterbury touched on a crucial component of Moroccan society: the degree to which political stability is contingent on economic and social justice. Given the heightened expectations associated with Mohammed VI's new reign—as well as enhanced stakes in the international arena—the new King may have even further to fall than his father. Economic or social promises will soon have to be delivered, or the closing of the political system may become even more pronounced. Minister of communication Nabil Ben Abdallah used a biological metaphor to explain this situation: "We need time to create a democratic culture. We are in a transitional period, which is naturally one of extreme fragility. It is like the period when reptiles molt, when they are at their most fragile. Morocco is in that period—coming out of one system and going into another."[62] As Morocco's transition continues, the fragility it experiences could indeed lead to a new openness. However, the fragility of the transition could also result in Morocco turning away from openness and leniency, and towards tighter restriction on political and civic life.

The legislative elections of 7 September 2007 appeared to defy the conventional expectation of the democratization literature. Logically, a consolidation of electoral reforms would prompt increased voter enthusiasm and turnout. Voters have a stake in the elections and, therefore, turn out at the polls. Other experiences of political liberalization in Africa and Eastern Europe have proven this empirical evidence. By contrast, the 2007 Moroccan elections saw a turnout of only 37 percent, a sharp decline from 52 percent in the 2002 election and 58 percent in 1997. In addition, the number of spoiled ballots increased to 19 percent from 17 percent in 2002.

The decline in voters turnout might be due to a combination of factors: the adoption of a system of proportional representation in 2002 that results in a fragmentation of party influence within the Majlis; voter disaffection stemming from apathy and distrust of party elites; sober assessments of the Majlis' political efficacy and influence; and insufficient media coverage and voter education efforts.

The Istiqlal Party won 10.7 percent of the vote, garnering 52 seats, an increase of 4 from 2002. The PJD won 10.9 percent of the vote, increasing its presence by 4 seats to 46. The pro-government People's Movement won 9.3 percent, increasing its holding of seats by 14 seats to 41. The National Rally of Independents earned 9.7 percent of the vote, resulting in 39 seats. The big loser was the USFP, which lost 12 seats from 2002. It earned 8.9 percent of the vote and now holds 38 seats; it left the governing coalition after that. The King appointed Istiqlal leader Abbas El Fassi as Prime Minister.

Notes

1 G. Joffé, "The Moroccan Political System after the Elections," *Mediterranean Politics*, 1998, vol. 3, no. 3, pp. 106–25.
2 J. N. Ferrié, "Chronique politique: Succession monarchique et désenchantement de l'alternance partisane," *Annuaire de l'Afrique du Nord*, Paris: CNRS, 1999.
3 Full text of the speech delivered by H. M. King Mohammed VI, 29 May 2003, Casablanca. Available at: http://www.mincom.gov.ma/english/generalities/speech/2003/casablanca_attacks.htm.
4 I. Dalle, "Espérances déçues au Maroc: Bilan de cinq ans de réformes," *Le Monde Diplomatique*, August 2004, pp. 18–19.
5 M. Le Gall, "The Historical Context," in *Polity and Society in Contemporary North Africa*, I. W. Zartman and M. Habeeb (eds), Boulder, CO: Westview, 1993.
6 A. Hammoudi, *Master and Disciple: The Cultural Foundations of Moroccan Authoritarianism*, Chicago: Chicago University Press, 1997; and J. Waterbury, *The Commander of the Faithful: The Moroccan Political Elite*, New York: Columbia University Press, 1970.
7 L. Anderson, "Absolutism and the Resilience of Monarchy in the Middle East," *Political Science Quarterly*, 1991, vol. 106, no. 1, pp. 1–15.
8 Text available at: http://www.mincom.gov.ma. See also G. White, "The Advent of Electoral Democracy in Morocco? The Referendum of 1996," *Middle East Journal*, 1997, vol. 51, no. 3, pp. 389–404.
9 T. Desrues and E. Moyano, "Social Change and Political Transition in Morocco," *Mediterranean Politics*, 2001, vol. 6, no. 1, pp. 21–47; R. Leveau, *Le fellah marocain: Défenseur du trône* 2nd edn, Paris, Presse de la Fondation nationale des sciences politiques, 1985; H. Munson, *Religion and Power in Morocco*, New Haven, CT: Yale University Press, 1993.
10 A. Richards, "Socioeconomic Roots of Middle East Radicalism," *Naval War College Review*, vol. 4, no. 4 (2002), pp. 22–38. The appellation *hittistes* emerged in Algeria in the early 1980s; they were very active in the tragic 1988 riots that shook Algeria.
11 Economist Intelligence Unit, *Country Report: Morocco 2004–05*. London: The Economist, 2004.
12 UNDP, *Human Development Report 1999: Globalization with a Human Face*, New York: Oxford University Press, 1999.
13 International Monetary Fund, *Staff Report for the 2003 Article IV Consultation: Morocco*, Washington DC: IMF, 2003.
14 G. Denoeux and A. Maghraoui, "King Hassan's Strategy of Political Dualism," *Middle East Policy*, 1998, vol. 5. no. 4, pp. 104–30; A. Maghraoui, "From Symbolic

Legitimacy to Democratic Legitimacy: Monarchic Rule and Political Reform in Morocco," *Journal of Democracy*, 2001, vol. 12, no. 1, pp. 73–86.

15 M. Ben Al-Hassan Alaoui, *La coopération entre l'Union Européenne et les pays du Maghreb*, Paris: Editions Nathan, 1994.

16 M. E. Combs-Schilling, *Sacred Performances: Islam, Sexuality, and Sacrifice*, New York: Columbia University Press, 1989.

17 H. Munson, *Religion and Power in Morocco*, New Haven, CT: Yale University Press, 1993.

18 M. J. Willis, "Morocco's Islamists and the Legislative Elections of 2002: The Strange Case of the Party That Did Not Want to Win," *Mediterranean Politics*, vol. 9, no. 1 (spring 2004), pp. 53–81.

19 Munson, *Religion and Power in Morocco*, op. cit.

20 S. Usher, "Moroccan Schools Teach Berber," BBC News, news.bbc.co.uk, 15 September 2003.

21 J. Mundy, "Neutrality or Complicity? The United States and the 1975 Moroccan Takeover of the Spanish Sahara," *The Journal of North African Studies*, vol. 11, no. 3, September 2006, pp. 275–306. See also, Y. H. Zoubir and K. Benabdallah-Gambier, "The United States and the North African Imbroglio: Balancing Interests in Algeria, Morocco, and the Western Sahara," *Mediterranean Politics*, vol. 10, no. 2, July 2005, pp. 181–202.

22 J. A. Mundy, "'Seized of the Matter': The UN and the Western Sahara Dispute," *Mediterranean Quarterly*, 2004, vol. 15, no. 3, pp. 130–48.

23 Economist Intelligence Unit, *Country Profile Morocco 2000/2001*. London: EIU.

24 A. Maghraoui, "From Symbolic Legitimacy to Democratic Legitimacy: Monarchic Rule and Political Reform in Morocco," *Journal of Democracy*, vol. 12, no. 1, 2001, pp. 73–86.

25 Ibid.

26 Available at: http://www.ier.ma.

27 C. Daure-Serfaty, *Letter from Morocco*, trans. P. R. Côté and C. Mitchell, East Lansing, Michigan State University Press, 2003.

28 M. Ottaway and M. Riley, "Morocco: From Top–Down Reform to Democratic Transition," Carnegie Papers: Middle East Series 71, September 2006.

29 J. J. Linz and A. Stepan, *Problems of Democratic Transition and Consolidation: Southern Europe, South America and Post-Communist Europe*, Baltimore, John Hopkins University Press, 1996.

30 Willis, "Morocco's Islamists and the Legislative Elections of 2002," op. cit.

31 Collected and compiled by the author from Moroccan newspaper reports in September–October 2002.

32 A. Jamai, "La gauche gouvernementale piégée au Maroc," *Le Monde Diplomatique*, September 2002, pp. 22–3.

33 L. Brand, *Women, the State, and Political Liberalization: Middle Eastern and North African Experiences*, New York, Columbia University Press, 1998; M. Charrad, *States and Women's Rights: The Making of Postcolonial Tunisia, Algeria, and Morocco*, Berkeley, CA: University of California Press, 2001.

34 B. Maddy-Weitzman, "Women, Islam, and the Moroccan State: the Struggle over the Personal Status Law," *Middle East Journal*, 2005, vol. 59, no. 3, pp. 393–411.

35 H. Amirah-Fernández, "Morocco is Failing to Take Off," Madrid: Elcano Royal Institute for International and Strategic Studies, 2004. Available at: http://www.realinstitutoelcano.org/analisis/609.asp.

36 N. MacFarquhar and S. Mekhennet, "In Morocco, a Rights Movement, at the King's Pace," *New York Times*, 1 October 2005, p. A1.

37 World Bank, "Morocco at a Glance," Washington DC: World Bank, 2006. Available at: http://www.worldbank.org/data.

38 The Economist Intelligence Unit, *Country Report Morocco May 2006*, London, EIU, 2006.
39 International Monetary Fund, *Staff Report for the 2006 Article IV Consultion: Morocco*, IMF Country Report # 06/413, Washington DC: IMF, December 2006.
40 Ibid.
41 I. Dalle, "Le Maroc attend le grand changement," *Le Monde Diplomatique*, June 2001.
42 Available at: http://www.groupe-ona.com/jsp/index.jsp.
43 UNDP, *Human Development Report 2006*. Available at: http://www.undp.org.
44 Ibid.
45 D. Bamford, "Morocco Bans Historical Conference," BBC World Service, 19 January 2002.
46 I. Dalle, "Espérances déçues au Maroc: Bilan de cinq ans de réformes," *Le Monde Diplomatique*, August 2004, pp. 18–19.
47 Ottaway and Riley, op. cit., p. 8.
48 S. Gränzer, "Changing Human Rights Discourse: Transnational Advocacy Networks in Tunisia and Morocco," in T. Risse, S. C. Ropp and K. Sikkink (eds), *The Power of Human Rights: International Norms and Domestic Change*, New York: Cambridge University Press, 1999.
49 F. Burgat, 1993. *The Islamic Movement in North Africa*, trans. W. Dowell, Austin, Center for Middle East Studies, University of Texas, 1993; M. Hamdi, *The Politicization of Islam: A Case Study of Tunisia*, Boulder, CO: Westview Press, 1998; and S. Waltz, "The Politics of Human Rights in the Maghreb," in J. Entelis (ed.), *Islam, Democracy, and the State in North Africa*, Bloomington, IN: Indiana University Press, 1997.
50 C. Marquis, "On North Africa Trip, Powell is Soft on Allies with Rights Blemishes," *New York Times*, 6 December 2003.
51 C. Powell, Interview with Fox News Sunday's Chris Wallace, 14 March 2004, Washington DC. Available at: http://www.state.gov/secretary.
52 G. White, *On the Outside of Europe Looking In: A Comparative Political Economy of Tunisia and Morocco*, Albany, NY, State University of New York Press, 2001; and G. White, "Free Trade as a Strategic Instrument in the War on Terror? The 2004 U.S.–Moroccan Free Trade Agreement," *Middle East Journal*, vol. 59, no. 4, fall 2005.
53 A. Cissokoi, "Accord de libre échange Maroc/UE: Un Mirage Économique," *Économie et Entreprise*, March 2004, p. 79.
54 Quoted in S. Katz, "Moroccan–US FTA," paper read at Tangier American Legation Museum, 30 May 2003.
55 See, for example, United Nations Development Programme, *The Arab Human Development Report 2002: Creating Opportunities for Future Generations*, New York: Oxford University Press, 2002.
56 T. C. Wittes, "The New US Proposal for a Greater Middle East Initiative: An Evaluation," *Saban Center Middle East Memo*, 2004, no. 2.; T. C. Wittes and S. Yerkes, "The Middle East Partnership Initiative: Progress, Problems and Prospects," *Saban Center Middle East Memo*, 2004, no. 5.
57 Dalle, "Espérances déçues au Maroc: Bilan de cinq ans de réformes," op. cit.
58 G. Denoeux and A. Maghraoui, "King Hassan's Strategy of Political Dualism," *Middle East Policy*, 1998, vol. 5, no. 4.
59 See: www.nadiayassine.net.
60 A. Maghraoui, "Country Report: Morocco," *Freedom House Countries at the Crossroads 2004*. Available at: http://www.freedomhouse.org.
61 Waterbury, *The Commander of the Faithful*, op. cit.
62 MacFarquhar and Mekhennet, op. cit.

6 Engendering Citizenship in Tunisia
Prioritizing Unity over Democracy
Larbi Sadiki

Bin Ali came to power in a bloodless coup in November 1987, ousting his predecessor, the octogenarian Habib Bourguiba, who had ruled Tunisia since the end of the French protectorate in 1956 (Moore, 1988). Bin Ali set two goals for his rule: democratization and national reconciliation (Hermassi, 1995, p. 109). This chapter addresses directly the issue of Tunisia's democratization. Tunisia largely meets with Western approval for being a post of moderation, stability, and liberal politics (Waltz, 1991, p. 29). But to an extent, there is a myth about the country's "liberal politics." Under the patrimonial Bourguiba's patrimonial regime (Krichen, 1992, pp. 32–41) single party rule was the order of the day (Moore, 1965). The North African country has an "electoral" democracy under his successor. But the resulting electoral regime that has been carefully controlled by the state is largely constrictive, uncompetitive, and illiberal (Murphy, 1999; Harik, 1992; Zartman, 1991). The "routinization" and consolidation of Bin Ali's hold on power has, however, generated greater stability than was the case with Bourguiba's last years at the helm (Ware, 1986, pp. 30–5). That stability has come at the expense of political pluralism, as will be elaborated below. But it is in the area of economic management that Tunisia seems to have established credibility (King, 1998, pp. 107–8; Economic Intelligence Unit, 1999). Economic liberalization, however, has gained more momentum than political liberalization or the implications of economic liberalization, for democratization remains uncertain (Murphy, 1997; Hermassi, 1994, pp. 227–42). In this vein, the extent to which economic development supports uniformity will be explored.

Tunisia Within its Maghrebi Context

At the start of the twentieth century the Maghreb, the Arab West, was in search of nationalist identity and liberty—self-determination in the face of external hegemony. The global climate then was emphatically shifting towards resistance and subsequent liberation from colonialism. At the turn of the millennium the Maghreb is in search of democracy—self-determination against internal hegemony. The current global climate is emphatically evincing global ethicism and legalism against authoritarianism.

The mirror images between past and present struggles are dazzling. The liberational ancestry's moral flame, emancipatory passion, and resistance against colonialism are deeply etched in Maghrebi common memory. The stands of Abd al-Kareem Al-Khattab, Abd al-Qadir al-Jaza'iri, Abdelhamid Ben Badis, Omar al-Mukhtar, Abd Al-Aziz Al-Tha'alibi, Allal Al-Fasi, amongst others, continue today to fire up the energies and protest politics of the second generation of citizenry born under independence—but dissatisfied with governance, principally its manifest democratic deficiency. The ancestry's struggles pitted *colon* against colonized, and European-Christian against Arab-Berber Muslim. Contemporary polarities point to dualistic tensions: state vs. society and ruler vs. ruled. However, one hallmark of Maghrebi post-colonial struggles is obviously conspicuous. In their quest for self-determination against a Maghrebi state that is still largely ruled by varying degrees of megalomaniac *asabiyyat* (singular *asabiyyah* or tribal solidarity) they deploy formerly contested discursive and technological artifacts of Westernism and modernism. These artifacts have ceased to be problematic. The notion of the European "state," especially in its Weberian form as territoriality, legal and political centralization, and monopoly over the legitimate use over coercion, is a given. So is the idea of "democracy," which may in some discourses be cloaked in the garb of *shura* (consultation). Rather, the contests are over whose morality best serves, on the one hand, the state's function of value assignment and allocation as well as of distribution of political power and welfare goods and, on the other, society's interests in equal citizenship, that is, civil rights of participation, contestation, identity, and economic welfare.

The mapping out of political community in the Maghreb proceeds against this background. In a milieu largely governed in the 1990s by new leaders with little or no contact with colonialism, Maghrebi old political myths around which the first generation of post-independence leaderships used to rally their newly independent peoples are today being either challenged by society, or revamped by the state, and in at least one case, completely superseded. Just as "*al-thawrah*" (revolution) in Algeria increasingly arouses derision, "Bourguibism" in Tunis has been assigned to the proverbial dustbin of history. In Tripoli the popular attachment in the masses' republic (*jamahiriyyah*) to the "Green Book" after the Lockerbie debacle can be surmised to be superficial even if it persists as the center's most fundamental rallying myth. In Rabat Sharifism is bound to shed its Mahdi and jihadi "cosmic" verities as it competes for reformism and pragmatism with visibly assertive currents of civic, Islamic, and syndicalist societal opposition. The peripheral Maghrebis of Mauritania remain locked in an Arabo-African tribalism whose political manifestation in statecraft is Hobbesian–Khaldounian. *Asabiyyah*'s breathtaking preponderance of power is held by those endowed with the brand of Khaldounian *jah* (hegemony) that comes from brute force (the army), rendering life for competing *asabiyyat* outside the state in strictly Hobbesian terms, i.e., "nasty, brutish, and short," a quasi "state of nature." Statecraft is serially coups and counter-coups. Whether the 2005 coup in Mauritania will herald a "democratic breakthrough" may be a tall order in a country still beset by parochialism in political organization, poverty, sexism, tribal forms of loyalty, and illiteracy.

The tests that afflicted Maghrebi statecraft under the first generation of nationalist leaderships have all met with varying degrees of failure. Algeria's statecraft atrophied in the 1990s; the upshot, a 10-year civil war that cost more than 120,000 lives and internecine strife for lack of cultural rights for the country's sizeable Berber minority. Because of the leadership's political miscalculations Libya suffered isolation and sanctions and subsequent hefty payments to the families of the Lockerbie victims. Morocco until the death of Hassan II reeled under draconianism that saw thousands disappear in desert detention camps—many are still missing—and the Western Sahara dispute impasse and subsequent war of attrition with the Algerian-backed POLISARIO Front point to both diplomatic and military failure. The 1957 Personal Status Code is not blameless in the degraded position of women in Morocco, where domestic violence is high and prostitution is on the rise. Bin Ali's Tunisia has consistently defended uniformity in the name of stability and piecemeal republicanism to the detriment of a free press, pluralism, and political equality. When Bin Ali vacates high office he will be remembered for illiberal democratization, despite some economic development and poverty alleviation.

As mentioned above there are reforms in response to crises in all Maghrebi states. However, there must be no illusion as to their democratizing effects. They have not placed the Maghreb on the cusp of a grand democratic turning point. As yet there are no systematic strategy or a consensually negotiated "pacted transactions" to garner the necessary dialogical, ethical, and political skill and energy of state and society for the purpose of ridding the Maghreb of authoritarian rule. The responses are simply opportunities for "decompression" with or without a liberalizing content or outcome. Algerian President Bouteflika scored a major victory in the September 2005 referendum, with voters massively supporting his Reconciliation Charter (*Mithaq al-Silm wa al-Musalahah al-Wataniyyah*). Whilst not as non-controversial, far-reaching, or wide-ranging as South Africa's model "Truth and Reconciliation" process, the Charter is nonetheless a confidence-building instrument that goes some way in reconciling Algerians and rebuilding state–society relations upon legal bases.[1] The Berber Civil movement's long-time fight for language rights paid off, as the state moved in 2002 to constitutionally enshrine "Tamazight" as a national language in addition to Arabic.[2] Morocco's February 2004 reforms to the country's Personal Status Law, or the *Mudawwanah*, have the potential of reducing inequality between the sexes on issues regarding divorce, child custody and guardianship, inheritance, and marriage. If the reforms are widely accepted and practiced by the public and the courts they will be an important milestone for both women's rights and the country's steady political liberalization under Muhammad VI.[3] Like Algeria, Morocco has its own "missing people" and the victims of torture under the late Hassan II. In creating the Equity and Reconciliation Commission (IER), a process of transitional justice in January 2004, Muhammad VI has produced probably the single most imaginative and original reform in the Maghreb and the wider Arab world. The IER's jurisdiction includes global regulation to the grotesque human rights violations committed during the reign of Hassan II, namely, enforced disappearances, extra-juridical killings, and unlawful detentions. The IER has three chief aims as part of a broader agenda to improve the state of human rights: propose recommendations that guarantee the non-repetition of the violations; remedy their effects (including some compensation); and re-establish confidence in the rule of law. However, this has not meant the end of torture or of violations reserved especially for Islamists after the 2003 Casablanca bombings (Stack, 2005; Ben Jelloun, 2004; Oufkir et al., 2002).

Gaddafi's dynasty will continue to rule Libya in the foreseeable future but the strongman's son and heir apparent, Sayf al-Islam, seems to be winning plaudits in the US and the EU for reforms that could not have been secured without his father's approval. These reforms are political (e.g., a rudimentary project of weapons of mass destruction was abandoned; compensation for victims of Libyan-sponsored terrorism; the right of return to Libya by regime opponents) and economic reverses (the indiscriminate opening of the country's markets to global investment). These measures are helping Libya, a country long stigmatized as a "rogue state," to rehabilitate itself after more than a dozen years of living in the shadow of international pariah status. However, worthy as they may be, the positive declarations and measures are engineered from within the ruling Gaddafi "dynasty," pointing to a quasi "possession" of the state. It is no coincidence that the only two proactive NGOs visible in a country with hardly any institutions are led by Gaddafi's son (Sayf al-Islam) and daughter (Aicha). So it would be fallacious to take liberal pronouncements by Gaddafi's son, pursuit of prisoner release, and compensation of victims of terror, as synonymous with a political liberalization in which Libyan society and opposition have little or no role. As yet there is no "paradigm shift" in Libya. Rather, quick fixes have been introduced to avoid a fate similar to that of Saddam's Ba'thist state. Thus far the "coup" in Mauritania that has put an end to illegal detentions and precipitated a process of state–society negotiations is no "Portuguese" coup (Linz and Stepan, 1996). Whether the military Council for Justice and Democracy reforms the country, as it committed itself to do in its declaratory policy to the world, it is too soon to determine.[4] As for Tunisia, as the ensuing analysis will show, discursively pluralism is commonplace. However, I shall argue that in practice uniformity survives as the centre continues with a brand of politics that relies on political corporatism. This bucks the Maghrebi trend, especially in Morocco and Algeria, of increased pluralism.

Cohesion First, Democracy Second?

The conventional wisdom within development and democratization theory has traditionally insisted on social and political, cultural, ethnic cohesiveness and unity as prerequisites for reproducible stability and democracy. This chapter does not share this wisdom. In Tunisia the straightjacket of national unity has historically compromised pluralism and plurality. Continuing with a model of electoral politics that is informed by the primacy of national unity offers nothing more than the reproduction of the status quo. Thus, elections cannot be considered an adequate test of Bin Ali's dicing with democracy.

Whatever the definitional requisites ascribed to the notion of democracy, it remains an essentially contested concept. There is no single definition or practice of democracy that can be taken as normative (Held, 1996; Sartori, 1987). However, a set of broad standards must obtain for genuine transition from authoritarianism to stand a good chance of success. The relevance and significance of proceduralism (periodic elections), legality (independent judiciary; fundamental liberties), and institutionalism (non-personalist institutions; separation of power) cannot be stressed enough when democracy is under construction. It is, however, the standard of equal opportunity for organizing and representing difference that renders a particular liberalizing experiment congenial to or at odds with democracy. Thus conceived, democratic community reads as "one which permits and perhaps also encourages every man and woman individually or with others to choose the course of his or her life, *subject to recognition of the right of others to do likewise*" (Parry and Moran, 1994, p. 4, emphasis added). The practice of political pluralism in key "liberalizing" Arab states is read as political conformism and monism. Salamé notes how insistence on national unity has meant persistence of authoritarianism in the Arab world (Salamé, 1994, pp. 4–6). National unity is seen as a prerequisite for stability and development. Thus, Owen notes how stability as a political value is more important than democracy in many Middle East polities (Owen, 1992, p. 245). No challenge therefore is perhaps greater than the building of an autonomously associational milieu that breathes life into the fledgling processes of democratization. Norton and Ayubi stress the importance of civil society for the maturity of democratization (Ayubi, 1995, pp. 396–9; Norton, 1995, pp. 5–9; 1993, pp. 205–16). The Arab state's "authoritarian corporatist" approach to ruling state–society relations interferes in this space theorized, from Hegel (1952) to Gramsci (Femia, 1981; Bellamy and Schecter, 1993), to be outside the state's coercive apparatus.

Democratization theory presents the student of Arab transitions with more problems than answers (Anderson, 1995, pp. 77–91; Brumberg, 1995 pp. 229–59; Hudson, 1995, pp. 61–76; 1988, pp. 22–37; Hermassi, 1993; Ibrahim, 1993, pp. 292–305; Esposito and Piscatori, 1991, pp. 427–40). Rustow's transitional model presupposes a set of three sequences for the realization of democracy (Rustow, 1970). These are authoritarian decay and collapse; institution building; and democratic habituation. However, a prerequisite for this transition is national cohesion. In practice, national unity has become symbiotic with an expectation by Arab ruling elites for their peoples to rally around the state, direct all loyalty towards central government, and be politically deferential. National unity is spelled "singularity."

Generally, there is broad consensus within democratic theory that homogeneity is far more conducive to democracy than heterogeneity. Like Rustow, Dahl in his *Polyarchy* (1971), as Przeworski notes, produces substantial empirical data correlating democracy with national and ethnic homogeneity (Przeworski, 1995, pp. 19–21). Multinational or multi-ethnic states are written off as good candidates for democratization, a view that Przeworski (1995, p. 20) rightly questions. The primordialist idea of being born into an identity suggests fixity and permanence. In a sense this view writes off the possibility of multiple layers of identity, and says very little about the imagining and constructing of identity. The view of a manipulable and changing identity strikes a chord with the instrumentalist conception of identification. This conception rejects anchoring identity in historical experience or reducing it to blood affinities or immutable loyalties. Identities are not objective givens operating outside space or time. They are constructed and mobilized by events and myths and myth inventors in specific contexts. They do not obtain from generalized categories. Reducing identity to a single underlying category, such as ethnicity, nationality, or religion, is both essentialist and reductionistic.

The analysis below turns to the question of how the political mapping of processes of inclusion and exclusion has been executed discursively and practically in Ben Ali's Tunisia (1987–present), comparing it with Bourguiba's Tunisia (1956–87). In both, discourse and practice of "citizenship" and "identity" are centrally controlled. They preclude alternative forms of self-identification, especially Islamist re-imagining (Hermassi, 1995, pp. 115–17). Islamists refer here to activists espousing ideologies that stress the implementation of Islam in public affairs (Esposito, 1992, pp. 2–16).

Imagining Identity and Community in Tunisia

In theory, at least, Tunisia's homogeneity makes for a solidaristic society. This homogeneity is *sui generis* a ready-made unifying force, an *esprit de corps* that links state and society. Ibn Khaldun, Tunisia's fourteenth-century philosopher of history, deploys the concept of *asabiyya* (social solidarity; tribal kinship) to impart his appreciation of the dynamic of social cohesiveness or lack thereof in the processes of state making and unmaking (Rosenthal, 1967, pp. lxxviii–lxxxi). Just as the social bond that obtains from *asabiyya* engenders state making and, subsequently, *umran* and *hadara* (sedentary culture), homogeneity in modern theory of democratic transition strongly implies stability and democratization, as stated above. The notion of *asabiyya* persists and is entangled in the political process in the modern Middle East (Salamé, 1994; Zubaida, 1989). For Salamé, modern *asabiyyat* (plural of *asabiyya*) complicate the search for democracy in the Middle East. The continuing legitimacy of community organization and identity is not always receptive to the individualism of Western democracy. Thus, the struggle for democracy in the Middle East can be directed concomitantly at the authoritarianism of the state as well as of the group (Salamé, 1995, pp. 9–11). For Zubaida traditional group solidarities have not disappeared and interpenetrate with nation-states, political parties, and parliaments (1989, p. 84). He argues that the constitution of political forces relates to various and shifting bases of social solidarities, which are themselves affected by changes in political and economic conjecture, including state structures and policies (1989, p. 90). In Tunisia, the dominant solidarity that has had more say in the shaping of national identity and political community is *baldi-Saheli*, which is *francisant* and bourgeois. This *asabiyya* built what Zartman calls a "bourgeois republic" (1998, p. 3).

The imagining of identity in a pre-nationalist and pre-modern stage rested on inherited conceptions of belonging that naturalized the image of identity as kinship or some form of clan or tribal *asabiyya*. In Tunisia, even post-independence, there were still vestiges of this genealogically based form of self-identification. Individual identity was cemented to clan or tribal collectivity. But the tribe or clan was not the only identity. There were significant identities attached to urban as opposed to rural dwelling, and to social groupings, such as the *baldi* (urban Tunisois families), *afaqi* (rural outsiders), *al-makhzan* (the state), and the *ulema* (learned scholars of Islam). The prefix *ouled* (kin of; literally, sons of) was as important as the name of the sire, male ancestor or clan chief it preceded (e.g., ouled jlas or simply al-jlas; (ouled) al-farashish; (ouled) al-hamama, etc.). It was an identity template. It denoted a genealogy that marked out for clan members the boundaries of belonging and identity. The tribal pluralism in that pre-nationalist milieu was a function of economic, physical, and psychological security. During colonization, imagining of community rested on a dichotomous formula: "us" vs. "them"—"French" vs. "Tunisian." But this dichotomy should not detract attention from the complexities of cultural assimilation among certain classes, and the importance attached by Tunisian élites to the modernizing impact of colonial rule. Nonetheless, the presence of an occupying force, France, not only made the drawing of lines between indigenous and non-indigenous a fairly uncomplicated exercise, but it also became identical with a historical moment in the imagining of community. "Tunisian-ness" had to be invented as a legal construct and a national identity (Sraieb, 1987). This marked the onset of state-oriented ethnic nationalism.

Thus, the marking out of national identity is essentialized, combining two different approaches. The first is derived from a liberal notion of identity predicated on the primacy and indivisibility of nation. This construction of identity conceives of identity as fixed and "objective," with ethnicity occupying a central place within it. Ethnicity entails commonalities of race, history, and language. When comparing ethnicity to other categories, such as class, some sociologists accord it endurance, comprehensiveness, and uniqueness in terms of common memories and histories. Hence ethnicity is affirmed to be endowed with "a greater affinity ... for sentimental elaboration of identity, and a larger capacity for reasserting exclusive loyalties, after long periods of increasing commitments to broader, more inclusive civic loyalties" (Kuper, 1969, p. 461). According to this conception, identity is a primordial given. Unlike the category of class, it does not follow from particular modes of capitalist production. The primordialism of this conception has been challenged by Anderson's seminal work, *Imagined Communities* (Anderson, 1991). The crux of his thesis is that nationalist identity is an artifice. It is the most articulate interrogation of naturalized representations of the nation as timeless and universal, extending from ancestry and sanguine relationships. Anthony Smith's equally important work stands somewhere in between primordialist and instrumentalist representations of identity. He neither naturalizes the conception of identity nor makes it so fluid and adaptive to material or political changes and pressures. He contends that any "modern" nation carries within it elements of a "premodern" ethnic group (1986, p. 18).

Whereas the first liberal conception of identity lays insufficient stress on religion, the second makes it inseparable from self-identification. Two useful concepts will be briefly invoked to understand the dynamics of identity construction and reconstruction: "ethnonationalism" and "ethnoreligiousness" (Ben-Dor, 1999, p. 1). If ethnonationalism is the endeavor to give ethnicity a territorially statist expression, ethnoreligiousness rests on the assumption of "an overlap of religious consciousness with some other characteristics of ethnicity—common origin, culture, or language." The resulting "ethnic activism" is not always territorially bound (Ben-Dor, 1999, p. 1). These two frames of reference intertwine a great deal when it comes to sketching the routes chartered by identity mapping in Tunisia.

The main catalyst for ethnonationalism was French colonization. In the *Mouvement Jeune Tunisien* (Young Tunisia), the nationalist movement had a precursor in the group Ali Bash Hamba founded in 1908 (Khairallah, 1957). Separateness and separation from colonial France were central to the group's imagining of identity. However, at that early stage in the struggle against colonization, ethnonationalism overlapped with ethnoreligiousness. The 1911 events of al-Jallaz, when resistance against a plan to build a road across a Muslim cemetery erupted into violent clashes with the occupying army, illustrated the strength of religious forms of self-identification. That plan, along with the attempt to place the administration of al-Jallaz cemetery under the jurisdiction of the Tunis municipality instead of its historical custodians, the *waqf* (religious endowments authority), was widely seen as a violation of religious identity and sensitivity. Again, in the 1932–34 *tajnees* (naturalization) campaigns introduced by the French to foster a policy of assimilation, the resentment to colonial rule, still simmering from al-Jallaz incidents, boiled over into renewed resistance to occupation. The overlap, as Ben-Dor puts it, of religious consciousness with some associate of ethnicity such as language and culture was visibly strong. It was strong enough to spawn the nucleus of anti-French "ethnic activism." Such an activism and the narrative supporting it resonated with traditionalism, grounding identity in a naturalized imaging of identity in Arabo-Islamic terms. The country's first political party, al-Hizb al-Destouri (Constitutional Party), co-founded in 1920 by Abd al-Azeez al-Tha'alibi and nationalists, including scholars from the Islamic al-Zaytunah Mosque-University, did not develop enough of a territorially bound identity.

Bourguiba's al-Hizb al-Destouri al-Jadeed (Neo-Constitutional Party—Neo-Destour) was bolder in the assertion of a territorially oriented identity. Ethnoreligiousness was relegated to a secondary status. Ethno-nationalism, be it one not devoid of religious idioms, was boldly pronounced. Unlike al-Tha'alibi, the *francisant* Bourguiba, a French-trained lawyer, had much use for the grammar of secular nationalism which was to inform his rule's mapping of identity in Tunisia (Salem, 1984). The shaping and reshaping of identity under pre-colonial, colonial, and post-colonial settings represented a continuous act of adjusting the ethnic imagery to politically value-laden narratives. But perhaps identity's most lasting and deepest disturbance was that caused by colonialism and post-colonialism. The first disturbance was wrought by the confusion of a violent encounter with an outside "otherness": Christian, European, mechanized, colonial, and secular. This led to the awakening or activating of ethnoreligiousness in the search of secure boundaries within which to ground identity. The French assimilationist politics of identity was retorted to by an indigenous manipulation of identity whose anchorage was Islam. From the indigenous perspective, succumbing under those particular colonial circumstances to the *colons'* assimilation would have been co-optation, not inclusion. Bourguiba and his fellow Neo-Destourians opposed assimilation at that time. But at the level of norms and ideology, Bourguiba and his Francophile allies did not reject French culture and had close contacts with the French Left in the 1930s (Micaud, 1964, pp. 74–5). After independence, they set about modernizing Tunisia by trying to copy the French model (Zghal, 1991, p. 207). Thus, Krichen criticizes Bourguiba's approach of mimicking Western modernization by mixing mutually exclusive fragments, such as of Occidental capitalism and Oriental pre-capitalism (1992, p. 49).

The second disturbance to the plurality of *asabiyyat* took the form of a systematic effort of self-identification calculated to create a collectively binding and overarching notion of national identity. In one sense, the identity reconstruction in this phase was geared to reclaiming what was thought to be a natural image of Tunisian identity, one that preceded the society and political community re-imagined by the nationalist leaders. What legitimized this identity mapping was its resistance to a colonially divided society. For the plurality of *asabiyyat* tilted the balance of power in favor of the hegemonic "other," the minority of *colons*, to the exclusion and exploitation of the indigenous majority. The appeal of the nationalist reconstruction of identity can be summed up in its symbiosis with emancipation and inclusion. But emancipation was double-edged: throwing the colonial yoke out, and then unshackling would-be *muwatinoon* (citizens) from the variety of *asabiyya*-based particularities. From the outset, the reconstruction of identity was, in theory at least, oriented toward a universal incorporation of *muwatinoon* into an indigenously governed order of *adala* (justice) *hurriyya* (freedom), and *musawat* (equality). By and large, all three remained intangibles in Bourguiba's Tunisia (Moore, 1988, pp. 179–80, 186–7). Colonial hegemony was substituted with an indigenous hegemony. For nearly three decades the new masters went about homogenizing society and polity. The nationalist ethnic imagery lacked a democratic imagery. Its democratic deficiency is beyond empirical doubt. The first book of its kind on Bourguiba's 30 years in power by one of his former *protégés* and ministers provides ample testimony to this deficiency (Belkhodja, 1998, pp. 241–66; Zartman, 1988; 1994). Krichen goes further by noting that the ruling culture was clientelistic in nature and that the notion of the "constitutional state" was more of a myth than a reality (1992, pp. 119–20).

Through the lens of the newly reconstructed identity, national unity continues until this day to be shorthand for political uniformity. The hegemonizing and homogenizing character of the state meant banning rival centers of power. After independence, this applied to the ruling party machine as well as to trade unions (Anderson, 1991, pp. 250–1, 257–9; Moore, 1988, p. 179). Before independence it applied to traditionalist and pan-Arab tendencies. Thus, Bourguiba's unmistakably Francophile and secular politics placed him at odds with Salah Bin Yusif, his rival nationalist leader (Moore, 1988, p. 177). In the then newly constructed nationalist identity, with its stress on uniformity, there could be room for only one identity narrative. Bin Yusif and the Yusifists' destiny was sealed in the 1955 Neo-Destour Party's Congress held in Sfax. Bourguiba's quasi Atatürkism was irreconcilable with the traditionalism and Arabism of Bin Yusif and al-Tha'alibi (Krichen, 1992, p. 35).

The Politics of Exclusion: Ethnos and Demos

The Tunisia bequeathed to Bin Ali was politically decaying, with a weak legal–rational basis. The break with Bourguiba's political practices has not been total. A few aspects of continuity deserve to be detailed. A naturalized image of Tunisian identity forms the cornerstone of the nationalist and territorial state under both Bourguiba and his successor. As a consequence, a key to the post-colonial state's transition from *ethnos* (pre-political community sharing kinship ties) to *demos* (nation constituted as a state) (Habermas, 1998, pp. 129–30) was the assimilation of clan *asabiyyat*. This task was achieved fairly easily, with the state using a combination of repression (e.g., Ouled Shirayyit in the country's south) and equalization through welfarist redistribution of goods—e.g., education, housing, health, employment—(Zartman, 1991, p. 30). In particular, state welfarism partly made the clan redundant. Dependence of individuals on the clan's safety net gradually decreased, and today it is almost nonexistent. Also, the breaking down of clan *asabiyyat* is due to a long history of centralized control over regional peripheries. And Tunisia's relatively large *Sahelian* middle class (Micaud, 1964, pp. 9, 81) and its higher prosperity helped foster welfare programs.

The democratic imagery leaves much to be desired. The regime has not yet transcended the political syndrome of Bourguiba's "first republic": political singularity. This singularity is the most salient feature of Bin Ali's "second republic" (Vandewalle, 1988). The difference between Bourguiba and Bin Ali is one of quantity, not democratic quality. In the early 1980s, Bourguiba's Tunisia, partly thanks to former Prime Minister Muhammad M'zali, committed itself to pluralism. On 10 April 1981, in the eleventh congress of the ruling Destour Socialist Party (PSD), Bourguiba reluctantly agreed to broad participation by all the different socio-political groups. There was a degree of seriousness on the part of liberal elements in the Bourguiba regime to steer an increasingly unstable country away from crisis point. The fact that the move towards pluralism should draw heavily on the turbulence of the 1970s is not surprising. Single-party rule was no longer suited to a country whose achievements in literacy and higher living standards, especially in the north and the Sahel, were constantly on the rise, necessitating political openings. Then there was the relative radicalization and pluralization of political life. Workers' syndicates, headed by the then powerful *Union Générale des Travailleurs Tunisiens* (UGTT) and its leader Habib Ashur, turned trade unionism into a fairly dynamic and autonomous, and at times confrontationist, branch of civil society. Disillusionment within the PSD led to a splinter liberal tendency headed by Ahmed Mistiri; later on it took the form of the Democratic Socialist Movement (MDS). An assertive student movement sprang up at the University of Tunis, with currents within it representing the new centrifugal forces within the polity and society. So did unofficial Islam in the form of the Association for the Preservation of the Holy Quran, the precursor of the Islamic Tendency Movement (MTI) and al-Nahdah (Hermassi, 1991). Increasing policing of universities, syndicates, and schools galvanized human rights activists into founding *la ligue Tunisienne des droits de l'homme* (LTDH) in 1977 (Waltz, 1995, p. 11; 1989). It is against this backdrop that Bourguiba committed his regime to letting diverse political organizations see the light of day (Belkhodja, 1998, p. 249).

But that commitment was never consummated. The 1981 elections were not fully multiparty, since the only opposition party legalized was the *Parti Communiste Tunisien* (PCT). No other party obtained the required 5 percent of the vote to be legalized. The political parties of the time had no funds, no significant power bases, and no access to the state-owned media. Also, the electoral system of first-past-the-post favored the ruling party. The elections were a strategy for regime consolidation, not a trial run of democratic procedures. Thus, the conduct of the elections did not confirm a genuine commitment by the PSD's machine to broaden political participation. The elections themselves were a disappointment. The PSD–UGTT coalition—the National Front—swept the board, winning 94.6 percent of the vote. The MDS was second with close to 4 percent (Belkhodja, 1998, p. 253). However, as Belkhodja confirms, illiberal elements within the PSD decided, apparently with Bourguiba's blessing, not to relinquish PSD hegemony over political life and rigged the results of the poll (1998, pp. 252–3).

The crises that beset the country in the 1970s were the driving engine of change in the 1980s. The 1970s witnessed the growth of the trade union movement into a political heavyweight in its own right, with dissident elements within it attempting to act as a formidable counterweight to the ruling PSD. Had it not been chastened by draconian interference, it would have animated political life at a time when Tunisia's civil society started to take shape (Alexander, 1997, pp. 34–5). It was, however, considered by some to be primarily a creation of the Neo-Destour Party (King, 1998, p. 118). Definitely, after independence the UGTT succumbed to corporatist pressures on the part of the state (Waltz, 1995, p. 50), becoming a vehicle for Bourguiba to mobilize support for the party and assume monopoly over labor issues. But for the greater part of its history, the UGTT depended on Bourguiba for status and thus never possessed any political power of its own. It remained, as Zartman, puts it a "potential opposition party" (Zartman, 1988, p. 83). Nonetheless, Belkhodja is right in noting that the UGTT in 10 years was transformed from a workers' movement into a dynamic and open rallying arena for intellectuals, professionals, and technicians and activists of all political colors. The PSD offered these cadres little or no space for democratic participation. As a result, Belkhodja suggests, the UGTT became a sanctuary for a new generation of highly educated cadres trained in France's *grandes écoles* and eager to change things radically (1998, p. 132). There was visible tension in the late 1970s between the PSD and UGTT. Not even the Social Pact of 1977 could glue the unions and the state together any longer, especially in the face of price hikes of staples. 26 January 1978 was "Black Thursday": the army interfered in an open and violent clash that pitted state against society, leaving hundreds dead in its wake.

Bourguiba's obsession with unity engendered hegemony and singularity. It was that very singularity that made him purge a comrade-in-arms, Bin Yusif, followed by the clans, Bin Salah, M'zali, amongst others. The same was true of organized politics, ranging from the UGTT to MTI. During some 50 years of Bourguibist domination of the political scene, the dogmatism with which *ethnos* and *demos* were blurred in Bourguiba's Tunisia rationalized the discarding of viable identities: religious, tribal, and democratic. That hegemony was embodied in *l'Etat-patron* (state as tutelary) and *l'Etat-parti* (party-state) (Belkhodja, 1998, p. 131). Bourguiba's brand of nationalism left no room for any free space for non-governmental or non-party actors. Rival centers of power were essentialized as fissiparous. Bourguiba ruled in a patrimonial fashion (Moore, 1988, p. 178).

Citizens and Denizens in Bin Ali's Electoral Democracy

The 7 November 1987 change led by Bin Ali was welcomed widely amongst Tunisians from all walks of life. But consensus over his advent to power was not universal. Many entertained skepticism about whether the new leader's military and security background would bode well for reversing the personalization, de-institutionalization, and privatization of the state he inherited from Bourguiba. Despite the modest "democratic" stirrings evident under his rule, exclusivity and singularity are once again intrinsic to the manufacturing of political community and ethnonationalism in Tunisia. The continuity of exclusivity and singularity is in conflict with the democratic plans Bin Ali articulated in his maiden speech (see text of speech in Chaabane, 1997, p. 18).

Quantitatively, at least, under Bin Ali Tunisia has moved from single-party rule and exclusivity. Following the 1999 and 2004 elections, the opposition holds 34 seats in the newly expanded 182-member National Assembly—15 seats up from the 1994 elections. The expansion of the *Chambre des Députés* (Chamber of Deputies) from 163 to 182 can be read in two ways: a gain for the opposition, and a further decrease in the government's domination of parliamentary politics. With 34 seats the opposition holds nearly 19 percent of the seats, a 7 percent increase from the last Chamber. King sees this as the regime's answer to increasing *pro forma* mediation after the oppression of the early 1990s (King, 1998, p. 121). However, in the newly created *Chambre des Conseillers* or Advisors Council, the upper chamber of the country's parliament, the RCD's domination is near total. Bin Ali's clients, including former Bourguibists, occupy seats. Tunisia's former Arab League Secretary-General, Chadhli El-Klibi, as well as ex-Prime Minister Hedi Beccouche, amongst other figures of the old regime, have been voted to the Chamber in elections noted for their boycott by some opposition parties and the union movement. The only transition has been from single-party rule to ruling-party hegemony. Electoral politics in this case has been about returning the incumbents to a monopoly of political power. Thus the regime continues to *possess the democratic process,* employing bureaucratic–corporatist strategies (King, 1998, p. 120; Waltz, 1995, p. 50). It has, more or less, appropriated and deployed all state resources to reproduce itself without much serious competition. Murphy has reservations about the prospects of democratic consolidation under Bin Ali, noting how he alone has been deciding "the pace, scope, and spheres of reform" (1999, p. 223).

Bin Ali took over the reigns of power in order to change the status quo. Up to now the monolithic machinery of the ruling Democratic Constitutional Rally (RCD) points to a singular trajectory. It is the PSD dressed in the *jibbah* (Tunisian traditional long garb) of democracy. The PSD was rebuilt with a view to making use of the Destourian and Bourguibist power base. The recycling did indeed involve more than substituting the epithet "socialist" for "democratic." The party was intended to be a *ruling party,* not one competitor amongst equals in the so-called era of *tajdeed* (renewal). In the July 1988 party *inqadh* (salvation) conference, Bin Ali lectured his audience on his plans to renounce single-party practice and mentality. He stated that "for all [the PSD's] massive heritage, its established history of resistance, its wide electoral base, cannot claim to represent all the political forces of the country" (Chaabane, 1997, p. 79). In practice Bin Ali has given *l'Etat-patron* and *l'Etat-parti* a lease of life. At no stage has he considered separating state and party (Tessler, 1990). The party was from the outset intended to fulfill two functions: serve both as a unifying force and a vehicle of stability. This signals a top-down approach to democratization. This approach was typical of the PSD, whose self-indulgence in its historical mission to unify, stabilize, and edify the masses downsized all viable political forces and identities.

The dyads *l'Etat-patron* and *l'Etat-parti* are today a massive support system that hegemonizes and homogenizes political life to the point of stultifying political life below the state. The figures below bespeak a reality of one-party rule, not a preparatory stage, for "post-one-party" political life:

> Today, in top form for the *competition*, [the RCD] stands as a force to be reckoned with on major political occasions, significantly boasting a following of almost a quarter of the country's university lecturers … Similarly, student membership of the party has risen from a few hundred in 1987 to better than 8,000 in 1995. In 1993, total party membership stood at 1,720,374.
>
> The party boasts 6,713 branches and 300 associations distributed across the Republic. There are 54,870 officials at branch level, 83,390 candidates having stood in the elections for local cell officials in 1993, i.e., 1.8 candidates per seat. Of that number, 4,400 were women, of whom 2,930 were elected—that is, 67% of the female candidates carried the day over their male counterparts.
>
> (Chaabane, 1997, p. 81, my emphasis)

With such impressive figures, talk of competition in the excerpt above cannot be serious. A case in point is the October 1999 elections in which Bin Ali won his third and theoretically last five-year presidential term. He ran "opposed," unlike in the two previous presidential plebiscites, by two hand-picked candidates from the opposition. Neither Muhammad Bilhaj Amor (leader of the Popular Unity Party) nor Abd al-Rahman Talili (head of Unionist Democratic Union) were presidential. Neither man volunteered his candidacy. Those who did in the past, such as human rights activist Moncef al-Marzouqi and Abd al-Rahman al-Hani, a known lawyer, were both prevented from standing (King, 1998, p. 121). This highlights Bin Ali's predilection for omnipresence and singularity in playing the role of Tunisia's new national mentor.

The rise of alternative identities, spatial or political, in the community manufactured by the regime is not only unimaginable, but also carries risk. (Article 19 Organization, 1991; Amnesty International, 1990, 1992, 1993, 1994; Waltz, 1995, pp. 175–85). In the words of a Tunisian academic, the country is akin to *"un commissariat"* (a police station), quintessentially a *mukhabarat* state. This *"commissariat"* has been justified by the exaggerated paranoia and fear of a "fundamentalist threat" (Simon, 1999a, p. 14). Bin Ali has used the Islamist threat to justify excessive policing (Murphy, 1997, pp. 121–2). The gradual breakdown of the Bourguiba–PSD legitimacy formula in the late 1970s to mid-1980s partly explains Bin Ali's exclusionary politics. Bin Ali (an ex-security chief) may be paranoid about loosening the reins. One way of explaining Bin Ali's authoritarian bent is the regime's deep fear of a region-wide Islamist threat, sharpened of course by the Algerian bloodbath. To an extent, the regime's behavior is exogenously driven. Zartman confirms the existence a kind of transnational anti-Islamist group (on the part of heads of state and ministers of interior) (Zartman, 1997, pp. 213–17).

The fault-line in Tunisia does not stem from manufacturing the polity and society at the expense of an ethnic group or particularity. Such a particularity does not exist. Rather, it happens at the expense of potentially viable political identities—especially Islamist—which cannot be mediated only through democratic rule. The blending of *ethnos* and *demos* in the name of social cohesiveness and unity has been undertaken within an authoritarian framework, precluding democracy as a harmonizing force. Here lies Tunisia's problem. Fierce contest over the interpreting of identity must not be underestimated as one source of the heightened antagonism between the regime and the Islamists. An Arab-Islamic identity must, for al-Nahdah, be reified through greater Islamization and Arabization of society and polity (Hermassi, 1995, p. 117). For the ruling élite, which itself does not reject Arabness and Islam in the shaping of Tunisia's identity, secular nationalism is the only route to modernity and development. Al-Ghannushi declares that the stand-off of his outlawed al-Nahdah with the regime has largely been oversimplified, with many analysts reducing it to a "race with the regime for the seat of power" (Author's interview, 20 November 1999).

As mentioned above, such construction and reconstruction of identity have vacillated between the poles of ethnoreligiousness and ethnonationalism. The swinging of the political pendulum between these two poles made and unmade élites, fixed and unfixed membership, and opened and closed political space. Politics as the art of the possible has been a continuous act of "leveling identities [something] pivotal to strategies of modernization and modernity" (Nisan, 1991, p. 22). This leveling of identities has definitely been visible in Tunisia. Both under Bourguiba and Bin Ali the state appears to have an ethnonationalist tendency and a strong secular–national basis. But under neither leader has the state lived up to its declaratory policy of privatizing religion—*al-din ila Allah, wa al-watan ila al-jami'* (religion is God's; the fatherland is for all). Bourguiba closed the well-known university-mosque, al-Zaytunah; in the 1970s he publicly declared his defiance to fasting during Ramadan, an act that he deemed inimical to development; and in the mid-1980s he issued "circular 108," which bans veiling (Chaabane, 1997, p. 32). Bin Ali reopened al-Zaytunah but, like Bourguiba's Ataturkist fashion, strictly bans veiling and the sporting of beards.

Democracy as Inclusion of Difference

The kind of polarization mentioned above over political rights regards an important friction over how to blur the boundaries between *ethnos* and *demos*. The idea of the nation-state is founded on the optimistic assumption that a "*demos* of citizens rooted in [an] *ethnos* of nationals" should translate into political freedom and equality (Habermas, 1998, p. 132). Yet ethnonationalism and the political associations resulting from it have everywhere, because of their insistence on ethnic commonality, victimized difference (Habermas, 1998, p. 142). In Tunisia this difference has been only marginally ethnic (e.g., the Berbers). In the main, political space has been denied to clan identities, religious forms of self-identification, and dissenting political discourses and practices. But two aspects that apply to Tunisia have complicated the question of juridical–political and cultural equity in the post-*demos* phase.

The first, Habermas points out, is that national independence does not automatically terminate discrimination. Discrimination demands inclusion and sensitivity to difference (1998, p. 145). Although the difference Habermas invokes here is cultural, individual, and group-specific, political difference is as essential. Habermas strongly advocates, especially in the case of multicultural societies, "difference-sensitive inclusion." The modalities of this inclusion range from compensatory policies to guarantees of cultural autonomy for minorities. While these modalities serve to consolidate democracy by way of including citizens in the *demos*, Habermas notes that political equity, especially in heterogeneous societies, should not be bought at the expense of the fragmentation of society (1998, pp. 145–6). The same principles should apply in largely homogenous societies. Independence in Tunisia did not lead to automatic civil and political rights. It is the absence of these rights that prevented the emergence of what Habermas refers to as "common political language and conventions of conduct to be able to participate effectively in the competition for resources and the protection . . . of a shared political arena" (1998, pp. 145–6).

The various paroxysms of the 1970s attest to the fact that the state-led corporatist project of social and political engineering never succeeded in engendering an inclusive citizenship, shared political space, and stability. Owen likens this brand of authoritarian corporatism in the Middle East to that of Mussolini's Italy. Both insist on national unity as a means of social and economic development. National unity entails political deference to the sate in return for welfare benefits (Owen, 1992, p. 225). In the same vein, Ayubi stresses the solidaristic character of corporatism, which creates a variety of clientelistic networks and places intermediaries under state patronage. Thus, the state has the ultimate say over political inclusion and exclusion (Ayubi, 1995, pp. 33–5). In Tunisia the homogenizing character of corporatism (Ayubi, 1995, p. 420) is bound up with state hegemony over the interpretation and allocation of cultural and political values. The repression of the late 1980s and the 1990s, on the other hand, shows that Tunisia is still a long way from a democratically conceived political community with shared political space and values. The verdict on Bin Ali's political reforms is that they are homogenizing Tunisia, not democratizing it.

The second aspect, which is inextricably linked with the first, is that citizenship rights and the refiguring of individuals into "legal subjects" do not "cut off people from their origins." Habermas elaborates this important point by arguing that the legalizing of subjectivity is not a neutral process. As he puts it, it affects "the integrity of the forms of life in which each person's conduct of life is embedded" (Habermas, 1998, p. 144). It is the extent of the assault on this integrity that sets the scene for fierce contests over not only identity but also political norms and values. Habermas further elaborates this political quandary of legalized identity:

In addition to moral considerations, pragmatic deliberations, and negotiable interests, this aspect of the law brings strong evaluations into play that depend on inter-subjectively shared, but culturally specific, traditions. Legal orders as wholes are also "ethically imbued" in that they interpret the universalistic content of the same constitutional principles in different ways, namely, against the background of the experiences that make up national history and in light of a historically prevailing tradition, culture and form of life. Often the regulation of culturally sensitive matters, such as the official language, the public school curriculum, the status of churches and religious communities, and the norms of criminal law … or the demarcation of the private from the public realm, is merely a reflection of the ethical–political self-understanding of a majority culture that has achieved dominance for contingent, historical reasons.

(1998, pp. 144–5)

The above quote is equally relevant to homogenous societies. The exclusion of the last four decades in Tunisia has triggered fierce contests over the kind of issues Habermas mentions. The Islamists resist privatizing religion. The lack of a shared political space has meant that there are rival political discourses to the dominant one. The dominant political language has been couched in the grammar of secularism and republicanism with a strong Francophile accent. That of the Islamists activates Arabo-Islamic idioms and metaphors, grounding Tunisian identity in additional frames of reference and origins that the post-colonial dominant political discourse and practice have marginalized. Thus, the political rhetoric of Ghannushi's Islamists in the April 1989 elections dwelled on the defense of the country's "Islamic identity" and "Arab-Islamic identity" (Hermassi, 1995, pp. 113–15). Identity is far more complex than the hegemonizing and homogenizing nationalist project has cared to imagine. The élites that began deforming and reforming identity in the colonial era proved how transactional and negotiable identity could be. Yet, after independence political discourse and practice abandoned negotiability, opting instead for fixed identity. Hybrid identity is the more reason why difference-sensitive inclusion must be essential for both homogenous and heterogeneous societies undergoing democratic transitions. However, it would be facile to ignore the role of economic development in maintaining political singularity, as will be discussed below.

Economic Development in the Service of Political Singularity

Tunisia's engineering of political development works in tandem with economic development. Political stability and the state's corporatism, which promotes political uniformity, are owed to the brand of *dirigisme*, central management, of economic affairs. A few features mark political engineering in Tunisia. These key features have implications for economic development. They are unity, centralized authority, and incremental reform. Unity is translated into perhaps the biggest success story of Bin Ali's rule: solidaristic ethics and practice of self-help that to an extent place state and society relations on a par. Institutionally, solidarity has been given expression in the country's successful National Solidarity Fund (NSF), also known by its informal name, "*Caisse 26–26*" (Fund 26–26). The state, for its part, manages the banking side of the Fund and the disbursement of financial aid to the needy, towards the financing through micro-credits of small projects, and the building of infrastructure in the poor urban space. Modern housing, roads, water, and electricity provision have been possible even in the slums. The statistics are impressive: close to 1bn dinars (US$ 700m) have been raised by the NSF since its inception in 1992; more than two million citizens have benefited from its services; close to 4,000km of roads have been built through the Fund, mostly in the country's shanty towns; and more than 60,000 small and medium projects have seen the light of day as a result of procurements from the Fund, creating jobs for technical graduates and retrained semi-skilled laborers. The thinking behind this successful poverty-alleviation scheme is not entirely economic. Its political economy derives from the secular ruling élite's view that slums constitute the urban space in which sympathy and recruitment for and subsequent membership of political Islam are incubated. That is, eradication of poverty serves both the communal obligation to instill the ethics of solidaristic networks for self-help and job creation through "*Caisse* 21–21" (Fund 21–21) and the prevention of the radicalization and politicization of Islam. This brand of state-led and grassroots-based financing is aimed at reducing inequality and nipping in the bud the rise of NGOs that could utilize charity as a springboard for political recruitment. In one sense, state control of the economy is being used to further entrench political quietism, whereby so-called "*khubzistes*" have no choice but to pay political deference to Bin Ali. It is a quasi-tacit contract between state and society whereby economic goods are exchanged for political deference. It is a quintessential example of economic reformism being put to the service of political particularism. As remarked by a Tunisian national, "in this country the 'deal' is simple. We leave politics for the president, and he, in exchange, lets us eat. We have even a term for this: '*khubzism*' … You eat and you keep quiet" (Simon, 1999c). It is an unmistakable trajectory towards a "strong" state at the expense of society. This is the reason why Tunisia's "over-stated" state has, since the mid-1990s, appropriated the major grassroots social welfare initiative project, Fund 26–26. It is now quasi-fully run and controlled by the regime. But to the regime's credit, the project has been dynamic in alleviating poverty and improving living conditions in the poor urban space, especially in the large cities. Society, the private sector, and government are the main donors. Another initiative building on the NSF is the creation in 1999 of the Tunisian Solidarity Bank (BTS). The BTS, founded on ideas of community development banking, procures small credits for the purposes of establishing small businesses or improving living conditions. Here the state's centralized authority looms large. On the one hand, the country is partially committing to transforming its inward-looking and centrally regulated economy into a market and export-oriented economy. On the other hand, such transformation stumbles upon the state's fear of losing its hegemony due to the potential of dispersion of power that a market economy—in which society plays a greater role in self-organization, self-regulation, and self-government—would inevitably engender. The state is not, as yet, prepared for such changes. Indeed, this resistance to change and incremental economic liberalization is motivated by protectionist impulses. Fast exposure to predatory competition, especially within the framework of the country's EU association agreement, may be more inimical than profitable. The Sahel bourgeoisie's reliance on agriculture and textiles for a livelihood could weaken, and this could force it to rethink its loyalty to the centre in the event of the country's adherence to the 2004 Agreement with EFTA states. The Agreement covers industrial goods, a reference to processed agricultural, fish, and marine products. The Agreement, concluded on the basis of Article XXIV of the GATT 2004, aims at total liberalization of trade in goods between Tunisia and individual EFTA states. This process is expected to culminate in the elimination of customs duties on most products by 1 July 2008. It remains to be seen whether the coldness in Arab–EU relations during the Madrid celebration of the tenth anniversary of the Barcelona Declaration, noted for the absence of Arab heads of state, will force a delay of the 2008 free trade zone in the case of Tunisia.

Having signed the first EU Association Agreement in 1995, Tunisia has committed to a process of Euro-Mediterranean partnership that stipulates continuous political and economic reform. Whilst the 1995 Barcelona Declaration facilitates aid and access to technical assistance in the fields of modernizing and restructuring the agricultural sector, it places limits on the country's export of products such as olive oil. Imports of agricultural products from Tunisia, and for that matter Morocco, have not followed global trends. Whereas the export of such products rose since the signing of the Barcelona Declaration in 1995 by 32 percent in international markets, it did so only by 20 percent in the case of Tunisia and Morocco. Worse still, the EU has increased its imports from other world economic regions at the expense of both countries, and Euro-Mediterranean partners in general. Whether the so-called Euro-Med Free Trade Area (EMFTA) to be created by 2010 and the Follow-up Committee for the Euro-Mediterranean Roadmap for Agriculture will in the long term benefit Maghrebi and Arab states remains to be seen. What is certain is the apprehension with which these states view agricultural and textile liberalization. Small and medium-sized business remains the mainstay of economic development in Maghrebi states. In the case of Tunisia, the Sahel and urban bourgeoisie have been loyal to the regime in return for protection of their interests, which may not be served by EU-instigated liberalization planned under the Euro-Mediterranean Partnership.

But there is an emerging nepotism and clan-type bourgeoisie closely related to the palace that appears to be illegally spreading its tentacles into the economy. Under the title "the families that pillage Tunisia," circulated anonymously in 1997 in Tunis, Bin Ali's in-laws have all been linked to corrupt activities, including the illegal appropriation of prime real estate and acquisition of formerly state-owned companies at substantially depreciated prices (Simon, 1999b). Regardless, the process of economic liberalization is occurring without parallel political democratization. Even Emma Murphy's enthusiasm for the success story of Tunisia's economic liberalization has reservations about the prospects of democratic consolidation under Bin Ali, noting how he alone has been "determin[ing] the pace, scope and spheres of reform" (Murphy, 1999, p. 223). After 20 years in power, the Bin Ali regime displays all of the "performative acts" which at face value suggest substantive liberalization is under way. However, proceduralism has not been coupled with principled commitment to democratic consolidation. All indications are that a return to singularity rather than plurality is under way. This almost amounts to a reverse of the democratic initiatives of Bin Ali's first three years in power.

Nonetheless, the regime has, by any standards, more success stories to tell on the economic than on the political front (Economist Intelligence Unit, 1997; General Agreement on Tariffs and Trade, 1994; World Bank, 1996). With an average annual growth rate of 5 percent over the last three years, 3 percent inflation, and a rising per capita GNP, Tunisia seems to be getting praise from the major international financial institutions and aid donors. Even *Le Monde*, whose trenchant criticism of Bin Ali's "police machinery" has not subsided, refers to the country's satisfactory economic performance as the "Tunisian exception," especially in comparison with its Maghrebi neighbors (Editorial, *Le Monde*, 1999b). But the economy is increasingly becoming an additional tool for tightening the regime's control over people's lives and political choice. Economic opportunity is being linked to political choice; and in Tunisia that choice is between Bin Ali and Bin Ali. That is more so, especially when a simple economic transaction of applying for an economic loan can turn into a test of loyalty to Bin Ali. A Tunisian speaking to *Le Monde* about his support for Bin Ali states: "I do not support him. I vote for him; that is different. The other day ... one of my friends went to the bank to apply for a loan. He was asked for his voting card; and you want us to have [political] choice" (Simon, 1999c, p. 14).

By and large, however, Tunisia's non-oil economy is on the way to greater diversification, especially as the country's competent technocrats are grappling with turning one of the Maghreb's smallest economies into a quasi "Asian-tiger." Thus, attention is directed towards the laying of the building blocks of an immaterial economy, a notion much used by the country's ruling élite. So-called "technopoles" are emerging in various regions and al-Ghazala "technopole" won some praise during the UN-sponsored World Information Systems Summit hosted by Tunisia during 16–18 November 2005. What is noteworthy in this economy is the developing of human resources, with Tunisia constantly improving its human development indices, as can be gleaned even from a perfunctory reading of the *UN Human Development Report 2004*. In particular, the Gender Development Index is, relative to the MENA region, encouraging; it shows female visibility socially, economically, and politically. The country has adopted the 1995 UN-sponsored Beijing World Women's Conference Final Communiqué's recommendation for a 30 percent quota for the inclusiveness of women in the political process. Investment in education remains among the highest in the world and modernization of the syllabus should yield results in the forms of either exportable skilled labor to select EU markets, such as Italy, or a highly mechanized labor force that helps boost industrial exports, especially in the fields of electronic and electrical goods. Already, industrial exports are showing promise as potential currency earners, surpassing agricultural goods in the last few years. The country's niche in tourism remains protected, even from emerging shopping destinations such as Dubai. Political stability has served tourism very well, with the country attracting more than six million visitors a year, one of the highest figures in the Arab world. Tourism remains important for job creation. In the long run, and with rising oil prices, the economy's sustained growth rates may not be sustainable. Salvation for this Maghrebi state lies in greater economic integration with its western neighbor Libya. It could produce mutual benefits for both. The former is oil-poor and human capital-rich; the latter is exactly the opposite.

Conclusion

Many specialists of transitions to democratic systems have taken national unity and the existence of a sovereign state as prerequisites for the development of democracy. Rustow (1970), as mentioned above, views national unity as the necessary background condition for a transition to democracy. His position is defended on the basis of the fact that "the vast majority of citizens in a democracy-to-be must have no doubt or mental reservations as to which political community they belong." It has been argued that Tunisia still provides an interesting contrast because, despite its ethnic homogeneity, it seems to be unable to democratize substantively. From this perspective, ethnic homogeneity is not a sufficient condition for genuine democratization. Under both Bourguiba and Bin Ali the state's concerted efforts to insist on national unity actually undercut possibilities for civic participation and good government. Appeals to national unity give the state an excuse to weed out would-be dissidents. That is, the presence of national politics that overemphasize unity often comes at the expense of tolerating political diversity, as the Tunisian case demonstrates. Corporatist strategies of co-optation and mediation as well as coercion (e.g., exclusion, purges, and imprisonment) have been used to reify unity and defend it against potentially viable political projects. Hence the discourse and practice of Tunisian identity nurtured by the state has been exclusionary in the main. Bin Ali's regime, like Bourguiba's, has worked hard to construct a certain Tunisian ethnonationalism, but it has surely limited success. Ghannushi's Islamists, with their opposition to secularism and excessive Westernization, do not buy it. Their vision for an Arab-Islamic identity figured strongly in their electoral program in 1989.

If citizenship is to be understood as "an instrument of equality in democratic states" (Oommen, 1997, p. 38) then nothing like it has yet evolved in post-colonial Tunisia. Furthermore, the idea of nationality and ethnicity constituting grounds for conferring or denying political equality by nation-states (Oommen, 1997, p. 38) corresponds with the empirical reality in Tunisia. So far, it seems, inclusion is conferred upon those willing to work within the straightjacket of either political deference or "loyal opposition," one aim of the 1988 National Pact (Anderson, 1991). As such, inclusion is read as "co-option." Tunisia's corporatist politics of inclusion and exclusion is authoritarian. Interest representation within it is limited to units or groups created or approved by the state. These groups are singular, non-competitive, and hierarchically ordered. Their political participation and articulation of demands must observe state controls, obey its discourse, and maintain support for them (Schmitter, 1975; Bianchi, 1989). Moreover, the brand of economic development engineered by the state seems to stress statism, centralized control, and incrementalism. All these elements make for a singular political order, as has been elaborated in the preceding section. In fact, Bin Ali's advent to power has sealed an inter-marriage not only between the army, the bureaucracy, and the urban agrarian and industrial Sahel bourgeoisie, but also between praetorianism and economic wealth. The president's wife, Madame Leyla Bin Ali, who hails from the wealthy mercantile Trabelsi family, is emerging as a powerful political figure in her own right. Twenty years after the deposition of Bourguiba, political singularity may for the first time in Arab history be exemplified in the passing of power from a male ruler to his female spouse. The couple's child is too young to inherit the state "*à la Syrienne.*" This transition may not be a bad thing for a country whose political ancestry included women such as Carthaginian Queen Dido, also called Elissa, and the Berber warrior princess, al-Kahina.

Notes

1 Bouteflika's amnesty plan follows from the 1999 Civil Harmony Law. The plan initially envisaged dropping charges against rebels who stopped combat after 13 January 2000. The first plan applied to all insurgents, but opposition to the controversial amnesty meant only a watered-down version could be adopted. The 97 percent "yes" verdict by 80 percent of the more than 18 million eligible voters has not stopped criticism that Bouteflika's amnesty whitewashes past crimes.
2 President Bouteflika states in his speech, 12 March 2002, that he took the measure "in total freedom and with full conviction."
3 In the newly reformed *mudawwanah* the minimum age of marriage for women is 18 (it was 15 in the original document of 1957 and after the amendments of 1993); divorce will now take place by mutual consent, thus ending the husband's practice of repudiation or unilateral divorce; polygamy, whilst still legal, will be more difficult as it will be subject to strict judicial vetting and control; parentage

and family are now equal responsibilities of both spouses; the old practice of the wife's duty of obedience to the husband is now rescinded; and women can now marry without the need for a male marital tutor or *wali*.

4 Military Council for Justice and Democracy, "Official Statement," 3 August 2005, Nouakchott, Mauritania. Available at: http://www.ami.mr/fr/Archives2005/aout/ 3/13.htm.

Part II
Regional Issues in the Contemporary Maghreb

7 Economic Reform in the Maghreb

From Stabilization to Modernization

Gonzalo Escribano and Alejandro V. Lorca

After the initial successes of the three central Maghrebi countries and Libya in macroeconomic stabilization, we have observed the attempted implementation of economic and administrative reforms since the 1980s in order to liberalize the economic system and enter a phase of sustained growth acceleration. The purpose of this chapter is to offer an analysis of the economic situation and the state of reforms in the Maghreb, as well as the region's economic prospects. The first section presents its geography as a unifying element of Maghrebi economies. Next, we analyze the development of its main economic features: growth, social indicators, development strategies, macroeconomic policies, and the foreign sector. Third, we examine microeconomic reforms, which basically consist of internal and external liberalization, privatization, and tax, administrative, and financial reforms. In the last section, we draw some conclusions which highlight the fact that the window of opportunity for implementing the reforms is narrow and that it is urgent to accelerate them so as not to jeopardize the region's credibility, the sustainability of its macroeconomic stabilization, the consolidation of its productive integration with the European Union (EU), and the encouraging, but fragile, economic growth acceleration of recent years.

The Maghreb's Geo-Economy

The Maghreb is a geographical concept encompassing diverse realities and which has several economic and political ruptures. Some analysts have even labeled the Maghreb as having a fractured geography.[1] The complexity can also be seen economically, with countries whose economy is based on income from oil and gas (Algeria and Libya) and countries more economically diversified, where export agriculture, industry, and tourism all play their part (Morocco and Tunisia). That complexity and fragmentation make it difficult to portray its economic reality as a whole. Using geography as a unifying element is a pragmatic approach since geography determines climate conditions and the nature of the soils, thus conditioning agriculture. The Western Mediterranean is protected from the cold, continental climates of Northern Europe by mountain chains, whilst in the south it borders on expanses of desert. Since it is an enclosed, sunny sea, the saline level of the water is high. The combination of both elements makes its climate warm and very regular, a regularity that also occurs in the composition of the soil. All this produces a Mediterranean agriculture in which crops are basically the same in the different countries on its shores, thus leading to a situation of apparent competition among them.

The orography and climate also influence the location of economic activities. Water resources and cultivatable land are concentrated in the coastal strip, sheltered from the rigors of the desert by mountain chains. Agricultural activity takes place mainly in these coastal strips, where the land is fertile and the rainfall, although irregular, makes Mediterranean agriculture possible. As a result, the population is concentrated on the coast, leaving the interior and mountainous regions sparsely populated. The colonial period exacerbated this territorial imbalance by locating industries in coastal urban areas with transport infrastructures. The Maghreb suffers from a double territorial imbalance: between the coast and the interior, on the one hand, and between the countryside and the cities, on the other. Bad living conditions in the rural areas have forced exodus to the urban centers, whose public services have been overwhelmed by the avalanche of rural migrants and by demographic dynamics.

From a European perspective, closeness to the Maghreb leads to trade, service, energy, migratory, and capital flows. Issues such as the Western Sahara conflict, drug trafficking, illegal immigration, energy interdependence, the rise of political Islam, or Jihadi terrorism become relevant to the EU as a result of its geographical proximity to North Africa.[2] Historically, the Mediterranean unifies rather than separates, and this geographical conditioning involves risks, but also opportunities, for the countries on its shores. The closeness of the EU exerts a great gravitational attraction over the Maghreb and turns it into a "natural trade block," to use Krugman's terminology.[3] The combination of geographical closeness, colonial links, and the size of markets is very effective, generating asymmetrical geo-economic interdependence. The proximity also enables migratory flows from the Maghreb and sub-Saharan Africa, as the trip is relatively easy and the colonial past has provided close linguistic and socioeconomic linkages.

In this context, it is necessary to provide a review of the EU's options based on its geographical situation.[4] In its first 40 years of existence, the European Community was only able to expand economically towards the south. These circumstances led to the first generation of Euro-Mediterranean agreements in the 1970s. In 1989, the fall of the Berlin Wall enabled the EU to start its economic expansion towards the east, which concentrated the majority of the Union's efforts, postponing any attention to the countries on the southern frontier, despite efforts made in this regard by Mediterranean member states. However, since 11 September 2001, priorities have changed. Jihadi terrorism is seen in the West as the materialization of Huntington's "clash of civilizations," and economic considerations on expanding markets and the production frontier have fallen into the background. The attacks in Madrid in March 2004 and London in July 2005 reinforced this trend.

The frontiers separating the northern and southern shores of the Western Mediterranean are diverse. The latest events favor the perception of cultural, religious, and political fractures, but the economic gap is essential in causing conflicts. For example, income differences between Spain and Morocco are among the highest in the world. From an international political economy point of view, the Western Mediterranean can be seen as a space for exchange, a geo-economic and geopolitical system where the Maghreb's economic weakness has an impact on the EU's vulnerabilities. These vulnerabilities do not manifest themselves directly in economic terms (given the small dimension of Maghrebi markets), but in their social consequences.

Aware of the need to promote sustained development in the Mediterranean, the EU launched the New Neighbourhood Policy in 2003, whose appellation itself demonstrated the extent to which it is dictated by geography. It consists of designing a new framework for relations with the Mediterranean and European neighbors of the enlarged EU, which, in principle, would involve shifting from the concept of frontier to that of neighborhood. For the Maghreb, the initiative is supported by the Euro-Mediterranean Partnership to form a "ring of friends" with which the EU wants to develop close and peaceful relations of cooperation. From an economic perspective, the instruments to achieve greater economic integration consist of further liberalizing trade so that the Mediterranean Partner Countries (MPCs) can participate in the European Single Market, besides an increase in technical and financial assistance.

The new development is based on the fact that these concessions are conditioned, in principle, by the MPCs' specific progress, which proves their willingness to undertake not only economic reforms, but also political and institutional transformations. On the basis of the MPCs' situation and their relations with the EU, Action Plans have been negotiated which establish priorities in the reforms to be adopted by the MPCs. In practice, conditionality has been substantially devalued and the measures stated in the Action Plans do not establish clear priorities, except in identifying a list of reforms that would lead to the *Europeanization* of these countries, but which is voluntary and not very operational.[5]

The Maghreb Economies

Social Indicators and Economic Growth[6]

The first observation is that the Maghreb has low human development indices that are explained primarily by the incidence of illiteracy, which mainly affects the rural population and women. Out of 177 countries, Algeria was in position 102, Libya 64, Morocco 123, and Tunisia 87 in

2005. In that year, income per capita in purchasing power parity was $6,603 in Algeria, $7,570 in Libya (although some estimates say it is much higher), $4,309 in Morocco, and $7,768 in Tunisia. Despite the fact that the Maghrebi countries spend a signifcant part of their GDP on education, the rate of literacy among adults is barely 70 percent in Algeria, 82 percent in Libya, 52 percent in Morocco, and 74 percent in Tunisia.

The reason for the stagnation in the per capita income and, consequently, in the public services the state is capable of providing, is twofold: strong demographic progression and an insufficient and volatile rate of economic growth. Despite a slowdown in recent years, demographic growth is still considerable. The fertility rate has gone down from 6–8 children per woman in 1970–75 to 2–3 in 2000–5, and the annual demographic growth has decreased from 2–3 percent, depending on the country, in 1975–2002 to forecasts of 1–1.8 percent for 2002–15. The Maghreb's demographic transition will have occurred in just one generation, whereas it took the West over a century. According to Philippe Fargues,[7] this demographic change involves important social transformations, which can have economic implications. The fertility rates in the Maghrebi urban environment are close to those in European countries. This fact advances human capital accumulation and raises the economy's growth rate in the long term, according to conventional growth theories. The problem is the existence of acute differences between the urban and the rural areas, the latter still recording high fertility rates, which prevent it from generating human capital and force the inhabitants in those areas to emigrate.

So far, GDP growth has not sufficed to generate the resources required by demographic pressure. In the long term, Maghrebi economies have grown below the rate of other developing countries. For example, Morocco and South Korea started with similar per capita GDP levels in 1960. According to data from the UNDP for the 1975–2004 period, the average annual growth rate of per capita GDP was 6 percent in South Korea compared with just 0.1 percent in Algeria, 1.4 percent in Morocco, and 2.3 percent in Tunisia. Growth was moderate in the 1960s, but it accelerated in the following decade, when expansion policies were implemented in line with the rise in raw material prices. The excesses of the 1970s turned into the recession of the 1980s and in the 1990s growth was very volatile, as can be seen in Table 7.1. In recent years, growth has become less volatile and there has been an acceleration, which, according to estimates, could be sustained in the future. Nevertheless, the reasons for the fragile nature of economic growth have not disappeared. In Algeria and Libya, this depends on the increase of oil prices, while in Morocco the importance of agriculture in the economy makes it more sensitive to droughts. Tunisia is showing a more sustained growth path based on a more diversified economy, but it is very dependent on the European economic cycle, just as Morocco is: European economic growth fosters Moroccan and Tunisian exports of goods and services, as well as remittances, while European stagnation reduces them.

Table 7.1 Real GDP Growth Rates (%)

	Algeria	Libya	Morocco	Tunisia
1995	3.8	0.7	−6.6	2.4
1996	3.8	3.1	12.2	7.1
1997	1.1	4.3	−2.2	5.4
1998	5.1	−0.4	7.7	4.8
1999	3.2	0.3	−0.1	6.1
2000	2.2	1.1	1.0	4.7
2001	2.6	4.5	6.3	4.9
2002	4.7	3.3	3.2	1.7
2003	6.9	9.1*	5.5	5.6
2004	5.2	4.6*	4.2	6.0
2005	5.3*	3.5*	1.7	4.2*
2006	4.9*	5.0*	7.3*	5.8*
2007	5.0*	4.6*	3.3*	6.0*

Source: IMF, *World Economic Outlook Database*.
Note: asterisk indicates IMF estimates.

The reasons for the lack of growth of Maghrebi economies stem, in the long run, from high demographic growth and the lack of physical and human capital accumulation. Economic policy mistakes in the past resulted in financial crises that have forced the Maghrebi countries to implement structural adjustment programs that have been very costly in social and economic growth terms, and to incur external debts which, despite being reduced in recent years, have mortgaged their growth. Libya is an exception, since its small population and its large hydrocarbon resources enable it to maintain the current expenditure of a subsidized economy. Besides a development strategy that is too dependent on hydrocarbons and bad economic management, its growth problems come from the cost of the US embargo and the UN sanctions.[8] When the sanctions were imposed in 1992, Libya's per capita GDP was $7,430. By the time they were suspended in 1999, the GDP per capita had decreased to $5,929.

Despite the growth problems, poverty did not become as evident in the Maghreb as it did in other developing countries, and it is mainly a rural phenomenon with large regional disparities. Between 1990 and 2004, 2 percent of the population lived on less than $1 per day in Algeria, Tunisia, and Morocco, compared with 4.4 percent in Mexico. Approximately 15 percent of the population lived on less than $2 per day in Algeria and Morocco compared with 6.6 percent in Tunisia and over 20 percent in Mexico. This lesser relative incidence is usually explained by institutional and cultural variables. The Muslim religion and its family and solidarity values provide a non-governmental social security network, which is sometimes used by political Islam to perform proselytizing strategies. Income distribution is also more balanced in the Maghreb than in Latin America or South Asia: the Gini index in Algeria is 35 (similar to Spain and Poland), and in Morocco and Tunisia it is close to 40, below Mexico, Argentina, and Malaysia (all around 50). Child malnutrition is also much less prevalent than in developing countries taken as a whole.

One of the main problems is unemployment, which is very high, especially among young people and women. In the rural areas, data are affected by a lack of statistics, hidden unemployment, underemployment, and subsistence activities. The labor market is incapable of absorbing the large number of young entrants, which is the result of demographic dynamics. This situation generates social tensions and is a factor leading to migratory flows. It is also an additional element of pressure on the economy, since strong rates of economic growth need to be attained to absorb those entering the labor market. By way of example, the World Bank estimates a 6 percent rate of growth for Morocco in order to absorb the new entrants in the labor market.

In Algeria, the rate of unemployment was 15 percent in 2005, a large drop from the 30 percent recorded in 2000 due to the expansion of public employment and the growth of the economy. However, estimates indicate that 35 percent of the manpower is unemployed or underemployed. In Morocco, the official figures for 2004 stood at 11 percent for unemployment (18.4 percent in the urban areas and 3.2 percent in the rural regions), but given that the official data only include a small proportion of rural unemployment, the overall rate is higher. Tunisia has official unemployment rates of 15 percent, but the real figures are probably higher, especially among young university graduates. There are no official data for Libya, but some estimates say that it is 30 percent, despite the fact that it has an immigrant population of close to a million people, as do other rentier economies.

Development Strategies

The usual sequence of development strategies can be seen in the Maghreb, from the export strategy of primary products to the promotion of exports, including import substitution. The implementation of these strategies created a network of economic structures and interests, which have substantially modified the initial balance of power among the different social sectors. In parallel, each strategy is a reaction to previous problems. However, once its implementation started, the profusion of ad hoc measures, economic policy errors, and conflicts of interest gave the strategies their own dynamics, which pushed them further away from the initial objectives and often made them fall into excess and inconsistency.[9]

The result of this export strategy of primary products was an excessive dependence on the income from this sector, squandering it, and the so-called "Dutch disease" (the exporting boom caused a spiral of inflation, public deficit, and exchange rate appreciation that resulted in unfavorable exchange terms for agriculture and industry). The whole Maghreb suffered from "Dutch disease," due either to hydrocarbon exports (Algeria and

Libya) or, in the 1970s, to phosphates (Morocco and Tunisia).[10] The governments' reluctance to sterilize the excess liquidity produced by the surplus in the current account, as well as bad macroeconomic management, made the abundance of natural resources almost a curse. As we shall see below, the countries in the region seem to have learned from their past mistakes and the macroeconomic management of the recent boom in the price of raw materials is proving to be more orthodox than in the past.

Agriculture deserves a detailed approach, because of its importance in terms of its contribution to GDP and working population. In Morocco agriculture occupies more than half the workforce, but it only contributes 10–15 percent of GDP, depending on rainfall, an imbalance shown by its low productivity. In Tunisia, the figures are more balanced, since it occupies 16 percent of the workforce and a similar percentage of GDP. In the rest of the region, the importance of agriculture is smaller, although Algeria has implemented an ambitious agricultural development plan that is promoting the sector in an attempt to decrease its large food dependence. In general, the Maghreb's agriculture has a dual nature: modern export agriculture with an emphasis on Mediterranean products (fruit, olive oil, vegetables) and traditional agriculture, based on cereals. This dual nature seriously limits liberalization.[11]

Export agriculture is more capitalized, uses irrigation, operates in favorable climatic conditions, and is marketed to the EU. It represents an important percentage of Morocco's exports and, to a lesser extent, Tunisia's (15 and 8 percent respectively in 2005). Traditional cereal-based agriculture obtains low yields; it is at the mercy of frequent droughts and subject to contradictory pressures from governments' price policies. On the one hand, it is penalized by consumer state price policies, which keep the price of basic food artificially low as a means of redistributing income towards urban population. On the other hand, producer prices are high in Morocco and Tunisia as a result of tariff protection, thus distorting relative prices.[12] In addition, there is still subsistence agriculture, based on self-consumption and barter. The combination of modern export agriculture and traditional, low-productivity cereal agriculture with strong rates of demographic growth and urban development has led to the increase in food deficits. All the countries in the Maghreb require a high level of food imports to feed their populations.

In the industrial sector, import substitution resulted in inefficient productive systems, incapable of competing and of supplying the population and companies with the most elementary consumer goods, intermediate products, and, of course, capital goods. In Algeria, import substitution was based on heavy industry, especially the iron and steel and the petrochemical industries, whilst in Morocco and Tunisia it occurred in light industry, basically in consumer goods and in the agro-food sector. Import-substitution industrialization paradoxically resulted in a large increase in imports and the overuse of scarce resources, such as physical and human capital. Its combination with the "Dutch disease" led to unsustainable external debts in the region (except in Libya), which are impossible to finance, and the need to implement stabilization and adjustment programs with support from the World Bank and the IMF.

The export promotion strategy, where it has been implemented (Tunisia and Morocco), has not been a panacea either. In the past, European protectionism could be blamed, but the current explanation is the inability of the majority of the exporting sectors to improve productivity or develop non-traditional exports. Furthermore, the exporting strategy became dependent on trade preferences established by the EU: competitiveness was not understood as the result of an improvement in productivity and a decrease in transaction costs, but as managing to have preferential access to European markets. World trade liberalization has led to a decrease in EU protection vis-à-vis more competitive economies, such as those in Asia or some in Latin America, thus eroding the trade preferences granted to the Maghreb. This has been evident in the textile sector, where the expiration of the Multifiber Agreement (MFA) has unleashed textile exports from Asia towards the EU, at the expense of Moroccan and Tunisian production, to the point that Morocco has been forced to sign an FTA with Turkey in order to import cheap inputs from that country and improve its competitiveness.

Currently, the three strategies overlap: the agro-food and consumer goods sectors are still protected to promote the consolidation of "infant industries" that do not mature; primary exports (energy, minerals, and agricultural products) are still a fundamental element of the external balance; and the export of light manufactured products, in which it has a comparative advantage (basically the clothing industry and, to a lesser extent, electronic components), comes up against competition from Asian countries and the low dynamism of international trade in both sectors.

Macroeconomic Situation[13]

The macroeconomic situation in the Maghreb has improved considerably; the imbalances in the 1980s made it necessary to implement stabilization programs. Inflation is better controlled today than it was in the recent past. Budgets show financeable tax deficits in Morocco and Tunisia, and there have been important surpluses in recent years in Algeria and Libya, due to the high prices of hydrocarbons; the situation for foreign accounts is more balanced and reflects moderate financing requirements (Morocco and Tunisia) or resource surpluses (Algeria and Libya), requiring a more prudent macroeconomic management. One of the most relevant matters is the type of fiscal adjustment implemented, which depends on the expenditure items it applies to. If the adjustment is made on current expenditure (public salaries and enrollment, and state transfers) and not on public investment, fiscal consolidation is more sustainable and less damaging for economic growth, although there is an important social and political cost in the short run.

The fiscal adjustment has been adequate in Tunisia, where the deficit decreased almost 4 points in the 1990s due to the drop in current expenditure. In Algeria, the increase in oil revenues led to a rapid reduction in the deficit of almost 10 percentage points in the 1990s to stand at around 2–3 percent of GDP recently. Until 2002, and despite the high significance of subsidies, current expenditure was under control. However, the boom in hydrocarbon prices has led to a sharp rise in both investment expenditure, by implementing a growth promotion plan, and current expenditure, especially the increase in staff and the salaries of civil servants and employees of state-owned companies. In Morocco, social demands over politically sensitive issues, such as public salaries and some subsidies, have forced current expenditure to rise. The budgetary deficit did not fall in the 1990s, and increases in current expenditure were compensated by stagnation in public investment, thus curbing growth and imposing a high cost due to the payment of public debt interest. At the moment, however, it has budgetary deficits of around 3 percent of GDP and it has successfully reduced the size of its external debt.

Algeria had a late start in macroeconomic stabilization. As a result of its economic structure, a very active macroeconomic policy management is necessary to prevent the current surplus generated by hydrocarbon exports from increasing prices due to excess liquidity. Tax policy has expansive slants since the prices of oil soared, and social unrest started to mount, leading to the riots of 2001. Despite the increase in expenditure, the rise in both oil prices and production has strengthened the Algerian fiscal position. The government is planning to raise capital expenditure considerably, although there are doubts about whether it has the capacity to implement the promised amounts. Forecasts are optimistic, as, although oil prices are starting to fall, fiscal income has the potential to increase because of the new energy facilities that will boost Algerian production capacity. Despite this rise in expenditure and liquidity, inflation is still contained. The main problem is sterilizing the excess liquidity from the national oil company, Sonatrach, revenue, the majority of which is in a state bank and subject to a prohibition on using it for extending credit. The development of this aspect is uncertain, but the result so far has been relatively positive in terms of inflation, although inflationist pressures seem to have surged in 2006.

In Morocco, the main difficulty is maintaining fiscal stability, which is threatened by current expenditure, made up of the total public payroll costs and consumption subsidies. This pressure prevents public expenditure from reaching the necessary investment levels in social issues and closing the infrastructure gap imposed by the fiscal restriction of recent years. On the income side, attempts at reform of the fiscal system did not materialize, due to political problems, and the income increase cannot maintain the rate of expenditure. If income from privatizations is not considered, public deficit is high, amounting to close to 6 percent of GDP. The tax impact from trade liberalization with the EU and the US remains to be seen. Although the rise in imports is compensating the fall in tariffs at the moment, the most sensitive tariff tranches still need to be liberalized. Therefore, it seems that budgetary weakness will remain in the future and will prevent the investments in infrastructures and modernization of institutions and public services which the country needs.

The dilemma in Morocco stems from combating poverty and deteriorating living conditions, at the same time as public expenditure should be curbed to improve the fiscal situation. So far, the government has financed current expenditure with privatizations, which prevents productive investment of these resources. In fact, the authorities adopted privatization as a fiscal requirement, but problems with trade unions and the bad condition of public companies make it difficult for this process to be intensified. Furthermore, inflation is controlled and monetary policy is stricter than in Algeria. The autonomy of the Central Bank with regard to monetary policy and supervision of the financial sector was strengthened in 2004, as it had been burdened by situations that infringe on prudent regulation, especially in public banking. Inflation has abated since the reduction in tariff protection and the subsequent drop in the price of imports, whose growth shows a deviation of internal demand towards EU imports. However, the concurrence of a possibly more expansive fiscal cycle, if a new government that is more sensitive to income redistribution comes on the scene, and the impact of oil prices if subsidies are eliminated, may lead to inflationist pressures in the future.

Tunisia's macroeconomic situation has improved, but it also has budgetary weaknesses (deficits of around 3 percent of GDP when privatizations are not included). The tax policy is committed to maintaining financeable deficits, but the political cost of reforming the oversized administration and decreasing current expenditure is causing obvious difficulties. As explained for Morocco, fears connected to the fall of tariff earnings after trade liberalization with the EU have proved to be unfounded, owing to an increase in imports. Also, there are serious obstacles for the reform of fiscal incentives and of the tax system, especially in the current context of economic expansion, which makes the revenue raised through income tax increase at a good rate. Privatization is a source of financing for current expenditure, which highlights the need to cut it. Monetary policy is prudent and inflation is controlled, although tensions over the price of oil can raise it in the future, besides increasing current expenditure in the form of fuel subsidies.

Libya's macroeconomic situation is as robust as any small rentier country's in the years when crude oil prices are high, with a budgetary surplus estimated at 15–20 percent of GDP. The Libyan budgetary law makes it obligatory to have a balanced budget, but the increase in oil proceeds has led to a considerable rise in public expenditure. In principle, the government is thinking of using 70 percent of this expenditure on development projects, but in practice a large part of it has been diverted to current disbursement, especially food subsidies, based on socio-political considerations. The lifting of the sanctions led to a deflationist cycle between 2000 and 2002 and inflation is currently at moderate levels. It is contained by price controls, which, although they have been relaxed in recent years for energy, are still keeping the prices of products and basic services stable. Expectations of strong growth and a restructured tax position cannot hide the productive weaknesses and peculiarities of the country's economic management, but they do not cause the macroeconomic challenges pointed out in the cases of Algeria and Morocco.

The Foreign Sector

Foreign trade in the Maghreb has a high geographical concentration in the EU, which, on average, was 64 percent of imports and over 70 percent of exports in the region in 2005. The comparative advantages are concentrated on basic products (agriculture, fishing, mining, and energy) derived from natural resources, or on labor-intensive manufactured goods with relatively low added value. Their development is disappointing, because there are hardly any exports of new products in the most dynamic segments of international trade. The substitution nature of some products in the different Maghrebi countries makes it difficult to implement intra-regional and intra-industry trade, which stands at very low levels. Exports to the EU are facing competition from enlargement countries and from other geographical areas: Asian countries for light manufactured products, Russia and the Central Asian republics for energy, and other Mediterranean countries (Turkey, Egypt) for agricultural and fishing products.

Morocco and Tunisia have structural trade deficits, while Libya and Algeria (the latter in years of high oil prices) have record surpluses. The trade deficit of Morocco and Tunisia translates into current account deficit when income from tourism and remittances and, in some years, foreign investment, is reduced. In macroeconomic terms, a current account deficit means that national savings are not enough to finance national investment and, therefore, this deficit in resources must be compensated by turning to foreign savings. This explains why Morocco and Tunisia have significant external debts, although improvement in external balances in recent years has substantially reduced them.

Tourism is very important for Tunisia and Morocco, while Libya and Algeria appear as less attractive tourist destinations, due to their political situations. The tourist sector is labor intensive, attracts foreign capital, and provides important compensation for trade deficits. Tourist potential in these countries is due to a rich combination of geography, climate, history, and culture. Morocco and Tunisia garner important revenue from tourism, equivalent to 5–6 percent of GDP. Traditionally, Tunisia has been more aggressive in its policies to attract tourists and the sector generates around

300,000 direct and indirect jobs. Morocco's tourism has recently increased greatly. Morocco has a strategic plan to make the country more attractive as a destination. This includes foreign investment, air traffic liberalization, and the construction of tourist complexes. Libya is also making a concerted effort to open up new tourist markets, which, to date, has not had many results.

In recent years, workers' remittances have been the main item to compensate for the trade deficit in Morocco, reaching 10 percent of GDP, although real figures could be double that due to the importance of unofficial flows. Remittances fluctuate in accordance with the European economic cycle, but also with the measures implemented by countries to attract them. In Morocco, for example, measures implemented to make migrant deposits more attractive have been relatively successful. The importance of remittances also depends on the rate of exchange, especially of the euro as compared with local currencies. Currently, with the euro's exchange rate strength, remittances are an important compensatory item in the balance of payments for the Maghreb (except for Libya), the greater part of which is being used for consumption. So far, the authorities have been more interested in their function of providing currencies with which to water-down the trade deficit than as a source of productive capital to modernize the Maghrebi economies. Only recently have both the receiving and issuing countries begun to explore a way to obtain more yield from these flows.

Lastly, the behavior of foreign investment is a fundamental variable for economic development and for establishing a Euro-Mediterranean Free Trade Area. The Maghreb enjoys important advantages, such as geographical proximity to the EU, preferential treatment for its exports, and, mainly, low labor costs. Despite this, political and institutional factors seem to be inhibiting greater European investment in the Maghreb. Nevertheless, those countries that have established active improvement mechanisms within an export-promoting strategy (Tunisia and Morocco) and which have opened their internal-services market up to foreign investment are receiving important investments as a result of these reforms.

As can be seen in Table 7.2, foreign direct investment (FDI) flows represent an important percentage of total investment in Morocco and Tunisia and FDI stock was 44 and 56 percent of the GDP in 2005, respectively. FDI has made a qualitative leap in Morocco in the current decade and its percentages, like those of Tunisia, are starting to be comparable with some of the main FDI destinations in the world, such as the EU enlargement countries or Chile. By contrast, in Algeria both indicators show that the country has not opened up as much to FDI. However, FDI in the Maghreb has followed a fiscal logic, based on obtaining proceeds from privatizations and the granting of licenses in public services, ignoring its productive modernization component and the strategy of climbing up the value-added chain.[14] This aspect can be seen to a greater extent in the shortage of FDI in dynamic exporting sectors, unlike what is happening in the EU enlargement countries, for example.

Table 7.2 FDI Flows and Stocks for Selected Countries and Regions

	FDI flows (% of gross fixed capital formation)			
	Annual average 1990–2000	2003	2004	2005
Morocco	8.1	23.1	8.7	22.1
Algeria	2.4	4.0	4.2	4.9
Tunisia	10.2	10.0	10.1	12.1
North Africa	5.1	10.8	9.9	19.5
Poland	11.8	11.6	28.4	14.6
Czech Republic	14.4	8.6	17.2	34.0
Chile	22.7	27.7	37.0	26.1
Latin America and the Caribbean	12.0	13.5	15.9	16.8
Developing countries	8.9	9.3	10.7	12.8

	FDI Stock (% of GDP)			
	1990	2000	2004	2005
Morocco	9.7	26.2	39.9	43.9
Algeria	2.5	6.4	8.9	8.1
Tunisia	61.8	59.4	63.2	56.1
North Africa	12.6	17.1	25.8	24.8
Poland	0.2	20.5	35.4	31.1
Czech Republic	3.7	38.9	53.5	48.1
Chile	30.0	61.1	64.3	64.6
Latin America and the Caribbean	10.3	25.8	37.6	36.7
Developing countries	9.8	26.3	27.9	27

Source: UNCTAD, *World Investment Report 2006*, Geneva, October 2006.

Liberalization and Other Microeconomic Reforms

Trade Liberalization

The economic fragmentation of the Maghreb can be seen above all in its trade policy, multilaterally, regionally, and sub-regionally. Morocco and Tunisia are subject to WTO discipline, but Algeria and Libya are not, although Algeria is in the process of joining the WTO and the EU would be prepared to support its candidacy; the United States is also assisting Algeria in accession to the WTO. The differences can also be seen in the EU's Association Agreements (AAs) with Tunisia, Morocco, and Algeria, which involve the creation of bilateral free trade areas (Table 7.3). Tunisia and Morocco were, with Israel, the first countries to negotiate and sign AAs, as well as the first countries where they came into effect. The AA with Algeria came into effect in 2005 and Libya only takes part in the Barcelona Process as an observer and has not negotiated an Association Agreement with the EU. The European Neighbourhood Policy involves more fragmentation of the southern Mediterranean shore, to the extent that it reinforces the bilateral

Table 7.3 Schedule of EU Association Agreements with the Maghreb

Country	Negotiation conclusion	Signature	Entry into force
Tunisia	June 1995	July 1995	March 1998
Morocco	November 1995	February 1996	March 2000
Algeria	December 2001	April 2002	September 2005
Libya	Observer in the Barcelona Process (since 1999)		

component and weakens its regional focus.[15] In the Maghreb, Tunisia and Morocco have Action Plans that have already been approved, but Algeria does not and Libya has not started negotiations, given that it has not even accepted yet the *acquis* of the Barcelona Process.

The new AAs with the EU introduce the concept of reciprocity, by which the MPCs can gradually liberalize their trade policies. Given that MPC-manufactured products already have free access to the community market, the bulk of the trade adjustment occurs in the Maghrebi countries, which are now forced to liberalize their imports from the EU without obtaining any significant improvement in access to the EU markets. The only sector in which the EU has protected markets and, therefore, has concessions to offer, is agriculture. Although the AAs have reciprocal agricultural concessions, they are limited, and, in cases such as that of Morocco, have necessitated an additional Agricultural Agreement. For Morocco and Tunisia, which have signed Action Plans, the neighborhood framework provides a new boost for liberalization and microeconomic reforms in general, since the objective is to gradually include the *acquis communautaire* (which involves modernizing their institutions and profound microeconomic reforms) to participate in the Single European Market.

The AA with Algeria forecasts the creation of a free trade area with the EU for 2017. The AA stipulates the gradual elimination of tariffs on imports of industrial products from the EU. Due to strong pressure from the EU and the IMF, Algeria has simplified its tariffs, using a system based on three categories of products: imports of raw materials and capital goods from the EU were subject to a unified tariff of 5 percent; intermediate products to one of 10 percent; and final products to one of 30 percent. However, to continue protecting domestic companies, the government imposed an "additional temporary rate" of 60 percent on a list of goods. Although this additional rate has gradually come down, in concession to pressures from protected sectors, it damages the credibility of the trade liberalization process.

In the first half of the current decade, Morocco has implemented a tariff reform based on reducing tariffs and decreasing the number of tariff types. The average unweighted tariff is around 25 percent, which compares favorably with the rest of the countries in the southern Mediterranean: only Jordan and Lebanon have lower tariffs, while Egypt, Tunisia, and Libya have tariffs that are 10 percentage points higher than those in Morocco. However, comparison with countries in the Gulf, Southeast Asia, or Latin America is much less favorable, with some tariffs being 20 percentage points higher in Morocco. The reforms also affect the institutional set-up, especially the modernization of customs management and infrastructures. Nevertheless, the WTO (2003) considers that there is room for more liberalization, especially in the services sector.

The EU's Association Agreement with Morocco came into effect on 1 March 2000 and aims at a free trade area by 2012. The agreement has plans for tariff-reduction schedules on the majority of products, but also for safeguard measures in the event of "serious disturbances" for the production of either of the two parties. The immediate and total exemption from customs duties only affected capital goods, which has had a very small impact, since they had very low tariffs (2.5 percent), and they could even be imported with the exemptions forecast by the Investment Code. Raw materials and goods not produced locally were completely liberalized at the end of 2003, but the impact has not been very large either, since customs systems offer an almost total tariff exemption for intermediate products used in export production. Tariff dismantling is more scaled for products made in Morocco, and tariffs will be eliminated for those products after 12 years, with a delay grace period of three years. The first tariff-reduction tranche started in 2003 and there has, therefore, not been enough time to assess its impact.

The Agricultural Agreement between Morocco and the EU reached at the end of 2003 is a "controlled" liberalization by Morocco, with the concession of preferential tariffs for cereals, meat, dairy products, and vegetable oils from the EU. Morocco obtained the extension of the preferential tariff quotas for certain products, above all the tomato. The most substantial modification as far as Morocco is concerned refers to the new import regime of soft wheat from the EU, the most sensitive product for Morocco.[16] To safeguard Moroccan producers without imposing excessive costs on consumers, the quotas will be reduced in good seasons, while in years of drought imports can increase to prevent excessive prices. In all cases, use of the safeguard clause for "serious disturbances" in the markets is planned. The use of exceptions and safeguards, as well as the effort to regulate agricultural flows, risks denaturalizing the liberalization process and making it less credible. Furthermore, in anticipation of the Agreement finally reached with the US, the EU ensured that any tariff concession to a third country would be implemented immediately for EU agricultural exports.

The 2004 Morocco–US free trade agreement came into effect in 2006, leading to internal political problems, to the point that Moroccan negotiators were virtually forced to negotiate in secret so as to avoid public opposition in the middle of the Iraq war. The three key points of the negotiations are acceleration of intellectual property reforms, improvement in the investment environment, and liberalization of agricultural markets. This agreement has aroused the mistrust of some European governments, which allege supposed incompatibilities between a free trade area with the US and the Association Agreement with the EU, particularly in agricultural liberalization, non-consideration of the cultural exception, and intellectual property commitments. Morocco is the third Arab country to reach a free trade agreement with the US after Jordan and Bahrain.

Tunisia's trade policy is multilaterally quite protectionist, but its commitment to the EU is demonstrated by having an AA that favors free trade. It was also the first MPC to negotiate and implement an agreement. There are 52 different dispersed tariff types that are very high on the most protected products, as well as numerous non-tariff barriers. However, given that over 70 percent of Tunisian imports come from the EU, the Most Favored Nation (MFN) tariffs are not very relevant. Tariffs with the EU have gradually decreased, as provided for in the AA. Since 2003, manufactured goods imports, which compete with local production, are subject to tariffs 44 percent below the 1995 level, while consumer goods, raw materials, and intermediate products are subject to tariffs that have been substantially reduced. Otherwise, the AA design and operation is similar to Morocco's. Service trade with the EU is not subject to additional commitments, reflecting Tunisia's also limited offers in GATS (General Agreement on Trade Services).

Libya's situation is an exception as far as trade liberalization is concerned. Until the UN sanctions (from 1992 to 1999) were suspended, and eventually lifted, and Libya accepted that it had to pay compensations deriving from the Lockerbie case (August 2003), the EU decided not to start normalizing relations. The UN sanctions damaged the Libyan economy more than the US embargo, which was replaced relatively easily with conditions more favorable for European companies, leading to important tension between the US and Europe. The UN sanctions, however, left the Libyan economy stripped of capital goods and the know-how needed to develop its hydrocarbon industry. In April 2004 the US lifted its embargo, so bilateral trade and financial relations have slowly started up again.

Libyan trade policy is not implemented using normal channels. The trade regime has traditionally been based on state trade, so tariffs do not provide an appropriate measure of protection. Since 1999, the laws regulating foreign trade, especially imports, have been reformed and there has been a certain amount of liberalization by making the limits companies faced for imports more flexible. However, control of imports is still severe, even when compared with the region's protectionist economies. Basic food imports are still handled by a state-owned company and, in general, the trade policy is very discretional, as it is not subject to any discipline, either multilateral, or regional.

With regard to the sub-regional scope, the paralysis of the Arab Maghreb Union (AMU) is a clear example of the Maghreb's trade fragmentation. The failure of sub-regional integration leads to important problems, both economic and political.[17] From an economic point of view, the absence of South–South horizontal integration makes it difficult for a sub-regional market to appear and to exploit comparative advantages and productive complementarities.[18] When the lack of sub-regional integration is overlapped by bilateral free trade areas with the EU, the result is a geo-commercial structure called a "hub-and-spoke" system, which means the EU can attract investment from companies that want to supply the MPC markets, since there is free access to the partner countries' markets from the EU. Meanwhile, the partner countries do not have the possibility of supplying the markets of other MPCs. From a political point of view, the absence of sub-regional economic flows decreases the opportunity cost of political conflicts.

Recently, other regional integration initiatives have been adopted, such as the Agadir Process, aimed at creating a free trade area between Egypt, Jordan, Morocco, and Tunisia. This initiative seems more promising from a technical point of view, considering that instead of establishing positive lists of goods to be liberalized, like the AMU, it is based on the community method of negative lists: it is not the products to be liberalized that are defined in the agreement, but the products that will not be. This focus is more liberalizing (everything liberalized except the products subject to schedules) than its alternative (nothing liberalized except the products agreed). The initiative adopts part of the *acquis communautaire* concerned with foreign trade as its own, which is a step towards "deep integration," going beyond mere tariff issues to enter the scope of harmonizing rules and standards. Having been signed (2005) and ratified (2006), it is expected to come into effect in 2007 after agreement on a roadmap for its implementation in the first half of the year. However, many observers are skeptical, due to political reasons already mentioned in relation to the AMU.

Privatization and Competition Policies

In Algeria, the results of privatization are disappointing. There is strong resistance, mainly from the energy sector, trade unions, and the elite in the public sector. The persistence of inefficient state-owned enterprises in a monopoly position is one of the most important challenges Algeria is facing in its reform process. The restructuring of the energy sector has stagnated after recent modifications to the hydrocarbon law, which have reinforced Sonatrach's control over projects in the hydrocarbon sector at the expense of foreign companies, which have been playing an increasingly important role in recent years.

In Morocco, regulation of prices and marketing conditions are quite widespread among subsidized products, monopolized markets, public services and certain other services, and goods considered to have social content. Despite the privatization, liberalization, and deregulation process of the 1990s, quite a few activities are still monopolized. The government has decided to make liberalizing and privatizing a large part of those activities one of its priorities. In recent years, the privatization and public concession process has gathered momentum, but there are now fewer and fewer state-owned enterprises that can be privatized and fewer concessions to grant. In addition, attempts have been made to improve the business environment, with more attention to competition policy and simplification of administrative processes, creating a one-stop regional procedure and regional centers to attract more foreign investment. Despite the efforts made, the regulatory framework of almost all the sectors is deficient and the legal insecurity of the investments, as well as corruption, lead to important transaction costs.[19]

In Tunisia, the privatization process has progressed slowly, with some important transactions in the banking and the energy sectors, but with a clear reticence to privatize and liberalize some key sectors, such as transport and public services. As a whole, the absence of regulatory agencies makes liberalization and privatization difficult. The measures implemented to improve the competitiveness of Tunisian industries vis-à-vis the AAs with the EU have received criticism due to their inefficiency and their concentration on the public sector and large companies. The difficulties that small and medium-sized enterprises (SMEs) have encountered resulted in the "*mise à niveau*" (upgrading) program being labeled as "counterproductive."[20] Bureaucratic obstacles and the adoption of "ad hoc" rules to benefit some local producers are still in force, which, together with the difficulty SMEs have in accessing sources of finance, diminish the country's competitiveness.

In Libya, state intervention in the economy is very prominent (the public sector concentrates around 70 percent of wage earners), the result of nationalization implemented by Qaddafi not long after he came to power in September 1969. The timid liberalization of the retail sector ended in 1996 with a purge of small traders, although the end of the sanctions has helped the private part of this sector come to the fore again. State monopolies are the norm in key industries and services, and they suffer from high costs, poor-quality services, and underdevelopment. The authorities have repeatedly expressed their desire to implement reforms to open up to competition and the private sector, but no significant progress has been noticed.[21] The political situation and bad quality of the institutions also make it difficult to implement the reforms without prior political and administrative reforms. There has been willingness to privatize a part of public banking. However, due to the circumstances of the Libyan economy, in particular its financial market, foreign investors have not shown very much interest. Despite the fact that the lifting of sanctions has led to a decrease in subsidies, especially for food, they still have more impact than in the rest of the Maghreb.

Fiscal and Administrative Reform

In Algeria the fiscal system is very complex, despite the reforms adopted since 1992 to introduce value-added tax (VAT), income tax, and corporate tax. This is due to the fact that revenue income is based on hydrocarbons and the system has a weak collection capability. Recently, some partial reforms have been implemented, like VAT simplification, the gradual elimination of some professional activity taxes, and a decrease in the rate of corporation tax. In 2000 an administrative reform program was started, but resistance encountered among the administrative elite and the directors and trade unions of state-owned enterprises presented serious obstacles for implementing it in a context of budgetary surplus.

In Morocco, fiscal reform has been conceived as a requirement of trade liberalization, given the dependence on tariff earnings. Measures have been sporadic and limited, concentrating on the granting of exemptions and reduced VAT rates for diverse sectors. The tax system has a decreased collection capacity of direct taxes, making it regressive and dependent on indirect taxation. Morocco has expressed its willingness to progress in reform of administration, which suffers from significant inefficiencies: it is oversized, inefficient, and opaque. State-owned enterprises are a source of inefficiency and losses for the treasury. Some of the recent measures include the containment of the total public payroll costs and a drop in hirings of new civil servants, as well as a moderate decrease in the importance of the public sector. The Moroccan government has implemented a reform based on decentralization and the improvement of human resources management, supported by the World Bank and the EU, to modernize the public sector and the administration. Customs have been the pilot sector, with reforms that have considerably improved performance.

Tunisia is, without any doubt, the most advanced Maghrebi country as far as tax reform is concerned. Based on a high dependence on tariff earnings, Tunisia has considerably increased its direct tax collection capacity. VAT has been introduced in the retail sector and measures have been implemented to discourage informal economic activity. In any event, the most important reform announced consists of the adoption of a budgetary process based on objectives and results, as in some Anglo-Saxon countries (US, United Kingdom). The new budgetary law involves a reform of administration and a change in focus of the state's role in the Tunisian economy. Some of the stated objectives are decentralization, more transparency, and public-sector accountability to society.

There are no substantial reforms in this area in Libya either. In connection with the budget, the law requires it to be balanced, but lack of transparency and a recourse to extra-budgetary items make it difficult to analyze the state of public accounts. In principle, oil proceeds are fixed by budgetary law: 30 percent for current expenditure and 70 percent for investments, of which the majority is for infrastructure, some of it wasteful, such as the "Great Man-Made River," an investment in unsustainable irrigation, since it does not have any renewable capacity. It is true that salaries in the public sector have not increased in keeping with oil earnings, but civil servants benefit from other privileges, such as housing or automobile subsidies.

Financial Reforms

The financial sector in Algeria has difficult problems to solve in the short term and requires a more pro-active focus by the government to solve the financial bottleneck that is affecting private activity. The market is being monopolized by public banking and its narrowness limits the development of instruments such as public debt or direct access of finance companies. The quality of the statistics is inferior and the payment systems are archaic. The state intervenes in the process of establishing interest rates, distorting credit allocation among alternative activities, often at the expense of more profitable activities. Thus, the financial sector is incapable of channeling savings towards the private sector and prefers to finance state-owned companies with deficits, with the subsequent problem of non-payments and non-performing loans, which have an impact on the financial system's solvency and performance.

Morocco has had a more positive experience in the reform of the financial sector. The modernization of the legal and regulatory framework has been considerable. The reforms include more independence and supervisory capacity for the Central Bank and improvements in the regulatory agency of the financial market. As far as the banking sector is concerned, specialized public banking is the most vulnerable segment, both in the quality of its portfolios and in its low compliance with banking regulations. Recently, economic authorities seem to have decided to tackle the problem and have introduced some improvements. The situation in the private sector is more solid. Despite improvement in the financial environment, access to credit by SMEs and the agricultural sector is still limited, which curbs the development of a dynamic business sector.

After the deterioration in the sector that led to the IMF's recommendation to decrease public banking, Tunisia introduced some reforms in 2003, both in the banking sector and in insurance, with more competition and reducing the role of the public sector. Despite this, the sector is still closed to international competition and, as occurs in Morocco, SMEs and the agricultural sector find it difficult to access credits under reasonable conditions. In Libya, the financial sector is still controlled by the public sector, as it has been since its nationalization in 1970. In 1993 a law was passed that allows private banks to be established, although their occurrence is still marginal and there is no relevant international presence of Western banks, except Maltese and, more recently, French financial institutions. The sector is characterized by a lack of transparency, the predominant public banking is very much in debt and there is no financial market as such. Although the authorities have expressed their willingness to privatize public banking, prospects of this happening on a significant scale are reduced.

Conclusion

The balance and prospects of microeconomic reforms and macroeconomic equilibriums present a mixed situation. Although conditions have greatly improved compared with the 1980s, the 1990s witnessed stagnation in the pace of reforms. Now, the same firmness in macroeconomic stability can be seen, with more dynamism in microeconomic reforms in Morocco and

Tunisia, where liberalization is progressing slowly and unequally among the sectors. In Algeria and Libya, promises to introduce microeconomic reforms have been systematically ignored. The boom in the price of hydrocarbons is, paradoxically, a serious obstacle for economic opening, since it strengthens the rentier sector and generates resources to maintain the state's clientelistic structure, diluting the need for reforms in the short run.

In the microeconomic field, regional liberalization (vis-à-vis the EU and, for Morocco, the US) and multilateral liberalization (WTO) require the acceleration of reforms and their extension to new spheres, so that Maghrebi companies can compete in their national and international markets. This pro-competitive pressure consolidates the reforms, but resistance is delaying the adjustment and implementation of policies that improve the investment environment and productivity. The window of opportunity for reforms is narrow, and will end with full industrial liberalization with the EU in 2012. If the reforms do not speed up, the implementation of safeguards will be seen as inevitable, damaging the credibility of the free trade area with the EU and, therefore, the urgency of the reforms. These are decisive years, above all in Tunisia and Morocco, for the Association Agreements to have the required effect of modernization of the Maghrebi economic structures and institutions. Algeria and Libya should also take advantage of favorable oil prices to start prioritizing reforms.

Macroeconomic policy has improved, but it is still quite fragile. In Algeria there are doubts about the capacity to manage hydrocarbon profits and to implement tax and monetary policies capable of controlling internal demand and current expenditure, but current crude oil prices generate high budgetary surpluses (8–9 percent of GDP). Libya, with a budgetary surplus close to 30 percent in 2005, is in a similar situation. In Morocco, tax consolidation has hardly progressed, current expenditure has increased, and public investment has stagnated, causing sustainability problems in the medium and long run. Public deficit without including privatizations was 6 percent of GDP in 2006, although forecasts point to a decrease in the deficit if the economic growth acceleration of recent years stays the same. Tunisia has more positive results, with a moderate tax deficit of 2–3 percent of GDP, although current expenditure may increase in the future to raise the regime's economic legitimacy. As with microeconomic reforms, tariff reduction in Morocco and Tunisia is a fiscal reform challenge that cannot be deferred any longer.

Foreign balances have also improved, despite the high non-energy commercial deficit. Only Tunisia has a persistent current account deficit, while Morocco is recording modest surpluses. Algeria and Libya are recording strong current surpluses due to the rise in crude oil prices, between 25 and 35 percent of GDP in 2005, respectively. This has allowed Algeria to pay a significant part of its external debt. Although debt interest has fallen substantially, it is still an important part of Maghrebi budgets, except for Libya and, to a lesser extent, Algeria, and jeopardizes the economic growth of

Tunisia and Morocco. Inflation is still controlled, although price increases on basic commodities have been recorded, above all on food, which have a negative impact on the purchasing power of the poorest segments of the population.

Poverty, unemployment, and the incapacity of public services to absorb demographic growth are the elements that generate most uncertainty for the Maghreb's economic (and political) future. Although poverty is not as intense as in other developing countries, living conditions in the countryside and in the outskirts of large cities are deficient. Fiscal difficulties, the public administration's inefficiency, and the volatility of economic growth have prevented ongoing improvement in the past in living standards, except in the case of Tunisia. Despite the fact that the demographic transition is going to slow down demographic growth, it will not start to remove pressure from the labor market and public services until after several years, so migratory movements and socio-political difficulties will not disappear, even though they will not worsen at the rate of past decades.

Lastly, the main uncertainty hovering over the Maghrebi economies at the moment is not economic in origin. Instead it is socio-political. There are doubts about the political willingness of some governments to carry out reforms speedily and to create a stable framework for investment when there is internal political instability. In the short run, governments may feel tempted to postpone microeconomic and institutional reforms and to miti-gate macroeconomic stabilization efforts to avoid exacerbating social dis-content and to maintain their legitimacy in the economic sphere, if not in the political one. Delaying these reforms may increase the cost of imple-menting them in the future, thus having a spiral effect, such as that which led to the economic crises in the 1980s.

In conclusion, microeconomic reforms and institutional consolidation have not occurred at the same rate as macroeconomic stabilization. This uneven result of economic policy can be explained by technical and political economy reasons. Technically, macroeconomic reforms are always simpler to implement. Their institutional requirements are, in general, smaller, since the number of decisions and players affected is relatively low, unlike micro-economic reforms, which involve a higher number of transactions and agents. From a political economy perspective, although macroeconomic stabilization also involves the appearance of winners and losers, structural reforms enable a more precise and visible income redistribution, so they raise more political difficulties. This difficulty is obvious in "pure" rentier economies, such as Algeria and Libya, but also in Tunisia and Morocco, where rent seeking is still a central element of the political scene.

In recent years there has been a modest and gradual change in Tunisia and Morocco in favor of accelerating reforms and the modernization of economic institutions. An example of that is the transition in economic policies towards more emphasis on microeconomic issues related to an increase in productivity and modernization of the productive apparatus and institutional environment. This shift from adjustment to modernization seems to be starting to bear fruit as far as economic growth is concerned, above all in Morocco. However, there is no reason to think this is irreversible. The window of opportunity to implement microeconomic and institutional reforms is narrow. It is urgent to accelerate them so as not to jeopardize their credibility, the sustainability of macroeconomic stabilization, the desired effects of the Association Agreements with the EU, and the incipient acceleration of economic growth in recent years.

Notes

1 See Kayser, B. (1996) *Méditerranée: une Géographie de la Fracture*, Aix-en-Provence: EDISUD.
2 Mañé, A. (2006) "European Energy Security: Towards the Creation of the Geo-energy Space," *Energy Policy*, no. 34, p. 3875. See also Jerch, M., G. Escribano, and A. Lorca (2002) "The Impact of Migration from the Mediterranean on European Security," in Vasconcelos, A. (ed.) *A European Strategic Concept for the Mediterranean*, Lumiar Papers no. 9, Lisbon, IEEI.
3 Krugman, P. (1992) "Regionalism versus Multilateralism: Analytical Notes," in De Melo, J. and A. Panagariya (eds), *New Dimensions in Regional Integration*, Cambridge University Press, pp. 58–84.
4 Lorca, A. and G. Escribano (1998) *Las Economías del Magreb. Opciones para el Siglo XXI*, Madrid: Pirámide.
5 By Europeanization (in economic terms) we mean the gradual adoption of the internal market *acquis communautaire*. See Escribano, G. (2006) "Europeanization without Europe? The Mediterranean and the Neighbourhood Policy," Working Paper of the Robert Schuman Centre for Advanced Studies, European University Institute, Florence, 2006/19. On this point, see also George Joffé's chapter in this volume on the European policy in the Southern Mediterranean (Chapter 15).
6 Unless otherwise stated, the data in this section come from the UNDP, *Human Development Report*, 2006.
7 Fargues, P. (2001) "La génération du changement dans les pays arabes," *Monde Arabe Maghreb-Machrek*, no. 171–2.
8 On the impact of the sanctions on the Libyan economy, see, Tim Niblock (2001) *Pariah States and Sanctions in the Middle East: Iraq, Libya, Sudan*, Boulder, CO: Lynne Rienner, in particular, pp. 60–92.
9 Richards, A. and J. Waterbury (1996) *A Political Economy of the Middle East*, 2nd edition, Boulder, CO: Westview Press, chapter 2.
10 Lorca and Escribano (1998) op. cit., chapter 3.
11 García Alvarez-Coque, J. M. (2002) "Agricultural Trade and the Barcelona Process: is Full Liberalization Possible?" *European Review of Agricultural Economics*, vol. 29, no. 3.
12 Lorca, A. *et al.* (2006) "Hacia un Pacto Agrícola Euro-mediterráneo," in *La agricultura y la Asociación Euro-mediterránea: retos y oportunidades*, IEMed, Barcelona, pp. 68–83.
13 The main references used in the sections that follow are from FEMISE (2005a, 2005b, 2006) and the *Economist Intelligence Unit*.
14 World Bank (2006) *Fostering Higher Growth and Employment in the Kingdom of Morocco*, Country Study, World Bank, Washington DC.

15 Johansson-Nogués, E. (2004) "A 'Ring of Friends'? The Implications of the European Neighbourhood Policy for the Mediterranean," *Mediterranean Politics*, vol. 9, no. 2.
16 Akesbi, N. (2006) "La experiencia Euro-marroquí. Enseñanzas y propuestas," in *La Agricultura y la Asociación Euromediterránea: retos y oportunidades*, IEMed, Barcelona, pp. 156–75.
17 Escribano, G. (2000) "Euro-Mediterranean versus Arab Integration: Are They Compatible?" *Journal of Development and Economic Policies*, vol. 3, no. 1, December. Also Escribano, G. and J. M. Jordán (1999) "Sub-regional Integration in the MENA Region and the Euro-Mediterranean Free Trade Area," *Mediterranean Politics*, vol. 4, no. 2.
18 Oualalou, F. (1996). *Après Barcelone ... Le Maghreb est nécessaire*. Casablanca/Paris, Toubkal/l'Harmattan, pp. 236 and ff.
19 Kingdom of Morocco (Ministry of Industry, Commerce, Energy, and Mines) and the World Bank (2002) *Morocco Manufacturing at the Turn of the Century: Results of the Firm Analysis and Competitiveness Survey*. Casablanca and Washington DC.
20 European Commission–Directorate General for Economic and Financial Affairs (2004) "Economic Review of EU Mediterranean Partners," Occasional Paper 6, February, Brussels.
21 Amirah-Fernández, H. (2004) "La vuelta de Libia a la escena internacional," *Anuario del Mediterráneo 2003*. IEMed-CIDOB, Barcelona.

8 Emigration, Immigration, and Transit in the Maghreb

Externalization of EU Policy?

Michael Collyer

In 1973, the Algerian government took the bold initiative of unilaterally banning emigration of its citizens to France. At the global level such a policy is rare; even 30 years later it continues to be mentioned in global overviews of migration.[1] Within the Maghreb, however, it is the sole example of absolute sanction in migration negotiations with European governments.[2] The French government brought an end to labor migration in 1974, which was a trend seen in migration policies across Western Europe at that time. Since the vast majority of international migration from the Maghreb is focused on Europe, European policy became the most significant control on Maghrebi migration. With the exception of Algeria's 1973 policy, migration from the Maghreb to Europe has been at the whim of apparently endless complications and revisions of European migration policies. Since 2000, those policies appear to have come full circle, and the relatively large-scale, legal migration of Maghrebi citizens to take up predominantly unskilled jobs in Europe is once again a reality.[3] At the same time, migration is being taken more seriously by Maghrebi governments, and there are new intergovernmental fora to discuss the migration issue. This chapter explores this new stage of Maghrebi migration governance to investigate whether it represents a genuinely new collaborative form of Mediterranean migration management, or simply a new stage in the development, or "externalization,"[4] of European migration policy.

The five countries of the Maghreb considered in this chapter have rather different experiences with migration. The first section examines the overall picture of Maghrebi migration. The second section examines policy responses provoked by migration, concentrating on the situation in the Maghreb and the bilateral and multilateral discussions in which Maghrebi governments are involved. The third section concludes with an analysis of the ongoing Mediterranean cooperation on migration issues. The development of migration policies in the Maghreb is a relatively new phenomenon and has therefore received relatively little attention in published work. In order to focus on the situation in the Maghreb, this chapter omits other important aspects of Maghrebi migration, such as the development of more general European migration policies[5] and the situation of Maghrebi immigrants in Europe,[6] or indeed in North America or the Gulf countries, where there are small but significant Maghrebi populations.

Changing Patterns of Migration Governance in the Maghreb

Since independence, North African states have been relatively uninvolved in migration governance. The few policies that existed focused on ensuring that migrants received adequate protection and on facilitating their remittances.[7] These limited policies generally addressed few other aspects of the migration process. This lack of involvement in forming a migration policy is due to two factors. First, North African governments have not been particularly interested in emigrants beyond their financial contribution, since until recently they were overwhelmingly unskilled, unemployed individuals from politically and economically marginalized areas. Secondly, North African governments have had little control of the significant policy regime, located in Europe, and European governments were unwilling to allow any external involvement in the formation of their own national immigration policies. Both of these factors are changing.

The profile of emigrants from North Africa has also gradually changed, in a similar way to international migration systems around the world.[8] Individual migrants now reflect all skill levels, employment categories, and regions of the Maghreb; more women are migrating autonomously, rather than as family members; and the migration process has become more complex, as means, motivations, duration, and direction of migrations have multiplied.[9] Scholars and policy makers have become aware of the attachments and commitments that migrants maintain with their place of origin, and are seeing migration less as a one-time, linear movement and more as an ongoing relationship with a place of origin.[10] Since the mid-1990s, North African countries have gradually become migration destinations themselves, which was previously the case only for Libya.[11] All of these changes have provoked significant reactions from policy makers. It is perhaps most surprising that migration has remained an important issue at all, since from the 1950s onwards it was always assumed to be a temporary phenomenon around the Mediterranean.

Along with changes in the profile of migrants, the policies of European states receiving immigrants have also been changing. European cooperation on migration issues began in the early 1970s and has been slowly gaining momentum. Throughout the 1980s and early 1990s, EU involvement in migration policy making predominantly consisted of advice and contained no real legal power.[12] This changed with the coming into force of the Treaty of Amsterdam on 1 May 1999, which, for the first time, empowered the European Commission to draft binding legislation regarding migration and asylum. The European Council meeting at Tampere in October 1999 outlined four themes to guide the process of policy making, including "partnership with countries of origin and transit."[13] By May 2004, sufficient measures had been approved by the European Council to constitute a "first stage" of "harmonized" legislation, although throughout this process the Tampere objective of partnership received the least attention of the four Tampere priorities. The Hague Programme, which replaced Tampere in November 2004 and is due to run to 2009, again calls for "a serious investment in relations with third countries" in the development of migration policies.[14]

In the Maghreb, the notion of partnership has been explored chiefly through EU regional policies, most famously, the Euro-Mediterranean Partnership, or Barcelona Process, which was launched in Barcelona in November 1995.[15] The prospects for peace in the Eastern Mediterranean then appeared to be improving, but during the second *intifada* (popular Palestinian uprising), the pace of Euro-Med discussions slowed. The "Barcelona + 10" conference in November 2005 may have breathed some new life into the discussions, but the 2003 European Neighbourhood Policy (ENP) had already attempted to find an alternative way forward. The revival of the Western Mediterranean Dialogue, or "5 + 5," in 2002 attempted another.[16] The "5 + 5" dialogue resulted from a desire to disassociate dialogue on the Western Mediterranean from the Middle East peace process. Migration has been an important consideration in Euro-Med and the first ENP Action Plans, published in 2004. Recent dialogue at the "5 + 5" level has focused almost exclusively on migration policies.

Despite their high public profiles, these multilateral initiatives have been more notable as fora for discussion, leaving the work to be carried out in the less public environments of bilateral negotiations and national policy making. At the national level, migration has acquired a growing importance in the Maghreb since the initiation of the "5 + 5" dialogue. Morocco, in December 2003, and then Tunisia, in February 2004, passed new legislation covering both immigration and emigration. The governments of Morocco, Tunisia, and Algeria now include ministers, or officials of ministerial status, responsible for migration issues. Migration has become a topic of media interest across the Maghreb, and Morocco, Tunisia, and Algeria have a variety of well-developed research centers specializing in migration. Migration has always been socially significant in the Maghreb, but since 2000 it has gained new importance at the political level as well.

Contemporary Migration Patterns in the Maghreb

The social make-up of the contemporary Maghreb is the product of migrations from the seventh century onwards. Many of the essential characteristics of the modern migration system originate from World War I or even earlier. Contemporary analysis of migration depends on data on numbers and characteristics of migrants, yet the empirical basis of such data is often shaky at best.

The Problem of Data in the Study of Migration in the Maghreb

The difficulty of obtaining reliable, comparable data on a large scale is a problem facing any empirical analysis of migration, but in the Maghreb this presents special difficulties. Wide discrepancies exist between different official sources, with variations as large as several million individuals due to the variety of counting methods employed across different European countries and within the Maghreb. For example, in most European countries migrants are counted as foreign-born individuals. In France, which remains one of the most significant destinations for Maghrebi migrants, only foreign nationals are counted as migrants and naturalized citizens are excluded from the statistics. The Moroccan government, by contrast, considers even the foreign-born children of Moroccan emigrants to have Moroccan nationality. According to the French government, there are barely 400,000 Moroccan migrants in France, but Moroccan sources cite almost a million.[17] This problem is compounded by the difficulty of accounting for undocumented migrants, who are absent from all official sources. Difficulties regarding data are even greater outside of Europe, where even official migrants between Maghrebi countries are not uniformly counted, and undocumented migrants have every incentive to avoid official contact. Basic data on the number of immigrants is unreliable and information on migrant profiles, such as gender, age, income, and qualifications, is impossible to acquire on a large scale. This sort of detailed data relies on periodic small-scale surveys.

Maghreb Migration to the European Union

Emigration from Morocco, Algeria, and Tunisia is substantial. According to the Organization for Economic Cooperation and Development (OECD), almost three million Moroccans, Algerians, and Tunisians reside in Europe, approximately two million have the nationality of a Maghrebi country, and one million have acquired European citizenship.[18] It is difficult to be precise regarding exact percentages, due to the difficulties previously mentioned, but certainly more than 90 percent, and probably close to 100 percent of the total Maghrebi emigrant population comes from these three countries. Mauritania is also a country of net emigration, but the emigrant population is too small to register in the OECD data. Estimates suggest that approximately 53,000 Mauritanians live outside of the country, though some commentators have suggested that the true figure is most likely higher.[19] According to the UN Population Division, net emigration from Mauritania consists of only 1,000 individuals per year.[20] Ever since the oil boom in the early 1970s, Libya has been a significant importer of migrants, though a small number of Libyans claim asylum in Europe.[21]

Morocco accounts for the largest number of migrants to the EU. Since the 1960s, Moroccans traveled to more European destinations than other

Maghrebi migrants, and this has been increasingly evident in recent years. Spain and Italy have emerged as significant destinations since the early 1990s. The most recent amnesties for undocumented migrants, in Spain (2005) and Italy (2002/03), provided nearly 1.5 million migrants with temporary status, and Moroccans were the largest group in both amnesties.[22] Moroccans are now amongst the top five most significant immigrant groups in Belgium, France, Italy, the Netherlands, and Spain. Every summer, "Operation Transit" prepares for the return of migrants from Europe to Morocco. In 2005, preparations were made for two million return visits.[23] The summer return of migrants is a ritual across the Maghreb, and in many rural communities the traditional agricultural seasonality of spring and fall has been replaced by the overwhelming significance of summer in village life.[24] The presence of Tunisians in Europe is significantly smaller than that of the Moroccans. Apart from the long-established community in France, Tunisians only represent a noteworthy number in Italy, although they were far less numerous than Moroccans in the 2002/03 amnesty.

The conflict of the 1990s has been a major factor in provoking emigration from Algeria, particularly since 1995. In 1990, 97 percent of Algerian emigrants lived in France. Since then, more than 100,000 Algerians have claimed asylum in Europe, fewer than 20 percent of them in France.[25] Although fewer than 10 percent of applicants received refugee or temporary protected status, not all those rejected have returned and an unknown but certainly significant number remain undocumented. France is still the dominant destination for Algerians, but most European countries now have a noticeable Algerian community.[26] There are many fewer asylum seekers from Libya, Mauritania, Morocco, and Tunisia.

Intra-Maghrebi Migration

Movement between Maghrebi countries is notoriously difficult and, within the Maghreb, the status of migrants is particularly precarious. The continuing difficulties of the Arab Maghreb Union (AMU) in arranging a meeting[27] suggest that facilitated movement and regional visa-free travel achieved in other African regional groups, such as ECOWAS,[28] remain unlikely prospects. Of the six land borders between AMU countries, one is officially closed (Algeria–Morocco), one is militarized (Morocco–Mauritania), and two are extremely remote (Algeria–Mauritania and Algeria–Libya), leaving only two borders across which some exchange is possible (Tunisia–Algeria and Tunisia–Libya). Even now, these are carefully controlled, as Tunisia has become an important destination for undocumented migration from outside the region and requires visas for most nationals of other Maghrebi countries. Historically, the situation of intra-Maghreb migrants has been precarious, as visible in the case of Libya's expulsion of Tunisian migrants in 1983. Although visa-free travel is now a possibility for Moroccans and Algerians for reciprocal visits, this was only reintroduced in

2004 and may change if any obstacle arises to disrupt the improving relations between the two countries. Labor migration is highly controlled and
any migrant intending to work in another Maghreb country requires a work
visa.

Most of the limited movement in the region is directed towards Libya.
Moroccans are the largest group of immigrants, with an estimated 200,000
working in Libya, followed by 60,000 Tunisians, and between 20,000 and
30,000 Algerians.[29] Tunisia, with its increasingly buoyant economy, is also a
significant destination for long-term Maghrebi migrants. Until the 1992
embargo on Libya, Tunisia was a popular business destination for Libyans.
It remains to be seen if this migration will increase again with the re-entry
of Libya into the global economy. Throughout the 1990s, given the extreme
difficulty for Algerians to reach Europe, Tunisia offered an opportunity of
brief respite for many. Indeed, with the closure of most European embassies
in Algiers from 1994 onwards, anyone wanting a European visa was obliged
to travel to Tunis. Net annual migration of Algerians into Tunisia rose to
more than 30,000 in 1994, before falling rapidly in 1997 following the
imposition of stricter visa controls for Algerian migrants.

Saharan Transit Migration

The migration of non-Maghrebi nationals, principally from sub-Saharan
Africa, through the Maghrebi states, with the aim of reaching Europe, has
gradually increased since the early 1990s and become a significant policy
issue since 2000. This is the area of greatest statistical uncertainty concerning migration in the region. The only data that are available come from
statistics on apprehensions, which are not public, and a small number of
published investigations, most of which come from Morocco,[30] though
some research has been conducted elsewhere.[31] The dangers of the crossing
of the Straits of Gibraltar or the journey to southern Italy and, more
recently, the Canary Islands, are now widely appreciated, though statistics
on fatalities remain uncertain. The desert crossing appears to be at least as
hazardous and even less information is available on the fate of migrants
there. Estimates of the number of migrants who have died on the entire
journey vary considerably, from official sources of a few hundred a year to
NGO reports citing figures of 5,000 and higher for the period 1995–2005.[32]

Largely due to the risks posed by these natural obstacles it is unusual for
migrants to make the journey unassisted and many pay for help from a
variety of smuggling operations, which may well bring additional dangers.
Much of the smuggling on this route does not match the media image of
large-scale international criminal organizations, though those certainly
exist.[33] Migrants interviewed in the few studies that have been published
typically report using much more ad hoc assistance, often paying other,
more experienced migrants to guide them on difficult stretches or across
single borders. Accounts of smugglers abandoning migrants in the desert

are relatively common. Security forces also pose a significant threat and, although this is usually even more difficult to research, several high-profile incidents have highlighted the role of security forces in migrant fatalities. These include accusations of violent deportations by Libya from 2004 onwards[34] and the alleged sinking of a crowded boat in an accident with an Italian naval vessel,[35] but by far the most reliable information available concerns incidents in Morocco.

A report published by Médecins Sans Frontières in July 2005 provides details of 9,350 medical consultations they had carried out over the previous two years in north Morocco.[36] Approximately 25 percent of these consultations concerned injuries sustained due to violence and 67 percent of all those were a result of the actions of security forces. In the first week of October 2005, 14 migrants were killed at the fences of Ceuta and Melilla, at least 11 of them shot by border-control officials. Many more were seriously wounded. These incidents attracted international condemnation and dramatically raised awareness of the plight of transit migrants. In a misguided response to this concern, Moroccan security forces caught an estimated 2,000 migrants and abandoned them in the remote southeastern border with Algeria, a desert region where their survival was uncertain.[37] The presence of a number of national and international human rights groups and a Spanish TV crew ensured that news of these events spread rapidly and the Moroccan security forces were obliged to return the following day with more than 60 coaches. Migrants were removed to temporary camps and those who could be repatriated were returned to their countries of origin. In July 2006 three more migrants were killed and in October 2006 Amnesty International reported that there had been no progress on the judicial inquiry into the 14 fatalities of the previous year.[38]

Although there is a considerable discrepancy in the studies of the nationalities of transit migrants, all agree that they are predominantly between 20 and 40 years old, and the majority are male. It is also clear that migrants typically remain in the Maghreb for increasingly longer periods of time, with periods as long as seven years reported.[39] Outside of Libya, paid employment is usually difficult to find, and living conditions are extremely poor. Libya is a significant exception in transit migration. There are an estimated 1.5 million non-Maghrebi migrants in Libya, mainly from sub-Saharan Africa.[40] The Libyan government has recently claimed that more than a million of these migrants are in transit in Libya,[41] but this number is most likely to be a politically motivated exaggeration, as Libya was an important destination for African migrants long before transit migration became an issue.

With the exception of the population of 175,000 POLISARIO refugees hosted by Algeria, and a handful of individuals granted protection on an ad hoc basis elsewhere, no Maghreb government has a working asylum system. Although the UNHCR has a presence in all Maghrebi countries and all except Libya have signed the 1951 Convention Relating to the Status of

Refugees, the UNHCR is only active in Morocco and even there it does not yet have a formal agreement with the government. Maghrebi governments are typically resistant to recognizing refugees. Although policies such as the Moroccan law 02/03 formally recognize the rights of refugees, in practice there is no distinction between asylum seekers and illegal migrants. The study conducted in northern Morocco by the French NGO Cimade[42] found that more than 50 percent of migrants interviewed cited protection as the reason for their migration. An estimated 80 percent of transit migrants in Morocco register an asylum claim and a likely minimum indication of those who require it is suggested by the results of the applications of those who reach Ceuta, where approximately 20 percent are recognized as refugees or granted temporary protection.[43] The development of asylum systems in the Maghreb is one of the most controversial aims of the ENP, and the outcome of ongoing negotiations will be a key indicator of the "partnership" aims of this policy.

Policy Responses and Institutions Concerning Maghrebi Migration

For most of the century, the development of the modern Maghreb migration system has been based on European policy responses, and the institutions have been located in Europe. This did not change significantly after North African independence. Since the late 1980s, a number of institutions have been founded in Morocco, and their continued development throughout the 1990s has yielded considerable experience and benefits in terms of financial transfers from migrants. In 2003, more than 40 percent of all migrants' remittances to the whole of Africa, as recorded by the IMF, went to Morocco.[44] However, it was not until 2003 that Morocco updated its precolonial migration legislation, and Tunisia followed in 2004.

EU Member States continue to play a dominant role in the regulation of Maghrebi migration. Many observers interpret the discourse on partnership, which has become commonplace since the 1999 Tampere European Council, as a smokescreen for the continual process of "externalizing" EU asylum and migration policy. Controversial plans for processing asylum seekers' claims to refugee status in centers outside of Europe have passed through many guises since 1999 and appeared in the Commission's June 2004 paper *Improving Access to Durable Solutions*.[45] The formal creation of such centers does not appear to be in the interests of either the Maghrebi states that would host them, or the migrants concerned; Libya is the only Maghreb state where such centers exist and even here their presence remains unofficial. Financial support for border reinforcement, such as the 45m euros granted to Morocco under the MEDA program[46] is forthcoming, although the details of this finance are not public and it is impossible to determine on what projects the money has been spent.

Despite the range of control measures sponsored by the EU, the EU discourse on partnership contains more than new repressive measures. The renewed popularity of debates on migration and development provides a subject on which the EU and countries of origin and destination can agree, at least superficially. Following a loss of interest in migration and development in the 1980s, the late 1990s onwards witnessed a widespread re-evaluation of the potential for emigrants to contribute to the social and economic development of their countries of origin, supported by empirical examples, such as the Moroccan experience.[47] There is thus a range of positive reasons for governments to take an interest in migration, beyond the more regressive concerns of reduction and control, although repression remains a dominant concern of the EU. The conclusions to the Euro-African conference on migration and development held in Rabat in July 2006 illustrate the ambiguity of these debates and the tendency to mix financial incentives with control and surveillance.[48] It is not yet clear how the Rabat "Action Plan" will translate into practice, or how it will fit alongside the already crowded international environment in which multilateral, bilateral, and national initiatives on migration are dreamed up with surprising regularity.

Multilateral Initiatives

Given the continued inactivity of the AMU, there are only two influential multilateral fora in which issues of migration and asylum are discussed in the Maghreb. Both are European initiatives: the Euro-Mediterranean Partnership and the "5 + 5" Western Mediterranean Dialogue.[49] From the Maghreb, the EU Mediterranean policy only includes Morocco, Algeria, and Tunisia. Relations with Mauritania fall under the broader framework of cooperation with African, Caribbean, and Pacific (ACP) states, and Libya has not yet been integrated into the Euro-Med process, despite the EU decision to engage with Libya taken at the October 2004 European Council.

The Mediterranean policy originates in Cooperation Agreements signed between Morocco, Algeria, and Tunisia and the European Union (or EEC, as it was previously) in the 1970s, which touched briefly on migration, guaranteeing fair treatment for workers residing in Europe. A gradual progression in European thinking about migration and the Maghreb is discernable in the recent evolution of Mediterranean policy. The Barcelona Declaration considers migration under the third pillar of social, cultural, and human affairs, and after a brief acknowledgement of the importance of migration it focuses on illegal migration as the topic of most concern.[50] Regular ministerial meetings have maintained this focus. Migration is far more significant in the Association Agreements, the bilateral tool for implementing the Barcelona Declaration, than in the earlier Cooperation Agreements, which they replace.[51] The agreements were signed by Tunisia in 1995, by Morocco in 1996, and by Algeria in 2002. The Tunisian and Moroccan agreements are identical in all the 96 articles. The Algerian agreement includes many similar articles, but is substantially different and contains 14 additional ones.

All three agreements identify illegal migration as the main problem in the area of migration, but the solutions offered are different. In earlier Moroccan and Tunisian agreements, the Maghreb is seen as a principal source area of migration, and one priority identified is "reducing migratory pressure, in particular by improving living conditions, creating jobs and developing training in areas from which emigrants come."[52] This interpretation of co-development, the notion that more development means less migration, has been substantially criticized.[53] The Algerian agreement, signed six years later, omits this article and focuses on readmission as the solution to the problem of illegal migration. The facilitation of readmission for Algerian nationals is explicit, and the agreement adds "If either Party considers it necessary, such [readmission] agreements shall cover the readmission of nationals of other countries arriving in their territory, direct from the territory of the other."[54] The Moroccan and Tunisian agreements do not mention readmission. They refer to "resettling those repatriated because of their illegal status,"[55] but this suggests that nationals of other countries are of no concern.

The shift of focus from nationals to transit migrants occurred later in Morocco. In 1999, the EU's High Level Working Group on Migration and Asylum produced a series of six Action Plans under the Tampere objective of "partnership with countries of origin and transit." The Morocco Action Plan was the only one that concerned the Maghreb.[56] Unlike the Association Agreements, the Action Plan focuses exclusively on migration, with an extensive introduction providing data, dealing especially with transit migration. The final section, reflecting a rather non-partnership-oriented attitude, is entitled "Action Required by the Community/Union," and contains two sections on Morocco as a country both of transit and of origin for illegal migrants. The transit section lists 11 measures that finalize a readmission agreement for third-country nationals who have transited Morocco, and that require Morocco to introduce visas for all West African countries. The section regarding origin presents only two areas for development cooperation. It is clear where the balance has shifted in the three years since the signing of the Association Agreement. Not surprisingly, this Action Plan was rejected by the Moroccan government, and the EU has yet to negotiate a readmission agreement of the required format.

The most recent stage in the development of migration in the EU's Mediterranean policy can be seen in the proposed Action Plans of the European Neighbourhood Policy, published for Morocco and Tunisia in December 2004.[57] "Asylum" appears for the first time in these documents referencing the need to implement the 1951 Geneva Convention.[58] Readmission and concern regarding visas remain issues, but any possibility of co-development becoming part of migration legislation has disappeared. The succession of documents, from the Association Agreements in the mid-1990s to the 2004 ENP Action Plans, reveals a developing vision of the

Maghreb as the most important region of origin for illegal migration, then as a transit region for illegal migrants and finally as transit region for potential refugees.

The Western Mediterranean Dialogue, or "5 + 5," offers a potentially more balanced approach to multilateral discussions on migration. Rather than the standard EU format of individual Maghrebi countries negotiating agreement details with all of the EU Member States, which produces tremendously imbalanced negotiations, the "5 + 5" format offers the possibility for group discussions. The meetings bring together European countries (France, Italy, Malta, Portugal, and Spain) with the five countries of the AMU (Algeria, Libya, Mauritania, Morocco, and Tunisia). After the initial conference in 1990, meetings faded with the embargo against Libya in 1992 and the difficulties within the AMU from 1994 onwards. A meeting in Tripoli in May 2002 gave rise to an initiative to organize a series of annual conferences on migration in the Western Mediterranean. The first meeting was held in Tunis in September 2002.

The meetings were organized with the support of the International Organization for Migration (IOM), which considers the Tunis meeting to be the "Founding Conference."[59] The "Tunis Declaration on the '5 + 5' Migration Dialogue"[60] established the willingness of countries to work together on issues such as information exchange, common training programs, priority actions to combat trafficking, migration, development, and gender equality. In 2003, a "Consolidating Conference," held in Rabat, identified three areas for further action: the joint management of the movement of people, the rights and obligations of migrants and migration, and joint approaches to development. The most recent meeting, held in Algiers in September 2004, established regional interest and support for the series of conferences. It was proposed that the dialogue should extend to encompass sub-Saharan sending states. Although the "5 + 5" dialogue remains at a relatively unthreatening level of information exchange and joint initiatives, rather than the hard policy proposals of the EU's Mediterranean Policy, it offers a welcome alternative framework for the discussion of migration issues in the Western Mediterranean. In the absence of an active AMU agenda, these meetings also have the advantage of providing a forum in which all Maghrebi governments can come together at the ministerial level to discuss migration.

At the time of writing there has not been a follow-up to the Algiers meeting in the context of the "5 + 5." The initiative for this dialogue has been somewhat superseded by the 2006 Rabat conference on migration and development, which, despite the title, concerned migration much more broadly. Although the resulting "action plan" makes widespread reference to development initiatives it appears to be focused on more control-orientated objectives. Article 13 of the Cotonou Agreement, signed between the EU and the African, Caribbean, and Pacific (ACP) states in June 2000, is cited as an "essential reference" for these policies. This article remains controversial as it essentially made development assistance to the 69 poorest countries in the world conditional on their cooperation in EU migration control policies. The conclusions to the 2002 Seville European Council, which make this policy more explicit, are also referenced. Significantly, Algeria was not represented at the Rabat conference, though a follow up conference was held very soon afterwards in Libya in November 2006 where all African and European countries were represented at ministerial level. This may mark the establishment of another multilateral discussion process concerning migration.

Bilateral Initiatives and National Migration Policies

Since the European Commission frequently represents the EU in negotiations with third-party countries, it typically refers to these negotiations as "bilateral," even if they effectively involve 26 states. More genuine bilateral relations between only two states are vital for policy making on Mediterranean migration issues. It is more difficult to gain precise information on the conduct and content of such discussions, since national governments typically do not post discussion documents on the Internet, as the European Commission does. Space does not permit a full inventory of available information on bilateral discussions on migration. They are most important for countries with significant migration exchanges, but some bilateral negotiations have a greater importance than others. Two recent examples are agreements between Italy and Libya on transit-processing centers and the successful conclusion of negotiations for the 2001 labor migration agreement between Spain and Morocco. These two pairs of countries account for the two most significant routes for undocumented migrants across the Mediterranean, and exemplify the opposing tendencies with which the development of migration policy in the region is now confronted.

In August 2004, Libya announced that 1.5 million undocumented migrants were waiting in Libya for the opportunity to reach Europe.[61] This figure seems to be exaggerated. Since the early 1970s, Libya has played host to a large number of sub-Saharan African migrants, and concurrently, the official government news source, *Al-Amn-Alam* (The Magazine of the Popular Committee of Libya's General Security), provided contradictory information that in 2003 only 4,308 migrants had been apprehended crossing from Niger, the Sudan, and Mali.[62] This exemplifies how migration can be used as a tool in political negotiations. In 2004, the Italian government came to an agreement with Libya by which Libya agreed to take back a large number of illegal migrants residing in Italy, to hold them in detention centers and to return them to their countries of origin. Libya is the only Maghrebi country that has not signed either the 1951 Geneva Convention on the Status of Refugees or its 1967 Protocol. In October 2004, 2,600 illegal migrants arrived in Lampedusa and the Italian government returned them to Libya, though claiming that migrants from Eritrea, Ethiopia, and

Somalia were allowed to stay.[63] Italy has been severely criticized for this agreement, due to the danger in which it puts refugees.[64] However, the strict surveillance policies appear to be making an impact: *Migration News* cites a figure of 9,985 migrants arriving illegally in Italy from July 2003 to June 2004, compared to 19,294 migrants in the previous year.

The Straits of Gibraltar is the other major route for illegal migrants to enter Europe. In 2003, more than 18,000 migrants were arrested along the Spanish coast (a similar number were stopped in Italy).[65] The Spanish government has attempted to negotiate with Morocco, as Italy has with Libya, to return third-country nationals, but Morocco continues to reject such suggestions. Agreement was reached on this issue in 1992 but this agreement has never been systematically implemented. In October 2005, during the confusion surrounding the mass expulsions from Morocco, 73 individuals were removed from Melilla and returned to Morocco via Tangier. This group included several asylum seekers, and in the face of international criticism Spain allowed a number of them to return, though the fate of the others is still unknown.[66] Given the failure of this initiative, and the public denial of the Moroccan government that the 1992 agreement was used at all, it seems unlikely that further removals will be carried out in this form.

Attempts to negotiate a temporary labor migration agreement with Morocco have been more successful. A new agreement was signed in 2001,[67] but it was then dissolved due to the rapid deterioration in relations between Spain and Morocco later that year. Following the victory of the Spanish Socialist Party (PSOE) in the 2004 elections, negotiations recommenced, and the agreement was implemented in May 2005.[68] The agreement allows Spain tremendous degrees of flexibility in employing Moroccan labor on short-term bases and includes no guaranteed number of employees, nor a specific duration for employment.[69] Flexibility is the key to temporary labor recruitment, given that it shifts the costs of unpredictability in labor demand to the worker. Undocumented migrants are used to meet these demands, and European countries are now in an ambiguous position regarding their requirement for flexible labor and their vigorous efforts to reduce illegal migration.

More recently, the reinforcement of migration control has moved south. At the national level, both Morocco and Tunisia have introduced new migration legislation. Morocco's law 02/03 (December 2003) is the first migration legislation since its independence. Morocco has been criticized for implementing parts of the 1999 Action Plan of the High Level Working Group, which it had officially rejected, without introducing protection guarantees for migrants.[70] However, there is much support for the fact that Morocco formed the new legislation. Tunisia also updated its 1975 migration legislation.[71] The new 2004 act increases the number of border-control officials to over 13,000 and provides military support where necessary. Joint patrols have been organized with Italy, partly explaining the increased popularity of Libya as a departure point for Italy. The literature on policy transfer regarding migration has typically focused on the degree of choice that states have in adopting new national legislation.[72] Considering the bilateral and multilateral migration negotiations throughout the Mediterranean in the years preceding the adoption of this legislation, and the range of other interests involved, such as trade, financial support, and fishing rights, the degree of freedom was certainly limited for Morocco and Tunisia.

Morocco, Tunisia, and Algeria have government ministers responsible for coordinating with their emigrant communities. The three countries operated through *Amicales* during the 1960s, but these were affiliated with their respective ministries of the interior at a time when the ministries were more interested in surveillance and control, rather than the support or encouragement of investment. The more recent establishment of national institutions responsible for coordination with emigrant communities represents a new generation of institutional investment.

In Tunisia, the Office of Tunisians Abroad was set up in 1988 to provide information and research data on Tunisians living overseas. The Hassan II Foundation for Moroccans Resident Abroad was established in Rabat in 1990. It provides a variety of support and information services for Moroccans abroad and supports research on Moroccan communities around the world.[73] In 1996, a similar organization was established for Algerians, the State Secretariat in charge of the National Community Abroad. This new institutional and legislative basis indicates an evolving vision of migration management, in terms of contact with emigrants and regulation of migration.

Migration policy in the Maghreb appears to be a continual response as much to European demands as to local needs, particularly with regard to the format of recent legislation. However, many of the initiatives sponsored by the institutions are viewed positively by emigrants, who are slowly beginning to build trust in governments that have been, and continue to be, viewed with considerable suspicion across much of the emigrant community.[74]

Conclusion: Towards Mediterranean Migration Management?

The system of international migration both to and from the Maghreb has been bound to Europe for more than a hundred years. Since the end of the twentieth century, this relationship has become increasingly significant for both sides. The continued growth in remittances, particularly to Morocco, has re-emphasized the importance of migration as a major source of investment that is vital in creating new employment in the Maghreb. Migration to North America and to other Arab countries is increasing slowly, but the bulk of financial and non-financial transfers still come from migrants based in Europe. Europe's dependence on the Maghreb is becoming clearer, both as a means of externalizing the costly obligations of responding to illegal migration and as a convenient solution to the growing requirements for labor caused by the continued decline in the birth rate across Europe.

The Australian response to the arrival of asylum seekers gained international notoriety in 2001, when the boat *The Tampa* carrying large numbers of people seeking refuge was turned away.[75] The migrants were isolated from Australian society, detained on a remote Pacific island where their claims for asylum were examined. This policy has become known as the "Pacific solution" and has been widely criticized by NGOs around the world, though the "solution" has become influential in policy-making circles. Recent developments in the externalization of EU asylum policy have demonstrated the beginnings of a "Mediterranean solution" to European asylum claims, where migrants are detained in the Maghreb while their claims are examined, and, if found to be refugees, are accepted into an EU Member State.

The various suggestions of establishing similar processing centers in the Maghreb have been strongly rejected by North African politicians and political commentators. Morocco's law 02/03 (December 2003) and the new Tunisian law (February 2004) introduced strict new controls that have at least partially succeeded in addressing the issue of transit migration. This was a prior concern of EU policy makers, as reflected in the later Association Agreements and Morocco's 1999 Action Plan. The publication of the proposed ENP Action Plans (December 2004) revealed that the emphasis on the intended EU "partnership" in these matters has shifted again to developing asylum policies in the Maghreb. Essentially, these centers already exist as informal camps at various points along the route through Algeria or Libya to Tunisia and Morocco.[76] Although, in policy terms, the acceptance of these informal centers is substantially different to a formal agreement, from the point of view of the migrants it may be difficult to distinguish. The Libya–Italy agreement (2004) formalizes the existence of such centers in Libya. However, they cannot be used for examining asylum claims until Libya has signed the relevant conventions.

The relative success of these new measures has come at a very significant human cost to the migrants concerned. Restricting illegal migration has affected migrants who require protection as well as those who do not. The establishment of a functioning asylum system in the Maghreb is likely to improve the situation by providing some protection for those recognized as refugees, though if this is successfully implemented it will likely have a negative impact on the readiness of EU states to accept refugees who have transited the Maghreb. There is considerable discrepancy in the number of transit migrants in the Maghreb with feasible asylum claims. Migrants who may not qualify for refugee status, but whose vulnerability has increased due to their situation, are likely to form a much larger group. Extended periods of time living in extremely poor conditions, without resources, and with no possibility of receiving state services for support or protection, makes these migrants easy victims to everything from health problems to attacks by fellow migrants or by members of security forces.

Despite the efforts of European and Maghrebi states to keep migrants out, migrants are economically important in Europe in filling a wide range of labor shortages. The Maghreb falls into what Ronald Skeldon has described as the labor frontier.[77] The traditional demand for men to work in the car factories and mines of Northern Europe has grown into a demand for both genders to work in a wider range of sectors, including agriculture, construction, and tourism in Southern Europe. Falling birth rates across Europe mean that in some countries the population would actually decline if it were not for migration. Birth rates in the Maghreb have fallen too. The 2004 census in Morocco revealed that the total population of Morocco has stabilized just below 30 million.[78] This was well below expectations, as population growth rates had fallen below replacement levels in many census districts. In Tunisia, each woman of child-bearing age has an average of 1.55 children, a rate as low as anywhere in Europe. However, due to the high birth rate in the late 1980s and early 1990s, the generation arriving on the job market will continue to grow until 2010.[79] Emigration will be the only solution in providing jobs for many individuals. Since the need for immigration and labor in Europe is also growing, there appears to be a balance of interests. In the short term, excess European labor demand could be met from the Maghreb, as it has been for most of the last century, but beyond 2010 migration to Europe will have to be met from other areas of the world from which Europe receives migrants.

The interdependency of the Euro-Mediterranean migration system is recognized as "partnership," which is a term employed regularly in trans-Mediterranean dialogue. Beyond the rhetoric, however, there is little indication that this is a true partnership amongst equals. When the EU can "require" the Maghrebi states to implement certain criteria, as in the case of the Action Plans, "partnership" appears to have little meaning in terms of practical approaches to policy making in the field of migration. The continued economic imbalance between the northern and southern Mediterranean shores remains one of the most important factors driving the migration system, and producing a parallel political imbalance. Though there are indications that more equal dialogues are taking place at less significant levels, in fora such as the "5 + 5" group, which has set the goal of "migration leadership" in the Mediterranean, an equitable system of collective migration management appears at least distant. This will form an important element of the developing EU migration and asylum policy, as indicated by the 2004 Hague Programme, but also enable the Maghreb to benefit more fully from the skills and capabilities of its population overseas.

Notes

1 S. Castles and M. Miller, *The Age of Migration: International Population Movements in the Modern World*, Basingstoke: Palgrave, 2003.

2 It is doubtful that the emigration ban had more than simply a symbolic effect, though the symbolic effect of moving beyond the former colonial power could not have been far from the mind of Boumedienne, as he took over the leadership of the non-aligned nations.

3 M. Collyer, "The Development Impact of Temporary International Labour Migration on Southern Mediterranean Sending Countries: Contrasting Examples of Morocco and Egypt," Development Research Centre on Migration, Globalisation and Poverty, 2004, Working Paper T6, University of Sussex. Available at: http://www.migrationdrc.org/publications/working_papers/WP-T6.pdf

4 S. Lavenex and E. Uçarer, "The Emergent EU Migration Regime and its External Impact," in S. Lavenex and E. Uçarer (eds), *Migration and the Externalities of European Integration*, Oxford: Lexington, 2002, pp. 1–13.

5 A. Geddes, *The Politics of Migration and Immigration in Europe*, London: Sage, 2003.

6 A. Al-Shahi and R. Lawless (eds), *Middle East and North African Immigrants in Europe*, London: Routledge, 2005.

7 P. Fargues, "Les politiques migratoires en Méditerranée Occidentale: contexte, contenu, perspectives," Tunis, Dialogue on Migration in the Western Mediterranean, 2002.

8 Castles and Miller, op. cit.

9 R. Van der Erf and E. Heering, *Moroccan Migration Dynamics: Prospects for the Future*, Geneva: IOM, 2002.

10 N. Al-Ali and K. Koser (eds), *New Approaches to Migration, Transnational Communities and the Transformation of Home*, London: Routledge, 2002.

11 M. Lahlou, L. Barros, C. Escoffier, P. Pumares, and P. Ruspini, "L'immigration irreguliere subsaharienne a travers et vers le Maroc," *Cahiers de Migrations Internationales*, 54F Geneva, ILO, 2002.

12 The rare exceptions, such as the Dublin Convention, implemented in 1997, took the form of International Conventions, rather than EU legal instruments.

13 The other three themes were: "the management of migration flows," "fair treatment of third country nationals," and "a common European asylum system."

14 European Commission "Communication from the Commission to the Council and European Parliament: The Hague Programme: Ten priorities for the next five years" COM(2005) 184 final, Brussels, 2005.

15 The Barcelona Declaration was initially signed by 27 countries: the EU-15 plus Algeria, Cyprus, Egypt, Israel, Jordan, Lebanon, Malta, Morocco, the Palestinian Authority, Syria, Tunisia, and Turkey. On 1 May 2004, Cyprus and Malta joined the EU along with eight Eastern European countries, making the total number of signatories 35. Libya has had observer status since 1999. Mauritania is not a member.

16 The Western Mediterranean Dialogue was founded in 1990 at the initiative of the French government, but following the Barcelona Declaration it only met at a ministerial level in 2001 in Lisbon. It is referred to as the "5 + 5": five European states (France, Italy, Malta, Portugal, and Spain) and the five states of the AMU. It is thus a more appropriate unit for the purposes of this chapter since it contains both Libya and Mauritania as full members.

17 M. H. Bekouchi, *La Diaspora Marocaine: une chance ou un handicap*, Rabat: La Croisée des Chemins, 2003.

18 SOPEMI, 2005.

19 Fargues, op. cit.

20 UN, 2002.

21 288 Libyans claimed asylum in the EU from 1999 to 2004 (UNHCR 2005).

22 A. Levinson, "The regularisation of unauthorised migrants: literature survey and country case studies, regularisation programmes in Spain and Italy," 2005

COMPAS Working Paper, University of Oxford. Available at: http://www.compas. ox.ac.uk/publications/papers/Country%20Case%20Spain.pdf

23 "Démarrage demain de l'Opération Transit 2005: Deux millions de Marocains traverseront le Détroit," *Le Matin,* 15 June 2005.

24 H. De Haas, *Migration and Development in Southern Morocco: The Disparate Socio-Economic Impacts of Out-Migration on the Toggha Oasis Valley,* published PhD thesis, University of Niimegen, Amsterdam, 2003.

25 The term "asylum seeker" has entered media language, but is not a strict legal term. It refers to someone who has requested refugee status. An individual is an asylum seeker only while their asylum claim is determined. State signatories of the 1951 Geneva Convention Relating to the Status of Refugees are obliged to consider any asylum claim that is registered, before any attempt to return an individual to their country of origin.

26 M. Collyer, "When Do Social Networks Fail to Explain Migration? Accounting for the Movement of Algerian Asylum Seekers to the UK," *Journal of Ethnic and Migration Studies,* 2005, vol. 30, no. 4.

27 C. Ouazani and R. Kéfi, "Union du Maghreb Arabe: Second souffle?" *Jeune Afrique/l'Intelligent,* 2005, no. 2315, p. 11.

28 Economic Community of West African States.

29 H. Boubakri, "Transit Migration between Tunisia, Libya and Sub-Saharan Africa: Study Based on Greater Tunis," paper presented at Council of Europe Regional Conference on Migrants in Transit Countries: Sharing Responsibility for Management and Protection, Istanbul, September/October 2004.

30 Lahlou *et al.,* op. cit.; A. S. Wender, M. J. Laflamme-Marsan, and H. Rachidi, *Gourougou, Bel Younes, Oujda: La situation alarmante des migrants subsahariens en transit au Maroc et les conséquences des politiques de l'Union Européenne,* Paris, Cimade, 2004; M. Collyer, "Undocumented sub-Saharan African Migrants in Morocco," Report for the Danish Institute for International Studies, November 2004.

31 H. Boubakri, op. cit.; A. Bensaad, "Agadez, carrefour migratoire sahélo-maghrébin," *Revue Européenne des Migrations Internationales,* 2003, vol. 19, no. 1, pp. 4–16; S. Hamood, "African transit migration through Libya to Europe: the human cost," American University in Cairo, Forced Migration and Refugee Studies Program, Cairo.

32 Médecins Sans Frontières, "Violence et immigration: rapport sur l'immigration d'origine subsaharienne en situation irrégulière au Maroc," 2005. Available at: http://www.msf.ch/fileadmin/user_upload/uploads/rapports/espagne_maroc/Informe MarruecosFran_aisDEF_2.pdf

33 M. Collyer, "States of Insecurity: Consequences of Saharan Transit Migration," COMPAS Working Paper 06-31, University of Oxford. Available at: http:// www.compas.ox.ac.uk/publications/working_papers.shtml

34 Amnesty International, "Immigration Cooperation with Libya: The Human Rights Perspective," AI EU Office, 12 April 2005.

35 ABC News Online, "Italy Probes Navy's Role in Migrant Boat Wreck." Available at: http://www.abc.net.au/news/newsitems/200608/s1719182.htm

36 Médecins Sans Frontières, op. cit.

37 Asociación Pro Derechos Humanos de Andalucía (APDHA), "Informe violaciones de los derechos humanos en Marruecos hacia las personas migrantes de origen subsahariano en tránsito," 2005. Available at: http://www.apdha.org/ documentos/inforsubsaharianos.pdf; Association des amis et familles des victimes de l'immigration clandestine (AFVIC) and Cimade, "Refoulements et expulsions massives de migrants et demandeurs d'asile: Récit d'une mission de l'AFVIC et de la Cimade," 2005. Available at: http://www.cimade.org/downloads/ expulsions%20Maroc%20rapport%20Afvic%20Cimade%2012-10-05.pdf

38 Amnesty International, "Spain and Morocco: Failure to Protect the Rights of Migrations – Ceuta and Melilla One Year On," AI ref EUR4100906, 2006.
39 M. Collyer, 2006, op. cit.
40 European Commission, "Technical Mission to Libya on Illegal Immigration," 2004.
41 See *Migration News*, 2004.
42 Wender *et al.*, op. cit.
43 M. Collyer, "Migration de transit et protection du voyage," paper presented at the conference of the Centre d'Etudes sur les Mouvements Migratoires Maghré-bins, Oujda, 9–10 November 2006.
44 International Monetary Fund (IMF), "Balance of Payments Statistics Yearbook," Washington DC, 2004.
45 EC, 2004.
46 The MEDA program is the EU's main financial instrument for cooperation in the Mediterranean region. Morocco was granted 5m euros to support the "circulation of people" in 2002 and 40m for "border control" in 2003, according to European Commission, "Maroc: programme indicative national 2002–2004," 2005, Annex IV. Amnesty International reports that Morocco was granted a further 10.5m in July 2006 but does not specify the source of this finance. See AI, 2006, op. cit.
47 N. Nyberg-Sorenson, N. Van Hear, and P. Engberg Pedersen, "The Migration Development Nexus: Evidence and Policy Options," *International Migration*, vol. 40, no. 5, 2002, pp. 49–71.
48 "Partenariat euro-africain pour la migration et le développement. Declaration de Rabat," July 2006. Available at: http://www.maec.gov.ma/migration/Doc/DECLARATION%20DE%20RABAT.pdf
49 There is a range of other intergovernmental fora in which migration is discussed, such as the Berne initiative launched jointly by the Swiss government and the IOM in 2001, or ICMPD's Dialogue on Mediterranean Transit Migration, established in 2002, as well as others, but these are often temporary or are focused at a large scale and never have universal representation at the ministerial level. Available at: http://www.icmpd.org/default.asp?nav=budapest &folderid=362&id=-1
50 B. Khader, "Immigration and the Euro-Mediterranean Partnership," in H. Amirah-Fernández and R. Youngs (eds): *The Euro-Mediterranean Partnership: Assessing the First Decade*, Madrid: Elcano Royal Institute for International and Strategic Studies and FRIDE, 2005. Available at: http://www.realinstitutoelcano.org/publicaciones/libros/Barcelona10_eng.pdf
51 Text of all Association Agreements, and their current status, can be found on the Barcelona Process web pages of the website of the External Relations DG of the European Commission. Available at: http://europa.eu.int/comm/external_relations/euromed/index.htm
52 See Article 71.1a in both agreements.
53 The key idea in this argument is the theory that, since it is rarely the poorest sector of society that migrates internationally, development will initially increase migration by providing potential migrants with the resources they require for migration. This creates what is known as the "migration hump." See Martin, 1993.
54 See Article 84.2.
55 See Article 71.1b in both agreements.
56 The remaining five Action Plans covered Albania, Sri Lanka, Somalia, Iraq and the surrounding region, and Afghanistan and the surrounding region.
57 Links to the full text of these Action Plans appear on the European Neigh-bourhood Policy homepage. Available at: http://europa.eu.int/comm/world/enp/index_en.htm. Neither Algeria nor Libya have begun negotiations to establish national Action Plans, and Mauritania is not involved in the ENP.

58 See Paragraph 43 for Tunisia; 46 for Morocco.
59 International Organization for Migration (IOM), *World Migration 2005: Costs and Benefits of International Migration*, Geneva, 2005, p. 81.
60 All documents on the "5 + 5" dialogue can be found on IOM's website: www.iom.int
61 *Migration News*, 2004.
62 IOM, op. cit., p. 79.
63 *Migration News*, 2004.
64 Amnesty International, 2005, op. cit.
65 IOM, op. cit.
66 Amnesty International, 2006, op. cit.
67 "Acuerdo sobre mano de obra entre el Reino de España y el Reino de Marruecos," Madrid, 25 July 2001.
68 *Boletín Oficial del Estado*, 13 May 2005.
69 M. Collyer, "The Development Impact of Temporary International Labour Migration on Southern Mediterranean Sending Countries: Contrasting examples of Morocco and Egypt," Development Research Centre on Migration, Globalisation and Poverty, 2004, Working Paper T6, University of Sussex. Available at: http://www.migrationdrc.org/publications/working_papers/WP-T6.pdf
70 A. Belguendouz, *Le Maroc Non-Africain, Gendarme de l'Europe? Alerte au project de loi no. 02/03 relative a l'entrée et au séjour des étrangers au Maroc, a l'emigration et l'immigration irreguiliers*, Rabat: Inter-Graph, 2003.
71 Act No. 2004-6 of 3 February 2004 amending Act No. 75-40 of 1975.
72 S. Lavenex and E. Uçarer (eds), *Migration and the Externalities of European Integration*, Oxford: Lexington, 2002.
73 Fondation Hassan II and IOM, 2003.
74 One indication of this trend is the attitude of diaspora-focused websites. Though they are typically highly critical of government initiatives, it is now increasingly common to see Internet links to government-provided information for emigrants regarding arrangements for summer returns or particular legislation. See, for example: http://www.bladi.net or http://www.tunisiancommunity.org
75 P. Mares, *Borderline: Australia's Response to Refugees and Asylum Seekers in the Wake of the Tampa*, Sydney: UNSW Press, 2002.
76 Wender *et al.*, op. cit.
77 De Haas, op. cit.
78 *Haut Commissariat au Plan*, 2005.
79 Fargues, op. cit.

9 Intra-Maghrebi Relations

Unitary Myth and National Interests

Miguel Hernando de Larramendi

The plan to create a united Maghreb has been present in the political discourse of North African leaders since their respective struggles for independence. The constitutions of the five Maghrebi states (Algeria, Libya, Mauritania, Morocco, and Tunisia) address regional unification, and official statements made by political leaders cite historic, religious, cultural, and economic reasons for creating a united Maghreb. Regardless of the official declarations, concrete results have not materialized. Political differences, distrust over security issues, and the Western Sahara conflict have brought the Maghrebi unification process to a standstill. Obstructions to unification have undermined the region's ability to negotiate as a bloc, resulting in economic isolation and political marginalization, equally highlighted by the tide of globalization.

The Failure of the Arab Maghreb Union

The political reforms introduced by the regimes at the end of the 1980s, in attempts to counter their lack of political legitimacy, were accompanied by the establishment of the Arab Maghreb Union (AMU) in February 1989.[1] This regional integration project was designed to enable the Maghrebi countries to tackle the challenges of economic globalization with the consolidation of regional blocs.[2] The easing of tension between Libya and Tunisia following Habib Bourguiba's removal from office on 7 November 1987, and the resumption of diplomatic relations between Algeria and Morocco in May 1988 after a 12-year hiatus, paved the way for the project's advancement. The AMU was presented as an embodiment of the unified Maghreb ideal that was forged during the struggle against colonialism.

The functioning of the AMU has been obstructed by political differences between its member states. The Algerian civil war in the 1990s and the conflict over Western Sahara since 1975 complicated relations between Algeria and Morocco, the twin engine of any regional integration project. The closure of the land border between the two countries in August 1994 blocked any further advancement. The international sanctions imposed in 1992 on Libya for its involvement in the Lockerbie affair demonstrated the limited scope of Maghrebi solidarity with Tripoli. Muammar al-Qaddafi's regime shifted the focus of its foreign policy towards Africa, distancing Libya further from a Maghreb union project for which it had demonstrated irregular and inconsistent interest. In 1999, Mauritania and Israel established diplomatic relations, which continued after the outbreak of the second *intifada* in September 2000, fueling tensions between Mauritania and its North African partners.

The performance of the AMU has also been impeded by its institutional structure. The Presidential Council is the only body with the power to make decisions, which must be agreed upon by the five heads of state.[3] The Council has not convened since the Tunis summit of February 1994. In 1995, Libya refused to shoulder the rotating presidency of the AMU after its partners complied with the international sanctions imposed on Tripoli. Algeria then assumed the presidency, which it did not hand over to Libya until 2003, when Tripoli was rejoining the international arena following the lifting of the UN sanctions. The AMU's activities have been at a standstill since 1994. The 36 conventions adopted in the AMU framework were all approved before the end of the year, but their ratification and implementation have been paralyzed by the political deadlock. Despite the hold on its activities, the AMU periodically organizes meetings of experts and, occasionally, meetings of ministers from the five countries. The Secretary-General, Habib Ben Yahia of Tunisia, represents the AMU at regional and international fora.[4]

Regional economic integration has made no substantial progress since the AMU was established. In 2002, interregional trade represented roughly 3 percent of total trade of the five member states, not taking into account the *trabendo*, or underground economy.[5] Trade between individual AMU member states and the European Union (EU) is greater than trade between the Maghrebi countries, a situation which has not changed since their independence. The flux of migrant workers at sub-regional level (for example, Tunisian workers in Libya) is insignificant considering the growing pressure of sub-Saharan immigration.[6]

Limited progress in the regional unification process has not stifled unionist rhetoric in speeches and official communiqués, although the sense of "Arabness" which underlines the unified Maghreb ideal faces increasing challenges from concurrent ideologies, such as political Islam and politicized Berberism.[7] Emphasis on the development of cross-border cooperation stemming from the exploitation of oil and gas reserves has often proved to be instrumental in counteracting the impasse of the AMU.[8] The project that raised the highest level of expectation was the Maghreb–Europe Gas pipeline (MEG) from Hassi R'Mel in southern Algeria, through Morocco, to Spain. It was expected to strengthen interdependence between Algeria and Morocco and contribute to sealing their bilateral reconciliation. In 1996, when the project was inaugurated with European funding, the border between Algeria and Morocco was closed. Since then, the pipeline has been operating without incident, crossing Morocco, but it has not contributed to dispelling distrust between the two neighbors. In 2002, Spain approved the construction of a new gas pipeline, MEDGAZ, directly connecting sizeable fields in Algeria to Europe via Almería.[9] This Algerian–European pipeline was conceived bilaterally between various European companies (Cepsa, Iberdrola, Endesa, Total, ENI, GDF, and BP) and Algeria's Sonatrach. Bilateral alliances of this nature, geared to ensuring direct supply from a Maghrebi country to European networks, take pride of place among regional actors in the energy sector. A number of recent projects can be cited in this respect, among which Gassi Touil (Algeria) between Sonatrach, Repsol YPF, and Gas Natural; and Damietta (Egypt) between EGAS, Unión Fenosa, and ENI. It is therefore unlikely that energy relations in the Maghreb will contribute to improving intra-Maghrebi neighborly relations.

The period of détente in 1999 following the suspension of international sanctions on Libya, coupled with the election of Abdelaziz Bouteflika as president of Algeria and the accession of Mohammed VI to the throne in Morocco, has not led to any meaningful developments in the regional integration process. Algeria's support of the POLISARIO Front remains an insurmountable obstacle to Algerian–Moroccan relations, which have also been strained by mutual mistrust over security issues. Political instability in Mauritania (attempted coups d'état in June 2003, and in August and September 2004) heightened tension between Nouakchott and Tripoli, which was allegedly supporting the rebels. The ousting of President Maaouiya Ould Sid'Ahmed Taya on 3 August 2005 did not elicit any official statement from the AMU, and Tunisia was the only member state to condemn the coup.

Attempts to reactivate the AMU have been unsuccessful. The meeting between Mohammed VI and Bouteflika at the UN headquarters in September 2003 seemed to pave the way for the Presidential Council to convene in Algiers that same year to discuss the creation of a free trade zone. The meeting was postponed until after the Maghrebi leaders had participated in the first "5 + 5" Dialogue Summit of the Heads of State and Government of the Western Mediterranean Countries (Algeria, France, Italy, Libya, Malta, Mauritania, Morocco, Portugal, Spain, and Tunisia), held in Tunis in December 2003. Mohammed VI's participation in the Arab League summit in Algiers in March 2005 fuelled hopes that the AMU would be reactivated. However, the proposed meeting of the Presidential Council in May was postponed indefinitely, due to the Moroccan king's refusal to attend in response to Bouteflika's statements supporting the Sahrawis.

The Challenges of Globalization

At the regional level, the advancement of globalization and the EU's eastward expansion have weakened the negotiating position of a divided Maghreb.[10] It was precisely this inability to present a unified front that led the Maghrebi countries to agree individually to the EU proposal to renew

Euro-Mediterranean relations in accordance with the Barcelona Declaration of 1995. The Euro-Mediterranean Partnership (EMP) set the goal to create a shared zone of prosperity on both shores of the Mediterranean Sea.[11] The proposed association agreements between the EU and each non-EU Mediterranean partner were ultimately geared towards the creation of a free trade zone by 2010.[12] In addition to emphasizing the need to accelerate unification in the south, the EMP has continued to perpetuate bilateral negotiations between each southern Mediterranean country and various EU bodies. Barely 10 percent of the MEDA funds, the principal financial instrument of the EU for the implementation of the Euro-Mediterranean Partnership, have been earmarked for regional action.[13] The European Neighbourhood Policy (ENP), launched by the European Commission in March 2003 to provide countries without the prospect of EU accession with a stronger framework for cooperation, strengthens the bilateral north–south relations through the signing of Action Plans, negotiated individually with each country.

Regional economic integration has been a US goal since the launching of the Eizenstat Initiative in 1999, later renamed the US North Africa Economic Program, now part of the Middle East Partnership Initiative (MEPI).[14] This initiative, which originally encompassed Algeria, Morocco, and Tunisia, is designed to strengthen US presence in the region by encouraging trade and investments, while promoting "the reduction in internal barriers among and between the countries of North Africa which have impeded the normal trade flows between those countries."[15] The Maghrebi countries that have benefited from the post-9/11 international climate to strengthen their ties with Washington are individually negotiating free trade agreements, the first of which was signed with Morocco in March 2004 and came into effect in January 2006. The signing of this agreement was not only geared to diversifying Morocco's trade relations but also to strengthening Rabat's role as a privileged partner of the US in the region.[16]

Attempts to revitalize the AMU since 1999 have been a response to globalization. The association agreement reached between Algeria and the EU in 2002 strengthened Algeria's interest in pursuing regional unification and thereby presenting a common front in negotiations. Technocratic elites are endorsing the resolution of political differences and the pursuit of regional economic integration in order to confront an increasingly globalized economy. Business leaders, entrepreneurs, and investors from AMU member states and overseas, and representatives of international financial institutions meeting in Casablanca in February 2002, expressed frustration that political differences continued to prevent private-sector cooperation in the region. They called on the political leaders to establish a Maghreb Central Bank (provided for in the AMU's founding treaty but never implemented) to ease the convertibility of local currencies.[17] This is addressed in a report issued by Morocco's Ministry of Finance and Privatization in 2003, which estimated that the benefits that could be obtained by removing trade barriers within the Maghreb could reach USD 4.6bn annually, the equivalent of 4.4 percent of the joint GDP of Algeria, Morocco, and Tunisia.[18]

To counter the political stalemate vis-à-vis Maghrebi integration, Morocco and Tunisia launched the Agadir Process in May 2001, together with Egypt and Jordan. All four countries signed partnership agreements with the EU with the aim of accelerating their trade liberalization schedule and creating a Free Trade Zone (FTZ). The absence of territorial continuity between the signatory states, which have no common land border, has sparked doubts concerning a sub-regional integration project whose entry into force has been postponed owing to delays in the agreement ratification process.

Political Islam

Although political Islam is linked with the internal social, economic, and political conditions of each individual state, in 1992 it extended to include the entire region.[19] The outbreak of violence in Algeria, following the cancellation of elections that the Islamic Salvation Front (*Front Islamique de Salut*, FIS) was poised to win, heightened perception of political Islam as a common threat. At the AMU summit in Nouakchott at the end of 1992, the Maghrebi leaders committed themselves to combating terrorism viewed as a product of religious fanaticism.[20] The Maghrebi governments were aware of the possibility of Islamist power to spread in the region if Algeria came under Islamist control. This view strengthened regional cooperation in security matters (information exchanges, border surveillance, and repression of Islamist groups' activities) between regimes. Algeria and Tunisia were the most outspoken in defense of anti-terrorist collaboration at AMU ministerial meetings. Coordination was not strictly bilateral, but encompassed regional and international cooperation, such as meetings of Arab interior ministers and the Organization of the Islamic Conference (OIC), which condemned Iran and Sudan for their support of Islamist movements.[21]

The Islamist threat fuelled mutual suspicions, becoming an element of interference in intra-Maghrebi relations. Radical Islamists were perceived primarily as a domestic threat and as an instrument neighboring countries could use to destabilize one another.[22] Libya may well have employed this tactic to put pressure on its regional partners for their lack of solidarity following the imposition of the 1992 sanctions. Tunisia accused Qaddafi's regime of attempting to destabilize the country. Algeria denounced the transfer of arms through Libya for Algerian Islamists. In 1993, Qaddafi offered to mediate between the Algerian regime and the imprisoned FIS leaders Abbasi Madani and Ali Benhadj, a proposal that Algeria interpreted as interference in its internal affairs.[23]

When Qaddafi's regime, weakened by the embargo, became seriously threatened by the Libyan Islamist opposition, Tripoli altered its strategy. In 1994, Libya pledged to cease all support for the Islamist opposition in

Algeria and began to cooperate with its North African neighbors with regard to security issues. In April 1996, when Libya's Islamist guerrillas were particularly active in the Cyrenaica region, Libya and Algeria agreed to jointly combat the Islamist threat. The agreement may have resulted in the handing over to the Algerian government of 500 FIS militants, who had taken refuge in Libya after the 1992 coup.[24]

The Algerian civil war also increased distrust between Algeria and Morocco. Hassan II, the late King of Morocco, had tried to offset Morocco's loss of geopolitical weight after the end of the Cold War by projecting the country as a "model of stability" in relation to Algeria. Morocco, he said, was a country where the drift towards violent religious extremism was countered by the existence of a religious monarchy which traces its lineage to the Prophet Mohammad. Preoccupied by internal conflict, Algerian leaders accused Morocco of supporting Algerian Islamist movements in an attempt to tip the scales of the Western Sahara conflict in Rabat's favor. At the end of 1992, following the assassination of Algerian President, Mohammed Boudiaf, the Algerian regime accused Morocco of turning a blind eye to arms trafficking, as well as granting safe haven to Algerian Islamists when the border between the countries was still open. Hassan II told the Saudi daily *Ash-Sharq al-Awsat* that the installation of an Islamist government would have constituted "an interesting laboratory experiment" in the Maghreb, a statement that only served to heighten Algeria's malaise.[25] The arrest in Morocco in June 1993 of the leader of the Armed Islamic Group (*Groupe Islamique Armé*, GIA), Abdelhak Layada, and his subsequent extradition in September 1993 to Algeria mirrored the distrust that existed between both countries against the backdrop of the Western Sahara conflict. According to General Khaled Nezzar, Morocco tried to make Layada's extradition conditional on Algeria ending its support of the POLISARIO Front.[26]

Algerian–Moroccan relations reached a low ebb in the summer of 1994 following the terrorist attack on the Atlas Asni Hotel in Marrakech, leaving two Spanish tourists dead. The Moroccan minister of the interior, Driss Basri, claimed the attack was carried out by a group of *beurs* (young North Africans born in France) and Maghrebi immigrants from a Paris suburb, hinting at the involvement of Algeria's military security in what was presented as an Algerian-orchestrated campaign to destabilize Morocco. Algeria closed its land borders with Morocco after Rabat imposed entry visas for Algerian citizens and citizens of Algerian descent.[27] Faced with the risk of civil conflict spilling over into the international arena following the massacres of thousands of civilians in the fall of 1997, Algeria reiterated its accusations that Morocco was sheltering the activities of Islamist groups. In the summer of 1999, security issues blocked the prospects of reconciliation that had been rekindled after Bouteflika attended Hassan II's funeral in July 1999. The arrest of nine members of the GIA, said to have perpetrated a massacre in Beni Ounif in southeast Algeria before allegedly returning to

Morocco, led the Algerian president to accuse Morocco of arming and financing Algerian terrorists.[28]

Regional Cooperation and Security

The regional distrust sparked by the security initiatives launched by Western countries after the end of the Cold War (creation of the Standing Naval Force Mediterranean by NATO in 1992 and the creation of Eurofor and Euromarfor by southern European countries in 1996) was replaced by a more cooperative attitude in the mid-1990s. Security cooperation was no longer considered taboo in regional relations throughout the Maghreb, and even less so following the attacks on 11 September 2001.[29]

The absence of intra-Maghrebi multilateral cooperation in the field of security has been offset by the participation of Maghrebi states in other sub-regional frameworks, such as NATO's Mediterranean Dialogue, launched in 1994 with Morocco, Tunisia, and Mauritania. Algeria joined in March 2000 after Abdelaziz Bouteflika became president. In the wake of the 9/11 attacks, Maghrebi countries collaborated in operation Active Endeavour, launched by NATO in October 2001 to counter terrorism and other illegal activities in the Mediterranean. They also welcomed the project approved at the NATO summit held in Istanbul in June 2004—far more enthusiastically than other Middle Eastern partners, such as Egypt—to enhance the operation and turn it into a genuine partnership.[30] Although the Mediterranean Dialogue was initially structured on a bilateral basis (26 + 1), it has since acquired a more multilateral dimension with the organization of periodic coordination meetings between heads of state.[31]

The five Maghrebi countries and five southern European countries (France, Italy, Malta, Portugal, and Spain) form the "5 + 5" framework for dialogue and collaboration. The first meeting of foreign affairs ministers took place in Rome in 1990, and the second in Algiers a year later. The effects of the Gulf War in 1990–91, coupled with the outbreak of civil war in Algeria and the imposition of international sanctions on Libya, paralyzed the initiative. The interruption of the political dialogue did not prevent the creation in 1995 of a forum for stronger internal cooperation, which has convened annually since then with the participation of Algeria, Libya, Morocco, and Tunisia since 1999, and Mauritania with observer status.[32]

The initiative was reactivated in Lisbon in January 2001 following the lifting of sanctions on Libya. Meetings of defense officials, as well as foreign ministers, have further broadened the discourse.[33] The "5 + 5" dialogue has also been extended to encompass heads of state, who held their first summit in Tunis in December 2003. All the Maghrebi heads of state attended this meeting, except the Mauritanian president, who sent his prime minister. The "5 + 5" dialogue seeks to strengthen stability in the region by providing a global perspective on issues such as North African integration, economic cooperation, human migration, and exchanges. The struggle against illegal immigration has become an increasingly paramount issue at ministerial meetings. Sub-Saharan migration via the Maghreb has been an issue since 2000. The strengthening of control mechanisms in the Western Mediterranean has turned the Maghreb into a transit point for sub-Saharan immigrants awaiting an opportunity to cross over to Europe. Despite using this as a negotiating element in their relations with the EU, Maghrebi countries have failed to strengthen regional cooperation in this field. Libya's re-entry in the Euro-African dialogue broadly hinged on its migration policy, which also served as a lever to lift the sanctions.[34] Algeria used Europe's demands for increased border control to its advantage by purchasing military surveillance material. Morocco also benefited from Europe's request by increasing European financial assistance.[35]

At the meeting of foreign ministers in Oran, in western Algeria, the Maghrebi countries rejected the creation of transit centers in North Africa for sub-Saharans waiting to immigrate to the EU.[36] In the fall of 2005, waves of sub-Saharan immigrants attempted to storm the fence surrounding the Spanish enclave of Melilla in northern Morocco, demonstrating the limits of Algerian–Moroccan cooperation in the field of migration.[37] Most sub-Saharans entered Morocco via the Algerian border, which has been officially closed since 1994.[38] Morocco accused Algeria of capitalizing on the immigration issue.[39] Moroccan foreign ministry officials made statements to the effect that Algeria was exploiting illegal sub-Saharan immigration in a bid to obstruct Spanish–Moroccan cooperation over the Western Sahara conflict.[40] In July 2006, Algeria boycotted the Ministerial Euro-African Conference on Migration and Development,[41] held in Rabat and jointly organized by Morocco and Spain, on the grounds that the issue of clandestine immigration should have been debated in the framework of the African Union, which Morocco had withdrawn from in 1984 after the Sahrawi Arab Democratic Republic (SADR) became a member.[42]

The War on Terror and the Sahel Region

The 11 September 2001 terrorist attacks against the United States permitted the Maghrebi countries to categorize their struggle against Islamist movements as part of the "global war on terror." The attack on the Djerba synagogue in April 2002 and the Casablanca bombings in May 2003 heightened the feeling of shared vulnerability to terrorism. After a decade of more open political systems, the regimes in the region have used the struggle against Islamist terrorism as an excuse to strengthen their authoritarianism.[43]

After 9/11, North African authorities expressed their willingness to join the fight against al-Qaeda. Maghrebi security services have actively cooperated with the US by providing information on citizens who had traveled to Afghanistan, and by collaborating with the dismantling of terrorist cells, such as the group that had planned an attack in the Straits of Gibraltar in June 2002, dismantled by Morocco. In exchange, they want the US to strengthen its military assistance and international support for their fight against Islamist movements.

Since the 9/11 attacks, the US has placed increased emphasis on the trans-Saharan region, including it within the context of its national security interests. It has actively sought to involve Maghrebi military forces in stabilizing and fighting regional terrorism. US defense officials claimed that the Sahel region was "the new front in the war on terror."[44] The activism of the Salafi Group for Preaching and Combat (*Groupe Salafiste pour la Prédication et le Combat*, GSPC) in the Sahel desert, the belief that the Madrid terrorist attacks of 11 March 2004 were prepared in Morocco, and the fact that a quarter of the Guantánamo detainees are North African, are among the arguments supporting the US claim.

Washington has sought a regional response to the terrorist threat while strengthening bilateral security cooperation with states vying for protection as US allies in the fight against international terrorism.[45] US foreign policy ensures that bilateral tensions between countries in the region do not jeopardize the struggle against terrorism. During his tour of the Maghreb in December 2003, former US Secretary of State Colin Powell appealed to the Maghrebi countries to cooperate in fighting radicalism and criminality.[46]

Although the US has strengthened bilateral cooperation with all five Maghrebi countries, Morocco has received preferential treatment. This is largely due to the support of neoconservative sectors in the US administration, which perceive Mohammed VI's Morocco as a forward-looking country and as a model for the US plan for political reform in the region, the so-called Broader Middle East and North Africa Initiative (BMENA). This is seen in contrast to the Algerian regime, whose leaders come from a generation of Arab nationalists linked with the past.[47] In June 2004, Morocco was designated a major non-NATO ally. It was also the only Maghrebi country selected to be a recipient of Millennium Challenge Account (MCA) resources, projected as part of the US long-term strategy in the "war on terror."[48]

Maghrebi leaders have been quick to benefit from US fear that al-Qaeda might regroup and reorganize in the Sahel region.[49] The Algerian regime has tried to link the GSPC, a splinter group of the GIA, with al-Qaeda. The allegiance sworn by one of the GSPC leaders, Nabil Sahraoui, to al-Qaeda in September 2003[50] and the actions of Abderrazak "El Para," a former Algerian special forces officer described by the Algerian army's secret services as "a lieutenant of Osama bin Laden," were presented by Algeria as evidence that it was an al-Qaeda target.[51] The elimination by Algerian security forces of a Yemeni citizen linked to al-Qaeda during an attack on a military convoy in January 2003 and the kidnapping in February and March of 32 European tourists in the Algerian Sahara heightened US concern over Northwest and sub-Saharan Africa. The region, whose oil reserves cover 15 percent of US requirements,[52] is one in which Washington hopes to set up military outposts in the framework of a renewed strategic deployment.[53]

The US government has put the GIA and the GSPC on the State Department's list of terrorist organizations and lifted the embargo for supplying anti-terrorist equipment to Algeria. Meanwhile, Morocco has tried in vain to link the POLISARIO Front and Sahel-based transnational terrorist organizations in an attempt to increase US support for its position in the Western Sahara conflict. Morocco claims that the POLISARIO Front is in the throes of disintegration and risks becoming a terrorist movement in the Sahel region. Mohammed VI said as much in a speech in November 2006 on the occasion of the thirty-first anniversary of the Green March.[54] In June 2005, an attack was launched on the Lemghayti military barracks, a remote outpost situated near Mauritania's border with Algeria and Mali. Morocco blamed the attack on the POLISARIO Front, which it claimed had formed an alliance with Islamist terrorist groups that had taken refuge in Mali; this was clearly a far-fetched accusation and no evidence was produced to support this claim. Mauritania tried to counteract the vulnerability of Ould Taya's regime, before it was toppled in August 2005, by reporting links between opposition Islamist movements and terrorist organizations linked to al-Qaeda,[55] such as the GSPC, accused of perpetrating the Lemghayti attack.

A number of studies have disagreed with what some consider an overstatement of the Islamist threat in the Sahel region, arguing that it is linked to US oil interests in Western Africa in the framework of a supply-diversification policy.[56] In 2002, the US earmarked USD 6.5m for launching the Pan-Sahel Initiative (PSI), designed to enhance border protection, track movements of people, combat terrorism, and enhance regional cooperation and stability. In 2003–4, US special forces in the EUCOM theatre of operations were deployed in the area to train security forces in these countries.[57]

In March 2004, the capture of GSPC leader "El Para," after a skirmish with the Chadian army, was presented as a concrete result of the PSI.[58] This incident remains relatively obscure, awaiting clarification. "El Para" was apparently captured by rebels from the Movement for Democracy and Justice (MDJT) in Chad, who may have kept him in the Tibesti region until turning him over to Libya, which in turn may have extradited him to Algeria. Tripoli exploited the incident to strengthen its commitment to the "war on terror" and its capacity as a mediator and interlocutor in Africa. In 2005, the PSI was replaced by the Trans-Saharan Counter Terrorism Initiative (TSCTI), which is more ambitious than its predecessor. The new initiative is better funded, with USD 500m over five years, and it has been expanded to include Algeria, Ghana, Morocco, Nigeria, Senegal, and Tunisia, in addition to the four African PSI countries. Of the five Maghrebi countries, only Libya is not directly associated with the TSCTI.

The Western Sahara Conflict

Although improved Algerian–Moroccan relations paved the way for the creation of the AMU in 1989, they did so against the backdrop of the still unresolved Western Sahara conflict.[59] Regional détente in May 1991 facilitated acceptance by Morocco and the POLISARIO Front of the UN Settlement Plan, which provided for a ceasefire in September 1991 and the holding of a referendum on self-determination in which voters could choose between independence or integration with Morocco.[60]

Morocco considered the referendum as a means of securing international legitimacy for its claim of sovereignty over Western Sahara. This has been the stance since Hassan II accepted the idea of a "confirmative" referendum at the Organization for African Unity (OAU) summit held in Nairobi in 1981. Tacit acceptance of the referendum has been accompanied by the quest for a political solution that would engender international recognition of Moroccan sovereignty over the territory and eliminate uncertainty of an unfavorable outcome. The referendum, initially scheduled to take place in January 1992, has been continuously postponed due to the difficulty of creating a voter list whose final structure could determine the outcome of the referendum.[61]

The delays coincided with political instability in Algeria, which in turn contributed to heightening the tension between the two main regional powers, effectively blocking progress in the Maghreb unification process. When Mohammed Boudiaf, a leader of the Algerian war of independence, was called after nearly 30 years of exile in Morocco to head the High Council of State in the wake of the 1992 coup, Rabat believed that a favorable solution to the Western Sahara conflict was perhaps finally in sight. During his brief mandate, Boudiaf indicated his willingness to find a bilateral solution to the conflict between Algeria and Morocco, going further than his predecessor, President Chadli Benjedid.[62] The Algerian leader distanced himself from the dominant stance taken by the country's top military officials, whose support of the POLISARIO Front was not merely political but also psychological, fueled by fear of Moroccan irredentism towards Algerian territory.[63] After Boudiaf's assassination in June 1992, the Algerian regime once again sought to make progress in the greater Maghreb integration process conditional on finding a solution to the Western Sahara conflict. It should be noted that Algerian public opinion had paid scant attention to this matter, unlike the army, which had been deeply involved since the years of Boumedienne's presidency.

Morocco suspected that Algeria's political instability would force it to adopt a more conciliatory tone towards the Western Sahara issue, thus strengthening Morocco's position. Despite reducing its assistance to the POLISARIO Front in the late 1980s and early 1990s, the Algerian regime continued to thwart Morocco's attempts to exploit its weakness and validate its annexation of the former Spanish colony.[64] Morocco attempted to win the support of the West by projecting itself as a counter-model to Algeria.[65] Knowing that Western powers feared that a POLISARIO Front victory in the self-determination referendum might destabilize Morocco, Hassan II presented himself as a buffer against radical Islamism and managed to convince the West to maintain the status quo in Western Sahara.

The "Third Way" and Baker Plan II

Changes in the region at the end of the 1990s did not translate into reconciliation between Algeria and Morocco. Bouteflika's pragmatism and his attempts to strengthen his autonomy and weaken the military's role in running the country rekindled Moroccan hopes of a bilaterally negotiated solution. Meanwhile, the former US Secretary of State, James A. Baker III, who had been appointed as Kofi Annan's personal envoy for Western Sahara in 1997, was trying to solve technical problems with the preparation of the census.

In Morocco, prospects of democratization had been fuelled by the accession of Mohammed VI to the throne in July 1999. The disturbances in Laayoune two months later tipped the scale in the new king's favor, enabling him to regain control of the Sahrawi dossier and dismiss Driss Basri, Hassan II's closest confidant, hitherto in charge of the Western Sahara dossier. Foreign ministry officials and diplomats began to speak openly about the possibility of autonomy for Western Sahara under Moroccan sovereignty.[66]

Anxious to avoid a repetition of the East Timor situation, where Indonesia, after decades of occupation, lost the referendum on self-determination in August 1999, Morocco secured the adoption of a "third way" via UN documents as of February 2000.[67] Without abandoning references to the Settlement Plan, the resolutions passed by Security Council began to reflect the growing skepticism of its members. The UN Secretary-General's personal envoy was invited to explore new political paths for resolving the conflict. The draft "Framework Agreement on the Status of Western Sahara" prepared by James Baker was based on a Moroccan plan and was included in Kofi Annan's June 2001 report to the Security Council.[68] The draft framework agreement distanced itself from the Settlement Plan by proposing a transfer of authority to inhabitants of the territory for a four- to five-year transition period; to be followed by a referendum deciding upon the final status of the territory, including the Moroccan settlers. The framework agreement also made provisions to distribute power in the territory between the populations of Western Sahara and Morocco.[69]

The POLISARIO Front and Algeria rejected Baker's proposal on the grounds that it was an obvious attempt to satisfy Morocco's aspirations and legitimize its illegal occupation of Western Sahara. Morocco, on the other hand, welcomed the proposal, given that it was virtually guaranteed sovereignty over the disputed territory at the end of the five-year period. Rabat was backed by France and the US, having convinced the two countries that it would never accept a referendum that risked endangering its territorial integrity and stability. It was this optimism that led Mohammed VI to declare in September 2001 that the conflict over Western Sahara had been solved.[70] A month later, Rabat signed offshore oil exploration contracts with TotalFinaElf of France and the US-based Kerr-McGee.

The proposal to partition the Western Sahara territory, according to the UN Secretary-General's report to the Security Council in February 2002, increased tension between Algeria and Morocco at a time when Morocco and Spain were in the throes of a profound bilateral crisis.[71] Moroccan authorities had fallen prey to regional isolation and geopolitical fragility due to a strengthening of relations between Madrid and Algiers, which actively exploited the post-11 September climate to make an international comeback.[72] Morocco accused Algeria of supporting a proposal that would allow it to create a microstate under its protection, thus giving it access to the Atlantic Ocean.[73]

Despite strong support from France, Rabat's perception of encirclement, coupled with the unlikely possibility that the Security Council would back the draft framework agreement, called so without ever having been agreed upon by the parties, strengthened Morocco's determination. On the twenty-seventh anniversary of the Green March in November 2002, Mohammed VI declared that the UN Settlement Plan had become obsolete because it was simply no longer feasible.

Faced with a stalemate, James Baker presented a new proposal for a political solution, the "Peace Plan for self-determination of the people of Western Sahara," details of which are set out in the UN Secretary-General's report of 23 May 2003.[74] The new draft, known as Baker Plan II, upholds the basic tenets of the framework agreement in the holding of a referendum among the settlers in the region after a four- to five-year period of autonomy. The new proposal is more detailed than the 2001 framework agreement, and slightly more balanced. It did not stipulate that the laws adopted by the Western Sahara Authority should be consistent with the Moroccan Constitution. Judicial authority would be implemented by the Supreme Court of Western Sahara, whose members should be appointed by the Chief Executive with the consent of the Legislative Assembly. These two bodies would be elected solely by voters who were eligible to vote in the abandoned referendum. The right to vote in the referendum to determine the final status of Western Sahara could be limited to those settlers who had resided in the territory since December 1999. In this respect, the plan stipulates that "the preservation of territorial integrity against secessionist attempts ... shall not authorize any action whatsoever that would prevent, suppress, or stifle peaceful public debate, discourse or campaign activity, particularly during any election or referendum period."[75]

Surprisingly, the POLISARIO Front and Algeria accepted Baker Plan II a few weeks before the Security Council convened. Morocco, which had actively contributed to designing the plan, rejected it. Algerian pressure may have been a key factor in securing the acceptance of the POLISARIO Front leadership after an internal debate that gave the Sahrawi movement a tactical advantage.[76]

Morocco, whose internal structure had been debilitated by the terrorist attacks of 16 May 2003, rejected the proposal, fearful of losing control of the territory during the autonomous transition period and of losing the referendum. Morocco submitted observations to the UN rejecting the new Baker Plan on the grounds that it would be necessary to modify the constitution in order to apply it to the so-called "southern provinces." The kingdom's main objection, however, was that one of the ballot choices in the referendum to determine the final status of Western Sahara was independence.

The POLISARIO Front's acceptance of Baker Plan II came a few days before Washington submitted a resolution supporting Kofi Annan's proposal for the Security Council to enforce the Baker Plan's acceptance by the POLISARIO Front and Morocco, while denying the parties the opportunity to negotiate the terms. Rabat felt as though it had walked into a trap laid by Algeria. Morocco attempted to prevent the UN Security Council from endorsing the plan, which was unanimously adopted in Resolution 1495 on 31 July 2003, as an "optimum political solution on the basis of agreement between the two parties."[77] Morocco could be grateful to France for replacing the word "endorsing" with the more moderate "support" in the text of the resolution, and the reminder in the preamble that the Security Council was acting under Chapter VI of the Charter of the UN, implying that Baker Plan II would not be imposed by force, as would have been the case under Chapter VII.

Baker's Resignation and Political Deadlock

James Baker's resignation as the UN Secretary-General's personal envoy to Western Sahara in June 2004 was interpreted by Morocco as a triumph that would enable it to shelve Baker Plan II[78] and reactivate a regional solution without putting its "territorial integrity" at risk.[79] The contents of this solution remain unclear. Autonomy, as far as Morocco is concerned, can only be envisaged as final, not as a transitional period. "The final nature of the autonomy solution is not negotiable," said Morocco's foreign affairs minister, Mohammed Benaissa. According to Morocco, any transitional period might result in "insecurity and instability for the whole Maghreb."[80]

The absence of a figure such as James Baker undoubtedly contributed to bringing the Western Sahara conflict to a standstill at the UN level. Alvaro de Soto's appointment to replace Baker was disputed by the POLISARIO Front and Algeria, who demanded the involvement of a diplomat, preferably from the US, with more political clout. Morocco, on the other hand, looked favorably on the new status quo, as the references to Baker Plan II gradually disappeared in subsequent reports by the Secretary-General and in Security Council resolutions. Morocco renewed its diplomatic efforts towards a bilateral solution negotiated between Mohammed VI and Bouteflika, who had strengthened his autonomy vis-à-vis the army since his re-election as Algerian president in April 2004. At the end of July 2004, Mohammed VI announced unilaterally the lifting of the visa requirements imposed on Algerian citizens since 1994.[81] Algeria, making no reciprocal gesture, was clearly irritated by its neighbor's unilateral announcement and redoubled diplomatic efforts geared to securing the involvement of the international community in the Western Sahara issue.

The establishment of diplomatic relations between the Republic of South Africa, the continent's leading economic power, and the Sahrawi Arab Democratic Republic (SADR) in September 2004 was attributed by Rabat to the diplomacy of a buoyant Algeria, supported by rising oil and gas prices.[82] This setback for Morocco mirrored the constraints of its African policy. After Mohammed VI received a letter from the South African President, Thabo Mbeki, in which he compared Sahrawis and Palestinians,[83] Morocco recalled its ambassador in Pretoria. Morocco reiterated its objection to Algeria's involvement in the Western Sahara conflict in a memorandum addressed to the UN Security Council, which came only days after Bouteflika described Morocco as a "colonial power" at the UN General Assembly.[84] The division widened following an exchange of accusations regarding troop movements along the Algerian–Moroccan border.[85] During this time of escalating tension, the POLISARIO Front threatened to take up arms again.[86]

The pressure exerted by Washington, Brussels, Paris, and Madrid may have contributed to alleviating the tension between Algeria and Morocco in the first quarter of 2005.[87] The participation of Mohammed VI at the Arab League summit in Algeria in March 2005 fuelled hopes of a reconciliation and reactivation of the AMU. Algeria responded by waiving visa requirements for Moroccans, reciprocating the measure adopted by Rabat eight months earlier. At his meeting with Bouteflika, Mohammed VI supposedly agreed to unblock bilateral relations and galvanize the regional integration process, leaving the Western Sahara conflict to the authority of the UN. Algeria was to establish a code of good conduct and a pact of verbal non-aggression, and to reopen the land border between the two countries.[88] Bouteflika, however, delayed reopening the border and even more forcefully defended the Sahrawi people's right to self-determination during a subsequent tour of South America. The last straw for Morocco was the congratulatory message Bouteflika sent Mohammed Abdelaziz, the secretary-general of the POLISARIO Front, on the movement's thirty-second anniversary, three days before the start of the AMU summit convened by Libya, and cancelled as a result.

The riots and pro-independence demonstrations that broke out in Laayoune and in other towns of Western Sahara at the end of May 2005 reignited regional tensions.[89] The focus of Sahrawi activism has shifted from the Tindouf refugee camps in Algeria to the Western Sahara territory and southern Morocco, where a politically aware civil society is openly clamoring for independence in what the POLISARIO Front has dubbed the "Sahrawi *intifada*."[90] The harsh repression and punishment of the Sahrawis who demonstrated in favor of independence (15 to 20 years of imprisonment) are a clear indication of Morocco's fear of unforeseen events. Morocco's official news agency (MAP) and pro-government press again trotted out a conspiracy theory, consisting of a plot instigated by Algeria and perpetrated by "the Tindouf gang of mercenaries."[91] Rabat subsequently accused the Algerian secret services of being behind the June 2005 attack on the Lemghayti barracks in northeast Mauritania.[92] Calls in the press for mobilization in the face of an "enemy" bent on destabilizing the country were accompanied by a diplomatic offensive to which all the political parties with parliamentary representation rallied, including the Islamist Justice and Development Party.[93] Outside Morocco, the campaign denouncing Algeria's involvement in the incarceration of 404 prisoners of war (POWs) on "Algerian territory" was intensified.[94] US diplomatic efforts succeeded in bringing about the liberation of the last Moroccan POWs in August 2005, under the supervision of the Republican Senator from Indiana Richard Lugar, Chairman of the Senate Foreign Relations Committee. The US promptly tried to broker a rapprochement between Algeria and Morocco, one that would give fresh impetus to regional relations, as well as defuse a potential crisis that looms ever larger on America's diplomatic agenda in the region.[95]

The death of a young demonstrator in October 2005 exacerbated tensions in Western Sahara. Political activism among a sector of young Sahrawis calling for independence from within the territory controlled by Morocco forced the Moroccan authorities to give the Sahrawi elite a hand in defining the "broad autonomy" project in the framework of Morocco's territorial integrity. During his visit to Western Sahara in March 2006, Mohammed VI announced that fresh impetus would be given to the Royal Consultative Council for Saharan Affairs (CORCAS),[96] whose 141 members represent 40 tribes in Western Sahara, as well as political activists and civil association officials.

Kofi Annan's report of April 2006 reflects the arguments brandished by Morocco, signaling the abandonment of Baker Plan II. The UN Secretary-General states that in the opinion of his new personal envoy, Peter van Walsum, the only way of breaking the deadlock is to allow direct negotiations, without preconditions, between Morocco and the POLISARIO Front, with the participation of Algeria and Mauritania as neighboring countries.[97]

In October 2006, shortly before the Security Council convened, the contents of the report of the OHCHR (Office of the High Commissioner for Human Rights) mission to Western Sahara and the refugee camps in Tindouf were released.[98] The report is highly critical of the human rights situation and the harsh repression that was meted out in the wake of the pro-independence demonstrations of May 2005 in Moroccan-occupied Western Sahara. In its recommendations, the report states that "the right to self-determination for the people of Western Sahara must be ensured and implemented without any further delay."

Although Morocco has notched up a number of diplomatic successes, such as the signing in June 2006 of an agreement with the European Union giving European fishing fleets access to Western Saharan waters, Rabat's tardiness in specifying the contents and details of the Western Sahara autonomy plan tried the patience of its allies. During the discussion of Security Council Resolution 1720 in October 2006, the US suggested winding up MINURSO,[99] whose mandate was finally extended to April 2007.[100]

However, under pressure from France and the United States, Morocco finally put forth its "historic initiative" of "enlarged autonomy" for a Saharan Autonomous Region (SAR), a plan Mohammed VI presented as an instrument that would spare the Maghreb, Mediterranean, and Sahel regions from Balkanization and instability.[101] In April 2007, in its Resolution 1754, the UN Security Council, although quite supportive of Morocco's SAR's proposal, urged Moroccans and Sahrawis to begin direct negotiations without preconditions. The first such direct talks took place in Manhasset, New York, in June and again in August 2007. Nothing tangible resulted from these talks, Morocco insisting on negotiating only its own autonomy proposal. The POLISARIO Front, with Algeria's backing, continues to argue that the peace plan for the self-determination of the people of Western Sahara is the only option unanimously endorsed by the Security Council, which continues to endorse technical resolutions devoid of any political content.

Conclusion

Regional integration has become a universal phenomenon, having gained tremendous momentum throughout the world in the last two decades. In the Maghreb, however, attempts to forge regional integration have failed miserably, surviving only on a formal level. The creation of the Arab Maghreb Union was a defensive reaction on the part of Maghrebi leaders in response to the expansion and consolidation of the European Union. Although greater political openness and the introduction of economic reforms since the 1990s have contributed to creating more favorable conditions for regional integration, this has continued to be thwarted by political issues linked with the struggle for regional leadership between Algeria and Morocco at a time when the structure of the international system is being recast. Algeria's civil war, the lack of Maghrebi solidarity with Libya after the embargo was imposed, and the Western Sahara impasse have combined to block the regional integration process in the Maghreb since the beginning of the 1990s. The election of Abdelaziz Bouteflika as president of Algeria in 1999, the coronation of Mohammed VI in Morocco the same year, and the lifting of the sanctions imposed on Libya have not served to advance intra-Maghrebi relations.

Security issues have been gaining weight in the regional agenda. The Islamist threat is no longer an element of interference in intra-Maghrebi relations, but rather an issue that is being exploited by the different regimes in the post-9/11 context to diversify their foreign relations by strengthening ties with Washington in the framework of the "war on terror." Distrust and the taboo nature of security cooperation with Western countries have progressively given way to cooperation in different fora, such as NATO's Mediterranean Dialogue and the "5 + 5" dialogue, fuelled by perception of terrorism and illegal immigration as a shared threat. The absence of institutionalized cooperation frameworks in the field of security has contributed to turning these fora into springboards for dialogue among the Maghreb countries, and between these countries and their partners in the North.

The Western Sahara conflict is still the main obstacle to economic integration and regional development. Sixteen years have passed since Morocco and the POLISARIO Front signed their ceasefire; the self-determination referendum has yet to take place, and the conflict remains deadlocked. In the 1990s, Morocco thought it could exploit Algeria's civil war scenario to achieve a favorable solution that would lend international legitimacy to its claims over the territory, on the basis of a political solution revolving around autonomy. Algeria's return to the international arena, coupled with rising oil and gas prices in recent years, makes this country less inclined to offer concessions in terms of its support of the POLISARIO Front and its defense of the application of the self-determination principle as the basis to solving the problem. Since May 2005, Morocco—which had always thought time was on its side—has been faced with a wave of pro-independence protests within the territory under its control. In a bid to secure the support of the US, which is showing increasing security interest in the region, Morocco is now conjuring up the specter of the instability that would be engendered there by the creation of a weak state, providing a platform for terrorist groups and other illegal networks.

Neither the agents of Maghrebi civil society nor the economic operators of the different countries have succeeded in galvanizing the integration process, now at a standstill owing to political differences. The benefits that could be obtained by removing trade barriers within the Maghreb have been estimated at an annual USD 4.6bn. Enhanced regional integration will yield substantial advantages, among which higher growth, lower unemployment, and greater capacity for negotiation with the European Union. All of this looks unlikely until the Western Sahara issue is solved.

Notes

1 Deeb 1989; Mortimer 1989.
2 Cammet 1999.
3 Mortimer 1999, pp. 178–82.
4 Available at: http://www.maghrebarabe.org/fr/index.htm.
5 Herce and Sosvilla-Rivera 2005, p. 1.
6 Barros, Lahlou, Escoffier, Pumares, and Ruspini, 2002; Coslovi 2006.
7 Stora 2003. See also Chapter 11 by Michael J. Willis in this book.
8 Optimists tend to recall the role the European Coal and Steel Community (ECSC) played in the European construction process. Algeria has been exporting

natural gas to Italy since 1983 via the trans-Mediterranean line. It crosses Tunisia, which is paid a transit fee of 900 million cubic meters of natural gas per year. In 1997, Algeria and Italy signed an agreement for the supply of an additional 400 million cubic meters per year until 2019. Algeria is also a member of the Arab Maghreb company for the transport of natural gas, created in Tripoli in 1988, and is presently studying the laying of an inter-Maghreb gas pipeline linking Algeria and Libya via Tunisia. In 1997, Tunisia and Libya signed an agreement to exchange Libyan gas and petrol for Tunisian products worth USD 250m.

9 Information on the Medgaz pipeline project is available at: http://www.medgaz.com/medgaz/index.html.
10 The creation of the AMU was interpreted by the then heir to the Moroccan throne as a response to the internal development of the EU and its expansion (Ben el Hassan Aloui 1994, p. 15).
11 Amirah-Fernández, Youngs 2005.
12 The three central Maghrebi countries have signed Association Agreements with the EU: Tunisia in 1995, in operation since 1998; Morocco in 1996, in operation since 2000, and Algeria in 2002, in operation since September 2005. Libya, under international sanctions, was not invited to join the Euro-Mediterranean Partnership but was given observer status in 1999. Mauritania's relations with the EU are covered by the Lomé Convention. Morocco and Tunisia are members of the World Trade Organization (WTO) and Algeria is presently negotiating its membership.
13 Available at: http://www.euoffice.metu.edu.tr/meda_en.htm.
14 Zoubir 2006b.
15 Eizenstat, S. E. 1999, Third Annual Les Aspin Memorial Lecture, Washington Institute for Near East Policy, Washington DC, 8 March.
16 Crombois 2005, pp. 219–23; White 2005, pp. 597–615.
17 *Tunisia Country Report*. The Economist Intelligence Unit, April 2002, pp. 16–17.
18 "Les enjeux de l'intégration maghrébine," Document de Travail no. 90, Ministère des Finances et de la Privatisation, July 2003. Available at: http://doc.abhatoo.net.ma/doc/IMG/pdf/f4.pdf.
19 The AMU had been concerned with finding ways and means of dealing with the Islamist issue since its creation (Soudan 1990). Some authors uphold the thesis, although exaggerated, that it was the rise of Islamist movements, perceived as a threat, which galvanized the Maghreb leaders into putting aside their differences and creating the AMU in February 1989 (Mezran 1998, pp. 1–34).
20 Zoubir 2004b, p. 158.
21 Algeria and Tunisia, together with Egypt, brought up the issue of Islamic terrorism for the first time at the OIC summit in Karachi in April 1993. Although the lack of consensus precluded the adoption of a resolution, the meeting did approve the creation of a code of conduct for Muslim states regarding terrorism (Visier 1994, pp. 708–9).
22 Faria 1994, pp. 36–7.
23 *Maghreb-Machrek* 142, October–December 1993, p. 83.
24 *Al-Hayat*, 5 June 1996.
25 *Le Monde*, 4–5 September 1994.
26 Zoubir 1999c, p. 201. This is also the stand taken by Abdelhak Layada in a letter sent to the Algerian president, Abdelaziz Bouteflika, in February 2005. *Le Soir d'Algérie*, 13 February 2005. Available at: http://www.algeria-watch.org/fr/article/pol/amnistie/fondateur_gia.htm.
27 Rouadjia 1996, p. 849.
28 Zoubir 2004b, pp. 167–8.
29 Benantar 2006, pp. 167–9. See also the chapter by Cherif Dris in this volume (Chapter 12).

30 Calderbank 2005.

31 The first meeting of heads of state took place in Brussels in November 2004.

32 Echeverría 2005b, pp. 90–1.

33 Coustillière 2005, pp. 76–83.

34 Three months before the embargo was lifted, Libya and Italy—then holding the presidency of the EU—concluded an agreement to control transitory migration between the two countries (Pliez 2004, p. 155); Balfour 2005, pp. 128–9.

35 Bensaad 2005.

36 The idea was discussed at the G5 meeting in Florence in October 2004, and it was endorsed by Britain, Germany, and Italy, but rejected by France and Spain (Echeverría 2005a).

37 Between 26 September and 6 October 2005, some 3,400 sub-Saharans tried to storm the Melilla fences in seven mass attempts, and another 600 tried to storm the Ceuta border fences. Of the roughly 1,000 who were successful, only 70 were sent back to Morocco for repatriation. In the course of these events, 13 immigrants died in conditions that have yet to be clarified. The Spanish government deployed the army to patrol the border perimeters of its two enclaves, while calling for more active collaboration from the Moroccan authorities in the fight against illegal immigration. Morocco transferred the sub-Saharan immigrants south to its border with Western Sahara, where they were separated into groups and abandoned without water and food, according to NGOs. Morocco raised its criticism of Algeria after the UN Mission for the Referendum in Western Sahara (MINURSO) joined the search for these immigrants, and some were rescued by the POLISARIO Front (Hernando de Larramendi, Bravo 2006).

38 *La Vanguardia*, 10 July 2006.

39 *Le Monde*, 11 July 2006.

40 Interview with a Moroccan Foreign Ministry official. Madrid, October 2005.

41 See: http://www.maec.gov.ma/migration/En/participants.htm.

42 *Liberté*, 10 July 2006; *L'Expression*, 8 July 2006.

43 Mohsen-Finan 2005, pp. 116–21.

44 International Crisis Group 2005a, pp. 25–7.

45 "American designs on the Sahel?" *Middle East International*, no. 721, pp. 26–9; *al Watan*, 16 October 2004.

46 *Middle East Economic Digest* 51 (2004), p. 16.

47 Henardt 2005, p. 30.

48 International Crisis Group 2005a, p. 29.

49 In March 2004, General Charles Wald, deputy commander of the US European command, claimed that members of al-Qaeda were trying to establish themselves in the Sahel region and North Africa: "They are looking for sanctuary as they did in Afghanistan when the Taliban were in power. They need a stable place in which to equip themselves, organize, and recruit new members." (Mellah and Rivoire 2005).

50 Smolan 2005.

51 The release of the European tourists after a payment of 5m and the GSPC's links with human and tobacco trafficking in the Sahel region has been met with a great deal of scepticism by most analysts who only see superficial connections between the GSPC and al-Qaeda (Saleh 2004, pp. 19–20).

52 Keenan 2004, p. 479.

53 In 2003, rumors, denied by the US administration, were circulating about the construction of a military base in Tamanrasset, Algeria. *Middle East International*, 19 March 2004, pp. 26–7.

54 The text of the speech is available at: http://www.maec.gov.ma.

55 International Crisis Group 2005b, pp. 11–12.

56 Keenan 2004; International Crisis Group 2005a.

57 Zoubir 2006b.
58 Landor 2005, pp. 21–2.
59 Mortimer 1993.
60 Zoubir and Volman 1993, pp. 227–36.
61 The Settlement Plan provides for the holding of a referendum based on the census of 74,000 voters drawn up by the Spanish colonial authorities in 1974. In July 1991, Morocco presented two additional lists of 76,000 and 45,000 alleged Sahrawis. In September 1991, ten days after the commencement of the ceasefire, 170,000 voting-age individuals entered the territory to be identified by MIN-URSO. This "second Green March" resulted in a revision of the identification criteria agreed upon by the two parties and the proposal by the then UN Secretary-General, Javier Pérez de Cuéllar, resulted in four new eligibility criteria. The Houston Accords of 1997, brokered by the UN Secretary-General's personal envoy, James A. Baker III, paved the way for a resumption of the identification process, which culminated in February 2000, with the publication of a provisional census of 86,425 voters. Morocco subsequently filed some 131,000 appeals, blocking the process once again (Pointier 2004, pp. 135–82).
62 Mohsen-Finan 1997, p. 143.
63 Zoubir 1999c, pp. 198–9.
64 Zoubir 1999c, p. 202.
65 Hernando de Larramendi 1997.
66 The decentralization/regionalization law passed in April 1997, just as negotiations were being reactivated, triggered speculation that Morocco was seriously starting to prepare the ground for autonomy in Western Sahara. A closer examination of this law, however, showed that it was underpinned by Morocco's fear of recognizing conflictive identities both in northern Morocco and in Western Sahara. The disputed territory ended up being splintered into three regions, with its most eastern reaches (Es Smara) being interlocked with the Tarfaya region, which Spain ceded to Morocco in 1958, and populated by the Ait-Ba-Amran confederation of tribes, which Morocco has tried to get MIN-URSO to identify as Sahrawis.
67 Report of the Secretary-General on the situation concerning Western Sahara, S/2000/131, 17 February 2000.
68 Shelley 2004, p. 148.
69 During the transitional period, the Kingdom of Morocco would have exclusive competence over foreign relations, national security and external defense, all matters relating to weapons, and the preservation of the territorial integrity against secessionist attempts. The territory would be run for four years by an Executive elected by voters eligible to vote in the abandoned referendum. The Executive would have competence over local government administration, territorial budget and taxation, law enforcement, internal security, social welfare, culture, education, commerce, transportation, agriculture, mining, fishing, industry, environmental policy, housing, and urban development.
70 *Le Figaro*, 4 September 2001. Available at: http://www.mincom.gov.ma/french/generalites/samajeste/mohammedVI/discours/2001/interview_lefigaro.htm.
71 Gillespie 2006.
72 José María Aznar was the first European head of government to make an official visit to Algeria following the election of Abdelaziz Bouteflika in 1999. The two countries signed a treaty of friendship, cooperation and neighborliness in October 2002, three months after the Moroccan–Spanish crisis over the Mediterranean islet of Perejil, in which Algeria took sides with Spain (Planet, Hernando de Larramendi 2003, pp. 133–40).
73 Pointier 2004, p. 171.
74 S/2003/565.

75 S/2003/565, paragraph 8.
76 The Algerian Prime Minister, Ahmed Ouyahya, joined his Foreign Affairs Minister and Algeria's UN ambassador Abdallah Baali at a meeting with the president of the Sahrawi Arab Democratic Republic (SADR) on 28 June 2003 to convince him to accept Baker Plan II. The POLISARIO Front representative to the UN, Ahmed Boukhari, claims that suggestions from other countries such as Spain, Mexico, and South Africa were also instrumental in causing the SADR to change its position (Boukhari 2004). This about-face did not go down well in the refugee camps. It was not until 12 August that the National Secretariat of the POLISARIO Front, after two days of deliberations, noted with satisfaction the adoption of resolution 1495 (Ruf 2004, p. 139). Baker Plan II was ratified during the XI Congress of the POLISARIO Front held on 12–19 October 2003 in Tifariti (Díaz 2004).
77 S/RES/1495 (2003).
78 The Moroccan Foreign Affairs Minister, Mohamed Benaissa, attributed Baker's resignation to "the tenacity of Moroccan diplomacy and its rejection of certain principles that put its territorial integrity at risk" (*El País*, 14 June 2004). At the end of his mandate, James Baker admitted that Morocco's attitude made it impossible to settle the question. According to him, "the Moroccans have talked about being willing to offer autonomy but they've never been willing to put a proposal on the table. They've simply said that they're willing to negotiate an autonomy arrangement." Interview with Former US Secretary of State, 19 August 2004. Public Broadcasting Service. Available at: http://www.pbs.org/wnet/wideangle/printable/transcript_sahara_print.html.
79 Beaugé, "Sahara Occidental: pour le Maroc, le plan Baker 'n'est plus à l'ordre du jour,'" *Le Monde*, 25 June 2003. The rejection of the self-determination referendum led Morocco's former Interior Minister, Driss Basri, to launch a media offensive in which he claimed that Mohammed VI was misinformed as to what he referred to as Western Sahara rather than Moroccan Sahara. He argued that the only solution was the referendum on self-determination that allows only the population of the Sahara the opportunity to declare itself either in favor of integration with Morocco or in favor of independence. *La Razón*, 5 September 2004; *al-Watan*, 18 November 2004; *al-Khabar*, 7 December 2004.
80 "Reply of the Kingdom of Morocco to Mr. Baker's proposal entitled 'Peace Plan for the Self-Determination of Western Sahara,'" in Report of the Secretary-General on the situation concerning Western Sahara, S/2004/325, Annex I; Bryne, "After Baker," *Middle East International* (2004), no. 728, pp. 23–4.
81 Speech by King Mohammed VI on the occasion of the Throne Day, 30 July 2004.
82 *El País*, 4 July 2005.
83 "Le Maroc comparé à Israel," *Le Journal Hebdomadaire*, 30 October 2004. Available at: http://www.lejournal-hebdo.com/sommaire/archives-d-cryptage2004/le-maroc-compar-isra-l.html. Thabo Mbeki's letter is available at: http://arso.org.site.voila.fr/MBK.htm.
84 "Memorandum of the Kingdom of Morocco on the regional dispute on the Sahara," 24 September 2004, addressed to the UN Secretary-General.
85 "Neighbors Clash," *Middle East International* (2004), no. 736, pp. 23–4.
86 "Rumblings in Western Sahara," *Middle East International* (2004), no. 741, pp. 28–9.
87 Ouzzani, "Une visite pour quoi faire?" *L'Intelligent/Jeune Afrique* (2005), no. 2305, p. 52.
88 Soudan, "La guerre des nerfs," *L'Intelligent*, 12 June 2005.
89 Shelley 2005, pp. 69–76.

90 Fibla, "El Frente POLISARIO califica de 'Intifada' los enfrentamientos que afectan a El Aaiún," *La Vanguardia*, 28 May 2005.
91 Mansur, "Pourquoi tant de haine?" *Maroc Hebdo International* (2005), no. 654, pp. 16–17. Canales, P. "Marruecos culpa a España y a Argelia de estar tras las revueltas saharauis," *La Razón*, 29 May 2005.
92 "Alger et Rabat en reviennent aux procès d'intention," *AFP*, 14 June 2005.
93 *El País*, 31 July 2005.
94 Protests were staged in front of Algerian embassies in Europe and Canada, and US senators and congressmen were lobbied. The Moroccan American Center for Policy sponsored a visit for a delegation of Moroccan former POWs to Washington DC in May 2005. Senator John McCain, a former pilot and ex-POW, promised to urge Congress and the Bush administration to exert pressure on Morocco and the POLISARIO Front.
95 Ghorbal, "Washington prend les choses en mains," *L'Intelligent*, 28 August 2005.
96 Available at: http://www.map.ma/mapfr/corcas/index.htm.
97 Report of the Secretary-General on the situation concerning Western Sahara, S/2006/249, 19 April 2006.
98 Soudan, "Tempête du désert," *Jeune Afrique*, 15 October 2006.
99 Available at: http://www.lejournal-hebdo.com/sommaire/maroc/sahara-la-situation-se-complique.html.
100 S/RES/1720 (2006).
101 Speech by King Mohammed VI on the occasion of the 31st anniversary of the Green March, 6 November 2006. Available at: http://www.maroc.ma/NR/exeres/B81E80AD-A849-4169-AF74-B2303AB7D2F0,frameless.htm?NRMODE=Published.

10 Women in the Maghreb

Stereotypes and Realities

Louisa Dris-Aït-Hamadouche

In recent decades, intellectual interest in women's issues has increased, especially since the "feminist revolution" of the 1960s. Women moved from the traditional positions in which they were restricted (housework, children education, transmission of traditional values, and the preservation of family cohesion) to sectors traditionally occupied by men (media, business, and security forces). Therefore, it became crucial for scholars to survey and to analyze this transformation from sociological and political perspectives.

In the United States, for instance, Margaret Anderson and Mary Crow Dog have examined women from a sociological perspective.[1] Wright Mills has associated "personal troubles" of individual women with "social issues."[2] Globally, the political–sociological perspective allows for better comprehension of the relationship between social structure, culture, religion, media, individual/collective agency on the one hand, and women's position in society with its different components (institutions, political parties, professional sectors, etc.) on the other hand.

As to the Maghrebi literature on this issue, it is not so rich despite the importance of the subject. However, some authors, such as Fatima Mernissi,[3] have gained prominence in dealing with women. Mernissi, who is also a sociologist, focuses on Arab women's rights and denounces their repression. Feriel Lalamai-Fates has also addressed the question; she has studied the phenomenon of violence against women. Kamara Djeynaba, for her part, considers the evolution of the role of women in Mauritanian society, especially in the economic sector. A few other analysts seek to explore this complex subject: Noureddine Saadi, Salima Ait-Mohamed, Keltoum Bendjouadi, Fatima Doukhan, Sakina Mdaoui, Haytham Manna, Imed Melliti, Sihem Najar, Zazi Sadou, and Leila Sebbar. In addition to scholars, a number of associations have taken concrete actions to give intellectual approaches a tangible dimension. Hence, "Positive Actions for Citizenship Rights of Women and Equality in the Maghreb" is a collective initiative that brings together associations, labor and NGOs in Morocco, Algeria, and Tunisia.[4]

Western media, for their part, frequently discuss women in the Muslim world, including North Africa.[5] Usually, the same issues are addressed and recurrent representations are used to describe and explain the situation of women, notably the veil, polygamy, and marriage, with a tendency to highlight abuses and injustices that women confront in their respective societies. Consequently, Western public opinion has developed stereotypes and prejudices which transmit a negative image of Muslim women. The existing perceptions raise important questions regarding the juridical status of women, their political representation and role in economic life, and the influence of religion in society. Comparisons between Western, African, and Arab countries will help to clarify these issues.

Common Regional Factors

The Role of Religion: Between Interpretation and Implementation

In the early Islamic period, women participated in social and political life and enjoyed rights as depicted in the first legal injunction of the Quran protecting females from infanticide (Sura 81:1–14).[6] Khadija, Prophet Mohammed's first wife, was a prominent businesswoman. Zaynab held the coveted position of inspector of social and political life. However, assumptions made about women's status in Islam depend on the interpreter, his/her culture, position as a traditionalist or a modernist, ability to rely on *ijtihad*,[7] and intentions. Certain Moroccan feminist movements call for more modern interpretations of Islamic law, while others maintain a secular approach to women's equality, arguing that women's status should be compatible with international and human rights covenants, and that the constitution should be reformed accordingly.[8] The current legal situation of women in Morocco is ambiguous since it is clearly indicated that this equality is textually *political*, which means that conservative religious scholars can remove the personal status from positive law for whatever does not relate to political rights. Article 8 of the 1992 Constitution states that men and women have equal political rights, but there are no specific references to women's equality in other domains. This ambiguity has allowed for religious authorities to exclude women's personal status from the equation, and to submit it strictly to religious interpretation. This religious interpretation can then take on another dimension, in supporting political ambition and strengthening a dominant status. For instance, Moroccan Islamists have tried to refute their sexist image by nominating Nadia Yassin as the spokesperson for *Al-'Adl wa-l-'Ihsan* (the Movement for Justice and Charity, led by her father, the charismatic Abd al-Salam Yassin). This illegal but tolerated movement calls for the abolition of the monarchy and the introduction of *Shari'a* (Islamic law) in Morocco. Nadia Yassin is viewed as a possible successor to the movement's leadership.[9]

The Moroccan king has proclaimed that he would protect women's rights, within the context of Islam and *Shari'a*. He has attempted to consolidate the middle and upper classes that support his regime, while leading his ideological fight against the Islamist opposition. The monarchy avoids head-on confrontation with Islamists and allows them a certain freedom of expression. The members of the association *Islah wa-tajdid* (Reform and Renewal), for example, have established a political party, and at times the government has even supported the Islamist position. The declarations made at the National Strategy for the Promotion of Moroccan Women in 2000 claim that: "free expression of female identity is anti-Islamic," that it is necessary "to challenge the foreign and imported image of women and treat this image according to a modernist Islamic version," and that to "reinforce awareness it is not necessary to adopt ways of life and behavior known in other societies where the values and aspirations differ from those of an Arab-Muslim society like Morocco."

Although expressed in an unusual way, the instrumentalization of religion also exists. As in Iran, Tunisian women are not free to dress as they wish. As in France, women wearing head scarves in Tunisia cannot occupy certain positions within the public administration, universities, and in the government.[10] The common point of these two different situations is the *hijab* (veil).[11] The Tunisian government launched a hostile campaign against the wearing of the *hijab*; the authorities use very harsh terms to criticize and condemn it. On the one hand, intellectuals and politicians have strongly criticized what is logically considered as a repressive measure against Iranian women (the obligation of wearing the headscarf).[12] On the other hand, many people have asserted that the Muslim community in France is a minority and must thus respect the laws of the state they live in (restrictions on wearing the headscarf). However, few, including human rights advocates, have disapproved of the Tunisian government's decision to forbid Muslims to exercise their faith freely in their own country. Have ignorance, impunity, and political manipulations in Tunisia eliminated the obvious difference between a religions action (wearing the headscarf) and a political one (militant engagement in an Islamist party)? Is the fear of Islamism wrongly assimilated to fundamentalism and terrorism stronger than universal principles for which democrats fight? The importance of external political considerations seems obvious if we observe that the same issue is differently evaluated in Turkey, where the media have widely reported the conflict between the Kemalist ideology (secularization/Westernization) and the opposition. In October 1998, four million protesters demonstrated in various Turkish cities in support of female students who had been suspended from their universities for refusing to remove their *hijab*. A wild campaign then denounced the police, who attacked thousands of demonstrators for participating in the protests staged at night.[13] According to some analysts, European critics of Turkey were and still are motivated less by the protection of women's right (wearing *hijab*) than by their opposition to Turkey's adhesion to the European Union.

Surprisingly, Morocco may be following in Tunisia's footsteps. Indeed, the government has made major changes to religious education, in particular regarding whether young girls should wear headscarves. A picture of a mother and her daughter wearing headscarves is being removed from the latest editions of a textbook. A verse from the Quran that requires women to wear veils has already been taken out of the books. Obviously, these measures are about politics. As in Tunisia, education ministry official Aboulkacem Samir says "the headscarf for women is a political symbol, in the same way as the beard is for men. But we in the ministry must be very careful that the books are fair to all Moroccans and do not represent just one political faction."[14] In Tunisia, Morocco, and Turkey, decision makers seem to ignore that the Algerian experience showed that the Islamist tendency is deeper than the appearance of dress. In 1990 and 1991, many young women wearing short skirts and tight jeans, and young men with long hair and piercings, voted in favor of the FIS, while many "*hijabiyat*" (women wearing headscarves) and bearded men were never attracted by Islamist parties because they refused to equate politics with religion.

Confronted with the instruments of religion, the women's movement has adopted a dual strategy. The first strategy consists of justifying the emancipation of women by examining the Quran and other sacred texts from a historical point of view. This approach has allowed them to contradict the non-historical approach of Islamist and traditionalist groups that impose a rigid and static interpretation. The second strategy calls for a progressive approach, based on a universal philosophy regarding individual rights. However, Islamists reject this universalism, considered as an indication of Westernization. Neither the first nor the second approach has successfully avoided opposition from either the government or the Islamists. Moroccan women's mobilization, particularly in 1992, was strongly condemned by Islamist organizations, which argued that questioning the *Shari'a* was not only a Western conspiracy against Islam, but also a crime punishable by death. The government adopted the same position through the official, conservative Council of Ulema. Religious leaders also rejected women's interference in religion. Finally, some experts think that the issue of women in the Arab world has become a bargaining chip to satisfy Islamists while limiting their influence.

The same process occurred in Libya. During the liberalization period of the late 1980s, Colonel Muammar Qaddafi publicly called for the reform of women's rights and ended measures such as the obligation for women to leave the house wearing a *hijab* and accompanied by a male relative. However, in the mid-1990s, when confronted with the Islamic threat, the Qaddafi government gave up attempts to ameliorate the rights of women, thus allowing Islam to claim a larger role in the law. The Socialist State party introduced revolutionary measures for the emancipation of women, but also emphasized the role of women as mothers and housewives, and has thus reinforced cultural resistance to substantial change.[15] To a large extent, this resembles the position the Algerian and Moroccan governments took, that is, the attempt to pre-empt rather than counter the Islamic opposition.

The potential for the negative impact of religious interpretations exists beyond the borders of the Maghreb and is openly criticized in Western countries with significant Muslim communities. In France, the media denounced the marked rise in violent crimes against women. Groups of young men impose their control and justify their aggressive behavior toward women in the name of religion. Consequently, many women only feel safe when they wear the *hijab*. Moreover, at least 70,000 young women have been pressured into accepting arranged marriages, according to France's Commission for Integration.[16]

Between Tradition and Cultural Changes

Resistance to improving the status of women is prevalent in the Arab world. There is a tendency to revert to the "roots and identity" of a nation, while there is a high level of suspicion towards any foreign influences, such as Western-modeled human development programs.[17]

What is the role of women in Maghrebi societies? One could say that women are like the pillars of a house: indispensable yet invisible. The woman is present in all daily tasks, doing the housework, supervising the children's education, working in the fields, and ensuring basic survival. However, as a pillar, the woman remains hidden. Decisions regarding the common interest are made in special meetings attended only by men. During difficult periods, North African men would emigrate alone, leaving the fate of their wives and children to family rules.

According to Mauritanian traditions, for example, women are required to work hard, be docile and submissive to the family, and to be patient and available for familial duties. In the past, a woman did not have the right to be educated or make decisions regarding marriage.[18] In Algeria, paradoxes and contradictions abound, especially among the Kabyles, who are known for their political militancy and their openness to political and economic matters. These characteristics are, in part, a direct cause of frequent travel and immigration both inside the country and abroad. However, despite this apparent openness, the Kabyles are also known for their extreme social conservatism. According to tradition, women do not even have the right to paternal inheritance. The reason for this is simple: a woman is the responsibility of her father, then her husband, and, subsequently, her sons. In other words, throughout her life a woman is always to be looked after by a male guardian.

However, Maghrebi societies are not unchanging and cultural progress has occurred, influencing behaviors as well as mentalities. An opinion poll conducted in November 2000[19] showed that 60 percent of men and 80 percent of women reject polygamy; 80 percent of the people questioned would like women to have the same right to divorce as men; 98 percent of Algerians want women to look after the children in the conjugal home; and 82 percent approve of parents sharing responsibility. This intellectual shift has had concrete effects on the lives of Maghrebi women, who are now having fewer children than in the past. Since the end of the 1990s, the total fertility rate (in the number of births per woman) has fallen from 7.5 to 2, more closely resembling the current birth rate in Europe.[20] Mauritania is an exception. Since 2000, the fertility rate has decreased: 6.22 percent in 2001; 6.15 percent in 2002; 6.08 percent in 2003; 6.01 percent in 2004; 5.94 percent in 2005; and 5.86 percent in 2006.[21]

The rising use of contraceptives has played a large role in influencing the birth rate in the Maghreb. The rate of women who use contraceptives in Tunisia increased from 5 percent in the 1960s to 60 percent in the mid-1990s; in Algeria it has increased from 8 percent in 1970 to 62 percent in 2001; and in Morocco it has increased from 5 percent to 59 percent since the end of 1960s.[22] The age of marriage rose considerably, a phenomenon which contributed to the drop in the fertility rate. In Tunisia, the age of marriage increased from 18 years in 1966 to 28 in 2001; in Morocco, from 16 years in 1960 to 26 in 1995; in Algeria, from 18 years in 1966 to 28 in 1998. More than 50 percent of Tunisian women between the ages of 25 and 29 were not married in 2001. Algeria and Morocco show the same trend.[23] The statistics show that the more women are educated, the more they postpone marriage in order to develop their careers and reach a level of financial security.[24] This tendency began in Tunisia and was followed by Algeria and later Morocco. Mauritania follows a similar trend, and the women are gaining more freedom, due to education. Eighty percent of young girls receive an education. Most of the women in southern Mauritania are farmers whose products are either sold or used for family consumption. However, a new phenomenon of female cooperatives has emerged. The Mauritanian government is giving more opportunities to women in the economic sector for insertion and reinsertion in the work force, but many black Mauritanian urban women still sell their products in the market place.

The contradiction between local tradition, religious values, and changing culture is not limited to Maghrebi societies, as the WLUML (Women Living under Muslim Laws)[25] has indicated, but extends to many regions around the world, as illustrated by the growth of the organization itself. The WLUML is an international solidarity network of individuals and organizations that provides information, support, and a collective space for women who live under Islamic laws or who are concerned by religiously derived customs. The WLUML was formed in 1984 by nine women from the Maghreb (Algeria, Morocco, and Mauritania), Africa (Sudan, Tanzania), and Asia (Iran, Bangladesh, and Pakistan). It now includes more than 70 countries from South Africa to Uzbekistan, and Senegal to France. It links women living in secular states, in countries where Islam is the state religion, and in countries where some groups call for the application of religious laws. It also includes women in immigrant Muslim communities and women married to Muslims. The organization deals with important issues, such as the impact of fundamentalism and militarization on the lives of women, violence against women, and discrimination. The WLUML puts women in direct contact with each other to facilitate a non-hierarchical exchange of information, expertise, strategies, and experience.

The Colonial Legacy

Despite different political aims to reduce the influence of the former colonial power, France's cultural influence persists in the Maghreb, particularly in those countries that were under French domination. France invaded Algeria in 1830, and established protectorates in Tunisia in 1881 and in Morocco in 1912. Furthermore, the presence in France of a large Maghrebi community which has maintained strong relations with the native countries reinforces this French influence. Economic immigration, coupled with French cultural policy, has created francophone Maghrebi elites. Using the same language, however, does not mean adhering to the same policies or cultural values. After the independence of Morocco (1956), Tunisia (1956), and Algeria (1962), the emerging ruling class was heavily influenced by French culture; however, some members within that class, especially in Algeria, strongly believed that French influence should be eradicated in their newly independent nations.

The unanimity imposed by authoritarian regimes is far from consensual; disparity emerged at high political levels as well as among civil society. Schematically, the reform of the status of women was included in the "progressive discourse" of the francophone elite, while Arabic speakers defended their traditions using a more "conservative discourse." The issue regarding women's status therefore became part of an ideological rather than a social battle. Supporters of the "progressive discourse" were accused of belonging to the former enemy and of being the "illegitimate children" of colonization, using language from the era of independence to do what the traitors failed to do with arms during the war. Supporters of the "conservative discourse" were described as extremists, reactionaries, and heirs of a past and close-minded era, thus refusing progress and science in the name of religion. According to the Moroccan sociologist Zakya Daoud, this radical polarization is the direct consequence of the "confiscation of historical initiative."[26] Unlike Western countries, the Arab-Islamic world was not allowed to mature, due to colonization, which interrupted its natural development. Western society in the Maghreb did not allow for mutual exchanges or influences, but instead was an imposed culture. The reaction of many Maghrebis was to turn inwards, developing strong loyalty to their own "traditional" and "authentic" culture.

Maghrebi women are victims of this polarization not only inside the Maghreb, but also in France, where it has become a complex social problem in the last few years. The various shaping elements make the issue complex. In French suburbs, economic as well as political and social problems have erupted. One of the best illustrations of this situation is the creation and the subsequent success of the movement *Ni putes ni soumises* (Neither whores, nor submissive), which strongly expresses the vicious circle in which young women find themselves. This dilemma highlights the conflict that stems from their double culture: the inherited and the acquired. Women are among second- or even third-generation immigrants who often have had no concrete contact with their ancestral country except through oral tradition. One language is spoken at home, while another is spoken both in the street and at school, where a biased version of history continues to be taught. After decades of confrontation between the private and public spheres, however, a reaction occurred, resulting in the incorporation of the private sphere into the public one. Young people, for example, have started to introduce Arabic words into their daily French language, to pray at mosques, and to change their style of dress, such as women wearing the veil. This change in particular has put women in an uncomfortable position. Perceived as the guardians of tradition, family, and morality, women were the first targets of a reversion towards original identity, which has indirectly renewed the notion of "submission." In this complex situation, rejecting submission would mean living as the French, dressing like them, going out, and claiming independence from their families at an earlier age. This behavior would subsequently label them as depraved. There have been several cases of brutality against young women, with tragic ends in the most serious situations.

The second level of the public conflict relates to economic and political issues. Unlike suburbs in US cities, French *banlieux* are synonymous with lower classes, where school dropouts, unemployment, drug dependency, delinquency, and criminality are present. As a result, strong laws have been adopted in an attempt to manage the "difficult districts," imposing rules such as the prohibition on congregating in front of a building's entrance. One should note that 80 percent of the suburbs' inhabitants are of rural origin, coming either from France or from its former colonies, such as the Maghreb, Senegal, and Mali.[27] According to experts, these suburbs have become cities within a city; they are excluded from national life. Unemployment has reached 75 percent in comparison to 25 percent in other districts. Violence in the suburbs has increased from 4 percent of global delinquency to 22 percent between 1950 and 2000.[28] Some statistics show that there are 132 "forbidden cities" in France, i.e., suburbs where state authorities and the police cannot enter. There are 55 such suburbs around Paris and eight around Lyon.[29] In 2005, France's suburbs drew attention to their unsettled history. Never before had this country known such urban violence and widespread clashes.[30] The authorities declared a state of emergency on 8 November 2005, before the situation returned to normal nine days later. Almost 3,000 people were arrested, and 9,000 vehicles destroyed, which represent damage estimated at 200m euros. One year later, some violent but sporadic action took place, to remind policy makers that poverty, discrimination, and the increasingly militaristic methods used by the police remain a reality. In addition to these repressive measures, the right-wing government has borrowed tactics from the far right, using its popular slogans and themes regarding security, immigration, national identity, and secularism (*laïcité*). This influence was seen in the first round of the presidential elections in May 2001, when the National Front of Jean-Marie Le Pen won a historic victory; the party did very badly in the presidential election of May 2007, and even worse in the legislative election a month later. The political situation has merely exacerbated the issues surrounding immigration.

The French perception and application of secularism is built on one basic idea: religious practice must be restricted to the private sphere. In other words, the public sphere, comprising administration, hospitals, and schools, is "neutral," in that it does not take any stance whatsoever, but instead it is firmly opposed to the presence of any religious sign or symbol.[31] The "veil affair" and the more recent "cafeteria affair"[32] exacerbated the feeling of unfair discrimination against Muslims.

Maghrebi societies are widely influenced by the European way of life, and the current generation of Maghrebi women is divided by the duality of cultures. Since the end of the 1980s, Western television has shown what life is like on the other side of the Mediterranean and has influenced and attracted many young people. Changes observed in consumerism, for example, provide undeniable evidence of Western influence. However, the trend towards a more conservative way of life is also quite appealing, and it stems from the idea that Western colonization has sown seeds of immorality and heresy. According to traditionalists, the solution to this conflict can be achieved either through returning society to the pre-colonial era or by emulating traditional Eastern Arab societies. This provides one reason why many women are more attracted to Arab television broadcasts from the Gulf or the Middle East, guaranteeing more "culturally [politically] correct" programs. In order to put an end to these contradictions in the lives of women, Ghita Al-Khayat, a Moroccan psychologist, suggests that with the elimination of colonization's influence "Maghrebi women must reinvent a new way of living as Muslims."[33] She uses the example of many women embracing an active and more aggressive form of Islam. Although they are submissive to male authority within the confines of religious values and reject Western feminism, women take part in almost all areas of societal activities. They work and practice politics wearing religious clothes. Generally, Islamist parties are known for having important and active women's sections within their organizations.

National Particularities

The Status of Women in Law: Comparing Family Codes

Personal status is ruled through a legal framework known as the *mudawwana* in Morocco, the Family Code in Algeria, and the Code of Personal

Status in Tunisia, Mauritania, and Libya. Morocco, Algeria, and Tunisia base their laws on Islamic jurisprudence of the *Maliki* rite and on the French legal system. Tunisia was undoubtedly avant-garde with a code that was ratified in 1956, the year of its independence from France. This code introduced reforms that were more progressive than the laws of many contemporary Western countries. The Moroccan *mudawwana*, endorsed in 1958, reinstated many principles of Islamic law and reinforced the traditional Moroccan patriarchal order. Its stipulations, such as the duty of a woman to be obedient to her husband or the need to acquire the husband's authorization in order to work, restricted the ability of women to exercise their rights as citizens. In 2003, the *mudawwana* was reformed by raising the minimum age of marriage for women from 15 to 18; establishing the right to divorce by mutual consent; placing polygamy and repudiation (unilateral divorce by the husband) under strict judicial control; making family the joint responsibility of both spouses; rescinding the wife's duty of obedience to her husband; and eliminating the requirement of a marital tutor (*wali*) for women before they could marry. However, according to the revised text, judges are still allowed to use religious principles and the most conservative religious interpretations in the numerous matters not covered in the text. The new law also assigns judges the role of overseeing mandatory reconciliation in divorce cases. Women's organizations argue that judges will prioritize reconciliation, in the interest of "family harmony," over the application of the reforms.[34]

In Algeria, the Family Code of 1984 was very restrictive for women, especially divorced women. For instance, women were denied access to the conjugal house regardless of whether they had custody of their children; the father had sole parental authority. Repudiation and divorce were easy for men to initiate; however, women were not granted the same rights. In Mauritania, statistics at the end of the 1990s showed a significant increase in cases of divorce (32 percent in 1995), which were almost exclusively initiated by men.[35] The divorce rate in the region is high, especially among older couples: 64.5 percent of marriages celebrated 30 years prior have been dissolved, and 18.7 percent of marriages of less than five years have been dissolved.[36] The divorce rate is higher in the Moorish communities and relatively low in the black communities. Statistics show that cases of divorce are more numerous when polygamy is rare.

As part of democratization and the fight against radical Islamism in the last few years, Maghrebi governments have reformed their legislation and introduced some positive changes, improving the status of women. Libya made some remarkable progress: admitting women into the judicial system and the armed forces; creating a center for women's studies; fixing a minimum age for marriage for both genders and restricting polygamy; correcting school books; setting up a department of women's affairs and supporting women's non-governmental organizations.[37] Regardless, the image of women in the media still needs to be improved. Similar to the Libyan government, the Mauritanian government launched a global campaign to promote women's status through political and legal measures. In 1992, the authorities created a Secretary of State for the woman's condition and in 1995 and 2002 elaborated on a national strategy for the promotion of women. In 2002, the National Assembly adopted a law imposing education for all children between the ages of 6 and 14, and ratified some international laws relating to children. After a long social debate, the government reformed the personal status code in 2001, making some important changes. For instance, a judge presiding over a divorce case must attempt to reconcile the couple before making the divorce legal (Article 83). Like its neighbors, the Algerian government has finally proceeded with the long debate concerning the conservative, discriminatory family code. Although the results did not meet the expectations of reformists, the 2005 new text includes some important revisions. For example, it sets conditions on the practice of polygamy, obliges the father to pay a pension to his ex-wife and children, guarantees a house for a mother with custody of her children, and recognizes the mother as a parental authority.

The Role of Women in Economic Life

A higher economic status is often considered to be the solution to the empowerment of women. This perception is based on the principle that modernization, development, knowledge, and welfare are interconnected and interdependent. Yet, women suffer most in countries with the highest per capita income.[38] Studies, however, show that the improvement of women's economic status is not dependent on wealth and high per capita income, but rather on development. In Algeria, the situation is improving. According to the National Economic and Social Council (CNES),[39] in 2004, 90.9 percent of girls between the ages of 6 and 15 were educated, compared to only 36.9 percent in 1966 and 80.7 percent in 1998. The gap between educated girls and boys decreased from 20 percent in 1966 to 3.6 percent in 2002. In 2004, 65 percent of baccalaureate graduates were girls, 10 percent more than in 1997. This trend has persisted at the university level, where, in 2007, two thirds of students are girls as compared to only 39.5 percent in 1991. Only 35 percent of Algerian women were illiterate in 2002, an improvement from the 85 percent in 1966. However, the UNDP 2005 *Arab Human Development Report (AHDR)* puts the rate of illiteracy among Algerian women at 60.1 percent,[40] a figure that seems too high.

Compared to the relatively high level of education in Algeria, Mauritania is improving slowly both in girls' education and in reducing disparity between the education of girls and boys. In 2000, girls constituted 48 percent of educated children, representing 82.2 percent of the total number of girls, versus 86.2 percent of boys. The gap between educated girls and boys is decreasing; in 1988, only 31 percent of Mauritanian women were literate and only 47 percent of men. In 2000, the literacy rate increased to 52 percent of

Table 10.1 Comparing Personal Status in the Maghreb

Country Year	Morocco (2003)	Algeria (2005)	Tunisia (1956)	Libya (–)	Mauritania (2001)
Guardianship	Banned	Maintained	Non-existent	Existent	–
Marriage age	18	18	17 women 20 men	17	18
Polygamy	Maintained with legal recognition and agreement of first wife	Maintained with legal recognition and agreement of first wife	Forbidden	Maintained with legal recognition and agreement of first wife	Maintained with agreement of first wife
Repudiation	Maintained with legal recognition	Maintained	Forbidden	Banned	Cancelled
Property	Separate	Separate	Separate	Separate	Separate
Divorce	Couple	Couple	Couple	Couple	Judge
Parental responsibility	Couple	Couple	Couple	–	–
Child custody	Mother with home and pension	Mother with home and pension	Mother with home and pension	Father	Pension

Note: Elaborated by the author from numerous sources quoted in the text and notes.

women and 63 percent of men.[41] In Morocco, female adult illiteracy remains high at 42 percent (38.3 percent according to the *AHDR*).[42] In Libya, the government provides free health-care and education to all Libyan citizens.[43] The World Bank estimated that nearly 100 percent of all boys and girls were enrolled in primary education in 1998, which shows significant progress. In 2002, adult female illiteracy had fallen to 29 percent from 35 percent in 1998, though it continues to exceed the 10 percent of illiterate men.[44] Moroccan female adult illiteracy is 64 percent, compared to 38 percent of males. In rural areas, it may be as high as 90 percent. Primary school enrollment is 86 percent of boys and 67 percent of girls.[45] Globally, the rate of illiteracy in Morocco decreased from 48 percent in 1998 to 43 percent in the period 2004–5.[46]

Education and Employment

Regardless of the increase in education, women continue to be underrepresented in the labor market, representing a meager 14 percent of workers. Although this figure is low, it has more than doubled since 1987, when women constituted only 6 percent of the labor force. Women are well represented with 45 percent in the public sector, and with 80 percent in education and medicine. In comparison, the participation of women in the economy is much higher in Mauritania (39.9 percent), and in Egypt (22.1 percent).[47] In Algeria, unemployment among women has increased by 11 percent between 1977 and 2003, and, according to the *AHDR 2005*, women's activity constitutes 31.6 percent of all economic activity (against 37.7 percent in Tunisia).[48] Female workers are urban at 70.35 percent, single at 58.26 percent, and married at 33 percent, which demonstrates that marriage is no longer an impediment to women being employed.[49] In order to increase the representation of women workers, Algerian legislation made a special provision in 2005 to protect women in the workforce. The act also ensures equality in wages and salary by specifying that men and women shall receive equal pay for equal levels of qualification and performance.[50] Tunisia has applied several measures to facilitate women's participation in the workforce; maternity leave policies and employment protection for mothers were established in 1966. The government has also sought to incorporate gender models in development planning.

Libyan men and women are guaranteed equality under the law, but due to the lack of application and control, there is continued gender inequality. Consequently, substantial discrimination continues to exist in the workplace, where women constitute less than 25 percent of the labor force.[51] There are also generational differences among Libyan women. For instance, women born before the 1969 revolution tend to stay at home and have a markedly lower level of education than the younger generations. Women under the age of 35 are more likely to receive public education and to participate in the public sphere. Moroccan women constituted more than one-third of the workforce in 2000 and 41.9 percent in 2003. Thirty percent of doctors and 25 percent of university professors in Morocco are women.[52] Women are well represented in agriculture, manufacturing, and employment performed at home.[53] Almost 50 percent of active women in urban areas work in the industrial sector, mainly in the textile industry, but the majority of them do contract work at home. Women workers in this industry do not belong to a labor union, they are between the ages of 12 and 32, single, and without social security. The working conditions are disconcerting: 50 percent receive the same salary for day or night work, 64 percent have no accident insurance, 30 percent of the women complained of being insulted by supervisors or employers, and 7 percent said they had been victims of physical abuse.[54] Women in Tunisia represent 31 percent of the total active workforce and hold 36 percent of the jobs traditionally reserved for women, such as the education and health sectors. It is estimated that 1,500 women hold senior positions in businesses,[55] while earned income is $3,840, more than Algerian women with $2,896, or Moroccan women with $2,299.[56] In Mauritania, only 25.4 percent of women in the country are classified as being employed, but many are active in unpaid and unofficial employment, as well as in agriculture,[57] where they hold 35 percent of the jobs in that sector. Although women generally do not own land or livestock, they are involved in all phases of the agricultural cycle, including planting, weeding, the protection and maintenance of fields, harvesting, conserving, storing, processing, and marketing the produce. Women play an important role in the processing and marketing of fish and fish products. All these tasks do not lighten the burden of traditional chores, such as household tasks, cooking, fetching water, and collecting wood.

The increased migration of males to the cities has augmented women's workload. Nevertheless, the men of the family are the major decision makers regarding land transfer and agricultural investments. They usually make decisions concerning the work for which they are responsible as well as their own income. This paradox between education and work is not surprising. According to the *AHDR 2003* survey, Arabs believe that education is as important for a boy as it is for a girl, but also think that a man has more right to a job than a woman. There is a cultural explanation to this way of thinking: in Arab societies, man alone must provide for his family. The wife has the right to keep her income and no one can oblige her to take part in household expenditures. This seems to be a new trend in North Africa, but also in the Middle East and in the conservative Gulf region, which has witnessed noticeable progress.[58]

The Role of Women in Politics

In modern times, the conservative Moroccan monarchy, the authoritarian Tunisian republic, and the conservative Libyan revolution have all allowed little space for women to enter politics. Was the progressive Algerian revolution

Table 10.2 Classification of Working and Educated Women

Country	Education (%)	Workforce (%)	Maternal mortality[59] (%)
Morocco	100	40	0.23
Algeria	91	14	0.22
Tunisia	99	31	0.07
Libya	100	22	0.08
Mauritania	82	25	–

Note: Elaborated by the author from numerous sources quoted in the text and notes.

different? Aside from women's role in the historical societies of North Africa, Algerian women participated in the war for independence from beginning to end. They acted as nurses, cooks, guides, and fighters. They confirm that revolutionary movements do not necessarily lead to revolutionary changes of mentality. This was seen not only in Algeria, but also in Europe (France and the UK) and in the United States. The Algerian war of liberation caused great disappointment with regard to the status of women. The Tripoli Congress in June 1962, just a month before independence, briefly recognized the existence of a "non egalitarian mentality about the role of women" and underlined the necessity of changing mentalities.[60] However, the fighters did not push for reform, thus compelling the *mujahidat* (women fighters) refugees in Tunisia to go on hunger strike to obtain the right to study and go out. The first national assembly had only two women.

Governmental Measures

Similar to the issue concerning the personal status of women, the need for democracy and the struggle against the Islamic threat have compelled governments to launch initiatives for progress for women. In Algeria, President Abdelaziz Bouteflika appointed the first female provincial governor and the first two female presiding judges. The number of female examining judges increased in August 2001 from 15 to 137 out of a total of 404 judges. It should be pointed out that if women represent fewer than 15 percent of the Arab judges, they represent 50 percent in Algeria (and in Morocco), against 22.5 percent in Tunisia.[61]

The 2002 legislative elections increased the number of female members of the Popular National Assembly from 13 to 25 of 389 total members (6.2 percent of the MPs and 7.2 percent of the functions linked to the Executive).[62] Both prime ministers Ali Benflis and Ahmed Ouyahia included five women ministers and secretaries of state in their respective governments.[63] Furthermore, the Vice Presidency of the National Council is held by a woman, Zahra Drif Bitat, who was active in the Algerian resistance against the French. The second Vice President of the House of Representatives is also a woman, Fatma Al-Kihel. All of the major political parties, including Islamist parties, also have women's divisions.

As a part of political reforms in Morocco, and prior to the September 2002 legislative elections, King Muhammed VI reserved 30 seats from the 325-seat House of Representatives for women. Every major political party provided female candidates. As a result, in 2006, there were 34 women in the legislature, making Morocco one of the few Arab nations where women make up 10 percent of the parliament. Women in the government at the ministerial level represent 5.9 percent (two ministers) of the total number of positions. The government has also set quotas for the election (30 out of 325 seats reserved for women). Explaining his decision, the king remarked that because women make up 50 percent of the population, they ought to have similar representation in the legislature. Muhammed VI has appointed three women to senior positions since coming to power, including a royal female advisor. He also appointed in November 2002 a new cabinet of 37 ministers, of whom three were women.[64] In 2003, the Secretary of the House of Representatives was a woman, Milouda Hazib, from the Democrat Constitutional Group.

In the late 1970s and early 1980s, Libyan women were mobilized in the military and in the revolutionary councils. The government established a Department of Women's Affairs as part of the secretariat for the General People's Congress, the national legislative institution. Overseen by an Assistant Secretary of the General People's Committee, the department collects information and controls the integration of women into all spheres of public life. The government also established the General Union of Women's Associations as a network of "non-governmental" organizations that address women's employment needs. Obviously, there still remains a strong governmental control over the issue. One of the few women to be appointed to a high political position is Salma Ahmed Rashid. Between 1992 and 1994, she was Assistant Secretary for Women and then Secretary in the General Secretariat of the General People's Congress for Women's Affairs (Deputy Chief of Government). In 1996, she was the first woman ambassador to the League of Arab States.

In Tunisia, the undeniably weak representation of women in politics is surprising; only 3 percent of the ministerial positions are held by women. The government tried to address this deficiency in representation by creating a number of governmental bodies to deal specifically with women's issues. These national institutions include the Ministry of Women and Family Affairs, the National Women's and Development Commission, and the National Council of Women and the Family. In the 1999 parliamentary elections, women won 21 of the total 182 seats. However, in 2006, the Tunisian Parliament boasted the highest percentage of women members in the Arab world. The percentage of Tunisian female members of Parliament, 11.5 percent, is in fact considered quite high by any international standards. It is a long way from the 1.8 percent of 1966. The ratio of elected women is even higher in local councils. More than one fifth (21.6 percent) of the members of the country's municipal councils are women. The ruling Democratic Constitutional Rally (RCD) has used its great influence to encourage the candidacy and the election of women to public office. The presence of women in the leadership bodies of the party is substantial; 22 percent of the members of the RCD's central committee are women.

Women have a higher level of representation at the local level, where 17 percent of municipal council members are women, and the second Vice President of the National Assembly was Chadlia Boukchina. In September 2006, the appointment of Naziha Zarrouk as Tunisia's new ambassador to Lebanon illustrates the increasing role of Tunisian women in diplomacy.[65] A former cabinet member, Zarrouk joined other women ambassadors who represent Tunisia in France, the Netherlands, and Norway. Another first in Tunisia's diplomatic establishment is the nomination of Saida Chtioui as secretary of state (junior minister) to the ministry of Foreign Affairs. Chtioui, a former ambassador to Switzerland, became one of six women cabinet members. Prior to the reshuffle, there were only four women cabinet members.

Feminist Militancy: Between Political Parties and the Government

Rights are never given; they are wrested, through different means. The Moroccan political parties generally refuse to engage in such sensitive conflicts. The "democratic" coalition called *Kutla*[66] refuses to promote women's political issues because it would pose a threat to the already fragile political consensus. The opposition, including the left-wing parties, is not willing to defend women's rights, not only because it would present a challenge to official religious discourse (the monarchy), but also because promoting women's rights would lead to a loss of power and legitimacy.[67] Furthermore, the issue of women's status is perceived as merely an extravagant demand from the upper-middle class of urban feminists; the issue is in fact far removed from the preoccupations of the overwhelming majority of rural women.

Women's associations have decided to change their strategy in an attempt to stop the marginalization of their issues inside political parties. Since the 1980s, they have distanced themselves from parties and trade unions in order to work through independent structures that are separate from the political system. Instead of re-examining their own stance, the political parties considered this change in strategy to signify a withdrawal of the issue from central political concerns. Subsequently, the issue was nearly erased from all political agendas. For instance, all political parties, without exception, neglected an initiative by the UAF (Union for Women Action) to reform the *mudawwana* in 1992.[68] The Istiqlal party, the USFP (Socialist Union of Popular Forces), and even the PPS (Party of Progress and Socialism, formerly the Moroccan Communist Party) actively opposed women on the *mudawwana* issue. By acting independently, the UAF obtained few results.[69] This disengagement, however, from the political sphere is not absolute and the women's movement is still ideologically tied to the Left. The feminist associations originating from political parties include the Democratic Association of Moroccan Women, the Union for Women's Actions, the Association 95 Maghreb for Equality, and the Moroccan Association for Women's Rights. These feminist organizations give priority to actions related to gender discrimination, such as inequality with regards to civil rights, violence against women, and sexual harassment. Traditionally limited to the private sphere and to specialists in theology, the main goal is to open a debate to the whole of society, as well as to introduce a long-term vision. These associations question the Personal Status code and civil rights as inscribed in the Constitution.

In Tunisia, women are represented in politics by a number of civil society groups that are more or less dependent on the government, although they remain outside of government institutions. The largest one is the National Union of Tunisian Women (UNFT), a nationwide organization that leads the national education campaign for women. The Tunisian Association of Women Democrats is active in debating and publicizing women's issues. One of the leading research centers on women in the Arab region, the Center for Studies, Research, Documentation, and Information on Women (CREDIF), is based in Tunisia. However, due to its authoritarian nature, the regime has denied representation of several women's organizations. Tunisia has stood out from its neighbors with respect to women serving in the military. As a step designed to enhance gender equality, the Ministry of Defense announced on 26 December 2002 that military service would become mandatory for Tunisian women. During the past few years some parliamentarians, including female members, have also called for mandatory military service for Tunisian women.[70] The Minister of Defense declared that women's recruitment would be gradually enforced. The professionalization of the army may push the rest of the Maghrebi countries to follow the Tunisian model. As for Algeria, the civil unrest of the 1990s created new conditions in which women now feel directly involved, especially regarding the consequences of terrorism, and anti-terrorism policy. Hence, Cherifa Kheddar became the leader of *Djazaïrouna* (Our Algeria), an association of victims of terrorism. Nacera Dutour leads an association that works for those who disappeared at the hands of the state or its agents. Both women are opposed to the national reconciliation policy that guarantees amnesty for abuses committed by security forces as well as to members of armed groups who surrendered and allegedly did not commit collective massacres.

Female militancy is also present in the Islamist movement. Islamist political parties do not subscribe to the same discourse on the place of women in society. For Ali Benhadj,[71] the number two leader of the FIS, most of the economic, social, and cultural problems of Algerian society are due to the fact that women no longer stay at home.[72] For Rachid Ghannouchi, exiled leader of Tunisia's Al-Nahda, development and defense against enemies are impossible if half of society is restricted to children's education, clothing, and food businesses. The Algerian MSP (Movement for a Peaceful Society) has a very active women's section inside the party and through the numerous non-political associations that the party controls. Three women from the MSP were elected to the National Assembly and one of them does not wear the veil. In Morocco, the Party of Justice and Development (PJD) has often displayed its feminine force. In March 2000, the party organized a big demonstration in Casablanca, with impressive women's participation, to denounce the reforms of the Abderrahman Youssoufi government, especially with respect to the status of women. In Tunisia, the semi-governmental opposition to Islamists includes female militancy. Nadia Selini (contributing author to the 2005 *Arab Human Development Report*) declared that Islamism was an obstacle to female progress, denying the distinction between moderate and extremist Islamists.[73] Globally, the report recognizes that because of their influence in society as a whole, Islamist movements can and have to be in the vanguard of women's economic and political development. This conclusion is confirmed in the 2006 *EuroMeSCo Report*. Elaborated for the European Commission, the report states that female Islamist militancy contributes to breaking down the patriarchal system and promoting an active political role for women more than the so-called "democratic parties" do.[74]

This phenomenon is due to the growing role of women in society. Globally, though, analysts consider that Islamist parties adapt their positions to the society they live in: they are inclusive and open to women, or exclusive and repressive, according to the way the whole society either integrates or marginalizes women.

Female Parliamentary Representation in the Maghreb

One of the main indicators of women's status is their political representation in a political institution, such as the parliament.

Table 10.3 Regional Representation of Women in Houses of Parliament

Region	Lower house %	Upper house %	Both houses %
Nordic countries	38.8	–	38.8
Americas	15.3	14.8	15.2
Asia	14.3	12.9	14.2
Pacific	11.6	25.4	13.5
OSCE	13.6	13.0	13.4
Sub-Saharan	11.5	12.9	11.7
Arab states	3.7	2.5	3.5

Source: http://www.undp.org/dpa/frontpagearchive/june00/9june00/carte%20anglais% 20OK.pdf#search='women%20in%20libyan%20parliament.

Compared to the rest of the world, women's representation in Arab governments is insignificant. The most developed regions are the Nordic countries, with a high representation of women in all sociopolitical sectors; their social democracy is quoted as being a success economically and politically. The American continent, Asia, the Pacific countries, the rest of Europe, and the sub-Saharan countries are similar in terms of their statistics for female representation in government. Female representation rates vary between 15.2 percent and 11.7 percent. Two political patterns emerge: first, developed countries are clearly divided into two groups: states that attempt to improve women's role in politics (38.8 percent) and states where women's role in politics is insignificant as well as neglected (an average of 15.6 percent); second, the division inside the underdeveloped or newly developing countries, where sub-Saharan countries are more involved in promoting women's status than Arab countries. There is an 8 percent difference in female representation in parliament between sub-Saharan and Arab countries and only a difference of 3.5 percent between American and sub-Saharan countries.

Table 10.4 compares the individual Maghrebi countries with both Arab and African countries. Representation of women in African parliaments far surpasses the representation of women in the Maghrebi countries. Most African countries are economically less developed than the Maghreb. However, female representation is better in most of them. Hence, in Rwanda, women Members of Parliament (MPs) represent 48.8 percent of the lower house and 34.6 percent of the upper house. In Mozambique, female MPs constitute 34.8 percent of the lower house, and in South America, they represent 32.8 percent of the lower house and 33.3 percent of the upper house. Most African countries with high female representation in parliament are English-speaking countries, whose past conflicts have not

Table 10.4 Representation of Women in the Houses of Parliament of the Maghreb Compared with the World, Africa, and the Middle East

Country	Lower house (%)	Upper house (%)	World rank	Africa rank	Middle East rank
Morocco	10.8	1.1	81	31	6
Algeria	6.2	2.8	107	44	6
Tunisia	22.8	–	32	9	2
Mauritania	3.7	5.4	118	46	8
Libya	12.5	–	70	20	3

Source: This table was made from a global table compiled by the Inter-Parliamentary Union on the basis of information provided by National Parliaments on 30 April 2005. A total of 185 countries are classified in descending order of the percentage of women in the "Lower or single House." Available at: http://www.ipu.org/wmn-e/classif.htm.
Note: The statistics for Libya come from the United Nations Development Programme. See: http://www.undp.org/dpa/frontpagearchive/june00/9june00/carte%20anglais%20 OK.pdf#search='women%20in%20libyan%20parliament.

prevented them from promoting the status of women. When classified among African countries, Tunisia is ranked in ninth position; Libya in twentieth; Morocco in thirty-first; Algeria in forty-fourth, followed by Mauritania in forty-sixth. The table shows that women have better representation in parliaments in the Maghreb than in the Arab East, but are under-represented when compared with African countries. This conclusion is not surprising, especially considering that the lowest level of female parliamentary representation in the world is in the Middle East with only 3.5 percent representation, versus 11.7 percent in sub-Saharan Africa.

Conclusion

Generalization, subjectivity, and relying on appearances have never been ideal ways to approach and understand the complex situation of women in the Maghreb. The first misconception is in the consideration that all Maghrebi societies are similar. Although these societies are similar in many respects, such as the strong presence of Islam, patriarchy, ongoing development, different levels of democratization, and different degrees of the Islamist phenomenon, they do not necessarily have similar regulations and beliefs as to the status of women. The second mistake is linking women's status to Islam. Analyzing the history of Islam and comparing Muslim countries, it is evident that religion itself has not deprived women of their political rights. Instead, politicians denied women their rights and continue to do so. The confusion between religious principles, conservatism, tradition, and Islamism, leads to misjudgment and misunderstanding. One can be faithful to one's religion, while being progressive and willing to renounce obsolete traditions. This is seen in Southeast Asian Muslim countries, as well as the urban classes of Maghrebi societies. Furthermore, local traditions in Mauritania and Libya can have a larger impact on society than abstract laws, which are endorsed in Tunisia, while Algeria and Morocco seek to find the best compromise between moral and political weight of tradition on the one hand and modern reforms on the other.

Third, the official stance towards Islamist opposition is also an important indicator in determining how far governments are willing to go in reforming and promoting the status of women, especially when this risks breaking the status quo. After independence, Tunisia adopted a modernist/Westernized legislation, surpassing the other Maghrebi countries with regard to the role of women.[75] However, the results are significantly more moderate in sections related to education. Furthermore, the question of the veil makes the list of repressive government measures against human rights even longer. Morocco, Algeria, and Libya have moved back and forth in opposing Islamists and making compromises with them. This process has resulted in strong and flexible legislation, which changes according to the balance of power, internal conjuncture, and international pressures. This is the reason why Mauritania, Morocco, and Algeria have reformed their personal status codes in 2001, 2004, and 2005, respectively. Overall, despite the fact that these reforms are relatively favorable to the promotion of women's status in the Maghreb, they remain frail and dependent on political conjunctures.

The last misconception occurs when discrimination and marginalization of women are limited to Arab societies. Statistics show that, regarding women's status, Maghrebi societies are more similar to African societies than to Middle Eastern ones. Furthermore, Maghrebi and African countries are not far from Asian, American, and southern European countries in female parliamentary representation, for instance. This simply means that, aside from northern European countries, the majority of countries, excluding Arab countries, have a weak female parliamentary representation of 13.4 percent on average. The issue of women's status and representation in government therefore appears not to be a cultural–regional problem, but rather a political–global one.

Notes

1 Margaret Anderson, *Thinking About Women*, Needham, MA: Allyn & Bacon, 2000; Mary Crow Dog and Richard Erdoes, *Lakota Woman*, New York: Harper Perennial, 1990.

2 C. Wright Mills. *The Sociological Imagination Fortieth Anniversary Edition*, New York: Oxford University Press, 2000, p. 187.

3 Fatima Mernissi is also the author of numerous books, such as, *Rêves de femmes*, Paris, Albin Michel, 1994; *Le harem politique*, Paris: Albin Michel, 1987; *Sultanes oubliées*, Paris: Albin Michel, 1990.

4 "Contre les crimes d'honneur et les violences faites au femmes," Nissa Souria Association. Available at: http://www.nesasy.com; "Actions Positives pour les droits de citoyenneté des femmes et l'égalité des chances au Maghreb," a partnership between different Maghrebi women's associations and NGOs. Available at: http://www.medespacefemmes.net; "Le collectif 20 ans barakat" fights for the family code abrogation in Algeria. Available at: http://20ansbarakat.free.fr/index.htm.

5 See Ben-Salah, "Profils de femmes: une typologie de conflits familiaux en contexte d'immigration," in *Femmes marocaines et conflits familiaux en immigration: quelles solutions juridiques appropriées?* Anvers: Edition M-C Foblets, 1998; J.-Y. Carlier, "Deux facettes des relations entre le droit et l'islam: la répudiation et le foulard," in *Facette de l'islam belge*, Louvain-La-Neuve, Bruylant-Académia, 1997; "Mauritanie: La Mauritanie lutte contre les violences faites aux femmes," *Africa Time*, 12 July 2005; "Mali: L'excision et les mariages précoces violent les droits de la femme," *All Africa*, 1 July 2005; "Pakistan: La justice du Pakistan rouvre le dossier d'un viol collectif," *Le Monde*, 30 June 2005.

6 Merve Kavakci, "Democratization of the Muslim World through Women," *Middle East Roundtable*, Edition 9, vol. 1, 4 September 2003. Available at: http://www.bitterlemons-international.org.

7 *Ijtihad* is a religious and scientific effort, which offers the explanation, interpretation, and adaptation of the sacred texts.

8 Morocco ratified the CEDAW Convention in 1993 with amendments, stating that Article 2 would only be applied if it is not contrary to *Shari'a* (Islamic law), and that Article 16 regarding marriage and its dissolution was also considered to be incompatible with *Shari'a* law.

9 See her book, Nadia Yassin, *Toutes voiles dehors – A la rencontre du message coranique*, Paris: Alter Editions, 2003. Note that she is a graduate in political science and is also a painter. She has been exposed to French culture from an early age and speaks perfect French.

10 The legal discrimination against French girls who wear head scarves starts in the public schools, where they cannot pursue their studies, and continues in all public institutions (administration, hospitals, universities, etc.) as long as they persist in wearing the scarf.

11 State employees are banned from wearing beards and workers can lose their jobs if they are spotted praying in public.

12 Just before and during the armed conflict, Algerian women living in the regions controlled by the FIS and later by armed groups were obliged to wear the veil to avoid being injured or even killed by Islamists.

13 Sahar Kassaimah, "The Shameful Conspiracy against Honorable Women in Tunisia and Turkey," 26 January 2001. Available at: http://www.islamonline.net/english/Politics/2001/02/article53.shtml.

14 Richard Hamilton, "Morocco moves to drop headscarf," BBC News, Rabat, 6 October 2006. Available at: http://news.bbc.co.uk/2/hi/africa/5413808.stm.

15 "Libyan Arab Jamahiriya," *The Committee on the Elimination of Discrimination Against Women*, Office of the United Nations High Commissioner for Human Rights, Geneva, A/49/38, par.126–185 (180), 12 April 1994.

16 Hayat Alvi, "The Human Rights of Women and Social Transformation in the Arab Middle East," *Middle East Review of International Affairs*, vol. 9, no. 2, June 2005, pp. 142–60.

17 Ibid., p. 143.

18 Kamara Djeynaba, "Changing Role of Women in Mauritania." Available at: http://www.maurifemme.mr/anglais.html.

19 "Collectif 95 Maghreb-Egalité." Available at: http://www.afrik.com/article 3974.html.

20 Dominique Lagarde, Mounia Daoudi, and Baya Gacém, "Le Mariage et les traditions dans le Maghreb Arabe: Tunisie, Algérie, Maroc, Mauritanie et Libye," *L'Express*, 25 January 2001.

21 *CIA World Factbook*. Available at: http://www.cia.gov/cia/publications/factbook/geos/mr.html

22 Dominique Lagarde, Mounia Daoudi, and Baya Gacém, op. cit.

23 Ibid.

24 Joblessness, housing shortage, economic hardship, and inflation also explain why marriages are deferred.

25 See http://www.wluml.org/english/about.shtml and http://www.wluml.org/english/publications.html.

26 Quoted by Dawn Marley, "Interactions between French and Islamic Cultures in the Maghreb." Available at: http://clio.revues.org.

27 Alain Hajjaj, "Quel avenir pour les banlieues?" *Sol & Civilisation – La lettre*, no. 4, December 1996. Available at: http://www.globenet.org/horizon-local/sol/sol4haj.html.

28 Kelly Walsh and Hélène Martin, "Les banlieues, la délinquance et l'exclusion." Available at: http://perso.wanadoo.fr/lycee_bossuet.lannion/rapport3.htm.

29 Véronique Fourault, "Pauvreté, ségrégation, violences urbaines." Available at: http://pweb.ens-lsh.fr/omilhaud/violences_urbaines.doc.

30 Violence in the suburbs is not new. In the 1980s, unrest spread throughout the suburbs of Paris and Lyon. In November 2004, the violence of the suburbs spilled over to the very heart of Paris when two rival gangs clashed on the Champs-Élysées.

31 Neutrality means to abstain from taking any position. Unlike American and British, French authorities are not neutral because they forbid the public expression of religiosity in the Republic's institutions.

32 The first controversy deprived several young girls of schooling, while the second tried to oblige Muslim children to eat meat and pork at the school canteen.

33 Dawn Marley, op. cit.

34 Stephanie Willman Bordat and Saida Kouzzi, "The Challenge of Implementing Morocco's New Personal Status Law," *Global Rights*. Available at: http://www.global rights.org/site/DocServer/Challenges_of_Morocco_s_New_Law.pdf?docID=663.

35 "Divorce: La règlementation suffira t-elle à mettre fin aux abus?" *Cheikh Sall*, no. 280, 14 November 2001.

36 Mohamed Ould Sidi, "Le divorce roi," *Espace Calme*, no. 5, May 1994.

37 "Libyan Arab Jamahiriya," op. cit.

38 Rima Khalaf-Hunaidi, former UN Assistant Secretary-General and Director of the Regional Bureau for Arab States in charge of publishing the *Arab Human Development Report 2002*, cited in Hayat Alvi, op. cit., p. 152.

39 Abdelmadjid Bouzidi, "La femme dans l'économie algérienne: beaucoup reste à faire," *Le Quotidien d'Oran*, 30 December 2004.

40 United Nations Development Programme, *Arab Human Development Report 2005*, New York, UNDP, 2006, p. 330.

41 Fond des Nations Unies pour la Population, "Genre et promotion de la femme en Mauritanie." Available at: http://mauritania.unfpa.org/gt_genre.htm.

42 *Arab Human Development Report 2005*, p. 330

43 On Libya's government policy toward women, see, Maria Graeff-Wassink, "Les relations hommes–femmes en Libye, hier et aujourd'hui," in Olivier Pliez (ed.), *La nouvelle Libye–Sociétés, espaces et géopolitique au lendemain de l'embargo*, Paris: Karthala-IREMAM, 1999, pp. 177–93.

44 The last *Arab Human Development Report* considers that female illiteracy remains at a very high level: 70.7 percent.

45 See: http://www.pogar.org/countries/gender.asp?cid=12.

46 *Maghreb Arabe Presse*, 15 October 2005.

47 Hayat Alvi, op. cit., p. 156.

48 The rate of women workers is only 18.68 percent, according to the National Center for Social and Cultural Anthropological Research, which does not take into account the informal sector. See, Naïma Hamidache, "Violence contre la femme en algérie," *L'Expression*, 26 December 2006.

49 Samar Smati, "Ce que ne veulent plus les femmes algériennes," *Liberté*, 25 December 2006.

50 This issue is very important, especially when developed countries, like France, still suffer from inequality between men and women at work.

51 See http://www.pogar.org/countries/gender.asp?cid=10.

52 See http://www.pogar.org/countries/gender.asp?cid=12.

53 Agriculture, which contributes approximately 20 percent of overall production, continues to be the largest source of employment, accounting for nearly half the active population.

54 The first study on women in the textile industry was undertaken by the Democratic League for the Rights of Women in April and May 1996. Quoted in Hanan Nasser, "Why Arab women are still in the slow lane of reform," *Daily Star*, 6 June 2005. Available at: http://www.dailystar.com.lb/article.asp?edition_id=10&categ_id=2&article_id=15672.

55 Ibid.

56 *Arab Human Development Report 2005*, p. 322.

57 See "Role of women in agriculture." Available at: http://www.fao.org/documents/show_cdr.asp?url_file=/docrep/V9324e/v9324e01.htm.

58 In December 2004, the economists elected Rola Dashti as chair of their profes-
    sional organization. Dashti, a Shiite active feminist, is the first woman to hold
    such a position in a mixed-gender non-governmental organization in Kuwait.
    She fought for women's right to own businesses and to host *diwaniyya* (salons) to
    discuss politics and business.
59 *Human Development Report 2002*, cited in, Hayat Alvi, op. cit., p. 153.
60 Claude Liauzu, "Djamila Amrane, Les femmes algériennes dans la guerre,"
    CLIO, no. 9, 1999.
61 "Les femmes en tant que participantes à part entière à la Communauté europé-
    enne-méditerranéenne d'Etats démocratiques," *Rapport d'EuroMeSCo*, April
    2006, p. 24. available at: http://www.euromesco.net/imgupload/index.php?option=
    com_content&task=view&lang=fr&id=237&Itemid=26
62 Erwin Delaplace, "La parité en marche," *Arabies*, September 2006, p. 49.
63 United Nations Development Programme: http://www.pogar.org/countries/gender.
    asp?cid=1.
64 See http://www.pogar.org/countries/gender.asp?cid=12.
65 *Middle East Online*, 17 September 2006.
66 The *Kutla* is a coalition of opposition parties, constituted in 1994, which cover a
    wide spectrum from the nationalist and pan-Arab left to the socialist and com-
    munist left.
67 Since the independence of Morocco, leftist parties considered women's equality
    would be achieved through class liberalization.
68 In 1992, the UAF launched the million signatures campaign for the following
    changes: 1) instituting equality and complementarities between husband and wife
    in the family; 2) according women, like men, legal competency when reaching the
    legal age of maturity; 3) giving women the right to marry without the need for a
    guardian after reaching the age of maturity; 4) placing divorce in the hands of a
    judge and granting women the same conditions as men for seeking divorce; 5)
    stipulating that both spouses have the same rights and obligations in marriage; 6)
    outlawing polygamy; 7) giving the wife the same right as the husband to guar-
    dianship over their children; and 8) establishing work outside the home and
    education as indisputable rights for man and woman.
69 For instance, in the marriage section, a woman who had reached the age of
    maturity and was an orphan, remained an orphan, but was allowed to contract
    her marriage without a tutor. The husband was required to inform the first wife
    of his desire to take a second wife, and was required to obtain the permission of
    a judge for such a marriage. In the divorce section, the new provision required
    the presence of two parties to register the divorce as well as the permission of the
    judge to implement the divorce, and to put some minor constraints on unilateral
    repudiation.
70 See http://www.pogar.org/countries/gender.asp?cid=20.
71 Abbasi Madani for his part declared that the woman has her place in social and
    economic life, and condemned in 1989 attacks against the "Westernized" girls in
    the streets.
72 In 1991 the FIS organized a big demonstration in Algiers in order to maintain
    the 1984 Family Code.
73 Ghania Khelifi, "Situation de la femme dans le monde arabe, des progrès mais . . .,"
    L'Expression, 9 December 2006.
74 EuroMeSCO, op. cit., pp. 29–30.
75 A study published by *The Economist* in April 2004, quoted in *Al-Watan*
    (Algiers), 14 April 2004.

11 The Politics of Berber (Amazigh) Identity

Algeria and Morocco Compared

Michael J. Willis

A notable feature of the Maghrebi political landscape since the 1990s has been the increased profile of the issue of Berber identity. There has been a rise in the number and influence of groups and organizations advocating greater rights for, and stressing the importance of the specificities of, the Berber-speaking populations of the region.[1] The governments of the two states with the largest Berber-speaking populations—Algeria and Morocco—have also made a series of considerable concessions to some of the main demands of these groups and organizations.[2] This chapter aims to explain the reasons for and implications of this apparently new development. These reasons and implications are fiercely debated not only by academics but also, significantly, by the leaders, political activists, and increasing numbers of citizens from the two states who recognize that the answers to these questions have potentially profound significance to important debates about the identity of Algeria and Morocco, the future political configurations in both countries, and even the Maghreb's relations with the wider world.

The Emergence of the Issue

The issue of Berber, or Amazigh,[3] identity gained prominence comparatively recently. This is perhaps surprising, considering the Maghreb's berberophone populations have existed alongside the majority arabophone populations for centuries. Until as recently as 30 years ago, opinion of all shades, from regional politicians to foreign academics, was united in the assertion that there were no meaningful political distinctions between Arab and Berber speakers in Algeria and Morocco. Such was the conclusion, most notably, of a major book that appeared in the early 1970s: Gellner and Micaud's, *Arabs and Berbers*, which drew together nearly all of the major scholars of the Maghreb in the Anglo-Saxon world. The contributors to the volume concluded not only that any Arab–Berber divide was absent from politics, but also that it was likely to remain so for the foreseeable future. The region was divided *linguistically* between those whose mother tongue was a form of Arabic and those whose first language was one of the recognized variations of Berber, but it was mistaken to assume that such a divide translated into any real social or, particularly, political distinction. Speakers of Berber, for example, did not primarily identify themselves as Berber speakers and, through that, as "Berbers." Instead they focused on markers of identity that were either broader or narrower than the essentially ethnic definition of identity as Berber. In this way, Berber speakers from northern Morocco would not think of themselves as "Berber" but rather as members of their particular tribe or of the Rif region. Simultaneously, they would also conceive of themselves as part of the wider Muslim *umma*. Identity was thus conceived of in local, tribal, and religious—rather than ethnic—terms.[4]

Evidence for asserting the unimportance of the Arab–Berber divide was also presented from history. Both Arabic and Berber-speaking dynasties had risen and fallen over the centuries in the Maghreb without the linguistic distinction appearing to have been of any political importance. More recently, there was also the experience of the colonial period, which witnessed significant attempts by the French colonial authorities to deliberately emphasize the differences between Arabs and Berbers. A product more of nineteenth-century racial ideology than of a strategy of "divide and rule," the French privileged their relations with Berber speakers over those with the Arabs. The Berbers were viewed as more trustworthy, more industrious, more democratic, and thus fundamentally more European than the Arabs. In this way, the French were making the mistake—referred to above—of taking the linguistic divide and assuming that it was fundamental to the region and was, moreover, indicative of two very different groups of people with different values, beliefs, and behavioral patterns. This misconception and the colonial policies that flowed from it came to be known as the "Berber myth." That it was a myth was amply demonstrated at the end of the colonial period when Berber speakers participated in equal, if not greater, numbers than the Arabs in the nationalist and liberation movements that fought to expel the French from the region. Therefore, French efforts to favor and form alliances with the Berbers appeared to have been an abject failure.

The Rise of Berberism

Given the evidence to the contrary, the question arises as to why Berber identity subsequently became a major political issue in the Maghreb. To understand the parameters of the debate on this question, it is perhaps useful to set out the two most opposed positions on the issue. One position argues that the revival of interest in a separate Berber identity represents simply a renewed and more successful attempt by Western states—with France at the forefront—to weaken and undermine the natural unity of the states of the region through the sponsorship and encouragement of notions of a separate Berber identity: a notable example of such efforts being the creation and expansion of "Berber studies" at French universities in the post-independence period. The diametrically opposed position to this view argues that the historical picture of Arab–Berber harmony was in fact itself a myth—Berber culture, history, and language having been crushed by Arab invasions of earlier centuries. The current interest in a distinct Berber identity is, therefore, only a culmination of centuries of struggle against Arab oppression finally beginning to bear fruit.

A more realistic evaluation of the question lies inevitably between these two positions, but with additional factors and nuances. Perhaps the most important point to acknowledge is the evolutionary nature of the issue: perceptions regarding the weight of importance attached to distinctions between Arab and Berber vary over time. What might have been true in the eleventh century might not have still been the case during the colonial period and in all probability is different again today. The two polemic positions described above perceive the issue in absolute terms, unchanging through history. However, as David Crawford and Katherine Hoffman have pointed out, the real issue is not whether distinctions between Arabs and Berbers are fundamentally historically true or false, but rather whether they are *perceived* to exist, not least by Berbers themselves.[5] Such perceptions can also shift over time.

Whilst it is difficult to examine the perceptions of Arab-Berber distinctions and their shifts throughout history, it is considerably easier to analyze them over more recent years, notably in the 30 years since the publication of the book by Gellner and Micaud. Such an approach also answers the more immediate question of elucidating the impact of the issue on contemporary politics in the Maghreb. It will be argued here that the rise of the Berber identity issue was indeed the result of changing circumstances both inside and beyond the Maghreb and that this pushed the evolution of the issue in directions unforeseen by Gellner and Micaud and the contributors to their volume.[6]

In the 1970s, there were two main factors—at the domestic and the international level—that changed the situation. Domestically, the emergence of movements demanding greater recognition of the distinctive aspects of Berber identity was, to a significant degree, a reaction to official policies that appeared to marginalize minority identity. Imported from the Mashreq (Arab East), where there was no Berber-speaking community, Arab nationalist ideas formed much of the discourse of the nationalist movements in Morocco and Algeria during the colonial period, as well as of the policy pursued by the post-independence regimes in both countries. There was also the policy of adopting classical Arabic as the state language and, from the 1960s, to "Arabize" the education and administration sectors. There was also an inherent suspicion on the part of the post-independence governments towards any discussion of Berber identity, given the divisive emphasis that it had been given during the colonial period.

During the same period, at the international level, there were more global movements converging with an increased interest in differentiated identity.

In the 1970s, particularly in academia, discourses of unity gave way to ones of difference and diversity—there being a growing argument that previous emphases on unity had really been a cover for the imposition of a single dominant identity over others. The presence of Maghrebi students and academics in universities in Europe and North America meant that the Maghreb did not remain insulated from this trend.

Algeria

Changes at the domestic and international levels were to have their impact first on Algeria and specifically on the country's largest Berber-speaking community, the Kabyles. The reason why it was the Kabyles, rather than any one of the other Berber-speaking communities in the Maghreb, is largely explained with reference to the colonial period. As the first and largest Berber-speaking group the French had encountered when they took their first steps in the colonization of the Maghreb in Algiers and its hinterland in 1830, the French based most of their observations on the Kabyles, which would later help create the "Berber myth." Although the Berber myth failed to translate into a coherent colonial "Berber policy" that favored the Kabyles, one consequence of contact with the French was that Kabyles became disproportionately exposed to French education. This occurred through a combination of lack of alternatives in mountainous Kabylia, the development of a strong tradition of migration to metropolitan France, as well as some conscious French efforts.[7] These educational links survived Algerian independence from France in 1962 and explain the high proportion of Kabyles amongst Algerian students and academics studying and working at French universities. It was amongst these groups that greater interest in Berber culture, history, and language grew, with an increasing number of students and academics alike studying these fields in departments in French universities as part of the global trend towards rediscovering and preserving diverse and minority cultures and traditions.

In the Maghreb itself, the Kabyles were particularly disadvantaged by the Algerian government's policy of Arabization, which had gained momentum by the 1970s. As the country's most accomplished francophones, Kabyles had initially been recruited in disproportionate numbers into the fully francophone educational and administrative structures abandoned by the French at Algerian independence. However, the official policy of Arabization of both these sectors put the recruited Kabyles under threat by the 1970s, since many Kabyles spoke only French and the Kabyle Berber dialect. The political difficulty of defending the use of the colonial language, French, meant that many Kabyles chose to present Arabization as a threat to the Berber languages. This was a task that was made easier by the fact that the Arabic being introduced was "high" classical Arabic, which is a language not used in everyday speech and noticeably different from the colloquial Arabic already used in Arabic-speaking areas. This allowed for

Arabization to be portrayed as the imposition of an essentially "alien" and "foreign" language.[8]

Not surprisingly, Kabylia was therefore the first region to experience the emergence of a defined Berber—or, as it often became known, Berberist—"movement." The strength of the movement was dramatically demonstrated in April 1980, when an official decision to cancel a lecture on Berber poetry at Tizi Ouzou University in Kabylia sparked protests and unrest that lasted several days. This event, which thereafter became known as the Berber or Kabyle "Spring" (a conscious reference to the Prague Spring of 1968), proved to be a political watershed in Kabylia even though few concessions were immediately won from the regime. The unrest marked the spreading of notions of Berber/Kabyle consciousness from the Kabyle intelligentsia to ordinary Kabyles and subsequently there was increased interest in Kabyle culture, history, and identity amongst Kabyles themselves. The Kabyle Spring also had implications for Algeria as a whole, since it marked the first major demonstration of popular dissent and dissatisfaction with the Algerian regime since independence. Accordingly, it damaged the image of the invincibility of the Algerian regime and opened the way for other dissident forces and voices in the 1980s—most notably the Islamists. Many Kabyle activists go further and suggest that 1980 paved the way for the political opening in 1989, when a new constitution allowed the creation of a multi-party political system and the holding of genuinely competitive elections. They argue that the push for greater cultural pluralism by organizations such as the Berber Cultural Movement (*Mouvement Culturel Berbere*—MCB) that emerged in Kabylia after the events of 1980 helped to prepare the ground for political pluralism.[9]

Following the political opening of 1989, which resulted from the countrywide unrest of October 1988, Kabyle politics came to be something of a sideshow to the central drama of the late 1980s and 1990s in Algeria that focused on Islamism, with the rise, electoral success, and then suppression of the Islamic Salvation Front (*Front Islamique du Salut*—FIS). Kabylia was one of the few regions that did not strongly support the FIS in elections in 1990 and 1991. The overwhelming majority of Kabyles voted for parties that had strong roots in the region: the Socialist Forces Front (*Front des Forces Socialistes*—FFS), a historic opposition party formed by Hocine Aït Ahmed, one of the Kabyle leaders of the liberation struggle against the French; and the Rally for Culture and Democracy (RCD), which originated during the 1980 Kabyle Spring and which emanated from a wing of the MCB. The failure of both the FFS and RCD to attract voters beyond Kabylia was, however, both a symptom and a cause of their being more generally perceived as specifically "Kabyle" parties.

As the violence from the civil war—unleashed by the banning of the FIS in 1992—began to decline substantially, Kabylia came to the forefront of Algerian politics once again. A renewed and much more sustained period of popular unrest in Kabylia grew out of clashes with the authorities in April

2001 during the annual commemoration of the events of spring 1980. Many, particularly external, commentators portrayed this new unrest as the latest stage in the Kabyles' struggle to secure official recognition for their cultural and linguistic rights as a region. This depiction seemed to be supported by the Algerian government's decision in 2002 to seek a revision to the constitution to make the Berber language—*Tamazight*—a national language. Such a picture was, however, rather misleading for several reasons.

The Algerian government had already made successive reforms in the 1990s that gave greater accommodation to Berber identity. These reforms included the establishment of an Institute for Amazigh Studies at Tizi Ouzou University in Kabylia in 1990, the broadcasting of nightly news bulletins in Tamazight on Algerian state television in 1991, the introduction of the teaching of Tamazight in berberophone regions in 1995, and a clause in the constitutional revision of 1996 that recognized Berber identity as one of the three constitutive elements of Algerian national identity alongside the already acknowledged Arab and Islamic components.[10]

Awarding Tamazight national status was only one on a list of demands from the representatives of the movement that emerged from the unrest in 2001, and which was formally presented in the al-Kseur Platform in June 2001. Moreover, it was the only demand that referred to Berber identity. In fact, the other 14 demands set out by al-Kseur were related to efforts to defuse the crisis in Kabylia and, more significantly, to proposals for reforms for Algeria as a whole. The latter category included demands to place "all executive functions of the state and the security corps under the authority of democratically elected bodies" and for "a state that guarantees all socioeconomic rights and democratic freedoms."[11] The national dimension of the al-Kseur Platform demands accentuated the fact that the mass movement emanating from the 2001 unrest was not one of regional particularism, but rather one that sought to spearhead change across Algeria.

A closer look at the events in spring 2001 and the al-Kseur Platform reveals that the impetus for the protestors was not unhappiness with suppression of their cultural rights, but rather anger at economic hardship, authoritarian rule, corruption, and injustice. These concerns were far from specific to Kabylia and indeed were common across the country. This, then, appears to explain why the regime only responded to the part of the al-Kseur Platform that referred to Berber identity; the regime hoped to portray the unrest as being fundamentally linked to particularist Berber demands, thereby preventing other regions of the country from responding to the example set by Kabylia in taking to the streets to protest against the shortcomings and failures of the state.[12]

Morocco

Compared to Algeria, the presence of a much larger Berber-speaking population in Morocco may suggest that Morocco would inevitably follow the path taken by Algeria.[13] Surprisingly, this has not been the case. The first reason for this has been the absence of a Moroccan region analogous to Kabylia. Morocco's Berber-speaking areas are more geographically dispersed and more remote than Kabylia in Algeria. Whereas the Kabyles are concentrated in the relatively compact regions of Greater and Lesser Kabylia and comparatively close to the national capital of Algeria, Morocco's berberophones are spread out through the Rif Mountains, the Middle, High, and Anti-Atlas, and in the southern Souss Valley—all rather distant from the capital city, Rabat, and the biggest city, Casablanca. During the French colonial period, attitudes towards the Berber-speaking populations were influenced by the Kabyle myth developed earlier in Algeria. The result was the formation of alliances with traditional leaders in Berber areas and the heavy recruitment into the French colonial army, rather than greater exposure to French education.

The second reason for the failure of Morocco's Berber populations to follow the example of Kabylia was the strategic alliance that the Moroccan monarchy formed with Berber notables (effectively continuing the policy of the French) in the aftermath of independence. The alliance was aimed to counterbalance the power of the main nationalist party—*Istiqlal*. The *Istiqlal* not only represented a threat to the political dominance of the monarchy in the post-independence era, but had also provoked resentment in rural, and thus mainly Berber, areas when its overwhelmingly urban and Arab cadres had sought to establish political offices and control in the countryside, disregarding the established and traditional rural leaders and administrators.[14] As a tangible expression of this alliance, Berber speakers came to dominate both the main royalist political party, the *Mouvement Populaire*, and the Moroccan military.[15] This alliance between the Berber areas and the Palace did not, however, translate into any "Berberization" of the state; neither the military nor the *Mouvement Populaire* developed an identifiably Berber agenda. The *Mouvement Populaire*, for example, was the major party in the governing coalition that introduced Arabization in Morocco in 1965.[16]

The strategic alliance between the Moroccan monarchy and the traditional Berber notables helped ensure that Morocco experienced no "Berber Spring" of its own equivalent to that which occurred in Kabylia in 1980. Nevertheless, by the 1990s the first indications arose signifying the beginning of an organized Berber movement in Morocco, as both the size and number of associations linked to Berber culture increased. This growth was attributable in part to the impact of similar global trends to those that had affected Algeria. The example and experience of Algeria was also of importance to the Moroccan cultural associations, which were clearly influenced by the growth of associations like the MCB in Algeria. The associations were also able to organize themselves by taking advantage of the gradual political and associational liberalization that the Moroccan regime had allowed since the beginning of the decade. In 1991, six Berber associations met in Agadir and issued a Charter advancing demands that included the constitutional recognition of Berber languages and their use in education, administration, and the media. Over time the associations federated themselves into a structured Amazigh Cultural Movement (*Mouvement Culturel Amazigh*—MCA) which expanded to include an estimated three hundred different associations by 2005.

The parallels to Algeria were evident. As in Algeria, these organizations were spearheaded by students, teachers, and university professors who were increasingly interested in their Berber heritage, many of them having studied in France or in other European or North American countries. Hostility to official policies of Arabization also played a part.[17] Similar to its Algerian counterpart, the Moroccan regime made various concessions to the demands of Berber identity during the 1990s. Daily news bulletins in the three main regional variations of Berber began transmission on state radio and television. In 2001, the Palace set up the Royal Institute for Amazigh Culture (*Institut Royal de la Culture Amazighe*—IRCAM) and two years later, in 2003, over 300 schools across the Kingdom began lessons in standardized Tamazight.

Another similarity with Algeria was the regional dimension. In Algeria, the failure of the country's other main Berber-speaking regions, notably the Chaouia of the Aurès mountains and the populations of the Mzab, to follow the path of Kabylia had been striking and indicative of Kabylia's peculiar history and experience. Although it was true there was no "Moroccan Kabylia," it was noticeable that certain Berber-speaking areas were more active in Berberist organizations. Measured by involvement in bodies such as the MCA and IRCAM, Berber speakers from southern Morocco (notably the Souss Valley) are the most involved, followed by Rifis from the north of the country. The least involved are Berbers from the center of the country and specifically the Middle Atlas. These differences can be attributed, in the case of the Rif, to a more defined and specifically Rifian sense of identity resulting from Spanish colonization rather than French and by subsequent (some would argue, consequent) alienation from the royal regime. In the case of the Middle Atlas, the continued influence of the *Mouvement Populaire* in these areas probably explains the relative absence from bodies such as the MCA and IRCAM.

There are, however, important apparent differences from the case of Algeria. The Berber cultural movement in Morocco is still largely the affair of the urban, the educated, and the expatriate, and there is yet to occur the spreading of "Berber consciousness" to the mass of ordinary Berber speakers (the majority of whom live in the more remote and mountainous areas). Nevertheless, there is anecdotal evidence that this may be gradually occurring through the efforts of educated and "conscious" Berber speakers returning to their home towns and villages, a process that can only be aided by the introduction of teaching in Tamazight into local areas.[18] Another difference from Algeria is the fact that the Berber cultural movement in

Morocco has not yet assumed a national vision of the sort that the leaders in Kabylia have in viewing their demands as part of a broader agenda for democratizing and reforming the Moroccan state for the whole of the population. This, however, may change with time.

Questions, Issues, and Challenges

The developments described hitherto present a range of questions, challenges, and issues to the modern Maghreb at both the domestic and the international level.

Domestic Level

Domestically, the primary question is the extent to which the rise of Berberist sentiment and organizations will affect existing political configurations in the region.

One major question concerns the impact that Berberism has on Islamism. In the 1990s, Algerian politics was dominated by the challenge mounted by Islamism, and Morocco has witnessed a significant rise in Islamist sentiment since the mid-1990s. Tensions have existed between Islamists and Berberists, most notably because many Islamists are hostile to what they see as Berberists' attempts to reduce the use of the Arabic language. Arabic being the language of the Quran, Islamists see the securing of its dominance as essential to the maintenance of the region's Islamic identity. This explains why many Islamists view Berberism as a Trojan horse for secular and Western neo-colonial agendas, particularly given the close links and educational backgrounds many prominent Berberists have in France and other Western states. The endorsement of secularism by the Kabyle-based RCD party in Algeria confirmed these suspicions for many Islamists and ensured extremely hostile relations between the RCD and the FIS during the latter's legal lifetime. For its part, the RCD viewed Islamism as a vehicle for the suppression of diversity and democracy and for the imposition of a uniform Arabo-Islamic culture. It was also one of the few parties to applaud the regime's decision to cancel elections in 1992 and dissolve the FIS.

In Morocco, the main Islamist party in the parliament, the Party of Justice and Development (PJD), has spoken against awarding Tamazight the status of an official language and was adverse to the idea (supported by most Berberists) that the Latin alphabet be used to teach the language in schools, arguing that the traditionally oral language had historically been taught using the Arabic script.[19] These tensions between Islamists and Berberists have been noted by the governments in both Algeria and Morocco, and the desire to use the Berberists as a possible counterweight to the Islamists undoubtedly explains in part the significant concessions the regimes in both states have made to the Berbers from the 1990s. Indeed, as early as the early 1980s, the Algerian government played the Islamists against the

Berberists and Leftists, a policy which resulted in bloody clashes between the two groups at the University of Algiers.[20]

In spite of the obvious tensions that exist between Islamists and Berberists, it should be stressed that the relationship is not one of total animosity. Many leading Islamists are Berber speakers themselves, most notably the leaders of Morocco's two largest Islamist organizations.[21] In Algeria, the leadership of both the FIS and some of the armed groups (including the extremist GIA) included Kabyles. At the political level, shared concerns about issues of justice, reform, and democracy have led moderates in both movements to believe they should cooperate. In 1995, in Algeria, the larger Kabyle-based political party, the FFS, collaborated with representatives of the dissolved FIS alongside other opposition parties to produce a common document, the Rome Platform, which set out proposals for a resolution to the armed conflict in Algeria and for the establishment of a democratic government. Significantly, the document also called for both the re-legalization of the FIS and the effective recognition of Tamazight (*Plateforme pour une Solution*).[22] Several writers have observed that both the Berberist and Islamist movements share the characteristic of being the only ones proven capable of mobilizing large numbers of the population in favor of major reforms of the regime.[23] Given the decline of the Islamist movement in Algeria in recent years, some have even seen the movements of Kabylia as potential inheritors of the popular political mantle of the FIS.

Another important question regarding the Berberist movement is its future political evolution. Many Berberists in Algeria would like to see it become a vehicle for the more general democratization and development of Algerian society. This explains the national scope of the platforms of the two main parties in the region, the FFS and the RCD, both of which have traditionally sought to portray themselves as national parties and have vigorously rejected being labeled "Kabyle" parties. It also explains the presence of demands relating to the whole of Algeria in the al-Kseur Platform. There are, however, questions as to whether the movement may evolve in a different direction. There are more radical elements in the movement that are pushing for specifically Kabyle-centered objectives, such as autonomy or even independence for Kabylia rather than reform of the broader Algerian state. In June 2001, advocates of autonomy established the Movement for Autonomy in Kabylia (MAK), led by the singer and political activist Ferhat Mehenni, a staunch opponent of both the regime and the Islamists. Azzedine Layachi has termed this development a move from civic nationalism to ethnic nationalism. In pursuing its strategy of portraying the unrest in Kabylia as being an entirely Kabyle affair, the Algerian regime has drawn attention to these more radical elements and, in doing so, has encouraged them.[24] Indeed, the prolonged, sporadic, and inconclusive negotiations that have occurred between the regime and the representatives of the al-Kseur Platform have served to divide and radicalize the latter.

In Morocco, both civic and more ethnic forms of nationalism are evident among the less-developed movement. One factor that may contribute to the development of a more ethnically based nationalism is economic. Morocco's Berber-speaking population remains concentrated in the kingdom's poor and rural areas, and the overlapping characteristics of being rural, poor, and berberophone have the potential to create a more politicized consciousness based on a sense of resentment and belief that marginalization is in some way connected to being Berber; as David Crawford observes: "Whatever the statistical reality, if rural Berbers come to see themselves as a group that is disproportionately impoverished, there will emerge real potential for a distinctly radical Berber politics."[25]

The Berber cultural movement in Morocco has its radical wing, and in July 2005, a number of Berber radicals announced the creation of the Moroccan Democratic Amazigh Party (*Parti Démocratique Amazigh Marocain*—PDAM); though unlike the MAK in Algeria, the PDAM is not a separatist or regionalist party and proclaims itself to be open to all Moroccans.[26] In taking such a stance, the party may be aiming to avoid the legal bar on regionally or ethnically based political parties. The newly elected secretary-general of the PDAM has also traditionally rebutted the charge of ethnic exclusivity by arguing that through centuries of intermarriage, all Moroccans have Berber blood in them and that, therefore, "there are no true Arabs in Morocco."[27] Accordingly, the PDAM appears to be advocating a national vision for Morocco: its founding declaration calls for the establishment of a fully democratic state with expanded social, political, and economic liberties.

International Level

Developments in Berber consciousness also have a potential impact beyond the borders of Morocco and Algeria. One significant development over the past decade has been the emergence of an international pan-Berberist movement and agenda.

In 1997, a first World Amazigh Congress was held in the Canary Islands, which brought together representatives from Berber associations and groups from across North Africa, as well as expatriate organizations in Europe and North America. Four such congresses have now taken place, the most recent having been held in the Maghreb itself, in Nador, in the Rif region of northern Morocco, in August 2005. These congresses represent the consolidation of Berber activism that transcends national boundaries and the concerns of individual Berber-speaking communities, and, in this way, a genuinely trans- and pan-"Berber consciousness" appears to have been created. Thus, this seems to transform the Gellner–Micaud assertion of the early 1970s that Berbers did not think of themselves as Berbers, but rather as Rifis, Kabyles, or Tuaregs and, beyond that, as Muslims. This transformation has been significantly facilitated by advances in globalized technology, most notably the Internet, that have enabled activists from all over the globe to communicate and cooperate and thus form—albeit largely in cyber-space—a common agenda and sense of community.[28] Indeed, it marks a change from the 1980s, when the events in Kabylia were very much a product of the particular experience of Kabylia, rather than of Algeria's wider Berber population.

The development of a transnational consciousness has wider repercussions for both the Maghreb as a region and its relations with the outside world. Many of the more committed and radical Berberists have developed a critique of their states that extends to foreign policy. A prominent call amongst many Berberists is for the teaching of Maghrebi history to be revised to accommodate and give credit to the contributions made by the Berbers both before and after the arrival of the Arabs, whose history many see as having unduly dominated official histories. In this way there is an attempt to shift the Maghreb away from its long-defined orientation towards the Middle East, Arab, and Islamic worlds. For some activists, the Maghreb should be redefined in its own specific and historical terms. For others, an alignment with Europe is more appropriate, given not just historic ties, but strong existing ones forged through trade and migration, which dwarf equivalent links with the Middle East.

In the process, some admittedly more radical Berber activists argue that Maghrebi states should abandon their preoccupations with and loosen their loyalties to the Middle East. They argue that it is a region that is remote from the Maghreb's concerns and from which the Maghreb has unnecessarily imported problems of violence, terrorism, and political and religious extremism.[29] Official attempts to encourage solidarity with Middle Eastern causes are not only viewed as damaging to the Maghreb's relations with the West, but also seen as serving domestic political ends.[30] Such a viewpoint remains restricted for now to only the most radical elements of the Berberist movement. Most ordinary Berber speakers in both Algeria and Morocco remain staunchly committed to international causes such as the Palestinian, not out of pan-Arab, but rather out of pan-Islamic, sentiment, which continues to be strong.[31] Nevertheless, if these radical Berber viewpoints were to become more mainstream among Berber speakers and subsequently in society as a whole, then this could have significant repercussions for regional and even international politics.

Conclusion

One of the most notable dimensions of the Berber identity issue in Maghrebi politics has been its dynamic and changing character. Any new attempts to predict the future evolution of the issue should therefore be made with substantial circumspection.

The roles played by the regimes in Morocco and Algeria will be of vital and central importance in the future. One prescient analysis of the events of spring 1980 in Kabylia concluded that "the relevant opposition is not: Kabyles vs. the nation-state, but: Kabyles vs. the regime in power. This is a very different matter."[32] This judgment holds true for the events of 2001 as a protest against the failures of the Algerian regime, rather than against the Algerian state. Being aware of this and of the mobilizing power of the FIS against the failures of the government, the Algerian regime has responded in a characteristically adroit fashion and has succeeded in splintering the political leadership of the movement that was created during the events of 2001 and has managed to contain it within Kabylia.

Conscious of Algeria's experience, the Moroccan regime decided to accommodate the kingdom's own nascent Berber cultural movement, influenced by concerns regarding the future possible radicalization of the movement. The damage inflicted on Morocco's Islamist movements by the suicide bomb attacks carried out by Islamist extremists in Casablanca on 16 May 2003 possibly lessened the regime's need to rely on the Berberist movement as a counterweight.[33] However, it could also be argued that just as the decline of the armed Islamist struggle in Algeria in some way opened the way for the popular protests in Kabylia of 2001, so the weakening of Morocco's Islamists might create a space for the kingdom's Berberists to criticize the regime. The greater Berber-speaking population in Morocco would make it potentially more difficult for the Moroccan authorities to contain such criticism in the way that their Algerian counterparts have done in Kabylia. An important part of the Berberist critique of the regime would likely be its failure to address rural poverty. All of the Casablanca suicide bombers came from the impoverished and marginalized shanty towns (*bidonvilles*) surrounding the city. These areas are regularly swollen by waves of migrants escaping the deprivations of the countryside, and this creates a potentially important link between issues of terrorism, poverty, the rural world, and thus the berberophone population.

Up to now, attempts by the regimes in both Algeria and Morocco to use and channel the energies of Berberist sentiment and organizations have largely been successful. In spite of this, the Algerian regime, in particular, must be conscious of the dangers of over-manipulating Berberism as a popular political force, since similar attempts to manipulate the Islamist movement in the late 1980s and early 1990s nearly ended in overthrow and disaster for the regime.[34] Equally, any attempt to repress Berberism, should it become too much of a threat as a political force, could well have consequences as disastrous as those that resulted from the Algerian regime's efforts to dispose of the FIS and Islamism after 1992. The ethnic dimension of Berberism and its strong links with Europe would ensure that any resistance to official repression would acquire more powerful support from Western countries than the Islamists were ever capable of attracting.[35] Indeed, the link with Europe is important not only because a disproportionate part of the large expatriate Maghrebi community in many European states is originally berberophone—notably Algerian Kabyles in France and Moroccan

Rifians in Spain. Bruce Maddy-Weitzman has observed that, while the development of a Muslim identity among Maghrebi migrants in Europe has received considerable attention, comparatively little attention has been paid to the development of a Berber identity there, despite the fact that expatriate Berber communities have played a vocal, leading, and often radicalizing role in Berberist movements.[36]

Ultimately, most developments still depend on the regimes. Survival has always been the primary instinct of the regimes in both Algeria and Morocco, and official responses to the growth of Berber sentiment and movements will be conditioned by this foremost concern. Therefore, it remains to be seen whether either regime fully appreciates that the strength of Berber sentiment—in common with Islamism before it—is substantially related to broader issues of poverty, governance, and justice; all of which must be addressed in order to secure long-term social and political peace.

Notes

1 The Berber-speaking populations of North Africa are descended from communities whose presence in the region significantly pre-dated that of the arrival of the Arabs in the seventh century AD. Of uncertain origin but thought to have originally migrated from Asia Minor around 2000 BC, these communities intermarried with the Arab population and over time embraced Islam. Although Arabic became the dominant language in the region, significant pockets of the population—notably in more remote mountainous and desert areas—have continued to use Berber languages and it is the use of these languages that most usually identifies someone as "Berber" (although family, cultural practices, and increasingly self-identification also play a part). The most important concentrations of these populations are in the mountainous areas of Morocco (the Rif and the Middle, High, and Anti-Atlas ranges), the southern Souss Valley in Morocco and the Kabyle and Aurès highland regions of Algeria. Much smaller communities can be found in other parts of Algeria as well as in Tunisia, Libya and Egypt. There are also the nomadic Tuareg tribes spread across southern Algeria, Niger, and Mali. Although each community has its own distinct dialect, all are recognizably related and seen as variations of "Berber."

2 Berber-speaking communities are present in most states of the North African littoral and the Sahel, but only those in Algeria and Morocco are large enough to have a substantial impact on domestic state politics.

3 "Amazigh" is the Berber word for "Berber." Most Berber speakers, particularly Berber activists, prefer using this term, believing the term "Berber" to have pejorative origins and connotations—notably a suggested link to the term "Barbarian."

4 E. Gellner and C. Micaud (eds), *Arabs and Berbers: From Tribe to Nation in North Africa*, London: Duckworth, 1973.

5 D. Crawford and K. E. Hoffman, "Essentially Amazigh: Urban Berbers and the Global village," in R. K. Lacey and R. M. Coury (eds), *The Arab-African and Islamic Worlds: Interdisciplinary Studies*, New York: Peter Lang, 2000, p. 119.

6 It should be noted that at least one contributor to *Arabs and Berbers* did correctly predict that rapid Arabization might lead to the development of "ethnic politics": see W. Quandt, "The Berbers in the Algerian Political Elite," in Gellner and Micaud (eds), op. cit.

7 P. M. E. Lorcin, *Imperial Identities: Stereotyping, Prejudice and Race in Colonial Algeria*, London: I. B. Tauris, 1995.

8 M. Brett and E. Fentress, *The Berbers*, Oxford: Blackwell, 1996, pp. 273–4.

9 S. Mezhoud, "Glasnost the Algerian Way: The role of Berber nationalists in political reform," in G. Joffé (ed.), *North Africa: Nation, State and Region*, London: Routledge, 1993.

10 International Crisis Group (ICG), *Unrest and Impasse in Kabylia*, Middle East/ North Africa Report No.15, 10 June 2003, pp. 7–8. Available at: http:// www.crisisgroup.org/home/index.cfm?id=1415&l=1.

11 Ibid., p. 38.

12 Ibid.

13 Although no official figures exist some 40 percent of the Moroccan population is usually thought to speak one of the Berber languages, compared to between a fifth and quarter of the Algerian population.

14 The behaviour of *Istiqlal* members led to complaints of "Fassi colonization" in several Berber-speaking areas—a reference to the fact that so many of the party's members and leaders came from the city of Fes. See J. Waterbury, *The Commander of the Faithful: The Moroccan Elite: A Study in Segmented Politics*, London: Weidenfeld and Nicolson, 1970, p. 235.

15 R. Leveau, *Le Fellah Marocain: Défenseur du Trône*, Paris: Presses de la Fondation des Sciences Politiques, 1985, pp. 83–7.

16 It is sometimes asserted that the two failed military *coups d'état* of the early 1970s represented attempts by Berbers to take control of the state, since all of the key figures involved were of Berber origin. However, such an assertion ignores the fact that the Berber origins of the plotters were simply a reflection of the domination of the military by Berber speakers. This meant that virtually all of the military officers who stayed loyal and resisted the coups were also of Berber origin.

17 Crawford and Hoffman, op. cit., p. 123.

18 One avenue for the spread of Berber "consciousness," which was particularly effective in Algeria, is popular music. In Morocco, one music group whose songs articulate ideas of Berber identity has sold 160,000 copies of its most recent cassette, mostly to young Moroccans (*Tel Quel*, 9 July 2005). At the more anecdotal level, in March 2001, the author encountered a youth in the central High Atlas in Morocco who refused out of principle to speak to him in Arabic. The youth stated that he was Berber and would only converse in Berber or a European language. Such a phenomenon has been common in parts of Kabylia in Algeria since at least the early 1980s.

19 Interview by the author with Saad-Eddine Othmani, Secretary-General of the Party of Justice and Development (PJD), Rabat, 12 April 2005; and with Mustapha Ramid, MP from the PJD, Rabat, 13 April 2005. A compromise on the issue of the script was found through the adoption of *Tifinagh*, an ancient script used by Berber speakers in parts of the Sahara.

20 Y. H. Zoubir, "Stalled Democratization of an Authoritarian Regime: The Case of Algeria," *Democratization*, vol. 2, no. 2, 1994–1995.

21 Abdeslam Yassin of the *Al-'Adl wa-'l-Ihsan* (Justice and Spirituality) movement and Saad-Eddine Othmani, head of the Party of Justice and Development (PJD) are both Berber speakers from southern Morocco.

22 Available at: http://www.algeria-watch.org/farticle/docu/platform.htm.

23 A. Layachi, "The Berbers in Algeria: Politicized Ethnicity and Ethnicized Politics," in M. Shatzmiller (ed.), *Nationalism and Minority Identities in Islamic Societies*, Montreal and Kingston: McGill-Queen's University Press, 2005, pp. 221–3.

24 ICG, op. cit., pp. 24–6; Layachi, op. cit., pp. 213–9.

25 D. Crawford, "Royal Interest in Local Culture: Amazigh Culture and the Moroccan State," in M. Shatzmiller (ed.), op. cit., p. 187.

26 *La Gazette du Maroc*, 8 August 2005.

27 Interview by the author with Ahmed Adghrini, Berberist activist and Secretary-General of the *Parti Démocratique Amazigh Marocain* (PDAM), Rabat, 2 July 2001.

28 Crawford and Hoffman, op. cit., pp. 119–22.

29 Ahmed Adghrini (now leader of the PDAM) has, for example, argued that "what threatens Morocco is the transfer of the Middle East conflict to North Africa. ... The true threat to our identity is the Arab-Islamic movement who import into here conflicts from outside" (*La Gazette du Maroc*, 15 April 2002).

30 One Berber newspaper in Morocco, for example, argued that official efforts to encourage solidarity with the Palestinians were aimed at undermining Berbers and Berber identity. *Agraw Amazigh*, 4 January 2001.

31 Crawford and Hoffman, op. cit., p. 126.

32 H. Roberts, (1982) "The Unforeseen Development of the Kabyle Question in Contemporary Algeria," *Government and Opposition*, vol. 17, 1982, pp. 312–34 (321).

33 Interview by the author with Abdeslam Khalafi, Member of the *Institut Royal de la Culture Amazighe* (IRCAM), Rabat, 8 April 2005.

34 H. Roberts, "From Radical Mission to Equivocal Ambition: The Expansion and Manipulation of Algerian Islamism, 1979–1992," in M. E. Marty and R. Scott Appleby (eds), *Accounting for Fundamentalisms: The Dynamic Character of Movements*, Chicago, IL: University of Chicago Press, 1994; M. Willis, *The Islamist Challenge in Algeria: A Political History*, New York: New York University Press, 1997.

35 Layachi, op. cit., p. 224.

36 B. Maddy-Weitzman, "Contested Identities: Berbers, Berberism and the State in North Africa," *The Journal of North African Studies*, vol. 6, 2001, pp. 23–47 (42).

Part III
Strategic and Security Relations of the Maghreb

12 Rethinking Maghrebi Security

The Challenge of Multilateralism

Cherif Dris

Bilateral relations define North African national security. Maghrebi states have failed to establish a multilateral mechanism, which determines for state behavior, as is the case in other areas such as Europe and Southeast Asia. Maghrebi states, therefore, manage their bilateral disputes without resorting to multilateralism or to multilateral mechanisms. This raises the question of whether or not the failure of Maghrebi states to create a multilateral system can be considered as an initial structural framework for regulating regional relations. This chapter will examine the factors and reasons that make the emergence of a multilateral security structure unrealistic. The influence of external factors on the security strategies in North Africa, as exemplified by NATO's Mediterranean Dialogue and the "5 + 5" forum, will also be analyzed. But before tackling these issues, it will be useful to introduce, albeit briefly, the theoretical framework of multilateralism.

Multilateralism: The Theoretical Framework

The multilateralization of security is a topic that has captured the interest of scholars in international relations since the end of the Cold War.[1] The management and resolution of regional conflicts and the promotion of peace and security in areas where the logic of balance of power has failed to do so increased the importance of multilateralism and collective action. Scholars from the neo-functionalist and liberal mainstream uphold the conventional wisdom that asserts that security dilemma—i.e., efforts undertaken to enhance one's security will often threaten the security of one's opponents[2]—shapes the behavior of states in some given areas, which explains the prevalence of regional tension. And if realists are convinced that no other mechanisms than the balance of power can mitigate these tensions and regulate the security relations between states, authors like David Mitrany and Karl Deutsch explore another path and promote instead the possibility that international and regional conflicts could be resolved through cooperation and integration. In his seminal work, *A Working Peace System*, David Mitrany advocated the importance of technical and functional organizations which are devoted to tackling economic and social issues. He proposed the substitution of hard political issues for low political issues as a key pillar in restructuring international relations. Mitrany's disciples, such as Karl Deutsch and Ernst Hass, went far beyond this in emphasizing the importance of economic and social issues as independent variables explaining the behavior of states and their tendency to cooperate among themselves. The emergence of the European Community and the transatlantic association symbolized by NATO gave more salience to the works of those two authors and to the works of neo-functionalist schools. Yet, the success of the Western European experience and the demise of the Soviet Union encouraged the authors of this school to use this model as the only reference deserving to be followed by other areas, since it depicts the transcendence of both national sovereignty and the limited conception of international relations reduced to the security dilemma.

The end of the Cold War made the settlement of multilateral structures more salient, because it became more difficult to resolve regional disputes by resorting only to bilateralism. As explained by John Ruggie, "multilateralism is the elementary institutional shape [form] of modern international life."[3] And by definition, multilateralism is the coordination of three or more states' national policies.[4] This means abiding by certain rules and norms that shape state behavior. The existence of such norms and rules aims at preventing hegemonic temptation and leadership rivalry. By abandoning part of their sovereignty to a supranational structure, states refrain from behaving unilaterally.

Furthermore, it should be noted that multilateralism raises the question as to whether a regional political identity is required. Such an identity exists in a given area when the respective actors composing a geopolitical space share certain values and a similar perception about the threats that may jeopardize their mutual security. In their seminal work on security communities, Emanuel Adler and Michael Barnett[5] stated that a collective identity represents a linchpin for the emergence of a security community, which is considered as the most developed form of multilateralism. This thesis is not new, since the first scholar to point out the importance of collective identity was Karl Deutsch when he asserted that security community-building is an exercise of identity formation.[6] Thus, one cannot imagine the creation of a multilateral security structure without the existence of a regional identity. More importantly, the emergence of this regional structure rests upon the actors' recognition that their national security depends on regional stability. The stability of the whole must prevail over that of the individual states.

The extent to which the Maghrebi countries are ready to abandon some part of their sovereignty to a transnational structure is questionable. We will try in this chapter to examine Maghrebi perception of regional security and the way cooperation in this field must be organized.

The Maghrebi Integrationist Project: Between Dream and Reality

The majority of the Maghrebi population still believes that a unified Maghreb is an illusion and that the regional integration project is out of reach. It is also questionable whether one should persist in hoping for the materialization of this idea when the national leaders do not display any political will to transcend their differences. Moreover, some intellectuals have overtly expressed the idea of forsaking the Arab Maghreb Union project and replacing it with a Western Mediterranean Union.[7] However, public opinion is less enthusiastic about supporting a project that does not reflect popular aspirations. The Algerians exchange more letters with France than with Tunisians and Moroccans. Despite the fact that the three countries of the central Maghreb share the same religion, Islam, the Arabic language, and the historical legacy of French colonialism, the economic and social connections are still weak, and nothing suggests that the situation may change soon. In its last report on economic perspectives in Central Asia and North Africa, the International Monetary Fund (IMF) pointed out the weakness of intra-Maghrebi trade, which does not exceed 2 percent, whereas trade between the Maghreb and the European Union (EU) amounts to over 66 percent.[8] And, if Europeans are able to cross their internal borders without presenting any document, Maghrebis still have to surmount administrative obstacles, such as an entry visa, thus preventing them from moving freely from one Maghrebi country to another. When a terrorist group assassinated two Spanish tourists in the Atlas Asni hotel in Marrakesh in summer 1994, the Moroccan government accused the Algerian secret services of being behind the attack and imposed entry visa requirements on Algerians and nationals of Algerian origin. The immediate response by the Algerian government was to close the border with Morocco. Only recently has the obligatory visa been unilaterally removed by Morocco,[9] considered a positive step in the process of normalizing relations between the two countries.

These measures demonstrate the importance of both Algeria and Morocco in the Maghrebi integration process. Indeed, like France and Germany in the process of creating the EU, both Algeria and Morocco are deemed to play a key role in regional Maghrebi dynamics. However, the conflict over Western Sahara, the "sand war" of 1963, and the delimiting of the common borders have frozen all attempts to open a venue for an integrated Maghreb. Until 1969, Morocco claimed Tindouf as belonging to its territory and some political leaders, even those who are in the opposition, such as Moumen Diouri, went far further by considering Béchar and Tlemcen as Moroccan territory. This explains why, in 1963, Morocco waged a limited war against Algeria to recover by force what France had promised in 1957, i.e., the re-ceding of Tindouf to Morocco in exchange for closing the FLN office in Morocco. But Mohammed V's plan was not to annex Tindouf by force after the decolonization of Algeria, nor was he eager to accept

France's proposal to withdraw support from Algerian militants. The 1963 "sand war" was King Hassan II's decision and the border issues between the two countries worsened with the territorial dispute over Western Sahara in 1975. Since then the Moroccan government has maintained its territorial claim over Saharan territory and rejected any solution that does not recognize its claim, and thus staunchly opposes the independence of Western Sahara.

Such a prerequisite reinforces the contentious role that the issue of Western Sahara plays in the evolution of Maghrebi dynamics,[10] notably in maintaining the salience of the bilateral character of Maghrebi relations, and thus shaping the region's security configuration. The efforts made in early 1989 with the creation of the Arab Maghreb Union (AMU) promoted multilateralism as a new way of regulating regional interactions, with the goal of diminishing the pressure exerted by bilateral relations. For Maghrebi leaders, this evolution implied rethinking Maghrebi security by favoring the promotion of multilateralism as a culture, and not as a substitute for bilateralism.

The Maghrebi Security Structure: The Weight of Bilateralism

The Maghrebi states have expressed no interest in becoming involved in any multilateral arrangement that could impose constraints. This lack of interest in multilateralism could be imputed to the regional leadership rivalry that has structured Maghrebi relations since the earlier years of independence. But it should be noted that this leadership rivalry has been fueled by the divergence that faced Maghrebi leaders on the way to achieving the nation-building process, and the role that each country should play on the regional scene. The persistence of border disputes inherited from the colonial era rendered the situation more complicated, for each country was convinced that the delimitation made by the French did not serve its interest. This explains why, in 1963, Morocco waged war against Algeria in order to annexe Tindouf as the first step in the realization of King Hassan's project to build Greater Morocco, with borders stretching from Tangier to the Senegal river. Moroccan leaders did not exhibit any will to resolve their frontier dispute with Algeria. The 1969 signing of the Treaty of Fraternity, Good Neighborliness, and Cooperation and the three 1972 conventions, especially that recognizing the de facto Moroccan–Algerian frontier as a legal boundary, were only a maneuver on the part of King Hassan II, who linked resolution of the issue to that of Western Sahara. For Morocco, as long as Algeria continues to oppose Morocco's claims over Western Sahara, the Algerian–Moroccan border issue will find no solution. King Hassan's decision to postpone the ratification of the 1972 border agreement until 1989, despite the fact that Algeria ratified it in 1973, was a clear demonstration of Morocco's determination to annexe Western Sahara.

However, Morocco was not the only country that contested the way borders with Algeria have been drawn. In 1957, just one year after independence,

Tunisia's President, Habib Bourguiba, asked the French government and the Algerian Provisional Government (GPRA) to arrange for a new delimitation of the Tunisian frontiers with Algeria. In 1964, Habib Bourguiba urged his Algerian counterpart, Ahmed Ben Bella, in vain to find a solution to this issue. The coming to power of Houari Boumedienne in June 1965 opened a door of opportunity for Tunisians who hoped for a final solution to the problem. Algeria's new leaders were very eager to address Tunisian claims; the two countries signed a 20-year treaty of Fraternity, Good Neighborliness, and Cooperation in January 1970. The problem was definitively solved in 1993, at a time when Algeria was struggling to contain the upsurge of terrorism.

The problem with Libya was more complicated than that with Tunisia, since Libyan leader Muammar Qaddafi had regional ambitions and considered the frontiers to be a product of colonization. Hence, he proclaimed their abolition and the deepening of Arab unity. The Libyan leader was not convinced of the necessity of creating a Maghreb union; this explains his refusal to sign a treaty with Algeria to delineate their common borders. Algeria retaliated against Libyan ambitions by opposing the extension to Libya of the Treaty of Fraternity and Concord signed in 1983 with Tunisia and Mauritania.[11]

Despite the resolution of border differences inherited from the colonial era, the alleviation of regional tensions was facilitated by the conclusion of bilateral treaties. None of the Maghrebi states was convinced of the virtues of multilateralism, and thus bilateralism remained the preferred way to interact within the Maghreb. This section will therefore focus on the different bilateral treaties signed between the Maghrebi states, with particular focus on intra-regional treaties, and later those between Maghrebi states and external powers.

The Friendship and Brotherhood Treaties

Algeria, Tunisia, Libya, and Morocco signed bilateral treaties in 1969, 1971, and 1973. However, due to their relevance, greater importance will be given to those concluded in 1983 and 1984. These treaties were ordained to meet the need of certain countries by strengthening their relations. The treaties also permitted the states concerned to better coordinate their policies and counter any external or internal challenge. Algeria and Tunisia, joined by Mauritania, signed the Friendship and Brotherhood Treaty in 1983 in response to their mutual need to tighten relations.

Many political analysts considered the treaty to be an alliance orchestrated by Algeria in order to isolate Morocco. Whether or not this was the case, the Algerian–Tunisian rapprochement reflected the mutual national intention to create a peaceful environment which would be conducive to a deepening of bilateral relations. The treaty entailed many clauses, but the most important related to non-aggression and respecting border demarcations.

The latter marked the resolution of the border disputes between Algeria and Tunisia. However, the question of borders in the Maghreb remains unsolved, as demonstrated by the lingering issue of Algeria's borders with Morocco. Since the early years of independence, Tunisia had claimed national sovereignty over part of eastern Algerian territory, namely the "*borne 243*" (i.e., milepost 243). However, unlike Morocco, Tunisia did not pursue its claim, perhaps due to its inability to sustain a rift with Algeria. This may explain why Algeria and Tunisia did not feel the need to cooperate militarily in an integration project, and maintained the isolation of Morocco. Though the 1983 treaty did not lead to a military alliance, Tunisian national defense policy increasingly resembled Algeria's.

Algeria and Mauritania signed a treaty the same year. The treaty contained the same clauses as were embodied in the treaty signed with Tunisia, and excluded military cooperation. In the case of Mauritania, this exclusion seems more justified, since Algeria feared that military cooperation with Mauritania could push Morocco to consider a military alliance with Libya; in which case, Algeria would be surrounded. Algeria's largest preoccupation was the need to preserve the regional balance of power, thus its strategy to isolate Morocco. While supporting the POLISARIO Front in the Western Sahara conflict against Moroccan domination, Algeria also attempted to keep Mauritania at a safe distance from its northern neighbor.

Morocco interpreted the Algerian ambition to strengthen its relations with Tunisia and Mauritania as an alliance and aggression against the kingdom. Accordingly, Morocco reacted rapidly to the Algerian strategy. On 13 August 1984, Morocco and Libya joined forces and signed a similar treaty. King Hassan II easily convinced the Libyan leader to remain aloof from Algeria and Tunisia and to join Morocco in its efforts to assert its sovereignty over the Western Saharan territory. Colonel Qaddafi was very interested in the Moroccan strategy because he feared that the rapprochement between Algeria, Tunisia, and Mauritania would reinforce Algeria's position as a regional leader. Moreover, due to the aborted integration project with Tunisia in 1974, Libya believed Tunisia was more eager to conclude a union with Algeria, and therefore responded to the Moroccan proposal. Qaddafi accepted the proposal because he thought that this could be the only way to promote Libya's interest and break the isolation imposed by the United States. But the United States neither appreciated this shift in Libyan Maghrebi policy nor approved of the Moroccan decision to strengthen its relations with Libya. The rift caused by the Moroccan–Libyan reconciliation paved the way for a honeymoon between Algeria and the United States, as illustrated by the visit of Chadli Benjedid to Washington in April 1985.

These treaties shed light on the logic of power ambition, reflected by alliance games in which each state needs the support of one of its neighbors in order to reduce the influence of its rival. These arrangements highlight regional interactions, and the balance of power is most evident in the case of rivalry between Algeria and Morocco. In addition to the persistence of their border disputes, both states are deeply involved in the Western Sahara conflict. The friendship treaty signed by Algerian President Houari Boumedienne and King Hassan II, on 15 January 1969, in Ifran, Morocco, failed to resolve the border dispute. Algeria ratified the treaty, but not Morocco, which still maintains irredentist claims over Algerian territory. In fact, each country tried to develop a strategy that aimed to marginalize the other. Indeed, the treaties signed by Algeria with Tunisia and Mauritania were intended to constrain Morocco from pursuing its claims over Western Sahara. These alliances mirrored what Paul Balta has described as the Maghrebi Cold War,[12] in which mutual distrust was the guiding rule of each country's foreign policy, which in turn instigated some Maghrebi states to conclude other treaties with external actors.

External Bilateral Agreements

The most obvious external bilateral agreements were signed by France with Tunisia on the one hand and with Mauritania on the other. No such agreement was signed between the United States and Morocco, but the two countries entered close military collaboration because the United States considers Morocco a key ally in North Africa. However, Algeria and Libya were not convinced of the need to associate their security with foreign powers through an accord. The nonalignment policy pursued by the two countries explains their opposition to military alliances, whatever their ideological implication. Their painful experience with colonialism may explain this attitude. Why, then, was this not the case for Tunisia and Morocco, even though both countries belong to the nonaligned movement?

Algeria and Libya strengthened their relations with a number of African countries by granting them military assistance. Algeria's inclination toward African countries was considered a pillar of its foreign policy. The support Algeria gave to liberation movements was motivated by its commitment, as a former European colony, to the achievement of national self-determination.[13] However, Algeria's endeavors toward some African countries stem from its aspiration to counteract Morocco, thereby gaining more support for Algeria's quest to help the Sahrawi people create an independent state.[14]

The military cooperation of Morocco, Tunisia, and Mauritania with Western powers has different motives. The aim of the military assistance the United States provided to Morocco was to strengthen the latter's position in the Western Sahara conflict. Since Morocco's independence in 1956, more than 3,000 Moroccan soldiers have received training in the United States. In 1979, the US administration decided to increase military assistance to Morocco by 100 percent. From 1989 to 1994, the US provided almost 30 percent of Morocco's arms supplies.[15] Currently, the amount of military assistance the United States gives annually to Morocco is over $20m. This assistance is aimed at helping the Moroccan security forces in their effort to stop illegal immigration and to fight terrorism.[16] However, this military assistance was not without strings attached to it: the United States used arms supplies to reinforce Morocco's capacity as a linchpin of US containment strategy in the Western Mediterranean. Gaining port access to Morocco provided the US with control of the western shore of the Mediterranean and the Atlantic Ocean, thus pre-empting possible Soviet incursions.

The French–Tunisian treaty did not imply military cooperation in a traditional sense. Though tacitly mentioned, neither country overtly committed to peaceful relations. Tunisia merely conceded its territory for France to use in undertaking certain operations, such as preventing Libya from exacerbating the crisis over the Gulf of Gafsa. The respective bilateral agreements clearly demonstrate the weight of bilateralism in Maghrebi relations. Multilateralism is therefore not critical in the national agendas of the Maghrebi states. The next section will examine the reasons for the aversion of Maghrebi states to multilateralism in their national security relations.

Maghrebi Security: Between the Logic of Westphalia and Transnational Requirements

All North African countries experienced several decades of European colonialism. With the era of decolonization, these countries entered a long and strenuous process of nation-state building. However, the common desire to build a strong state did not imply a common development strategy. Morocco and Tunisia chose the capitalist model, while Algeria, Mauritania, and Libya opted for the socialist system. But the differences in the national development process did not mean the absence of a common denominator. All five countries share the tendency to centralize the decision-making process, which excludes any participation on the part of civil society actors. Nothing is more striking in this tendency to centralize public affairs management than the way foreign policy is conducted. As former colonies, Maghrebi countries, like others, are very jealous of their sovereignty and national independence. In the case of developing countries, this feeling is expressed more acutely. The Maghreb countries remain faithful to the Westphalian logic and were thus not eager to get involved in any kind of transnational action, with all that this term implies. The preoccupations related to the tasks of nation-state building process are often presented as a justification for refusing any multilateral security arrangements.

As the process of nation-state building in the Maghreb has just begun, the ruling elites fear that Maghrebi security multilateralism would jeopardize their domestic integrity and national development process. Accordingly, colonial legacy shaped the way the states envisage the legal use of violence. The national security doctrine of those states was thus elaborated to pursue the objective of preserving territorial integrity and national independence. What also made the engagement of Maghrebi states in a multilateral security enterprise less realistic was the nature of ruling regimes that were dominated by the military establishment. Consequently, the culture of secrecy and the politicization of the military became cardinal pillars in sustaining the philosophy of the political systems of these countries. Thus, the transfer of some fragments of state sovereignty to a transnational security institution proved impossible to realize.

The national security of these countries is more often than not linked to the security of the regime. What is often considered as a threat to national security is in fact a threat to the continuity of the regime. The Maghrebi ruling elites have been more preoccupied with the activities of the opposition than with any external threat. The persistence of the regime security shows the weight of the Westphalian culture in Maghrebi politics. The case of North Africa is also illustrative of the general situation prevailing in the Arab world, where Arab leaders express an exacerbated nationalism. The logic of Westphalia therefore still persists.

The Geopolitics of the Maghreb and Hegemonic Rivalry

As a sub-regional system, the Maghreb is linked to three geopolitical areas: Africa, the Mediterranean, and the Arab world. To these areas should be added the highly strategic access to the Atlantic Ocean enjoyed by both Morocco and Mauritania. These three areas provide the Maghreb countries with the opportunity to envisage a multidirectional policy.

Given this geopolitical location, each Maghrebi country is trying to pursue a national policy that promotes its interests in the best way possible. However, the ability of these countries to be present in these three areas depends on their power resources. The only countries that possess the capacity to develop a multidirectional policy are Algeria and Libya, and to a lesser extent Morocco. Therefore, Algeria is involved in the Arab world, Africa, and the Mediterranean. But Algerian diplomatic activism in Africa and the Mediterranean is more important than in the Arab world. After almost a decade of isolation (1992–2000), Algeria has tried to regain the ground it lost due to its internal crisis. Algeria's neighbors are following the same path.

The case of Libya deserves particular attention. Libyan foreign policy, since the coming to power of Colonel Muammar Qaddafi on 1 September 1969, moved from Arabism to Africanism. The Libyan leader considers his country to be linked more to Africa than to the Arab world. Indeed, on many occasions the Libyan leader has displayed his disdain for any effort to boost common Arab action by making declarations that discredit certain Arab leaders.[17] The center of gravity of Libyan diplomacy seems to be Africa, where Libya's level of investment is highest. Libyan efforts to encourage Islamic preaching by financing the construction of mosques and Islamic centers in many sub-Saharan countries should also be emphasized. The proselytizing clashes, however, with Saudi Arabian interest in Africa, are even more important. Though there is a similitude in the objectives of both countries, Saudi Arabia considers Libyan initiatives in Africa as threatening its efforts at spreading Wahhabism, a very conservative, *salafi* form of Islam, in this area. Morocco is also trying to reinforce its presence in Africa, at least in the Sahel region, and in the Mediterranean. However, Morocco is clearly more interested in an active presence in the Mediterranean basin than in the African continent. Announced in 1987 by former King Hassan II, Morocco's appeal to conform to European community standards is an indication of the lack of interest toward an integrated Maghreb region. In 1993, Morocco's former foreign minister, Abdelatif Filali, declared that Morocco is entitled to a special relationship with the EU because it is the country closest to Europe in the orientation of its economy, diplomacy, and internal policies.[18]

The quest of each North African country to reinforce its presence in one of the three areas mentioned will undoubtedly create leadership rivalry. The bilateral disputes outlined above can be considered a direct result of the animosity that characterizes relations between the national leaderships. The balance of power in this region depends upon the evolution of bilateral relations, primarily between Algeria and Morocco. Leadership rivalry is not a characteristic peculiar to the Maghreb. In Europe, Latin America, and Southeast Asia some countries embarked upon competition to enhance their leadership. The case of Southeast Asian countries deserves particular attention. Although they have coalesced as a regional forum, the Association of Southeast Asian Nations (ASEAN), these nations are not exempt from leadership rivalry, exemplified primarily between Indonesia and Malaysia. Unlike the Maghrebi region, the problem in this area is slightly different. The Southeast Asian geopolitical game is played in such a way that no country in the region can develop a multidirectional policy. Except for Indonesia, which has access to the Indian Ocean via the straits (Malacca, Sonde, and Lambok), the other Southeast Asian countries are land-locked, and do not have any maritime connection to other areas. This may explain why they can overcome disputes and thus create a regional structure based on principles and rules that guide the regional interactions.

Considering these factors, multilateral security-building in the Maghreb is currently not feasible. The absence of a common threat renders the project unnecessary. Some may argue, however, that Maghrebi countries share the same security preoccupation, particularly the Islamist upsurge. During the last decade, Islamist movements appeared as the main political actors that could threaten the stability of the Maghrebi states. In Algeria, the interruption of the electoral process in January 1992 laid the ground for the radicalization of some Islamist movements. The other wing of political Islamism, represented by Hamas and Enahda, stood back from the violence, preferring participation in the political process. The way those two parties managed the interruption of the electoral process and the ensuing crisis was very beneficial to the political and military establishment, since it strengthened the legitimacy of the decision made on 11 January 1992. It should be noted, however, that Morocco and Libya did not perceive the irruption of terrorism in Algeria in the early 1990s as a direct threat to their own security. In fact, King Hassan stated that what happened in Algeria could be considered as a laboratory, suggesting that Morocco would not be opposed to an Islamist regime in Algeria. Qaddafi seemed to share the same view. It is no secret that both Morocco and Libya facilitated the action of Algerian terrorist groups; they imposed no restriction on their movement across their respective borders. This attitude shows how different those countries' perceptions of the Islamic threat were in the early 1990s.

Moreover, respective national interests still guide foreign policies and thus take precedence over a Maghrebi regional policy. In the absence of a common regional threat and due to these factors, the construction of a regional security structure in the Maghreb is highly unlikely. However, North African countries do share many values, which translate into a common regional political identity. This regional identity has led to the creation, in February 1989, of the Arab Maghreb Union (AMU), but it remains unclear whether the AMU can be the keystone to multilateral security in the Maghreb.

The Arab Maghreb Union and the Problem of Multilateral Security

The AMU was not created as a result of security preoccupations. Given that no external threat endangered regional security—the Islamist threat having appeared after the creation of this structure—the five Maghrebi states felt no need to elaborate a transnational security strategy which would impose many national constraints. Therefore, multilateral national security was not included in the AMU agenda. The reason for the creation of the AMU was the mutual fear among Maghrebi states that EU enlargement eastward would increasingly marginalize them. The Maghrebi states thus responded to these changes in the international system.

When the Maghrebi states launched this regional initiative, they were committed to respecting certain rules of conduct to prevent destabilization of the balance of power in the Maghreb. These rules are embodied in articles 14 and 15 of the AMU treaty. Article 14 states that "any aggression targeting one of the member states will be considered as an aggression against all members." And article 15 claims that "no member state should engage in any military or political alliance that may threaten the territorial independence of the other members." As demonstrated by these two articles, the AMU cannot be considered as a security bloc or a military alliance, but article 14 also seems to suggest the opposite.

The example of NATO is not all that different. Article 5 of NATO's charter stipulates a similar meaning to that of article 15 of the AMU treaty. When the United States was attacked on 11 September 2001, all members of NATO expressed their solidarity with the United States and mobilized their commitment to assist their allies, as specified by article 5. In the North African context, solidarity is not the rule. When an international embargo was imposed on Libya by the UN Security Council, following the explosion of the Pan Am airplane over Lockerbie in Scotland in December 1988, no Maghrebi state went beyond denouncing the embargo. Furthermore, the current circumstances do not suggest that the solidarity stated in article 14 will be applied. The reason for this is that the AMU treaty does not contain any clauses that would permit a preliminary discussion.[19] The disposition forbidding any member state from engaging in a military or political alliance did not prevent the Maghrebi countries from cooperating with external powers and creating internal military alliances, thus effectively pursuing some objectives that overlooked those embodied in the AMU charter. NATO's Mediterranean Dialogue and the "5 + 5," which gathers five countries from the northern Mediterranean shore and five countries from the southern shore, are equally indicative of this contradiction between the theory and practice of Maghrebi security realities.

With the exception of Libya, the adherence of Maghrebi states to the Mediterranean Dialogue since 1994 represents a break with the typical Maghrebi security discourse. Until then, the Maghrebi states had never been involved in such a multilateral security structure. A process of rethinking the way Maghrebi security should be perceived has stemmed from the different multilateral security forum approach. The prerequisites for paving the way to the multilateralism of Maghrebi security are equally important.

Multilateralism and Regional Political Identity

As noted above, regional political identity could be considered as a prerequisite for a multilateral construction, especially if this construction takes the form of a security community. As a security community, Western Europe fulfills this condition because the members composing the community share many common values, priorities, and threats.[20] What about Maghrebi countries?

In the Maghreb, common values still exist: the five countries practice the same religion, speak the same language, and have the same historical legacy of European colonialism. The other common feature is the existence of a Berber identity. The Berbers are present in all five countries. They are therefore considered a predominant component of North African identity. These features may suggest the existence of a common Maghrebi political identity. But, as Michael Barnet claims, "There is no reason to assume that those who share a common identity will necessarily have a conflict-free environment."[21] Along the same lines: "States that share a basic identity and attempt to organize themselves into a self-constituted group may hold rival interactions concerning a desired regional order."[22]

As a consequence, a common identity does not necessarily imply a common perception of the regional security order that should prevail.

Algeria and Morocco, for example, have a deep Islamic heritage, pertaining to the same religion and to the same political entity under the Almoravid and Almohad dynasties of the twelfth and thirteenth centuries. However, this has not prevented either state from maintaining a mutual distance, even from engaging in border disputes and a protracted conflict over Western Sahara. The multilateralism of Maghrebi security therefore implies setting rules and norms to guide the national conduct of the state actors. Yet, thus far, the Maghrebi states seem incapable of developing a similar perception about the nature of a national security threat, and currently no external power threatens Maghrebi regional security.

Maghrebi Threat: Conflicting Perceptions and Mutual Distrust

The power ambitions of some external actors, like Europe and the United States, have never been considered as a threat to the security of the Maghreb. However, there is no regional power with the ability to impose its will over the rest of the Maghreb. Characteristically, the North African states have belonged to a category of "small" countries which lack the capacity to influence other countries or to shape the regional balance of power with a pursued national policy. When the Southeast Asian states took the decision in 1967 to create ASEAN, they did so because they felt threatened by Chinese expansion. Indonesia and Malaysia perceived the Chinese threat as greater than that from any other state. The Southeast Asian states clearly agreed that the containment of Chinese communism was in their mutual interest. This does not mean that bilateral and local tensions did not exist, but rather that China was perceived by the Southeast Asian states as the primary threat. In the Maghreb, as mentioned earlier, the situation is quite different, and the perception of the threat remains largely domestic.

The Maghrebi states do not face any secessionist movement, as is the case in other countries. Although Maghrebi societies entail some ethnic and racial elements, represented mainly by the Berbers, no secessionist movement has emerged. When they obtained independence, the Maghrebi states imposed national unanimity that prevented any pluralistic expression. The Maghrebi states have internal preoccupations, and the threats to national security are domestic in nature. Most Maghrebi states had one-party systems which barred political pluralism, and thus excluded the rise of opposition parties, which have been largely oppressed. The wave of democracy that swept the world pushed the ruling elites in these countries to open up the political arena to legal opposition parties. The Islamic movement was the great beneficiary of this democratic opening; its large social bases allowed it to strengthen and enlarge its presence and thus appear as a leading political force. The local and legislative elections held in 1990 and 1991 in Algeria confirmed this trend.[23]

However, the interruption on 11 January 1992 of the second phase of the legislative elections in Algeria pushed radical Islamists, represented by the

Front Islamique du Salut (FIS), to resort to violence, which was labeled terrorism and became the primary threat to the national security of Algeria. The other North African states faced the same Islamic challenge, but to a lesser degree. The radicalization of Moroccan and Tunisian Islamists did not lead to large-scale terrorism. Algeria therefore represents an exception, for the resurgence of terrorism in Morocco and Tunisia dates only from 2002 and 2003, with the attacks in Jerba in 2002 and Casablanca in 2003.

The three countries perceive terrorism as a main security threat, but this does not mean that they act according to the same policy. The national definition of terrorism is also different. Morocco thus considers the POLISARIO Front as terrorist movement and claims Western Sahara to be a domestic concern, whereas Algeria, like most African countries, categorizes the POLISARIO as a liberation movement struggling for independence. Moreover, the fact that Algeria and Morocco are facing the same threat does not exclude a mutual distrust. Algeria's leaders constantly accuse Morocco of allowing Algerian terrorist groups to use Moroccan territory as bases and are convinced the Moroccan government has done nothing to put an end to the activities of terrorist groups along the borders. In 1999, Abdelaziz Bouteflika publicly accused Morocco of supporting Algerian terrorists and encouraging the drug trade in Algeria. Morocco also accused Algeria of orchestrating a campaign of destabilization by allegedly permitting the 26 August 1994 terrorist attack which targeted the Atlas Asni Hotel in Marrakech.[24]

These reciprocal accusations clearly demonstrate the prevailing distrust between the two states. This mutual distrust pushed the two countries to develop a different strategy for national policy. The Algerian security doctrine therefore has been elaborated since the earlier years of independence according to the Moroccan parameter. The Algerian security interest focuses mainly on its southern borders. This explains the importance given by Algerian military authorities to its ground and air forces.[25] Similarly, in Morocco, the Western Sahara conflict and the border problem with Algeria represent key determinants in the formulation of the national security doctrine.

The difference in perceptions explains the Maghrebi countries' difficulties when confronted with coordinating their foreign and security policies. It goes without saying that even in the police and customs fields Maghrebi countries have failed to display any kind of goodwill to coordinate their efforts. Cooperation between the police of the Maghrebi states is still lagging behind, ever since the setting up of the AMU. The few common security challenges and stakes have not created an incentive for police cooperation because of national logic fed by the distrust they feel for each other. Indeed, article 15 of the AMU treaty stipulates that the member states should not allow any kind of activities that could harm the security and territorial integrity of one member state, but this commitment remains an unfulfilled promise.

However, the proliferation of some threats like drug trafficking, illegal migration, money laundering, and terrorism rendered police and customs cooperation between Maghrebi states more than necessary. During the 24th session of the Maghrebi Foreign Ministers' Council, held on 1 June 2006 in Tripoli, it was agreed that the member states should strengthen their efforts in order to contain the spread of illegal migration. But this too remains wishful thinking. In reality, there was no common regional strategy to tackle such issues. The reason explaining this vacuum may be found in the absence of political will on the part of Maghrebi leaders who seem more keen to tackle these common issues on a bilateral basis. Accordingly, Algeria and Libya agreed last year to coordinate their efforts in order to fight illegal migration and, in particular, drug trafficking, which has spread in an unprecedented manner during recent years. The two countries are considered as a transit area for these underground activities and share a long border. Both are not only seeking the exchange of experiences, information, and practical methods, but also trying to develop a common strategy to eradicate drug trafficking, which may include other AMU members. The other bilateral initiative in this area was taken by Algeria and Mauritania, whose two police institutions concluded, on 22 February 2006, an agreement that allows Mauritanian police to receive adequate training and equipment to fight terrorist groups and drug trafficking bands. The assault against a military barracks in Chenguiti, 150 km away from the capital Nouakchott, has, in fact, induced the Mauritanian government to seek police cooperation with its Algerian counterpart.

As shown by these examples, Maghrebi countries are not very interested in multilateral cooperation, which may limit their movement by imposing constraints on them, even though the problems mentioned above are becoming a serious threat to regional security. The absence of a Maghrebi security framework paved the way for an exogenous security framework to fill this vacuum. NATO and the European Union are trying to bend the Maghrebi region to their area of influence. This implies reshaping Maghrebi security behavior by encouraging the five countries to abandon their selfish attitude and act collectively by adapting their foreign and security policies to these of NATO or the European Union. But even in this area, Maghrebi states conform to NATO's Mediterranean Dialogue individually, not as a cohesive bloc. The same observation is made about the Maghrebi police structures, which cooperate separately with European police (Italy and Tunisia, Italy and Libya) for extraditing illegal immigrants. This multilateral security forum and the "5 + 5" forum will undoubtedly have consequences for Maghrebi security. These security frameworks will compel the Maghrebi states to rethink ways of instituting regional security. Now, the question is how this reformulation can occur.

External Factors and the Restructuring of Maghrebi Security

External factors refer to the Mediterranean multilateral security framework initiated by foreign powers. This security framework refers essentially to

NATO's Mediterranean Dialogue and the "5 + 5" forum, which brings together five countries from the northern Mediterranean shore and five from the southern shore.

NATO's Mediterranean Dialogue

Initiated in 1994, NATO's Mediterranean Dialogue is merely a multilateral congregation framework that does not open the door of adhesion to the southern partners. Many reasons lie behind NATO's decisions to launch this dialogue. But the most important remain the fears expressed by the southern countries about the future intentions of this multilateral security organization. After the demise of the Soviet Union, the southern countries began to raise questions about the future strategic concept that will shape NATO's policy for the third millennium. The quest for a new enemy fed the fears of the southern countries that NATO's threat perception would be dominated by what will happen in the south. The northern security discourse indeed reinforced this conviction, and certain Western leaders clearly declared that Islamic fundamentalism will be the next threat for NATO. Therefore, what leads the Atlantic Alliance leaders to bridge the gap with the southern countries is their desire to mitigate their apprehensions about the future directions of NATO. In this respect, NATO's Mediterranean Dialogue can be viewed as a public relations operation whose unique aim is to correct NATO's image and project the image of a peaceful organization in the south.[26]

The elements of NATO's Mediterranean Dialogue cannot be regarded as a foundation for adherence to the Atlantic Alliance by the southern Mediterranean states, and nothing suggests that this perspective is foreseeable in the future. However, the contents of NATO's dialogue are similar to the partnership for peace with former Eastern European countries. It entails a military cooperation program that includes joint exercises, visits, and training sessions for military institution members of the southern countries at NATO. Military cooperation has been broadened and intensified in such a way that military exercises on high seas became a routine and the docking of NATO's fleet in southern countries' ports became routine.

After more than ten years of existence, NATO's dialogue is now on the way to taking the form of a partnership. The members of the Atlantic Alliance have taken the decision, during their summit in Istanbul in June 2004, to promote the dialogue with the southern Mediterranean countries as a kind of partnership. This evolution of the dialogue is a clear indication of the Atlantic Alliance's determination to involve the countries of the southern shore in what they have undertaken since the end of the Cold War: crisis management and the fight against terrorism. Beyond this qualitative evolution, the Istanbul summit testifies to the Alliance's desire to overstretch its geo-strategic borders. Several NATO leaders have declared that nothing could prevent the Alliance from enlarging its security area to the south. More importantly, the promotion of NATO's dialogue members to the status of partners could not be dissociated from the US ambition to reshape the geopolitical map of the Middle East by incorporating some non-Arab countries, like Pakistan, Israel, Turkey, and possibly Iran. The broader Middle East that encompasses North Africa requires from NATO an adaptation of its missions by putting more emphasis on the promotion of democracy in the region. It remains to be seen whether the US project will receive full acceptance from the other allies.

The "5 + 5" Dialogue

Needless to say, the United States' desire to redirect NATO's missions toward what can be termed as soft powers-related priorities may not easily be accepted by some Alliance members. France appears to be the least inclined to back the US effort to spread democracy through the Middle East. The dynamism of the dialogue that gathers five countries of southern Europe (France, Italy, Malta, Portugal, and Spain) and the five states from the Maghreb could not be dissociated from the US dynamism in the Middle East since 11 September 2001. It seems that the southern European countries fear that the US project will exacerbate their marginalization in the region, especially as Europe's role in the peace process is peripheral compared to that of the United States. The "5 + 5" dialogue therefore represents an opportunity for France and its neighbors to reaffirm themselves in the region as major players that can influence the regional balance of power. What is the nature of this dialogue? Does it entail the same content as that of NATO?

Similar to the NATO dialogue, the "5 + 5" gathering is a consultation framework and thus does not entail any binding rules. The main difference between these two frameworks is that the "5 + 5" dialogue lacks a civil–military cooperation program. This Euro-Mediterranean security framework was reactivated recently, even though the idea is not novel. In 1983, French president François Mitterrand proposed the creation of the Mediterranean Security and Cooperation Council that brought together Algeria, France, Italy, Morocco, Spain, and Tunisia. However, the French proposal was short lived because Algeria rejected it on the ground that it closed the door to other countries such as Yugoslavia and Libya.

For many years, the dialogue was frozen due to the bloody strife in Algeria and the Lockerbie affair, which brought Libya into opposition to the US and the UK. The ten countries involved in the "5 + 5" gathering held two meetings in Lisbon and Algiers between 1990 and 2001. However, it is worth emphasizing that the launching of the Barcelona Process in November 1995 made the usefulness of this dialogue more questionable. The Euro-Mediterranean Partnership diverted the European countries' priorities from socioeconomic questions to issues of regional security. Additionally, the creation of Euromarfore and Eurofore in 1995 accentuated the Maghrebi states' distrust of European intentions. Contrary to NATO's Mediterranean Dialogue, the "5 + 5" ambitions do not extend beyond the geopolitical scope of the western Mediterranean. The *raison d'être* of this dialogue is the five southern European countries' desire to forge a Euro-Mediterranean security identity to diminish Euro-Atlantic domination. France seems to be the most adamant defender of this idea by trying to convince the Maghrebi countries to stay closer to Europe. Indeed, during the Tunis summit of 2004, France deployed intense diplomatic effort in order to restrict US influence in the Maghreb. This dialogue represents for France a lever that allows it to ensure its continued influence in the Maghreb.

However justified the French distrust of NATO's intentions may be, which could be considered as the main reason behind the decision to reactivate the "5 + 5" dialogue, this forum remains the most important multilateral security framework on the southern shore of the Mediterranean. The question remains: how far do the Euro-Mediterranean security framework and NATO's dialogue constitute an impetus for multilateral Maghrebi security?

Conclusion: Multilateralism or Denationalization of Maghrebi Security?

The involvement of the Maghrebi states in a multilateral security framework requires a readjustment of their internal security policies to cope with changing external factors. Encapsulated in NATO's dialogue program, the measures the Atlantic Alliance aims to reach are strategic homogeneity with the Mediterranean states. This implies that the Maghrebi states will adopt the same military norms as the allied members' armies. NATO is thus seeking to develop inter-operational capabilities between its army and the armies of the dialogue participants. However, the objective of the Atlantic Alliance surpasses the establishment of strategic homogeneity. NATO wants to incorporate the Maghrebi states into a new transnational security structure, the borders of which would stretch from Morocco to Pakistan. What happens then to the Maghrebi security structure?

Once the dialogue was launched, the Maghrebi states adapted to NATO's *modus operandi* by participating in several joint military operations. These operations tend to prepare Maghrebi armies to partake in NATO-led missions or in those in which the Atlantic Alliance is reluctant to become involved directly. These are mainly stabilization missions that require a minimum degree of inter-operational cooperation. Though some Maghrebi armies had previous experience with these kinds of missions, the military cooperation implied overall a qualitative evolution in the life of the Maghrebi armies. The case of Morocco's army is worth emphasizing because it participated in many stabilization missions or peace-making operations, such as in Bosnia in 1994. In the past, Algeria has also participated in peace-keeping operations (Cambodia). The integration of Maghrebi states into NATO's security network implies, undoubtedly, a more active participation by Maghrebi armies in stabilization missions. More importantly, after the closure of American bases in Germany, the North Atlantic Alliance intends to implement an outsourcing logic with the Maghrebi states by gaining military facilities in the Maghreb. The support given to Maghrebi states involved in the fight against terrorism in the Sahara is most illustrative of NATO's new way of working. The leaders of the Atlantic Alliance do not want their armies implicated in the Maghreb. Therefore, they prefer to entrust the Maghrebi armies with matters of security, assuming they be prepared for the stabilization missions envisioned.

The involvement of Maghrebi countries in stabilization missions will become a determining parameter in the security policy-making process for the Maghreb. Consequently, the Maghrebi states will resort to a transnational structure guided by different strategic objectives. The risk, however, is that this denationalization of the security policies of the Maghrebi states may lead to the dissolution of the regional Maghrebi security identity. Considering these factors, is it possible to envision another Maghrebi security system?

Due to its geopolitical location, the Maghreb is torn between Europe, Africa, and the Arab world. This geopolitical specificity pulls Maghrebi security identity between a Mediterranean security logic, which is closer to the European security, and a transatlantic strategy, which is more preoccupied with the broadening of the Middle Eastern geopolitical borders by incorporating some non-Arab states, such as Israel, Pakistan, and Turkey. As such, the Maghrebi countries will have to choose between the two strategies. The task will not be easy, owing to the different orientations dividing the ruling elites of the Maghreb. While some elites are more inclined to strengthen the relations of their countries with the West, others prefer to reinforce their ties with the Arab world. The most difficult result that could possibly ensue would be forging an independent security identity based on multilateralism in the Maghreb.

Rethinking Maghrebi security along the lines of reducing the weight of bilateralism and initiating a new security approach to multilateralism is a difficult endeavor. Maghrebi security policies remain defined by national self-interest and the weight of certain perceptions of the past that prevent them from developing a new and common vision of the future. This constant characteristic is the main factor that explains leadership rivalry, which in turn sheds light on why the Arab Maghreb Union remains deadlocked. The multilateralism of Maghrebi security depends on the prerequisites discussed earlier, which currently are not present. Shared values have not sufficed to generate a regional security identity because each Maghrebi state continues to perceive a national threat to its security and its strategic interest in the narrowest geographic sense. Moreover, many questions are still pending. The role of civil societies, the Maghrebi economic disparities (Libya and Algeria have larger supplies of oil and natural gas than do Tunisia and Morocco), the adherence to the norms of the World Trade

Organization (WTO) and its impact on Maghrebi security policies, the exclusion of elites from political participation, and the national identity crises are all elements of great importance and may play a critical role in the process of restructuring Maghrebi security.

Notes

The author would like to thank Professor Belkacem Iratni of the University of Algiers for his comments on an earlier draft of this chapter.

1 See, for example, the works of John Gerhard Ruggie, *Multilateralism Matters: The Theory and Praxis of an Institutional Form*, New York: Columbia University Press, 1993; Lisa L. Martin, "Interests, Power and Multilateralism," *International Organization*, vol. 64, no. 4, fall 1992, pp. 765–92.

2 Seyom Brown, *International Relations in a Changing Global System*, Boulder, CO: Westview Press, 2nd edn, 1996, p. 34.

3 Quoted in Brian L. Job, "Multilatéralisme et résolution des conflits régionaux: les illusions de la coopération," *Etudes Internationales*, vol. 26, no. 4, December 1995, p. 668.

4 Ibid., p. 668.

5 Michael Barnett and Emanuel Adler (eds), *Security Communities*, Cambridge and New York: Cambridge University Press, 1998, Chapters 1 and 2, pp. 3–67.

6 Quoted in Amitav Acharya, "Collective Identity and Conflict Management in Southeast Asia," in M. Barnett and E. Adler (eds), *Security Communities*, op. cit., p. 205.

7 A former Algerian ambassador developed this point of view: Khalfa Maameri, "De l'UMA à l'UMO," *El Watan*, 26 December 2004.

8 Salah Slimani, "Echanges commerciaux intermaghrébins: le FMI appel à plus de coopération," *El Watan*, 1 October 2006.

9 The Algerian government still maintains its decision to keep the border with Morocco closed. This decision was based on the fact that Morocco's decision to reopen the frontiers was taken unilaterally. But it is also a means to compel Morocco to agree to discuss other bilateral issues.

10 For more details concerning the Western Sahara, see Yahia H. Zoubir and Daniel Volman, *International Dimensions of the Western Sahara Conflict*, Wesport, CT: Praeger, 1993; Khadija Mohsen-Finan, *Le Sahara occidental: les enjeux d'un conflit regional*, Paris: Presses du CNRS, 1997; Erik Jensen, *Western Sahara: Anatomy of a Stalemate*, Boulder, CO: Lynne Rienner Publisher, 2005.

11 For further details about bilateral conflicts between Maghrebi countries, see John Damis, "The Maghreb Union and Regional Reconciliation," in George Joffé (ed.), *North Africa: Nation, State and Region*, London and New York: Routledge, 1993, pp. 288–96.

12 Paul Balta, *Le grand Maghreb: des indépendances à l'an 2000*, Paris: Editions La Découverte, 1990, p. 201.

13 For more details about Algeria's Africa policy, see Slimane Chikh, *L'Algérie porte de l'Afrique*, Algiers: Casbah Editions, 1999.

14 Abdennour Benantar, *The Mediterranean Dimension of Algerian Security: Algeria, Europe and NATO* (Al Boud Al Moutaouassiti Li al Amn Al Djazairi: Al Djazair, Europa oua Al Hilf Al Atlasi), Algiers: Al-Maktaba Al-Assria, 2005, p. 43.

15 For more details about US military aid to Morocco, see Daniel Volman, "Foreign Arms Sales and Military Balance in the Maghreb," in Yahia H. Zoubir

(ed.), *North Africa in Transition: State, Society, and Economic Development in the 1990s*, Gainesville, FL: University Press of Florida, 1999, pp. 212–27.

16 Yahia H. Zoubir, "La politique étrangère américaine au Maghreb: constances et adaptations," *MERIA, Journal d'Etudes des relations internationales au Moyen-Orient*, vol. 1, no. 1, article 8, July 2006. Available at: http://meria.idc.ac.il/journal_fr

17 During the fifteenth summit of the Arab League in March 2003, Qaddafi publicly insulted the then crown prince of Saudi Arabia, Prince Abdallah and accused him of being a servant of the United States.

18 Quoted in Robert A. Mortimer, "The Arab Maghreb Union: Myth and Reality," in Yahia H. Zoubir (ed.), op. cit., p. 185.

19 Marie-Lucy Dumas, "Méditerranée occidentale: coopération et sécurité," *Fondation pour les Etudes de Défense Nationale*, Paris, May 1992, p. 209.

20 For more details concerning Western Europe as a security community, see Ole Weaver, "Insecurity, Security, and Asecurity in the West European Non-war Community," in M. Barnett and E. Adler (eds), *Security Communities*, op. cit., pp. 69–118.

21 Michael Barnet, "Regional Security after the Gulf War," *Political Science Quarterly*, vol. 111, no. 4, winter 1996–1997, p. 599.

22 Ibid.

23 In the 1990 local elections, the Islamic Salvation Front (FIS) obtained 4,331,472 votes (57.44 percent), and in the December 1991 legislative elections almost three millions votes (47.26 percent).

24 The former Moroccan minister of the interior, Driss Basri, rejected these accusations in an interview with the Algerian newspaper *Al Khabar*, Algiers, 8 December 2004.

25 Abdennour Benantar, op. cit., p. 36.

26 Alberto Bin, "NATO's Mediterranean Dialogue: A Post-Prague Perspective?" *Mediterranean Politics*, vol. 7, no. 2, summer 2002, pp. 115–20.

13 The United States, Islamism, Terrorism, and Democracy in the Maghreb

The Predominance of Security?

Yahia H. Zoubir

In recent years, the Maghreb has undoubtedly become a region of great interest to the United States. The main reasons for this heightened interest are divided into two broad categories: 1) economic and political interests, and 2) military and security interests. The first are linked to America's energy needs, mainly oil and gas in Algeria and Libya, and now Mauritania, as well as the regionalization that could provide a potentially important market for US corporations. The second set of motives is related to the consequences of the attacks on America on 11 September 2001, which have increased the need for a new form of management of the questions of security, Islamism, terrorism, and democratization. These questions fall within the Broader Middle East and North Africa Initiative (BMENA) that the Bush Administration launched in 2003.

Given the ambiguity of US policy toward the question of Islamism, especially its radical form, this chapter will examine the functionality of the phenomenon in defining policy and how and/or whether Islamism, at least its "moderate" form, can be integrated into the democratization process in the BMENA. The main objective is to show how the United States has sought in recent years to contain Islamist extremism while purportedly tackling its main causes, i.e., the lack of democracy, socioeconomic conditions, education, and the absence of vibrant civil societies in the region. The chapter will also study US security policy in the Maghreb region and how it seeks to consolidate American military presence to fight "terrorism" and to assist the regimes in combating armed opposition (Henry's chapter in this volume, Chapter 14, deals with the "dividends" that the regimes in place have extracted from the events of 9/11 and US security policy in the region since then).

The question, however, is to assess whether US plans have any chances of materializing in the Maghreb, especially in light of the wave of anti-Americanism in the region.[1] Indeed, the occupation of Iraq, the treatment by the US military of Muslim prisoners in Guantánamo and in Abu Ghraib, support for Israel in its destructive war against Lebanon, the outsourcing of torture of Muslim prisoners, and the support for authoritarian Arab regimes, are factors which have discredited US claims to be spreading democracy around the world. Anti-Americanism also derives from the perception that the United States government is anti-Muslim and intent not only on humiliating the Muslim world in a "clash of civilizations" of sorts, but also on preventing the Arab-Islamic world from ever making technological progress, as illustrated in the fact that the US overlooks Israel's nuclear capabilities but seeks to prevent the Islamic Republic of Iran or any other Islamic or Arab country from developing nuclear energy, even for peaceful purposes. The problématique for American policy makers is how to promote a process of democratization, no matter how genuine, while its policies in the region at large suffer from considerable disrepute.

Evolution of America's Policy toward the Maghreb

The main reason why Europeans and Maghrebis are surprised, some even concerned, about growing US interest in the region[2] springs out of decades during which American policy makers paid little attention to the Maghreb, considering the region as falling within Europe's sphere of influence. Of course, there were periods when the US exhibited heightened economic and political interest. One can identify a few such periods: World War II, the era of decolonization in the 1950–60s, and the conflict in Western Sahara from the 1970s until the end of the 1980s, and again in recent years. During the Cold War, the United States did not perceive the Maghreb, despite its geopolitical significance, as a regional entity, preferring instead bilateral relations with each Maghrebi state. Although it constitutes a subsystem of the Middle East, the strategic weight of the Maghreb was insignificant compared to that of the Levant (Arab–Israeli conflict) or the Gulf (immense oil wealth). Furthermore, the US left the Maghreb to European, especially French, influence. The Maghreb was of consequence only insofar as the problems that dominated it could spill over and affect the stability of southern Europe, NATO's southern flank. The main objective during the Cold War was to contain Communist, mainly Soviet, influence. And, despite privileged security, military, and political relations with Morocco and Tunisia, the US relied on France to play the dominant role in the Maghreb. Probably the main reason that compelled the US to pay greater attention to the Maghreb in the post-Cold War era was the highly volatile situation in Algeria throughout the 1990s. The Islamist armed insurgency in Algeria, and the mayhem that analysts anticipated as a result of the weakening of the state,[3] compelled the US to play a more active role in the region, namely the protection of the regimes in Morocco and Tunisia, and to cooperate more closely with France on Maghrebi matters.

With the relative recovery of the Algerian state and the quelling of the Islamist insurgency in the late 1990s, US policy makers expressed strong interest in the emergence of a regional, market-based Maghreb entity, an objective it has yet to achieve due to the non-resolution and perpetuation of the conflict in Western Sahara, which remains a source of tension in the region and constitutes the main area of discord between Algeria and Morocco, the backbones of the regionalization process.[4] Yet, it remains clear that the United States, since the collapse of the Soviet Bloc and in its new role as hegemonic power, has developed a quasi-regional policy, dictated by the necessity of globalization, seeking the integration of the Maghreb as a trading bloc into the capitalist world market. Americans view favorably a North African market that extends from Morocco to Egypt and would eventually connect with the rest of the Levant and Gulf regions. The normalization of relations with Libya, a major oil producer, has strengthened US determination to achieve its objectives in the region. Undoubtedly, 9/11 represented the most significant event that heightened US attention to the Maghreb. There is considerable, quite exaggerated concern among some US government officials over the Maghreb, and by extension the Sahel,[5] becoming an al-Qaeda recruiting area and a potential backdoor into Europe, particularly since many members of the al-Qaeda terrorist network, the so-called "Arab Afghans," are of Maghrebi extraction. A number of events in the Sahel region, which borders the southern extremities of the Maghreb, provided further justification for US presence in the area.

Before the events of 9/11, under the Clinton administration, the United States declared that it "seeks the stability and prosperity of North Africa" and "to strengthen our relations with Morocco, Tunisia, and Algeria and to encourage political and economic reform."[6] Obviously, there have been additional objectives since the publication of the National Security Strategy 2000. Before 9/11, the key US interest in the Maghreb was primarily economic; the clearest indication being the so-called Eizenstat Initiative, as well as the multiplication of American–Maghrebi chambers of commerce.[7] Indeed, the US launched in 1999 the US–North Africa Economic Partnership or Eizenstat Initiative, named after its main advocate Stuart Eizenstat, then Undersecretary of State for Economic, Business, and Agricultural Affairs. The objective of such an initiative—later renamed the US North Africa Economic Program—was

> to link the United States and the three countries of North Africa much closer together in terms of trade and investment, to encourage more trade between our countries, to encourage more US companies to invest in the region and create good-paying jobs … and to encourage the reduction in internal barriers among and between the countries of North Africa which has impeded the normal trade flows between those countries.[8]

Implicit in this statement was clear encouragement for the three Maghreb countries to revive the moribund Arab Maghreb Union (AMU) and the reopening of the Algerian–Moroccan border, closed since 1994.[9] Undoubtedly, from an economic perspective, the United States wishes to look at the Maghreb as an integrated whole, which could potentially expand eastward.[10] With recent developments in US–Libyan relations, such expansion might soon become a reality. Furthermore, US policy makers do not regard the Maghreb entity as an end in itself but as an integrated region that would eventually include America's strong ally, Egypt,[11] which already holds observer status in the AMU. In US eyes, the inclusion of Egypt would undoubtedly serve as a link in the chain of states normalizing relations with Israel. The US North Africa Economic Program is now an integral part of the Middle East Partnership Initiative (MEPI) that the United States launched in late 2002.

Throughout the 1990s, the greatest concern of US policy makers with respect to the Maghreb was the extremely unstable situation in Algeria.[12] The possibility of radical Islamists coming to power or the conquest of power by Islamist extremists frightened not only local and European governments, but also the United States, which sought to avoid the chaos that experts predicted would occur in this eventuality. The situation in Algeria compelled the United States and European powers to protect Algeria's neighbors, more particularly Morocco, a strategic ally in the region then considered a bulwark against radical Islamism. There was genuine fear in the United States and Europe that destabilization of Algeria and Morocco could have devastating spillover effects. The prevailing opinion was that a weakened Morocco would allow the emergence of radical Islamism there, which would create yet another wave of migration toward Europe. Indeed, the crisis in Algeria, especially in 1992–96, when Islamist terrorism ravaged the country, witnessed massive emigration of mostly educated people toward Europe and North America.[13]

Islamism, Democracy, and US Policy in the Maghreb

Two observations should be made about US policy toward Islamism: 1) there is no one definition of the phenomenon, and 2) ambivalence characterized US policy toward this movement precisely because of the lack of consensus on a definition. However, the events of 9/11 have made the US more careful in its dealing with Islamism. The contention in this chapter is that the events of 9/11 have not totally altered the strategy with respect to the juxtaposition of Islamism and democratization, and, in fact, have instead consolidated it in some countries in the Middle East and North Africa (MENA), where the US encourages the co-optation of a certain type of Islamists into the political process. Two dimensions must be taken into account when analyzing US policy toward Islamism. The first dimension relates to broader US interests in North Africa and toward each individual country. The second dimension needs to be associated with US perception(s) of Islamism and the way American policy makers have managed this phenomenon. The juxtaposition of the two factors has resulted in the making of a variable policy, where adaptation and change cohabit with conventional American interests. This was most noticeable during the Algerian crisis (1991–99). Indeed, policy makers were divided between conciliators and confrontationists[14] until it was clear that US interests were better served by siding with the incumbent regime, which was no longer on the brink of collapse, and when it also became obvious that Islamists had no chance of seizing power through the ballot box or through armed insurrection.[15] Of course, the US would continue to pay lip service to the necessity of allowing "moderate" Islamists to partake in the political process—as a sign of democratization—but in reality, the driver of policy remains US national interests, although the local regime's inclusion of such moderates comforts the US position. Nowadays, such integration of "moderate" Islamists plays a significant role—at least in terms of projection of perceptions—in the BMENA. Indeed, this initiative aims at reforming the regimes and to prove that there is no incompatibility between Islam and democracy. As President George W. Bush put it, "The peoples of the Islamic nations want and deserve the same freedoms and opportunities as people in every nation. And their governments should listen to their hopes."[16] In the current American conception of democracy, democratization and religious freedom are closely associated. Actually, the core idea of the American project is to think of Islamic countries as any other countries that can change political rules, and adapt them to liberalism without upsetting the local culture and sacred religious values.

The United States' versatility regarding Islamism derives from the fact that there are several "definitions" of this phenomenon, as well as an ambivalence vis-à-vis Islamism that has marked US policy for decades, which can also be tied to the Arab–Israeli conflict within US administrations, as clearly illustrated on the morrow of the democratic election of the Palestinian Hamas in the December 2005 legislative election. Hence, US policy depends on the category in which a given Islamist movement has been classified. Endorsing the reality of "moderate" Islamists provides the de facto linkage between Muslim societies and their potential democratization. This kind of democratization is considered like any legitimate political process in other democratizing countries in the world, without preconceived notions. In other words, Muslim countries are subject to the same conditions and the same principles in order to change their political regimes.[17] In this approach, the principles of democratization boil down to three essential points: first, there are many models of democracy; second, democracy takes time; and, third, democracy can be encouraged from outside, but is best built from within.[18] Of course, American policy makers decide, sometimes quite subjectively, which countries are on the right course of democratization. Thus, countries like Morocco, a longtime friend of the United States, would obtain high marks regardless of the limitations of the democratization process.

However, the approach on Islamism, albeit of the moderate kind, has also created a remarkable dilemma for US policy makers, a dilemma with considerable policy implications. Indeed, while the United States encourages its friends in the region to open up their political systems and respect human rights, the main beneficiaries from such democratization would be the Islamists whose views are often antithetical to US interests, especially those related to the Palestinian question, the situation in Iraq or Lebanon (summer 2006), or to US military presence in the Gulf. Thus, with respect to the Maghreb, as in the rest of the Arab world, the question that arises for US policy makers is how to encourage these friendly governments to participate in a genuine democratic process when such a process would undoubtedly bring to power Islamist political parties. The issue is even more complex when, from the perspectives of the United States and of the regimes in place, security is considered to be paramount. Assuming that interest in democratization is genuine, there also remains the question of the real commitment of the "moderate" Islamists to democracy and democratic values. The next sections will look at US policy toward the Maghrebi countries. While it is certain that American policy makers are aware that democratization in North Africa, like in the rest of the Arab world, will most certainly result in Islamists coming to power, they are also aware that the status quo that served the US so well for decades is no longer tenable. Support for authoritarian regimes breeds the very same instability that the US seeks to thwart. The US is quite cognizant of this reality, which explains why, at least in rhetoric, there was such a push for democratization. Indeed, President Bush himself declared that,

> Sixty years of Western nations excusing and accommodating the lack of freedom in the Middle East did nothing to make us safe—because in the long run, stability cannot be purchased at the expense of liberty. As long as the Middle East remains a place where freedom does not flourish, it will remain a place of stagnation, resentment, and violence ready for export. And with the spread of weapons that can bring catastrophic harm to our country and to our friends, it would be reckless to accept the status quo.[19]

But, it seems that the United States is still willing to support semi-authoritarian regimes that can serve US interests rather than to alienate these regimes whose support is essential in the global war on terrorism and whose hydrocarbon resources are so vital to the United States.

Algeria: Energy and the War on Terrorism

While US–Moroccan and US–Tunisian relations—with few occasional tensions[20]—have been steady for decades, US–Algerian relations have been quite complex. Historically, Algeria's relations with the United States were marked by misunderstandings, suspicion, and at times great antagonism as the two countries collided over the Arab–Israeli conflict, Vietnam, Western Sahara, Nicaragua, Cuba, and Grenada. Until the late 1980s, Algeria's radical foreign policy and its position of leadership in the Non-Aligned Movement, the Organization of African Unity (OAU), and other international organizations often contradicted US policy objectives and interests. Worse still, Algeria's privileged relations with the Soviet Union, America's global rival, placed the two countries on a collision course. Although commercial relations were excellent, especially in the hydrocarbons sector, the lack of political, military, and ideological ties prevented the United States from wielding more than negligible influence in Algeria. Furthermore, the United States provided insignificant bilateral foreign assistance to Algeria. Thus, unlike Morocco or Tunisia, Algeria never was a close friend of the United States. The traditional facilitating instruments were simply missing. The fact that Algeria was never vital to US strategic, economic, and political interests and that the United States has practically had little influence in that country provide a partial explanation as to why Washington had pursued a seemingly ambivalent policy during the civil conflict that destabilized Algeria until the late 1990s.[21]

The civil unrest that began in the early 1990s compelled the US government to pay greater attention to developments in Algeria; this coincided with a period during which the US became cognizant of the rise of radical Islam as a threat to America's interests. Yet, as far as Algeria was concerned, important groups within the government felt that perhaps the coming to power of "moderate" Islamists, provided they were not opposed to US interests (acceptance of Israel, free flow of oil, and the liberalization of markets), would be in US interest. In fact, those who were not opposed to moderate Islamists coming to power felt that it would in fact be a way of democratizing the authoritarian regime in Algeria—as well as in other countries in the Arab world. One can even speculate—with good reason—that the United States was considering using Algeria as a laboratory for a "moderate" Islamist regime and establishing good rapport in the hope of "revamping our [US] image in the militant Islamic world."[22] In that period, not only was exiled FIS leader Anouar Haddam allowed to speak freely in Washington, but the US government consulted Mahfoud Nahnah, the leader of the moderate Movement of a Peaceful Society (formerly HAMAS) and candidate during the presidential election in November 1995, on his party's program and position on various issues. In 1995, he held talks with Martin Indyck at the National Security Council. Permanent contacts have continued ever since.[23] The forces favorable to using Algeria as a laboratory or model exhorted the Algerian government to seek compromise with the Islamic Salvation Front (FIS), perceived in Washington as a "moderate" party. They believed that such compromise would not only isolate Islamist extremists but would also end the bloodshed in the country. While encouraging a compromise between the regime and FIS Islamists, the US government was quite critical of the authorities for failing to carry out market reforms, to respect human rights, and to establish a more democratic system. Furthermore, while suspicious of the Islamist movement, some US policy makers downplayed the possibility of an Islamist domino effect in the region. This, of course, was not a shared opinion; other policy makers held the opposite view and believed that it would be a mistake to allow Islamists to come to power. In April 1995, a hearing in Congress illustrated this evolution, and is quite reminiscent of the arguments the neoconservatives and others made after 9/11. Rep. Ileana Ros-Lehtinen, who needs to be quoted at length, stated unambiguously that:

> The crisis in Algeria ... is but a microcosm of a larger problem. There are many US policymakers, some perhaps at the State Department, who emphasize that Islamic extremism is too diffuse to be called a movement ... They must not be listening to the statements made by these Islamic militant groups. They may not answer to a single individual; however, they do have a common theme, a cause which drives them to take any risk necessary to achieve their end. They believe that frontiers could never divide Muslims because they are one nation. They will always remain one entity. They are sworn to fight the "Great Satan America" for the global supremacy of Islam. In this context, it is clear that Islamic extremism and militant groups pose a direct threat to regional stability, to the fragile democracies of the African continent, and to US security interests. They overtly challenge US leadership and that of its allies by making them primary targets of their hatred and their hostility. For those who state that this is not an international problem, that the United States is beyond the reach of these terrorist groups, I can only respond by saying—remember New York! Remember the World Trade Center! For those who reiterate this is not a problem in Africa, I can only remind them that a majority of the defendants in the New York bombing trials are from African countries.[24]

Nevertheless, even those opposed to Islamists blamed the government for the conditions that gave rise to the instability in Algeria. But a variety of factors, namely the presidential election in Algeria in November 1995; the brutality of radical Islamists; fears of the neighbors as well as inside NATO; the belief that the armed Islamists were no longer able to bring down the regime which the population now preferred as a lesser evil to Islamists; and the successes scored by the security forces in the antiterrorist combat, convinced the US government to provide "positive conditionality" to the authorities in Algiers as long as they carried out the reforms called for by the US.[25] In sum, they encouraged a policy of reconciliation with and inclusion of "moderate" Islamists.[26]

No analyst in the 1990s could have imagined the reversal that US–Algerian relations have taken since the events of 9/11. True, in addition to the factors cited above, the oil discoveries in Algeria in the mid-1990s rendered Algeria more important in US eyes. Bouteflika's policy following his election in 1999, despite a testing start, also helped improve US–Algerian relations. But this still could not suffice to explain the incredible importance that Algeria currently holds in US policy in the region. Indubitably, 9/11 and the subsequent global war on terrorism are the main factors that set off US–Algerian relations on a new course at all levels shortly before 9/11, the best illustration being President Abdelaziz Bouteflika's official visit to the United States in July 2001. In addition to the success of the policy of Civil Concord, which the US strongly endorsed, Algeria had scored some other good marks in Washington. Even with respect to the Middle East, Washington nudged Algerians to establish lines of communication with Israel. Most importantly, the US saw the necessity of cooperating with Algeria on matters of global terrorism; in fact, Algerian security services enjoyed close cooperation with the FBI, CIA, and National Security Agency (NSA) well before 9/11.

Security, Political, and Economic Cooperation with Algeria

The 9/11 attacks on the US brought Algeria and the United States closer, particularly in regard to security cooperation. Algerian authorities condemned unequivocally the attacks and agreed to join the US-led international coalition; they handed Washington a list of hundreds of suspected Algerian militants on the run in Europe and the United States and offered their cooperation in security and intelligence matters. President Bouteflika visited Washington again on 5 November 2001. His objective in meeting with President Bush was to convince the latter that US–Algerian relations should be strengthened, but also to persuade him that the fight against terrorism would be in vain unless the roots were dealt with, that is, the poverty and inequality that, in his view, globalization exacerbated. This paralleled the view of even the neoconservatives who made democracy and economic prosperity one of their mottos; in fact, the Bush administration has made the promotion of democracy in MENA a national security priority, arguing that greater political freedom would undermine radical Islamism and its ideology.

With respect to the fight on terrorism, the CIA, FBI, and the NSA have continuously sought and obtained assistance from Algerians who have acquired valuable experience in this domain. More importantly, although it was reluctant to sell Algeria lethal weapons, to avoid upsetting the military balance with Morocco, the United States decided to provide Algerian security forces with effective equipment to assist them in eliminating the "remaining pockets" of armed militants in rural areas. This decision is a logical result of the objectives stated in the National Security Strategy 2002, which stipulates that: "We will continue to encourage our regional partners to take up a coordinated effort that isolates the terrorists. Once the regional campaign localizes the threat to a particular state, we will help ensure the state has the military, law enforcement, political, and financial tools necessary to finish the task."[27] In October 2003, Assistant Secretary of State for Near East Affairs William Burns, during his two-day visit to Algiers, declared that "Our bilateral relations never were so strong in the last forty years [i.e., since Algeria's independence] as they are today." With respect to security and military cooperation, Burns stated that "the United States supplied non-offensive military equipment to Algeria," while emphasizing that "military cooperation has witnessed continuous and stable growth." Burns acknowledged that cooperation between the two countries has been not only "remarkable" and "of great value," but that "Algeria's assistance (to the United States) helps in saving American lives and we are grateful." As to the American side, "we are doing our best to help Algeria put an end to the terrorist phenomenon which has devastated Algeria for 10 years."[28] Shortly after Burns' visit to Algiers, Colin Powell went to the region to discuss with the Algerians issues of military cooperation and economic exchanges. This was quite a change from the 1990s, when the United States decided, following the lead of other Western nations, not to provide any military equipment to the Algerian authorities, confronted with a savage guerrilla war. Undoubtedly, Powell's trip confirmed Algeria's status as a credible partner in the region. Undoubtedly, the geo-strategic transformations that 9/11 caused contributed greatly to the strengthening of Algeria's role in the Mediterranean.

As shown in Henry's chapter in this volume, US–Algerian security relations have taken on considerable dimensions. However, the question of US bases in the Algerian desert—to allegedly combat Islamist groups affiliated to al-Qaeda—has been the most interesting, and even puzzling, since both sides deny their existence. An analysis of US military objectives in the region, however, demonstrates that there is no need for permanent bases as in the past, or that those bases be identified as American bases. What is important is that US troops can utilize those bases whenever the need arises.[29] During his visit to Algeria in November 2006, Deputy Assistant Secretary of Defense for International Security Peter Rodman corroborated the above analysis:

> The United States does not want military bases in Algeria. We wish to increase the capacities of the local forces, not to open bases. We are interested in a strategic and military partnership, the training of officers and security cooperation, joint military exercises, exchange of information, purchase of military equipment, and exchanges between our officers.[30]

In private, though, some US officials have confirmed the existence of at least one such operational base in southern Algeria that fits this profile. But following the announcement on 7 February 2007 by the United States of the creation of AFRICOM,[31] the regional command for the Maghreb–

Sahel, contrary to the Moroccans, the Algerians made it plain in March that they would never agree to the establishment of foreign bases on their soil, for this would be, as Foreign Minister Mohammed Bedjaoui put it, "incompatible with Algeria's sovereignty and independence," and Algerian territory would not be integrated in this command.[32] Algerians argue that the African Union has the necessary collective security mechanism to deal with security issues on the continent.[33] However, this has not diminished US determination to keep trying to set up such a Command by October 2007 and make it operational by October 2008 at the latest. In July 2007, unofficial reports indicated that the United States was negotiating with Morocco to establish AFRICOM in the kingdom. Undoubtedly, Morocco hopes that if AFRICOM were established on its territory, it would terminate the Sahrawi independence movement, the POLISARIO Front, which it has sought, unsuccessfully thus far, to associate with al-Qaeda, and to weaken Algeria's role in the region. Others have argued that in fact AFRICOM might be spread over a number of African countries. Whatever the truth, the issue has created some unease in US-Algerian relations.

In Algeria, some politicians and journalists accused the United States of having had a hand in the bombings on 11 April 2007 of the Government Palace in Algiers and the police station in Bab Ezzouar, near Algiers Airport.[34] They argued that the US seeks to amplify the terrorist threat so as to penetrate the region and establish a presence in the Maghreb to control the natural resources, mainly hydrocarbons, there. Although the Algerian government saw a foreign hand behind the bombings, it made no accusation against any country but reacted vigorously to the US Embassy's warning of other oncoming bombings on specific sites. The authorities reacted firmly and asked that the US respect Algeria's sovereignty and avoid interfering in its domestic affairs. Condoleezza Rice dispatched US Itinerant Ambassador John Clint Williamson to Algiers in order to calm what seemed like a looming crisis. The tension subsided but it revealed the fragility of US–Algerian relations, due perhaps to the newness of the special relationship. The strain in relations was also due to the US siding with Morocco on the Western Sahara before the UN Security Council meeting on that question in late April 2007.

There has been much speculation regarding US supplies of weapons to Algeria. Many US officials, including Donald Rumsfeld, who visited Algeria in February 2006, indicated American willingness to consider Algerian arms purchases from the United States. However, there is no evidence that Algeria is interested in large purchases from the US other than sophisticated night-vision equipment and specific types of radar. Following the conversion of its debt with Russia in 2006, Algeria spent $7bn to buy arms from Russia, including MiG 29 aircraft, tanks, and other lethal weapons to revamp its armed forces beginning in 2007. Despite the undeniably close cooperation with the US, two points must be made:

1) the Algerians are not willing to have military cooperation with the United States that is conducted on US terms,[35] and 2) Algeria refuses to become dependent on the US for its military hardware, which explains the diversification of its arms purchases from Russia, China, France, South Africa, the US, the former Communist bloc, and Turkey. Furthermore, US close alliance with Morocco, Algeria's immediate rival in the region, perpetuates Algeria's suspicion vis-à-vis the United States. Algerian officers are also resentful of US attempts to involve them with Israelis, using special sessions at NATO to induce the Algerians to participate alongside Israelis.[36]

The National Security Strategy 2002 document devotes a large section to economics, reiterated in the National Security Strategy 2006, entitled "Ignite a New Era of Global Economic Growth through Free Markets and Free Trade," because "a strong world economy enhances our national security by advancing prosperity and freedom in the rest of the world." With respect to MENA, the United States has devised the BMENA, an "initiative [that] strives to link Arab, US, and global private sector businesses, non-governmental organizations, civil society elements, and governments together to develop innovative policies and programs that support reform in the region." The objective of such economic interest is obviously to create an integrated Maghreb economy that is open to US and European investments.

However, in spite of a positive evolution in American–Algerian relations, US investments outside the hydrocarbons sector remain relatively small, although North Africa in general has an insignificant world share of FDI, estimated at $5bn annually.

Libya: The "Rogue" Turned "Good Fellow"

After decades of animosity and direct confrontation, the United States and Libya have normalized their relations in a very short time span.[37] The final settlement in 2003 of the Lockerbie affair (the bombing of Pan Am flight 103 in December 1988 over Scotland, allegedly by Libyan operatives) marked the culmination of the process begun in 1999, followed by Libya's astonishing proclamation on the eve of Christmas 2003 that it had decided to dismantle its weapons of mass destruction (WMD) programs and MTCR-class missile systems. Cooperation on WMD opened the way for normalization in relations; hence, in June 2004, the United States officially opened a two-person Liaison Office in Tripoli, marking the resumption of direct US diplomatic presence in the country. The Libyans opened a Liaison Office in Washington the following month. In May 2006, the United States announced its decision to upgrade its diplomatic presence to ambassadorial level and full diplomatic relations were restored on 31 May 2006. The US also began the process on 15 May of removing Libya from the list of countries that support terrorism, and excluded Libya from the annual list of countries not fully cooperating with US antiterrorism efforts.

The United States and Libya have since 2003 extended negotiations to widen discussions connected with policies on Africa, terrorism, human rights, and economic reforms in Libya. The discussions on oil and commercial questions resulted in extremely lucrative deals for American companies; those companies had carried out ceaseless lobbying with US authorities throughout the 1990s to lift the embargo and for the companies to be able to resume their activities in Libya.

Many officials and opinion makers argue that fear of US retaliation after 9/11 is what enticed Libya to abandon its WMD. Nothing can be farther from the truth; while there is no doubt that Qaddafi was extremely concerned about US intentions after 9/11, US–Libyan negotiations on WMD, albeit secret, had begun in the late 1990s. In fact, Libya had been willing to discuss that issue with the US back in the late 1980s and early 1990s, for Libya had its own reasons for abandoning its WMD programs.[38] From the US perspective, Libya's decision came at an opportune time for the US to use Libya as a model for Iran and North Korea.[39] Furthermore, the US could also brandish Libya as a "rogue state turned good fellow" or a "sponsor of terror turned to example partner."

The normalization of relations with Libya demonstrated that the US was no longer making democracy a *sine qua non* of its relations with autocratic regimes in MENA. But, from a realist point of view, there is no shame in sacrificing human rights principles for abundant oil. Libya boasts the largest reserves of oil in Africa, estimated by OPEC at 41,464 million barrels, and the eighth largest reserves in the world. Given US thirst for oil, normalization with Libya, at no real cost for the regime, should have come as no surprise. The return of American companies to Libya has accelerated since 2004. Not surprisingly, in January 2005, Occidental and Chevron secured 11 of the 15 contracts in Libya's first open competition for oil contracts.[40] In December 2005, Exxon Mobil Corp signed agreements for the exploration and production of oil with the Libyan National Oil Company (NOC). In any event, Libya's energy resources are considerable, particularly since much of the oil and gas wealth remains untapped. The problem, of course, is that this wealth, far from encouraging reforms, strengthens the authoritarianism of the regime and provides little incentive for democratization. While oil and natural gas are important incentives for US businesses, other sectors are also extremely attractive, especially since Libya is earmarking billions of dollars for the revamping of the country's infrastructure, housing construction, and civil and military aviation.[41] The authorities are also seeking to attract billions in foreign investment.

The other area of interest for the US is Libya's role in the global war on terrorism. Even before 9/11, Libya cooperated with the United States on matters of terrorism,[42] since Libya itself was also confronted by Islamist groups. Thus, Libya's reaction to 9/11 was not surprising; the authorities condemned the attacks in no uncertain terms and supported the US decision to attack the Taliban in Afghanistan.[43] In mid-October 2001, a CIA agent, Ben Bonk, a former classmate of Musa Kusa, head of Libya's intelligence, told Kusa: "Two things. We're going to need you to give up your destructive weapons. And, most importantly, we'll need assistance to fight the terrorists." Apparently, that very same evening, Kusa gave Bonk a list of key al-Qaeda operatives.[44] Since then, the Libyan regime has cooperated fully in the global war on terrorism. The US not only acknowledged Libya's close cooperation but Bush himself, in his speeches, in 2002 omitted Libya as part of the "axis of evil," which included North Korea, Iran, and Iraq. The United States recognized the importance of Libya's cooperation and would like to co-opt it into the security network that the US has built in the Maghreb–Sahel region. Indeed, the US would like to add Libya to the nine North and West African countries that make up the Trans-Sahara Counter-Terrorism Partnership. General Charles Wald, deputy chief of the US European Command (EUCOM), declared in April 2005 that the reestablishment of military relations with Libya would greatly assist the United States in its efforts to counter the forces of instability in North Africa.[45] The integration of Libya in the Trans-Sahara Counter-Terrorism Partnership (TSCTP) is a matter of time, as Libya has already indirectly contributed to this structure. Washington seems concerned about the activities of the Libyan Islamic Fighting Group and that al-Qaeda might be seeking safe haven in TSCTP territories. However, although the United States has not made any request for the use of Ukba ben Nafi Air Base (formerly Wheelus AFB), Libyans have argued that a US military presence in Libya cannot be contemplated. A Libyan official interviewed in February 2006 stated bluntly, "We will never compromise our sovereignty to have someone back into our country."[46] However, time will tell whether Libyan "nationalism" can resist the influence of realism. Continued pressure from the US Congress for Libya to resolve some past issues (e.g. the Berlin bombing) may force Qaddafi to display once again his surprising pragmatism when survival of the regime is at stake.

Mauritania: The Israeli Connection, the Road to America

US interest in Mauritania is a recent phenomenon. Until the late 1990s, Mauritania and the United States maintained ordinary, albeit cordial, bilateral relations. A few events, such as the war in Western Sahara in the 1970s, the creation of the Arab Maghreb Union, Mauritania's conflict with Senegal, Mauritania's alignment with distant Iraq, and the flagrant abuses of human rights in the 1990s, attracted US attention. Mauritania is a very poor country and depends on foreign assistance despite its rich fisheries and minerals. However, Mauritania gained prominence with the US global war on terrorism, the discovery of oil, and its relationship with Israel. One can only agree with Mauritania expert Mohameden Ould-Mey that the country gained its new status in US policy in the region through the establishment of full diplomatic relations with Israel; this was the third Arab country to do so. "The US government pressured the Mauritanian government to recognize Israel through the US assistance programs, the US leverage over loans from international financial institutions, and the US annual country reports on human rights."[47] The signing in October 1999 of the decision to establish full diplomatic relations with Israel was held in Washington under the auspices of US Secretary of State Madeleine Albright.[48] Shortly thereafter, Mauritania secured debt relief from the Highly Indebted Poor Countries (HIPC) initiative in the amount of $1.1bn.[49] Despite the authoritarian nature of the regime of President Maaouiya Ould Sid'Ahmed Taya, the United States extended political and economic support as well as military cooperation and training. During his African tour, President Bush declared in a speech he gave in Abuja, Nigeria, on 12 July 2003, "The United States is also supporting the efforts of good friends all across this continent, friends such as Mauritania. We will not allow terrorists to threaten African peoples, or to use Africa as a base to threaten the world."[50] This was at the time when Mauritania had joined the Pan-Sahel Initiative.

The various coup attempts worried the United States, for Taya's regime was a reliable friend. Taya himself was astute in waving the flag of "al-Qaeda-affiliated Islamists" whenever any opposition threatened his rule. When Colonel Ely Ould Mohammed Vall overthrew Taya on 3 August 2005, the US government condemned the coup and the seizure of power by the Military Council for Justice and Democracy (MCJD). The US called for the return of constitutional government and free elections.[51] Undoubtedly, what worried the United States the most was the possible overturn of Mauritania's close relations with the United States and Israel. However, the assurances that the new leader gave to the United States that Mauritania would maintain its good relations with the US, would not sever ties with Israel, and would continue the "war on terror,"[52] alleviated American and Israeli fears. Mauritanian authorities promised also to honor the contracts that had been made with oil companies.[53] While security issues and oil undoubtedly predominate, the US government nonetheless stresses the need for a democratic transition in Mauritania. The US congratulated Mauritania for the holding of clean legislative and municipal elections in November 2006,[54] and for a successful repeat of the second round of those elections in early 2007, as well as for the presidential election in March 2007. This rhetoric fits well within the context of MEPI. However, what seems to be missing in US analysis is that the population in Mauritania is by and large opposed to relations with Israel—as demonstrated during the visit to Mauritania of Israeli Foreign Minister Sylvan Shalom in May 2005[55]—especially in view of brutal Israeli actions in the occupied territories and their devastating war against Lebanon in summer 2006. The new president, Sidi Mohamed Ould Cheikh Abdallahi, has already insinuated that Mauritania may submit the decision to continue relations with Israel to popular referendum.[56]

Morocco: "The Best Democratic Experiment in the Middle East"

In the American establishment discourse the notion of "pro-Western" and "friendly country" generally applies to countries like Morocco or Tunisia. American policy makers at the highest levels describe the Kingdom of Morocco as an example of Islamic democracy. In the past, American officials had portrayed King Hassan II as a visionary leader in the Arab world and, in 2004, they designated Morocco, under the rule of his son Mohammed VI, as a major non-NATO US ally. President Bush bestowed such recognition on Morocco because of the country's involvement in the global war on terrorism and the longstanding, close relationship with the United States.

The Islamist terrorist attacks in Marrakech and Casablanca in May 2003 consolidated this perception of Morocco as an ally who deserved assistance and backing. Hence, the immediate international reactions to the attacks were to show strong defense of Morocco; most countries condemned the terrorist groups that carried out those attacks. Most noteworthy, and unlike what took place in Algeria throughout the 1990s, was the fact that most declarations linked those attacks to international terrorism and thus considered that the international community and Morocco were engaged in the same fight against a common enemy.

While during the Cold War Morocco was perceived as a bulwark against communism in North Africa, it now is seen as playing the role of a rampart against radical, "obscurantist" Islamist forces. American officials appreciate Morocco's ability to repress radical Islamists while institutionalizing "moderate" Islam. In fact, this was the model that inspired the conciliators in the US administration, such as former Assistant Secretary of State Robert Pelletreau, who had urged in the 1990s a compromise between the Algerian regime and moderate Islamists.

Regardless of the astonishing development of US–Algerian relations, Morocco remains the main support for the American presence in North Africa, especially for the US Sixth Fleet in the Mediterranean. With the notable exception of Egypt, Morocco has, since its independence in 1956, received more US aid than any other Arab country. And, since the start of the war over Western Sahara in 1975, Morocco has obtained more than one-fifth of all US aid to the continent, totaling more than $1bn in military assistance alone. The US played a major role not only in the handing over to Morocco of the former Spanish colony,[57] but also in reversing the war over Western Sahara in Morocco's favor through large-scale economic and military aid, military advisers, and logistical assistance. The specter of a radical Islamist revolution in North Africa during the Algerian crisis placed Morocco once again in the role of bulwark against extremist, anti-Western forces. King Hassan II's success in curbing radical Islamist movements in his own country made him a particularly useful buffer against such forces. The United States supported Morocco also because of the increase in free-market economic reforms, which include large-scale privatization that coincides with American ideological goals.

US policy in Morocco seeks to safeguard the very old friendship and cooperation with the kingdom, which is still perceived as a stable state in the Maghreb region. Support for Morocco in the US Congress is also significant, not least because Morocco is not antagonistic to Israel. It is Morocco's position toward Israel and its pro-Western orientation that various American administrations have appreciated. Under the Clinton administration, US officials gave high marks to the changes taking place in Morocco. Hence, Edward Gabriel, US Ambassador to Morocco, stated that, "with regard to Morocco, we're very excited about its democratic experiment. We in the US State Department believe that Morocco probably is the best democratic experiment that currently is going on in the Middle East."[58] President George W. Bush reiterated appreciation for Morocco in April 2002, reaffirming the strong ties between the two countries during a conversation with Mohammed VI. William Burns for his part argued that, "The historic steps Morocco has taken toward political, economic, and social modernization demonstrate its strength and reinforce its standing in the community of nations. The United States will continue to be the closest possible partner and ally to Morocco as it takes the necessary steps to ensure peace and prosperity for the future generations in this region."[59] Indeed, the US has assisted Morocco, through various programs, to implement the reforms.[60] While it is true that Bush's positive characterization of Morocco is part of diplomatic discourse, one can still raise the question as to the type of democracy Bush and other officials are referring to. Questioning Clinton and Bush's description of Morocco as a democracy is legitimate because the path to democratization in Morocco has not been as genuine. Although attempts to address the rights of women and the adoption of the new family law are praiseworthy, violations of human rights in Morocco and in occupied Western Sahara—which the US Department of State reports yearly—are a reminder of Moroccan reality. Indeed, while the US Department of State's *2005 Country Report on Human Rights Practices* for Morocco acknowledges some progress it also recognizes that "the human rights record remained poor in many areas."[61] The report lists 15 areas of abuses, including the inability of citizens to change fully their government, excessive police force resulting in deaths of demonstrators and migrants, unresolved cases of disappearance, police and security force impunity, lack of judicial independence, and restrictions on freedoms of speech and of the press, to name but a few. But issues of human rights do not seem to outweigh the excellence of relations between the two countries. And, despite the flagrant abuses of human rights in occupied Western Sahara, the United States supports Morocco in its attempts to circumvent international legality regarding the disputed territory.

Integration of Moderate Islamists as Model for Arab Democracies

The United States viewed positively the cooptation of moderate Islamists in Morocco and their inclusion, albeit strictly controlled, in the political system. As long as Islamists do not question the legitimacy of the monarchy and the king's role as "Commander of the Faithful," they are allowed some political activity. This strategy of inclusion is also aimed at curbing the appeal of jihadism among the youth in the poverty-stricken areas in the cities and countryside. In the last decade, the *Parti de la Justice et du Développement* (PJD) increased its participation in politics. Unlike the more radical and more grassroots, *Al-'Adl wa-'l-Ihsan* (Justice and Charity), the PJD, dubbed the *parti islamiste du palais* (Palace's Islamist party), not only recognizes the legitimacy of the monarchy but has even refrained from winning too many votes,[62] to avoid a situation similar to what had occurred in neighboring Algeria.

Because the United States wishes to use the reforms in Morocco as a model for democratization and liberalization in MENA, it has granted Morocco financial support through various channels, such as MEPI, the Millennium Challenge Account, US AID, and BMENA. This support is exclusive of the military and economic assistance that Morocco receives regularly. The assistance to help ensure the success of the reforms in various areas (health, education, job creation, and women's rights) has the double effect of backing the reforms but also of alleviating the severe socio-economic problems which may derail the process of change. Of course, given the closeness of its relationship with Morocco, the United States seeks gradual reforms that do not jeopardize the stability of the monarchy. Since the PJD, which enjoys popular support, is quite involved in political and economic activities, its participation in US programs is inevitable. In fact, the PJD partakes in international seminars organized by various NGOs, such as the National Democratic Institute or the International Republican Institute, and think-tanks, like the Carnegie Endowment for International Peace.[63] There is evidence that the US government has engaged the PJD, an initiative encouraged by US diplomats in Morocco.[64] The fact that the PJD not only does not question the legitimacy of the monarchy, but also that the latter actually seeks to integrate it in the political system, facilitates US engagement with the PJD. However, divisions within the party, due to US policies in the Middle East and unconditional support for Israel against the Palestinians and in summer 2006 against Lebanon, tend to radicalize the PJD. As Abdeslam Maghraoui explained, the PJD's dilemma is that it "must negotiate its moderation with its conservative popular base."[65] The dilemma for the United States is that its contacts with the PJD may be interpreted as support for Islamists, an action about which anti-Islamists in Morocco and in the US are quite critical, for they believe that this policy will result in sending the wrong message to Islamists. At the same time, US encouragement can also be detrimental to the PJD, for any effort the US takes is viewed suspiciously not only by the more radical Islamists but also by the Moroccan population at large, resentful of American policies.

Undoubtedly, the rise of Islamism in Morocco is in great part the result of the lack of determination of the monarchy to bring about genuine, sweeping reforms. Despite the high praise that Morocco receives from the West, one should remember that the monarchy constitutionally holds all powers and has remained the principal political force since the country's independence in 1956. Thus, while it is true that the monarchy is seeking to co-opt the PJD, it still warns against the less-tamed Islamists in the country and it is precisely the fear of the rise of "radical Islamists" that has allowed Morocco to continue receiving strong US support in the post-Cold War era and more particularly since 9/11 and the bombings in Casablanca in May 2003. The talented Moroccan journalist Aboubakr Jamai insightfully observed that, "As it leveraged the danger of the Communist peril to gain the support of the West during the Cold War era, it [the monarchy] is now attempting to use the Islamist threat to justify the eternal postponement of true democratic reforms in Morocco."[66]

Clearly, the United States maintained the same policy vis-à-vis Morocco and the Bush administration strengthened economic and military cooperation with the kingdom. In October 2003, William Burns announced

> our intention to more than quadruple our non-military assistance to Morocco ... We will seek to provide approximately $40 million in assistance, a number we will look favorably to augmenting in the years ahead. These monies will help strengthen Morocco's efforts to open up greater economic, educational, and political opportunities for all its citizens. Some of these monies will also assist Morocco to enhance its fight against terrorism.

He also announced US "intention to double our Foreign Military Financing to Morocco to reach $20 million next year ... to increasing Morocco's abilities to update its equipment and police its shores."[67] In December 2003, during his trip to the Maghreb region, which included Morocco, Secretary of State Colin Powell restated US willingness to assist Morocco at all levels. Powell expressed the administration's satisfaction with respect to the social, economic, and political reforms that Morocco has undertaken.

In sum, US–Moroccan relations remain quite strong even though the old perceptions of Morocco as a pole of stability in the Maghreb were shattered. The unmistakable rise of jihadism in the country, the Islamist suicide bombings in Casablanca in May 2003, as well as the terrorist attacks in Madrid in May 2004, perpetrated essentially by Moroccans, may induce a shift in the US perception of Morocco as a stable country. Whatever the case may be, support for Morocco remains solid. Thus, in 2002, Morocco received 72 percent of total American assistance to the three central Maghreb countries. In 2005, this aid accounted for 81.8 percent, nearly

$58m.[68] Military aid has now risen to $20m in order to help Morocco not only to curtail clandestine immigration but also, and above all, to be able to protect its borders and to continue the fight against terrorism. More importantly, the United States and Morocco signed in 2004 a bilateral free trade agreement, which entered into effect in January 2006. It is, however, noteworthy that Morocco did not succeed in getting the United States to include Western Sahara in the accord. The US made it clear that the trade agreement "will cover trade and investment in the territory of Morocco as recognized internationally, and will not include Western Sahara."[69] This unambiguous stance allowed the FTA with Morocco to be approved by Congress. Such decision was made to avoid conflict with US congressmen who are in favor of holding a referendum in the disputed territory, but also to avoid alienating Algeria, which supports Sahrawi nationalists and does not recognize Rabat's occupation of Western Sahara, and whose support in the war on terror has been deemed critical. Furthermore, despite Moroccan requests that the United States impose a solution favorable to Morocco in the dispute, the US has rejected such a proposal. In 2006, the United States repeatedly asked that Morocco make a serious proposal to help solve the conflict. Gordon Gray, Deputy Assistant Secretary of State for Near Eastern Affairs, declared recently that with respect to Western Sahara

> the United States continues to seek an acceptable political solution, within the United Nations framework, and has no desire whatsoever to impose a solution ... The Moroccan government has recently expressed its willingness to write up an autonomy plan for Western Sahara; the United States encouraged Morocco to present a credible proposal so that all parties can analyze it.[70]

American policy makers are so enthused about the reforms in Morocco, which they have elevated to a model in MENA, that they seem to overlook the fact that the monarchy is not willing to push the reforms beyond certain limits. There is evidence that Moroccan officials are annoyed with what they see as American interference in the country's internal affairs.[71] The monarchy is quite apprehensive about US support for Moroccan NGOs and the cozy relationship it has with the PJD, regardless of how subservient to the palace the PJD is. Furthermore, the PJD, no matter how moderate, is not willing to accede to one of the US's long-term wishes: recognition of Israel. Indeed, in November 2005, the PJD "rejected categorically" any form of normalization with Israel whatever the motives.[72]

Tunisia: "The Sweet Little Rogue"[73]

Since its independence in 1956 and up until 2003, Tunisia had a privileged position on the list of countries friendly to the United States. Tunisia's pro-Western stance proved extremely attractive, as did its model of political, economic, and social development. In the 1990s, American policy makers presented Tunisia as an example of a success story: reforms, market liberalization, secularism, promotion of women's rights, unconstrained use of birth control, and elimination of illiteracy. Until the early 1990s, the State Department presented the Tunisian Islamist movement as a moderate movement. But the determination of the Tunisian government to eradicate the Islamist organization, coupled with the very unstable situation in neighboring Algeria, led the US government to abandon Tunisia's Islamists and to stop contacts with Rachid Ghannouchi and his moderate Al-Nahda movement.

The United States favors Tunisia for security reasons, as proved by the number of joint military operations carried out each year. During the decade-long Algerian crisis, Tunisia, just like Morocco, benefited from strong American support in order to prevent the propagation of radical Islamism and also to dissuade Libya from any attempt to destabilize its Tunisian neighbor. Taking into account its strategic importance, Tunisia has managed to escape, at least publicly, criticism regarding the serious violations of human rights. In contrast to the criticism that the United States leveled against the Algerian government in the 1990s, Tunisia was spared because, like Morocco and Egypt, it justified repression in the name of maintaining the stability and the survival of the government against "radical" Islamist forces hostile to the Western world.

Two recent exceptions to American indulgence toward the Tunisian government are notable. During his visit in November 2003, Secretary of State Colin Powell criticized the violations of human rights in Tunisia. In February 2004, President Bush said to a baffled Zine al-Abidine Ben Ali that it was necessary for Tunisia to undertake reforms in the areas of freedom of the press and of the legislative system, both legal and electoral. However, apart from these specific reprimands, Tunisia continues to benefit from Washington's leniency and tolerance of its authoritarian regime.[74] In fact, right after criticizing Tunisia on freedom of the press, Bush added that "Tunisia can help lead the greater Middle East to reform and freedom, something that I know is necessary for peace for the long term."[75] Thus, it is not surprising that Tunis hosts one of MEPI's regional bureaus, which is "responsible for coordinating MEPI activities in Algeria, Egypt, Lebanon, Morocco, and Tunisia in close coordination with the American Embassies in those countries."[76]

Tunisia enjoys particularly strong support in the Defense Department, whose leaders wish to maintain Tunisia on the side of the United States. As an official at the State Department put it, "The Department of Defense serves as a lobby for Tunisia in Washington DC; here at State, we were serious about putting pressure on the Ben Ali regime, but DOD persuaded the White House otherwise."[77] Like the other Arab governments, Tunisia benefited from the events of 9/11 and their aftermath and thus succeeded in obtaining support from the United States through its participation in the global war on terror, help to Iraq, recognition of the Iraqi Council of government, and participation in peace-keeping operations. Of course, Tunisia is an active member of the Trans-Saharan Counterterrorism Partnership, which replaced the Pan-Sahel Initiative, along with Algeria, Chad, Mali, Mauritania, Morocco, Niger, Nigeria, and Senegal. The security relationship is paramount; the US has consolidated it military cooperation with Tunisia, whose armed forces are equipped more than 70 percent with US weaponry. In 2005, the US authorized the export of defense articles and services worth $25,397,490 for Tunisia.[78]

During his visit to Tunisia in February 2006, Donald Rumsfeld announced that the US and Tunisia were "working on a Status of Forces Agreement, a SOFA, and that's moving along, and that would create a situation where we would be able to do more things, exercises and that type of thing."[79] The SOFA usually specifies the terms under which foreign military operates in a given country. As of yet, it is not clear whether or to what extent Tunisia will allow the stationing of US troops on its soil. What is certain is that the United States is keen on strengthening its military cooperation with Algeria, Morocco, and Tunisia, and eventually, Libya.

In order to attenuate US criticism on human rights, Tunisians, in addition to consolidating military cooperation with the US, played the "Israeli card"; thus, in February 2005, they invited Israeli Prime Minister Ariel Sharon to come to Tunis. This could have played well in Washington, where Tunisia also benefits from strong support among most congressmen, all impressed with Tunisia's social system. In the meantime, the regime's repressive and anti-democratic measures elicit little criticism from its US ally.

Conclusion

The main argument in this chapter has been that US policy in the Maghreb under Bush's presidency has been driven primarily by security concerns. Focus on security and the global war on terror has found receptive ears in the Maghreb, where the regimes in place are still reluctant to carry out authentic democratic reforms that would allow for greater participation and more democratic representation. There is no doubt that repressive measures, abuses of human rights, absence of freedoms, and the lack of accountability toward citizens are greatly responsible for the rise of radical Islamism. Assuming that the US push for democracy in the region is genuine, any democratization process is likely to bring to power Islamists, for they constitute the most organized opposition force to the regimes in place. American policy makers face a real dilemma: pushing for democracy would result in the coming of Islamists to power. The contention here is that the types of Islamists acceptable to the United States are those that resemble the Saudi regime which is compliant with US wishes. In other words, the United States seeks to promote "moderate" Islamist parties that do not counter US interests: free access to oil and natural gas resources and support for Israel.

The problem, however, is that the main opposition to US presence in the region derives precisely from US policies in MENA, and in particular its support for Israel. Even the most moderate Islamist parties, such as the Algerian MSP, are critical of US one-sided support for Israel. The party was also baffled by the US decision not to recognize the democratic election of HAMAS in Palestine. Unlike the US and despite their moderation, MSP supporters do not perceive HAMAS as a terrorist organization but as a movement of resistance to Israeli occupation.

It seems that, faced with this dilemma, the US has lowered its demands for genuine democratization, preferring instead to support the regimes in place provided they initiate a modicum of change and co-opt "moderate" Islamists who do not endanger US interests. This approach has little chance of success, for it does not tackle the root causes of the rise of radicalism and anti-Americanism in the region. One can only agree with Anthony Cordesman that, "the United States needs to understand that it can only use its influence and its counterterrorism and military capabilities if it changes its image in the Islamic world. The importance of changing the US image does, however, go far beyond public diplomacy."[80]

Having close relations with the regimes in place, even while encouraging them to democratize, will not change the US image, which has gone from bad to worse. The PEW survey released in June 2003 showed that only 23 percent of Moroccans viewed the US favorably, while the figure was 77 percent in 2000.[81] And a Zogby International survey carried out in June 2004 found that 88 percent of Moroccans surveyed held a negative view of the United States because of its "unfair foreign policy."[82] Even middle-class Moroccans hold a negative view of the United States,[83] and all reports show that this is a view shared by most Maghrebis.

Furthermore, current US policy is dominated by actors and agencies more obsessed with security than with socioeconomic and political transformations or with changing course on policies so offensive to the peoples in the region. Also, it seems that the forces in the US government that are more favorable to an alliance with autocratic regimes have the upper hand over those seeking to put pressure on Maghrebi regimes for genuine democratization. With such a state of affairs, it is hard to see how the US can establish positive influence in the region.

Notes

1 Yahia H. Zoubir and Louisa Aït-Hamadouche, "Anti-Americanism in North Africa: Can State Relations Overcome Popular Resentment?" *Journal of North African Studies*, vol. 11, no. 1, March 2006, pp. 39–58.
2 Cécile Jolly, "Ambitions américaines en Méditerranée," *Arabies*, Septembre 1999; Fayçal Oukaci, "Euromed contre plan Eizenstat-Guerre d'influence au Maghreb," *L'Expression* (Algeria), 14 December 2005. Hamida Ben Salah, "Le Maghreb suscite l'intérêt grandissant des Etats-Unis," *Le Quotidien d'Oran* (Algeria), 3 February 2004; Sarah Raouf, "Maghreb: Les regards identiques de

Paris et Washington," *Le Quotidien d'Oran*, 8 December 2003; Moussa Hormat-Allah, "USA-Maghreb: Les dessous des cartes," *L'Opinion* (Morocco), first part 16 January 2003 and second part 11 February 2003.

3   One recalls the fear-provoking book by Graham Fuller, *Algeria: The Next Fundamentalist State?* Santa Barbara, CA: Rand Corporation, 1996. The argument in the book suggested that the question was not whether the Algerian regime would collapse, but how soon. Despite the often fanciful analysis of the book, the author was taken seriously.

4   Yahia H. Zoubir, "Algerian–Moroccan Relations and their Impact on Maghrebi Integration," *Journal of North African Studies*, vol. 5, no. 3, fall 2001, pp. 43–74.

5   International Crisis Group, "Islamist Terrorism in the Sahel: Fact or Fiction?" *Africa Report* no. 92, 31 March 2005. Available at: http://www.crisisgroup.org/home/index.cfm?l=1&id=3349.

6   *U.S. National Security Strategy Document*, The White House, Washington DC, 7 February 2000.

7   Cécile Jolly, "Ambitions américaines en Méditerranée," op. cit., p. 35.

8   Stuart E. Eizenstat, Undersecretary for Economic, Business, and Agricultural Affairs, *Third Annual Les Aspin Memorial Lecture*, Washington DC: The Washington Institute for Near East Policy, 8 March 1999.

9   Yahia H. Zoubir and Karima Benabdallah-Gambier, "The United States and the North African Imbroglio: Balancing Interests in Algeria, Morocco, and the Western Sahara," *Mediterranean Politics*, vol. 9, no. 1 (July 2005), pp. 181–202.

10 Interviews author conducted with US officials at Department of State and Department of Commerce, Washington DC, May 2000.

11 See statement of Secretary of Commerce Sam Bodman during his trip to the Maghreb that the Bush Administration "[is committed] to a strong partnership of trade and investment with the region and achieving the goal of integrating Egypt and the Maghreb into the global economy." Available at: http://www.commerce.gov/opa/press/Secretary_Evans/2002_Releases/Sept_20_Bodman_trip.htm.

12 Yahia H. Zoubir, "Algeria and U.S. Interests: Containing Radical Islamism and Promoting Democracy," *Middle East Policy*, vol. 9, 1 March 2002, pp. 64–81.

13 See Mourad Saouli, "Algérie: Fuite des cerveaux," *Arabies*, October 2003.

14 For these categories applied to the US foreign policy establishment, see Fawaz A. Gerges. *America and Political Islam. Clash of Cultures or Clash of Interests*, Cambridge: Cambridge University Press, 1999. In "Algeria and U.S. Interests," I used "accommodationists" and "confrontationists," categories that corresponded to the actors in the Algerian military–political establishment and in civil society who either sought conciliation with or eradication of radical Islamists. I argued that they had their counterparts in the United States. In his analysis of the Algerian crisis, Hugh Roberts applied those categories only to the Algerian actors: "Algeria between eradicators and conciliators," *Middle East Report*, no. 189 (July–August 1994), pp. 24–7.

15 Zoubir, "Algeria and US Interests," op. cit.

16 President George W. Bush's statement during a speech he gave to graduating seniors at West Point in June 2002. Louisa Aït-Hamadouche, "Les Etats-Unis à l'aube d'une nouvelle doctrine stratégique?" *La Tribune* (Algiers), 19 November 2002.

17 Richard N. Haass, "Toward Greater Democracy in the Muslim World," *The Washington Quarterly*, vol. 26, no. 3 (summer 2003), pp. 137–48, pp. 145–6.

18 Ibid., p. 143–8.

19 "President Bush Discusses Freedom in Iraq and Middle East," remarks by the President at the 20th Anniversary of the National Endowment for Democracy, Office of the White House Press Secretary, 6 November 2003.

20 The worst tension in US–Moroccan relations occurred in 1984–86 when Morocco, for regional reasons, entered an alliance with Libya, then America's archenemy in North Africa. The Israeli attack on the PLO headquarters in Tunis, which could not have taken place without US approval, infuriated pro-Western Habib Bourguiba, who almost broke off diplomatic relations with the US over that attack.

21 Zoubir, "Algeria and US Interests," op. cit.

22 Edward G. Shirley, "Is Iran's Present Algeria's Future?" *Foreign Affairs*, vol. 74, no. 3, May–June 1995. Edward Shirley is the penname of a former CIA official.

23 Author's interview with Abdelkrim Dahmen, Deputy, member of MSP parliamentary group and member of the party's national leadership in charge of foreign relations and emigration, 24 January 2007.

24 *The Threat of Islamic Extremism in Africa. Hearing before the Subcommittee on International Relations, House of Representatives, One Hundred Fourth Congress, First Session, April 6, 1995*, Washington DC: U.S. Government Printing Office, 1995, p. 1.

25 A detailed analysis is provided in, Zoubir, "Algeria and US Interests," op. cit.

26 "US policy toward North Africa," statement made by Robert H. Pelletreau before the House Foreign Affairs Committee's Subcommittee on Africa on 28 September 1994. Available at: http://www.findarticles.com/p/articles/mi_m1584/is_n40_v5/ai_15889460/

27 The White House, *The National Security Strategy of the United States of America 2002*, Washington DC: The White House, September 2002.

28 H. B., "W. J. Burns se prononce sur la prochaine présidentielle," *Le Jeune Indépendant* (Algiers), 26 October 2003.

29 See, Anthea Jonathan, "US eyes North Africa," *Politics*, 10 March 2004. Available at: http://www.news24.com/News24/Africa/News/0,2-11-1447_1496197,00.html; Giles Tremlett, "US sends special forces into North Africa," *The Guardian*, 15 March 2004.

30 Fayçal Oukaci, "Washington disposé à armer l'ANP," *L'Expression*, 11 November 2006, p. 2. See also, Carmen Gentile, "US eyes Algeria as key partner in war on terror," *ISN Security Watch*, 15 December 2006. Available at: http://www.isn.ethz.ch/news/sw/details.cfm?id=17052.

31 Ryan Henry, Principal Deputy Undersecretary of Defense for Policy and Army Lt. Gen. Walter L. Sharp, Director, Joint Staff briefing, in US Department of Defense Office of the Assistant Secretary of Defense (Public Affairs) News Transcript, 7 February 2007. Available at: http://www.globalsecurity.org/military/library/news/2007/02/mil-070207-dod02.htm.

32 Ghada Hamrouche, "M. Mohammed Bedjaoui l'a affirmé hier 'Pas de bases militaires étrangères sur le sol algérien,'" *La Tribune* 4 March 2007. US Ambassador to Algeria Robert Redford said that the United States has not asked Algeria for a US military base there. See, Fayçal Oukaci, "Washington n'a pas demandé à établir une base militaire en Algérie," *L'Expression* (Algiers), 5 March 2007, p. 3.

33 Fayçal Oukaci, "Divergences entre Alger et le Pentagone sur l'Africom," *L'Expression* (Algiers), 12 June 2007, p. 6.

34 "Attentats d'Alger-Louisa Hanoune accuse les Etats-Unis," *Le Soir d'Algérie*, 18 April 2007; Nordine Grim, "Attentats au Maghreb sur fond de lutte géopolitique," *El Watan*, 15 April 2007.

35 Interview with high-ranking Algerian officer, December 2006.

36 Interview with high-ranking Algerian officer, December 2006.

37 See Yahia H. Zoubir, "The US and Libya: From Confrontation to Normalization," *Middle East Policy*, vol. 13, no. 2, summer 2006, pp. 48–70; Yahia H. Zoubir, "Libya in US Foreign Policy: From Rogue State to Good Fellow?" *Third*

World Quarterly, vol. 23, no. 1, February 2002, pp. 31–53; and Ronald Bruce St John, *Libya and the United States—Two Centuries of Strife*, Philadelphia, PA: University of Pennsylvania Press, 2002.

38 Zoubir, "The US and Libya: From Confrontation to Normalization," op. cit., pp. 63–4.

39 C. David Welch, Assistant Secretary for Near Eastern Affairs; Coordinator for Counterterrorism Henry A. Crumpton; Assistant Secretary for Verification, Compliance and Implementation Paula A. DeSutter On-the-Record Briefing Washington DC, 15 May 2006. Available at: http://www.state.gov/p/nea/rls/rm/2006/66268.htm.

40 Willa Thayer, "Libya Awards Oil Contracts," *Associated Press*, 20 December 2006.

41 "Libya to Spend $40 Billion on Infrastructure, Housing Projects; Invites U.S. and International Companies to Partner With Libyan Firms," 20 December 2006. Available at: http://newsblaze.com/story/20061220008530000001.sp/topstory.html.

42 Ronald Bruce St John, "'Libya Is Not Iraq': Preemptive Strikes, WMD, and Diplomacy," *Middle East Journal,* vol. 58, no. 3, summer 2004, pp. 391–2.

43 Peter Slevin and Alan Sipress, "Tests Ahead for Cooperation on Terrorism: Several Countries on Blacklist Have Helped US, but Only Marginally So Far," *The Washington Post*, 31 December 2001. See also, Yahia H. Zoubir, "The Maghreb States and the United States after 9/11: A Problematic Relationship," in Sigrid Faath (ed.), *Neue geopolitische Konstellation im Nahen Osten nach dem 11 september 2001*, Hamburg: Deutsches Orient-Institut, 2003, p. 177.

44 Ron Suskind, "The Tyrant Who Came In From the Cold," *Washington Monthly*, vol. 38, no. 10, 1 October 2006.

45 Robert Burns, "General: US Gains From Ties with Libya," *Associated Press*, 21 April 2005.

46 Author's interview with high-ranking Libyan official, London, 18 February 2006.

47 Mohameden Ould-Mey, "US–Mauritanian Relations and the Coriolis Force of Normalization with Israel," in *Les Cahiers du CREAD* (Algiers), forthcoming. The author would like to thank Dr. Ould-Mey for sharing the manuscript with him before publication.

48 Israeli Ministry of Foreign Affairs, *Remarks at Ceremony on Signing of Diplomatic Relations between Israel and Mauritania Washington DC, 28 October 1999 Secretary of State Madeleine K. Albright, Minister of Foreign Affairs of Israel David Levy, and Minister of Foreign Affairs and Cooperation of the Islamic Republic of Mauritania Ahmed Ould Sid'Ahmed*. Available at: http://www.mfa.gov.il/MFA/Government/Speeches%20by%20Israeli%20leaders/1999/Remarks%20at%20Ceremony%20on%20Signing%20of%20Diplomatic%20Relat.

49 See, International Monetary Fund, "Mauritania Qualifies for US$1.1 Billion Debt Relief under HIPC to Support Poverty Reduction," Press Release no. 00/9, 10 February 2000. Available at: http://www.imf.org/external/NP/SEC/PR/2000/pr0009.htm.

50 "President Bush Concludes Week Long Trip to Africa Congress Hall, Abuja, Nigeria." Available at: http://www.whitehouse.gov/news/releases/2003/07/20030712.html.

51 Ahmed Mohamed, "Coup Leader Meets First With US, French Envoys," *Associated Press*, 4 August 2005.

52 Ahmed Mohamed, "Mauritania's junta leader determined to fight terrorism and maintain relations with Israel," *Associated Press*, 9 October 2005. See also, "US Relations with Post-Coup Mauritania," *AllAfricaNews*, 10 October 2005.

53 Christopher Thompson, "Mauritania. Putting Oil before Refugees," *The New Statesman*, 19 September 2005, p. 26.

54 Press Statement. Mauritanian Elections. Tom Casey, Deputy Spokesman. Washington DC. November 30, 2006. Available at: http://www.state.gov/r/pa/prs/ps/2006/77161.htm.
55 "Israeli Foreign Minister Arrives in Mauritania Amid Violent Street Protests," *Associated Press*, 3 May 2005.
56 "Ould Cheikh Abdallahi organiserait un référendum sur les relations diplomatiques avec Israël," 8 April 2007. Available at: http://www.fr.alakhbar.info/page1.php?id=511&catid=2; the original interview is available in Arabic in the Algerian newspaper, *El-Khabar*, 8 April 2007. Available at: http://www.elkhabar.com/dossiersp/lire.php?ida=65048&idc=45&date_insert=20070407.
57 Jacob Mundy, "Neutrality or Complicity? The United States and the 1975 Moroccan Takeover of the Spanish Sahara," *The Journal of North African Studies*, vol. 11, no. 3, September 2006, pp. 275–306.
58 See: http://usembassy-israel.org.il/publish/peace/archives/2000/november/me1117a.html.
59 Press Conference, Ambassador William J. Burns Assistant Secretary of State for Near Eastern Affairs at Villa America Rabat, Morocco, 28 October 2003. Available at: http://usinfo.state.gov/mena/Archive/2004/Feb/04–648008.html.
60 On US programs to support Moroccan reforms, see, Haim Malka and Jon B. Alterman, *Arab Reform and Foreign Aid-Lessons from Morocco*, Center for Strategic and International Studies, Washington DC, 2006, pp. 62 ff.
61 United States Department of State. *Country Reports on Human Rights Practices–2005*, Bureau of Democracy, Human Rights, and Labor, Washington DC, 8 March 2006. Available at: http://www.state.gov/g/drl/rls/hrrpt/2005/61695.htm.
62 Michael J. Willis, "Morocco's Islamists and the Legislative Elections of 2002: The Strange Case of the Party That Did Not Want to Win," *Mediterranean Politics*, vol. 9, no. 1, spring 2004, pp. 53–81.
63 Saad Eddine el-Othmani, General Secretary of the PJD and a Member of the Parliament participated in May 2006 in a seminar organized by the CEIP in which he presented the party's program. Available at: http://www.carnegieendowment.org/events/index.cfm?fa=eventDetail&id=883.
64 Jeremy M. Sharp, "US democracy Promotion in the Middle East: The Islamist Dilemma," *CRS Report for Congress*, Washington DC: Library of Congress/Congressional Research Service, 15 June 2006.
65 "Morocco: Top–Down Reform to Democratic Transition," Carnegie Endowment for International Peace, seminar, 1 November 2006. Available at: http://www.carnegieendowment.org/events/index.cfm?fa=eventDetail&id=931&&prog=zgp&proj=zdrl,zme.
66 See, Aboubakr Jamaï, "As Monarchy Falters, Islamism Rises," November 2006. Available at: http://blog.washingtonpost.com/postglobal/jamai_aboubakr/2006/11/moroccos_monarchy.html. In January 2007, Jamai was forced to resign to avoid the closing of the independent weekly *Le Journal Hebdomadaire* which he published; see, "Prominent Moroccan Publisher Resigns in Bid to Save Weekly," New York, Committee to Protect Journalists News Alert, 18 January 2007. Available at: http://www.cpj.org/news/2007/mideast/morocco18jan07na.html.
67 Press Conference, Ambassador William J. Burns Assistant Secretary of State for Near Eastern Affairs at Villa America Rabat, Morocco, October 28, 2003. Available at: http://usinfo.state.gov/mena/Archive/2004/Feb/04-648008.html.
68 These figures were calculated from the statistics provided in US Department of State Congressional Budget Justification for Foreign Operations, Fiscal Years 2004 and 2005.
69 Letter from Robert B. Zoellick, United States Trade Representative, to Congressman Joseph Pitts, 20 July 2004. Author's personal file.

70 Gabriela González de Castejón, "Entretien avec Gordon Gray," *Revue Afkar/ Idées*, no. 9, winter 2006, p. 15.
71 Aboubakr Jamaï and Taieb Chadi, "Pourquoi l'Amérique fait peur au régime," *Lejournal-Hebdo* (Morocco), no. 253, 29 April–5 May 2006. Available at: http:// www.lejournal-hebdo.com/article.php3?id_aricle=8031.
72 Statement available on PJD's website: http://www.pjd.ma/article.php3?id_article=503.
73 I borrowed this expression from Clement M. Henry, "Tunisia's 'Sweet Little Rogue' Regime," in Robert Rotberg (ed) *Worst of the Worst: Dealing with Repressive and Rogue Nations*, Washington DC: The Brookings Institution Press, 2007.
74 Shortly after criticizing Tunisia, Powell praised it for the changes that were taking place there. See, Colin Powell on Fox News Sunday, 14 March 2004. Available at: http://www.foxnews.com/story/0,2933,114159,00.html.
75 "President Bush Discusses War on Terrorism with Tunisian President," The White House, Office of the Press Secretary, 18 February 2004. Available at: http://www.whitehouse.gov/news/releases/2004/02/20040218-2.html.
76 See: http://www.state.gov/outofdate/bgn/t/47575.htm.
77 Interview with the author, Washington DC, May 2004.
78 See: http://www.state.gov/t/pm/64779.htm.
79 Al Pessin, "Rumsfeld Discusses Expanding Military Ties with Tunisia," 11 February 2006. Available at: http://www.globalsecurity.org/military/library/news/ 2006/02/mil-060211-voa03.htm.
80 Anthony H. Cordesman, "Winning the 'War on Terrorism': A Fundamentally Different Strategy," *Middle East Policy*, vol. 13, no. 3 (fall 2006), p. 102.
81 See: http://people-press.org/presentations/PewGlobalAttitudesViewsofaChanging World.pdf.
82 Dafna Linzer, "Poll Shows Growing Arab Rancor at US," *The Washington Post*, 23 July 2004, p. A26.
83 Craig Charney, "Morocco: The price of anti-Americanism," 7 January 2005. Available at: http://dir.salon.com/story/news/feature/2005/01/07/morocco/index_np. html.

14 Reverberations in the Central Maghreb of the "Global War on Terror"

Clement M. Henry

This chapter examines how the regimes of Algeria, Morocco, and Tunisia managed to take advantage of new opportunities offered by the Bush administration's "global war on terror" (GWOT) while minimizing the risks. Stepped-up US aid and military cooperation strengthen the regimes' coercive capabilities but risk distancing them further from their respective publics, which view the United States as most responsible for the bloodshed and military occupation of Iraq and, even worse, complicit in the Israeli occupation of Palestine and destruction in the summer of 2006 of parts of Lebanon.[1] The chapter also discusses how the GWOT has redefined the region's "strategic rents" and suggests how the United States might re-evaluate them if promoting democracy were really taken to be a central strategy of the GWOT.

Opportunities and Risks of the GWOT

A confluence of factors has enhanced the Maghreb's importance to the United States. Even before 11 September 2001, the neo-conservatives were already advocating new and more global patterns of troop deployment. The Project for a New American Century (PNAC) published a detailed plan in 2000, before the presidential election, for extending America's security perimeter well beyond the old Cold War limits of Central Europe in thinly staffed forward bases that could be activated in times of crisis with forces normally based in the US. The GWOT only accelerated the redeployment of American forces, and the search for new basing sites may have driven the Pentagon as much as any weapons of mass destruction to focus on Iraq after 9/11. The Afghanistan campaign accelerated American troop redeployments in the Caspian region that had already been initiated for other reasons.

Two related objectives underlay the extension of America's security perimeters: containing China and securing the flow of oil to the United States and its allies. By mid 2002 both Pentagon and State Department officials were stating that Africa had strategic importance. In a Pentagon press briefing on 2 April 2002 the Assistant Secretary of Defense for African

Affairs observed that 15 percent of US oil imports came from West Africa, and he observed "this is also a number which has the potential for increasing significantly in the next decade."[2] Table 14.1 shows that US imports indeed increased in 2005, even as US production decreased to little more than half of total imports. Along with Algeria and Libya in North Africa, Angola and Nigeria were viewed as particularly promising, together with offshore deposits in the Gulf of Guinea, where the US Navy has increased its presence in recent years.

China, also ever more in need of imports, was seeking new supplies as far afield as Venezuela,[3] where Hugo Chávez has slightly cut exports to the United States.[4] While China so far has only one major African supplier, Sudan, it is actively seeking other partners in the region. Indeed, an African "oil rush," as Michael Klare and Daniel Volman call it,[5] seems to be accelerating. They also detect a military pattern similar to the one that had resulted in a US military build-up in the Caspian region a decade earlier, subsequently accelerated by post-9/11 operations in Afghanistan. First the Pentagon launched a Pan-Sahel Initiative in 2002 to seek out any terrorists escaping across Africa from Afghanistan and Somalia. This was originally "a U.S. State Department funded program in the northern African countries of Mali, Mauritania, Niger, and Chad designed to enhance border

Table 14.1 Sources of US Oil Imports 2004–2005

Sources	2004	2005	2004	2005	Reserves	R/P (yrs)*
	(mm barrels/day)		(%)	(%)	(% total)	
Canada	2,119	2,172	16.4	16.1	1.4	14.8
Mexico	1,642	1,647	12.7	12.2	1.1	10.0
South and Central America	2,647	2,868	20.5	21.2	8.6	40.7
Europe	987	1,100	7.7	8.1		
Former Soviet Union	282	473	2.2	3.5	10.2	28.4
Middle East	2,505	2,345	19.4	17.3	61.9	81.0
North Africa	476	547	3.7	4.0	9.5	31.8
West Africa	1,637	1,943	12.7	14.4	(included above)	
East and Southern Africa	–	–	0.0	0.0		
Australasia	28	14	0.2	0.1	0.3	20.0
China	20	32	0.2	0.2	1.3	12.1
Japan	8	–	0.1	0.0		
Other Asia Pacific	145	170	1.1	1.3	1.8	13.0
Unidentified *	400	214	3.1	1.6		
Total Imports	12,898	13,525	100.0	100.0	1.2 trillion barrels	

Source: BP Statistical Review of World Energy June 2005 and June 2006
Note: *R/P is proven reserves to production ratio, or the number of years of reserves at current production rates.

capabilities throughout the region against arms smuggling, drug trafficking, and the movement of trans-national terrorists."[6] Its proponents further explain:

> The key point of the Pan Sahel Initiative was to foster regional coop-eration and coordination; to counter terrorist elements that are operat-ing and cooperating in the region now; and to bolster EUCOM's interest in the regional [sic]; to make a US policy statement using active US forces. It was a kind of door opening exercise over a few years with every intent to broaden this program.

Indeed, with "intensive lobbying" the Pentagon established a more gener-ously funded Trans-Sahara Counterterrorism Initiative (TSCTI) in March 2004. In addition to the original African Sahel countries, it includes Algeria, Morocco, Nigeria, Senegal, and Tunisia. As the TSCTI officials justify this new display of American hegemonic domination, "Africa is an emerging haven for our enemies in the Global War on Terrorism."[7] It is not so much democracy as border control with help from US Special Forces that will secure those "vulnerable" spaces in the African Sahel between the oil and gas of Algeria and Nigeria. Africa has become a focal point of the GWOT, or really a series of them. One Pan-Sahel Initiative map highlights Algeria and the four Sahel countries and displays arrows of Special Forces uprooting any "terrorists" from their "indigenous habitats" and pushing them southeast, while other Special Forces press southwest from Egypt and the Horn of Africa to converge—catching terrorists in a pincer move-ment?—in the Lakes Region and Tanzania.[8] Claiming that "terrorists oper-ate throughout the Sahel," another map also notes that the region is "safe haven for extremists; borders are unable to be regulated or patrolled due to enormous size" and "interiors are too large to enforce laws."[9]

Hence special mobile operations were needed. Militarily, the principal activity, called Operation Enduring Freedom-Trans Sahara (OEF-TS), is an "unconventional Warfare line of operation ... conducting a broad spectrum of military and paramilitary operations of longer duration, predominantly conducted through, with, or by indigenous and/or surrogate forces."[10] An important by-product is the training of the US Special Forces, now that they have trained their counterparts of the former Warsaw Pact countries, after those "'lean years of the 1970's [that] saw an absolute decrease in the number/frequency of operational deployments."[11] Operation Flintlock in June 2005 convened assortments of US Special Forces training with local counterparts in Algeria and Senegal, as well as the original Sahel coun-tries of Mauritania, Mali, Niger, and Chad. Without minimizing the role of the Senegalese, who policed the region in French colonial times, the cri-tical "surrogate force" was bound to be Algerian, certainly not Moroccan or Tunisian. Algeria inherited the longest of France's Saharan borders and also provided the TSCTI with its only known terrorist enemy, the

Salafist Group for Preaching and Combat (GSPC), posted on TSCTI's website and without which the Special Forces' "boots on the ground" would lack legitimacy. All three Maghreb countries were assuming a new geopolitical significance and acquiring new strategic "rents" from the United States.

Closer relations with the United States, however, may put any Arab regime at risk. However authoritarian a regime may be, it must also be sufficiently sensitive to public opinion to retain the support of its key constituents, cadres, and security services. Regimes of the central Maghreb display interesting variations in their sources of support and consequently in their abilities to balance their international and domestic commitments. Practicing a finely tuned degree of political pluralism with seasoned political parties, the Moroccan monarchy enjoys a tactical advantage over its more monolithic neighbors. It may conjure up massive demonstrations to relieve any public pressures against the very policy it pursues, as in 1990, when Morocco sent a contingent of troops to join the American-led coalition to liberate Kuwait from Iraqi occupation. So also in 2003, the monarchy enjoyed similar latitude in coping with mass protests against the US invasion and occupation of Iraq. Algeria, by contrast, permitted just one demonstration of protest, not in the streets but inside a conference room chaired by the marginal female leader of a leftist splinter party. Official Algerian and Tunisian opposition parties enjoy considerably less credibility than their Moroccan counterparts, however chastened and weakened the latter became after many years of "use." In addition, Morocco has a relatively vibrant field of NGOs, compared to very small numbers in Algeria and Tunisia that are not heavily penetrated by the regime.

The United States has compounded the pressures on these regimes by trying to promote democracy as well as allegiance to the GWOT. Although GWOT took precedence over efforts to promote democracy, the Bush administration justified upgrading the political initiative, inherited from previous administrations, as a means of combating terrorism by eliminating the repressive conditions that breed terrorists—draining swamps, so to speak, to dry up the breeding grounds for mosquitoes. Its Middle East Partnership Initiative (MEPI) contains a well-funded political reform pillar that promotes a variety of piecemeal reforms. Given prevailing public opinion in the Maghreb, however, real democracy could seriously compromise the participation of any of these regimes in America's GWOT. Polls show that majorities fear the United States as much as al-Qaeda. But MEPI-style reforms are perfectly congruent with a Moroccan strategy of gradual (never-ending?) transition to democracy.[12]

Morocco indeed seems to be positioned to derive more benefits from the GWOT with less risk than its neighbors, and it enjoys a deeper history of diplomatic relations, having been one of the first countries to recognize the United States when the rest of North Africa was still nominally under Ottoman rule. Tunisia, however, has used its enhanced status as regional center of the MEPI to its advantage, citing it as proof that Ben Ali's regime must be progressive and respectful of human rights since it enjoys the blessings of the United States. And Algeria, historically the least aligned with the United States, joined the US Sahel counter-insurgency initiative and devised scenarios of common enemies in the GWOT. Its discreet military collaboration with the United States has gained it not only military equipment but also a measure of legitimacy for its prolonged internal state of emergency. This chapter will suggest, somewhat counter-intuitively, that Algeria may well be deriving the greatest benefits from the GWOT and that Tunisia could regain its status as the *état pilote* of the region if the United States and the EU were to follow through on its status as a regional center and select it as the region's testing ground for real democracy promotion.

Algeria

While each regime has used the GWOT as an excuse to tighten security and repress opposition, Algeria had the greatest need for it. The GWOT serves the regime in two ways. It justifies a continued state of emergency at home, enabling the regime to bottle up protest,[13] and it wins the regime a measure of international legitimacy, or at least dampens external criticism of its human rights abuses. The events of 11 September 2001 enabled the Algerians to identify with the United States and to claim that they had been struggling alone for years against the common global enemy. In October 2002 the government convened an international conference on terrorism in Algiers to explain its position. One military reporter noted that the "Afghans," Algerians returning from Bin Laden's "base" (al-Qaeda), were already launching terrorist operations against the Algerians before the December 1991 parliamentary elections were held.[14] On this interpretation, Bin Laden had selected Algeria as the vulnerable battleground, whereas the Algerian generals' decision to cancel the elections after the first round of voting was a purely defensive response to the terrorists. Algeria's armed forces were depicted as standing alone fighting the GWOT in the 1990s—like Churchill facing down the Nazis in 1940–41—and they now sought international recognition for their brave deeds. In October 2002 the Algerian armed forces and police were taking credit for saving the country in the mid-1990s, when many external observers had thought that the triumph of the Islamic Salvation Front (FIS) was inevitable.

It was payback time for Algeria. The GWOT, coupled with Secretary Rumsfeld's modernization of the American military, was altering the nature of strategic rents in the Mediterranean. While military bases, port facilities, and joint naval maneuvers, the matters of Cold War exercises, remained important, these rents were depreciating relative to new ones associated with the new conditions of warfare. The perpetual GWOT was one of constant movement and clandestine operations, using mobile Special Forces in need only of rough landing strips, communications facilities, and some storage space with a minimum of upkeep and local maintenance. If the writings of Jeremy Keenan, a British anthropologist who patrols the Sahara, are even broadly on target, the Algerian military's *Département du Renseignement et de la Sécurité* (DRS), successor of the dreaded *Sécurité Militaire*, is America's principal ally in the African Sahel.[15] In that sense, Algeria has cleverly exploited its geopolitical position commanding the Sahel.

The only successful counterterrorist operation registered to date in the Sahel concerns "Abderrazaq El Para," as the Pentagon cites him in one brief paragraph.[16] Perhaps now that five years of funding were committed to TSCTI it was no longer necessary to discuss the "enemy" in more than perfunctory terms. "El Para," turned over to the Algerians in 2004 in what the Pentagon claimed to be one of the "biggest successes" of the Pan-Sahel Initiative, was subsequently downplayed on the TSCTI's website, which offers some brief background on the GSPC.[17] The TSCTI's advocates also cryptically comment that "Some of the governments have embraced counterterrorism as a means of suppressing legitimate dissent and Islamic groups," but go on oddly to discuss Chad,[18] not Algeria or other prime manipulators of the GWOT like Mauritania (until the removal of President Taya in early August 2005) or Tunisia.

The only real connection between Chad and the GWOT was the capture in this distant country of "El Para," not by Americans or Algerians but by rebels against Chad's government who subsequently negotiated with the Algerian military's DRS. *Le Monde Diplomatique*, a more credible source than either the Algerian press, manipulated by the DRS, or Pentagon sources fed by the Algerians, questioned whether the Algerian government could be "arranging events, such as the kidnapping of foreign tourists in the Sahara and inventing its own Osama bin Laden, to capture Washington's attention and ensure attendant arms sales."[19] In its February 2005 issue, Salima Mellah and Jean-Baptiste Rivoire demonstrate the involvement of the Algerian military in the kidnapping of the tourists, supported by evidence from some of the subsequently freed hostages. Most telling of the politics behind the drama is a commentary they cite, when "El Para" was still in the hands of the rebels, from one of Algeria's most manipulated newspapers: "the sole justification for an American presence in the region is the GSPC. If El Para is killed and officially identified, or is captured and handed over to a third country, many things may have to be reassessed."[20] Fortunately for the Algerians and the Pentagon, he was back in Algerian custody by October, but he was no longer useful after an earlier attempt had failed to have the GSPC ransom him from the rebels. Apparently he was being replaced by Mokhtar Belmokhtar (alias One-eyed), another former Algerian soldier.[21] Presumably, however, there were elements of the GSPC loyal to al-Qaeda and not infiltrated by the DRS, because they claimed responsibility for an attack on a Halliburton subsidiary in December 2006 that wounded four Britons and one American as well as four Algerians.[22]

Meanwhile Americans appear to have bought at least part of the DRS line, for General Charles Wald, deputy commander of the US European Command (EUCOM), claimed in March 2004 that terrorists "in the northern part of Africa, in the Sahel and the Maghreb," were "looking for sanctuary as they did in Afghanistan when the Taliban were in power. They need a stable place in which to equip themselves, organize, and recruit new members."[23] By the time "El Para" was exposed as a fraud, the GWOT had taken institutional form in the TSCTI, featuring Operation Flintlock and other military activities of special benefit to both the Algerian and American administrations. Whether or not there were any terrorists independently roaming around in the African Sahel, geopolitical considerations had given them a status not unlike those Weapons of Mass Destruction in Iraq, a sort of reality that could only be disproved with more armed forces on the ground.

Strategic Rents of the GWOT

The mutual deceptions of the GWOT may exact higher strategic rents than those of more conventional military strategies. Algeria does not even appear to be winning any significant conventional rents, but Morocco and Tunisia were not receiving much more. Congress, which is notified of most arms sales including Pentagon giveaways, received only four notifications of US arms to Algeria between 2002 and May 2006, all of them repairs and communications and surveillance, not heavy weapons, missile systems or even excess ammunition, staples of the diet of military assistance fed to Morocco and Tunisia in previous years. After 2002, in fact, Tunisia was left pretty much out in the cold, while Morocco did a bit better, receiving helicopter servicing along with excess ammunition and some communications equipment.[24] Most traditional military aid, having dried up in the 1990s, increased in the GWOT years from very low levels in 2001. Table 14.2 tells the story of overall US military and economic assistance to the three countries.

Not included in these numbers, however, are either the Middle East Partnership Initiative, discussed below, nor the $1.6m allocated by the Pentagon in 2006 and 2007 for the training and education of Algerian military associated with the GWOT.[25] But perhaps the most important rent Algeria received from the United States has been the international legitimation of its regime, a principal goal of the military decision makers in the first place for selecting Abdelaziz Bouteflika to run for president in 1999. By 2003 Algeria was in the enviable position of being courted by both France and the United States. One sign of the regime's ability to placate both its internal supporters and the United States is the handling of new oil legislation proposed by Chekib Khalil, Bouteflika's oil minister, who had spent many years at the World Bank in Washington before being recalled to serve his longtime friend Bouteflika. The legislation was designed to attract large transnational oil companies, such as Exxon, to explore and develop Algerian oil and gas. When Bouteflika faced re-election in April 2004, it was only prudent to put the legislation on the back burner, despite

Table 14.2 US military and Economic Assistance to Algeria, Morocco, and Tunisia, 2001–2007 (USDm)

	FY 2007 Request	FY 2006 Estimate	FY 2005 Actual	FY 2004 Actual	FY 2003 Actual	FY 2002 Actual	FY 2001 Actual
Military aid							
Algeria	0.840	0.743	0.920	0.722	0.612	0.067	0.121
Morocco	14.5	14.3	17.0	11.9	6.5	4.5	3.5
Tunisia	10.5	11.9	12.3	11.7	6.4	4.5	4.5
Training							
Algeria	0.840	0.743	0.920	0.722	0.612	0.067	0.121
Morocco	2.0	1.9	1.9	2.0	1.6	1.0	0.999
Tunisia	2.0	1.9	1.9	1.9	1.5	1.0	0.968
Economic aid							
Algeria	1.100	0.065	0.482	n/a	n/a	n/a	n/a
Morocco	29.4	24.5	34.0	8.9	9.1	13.1	12.8
Tunisia	0.755	1.3					
Anti-terror							
Algeria	1.075						
Morocco	1.317	0.774	2.1	0.35			
Tunisia	0.755	1.206					
Total aid							
Algeria	1.940	0.808	1.402	0.722	0.612	0.067	0.121
Morocco	43.9	38.8	51.0	20.8	15.6	17.6	16.3
Tunisia	11.255	13.2	12.3	11.7	6.4	4.5	4.5

Source: Middle East Desk. Available at: http://middleeastdesk.org.

diplomatic pressures from Washington. After he was re-elected, he pushed the legislation through the Algerian parliament with virtually no discussion in March 2005. But then, as higher oil prices and America's predicaments in Iraq further enhanced Algeria's strategic value, the government virtually nullified the reforms. The decrees needed to implement the legislation increased the participation of Sonatrach, the national oil company, to 51 percent of any new discovery, so that it would exercise full control over any foreign partner. Although new regulatory agencies divested Sonatrach of certain powers, it kept the state monopoly over upstream operations.[26]

Perhaps domestic politics and high oil and gas prices better explain Algeria's backtracking on reforming the petroleum sector, but surely the country's increased strategic rents associated with the GWOT helped it face down any diplomatic pressures from Washington (where Pentagon interests were trumping any oil diplomacy). Even more telling of Algeria's new strategic value was the major shift of fortunes in its conflict with Morocco over the former Spanish Sahara. By 2001 the United Nations was on record as supporting a "third way," that is, an eventual autonomy that Morocco could control and that POLISARIO, the Sahrawi nationalist movement, and

Algeria consequently rejected. But then, in 2003, James Baker, the UN's chief mediator, devised a new plan that was more acceptable to the Sahrawis and Algerians, for it included a referendum on self-determination after a five-year transition period. When Morocco rejected it, Baker resigned a year later, but the point was made. Although Baker ostensibly represented only himself, not the US government, it is hard to believe that the United States, perhaps encouraged by oil interests that the Bush administration appreciated, was not reversing a policy that had systematically favored Morocco since 1975, when the conflict started. Possibly strict neutrality still favored Morocco in the long run, building ever more facts on the ground, but the apparent US policy shift was a further illustration of the marginal advantages accruing to Algeria from the GWOT. A trial balloon in the Moroccan press, "Can Morocco lose the Sahara?" would have been unthinkable in earlier years.[27]

Morocco

Although the United States increased military and economic aid to Morocco as part of the GWOT, the financial support was minimal. Morocco relied primarily on the EU's Mediterranean Economic Development Assistance program (MEDA) and on bilateral French assistance. Morocco also earned special praise from Washington in 2004 "in recognition of the close US–Morocco relationship, our appreciation for Morocco's steadfast support in the global war on terror, and for King Mohammed's role as a visionary leader in the Arab world."[28] The new status as "major non-NATO ally" in 2004 allowed Morocco to have access to weapons facilities from the Pentagon. But neither the new title nor a Free Trade Agreement (FTA), also signed in 2004, and entered into effect in January 2006, could help resolve the Western Sahara issue. In fact the FTA explicitly excluded the disputed territory. To the extent that strategic rents in the Maghreb are a zero-sum game, Algeria's gain was Morocco's loss.

Domestically, moreover, the GWOT was probably placing greater strain on the Moroccan political fabric than on Algeria's.[29] This blog conveys some of the differences, reflecting on Defense Secretary Donald Rumsfeld's visit to the Maghreb in February 2006:

> Demonstrations took place everywhere before Iraq war, or the publication of Abu Ghraib photos all over the world, except Algeria. You never ever hear of a demonstration in Algeria when Palestinian kids are shredded to pieces in Khan Younes or the Balata Refugee camp. Not a care in the world. About the [Danish] cartoons? Not a peep, no condemnation, no demonstration, not even a condemnation on an Algerian blog: they seem to be dead inside. I can't explain it.
>
> Yesterday Rumsfeld left Algeria to go to Morocco. Thousands of Moroccans were standing in front of the Moroccan Parliament with

placards of Rumsfeld and Bush that said: "wanted," or "war criminal," etc. Men, kids, women were demonstrating for the arrival of Rumsfeld (who apparently had a peaceful pleasant trip to Algeria) [30]

Worn out by years of strife, the Algerian public was more containable than Morocco's, but conversely the monarchy was more adept than the police state in manipulating the diverse political forces at play in Morocco. In a certain sense, too, the tragic events of May 2003 in Casablanca, when jihadist suicide bombers struck downtown, killing scores of people, relieved some of the pressures. After years of apologies (without any personal accountability) for police brutality under Hassan II, the Ministry of the Interior could freely resume its activities in concert with the GWOT.[31] At the same time, however, Mohammed VI's monarchy was sufficiently flexible to take full advantage of opportunities offered by MEPI and other programs designed to promote democracy, or at least to promote better governance.

Morocco was in the forefront of the Arab countries receiving MEPI technical assistance in sensitive political areas, such as elections and "political process strengthening," and "legislative strengthening." "Civil society and reform advocacy" was another area in which Moroccan NGOs could gain international support and embellish the regime's reform image. While getting at least its fair share of the MEPI funds earmarked for its political, economic, an education "pillars," Morocco did especially well with the "women pillar." In fiscal years 2003 and 2004 MEPI invested over $12m in various programs designed to promote women's rights in the region. Morocco received a good third of it in direct bilateral programs for publicizing its new legislation on the family and other reforms, in addition to multilateral benefits. In fact over $28m of MEPI funds went directly to Morocco during this period, as well as a fair share of some $250m in multilateral program aid. In programs related to civil society development and corporate governance Morocco was exceptionally well placed to benefit, for it was the only country in the region, apart from Lebanon, to sponsor a fully recognized branch of Transparency International. A measure of political liberalization was not incompatible with collaboration with the United States in the GWOT because political forces were structured so as to moderate their demands for fear of less tolerant oppositions.[32] As Guilain Denoeux observed, King Mohammed VI "has managed to 'dehassanize' significantly the system he inherited, while at the same time keeping its basic logic intact."[33]

Tunisia

The regime that was most vulnerable was the one with the fewest strategic rents, namely Tunisia. Selected by the United States to be a regional center for the MEPI, Tunisia was potentially the most exposed to democracy promotion and human rights programs but the least able to tolerate them. The police state was brittle because it had undermined its own safety valves of political expression and discussion. The few organizations that attempted to preserve any autonomy were continually harassed, and the police, increased fourfold since the presidency of Habib Bourguiba (1957–87), had transformed the country into a vast surveillance camp.[34] Tunisia did not have Morocco's safety valves of parliamentary and other forms of expression and consequently seemed to be inviting Islamist violence. In January 2007 the police finally triumphed after ten days of gun battles in the capital's southern suburbs over a gang of at least 27 armed men. Arguably, "Many people are convinced that the policy of anti-Islamist repression conducted since the early 1990s by Ben Ali has, in fact, radicalized youths."[35]

Ben Ali's regime, efficient as always, originally took quick advantage of the GWOT in December 2001 by announcing to the Counter-Terrorism Committee of the United Nations its intention of enacting "a comprehensive national law on counter-terrorism." Amnesty International observed that the legislation, eventually approved by Tunisia's Constitutional Council on 4 June 2003, was "based on a broad definition of 'terrorism' [that] may further undermine human rights, including ... further serious restrictions on freedom of expression and belief."[36] The bombing by al-Qaeda of a synagogue in Djerba on 11 April 2002, killing 21, including 14 German tourists, served—like the subsequent Casablanca bombings in Morocco in May 2003—to marshal strong domestic support for the regime and participation in the GWOT.

Indeed a "global war on terror" seemed to fit perfectly the authoritarian trajectory that Ben Ali had traced since 1989, when he responded to legislative elections in which opposition Islamists, running as Independents since their party was not officially recognized, garnered surprising support, perhaps more than the official 15 to 20 percent of the vote that was credited to them.[37] Ben Ali's strategy had been to play upon middle-class Tunisians' fears of rabid Islamist extremists, who allegedly lit fires and torched people,[38] so as to justify his crackdown in 1991–92 on the only opposition to his regime that could display organized mass support. The fact that his war on these "terrorists" had become global gave Ben Ali an international respectability that Tunisians crave, recalling as it does the image of their country as a *état pilote* or model of development, so cultivated and cherished in the golden Bourguiba years but so tarnished at the end by pictures of a doddering dictator.

Although the GWOT gave the regime a new lease on life, Tunisia's human rights problems would not go away. As the smallest country in the region and the one least endowed with strategic rents, Tunisia was also the most vulnerable to external pressures for reform yet was also, by mid-decade, as the Algerian insurrection wound down, the most repressive of the three countries. Even after scores of political prisoners were released in

2006, Tunisian jails still contained more prisoners, at least on a per capita basis, than its neighbors' to the west. Greater administrative efficiency and police density, moreover, meant that those who were released suffered internal exile, "social death," as Béatrice Hibou describes their condition.[39] Human rights activists could also lament the degradation of the Tunisian media. The condition of the country's newspapers was abysmal even by regional standards: readership plummeted after the exciting transition period following the forced retirement of Bourguiba, so that by 2003 Tunisia tied with Syria for last place among lower middle-income Arab states. A cyber-police disciplined the Internet as well as fax machines, and all international connections ran through a central control. People close to the president, including a daughter, owned the two private sector service providers. In its desire to gain international recognition, the regime had wooed the organizers of the World Summit on the Information Society (WSIS) into hosting its second phase in Tunis in November 2005, only to focus international attention on the system of local information repression. An international study of Tunisian Internet practices concluded that the national filtering system blocked not only politically controversial sites but also those where surfers could enjoy anonymity and be free of cyber-police surveillance.[40] At least three groups of young Internet surfers were caught, imprisoned, and in some cases tortured in 2002 before being subjected to trials and long prison sentences.[41] Released in 2005, the Zarzis group remained deprived of educational opportunities and under virtual house arrest. Consequently Internet usage in Tunisia stagnated; by 2004 only 84 Tunisians per 1,000 people were connected, compared to 117 per 1,000 in Morocco, despite its poorer and less-educated public.[42]

The situation was hardly conducive to the sorts of regional business operations that the country's efficient administration might otherwise have harbored. Indeed, Tunisia was not getting the foreign direct investment it needed, and its international debt was reaching alarming proportions: the World Bank calculated that the value of the debt in 2004 had reached 78.5 percent of gross national income.[43] The ruling family, reputed for its rapacity,[44] received even worse publicity than usual in 2006. Indeed, members of the ruling family were implicated in corruption and other illegal activities, such as the president's nephew Imad Trabelsi's involvement in a bizarre affair in France in summer 2006.

More serious for Ben Ali's regime would be the EU's concern for human rights in Tunisia if a post-Chirac France were to abandon its protection, so reminiscent of the French Protectorate (1882–1956), of the police state. In addition to the usual criticisms of theft and corruption within the president's entourage, the regime faced numerous complaints about human rights and reacted in ways that may further heighten EU concerns. In May 2006 the regime was especially heavy-handed. First the police broke into the office of the head of the Tunisian Bar Association and attacked lawyers protesting a new law that threatened the profession's independence. Then, on 11 May, security forces detained the head of the newly formed Syndicate of Journalists for holding a secret meeting. A week later the police even prevented members of the family of a deceased human rights activist from entering the headquarters of the Tunisian League for Human Rights (LTDH) to attend a memorial ceremony in his honor. Then, on 21 May, they detained a Swiss representative of Amnesty International who was attending a meeting of the Tunisian section, and asked him to leave the country. A week later, in the presence of foreign guest observers, including Hélène Flautre, Chair of the European Parliament's Human Rights Committee, police physically blocked LTDH delegates from holding their congress. They even snatched Flautre's cell phone from her, returning it only hours later. A further incident not calculated to please the EU's partnership program for its southern partners occurred in September, when the Tunisian authorities blocked all hotel facilities to prevent an EU-sponsored study group from convening its "International Conference on Employment and the Right to Work in the Euro-Mediterranean Region" (after many of the European and other North African participants had already arrived). The authorities evidently resented the protection being provided for a number of Tunisian human rights activists.[45]

Fortunately for the activists, their country is still too close to France for their suffering to be totally ignored. Online and in France, various opposition groups publicly engage in exile politics and support Tunisian human rights. The ruling party insulates the masses from the small elite of human rights activists at home, however, and the only serious threat to the regime would be if internal dissidents within the ruling apparatus were to join forces with those activists. Strangely, the regime acts as if it is constantly being threatened. Reminiscent of Stalin's Soviet Union, its football coach prevented a journalist from the Qatari *Al-Jazeera* TV from interviewing Tunisian players practicing in Switzerland for the World Cup in 2006. But unlike the old Soviet Union, the regime curries international favor and hires public relations teams in the hope of again being seen as a model, an *état pilote*, for the universe of developing countries, rather than a laughing stock.

Conclusion

Tunisia could indeed regain its status as a model for the region, were the EU and the United States to single it out for special attention and demand that it meet international human rights standards. Tunisia deserves special attention because it is better situated than its neighbors to support substantive political reform. It has a large middle class—80 percent of its population, if President Ben Ali is to be believed[46]—and an efficient public administration to see to its record numbers of private home owners. It also has a political history of strong political organization and grassroots activity that Ben Ali's RCD has perpetuated, along with a trade union history that cannot be repressed. Overt pressures, especially those coming from France and the EU rather than from the discredited Bush administration, would be bound to have a constructive impact on Tunisia's ruling elite as well as its human rights activists. The probabilities of this happening may be minimal, but the potential benefits to both Tunisia and the West are worth imagining.

Tunisia has minimal strategic rents as the GWOT is currently conducted, whereas Algeria's are maximized. Each regime gains in the short run because it is given excuses to enhance its authoritarian controls. Imagine, however, a Tunisia that includes its Islamists (the An-Nahda Party) in a more tolerant, pluralist regime. In place of a pervasive police it would gain the "soft power" that comes with moral authority.[47] Imagine, too, a United States that reconsiders its strategy, once enough of its leadership realizes that the GWOT is really a political contest over the hearts and minds of Muslim publics and has no military solutions, that the principal means of combating the jihadists, whether in Africa, the Middle East, or Europe, is through the soft power of surrogate Muslim authorities, not the force of arms. Anti-terrorist actions by police or Special Forces may sometimes be necessary, but they need to be perceived as legitimate, not further exercises in Western imperialism. A winning Western strategy will rely primarily on soft power, enhancing Tunisia's strategic rents. A more democratic Tunisia would be hostile to the Bush–Cheney administration but would be positioned to benefit from overdue changes in America's conduct of the GWOT.

An American change of policy would of course also relieve the pressure on the other North African regimes, torn between alliances with the United States and public opinions hostile to the close relationships. Although certain opportunities offered by the GWOT would be foregone, so also would be the risks of further internal disorder associated with imaginary GWOTs and overly close relationships with the United States. A better American understanding of potential strategic rents might also gently reinforce the forces for political reform in Morocco.

Notes

1 The American Arab Institute/Zogby International poll released on 14 December 2006 points to increasing disaffection with the United States by publics sampled in Egypt, Jordan, Lebanon, Morocco, and Saudi Arabia. Opinion in Algeria and Tunisia was not sampled but can be assumed to follow the regional trend. For the poll results see: http://www.zogby.com/NEWS/ReadNews.dbm?ID=1220.

2 Cited by Michael Klare and Daniel Volman, "America, China and the Scramble for Africa's Oil," *Review of African Political Economy*, no. 108, June 2006, pp. 298–9.

3 Gabe Collins and Carlos Ramos-Mrosovsky, "Beijing's Bolivarian Venture," *The National Interest*, 1 September 2006. Available at: http://www.nationalinterest.org/Article.aspx?id=11912.

4 Venezuela exported about 2.2 million barrels per day in 2005, of which only 40 percent went to the United States. In 2004 it had exported little more than 1.5

million barrels per day, two-thirds of it to the US. Venezuela exported about 130,000 barrels per day less to the US than in 2004, about as much as China gained, but, whatever future plans for China may be, Venezuela's increases in exports went principally to Latin America and Europe.

5 Michael Klare and Daniel Volman, "America, China and the Scramble for Africa's Oil," p. 304.
6 As indicated on its web page: http://www.globalsecurity.org/military/ops/pan-sahel.htm.
7 See: http://www.globalsecurity.org/military/ops/tscti.htm.
8 See the map: http://www.globalsecurity.org/military/ops/images/psi-map2.gif.
9 See: http://www.globalsecurity.org/military/ops/images/psi-map.jpg.
10 See: http://www.globalsecurity.org/military/ops/oef-ts.htm.
11 See: http://www.globalsecurity.org/military/ops/flintlock.htm.
12 Thomas Carothers, "The End of the Transition Paradigm," *Journal of Democracy*, vol. 13, no. 1, January 2002, pp. 5–21.
13 General Mohammed Lamari, former chief of staff, declared in 2004 that the state of emergency was no longer necessary.
14 In his report "Le Terrorisme: le précédent algérien," Lt. Col. Zerrouk referred to the overrunning by Algerian veterans of the Afghanistan war (the so-called "Afghans") in June 1991 as evidence that the Islamists had already chosen "bullets over ballots" to gain power.
15 Jeremy Keenan, "Waging war on terror: the implications of America's 'New Imperialism' for Saharan peoples," *Journal of North African Studies*, vol. 10, no. 3–4, fall–winter 2005, pp. 610–38; J. Keenan, "Security and Insecurity in North Africa," *Review of Political Economy*, vol. 33, no. 108, June 2006, pp. 269–96.
16 "One of the program's biggest successes was the capture of Abderrazak al-Para, a key figure in the extremist Salafist Group for Call and Combat, who was turned over to the Algerian government in 2004." Available at: http://www.global security.org/military/ops/pan-sahel.htm. In fact, he received the name El Para for having accomplished military service with the Algerian paratroops, but was also variously known as Abderrezak Lamari, Amari Saifi, and Abou Haidara.
17 See: http://www.globalsecurity.org/military/world/para/gspc.htm.
18 "Chad's leaders assert that the transnational networks of anti-Western Islamic extremists feared by America are not their main problem. Rather, they cite foreign-backed rebels as their main terrorist threat. They believe that Sudan and other countries are supporting a group of about 4,000 anti-government rebels near Chad's eastern border with Darfur." Available at: http://www.globalsecurity.org/military/ops/oef-ts.htm.
19 Salima Mellah and Jean-Baptiste Rivoire, "El Para, the Maghreb's Bin Laden," *Le Monde Diplomatique*, February 2005. Available at: http://mondediplo.com/2005/02/04algeria.
20 *L'Expression*, 6 June 2004, cited by Mellah and Rivoire, "El Para."
21 The name is reported in *L'Expression*, 27 December 2004, and the alias is reported on the MIPT Terrorism Knowledge Base. Available at: http://www.tkb.org/KeyLeader.jsp?memID=5878.
22 "Qaeda-Linked Group Claims Algerian Attack," *New York Times*, 13 December 2006.
23 *Le Quotidien d'Oran* (Algeria), 6 March 2004, cited by Mellah and Rivoire, "El Para." See also General Charles Wald's talk to the American Enterprise Institute, Washington DC, 14 April 2004. Available at: http://www.aei.org/docLib/20040414_Wald.pdf. The GWOT and African oil were principal themes, esp. pp. 14–16. The two themes were spontaneously conflated in these remarks: "Now, are they [the GSPC] al-Qaeda? No. But are they a problem? Yes. Do we have to do something about it? Well, I'll tell you one thing, I think the United States

learned a lesson in Afghanistan. You don't let things go. You can't let it happen. So we're working with these countries to go ahead and try to have some capability for their militaries to do a better job of solving the problem of ungoverned spaces in that area. They're very dangerous. This has been beaten to death, but we believe it in strongly. If you look at the Gulf of Guinea, for example, and the oil revenues, and the hydrocarbons that are going to come out of there over the next 10, 12 years, it's going to be more than we get out of the Middle East." Earlier he commented that in the coming 10 years the United States would be receiving 30 percent of its oil imports from areas around the Gulf of Guinea (including Nigeria).

24 Federation of American Scientist, Database of Notifications to Congress of Pending US Arms Transfers. Available at: http://www.fas.org/asmp/profiles/world.html.

25 Carmen Gentile, "US Eyes Algeria as Key Partner in War on Terror," *ISN Security Watch*, 12 December 2006. Available at: http://www.isn.ethz.ch/news/sw/details.cfm?id=17052. Gentile mistakenly gives the figure of $1.6bn instead of $1.6m. Earlier, in May 2006, it had been understood that Section 1206 of the 2006 Defense Authorization law included $200m outside the formal Foreign Military Assistance framework to be divided up among a number of countries, including Pakistan, Indonesia, and Nigeria, as well as all three central Maghrebi states.

26 François Krotoff and Nicolas Bonnefoy, "Hydrocarbons Legislation in Algeria: Back to Square One?" *Advisor* (Association of International Petroleum Negotiators), no. 269, October 2006, pp. 10–15.

27 Abdellatif Mansour, "Can Morocco lose the Sahara?" *Maroc Hebdo* (International Edition, retrieved 13 October 2006 by the BBC and distributed by Lexis Nexis).

28 BBC News Service, 4 June 2004.

29 The Arab American Institute/Zogby International poll released on 14 December 2006 indicated that Moroccan opinions of the United States had declined sharply since 2002 and even since 2005, when 64 percent of those polled had negative views, compared to 87 percent in 2006. Only in Jordan, among the five Arab countries being surveyed, had opinion hardened so much against the United States, but Algeria was not included in the study. For a summary of the poll results see: http://www.zogby.com/NEWS/ReadNews.dbm?ID=1220.

30 Rumsfeld was in Algiers for 5 hours, after visiting a US Word War II cemetery in Tunisia, and then flew on to Morocco to visit the king's horse ranch and meet Moroccan politicians. I have edited the blog and cited it selectively because it was not all fit to print, but the unexpurgated version is available at: http://community.channel4.com/eve/forums/a/tpc/f/503603557/m/5010009804.

31 Human Rights Watch, *Morocco: Human Rights at a Crossroads*, vol. 16, no. 6(E), October 2004. Available at: http://hrw.org/reports/2004/morocco1004/index.htm.

32 Ellen Lust-Okar, *Structuring Conflict in the Arab World*, Cambridge: Cambridge University Press, 2005.

33 Guilain Denoeux, "Paradoxes of Reform in Morocco," *The Middle East in London*, vol. 3, no. 5, November 2006, p. 10.

34 Béatrice Hibou, "Domination and Control in Tunisia: Economic Levers for the Exercise of Authoritarian Power," *Review of African Political Economy*, no.108, June 2006, pp. 186–206.

35 Kamal Labidi, "Ben Ali's dictatorship is creating more Islamists," *Daily Star* (Beirut), 26 January 2007.

36 Report S/2001/1316, 26 December 2001, cited by Amnesty International, "Tunisia: New draft "anti-terrorism" law will further undermine human rights,"

Briefing to the European Union EU–Tunisia Association Council, 30 September 2003. Available at: http://web.amnesty.org/library/Index/ENGMDE300212003?open&of=ENG-TUN.

37 Selective restrictions on voter registration also helped to increase support for the ruling party. See Clement Henry Moore, "Political Parties in North Africa," in I. William Zartman and William Mark Habeeb (eds), *Polity and Society in Contemporary North Africa*, Boulder, CO: Westview, 1993, pp. 42–67.

38 At least one night watchman of a ruling party local bureau in Bab Souika, Tunisia, died in a fire set by dissidents. It was alleged that the Islamist radicals of Rashid Ghannouchi's Nahda Party had deliberately murdered him, although a lawyer associated with the case told me that nobody intentionally killed anybody. The Bab Souika incident served as a pretext, followed by an alleged Islamist plot in the summer of 1990 to seize power, to unleash massive force against the Islamists. Tens of thousands of Islamist members and sympathizers were arrested in 1991–92, many of whom spent long years in jail.

39 Béatrice Hibou, "Domination and Control in Tunisia," pp. 188–9.

40 "Internet Filtering in Tunisia in 2005: A Country Study." Available at: http://www.opennetinitiative.net/studies/tunisia.

41 Six youths and a minor were arrested in Zarzis in late 2002 on grounds of "forming a band with the object of preparing armed strikes." They claimed simply to be surfing the net for information about the political situation in the Middle East. Tried and originally condemned to sentences ranging from 19 to 26 years in jail, they gained slight reductions, down to an average of 13 years on a prison farm, on appeal in July 2004. See, *Le Monde*, 8 July 2004, p. 3; the International League of Human Rights, "Tunisie: Condamnation des 'Internautes de Zarzis' à de Lourdes Peines au Terme d'un Procès Entaché d'Irrégularités," 7 July 2004. Available at: http://www.fidh.org/article.php3?id_article=1558.

42 World Bank, *World Development Indicators 2006*.

43 The present value of debt is defined as "the sum of short-term external debt plus the discounted sum of total debt service payments due on public, publicly guaranteed, and private non guaranteed long-term external debt over the life of existing loans. The GNI denominator is a three-year average." The definition unfortunately does not specify the discount rate used in the calculation. See World Bank, Development Gateway, Tunisian country profile, accessed at: http://www.developmentgateway.org/DataStatistics. Presumably using the same discount rate, the present value of Morocco's debt, historically heavier than Tunisia's, was only 39.2 percent of GNI, while Algeria's, constantly diminishing with the help of substantial oil and gas revenues, was 32 percent in 2004.

44 See Nicolas Beau and Jean-Pierre Tuquoi, *Notre Ami Ben Ali: L'envers du "miracle tunisien*," Paris: Editions La Découverte, 1999, esp. pp. 152–7.

45 Vanya Walker-Leigh, "Tunisia under Fire for Ban on NGO Meet," 18 September 2006, Interpress News. Available at: http://ipsnews.net/news.asp?idnews=34757. See also Omar Mestiri, "La Benalie 'terre d'accueil et d'ouverture,'" *Kalima*, no. 45, 3 September 2006.

46 Interview in *Washington Report on Middle East Affairs*, April 2005. Available at: http://www.tunisiaonlinenews.com/interviews/wrmea_0405.html.

47 Joseph Nye, *Soft Power*, New York, Public Affairs, 2004, pp. 1–32. For a summary see his "The new Rome meets the new barbarians," *The Economist*, 21 March 2002.

15 European Policy and the Southern Mediterranean

George Joffé

In November 2005, the European Union, together with its partners in the Southern Mediterranean basin,[1] reviewed the progress of its major policy initiative there, the Euro-Mediterranean Partnership, 10 years after it was initiated. At the founding conference of the Partnership in the city of Barcelona in November 1995, the new policy had been lauded, through the Barcelona Declaration, as an attempt to create a region of shared peace, prosperity, and stability in the Mediterranean basin. The normative objective, of course, concealed the real purpose of the policy, which was to apply the principles of soft security to enhancing European security along its southern periphery. The soft security objectives were to be achieved primarily by stimulating economic development in Southern Mediterranean countries in order to minimize labor migration into Europe, seen at the time as a major source of internal social, political, and economic tension in both Europe and the countries concerned, given the demographic pressures they faced.

There were other aspects to the policy, too, for it sought to provide a holistic response to the ills of the Mediterranean basin. Thus problems of regional security were to be addressed by a collective security approach; an ambition that was to be frustrated by the failure of the Middle East Peace Process after the 1993 Oslo Accords. Issues of governance were addressed by measures designed to increase democratic governance and respect for human rights in the Southern Mediterranean region. Mutual social and cultural misperceptions and ignorance were also to become the objects of initiatives designed to improve awareness on both sides of the Mediterranean.

These three baskets of measures provided a genuinely innovative European initiative designed to engage the Southern Mediterranean in measures which both enhanced European security and promoted development in the Union's chosen partners through a holistic confidence- and later partnership-building measure. Despite the initial Eurocentric nature of the policy, it was anticipated that the measures proposed would both promote closer economic integration amongst the southern partner-states and encourage improvements in governance and mutual socio-cultural awareness so that, over time, European dominance over the process would be dissipated by Southern Mediterranean progress. As the review conference in November 2005, halfway through the 20-year purview of the new policy, was to acknowledge, these aspirations are unlikely to be fulfilled to any substantive degree.

Europe's Mediterranean Policies

The initiative was, nonetheless, quite unlike the policy initiatives that Europe had adopted towards its southern periphery previously, which had in large measure stemmed from the colonial inheritance. Britain and France had been the major colonial powers in the Middle East and North Africa, although Italy had first colonized Libya before being expelled during the Second World War, and Spain had had interests in Northern Morocco and in Western Sahara. This had left a legacy of economic dependence on Europe, as well as ambiguous cultural relationships, which the Union and its predecessor, the European Economic Community, had tried to address in a series of bilateral economic agreements from 1969 onwards, starting with North Africa and then, in 1976, extending to the Middle East Mediterranean littoral. With Israel and Turkey there had been separate but parallel agreements dating from the mid-1960s. There was also a growing problem of migration into Europe, mainly from Turkey and North Africa but later, too, from Egypt, which European states found difficult to digest in social and cultural terms, despite the growing demand for migrant labor and the growing need of the countries of origin for the remittances it generated. Parallel to this were accelerating flows of asylum seekers, reflecting deficiencies in governance in the Southern Mediterranean region.

Now the new Partnership, more colloquially known as the Barcelona Process, swept all of these into a single policy. Inevitably, the economic dimension of the policy was the most detailed and comprehensive, not least because this approach had underlain the construction of the Union itself. It was also an extension of the original bilateral agreements that had been negotiated between Europe and the Southern Mediterranean states. However, whereas these had provided for free access to the European market for industrial goods and restricted access for agricultural produce, the new economic policies converted these trade agreements into free trade agreements, in which European industrial products would also be granted free access to Southern Mediterranean markets after lengthy transition periods when tariff and non-tariff barriers would be gradually reduced.

The detailed policy anticipated the organization of a series of bilateral free trade arrangements between individual Southern Mediterranean states and the European Union in industrial goods, thus exposing their industrial sectors—seen as the primary potential generators of growth and employment—to unfettered competition with European industry. This, it was anticipated, would force an optimal use of resources in the countries concerned and ensure appropriate economic reforms to meet the European challenge by modernizing their economies. It was an approach that recalled the principles behind the European Union's own construction, culminating in the Single European Market. It was also paralleled with a series of multilateral partnership measures based on the confidence-building approach established by the Conference on Cooperation and Security in Europe, held in Helsinki in 1975 to initiate the process of *détente*, and repeated in the Italian–Spanish non-paper of 1990 which proposed a similar Conference on Cooperation and Security in the Mediterranean. This, together with free trade, provided the innovative elements of the new policy and would construct the shared zone of peace and stability whilst the integration of Southern markets would provide a shared prosperity.

However, although the new policy was based on the principles of economic integration, with the implied assumption of free movement of capital and goods, it remained faithful to its underlying purpose and did not include the essential third freedom, that of labor. Borders and divisions, in short, were to be preserved for economic and political reasons. Indeed, to this extent, it faithfully replicated the underlying principles of *détente* which had sought to create confidence-building measures designed to reassure the Soviet Union against its fears of military threat but not to assimilate it, with its alien political system, into Western Europe or the wider Western sphere. That would have to await internal change and the spontaneous disintegration of the Socialist Bloc in 1989 as the Cold War came to an end. In the same way, the Barcelona Process was designed to promote economic, social, and political change within established boundaries and indirectly reinforced their effectiveness, thus primarily serving the objective of European security through Europe's preferred diplomatic instruments.

Thus, as outlined above, the basket of economic measures designed to set up the bilateral free trade areas with the Union—which were eventually intended to be integrated into a single Southern Mediterranean market to match the Single European Market—was matched by two other baskets of measures. One basket dealt with common security concerns in the Mediterranean with the objective of constructing a cooperative security regime, an objective that, given the ongoing crisis in relations between Israel and the Palestinians, has remained stillborn. It also advanced the prospect of democratic governance and institutional respect for human rights as an essential part of the modernization package. The other basket addressed measures directed at creating mutual public appreciation of cultures and societies, alongside others designed to stimulate the development of civil society in the Southern Mediterranean.[2] It has to be said that there has not been much progress on either objective, both because of the timidity of European politicians and because of Southern resentment of European xenophobia at home and interference abroad, not to speak of the wider implications of Western policy after the events of 11 September 2001 in the United States.

What the Euro-Mediterranean Partnership did not do was to resolve the inherent contradiction between closer economic cooperation and the persistence of political division. This focused around the issues of migration and visas. Migration had originally been treated by the Union on the basis of a zero inward-migration policy and seen as part of the Justice and Home Affairs pillar of the Maastricht treaty. By the end of the 1990s, however, Europe had come to recognize that it had become an immigration area and that a policy of managed migration would be necessary—a concern of the Common Foreign and Security Policy because it would involve state-to-state negotiation.[3] Even though this implied that migration, and thus labor flows, would be permitted, it was still based on the idea that this would take place between states and thus across borders normatively defined as impermeable.

European visa policy maintained this, whether inside the Schengen Area or outside it, so that the difficulties in obtaining a visa began to become a major theme of complaint from the South to the North of the Mediterranean. Similarly, the rapidly increasing flows of illegal migration and asylum seekers from the South highlighted the reality of the European external border and the growing tensions that it caused—as President Jacques Chirac learned on his famous official visit to Algeria in August 2003, when he was greeted by the mass chanting of "visas, visas!" by the crowds who welcomed him. Their cries were also a salutary warning to European politicians of the potential failure of the Barcelona Process to achieve its declared objectives, as illegal migration into Europe rose inexorably towards 400,000 to 500,000 a year.[4]

The failure to control migration, however, has not been the only failure that has confronted the Euro-Mediterranean Partnership since its inception in 1995. As mentioned above, the security agenda was stymied by the continuing violent confrontation between Israel and the Palestinians. This meant that no consensus could be reached over a Charter for Peace and Stability in the Mediterranean, the embodiment of the Barcelona Process and its aspiration for cooperative security in the region, at the Marseilles Summit in November 2000 and the matter has now been postponed indefinitely.

The European Commission has also been unwilling to invoke the sanctions provided in the bilateral Association Agreements it has signed with its Southern Mediterranean partners over progress towards democratic governance, and particularly over the issue of human rights observance, despite blatant abuses committed in Algeria during its civil war between 1992 and 2000; in Tunisia; or as a result of the conflict between Israel and the Palestinians in the Occupied Territories. It has argued that it is more effective to act quietly through diplomatic channels in a process of constructive engagement and that this has been done. There have not, however, been any evident positive outcomes and it is difficult to avoid the conclusion that the political and security basket of the Barcelona Process has had little effect.

More obvious has been the failure of the basket of economic measures contained in the bilateral Association Agreements and the objective of integration of economies in the Southern Mediterranean. Bilateral free trade areas have been created through the Association Agreements and parallel reforms have taken place in the Southern Mediterranean states concerned. Primarily, this has involved the gradual phasing-out of tariff barriers to imports and the replacement of lost customs revenue to the state by the imposition of value-added tax. In parallel to this, economic restructuring has taken place. This has been designed to liberalize the economies concerned, in terms of their external trade, monetary policies, and exchange control regimes, together with the withdrawal of the state from the economic process and the development of institutions—domestic financial markets and legal systems—designed to encourage foreign private direct and equity investment.

These changes, which mirror precisely the prescriptions of the IMF and the World Bank, were intended to improve the climate for foreign investment which was seen as the necessary driver for industrial expansion and job creation. Unfortunately, except for the one-time realizations of privatization receipts, inflows of investment have been disappointingly low. This has proved to be the pattern of the region overall, which has not only had the second lowest level of foreign investment worldwide on average in recent years—only Africa received less—but has also seen its share of investment actually decline in proportion to global investment flows.[5]

The main reason for this has been the region's lack of comparative advantage in a world where low-cost Asian producers are now a dominant force. The implications of this were underlined in January 2005 when the end of the multifibre agreement meant that Southern Mediterranean textile exports to Europe—one of the mainstays of the expected growth in industrial exports—collapsed precipitously. In the first three months of the year, Moroccan textile exports to Europe, for example, dropped by 30 percent. The consequences of this in terms of job creation have been compounded by the continuing demographic boom for, even though birth rates in the last decade have fallen significantly, the massive bulge in population created in the twentieth century is now approaching the age range when it will be potentially economically active, but the potential for job creation is simply not there.

This implies that one of the main, if unexpressed, objectives of the Barcelona Process—the creation of economic opportunity and employment to soak up the potential well of emigrants—has simply not been achieved. Of course, had agriculture formed part of the original economic package, this would have provided a further outlet for the economies of the Southern Mediterranean, as had been the case with the agreements drawn up before 1995. Yet, even here it is not clear that this would have been the case, for the highly mechanized, capital-intensive agriculture of the European Union with its subsidized production costs could have done untold damage to the protected cereal markets of the southern peripheral states—a problem they now face in relation to the United States.

Challenges

The reality of this potential failure has been highlighted by two other developments that further reinforce it, despite their innate contradiction with the normative values of the Euro-Mediterranean Partnership. The first of these has been the European reaction to both this implicit failure of the Barcelona Process and the challenge to it offered by similar American policy proposals such as the US–Middle East Partnership Initiative (USMEPI) or the Broader Middle East and North Africa Initiative (BMENA). The second has been the increasing securitization of Europe's Common Foreign and Security Policy in response to the perceived threat of global terrorism in the wake of the Madrid train bombings in March 2004 and the London bombings of July 2005. This tendency had begun long before, after the events of September 2001, but it has accelerated dramatically in recent years and is now conditioning all other external policies.

Its significance lies in the fact that it targets an internalized enemy, Europe's poorly integrated migrant communities, and because it is increasingly being seen at the demotic and instinctive level as a cultural confrontation. Ironically enough, it was to these very problems that the social and cultural basket of the Barcelona Process was addressed and the ongoing social crisis within Europe is yet another testament to the wider policy failure described above. Indeed, it could be argued that these tensions go even further back, into the heart of the European project itself with its own normative values of political secularism and intellectual tolerance. In many respects, these are being inverted into statements of cultural intolerance in that, unless they are accepted in their entirety by alien non-European groups within the Union— whether or not they are in the process of being Europeanized through assimilation or integration—such groups are to be excluded from the European project despite their residence in Europe, in a deliberate process of migrant cultural and social "ghettoization."

This was, after all, the inherent significance of the message issued by Pim Fortuyn, the charismatic Dutch politician who was assassinated in 2002. His political party, the *Lijst Pim Fortuyn*, was predicated on the assumption of a cultural clash between European principles and Islamic values which he saw as an inherent threat[6]—multiculturalism as a threat to Dutch traditional tolerance.[7] Although he was roundly criticized in Europe for his attitudes towards immigrants, he articulated very well a widespread European prejudice against those who did not accept European principles of democratic governance and human rights observance and who, for that reason alone, should be excluded from the European cultural space. It is an argument that has resurfaced violently in the wake of the murder of the

Dutch film and television director, Theo Van Gogh, by a Moroccan Islamist resident in Holland in 2004.

In this respect, if not in others, he did mirror very widely felt views in Europe about the supremacy of European values, views which acted as a respectable counterpart to the even more widespread xenophobia that has, to official embarrassment, often emerged in recent years. Such approaches, of course, as with the securitization of foreign policy in the face of an alleged terrorist threat, inevitably provoke a response from those perceived to be responsible. The response is often complex but, at one level it involves alienation, either overt or covert, in which both the migrant community and the multi-cultural object of the project itself—Islam—are targeted in a complete inversion of the normative principles lying behind the Barcelona Process. Part of the reason for this is the degree to which, despite tensions over neo-conservatism and the invasion of Iraq, current European and American agendas share common values and approaches.

American Soft Security Alternatives

In essence Europe and the United States have a common interest in shaping the Mediterranean environment to enhance their security interests although those interests differ. For Europe, as described above, the dominant concern relates to the Southern European periphery and seeks to ensure border security within an environment of controlled migration. That concern has now been complicated by the growing security threats within Europe itself, which are linked, in part, to the external political environment and to the European reaction to it. The result has been an increasing tendency to internalize these political concerns and to redefine them in terms of a cultural confrontation within and outside Europe that manifests itself as globalized terrorism.

For the United States, the security concern is quite different in that threats in the Mediterranean remain geographically external to the United States itself and relate to its wider strategic concerns. These reflect the security of strategic lines of communication through the Mediterranean itself,[8] given the fact that these are dominated by a series of choke-points, and the situation in the Eastern Mediterranean with respect to Israel and the Persian Gulf. Of course, in the wake of the events of 11 September 2001, the United States has, in effect, adopted Samuel Huntington's concept of the clash of civilizations[9]—an essentially culturalist interpretation of security threat.

This has not, however, been internalized as is the case with the European Union, but it has emphasized a coincident geographic and cultural boundary, particularly with respect to Israel, to which the United States, in addition to its hard security response in the "war on terror," has now adopted soft security responses in a similar fashion to the European Union. This, in essence, argues—as does Europe—that the adoption of certain specific cultural and political values and practices could eliminate the security threat, provided that innate and indigenous parallel values are discarded. Despite superficial differences between the two projects—European and American—at root, they are surprisingly similar, even if articulated in different ways.

Thus, on 12 December 2002, the then secretary-of-state, Colin Powell, in an address to the Heritage Foundation in Washington introduced a new soft security policy for the Mediterranean.[10] This, the US–Middle East Partnership Initiative, was designed to compensate for deficiencies in governance, economic development, educational approaches, and the empowerment of women, to which Congress had committed $302.9m over a four-year period for the multilateral initiatives, in addition to the $1bn-worth of bilateral aid that the United States supplies to the region every year,[11] quite apart from the special aid programs for Egypt and Israel. In 2004, the United States opened two regional offices, in Tunis and Bahrain, to manage this initiative and has negotiated bilateral free trade areas with Jordan, Tunisia, and Morocco. The initiative is also the vehicle through which the individual programs of the Broader Middle East and North Africa Initiative, proposed by the United States and adopted by the G-8 group of states at the Sea Island meeting in 2004, are put into operation.

The interesting feature of this new American policy is that, even though its security justification is quite different, it is in direct competition with the Barcelona Process, at least as far as governance and economic development are concerned. At best, such duplication causes confusion and at worst it provides a mechanism by which Southern governments can avoid commitments they do not wish to undertake by playing off the European Union against the United States. It is not clear why cooperation between both major regional powers was not encouraged when the United States decided to adopt a soft security approach and, although Commission officials today claim that there is no conflict, the Commission presidency in 2002 had no doubt at all that the American initiative was designed, in part at least, to challenge Europe.[12] After all, the United States had been sidelined when the Barcelona Process had been introduced in 1995.

It is also clear that the American initiative also emphasizes the existence of a cultural barrier between a realm of assumed secular democratic tolerance and an external arena of cultural otherness characterized by violence and threat. This is to be corrected by the introduction of cultural and political change in a rather more intrusive fashion, particularly with respect to education and the status of women, than that practiced by the European Union, although the underlying assumptions are the same in both cases. Both arise from shared perceptions of a new international order, created by the hegemony of a single hyper-power, to use Hubert Védrine's term,[13] in which Europe must find its place, despite the contradictions this may create with its underlying interests, given the presence of domestic migrant communities and a turbulent periphery in which the turbulence is, in part, a consequence of the attitudes and policies of its dominant partner, the United States.

A New International Order

The policies of both the United States and the European Union towards the Middle East must, however, be seen against the wider context of the contemporary international order. Most analyses of international relations today start with an assumption that a new world order was essentially established upon the ashes of the Cold War. With the destruction of the prolonged stability of the Cold War, a new kind of stability emerged, predicated on the predominance of the United States in security and economic terms—a kind of uni-polar hegemonic stability—and on the universalization of the liberal democratic model and the market economy—the modern version of globalization.[14] The first airing of this new world order occurred in the aftermath of the expulsion of Iraq from Kuwait by the Multinational Coalition under the leadership of the first Bush presidency and the aegis of a revived United Nations, now set, apparently, to operate as its founders had intended. Intellectually, the spirit of the new age was captured by Francis Fukuyama's concept of the "End of History"[15] and Adam Robert's vision of a developed world as a "Grotian one, observing norms of cooperation, and perhaps even has its Kantian element: a civil society of civil societies."[16]

There were, of course, competing visions, hinted at by Adam Roberts when he went on to remark that, outside this normatively ideal focus, "parts of the world beyond are still Hobbesian, with force still a very active final arbiter within and between countries, and sovereignty loudly proclaimed." It was a vision that was to be given sinews by Samuel Huntington in his famous article, later amplified by an influential book entitled *The clash of civilizations*, in which civilizational conflict would replace war based on national interest. At the time, this view was swamped by the confident belief that the Westphalian system was coming to an end, that a world community based on idealistic concepts of an international society ordered through international law and the United Nations was coming into being, and that geo-economics[17] would sweep away the neo-realist concept of geo-politics as a definition of the new world order.

During the 1990s, furthermore, a series of new ideas began to emerge, building in part on new, postmodernist concepts of sovereignty. These allowed for intervention in the internal affairs of a state, indeed encouraged it, if the state in question in some way abused universal principles of human rights or, because it repressed its own population, could be considered to have forfeited its right to rule, since sovereignty was an expression of general will or collective legitimacy, not solely of the power of the state.[18] By the end of the decade, this had blossomed into a full-blown ideology of intervention, particularly in the Anglo-Saxon world, as typified by

Tony Blair's Chicago speech on 22 April 1999.[19] These ideas were given intellectual substance by Robert Cooper, a British diplomat, who first argued that the postmodern state would be a construct of a state within an ordered international community where sovereignty was voluntarily derogated. He subsequently proposed a reification of interventionism under the rubric of "reluctant imperialism," which turned out to be suspiciously similar to concepts of liberal imperialism as developed at the height of the Victorian era.[20]

Such ideas meshed well with those that were to emerge when the Bush administration came to power in 2001 and the neo-conservative agenda came to dominate the foreign policy process. The new concepts not only involved the longstanding American conservative vision of the projection of national interest at a global level—first proposed and justified by President Reagan in the 1980s, as a kind of inversion of the moral status of American democracy into the international area as a justification of the practice of diplomatic neo-realism—but also added its own unique assumptions. These involved the practice of unilateral force where necessary, on a pre-emptive basis if need be, to establish an international democratic environment sympathetic to and supportive of the United States and its allies. The neo-conservatives rejected the restraining influence of international organizations or of an international, law-based community.[21] They also distanced themselves from the European Community's endorsement of such an approach and its innate preference for soft security and the preferred European diplomatic technique of constructive engagement.[22]

The neo-conservatives were a product of the frustrations felt by the United States during the 1990s and of the underlying American distaste for any kind of restraint on its diplomatic activities. As such, they were well within an American tradition reaching back, ironically enough, to Woodrow Wilson as well as to his Congressional critics at the time, who had refused to endorse the international institutions created by the Treaty of Versailles. They also reflected many of the assumptions behind the geo-economics of the Clinton era, much though they decried Clintonian foreign policy. In a sense, they combined the universalism of Francis Fukuyama's vision and the skepticism of Samuel Huntington. Even more surprisingly, they echoed many of the assumptions behind the New Right in Europe, even though they rejected the European project.

Indeed, in many respects, their arrival to power, as articulated through the Bush administration and, subsequently, in the new national security doctrine enunciated by the new administration,[23] marks the end of a long period of transition from the Cold War to a genuinely new world order. This has little to do with a rule-based international society and much more to do with the revival of a neo-realist approach to the international arena, albeit now against a globalized economic background. And, of course, it is this conundrum that Europe is now struggling either to digest or to reject because of the contradiction between innate, if rarely voiced, European sympathy for such a project and overt European preference for international law as the leaven for international relations. It is a crucial contradiction, for it provides the intellectual counterpart to the internalized cultural boundary that has emerged in recent years as a result of terrorist violence. The irony is that, despite the reverses that the neo-conservative vision has suffered in recent years, both in Iraq and in the wider Middle East, the essential principles of the ideology itself have been increasingly integrated into the contemporary general European *weltanschauung*.

It is against this intellectual environment that the implications of the events of 11 September 2001 should be seen. Ironically enough, they acted as a catalyst for the application of the neo-conservative agenda to the Middle East and for the development of the associated "war on terror" which now applies to the whole region, together with Southeast Asia, Afghanistan, and Pakistan. They have resulted in profound changes in regional politics and geo-politics, as well as in the underlying assumptions behind American and, to a lesser extent, European regional diplomacy. They have also generated a competition over soft security, as opposed to hard security, responses in the Mediterranean region and in the Gulf. Most strikingly of all, they have nourished the development of a major, dispersed, and fragmented terrorist threat, exploiting modern means of communication and benefiting from access to a coherent intellectual background that has profoundly affected the internal politics and security assumptions of states throughout Europe, as well as in the United States. And, most importantly, both sides in this conflict are increasingly interlinked through a dialectic of antiphonal, mutually reinforcing violence—a reification, as it were, of the "clash of civilizations." It is this that forms the background to both the failure of the Barcelona Process and the emergence of a parallel American policy which is unlikely to be more successful.

The European Response

In the past five years, Europe has had to respond to these new challenges, as well as to some old ones. It has had to face the fact that the Barcelona Process has failed to realize its early promise; it must confront the challenge of American soft security policies in the Mediterranean; and it has had to confront the issue of terrorism within its external frontiers. It has also had to face the implications of Enlargement, especially in the East where new states now share its common external frontier, many of them also having gained membership of the Union itself.

The issue began to be faced in 2002, at the Copenhagen summit of the Council of the European Union. A fully developed policy was produced by the European Commission in May 2004[24]—the month of Eastwards Enlargement—directed towards the new frontier states of the Ukraine, Belarus and Moldova (Russia was excluded at its own request) as well as the 10 remaining partner-states in the Barcelona Process (Turkey was excluded because of its imminent accession negotiations but Libya was included because of its expressed desire to join the Euro-Mediterranean Partnership). Finally, in June 2004, the states of the Caucasus also joined the new frontier policy[25] as a result of a decision taken by the European Union's Council on 17 June 2004.

The policy is designed to create a "ring of friends" around the European Union and to respond to the problem that Enlargement cannot be indefinitely extended, although European security depends on political and economic change in neighboring states, something which, therefore—as in the Barcelona Process—the Union would wish to encourage. As such, although much of the policy is copied from the Enlargement experience,[26] its roots lie in the European Security Strategy, developed in 2003.[27] In other words, in security terms, the new policy is primarily concerned with trafficking of drugs and people, organized crime, terrorism, and similar trans-border issues, including the environment. This was, of course, inevitable, once the decision was taken in Brussels to limit future Enlargement, although the fact that boundaries between the neighbor states concerned and the European Union are to be maintained is to be mitigated by encouraging cross-border cooperation.

The logic behind the policy is, however, unchanged from that behind the Barcelona Process or, indeed, behind the parallel American initiatives; namely, that neighborhood states must accept European values in terms of governance and economic policy to enable them to become "friends" and "neighbors," but that doing so only provides proximity to the European Union, not access. Thus the policy proposes that a series of individual bilateral relations be established between the Union and each state in which the non-European partner is encouraged to adapt its political and economic policies towards the norms of the European Union and, as this occurs, greater and greater access is provided to the instruments of the Union itself, except that participation in the actual governance of the Union will not be part of the agreement. In other words, through a process of positive conditionality, neighborhood states are to be encouraged to apply the European *acquis communautaire*,[28] on the assumption that this will reduce potential security threats as, in effect, such states adopt the Copenhagen criteria which lie at the root of the Enlargement process.[29]

The policy itself is articulated through a series of Action Plans. These consist of bilateral agreements between the Union and individual states in which a program of action, over three to five years, is laid out to achieve the overall objective. The state concerned, in negotiation with the Commission, determines the content of the Action Plan, thus establishing what it would consider a reasonable program, whilst the Union monitors progress through a process of benchmarking and provides political, administrative, and financial support. Since 2007, the old Barcelona MEDA (*Mesures d'Ajustement*) financing program which provided funding for the Euro-Mediterranean Partnership, together with the old programs for funding political and economic change in the East, such as the TACIS program, have been absorbed into a new financial instrument designed specifically for the European Neighbourhood Policy.[30]

What, then, happens to the Barcelona Process? It seems clear that the new European Neighbourhood Policy runs directly counter to the underlying principles of the Euro-Mediterranean Partnership, for it promotes bilateral relations between neighbor-states and the European Union, rather than the horizontal integration which was the ultimate purpose of the Barcelona Process. The Commission is determined to reject such a conclusion and, in the regulations laying down the final policy,[31] published in October 2006, it states that (paragraph 13) "For Mediterranean partners, assistance and cooperation should take place within the framework of the Euro-Mediterranean Partnership ... " It argues that, in effect, the European Neighbourhood Policy will enable states to enter the European Economic Area (paragraph 18) and thus, supposedly, they will enjoy all the benefits offered under the Barcelona Declaration's "zone of shared peace, prosperity, and stability" proposed in 1995.

The problem is twofold: firstly, all the measures to be adopted under the new European Neighbourhood and Partnership Instrument in reality emphasize the bilateral relationship between neighbor-states and the Union and undermine the South–South relationships which were the key to the Barcelona Process, and secondly, neighborhood states have no compulsion for reform. Instead they set the reform agenda by negotiation with the Commission and suffer no inconvenience if they do not achieve the objectives they have set for themselves. It is true, of course, that there are rewards for states that do achieve their targets, but no price is paid if they do not. Thus, clearly, if a foreign government feels that its priorities require that the priority accorded to the Neighbourhood Policy should be downgraded, it suffers no disadvantage in consequence.

In essence, therefore, unlike the Barcelona Process, the old principle of horizontal integration has disappeared and the new policy is resolutely bilateral in its conception, rejecting the multilateralism inherent in the Barcelona Process as a complicating factor which led in part to the failure of the Euro-Mediterranean Partnership. It thus entrenches the "hub-and-spoke" concept which the Barcelona Process considered to be a temporary stage, to be overcome by horizontal integration in the political, security, and social spheres, once economic integration had been achieved in the South. In security terms, it seeks to build what Attinà regards as an amalgamated security community, as defined by Karl Deutsch.[32] As William Wallace has said, "Western Europe faces the uncomfortable choice of importing insecurity from its neighbors, or of exporting to them security— which necessarily involves prosperity and stability."[33] The policy is thus overtly Eurocentric, avoiding any of the linguistic moderation of the Euro-Mediterranean Partnership, even if its underlying purpose is little different.

Conclusion

In a sense, the policy wheel has come full circle, although the European Commission insists that the global and holistic features of the Euro-Mediterranean Partnership will not be over-ridden by the European Neighbourhood Policy when the two are amalgamated after 2007. Whether this is true or not will depend on the degree to which the political–security and cultural–social baskets of the Barcelona Process are sustained under the new, combined policy. In economic terms, however, the hub-and-spoke arrangement of independent bilateral agreements with the European Union will dissipate hopes of integration of the economies in the Southern Mediterranean into a single market to partner the European Single Market, through initiatives such as the Agadir Agreement and the moribund Arab Maghreb Union (AMU). Yet that, of course, was one of the major justifications for the Barcelona Process; that it would generate economic integration in the South that would provide a sustainable economic region that could ensure endogamous economic growth.

Yet the real question is whether or not the new initiatives can achieve the aspirations of the Barcelona Declaration, of creating a zone of shared peace, stability, and prosperity, and thus of providing Europe with the security it needs from uncontrollable immigration from the Southern Mediterranean and from the spill-over effects of regional violence as a result of economic and political failure there. In part, of course, this depends on the ability of Western policy to defuse, not exacerbate, regional problems and tensions. In part it depends, too, on the development of stable, participatory government there as well. Both, in turn, depend on resolving the two great crises in the region—the aftermath of the invasion of Iraq and the continuing crisis in the Palestinian territories—and that, too, is a European and American responsibility. And, increasingly, both are becoming tributary to the securitized obsessions inherent in the "war on terror."

However, even if both issues—and even the "war of terror"—were addressed by appropriate policies, in which the European Union, because of its lack of effective, integrated military force, could only play a subsidiary role, this will still not resolve the underlying economic crisis. Here, even given the indulgence inherent in the European Neighbourhood Policy, which does not prescribe economic restructuring as the Barcelona Process, in parallel to the Washington Consensus, did, success seems unlikely. In large part this is because of the dimensions of the economic challenges that exist and because of the theoretical and ideological implications of the responses proposed. The European experience, even that of the Accession countries, does not necessarily apply in the Southern Mediterranean and attempts to force the region into the European mould will almost certainly fail. The danger will then be that frustration in the region will produce violence and extremism so that policies intended to dissipate security threats may well create them instead.

Appendix

Trade and Investment Statistics for the EMP Southern Partner Countries

Table 15.1 Direct investment

€ billion	2001		MED-9	MED-12	2002	MED-9	MED-12
Flows	Inflow		0.4	1.2	Inflow	0.7	0.6
	Outflow		1.5	3.2	Outflow	1.3	4.0
	Balance		1.1	2.0	Balance	1.2	3.4
Stocks	Inward		4.1	7.9	Inward	4.6	8.5
	Outward		15.0	26.5	Outward	16.9	30.5

Note: The MED-9 consists of Morocco, Algeria, Tunisia, Palestine, Egypt, Jordan, Israel, Lebanon, and Syria. The MED-12 consists of these states and Turkey, Malta, and Cyprus. There are no statistics included in these figures for Palestine.

In 2002, the MED-12 group provided 0.7 percent of the Union's inflows of direct investment and absorbed 3.07 percent.

Table 15.2 External trade: services

€ billion	2001		MED-9	MED-12	2002	MED-9	MED-12
	Imports		13.1	20.4	Imports	11.3	19.3
	Exports		11.5	14.2	Exports	10.4	13.4
	Balance		−1.6	−6.1	Balance	−1.5	−5.9

Note: In 2002, the MED-12 group provided 6.31 percent of the Union's imports of services and absorbed 4.09 percent of its services exports. The MEDA-12 group represented 5.2 percent of the Union's total trade in services, compared with the MEDA-9 at 3.5 percent, America at 37.5 percent, Switzerland at 11.2 percent, and Japan at 4.5 percent.

Table 15.3 External trade: goods (European Union)

European Union	1980		1990		2002	
€ billion	MED-9	MED-12	MED-9	MED-12	MED-9	MED-12
Imports	13.0	14.7	20.3	27.7	43.0	66.3
Exports	17.8	20.9	24.0	34.7	50.2	80.2
Balance	4.8	6.3	3.7	7.0	7.3	13.3
Share in European Union total (%)						
Imports	4.6	5.2	5.0	6.9	4.3	6.8
Exports	8.4	9.9	6.8	9.8	5.0	8.0

Note: MED-12 trade with the European Union grew on average by 7.14 percent per year between 1980 and 2002. The MED-12 group generated 6.75 percent of the Union's imports in 2002 and absorbed 8.04 percent of its exports.

Table 15.4 External trade: goods (World)

World	1980		1990		2002	
€ *billion*	*MED-9*	*MED-12*	*MED-9*	*MED-12*	*MED-9*	*MED-12*
Imports	30.6	32.1	62.2	65.7	164.2	176.0
Exports	24.0	24.6	41.4	43.0	113.4	123.2
Balance	−3.3	−7.5	−12.7	−22.7	−28.1	−52.8
Share in European Union total (%)						
Imports	2.3	3.0	2.2	3.3	2.1	3.3
Exports	2.2	2.4	1.6	2.3	1.7	2.5

Note: The Southern Mediterranean's trade dependence on Europe has not lessened significantly in recent years, indeed, if anything, it has increased. In 2002, 30.57 percent of MED-9 imports and 45.57 percent of MED-12 imports came from the European Union, which also absorbed 26.18 percent of MED-9 and 53.81 percent of MED-12 exports.

Table 15.5 External trade: commodities

€ *billion*	*Agricultural produce*	*Energy*	*Machinery*	*Transport materials*	*Chemicals*	*Textiles*
MED-9						
Imports	3.0	16.4	3.8	0.8	2.6	7.0
Exports	4.5	1.1	12.3	5.8	6.7	4.7
Balance	1.5	−15.3	8.5	5.0	4.1	2.3
MED-12						
Imports	5.3	16.6	7.3	4.2	3.1	16.3
Exports	6.4	2.0	21.6	10.3	11.9	6.4
Balance	0.7	−14.6	14.3	6.1	8.8	-9.9

Sources: http://www.trade-info.cec.eu.int/doclib/docs/2004/fed/tradoc_113276.xls; http://www.trade-info.cec.eu.int/doclib/docs/2004/fed/tradoc_113468.xls.

Table 15.6 European Union MEDA support

€ *million*	*MEDA-1 (1995–1999)*	*MEDA-2 (2000–2004)*	*MEDA 1 and 2 (1995–2004)*
Bilateral funding			
Algeria	164.0	232.8	396.8
Palestine	111.0	350.3	461.3
Egypt	686.0	353.5	1,039.5
Jordan	254.0	204.4	458.4
Lebanon	182.0	73.7	255.7
Morocco	660.0	677.1	1,337.1
Syria	101.0	135.7	236.7
Tunisia	428.0	328.6	756.6
Total bilateral	**2,586.0**	**2,356.1**	**4,942.1**
Regional funding	471.0	739.8	1,210.9
Total funding	**3,057.0**	**3,095.9**	**6,152.9**

Source: Europe Aid.
Note: According to the MEDA budget projections, funding under MEDA I (1995–1999) was set at €3,435 million, with an additional €4,808 million in soft loans from the European Investment Bank. Funding under MEDA II (2000–2006) will have totalled €5,350 million, with European Investment Bank loan funding up to 2007 of €6,700 million.

Table 15.7 American financial support under the USMEPI program

$ *million*	*2002*	*2003*	*2004*	*2005*
Economic development	6	38	32	23
Political development	10	25	20	22
Educational development	8	25	22	14.4
Women's empowerment	5	12	15.5	15
Total	**29**	**100**	**89.5**	**74.4**

Source: http://mepi.state.gov/mepi

Notes

1 The original members of the Partnership were Morocco, Algeria, Tunisia, Egypt, Jordan, Israel, the Palestinian National Authority, Lebanon, Syria, Turkey, Malta, and Cyprus. In 2004, Malta and Cyprus became members of the European Union and Turkey began Accession negotiations. Libya was not originally a member because of its isolation through United Nations sanctions over the Lockerbie affair, although in 1997 it was invited to become an observer as a guest of the European Commission presidency. This continues to be the case, although Tripoli is said to be considering full membership although it appears to be reluctant to accept the *acquis communautaire* and the implications of democratic governance that membership would require. There is also a similar agreement with the states of the Gulf Cooperation Council—Kuwait, Qatar, the United Arab Emirates, Bahrain, Oman, and Saudi Arabia—although it is primarily concerned with economic relationships.

2 There is now an extensive literature on the Euro-Mediterranean Partnership, the correct title for the Barcelona Process. Two short introductions to it and to its main activities over the past 10 years are provided by the European Commission and the Euro-Mediterranean Human Rights Network. See: http://europa.eu.int/comm./external_relations/euromed;   http://www.euromedrights.net/english/barcelona-process/main/html.

3 Aubarell, G. and Aragall, X. (2005), *Immigration and the Euro-Mediterranean Area: Keys to Policy and Trends*, EuroMeSCo Paper no. 47, IEEI (Lisbon), pp. 8–9.

4 Jandl, M. (2004), "The Estimation of Illegal Migration in Europe," *Studi Emigrazione/Migration Studies*, vol. XLI, no. 153, March 2004, p. 150.

5 UNCTAD (2005), *World Investment Report 2005*, Table 1 (FDI flows by region and selected countries 1993–2004), pp. 10–11.

6 See Fortuyn, P. (1997), *Against the Islamization of our Culture: Dutch Identity as a Fundamental* (Leiden).

7 Cherry, M. (2002), "Have those lovely liberal Dutch finally lost the plot?" *New Humanist*, vol. 117, no. 2, June 2002.

8 Strategic lines of communication, as defined by the Pentagon, carry 99 percent of global maritime trade by volume. Four of the nine critical choke-points for global trade exist in the Mediterranean system—the Bosporus and the Dardanelles for access to the Black Sea; the Bab al-Mandab and the Suez Canal which control access to the Red Sea; and the Straits of Gibraltar which controls access to the Atlantic. To these could be added the Straits of Hormuz which controls access to the Persian Gulf and 70 percent of the world's oil reserves. The Mediterranean itself, of course, is a major pathway for the transfer of oil to both Europe and the United States. A choke-point is defined as a waterway narrow enough to be closed by simple military action involving artillery, air, or naval power. These issues are studied in detail in Nincic, D. J. (2002), "Sea lane security and US maritime trade: choke-points as scarce resources," in Tancredi, S. J. (ed.), *Globalization and Maritime Power*, Washington DC: Institute for National Strategic Studies, National Defense University.

9 Huntington, S. (1993), "The Clash of Civilizations," *Foreign Affairs*, vol. 72, no. 3, summer 1993.

10 See: www.state.gov/secretary/former/powell/remarks/2002/15920.htm.

11 The detailed commitments are given in the appendix to this chapter and can be compared with funding levels under the MEDA programs for the Euro-Mediterranean Partnership, also given in the appendix.

12 Personal communication.

13 The original use of the term was by Peregrine Worsthorne in the *Daily Telegraph* in 1991. It was, however, revived in 1998 and popularized by Hubert Védrine,

then French foreign minister, in a speech to the Association France-Amériques in Paris on 1 February 1999.

14 Globalization, of course, is no new phenomenon but, in its contemporary guise, based on deregulated global financial markets powered by information technology, together with free trade dominated by the Triad of the United States, Europe, and Japan, it has some quite unique characteristics. See Barber, B. R. (1995, 2001), *Jihad vs. McWorld: terrorism's challenge to democracy*, New York: Ballantine Books.

15 Fukuyama, F. (1989), "The end of history?" *The National Interest*, summer 1989.

16 Roberts, A. (1991), "A new age in International Relations?" *International Affairs*, vol. 67, no. 3, July 1991.

17 Geo-economics, the concept that factors related to economic globalization would determine international relations, with the United States seeking to dominate the globalized world economy.

18 See, for example, Weber, C. (1995), *Simulating sovereignty: intervention, the state, and symbolic exchange*, Cambridge: Cambridge University Press.

19 A useful and sympathetic review of the speech and its subsequent implications is provided by Bentley, T. (2003), "Countdown to war: Tony Blair, issue by issue," *Le Monde Diplomatique* (English version), February 2003.

20 Cooper, R. (1998), *The post-modern state*, London: Demos; Cooper, R. (2003), *The breaking of nations: order and chaos in the 21st century*, London: Atlantic Books.

21 See Halper, S. and Clarke, J. (2003), *America alone: the neo-conservatives and the global order*, Cambridge: Cambridge University Press, pp. 76–81 and 254–7.

22 Kagan, R. (2003), *Paradise and power: America and Europe in the New World Order*, London: Atlantic Books.

23 *National Security Strategy of the United States of America*, The White House, 17 September 2002.

24 See Commission of the European Communities, *European Neighbourhood Policy: Strategy Paper*, COM (2004) 373 final, Brussels, 12 May 2004.

25 Smith, K. (2005), "The outsiders: the European Neighbourhood Policy," *International Affairs*, vol. 81, no. 4, p. 760.

26 See Kelley, J. (2006), "New wine in old wineskins: policy adaptation in the European Neighbourhood Policy," *Journal of Common Market Studies*, vol. 44, no. 1.

27 Aliboni, R. (2005), "The geopolitical implications of the European Neighbourhood Policy," *European Foreign Affairs Review*, vol. 10, no. 1, p. 1.

28 The body of European regulation that goes to make up the shared legal system of the European Union and makes access to the Single European Market possible, as well as, in the case of members, access to the Union's policy-making and administrative activities. The implications of this could be very costly. See Tocci, N. (2005), "Does the ENP respond to the EU's post-Enlargement challenges?" *The International Spectator*, vol. XL, no. 1, p. 30.

29 These were laid down at the Copenhagen summit in June 1993 as the basis upon which Enlargement could proceed as they determined the conditions Accession states would have to fulfill to actually join the Union. They are:
- political: stable institutions guaranteeing democracy, the rule of law, human rights, and respect for minorities;
- economic: a functioning market economy;
- incorporation of the Community *acquis*: adherence to the various political, economic, and monetary aims of the European Union.

See: http://europa.eu.int/scadplus/glossary/accession_criteria_copenhague_en.htm.

30 The figures for the new financial instrument, known as the European Neighbourhood and Partnership Instrument (ENPI), in constant 2004 prices, are taken from Smith, op. cit., and given below:

Year	2007	2008	2009	2010	2011	2012	2013	Total 2007–2013
€ million	1,433	1,569	1,877	2,083	2,322	2,642	3,003	14,929

This can be compared with the budget for the East and the Mediterranean in 2004 (€1,420 million with €953 million for the Mediterranean) but the figures are not fully comparable.

31 Official Journal of the European Union, 9 November 2006, Regulation (EC) no. 1638/2006 of the European Parliament and of the Council of 24 October 2006 laying down general provisions establishing a European Neighbourhood and Partnership Instrument, Brussels.

32 Attinà, F. (2004), "European Neighbourhood Policy and the building of security around Europe," in Attinà, F. and Rossi, R. (eds), *European Neighbourhood Policy: political, economic and social aspects*, Catania: Jean Monnet Centre, University of Catania, pp. 16–17. Deutsch's concept of an amalgamated security community is one in which the community considers war as an obsolete instrument of conflict resolution. Deutsch, K. *et al.* (1957), *Political community in the North Atlantic area*, Princeton, NJ: Princeton University Press.

33 Quoted in Balfour, R. and Rotta, A. (2005), "The European Neighbourhood Policy and its tools," *The International Spectator*, vol. XL, no. 1, p. 9.

16 France and the Maghreb

The End of the Special Relationship?

Jean-François Daguzan

In approaching the Franco-Maghrebi "special relationship," one should raise the question whether such a "special relationship" is not mere myth? For 40 years France tried to impose a vision of its foreign policy regarding North African countries as a positive exception in the global framework of world diplomatic relations. How true is such an assertion?

Of course, any foreign observer having followed Franco-Maghrebi relations for more than 40 years may consider the strange "marriage" of France with Algeria, Morocco, and Tunisia, respectively, improbable. Indeed, such complex bonds have rarely been established between sovereign nations. Other regions have experienced decolonization from the British, Portuguese, or Russian colonial powers, but none has engendered this mix of passions and misunderstandings, punctuated by breakdowns. Undoubtedly, this phenomenon was caused in large part by the longstanding and in many ways definitive decision by France to use its relations with Algeria as a model for the international community. However, this is not the only factor.

This chapter aims to present the global framework of Franco-Maghrebi relations (including Libya but not Mauritania), to analyze the different bilateral relations with each Maghrebi country and discuss the ongoing strategies to maintain such "special ties" through an enlarged cooperation framework in the post-9/11 era.

Regarding the connection between France's Maghreb policy and the theories of international relations and geopolitics, one could link General De Gaulle's creation of Arab policy in the context of the realist paradigm as expounded in Raymond Aron's work.[1] That is to say, France should accept the decolonization process as inevitable and later play a role to counterbalance the influence of the Soviet Union and the United States in the diplomatic sphere—the US accepting more or less graciously a form of burden-sharing for the control of Africa. Successive policy makers tried to balance the pure Gaullist-realist approach with a mix of idealism, organizing the cooperation with Maghreb countries more or less as a model of North–South relations. The first period of François Mitterrand's first mandate (1981–1987) was the best illustration of the temptation to launch a socialist/internationalist model of international relations based on the recognition of and redressing the unequal exchange in trade relations. The signature of an especially advantageous gas supply "super contract" with Algeria served for a short time as the symbol of such a policy.[2] Also, one can speak of "geo-political deployment," referring to the construction of the post-colonial security of France following Algeria's independence in 1962. Pascal Lorot and François Thual see "geopolitical deployment" as, "at a given stage, the state hierarchy of priorities in term of objectives and counter-objectives."[3] In the early 1960s, this implied loosening the alliance with Israel (useful during the Algerian war and the global struggle against decolonization) and the reorganizing of relations with the Arab states through an "exemplary" new policy with the Maghreb countries seen as a "flagship" of the positive French evolution.

Structural Factors

This unique relationship also has structural strength, which has several roots. Naturally, the presence in France of a long-established and large Maghrebi minority contributes to this unusual situation; unofficial reports estimate that there are currently between four and five million Maghrebis in France,[4] plus another 1.5 million (*"pieds noirs," Harkis,* and Jews)[5] repatriated from North Africa, primarily from Algeria. Their presence in France has affected French policy towards the region, but their influence is decreasing with time, due to the effect of demographic attrition. This situation makes the management of Islam in France quite distinctive and a touchy issue.

The other structural factor is the question of human rights in the Maghreb. In order to maintain a special relationship and because of its own actions during its colonial past, France is quite reluctant to address the question of human rights. Given the demands that it makes on other countries with respect to human rights, France's lenience toward Maghrebi countries on this dramatic question does make the relationship very special indeed.

The Question of Islam in France

Concerning the Maghreb, the question of Islam in France has been encapsulated in the prolonged dispute with Algeria. The situation revolves around the control of the Paris mosque and the appointment of its Rector. Despite the presence of a highly talented Franco-Algerian Rector, Dalil Boubakeur, who was rushed in to rescue a weakened institution, Algerian influence has diminished since the mid-1980s. Since then, ties with the Algerian authorities have been considered too strong for the prospective faithful but, more importantly, the sermon at the Paris mosque is primarily a political instrument used by the French authorities, who have little contact with the Islam practiced in improvised places of worship or in the suburbs, or with African Islam. Over the last 20 years, the sermons of fundamentalist movements financed by Saudi Arabia and other proselytizing organizations, such as the

Pakistani Tabligh or the Muslim Brotherhood along with the powerful Union of French Islamic Organizations (UOIF),[6] have found a genuine audience among peoples with an identity crisis and bearing the brunt of economic predicament. Black African populations in particular are participating in this movement and are not interested in Maghreb "minaret wars." For his part, Moroccan King Mohammed VI is doing his best to retain control over a community more closely knit than others, but the limits of his strategy are becoming increasingly evident, as shown by the steady progress of the agenda of radical Moroccan groups in Morocco and in Europe.[7]

Inspired in 2003 by the then French Minister of the Interior Nicolas Sarkozy, the elections and the organization of the French Council of Muslim Faiths (CCFM) have thrown those with a hidden agenda into confusion. The election of Dr. Dalil Boubakeur was achieved with great difficulty and marked a sharp decline of traditional forces in favor of new and more radical organizations.[8] In reality, there is perhaps a "de-maghrebization" of Islam in France, or the extraction of religion from state control. This "French" Islam must find its path between a French way, emerging amid a power struggle having little to do with religion, and the various siren calls of active fundamentalism.[9] Although the second set of elections for the CCFM in June 2005 confirmed this basic tendency and the decline of the Paris mosque by its distancing itself again from public authorities, the elections also illustrated Moroccan influence on the French Muslim community by reinforcing the National Federation of French Muslims (FNMF). But how much influence does Morocco still have over French Muslims?

The management of French Muslim affairs is departing increasingly from its historical ties with the countries of origin. Nowadays, the influence of these countries on France still exists, but a new and more independent force is emerging. This is leading to two possible scenarios: either the emergence of a coherent French national Muslim identity or the fragmentation into ineffective competing groups. The intermediate options cover a palette including "soft" African *Marabouts*, through Islamic *Salafism*, to secular Muslims who have begun to voice their opinions. As Samir Amghar notes, "The French Islamic connection covers a wide spectrum of social practices and a plurality of religiosities, which runs from a cultural relationship with the Muslim religion to more demanding religious forms."[10] This does not necessarily imply that the link with the country of origin is weakening: the need to "return to the village" for holidays, or to be buried there, remains very strong among all generations. But the tendency today is towards an "Italian" or "Spanish" attitude, in which the link with the country of origin is of a sentimental, familial, and historical nature.

The Question of Human Rights

France has had diplomatic conflicts with each Maghrebi state, especially over human rights; and each time, bilateral relations were affected. Initially, the principle of non-interference was scrupulously applied, but subsequently, each country was subject to individual treatment without a particularly developed or detailed policy.

In the case of Tunisia, the Quai d'Orsay (France's Ministry of Foreign Affairs) did not explicitly disapprove of Habib Bourguiba's repeated repression or of Zine al Abidine Ben Ali's prison system. Only with the end of the Lionel Jospin government in the summer of 2001 did French authorities discreetly but significantly change course.[11] Due to the Global War on Terror in the post-9/11 period, repression of any forms of opposition and the abrogation of democratic and human rights have currently found justification.

In Algeria, the situation is more contrasting. The years of Houari Boumedienne (1965–1978) and Chadli Benjedid (1979–1992) were quietly ignored. The ferocious repression of the October 1988 riots hardly aroused any signs of concern. The interruption of the democratic process in 1992 and the quasi-civil war, the so-called "red decade," plunged successive French governments and the political elites into confusion and division. Overall, France proved incapable of balancing a strict defense of human rights (opposition to arrests, arbitrary detention, and suspicious deaths) with the eradication of an extremely cruel brand of Islamic terrorism.[12]

The debate over the so-called *"qui tue qui?"* (who is killing whom?), which tended to place the active or passive responsibility for village massacres on the Algerian army, reached its apogee in 2001. General Major Khaled Nezzar, considered the conscience of the Algerian army, tried to bring the matter to court, where no subsequent action was taken. The final act came with the complaint by Nezzar before the seventeenth court of the Paris magistrate from 1 July to 27 September 2002. This court process led to the surrealist sight of Algerians violently confronting each other before French judges, who eventually left both sides to the judgment of history.[13] Any remark, whether or not couched in diplomatic or coded terms, is perceived in Algiers as external interference in Algeria's internal affairs. The debate on human rights is therefore neutralized by this structural factor of opinion. Only through other venues, such as the European Union, can France make its view heard in Algiers.

In Morocco, nothing substantial was said about the regime's secret prisons and illicit arrests and violence. The silence was broken when Danièle Mitterrand raised the case of the opposition trade union leader, Abraham Serfaty, and the military Cadets involved in the Kenitra coup attempt against King Hassan II in 1971.[14] Although this intercession was non-official, it caused a freeze in diplomatic relations between France and Morocco. There is general embarrassment in Paris over the question of human rights in the Maghreb. The modernization of these relations will require a courageous revision of French policy.

Jealousy, competition, or conflicts between the three Maghrebi states make a global policy difficult for France. Algiers accuses France of supporting

Morocco in the Western Sahara dispute. Tunisia feels that France has always shown more interest in Algiers for historical and economic (hydrocarbons) reasons. The real Maghrebi policy is more than the sum of three bilateral policies more or less linked to the same historical fate and to the French language (*francophonie*). The Maghreb countries' incapacity to create a community of interests through the Arab Maghreb Union (AMU), even limited to economic issues, demonstrated the limit of a global approach. Finally, the Maghreb policy means essentially, for France, the management of immigration, the "*francophonie*" policy, the tolerance of human rights violations, and the defense of French economic interests. Despite the vision of the Maghreb as a regional entity, the reality of relations is bilateral.

France–Tunisia: The Big Hush

France appears to have decided to avoid criticizing Tunisia. The measured boldness of the Jospin government was quickly forgotten. On a state visit in December 2003, President Jacques Chirac declared in a lyrical flight of fancy that "the first human right is to have bread," thus giving President Ben Ali a stamp of "democratic" approval and ratifying the 94.48 percent of votes that Ben Ali "garnered" at the last presidential election in 2004. Vincent Geisser and Eric Gobe claim that "the hopes of the Palace of Carthage have not been disappointed." Chirac agreed not only to "resolve" all the problems between Paris and Tunis but also to provide decisive backing to the "new security policy" of the Tunisian regime, by deliberately staying away from "upsetting questions," notably those concerning human rights and public liberties.[15]

Is this a return to a bold post-Iraq-war French Gaullism? More prosaically, France is, in fact, defending its most recent positions. Ben Ali has always known how to use threats when dealing with Paris: forbidding the use of French and emphasizing his ties with the United States are well-known examples of such threats. France prefers to ignore what is happening on the other side of the Mediterranean in order to defend its economic and political interests, while pursuing modest military cooperation as well. Paris therefore is satisfied with appearances even when they are crumbling rapidly. This is exemplified by the current resurgence of repression in all areas, based on a banking crisis and a series of bankruptcies due to the drastic application of structural reforms imposed by the European Union within the framework of the Euro-Mediterranean Partnership. One wonders how long it will take France to face reality.

Algeria: The Unending Lovers' Quarrel

The position taken by France with regard to the 2003 Iraq war increased the popularity of Jacques Chirac and strengthened ties between France and

Algeria. The state visit by the French President to Algiers on 15–16 March 2003 was a historic event. However, the phenomenal success of this first state visit did not diminish the *cri du coeur* of the crowd, which chanted continuously during procession of the delegation "visas, visas," thus symbolizing the malaise of the entire society.[16] Nonetheless, Chirac's visit to Algiers inaugurated two years of improved relations between the two countries. President Bouteflika even announced a resumption of the generalized teaching of French in Algerian schools. This rapprochement with France is now taking various forms. The most symbolic event was the visit by the Minister of Defense, Michèle Alliot-Marie, which was the first visit of its kind to Algeria. Relations in the area of defense became a little closer and the two countries agreed to sign a treaty of friendship in 2005, which, as of early 2007, has not yet been signed because Algerians demand that France apologize for its colonial past.

Most recently, relations between the two countries have taken another turn. President Bouteflika's position was strengthened when oil prices increased dramatically, thus giving his government a margin of economic maneuver which had not existed since 1988. The President has disposed of the old guard of the military establishment which exerted formidable power in the political sphere. Among other changes, the powerful Major-General Mohammed Lamari was pushed into retirement, and General Larbi Belkheir was transferred from the President's cabinet to the Rabat embassy. This favorable conjunction of events was used by President Bouteflika to denounce France's involvement in Nazi-like crimes, such as the use of lime kilns to burn the corpses of Algerians who rose up during the Sétif riots in 1945, as well as to make accusations of latent genocide. This outburst was either a tactic used by the Algerian President to temper the attacks of the opposition, which is always quick to brandish the easy specter, the slogan *hizb França* (partisan of France),[17] or may mean that when the Algerian government has diplomatic and political freedom of maneuver, then France no longer figures heavily in the equation of Algeria's diplomatic game. This is as much due to its new revenues as to the ever-closer alliance which appears to be taking shape with the United States. How valuable then is the Treaty of Friendship in this situation?

The French review *Damocles* identified four bilateral challenges for France and Algeria: "the definition of their national identity, their reciprocal fascination, and their move from confrontation to a new friendship; forgetting past wounds; curing xenophobia and blending the values of French and Arab culture; and finding a counterweight to American globalization."[18] The problems affecting bilateral relations between France and Algeria have rarely been put so well.

The question that deserves to be raised is whether Bouteflika's new declaratory policy has a tactical value or whether it heralds a new "freeze" in Algerian–French relations. Traditionally, in accordance with French national interest, Paris is prepared to make concessions and even to endure humiliation. However, France is currently overwhelmed by its old demons. On the one hand, France has made great efforts to acknowledge its past errors, though isolated acts still occur, such as the erection of the monument in the southeastern city of Marignane, commemorating members of the Organization of the Secret Army (OAS) which violently supported a French Algeria. On the other hand, the government's parliamentary majority approved mentioning in school programs the "positive role of the French presence overseas and especially in North Africa."[19] This political scandal reached the immigrant population and caused an uncomfortable resurgence of France's colonial past. Coincidentally, the debate erupted during the long hospitalization of President Bouteflika in Paris. This is an excellent example of the schizophrenic relationship between both countries.

The relationship between the two countries has begun to deteriorate seriously since then. President Bouteflika initiated an aggressive process to oblige France to repent of the "crimes" it committed during the colonization period and spoke about "cultural genocide."[20] As seen earlier, the Algerian president emphasized the alleged use of lime kilns as crematory kilns during the repression of the Sétif riots in May 1945, establishing implicitly a symbolic link with the extermination of Jews during World War II.[21] Now the situation is blocked: France dodges Bouteflika's imprecations but refuses to offer any excuse and nobody can identify any foreseeable exit to the crisis. Some observers attribute Bouteflika's anger either to his illness or to the preparation of a third presidential term in office and the failure of the reconciliation process domestically. Linked to the recent call for the arabization of the Algerian educational system, the crisis between the two countries could be a long one, although there are attempts on both sides to alleviate it. The last visit of the French Minister of Interior, and then candidate to the Presidency of the Republic, Nicolas Sarkozy, avoided addressing the disturbing topics and focused instead on the visa question for Algerians, a question of greater importance for citizens' bilateral relations.[22]

Morocco: A Muted Harmony

In the case of Morocco, relations between the two countries were particularly good during the presidencies of George Pompidou and Valéry Giscard d'Estaing. Pompidou's foreign affairs minister, Michel Jobert, was born in Morocco. He helped in bringing the two countries closer after a long-term freeze following the kidnapping in France of Moroccan opponent Medhi Ben Barka during De Gaulle's presidency. Under Giscard's presidency the crisis, then the war over Western Sahara, made France a discreet military and fervent diplomatic ally of Morocco and Mauritania.[23] But relations with France were subdued during the François Mitterrand era. Although official relations matched the criteria of traditional and necessary friendship and cooperation, the permanent agitation of French organizations for the defense of human rights in Morocco set the real mood between the two countries. In fact, the liberation of the political activist Abraham Serfaty, the discovery of the secret Tazmamart prison, the flight of the Oufkir family, and the publication of Gilles Perrault's scathing book *Our friend the King*, marked painful episodes for the Moroccan monarch with France and with the Moroccan elite in Rabat, which he accused of permanent plotting.[24]

Jacques Chirac's election in 1995 completely changed the bilateral relationship. Chirac is very attached to Morocco and had a particularly close relationship with King Hassan II. The two men appreciated each other and frequently worked together. The networks of pro-Moroccan Gaullists were reactivated. Thus, the strong relationship flourished until Hassan II's death in July 1999.[25]

The coming to power of Mohammed VI, believed to be a modern and dynamic monarch, was perceived in France as a good opportunity to simplify and perhaps ease bilateral relations. Certainly, several cordial visits by the young king have taken place, but substantial political results are not forthcoming. The Leila/Perejil islet affair in summer 2002 and the humiliating expulsion of Moroccan soldiers by Spanish special forces not only depicted a profound state of political immaturity, but also posed a severe problem for France, which now had to decide between Morocco and Spain. Though perceived as purely formal, solidarity with Europe eventually outweighed ties with North Africa, although it was not perceived as such in Spain. Moreover, Mohammed VI's "resistance" to Chirac's advice and the growing French feeling of inconstancy in the management of the Moroccan state increasingly, albeit slowly, strained the relationship.[26]

The real preoccupations remain at the political and social levels. The rise of Islamism, which the state struggled to conceal for years, is emerging as a structural factor in Moroccan society and is strongly opposed to reform. After the failure of the socialist Prime Minister Abderrahmane Youssoufi experiment, which was unable to pull Morocco out of economic stagnation, Islamists now represent the principal political force, which also controls universities and the slums of Morocco. A fully transparent election would most probably lead to an Islamist victory. However, an agreement negotiated with the Palace (*Makhzen*) currently confines Islamists to 20 percent of parliamentary seats. The true question now is the capacity of the Islamists, essentially the Justice and Development Party (*Parti de la justice et du développement*—PJD) to reject the agreement and go to the polls without limitations. Recent declarations by the leaders announced such a position. But it is difficult to analyze the level of bluff and the capability of the party to test the resolve of the *Makhzen*.[27]

Islamic terrorism has brutally established itself through a series of coordinated suicide attacks in Casablanca and Madrid, which have implicated and linked Morocco to international radicalism, thus shattering the benign image the authorities had worked to create over the years. The *Makhzen* also seems to have rediscovered its old reflexes by directly attacking press criticism of the regime, resulting, for example, in the imprisonment of the journalist Ali Lamrabet for "outrage against the person of the King."[28] The struggle against radical Islamic terrorism undoubtedly facilitates the return of these practices.

The progressive steps undertaken by Mohamed VI (regarding the status of women, for example, *Moudawwana*)[29] cannot conceal the basic problems of Morocco. As Jean-Claude Santucci notes:

> By its awareness and the reform initiatives intended to restore social cohesion, the state has taken refuge in the logic of total security while firmly restating, through the voice of the sovereign in his speech from the throne, that there is no place for political parties which monopolize Islam.[30]

Perceived from Paris, developments in Morocco cause some concern, but France remains incapable of elaborating a policy.

The radical realignment of Morocco with the United States (see Chapter 13 by Yahia Zoubir) has been demonstrated by its total adherence to the US project for the "Greater Middle East" and America's active participation in its events, such as the Rabat Forum. In December 2004, this Forum brought together the regional states and the G8 members and produced proposals intended to be useful in the area of democracy and development.[31] In these conditions, France's room for maneuver has greatly diminished. Behind an appearance of constant serenity reigns a vague feeling of diplomatic attrition. In spite of France's goodwill vis-à-vis Morocco, the radicalization of the Moroccan position with regard to Western Sahara has not helped thaw the tense bilateral relations. Officially, the French position towards the Western Sahara dispute is neutral. During a meeting with the Moroccan press on 25 September 2005, Prime Minister Dominique de Villepin (also born in Morocco), stressed the necessity of a "political solution mutually acceptable by the parties" within the UN framework.[32] However, despite such seeming balance, the truth is that France is decidedly on Morocco's side. As Aeschimann and Boltanski say, "the most beautiful gift given to Hassan II was Chirac's absolute support to the Moroccan position on the Western Sahara."[33] Of course, France does not provide the same military assistance as in the 1970s, but works discreetly to provide Morocco with efficient support at the United Nations, and working within the international groups of negotiation for a final solution. Naturally, this position is well known in Algiers and contributes to the points in dispute between Paris and Algiers, which considers the Western Sahara affair a question of principle.

Libya: The Race to the Market

Relations between France and Libya followed an erratic path after the failure of the annexation of the Fezzan region in 1945. France had few relations with the new, artificial kingdom created by the United Nations. When Colonel Qaddafi came to power in September 1969, the Pompidou government, analyzing the new and young leader as modern and progressive, saw an opportunity to supplant British and US influence over the country. Foreign Minister Michel Jobert signed a "colossal" armament contract in 1971, thus laying the foundation for an increasingly excellent relationship. But the question of Chad in the 1980s led to the deterioration of the good ties between Paris and Tripoli. Libyan support for the Chadian insurgency and the dispute over the border territory, the Aouzou strip, made confrontation inevitable. An informal war began in the 1980s between France and Libya (including the use of terrorist methods), which lasted until the definitive Libyan defeat in 1987.[34]

The events of 11 September 2001 have also had considerable repercussions for Libya (see Chapter 3 by Ronald Bruce St John). Colonel Qaddafi's new and rejuvenated team simultaneously perceived the nature of the change in international relations and the logic of globalization.[35] From both a political and an economic point of view, Libya could no longer remain on the margin of world events. The fact that the Libyan government had produced the first international arrest warrant against Bin Laden in March 1988, and had resolutely committed itself alongside the United States after 9/11, acted in its favor.[36] Saif al-Islam Qaddafi established himself as the *Missi Dominici* of his father, the "Guide," and started a long process of winning the rehabilitation of Libya in Western capitals. The return to normality included the resolution of financial disputes connected with the Lockerbie and UTA aircraft terrorist attacks. The Lockerbie affair was quickly brought to an expensive conclusion. France was not compensated as equitably, and there was a delay in receiving the compensation; the Libyans also procrastinated in admitting their responsibility in the event; but a favorable outcome was achieved on 9 January 2004.

However, the most dramatic turn of events came on 19 December 2003, with the Libyan announcement that it was renouncing its programs for the development of weapons of mass destruction, and the subsequent placing of sites and other production facilities under the control of the IAEA and other international disarmament institutions.[37] This agreement was negotiated secretly with Great Britain and the United States, and effectively excluded France.[38] Obviously, this strategic policy relies on the enormous markets available for the reconstruction of a country ruined by years of sanctions. Libyan oil reserves, in view of the high price of oil, make the country a new *El Dorado*.[39] France has therefore sought to get back into the good graces of a country which for years was its primary African adversary during the Chad affair.

The French desire to revamp bilateral relations with Libya was demonstrated at the highest level by President Chirac's state visit in November 2004. This was the first of its kind since Libya's independence in 1951, and the level of success was mixed. The two countries were officially reconciled, but the "Guide" did not refrain from criticizing the presence of France in Africa. However, he eventually proposed a joint policy for Africa.[40] The French President suggested that Libya join the Euro-Mediterranean Partnership; however, the parties parted without issuing a joint communiqué. Regarding the economic arena, vague letters of intent were signed concerning the sale of civilian air-traffic-control radar, Airbus aircraft, and confirming French participation in the Great Man-Made River—the giant pipeline which will take water from the fossil reserves of the Sahara to major Libyan cities and towns.[41]

This restrained visit largely reflected the state of bilateral relations since the huge contracts of the 1970s. Despite the conquest of the Fezzan by General Leclerc during the Second World War, Libya is unfamiliar territory to France. From a strategic point of view, the United States has become the primary actor. This confirms the balance of forces resulting from the Iraq War and the current level of influence of the various powers.[42]

Relations after 11 September: A Security Premium?

Significant developments in the official discourse of human rights perhaps reached their limits with the events of 11 September 2001. The struggle against terrorism now tends to structure relations between Europe and the Maghreb as it does those between the United States and the Maghreb (see Zoubir's and Henry's chapters, 13 and 14). The Algerian government has emerged from its position as a pariah by posing as a front-runner in the war against radical Islamism. This position is now universally supported. In Tunisia and Morocco, hesitant and modest official and unofficial admonitions have given way to appeals for the suppression of terrorism. The fact that both countries became targets of Islamist terrorism intensified such appeals. The attacks of 11 April 2002 in Jerba, Tunisia, and the series of attacks on 16 May 2003 in Casablanca, Morocco, were only a year apart. The attack in the Atocha train station in Madrid, Spain, on 11 March 2004 must be included as well, because almost all the perpetrators were Moroccans or Spaniards of Moroccan origin, thus demonstrating the ever-closer ties between the two shores of the Mediterranean Sea.

Though it is difficult to correlate a "local" attack such as Jerba (linked to al-Qaeda), with the impressive organization of the Casablanca and Madrid attacks, both Morocco and Tunisia attempted to transmit an image of internal control, yet suffered dramatic consequences to their tourist industry due to the damage to their overseas image. In fact, the Ben Ali regime flaunted repression as a guarantee of security and Morocco concealed Islamic progress behind the constitutional quibble of the duality of the sovereign—being both political leader and commander of the faithful (*Amir al-mu'minin*)—and thus sheltered from all religious threats. The current police control imposed by the Tunisian and Moroccan regimes on their respective societies is buttressed by the justification of the struggle against radical

Islamic terrorism. In 2003, the King of Morocco even announced the "the end of the era of leniency."[43]

For three years, Paris decided to underline the minor initiatives at the end of the Jospin government and to reorient itself towards reinforcing political and economic ties, as demonstrated by the numerous visits to the Maghreb in recent months by various important ministers, including Nicolas Sarkozy and Michèle Alliot-Marie. President Chirac's personal involvement was also reinforced by the French position regarding the Iraq War. The control of security therefore tends to emerge as a long-term structural factor in the three countries, with the tacit blessing of the West and of France in particular.

However, after Chirac recognized Ben Ali's stance in 2003 regarding human rights in Tunisia, the French foreign minister, Philippe Douste-Blasy, stressed the need to build upon the earlier UN Summit on Information Societies: "France considers human rights as a component of the political dialogue between our two countries ... but also with [the] European Union." France also congratulated Algeria for the referendum victory on the Civil Concord in September 2005, with 79.6 percent in favor of the government's policy. Unhappy over such support, some analysts blame French complacency regarding Algeria.[44] This merely reveals the difficulty of establishing a normal dialogue between the countries.

A French Foreign Policy for the Maghreb?

Does France have a foreign policy with regard to the Maghreb? The answer is that it is an aspiration and a goal rather than a substantial course of action. The three francophone Maghreb states claim a privileged relationship which excludes others. This certainly exists, subject to the reservations declared at the launch of initiatives such as the "5 + 5" or the Barcelona Process. The Maghrebi states perceive the Barcelona Process as a threat to their uniformity. The failure of the Arab Maghreb Union (AMU), which stalled in the 1990s, prevents any renewal of valid Franco-Maghrebi or Euro-Maghrebi dialogue. The choice made by France after the 1991 Gulf War to favor the path of an overall Mediterranean vision excluded, *a priori*, a sub-regional multilateral union.

Until Nicolas Sarkozy's election in June 2007 as president of the French Republic and his reaffirmed proposal for a Mediterranean Union, the return to a sub-regional approach, such as the "5 + 5," seemed to be a useful alternative to the paralysis of the Barcelona Process and to the state of shock caused by the Iraq War. If the US freezes the political map of the Middle East, as already seems to be the case, then renewed political and economic cooperation within a more restricted framework can be envisaged. This framework would be less subject to the problems of the Eastern Mediterranean; but the Western Sahara conflict still spoils Algerian–Moroccan relations. Although heavily influenced by the Iraq War, the ministerial meeting of the "5 + 5" dialogue in Saint Maxime on 9–10 April 2003 allowed for the disclosure of mutual preoccupations: the struggle against terrorism was emphasized, as was the implementation of increased cooperation between the Southern European Union countries and the Maghreb countries. Since 2003, different ministries or official bodies have met to engage concerted processes of cooperation: foreign affairs (every year), interior (2004), social affairs (2004 and 2005), tourism (2006), Presidents of Parliaments (2004), and ministries of defense (2004 and 2005).

On 10 and 11 July 2007, the new French President, Nicolas Sarkozy, visited Algeria and Tunisia respectively. While a candidate, in a speech in Toulon on 7 February 2007 Sarkozy proposed, the creation of a Mediterranean Union. This was precisely the question that dominated his discussions with his Algerian and Tunisian counterparts. The content of the Mediterranean Union remains rather vague, but it is known that it is aimed at countries on both sides of the Mediterranean, that it would have a small secretariat to support G8-type meetings, and that the Council of Europe would be its model. The Mediterranean Union would focus on salient issues, such as sustainable development, police cooperation, and terrorism. Economic questions were also high on the agenda, especially since France is no longer the dominant investor; it is now being rivalled by new entrants in the Maghreb market from the Gulf and Asian countries. Furthermore, France may extend to Algeria a civilian nuclear cooperation agreement to supplement the bilateral civilian nuclear accord signed between Algeria and the United States at the end of June 2007. Nicolas Sarkozy's visit highlights once again the difficulty that France faces in conducting a global approach in the Maghreb. Indeed, while the French presidential delegation had scheduled a brief trip to the Moroccan capital Rabat, the Royal Palace indicated that Sarkozy's visit was not well-timed and that it would be more appropriate to host an official visit of high importance in October 2007. This demonstrates yet again that France's Maghreb policy rests as always on three distinct policies. Will the Mediterranean Union succeed in bringing them closer? Only time will tell.

Conclusion: Will France Resurface Through the "5 + 5"?

The Arab Maghreb Union (AMU) is paralyzed by inter-member disagreements. Paradoxically, the fertile soil of the Maghreb renewed the "5 + 5" dialogue, as hoped for by France after the stalling of the Euro-Mediterranean Partnership. Originally a French initiative launched in 1983, then progressively supported by Western Mediterranean parties, the "5 + 5" project was overshadowed by the 1991 Gulf War, the international embargo affecting Libya, and then by the launch of the Euro-Mediterranean Partnership as an integral part of the Barcelona Process. The "5 + 5" has been revamped in recent years. The loss of momentum of the Euro-Mediterranean Partnership called for a renewed sub-regional attempt to improve the Western Mediterranean region, which is already less "polluted" due to the absence of the Israeli–Palestinian conflict, but also because it embodies more coherence between the northern and southern partners.

The process was relaunched in January 2001, at a meeting of foreign ministers. Despite a difficult start, the meetings have become an annual event. The "5 + 5" also reopened activities with a great symbolic act, the Chiefs of State and Governments meeting in Tunis (5–6 December 2003 in Tunis). However, the real progress was establishing meetings of the ministers of defense, which represented a unique advance never before achieved by the Euro-Mediterranean Partnership. Suggested by the French minister of defense in Lisbon in 2003, a first meeting of experts took place in Paris in September, followed by one in Rome in November 2004 to prepare the 21 December 2004 summit, which brought together the ministers of defense of Algeria, France, Italy, Libya, Malta, Mauritania, Morocco, Portugal, Spain, and Tunisia. This meeting led to the signing of a declaration of intent for a pragmatic and constructive partnership and for the development of an action plan for the deepening of cooperation on maritime surveillance, civil defense, and air safety. A steering committee met in Algiers in March 2005 to prepare the ministry of defense meeting held in Algiers on 12 December 2005, with the goal of developing further topics of mutual interest. An action plan was been established up to 2006, which included, *inter alia*, actions on civil protection, and the creation of a *"Centre euromaghrebin d'études statégiques"* in Tunis in 2007, proposed under a Franco-Tunisian initiative.[45]

Why does a cooperative process work when involving European countries, yet fail when the Maghrebi countries are confronted with each other? One explanatory factor can be highlighted: the desire for cooperation comes primarily from the North. The objectives are certainly accepted by the South but the process is not initiated from there. The pressure and the will to cooperate come from Europe. This poses the problem of keeping cooperation within boundaries, whether it be the "5 + 5" or the larger Euro-Mediterranean Partnership. Concerning the Maghreb, collective action becomes possible when Europe or some of its representatives (those of the Western Mediterranean in this case) represent a neutral intermediary. This causes individual national initiatives to be neutralized as well, as is the case for France. Difficulties between the Maghreb states are thus postponed within a self-contained framework separate from bilateral disputes, including areas such as defense and security. This would be impossible within a bilateral arena involving Paris, for example, but is possible in the more general framework mentioned. Paradoxically, the EU is the sponsor of the only collective process possible in the Maghreb.

Since the 2003 Iraq War, has France developed a new foreign policy for the Maghreb? If there has been one, as authors such as Geisser and Gobe believe, then the policy has only been operative for a short period, corresponding approximately to the length of the Franco-American crisis when France benefited from the positive reception of Dominique de Villepin at the UN Assembly. Nonetheless, Paris's room for maneuver was too narrow for substantial results to be produced. The Maghreb states, including Libya, quickly saw the internal and external political advantages of expressing a minimal level of criticism, intended for public consumption, while taking no steps that could reflect valid opposition to the United States. This was demonstrated most clearly by the dramatic failure and coolness of the meeting of the Arab League at Tunis in May 2003.

France's policy towards the three francophone Maghrebi countries is in accordance with her traditional interests in the region. In Libya, for example, the interest is predominantly economic. A French policy, therefore, can increasingly be found in collective policies such as, primarily, the Euro-Mediterranean Partnership and, since 2003, the "5 + 5" project. However, after the modestly successful Barcelona conference in November 2005, the Euro-Mediterranean Partnership has not succeeded in rejuvenating its commendable initiative. The "5 + 5" project is the latest promising path for an alternative policy, given the schizophrenic French relationship with the Maghreb states. The margin of maneuver for France continues along narrow straits, and the possibility of national normalization remains a dream: the "special relationship" will continue.

Notes

1 Raymond Aron, *Paix et guerre entre les nations*, Paris: Calmann-Lévy, 1962, 1984.
2 Jean-François Daguzan, "Les rapports franco-algériens, 1962–1992, réconciliation ou conciliation permanente?" *Politique étrangère*, winter 93/94, p. 890.
3 Pascal Lorot and François Thual, "Dispositif géopolitique," in *La géopolitique*, Paris: Montchrestien/Clefs, 1997, p. 71.
4 All census statistics on faiths being prohibited in France, estimates of the Haut Conseil à l'Intégration are thus used. See, *Libération*, 19 December 2002, p. 14.
5 "Pieds-noirs" is the nickname given by the Arabs to the French settlers, due to the black boots worn by French soldiers in the initial invasion of 1830. The *harkis* are Algerians who were and are sympathetic to French culture, and thus to the presence of France in Algeria. They also served as auxiliaries to French forces during Algeria's war of independence in 1954–1962.
6 In French: *Union des organisations islamiques de France.*
7 Khadija Mohsen-Finan and Remi Leveau (eds), *Musulmans de France et d'Europe*, Paris: CNRS Editions, 2005.
8 "Défaite de la Mosquée de Paris au Scrutin pour le Conseil Musulman," *Le Monde*, 14 April 2003.
9 Catherine Coroller, "Le Conseil du Culte Musulman ensablé dans ses courants," *Libération*, 8 September 2005, p. 15.
10 "Les nouvelles voies de l'Islam de France," *Maghreb-Machrek*, no. 183, spring 2005, p. 11.
11 See "France, Democratization and North Africa," in Richard Gillespie and Richard Youngs (eds), *The European Union and Democracy Promotion: The Case of North Africa*, London and Portland, OR: Frank Cass, 2002, p. 139.
12 See Jean-François Daguzan, "Les rapports franco-algériens, 1962–1992: réconciliation ou conciliation permanente?" *Politique étrangère*, winter 93/94, pp. 885–896;

and Jean-François Daguzan, "Les relations franco-algériennes ou la poursuite des amicales incompréhensions," *Annuaire français de relations internationales 2001*, Bruxelles: Bruylant, Vol. II, 2002, pp. 438–50.

13 See the partial, but relatively full, minutes of the debates: General Nezzar and Mohammed Maarfia (eds), *Un procès pour la vérité: l'armée algérienne face à la désinformation*, Algiers: Editions ANEP, 2002.

14 Christine Daure-Serfaty, *Tazmamart, une prison de la mort au Maroc*, Paris: Editions Stock, 1992, p. 104.

15 "Le Président Ben Ali entre les jeux de coteries et l'échéance Présidentielle de 2004," *Annuaire de l'Afrique du Nord, Vol. XII, 2003*, Paris: CNRS Editions, 2005, p. 313.

16 Florence Beaujé and Jean-Pierre Tuquoi, "Les leçons d'une visite à Alger," *Le Monde*, 15 March 2003, p.16.

17 "Parti des Français," a derogatory expression aimed at attacking the credibility of an opponent—more or less equivalent to "collaborator" referring to Vichy France.

18 Stéphane Petit, Michel Robert and Patrice Bouveret, *Damoclès*, no. 93, February 2002, p. 1.

19 Appendix to Article 4 of the Law of 23 February 2005.

20 18 March 2006. Available at: http://tf1.lci.fr/infos/monde/0,3296966,00.html.

21 Bouteflika said during the celebration of the 60th anniversary of the massacres in Sétif, eastern Algeria: "Qui ne se souvient des fours de la honte installés par l'occupant dans la région de Guelma au lieu dit 'El hadj Mebarek' ... Ces fours étaient identiques aux fours crématoires des nazis ... De telles pratiques se sont multipliées notamment durant la deuxième moitié du 19e siècle sans oublier les affres endurées par la population durant la guerre de libération, l'ennemi ayant perfectionné ses moyens de torture, d'extermination et de destruction faisant de l'Algérie un gigantesque camp de la mort et de la torture ceint de fils barbelés et de champs de mines." Available at: http://politiquearabedelafrance.blogspot.com/2005/05/dshonneur_10.html.

22 S. Raouf, "Les Algériens attendent pour voir," *Le Quotidien d'Oran*, 13 November, 2006.

23 See Martine de Froberville, *Sahara Occidental, La confiance perdue*, Paris: L'Harmattan, 1996, p. 88.

24 "France, Democratization and North Africa," in Richard Gillespie and Richard Youngs, op. cit., pp. 136–8.

25 See Jean-Pierre Tuquoi, '*Majesté, je dois beaucoup à votre père ... ' France–Maroc, une affaire de famille*, Paris: Albin Michel, 2006, pp. 63–75.

26 Eric Aeschimann and Christophe Boltanski, *Chirac d'Arabie, les mirages d'une politique française*, Paris: Grasset, 2006, pp. 376–84.

27 See Michael J. Willis, "Justice and Development or Justice and Spirituality? The Challenge of Morocco's Non-Violent Islamist Movements," in Bruce Maddy-Weitzman and Daniel Zisenwine (eds), *The Maghrib in the New Century: Identity, Religion and Politics*, Gainesville, FL: University of Florida Press, 2007.

28 *Le Monde*, 15 May 2003, p. 4.

29 Alain Roussillon, "Réformer la Moudawana," *Maghreb-Machrek*, no. 179 (spring 2004), pp. 79–100.

30 "Le pouvoir à l'épreuve du choc terroriste: entre dérives autoritaires et tentation de l'arbitraire," *Annuaire de l'Afrique du Nord*, vol. XII, 2003, Paris: Editions du CNRS, 2005, p. 246.

31 Yemen and Bahrain proposed creating a development fund for private firms in the International Finance Corporation (IFC) to provide technical and financial support to small enterprises. $60m (out of $100m initially envisaged) were promised for this purpose, of which $15m were offered by the United States. Turkey,

Yemen, and Italy also proposed creating a "Democracy Assistance Dialogue" to promote exchanges and debate between civil society groups and governments in the region. France espoused the creation of a center for micro-financial training in Jordan to work with NGOs to improve access to loans for entrepreneurs who had no access to the banking sector.

32 Entretien du Premier Ministre, M. Dominique de Villepin, avec la presse marocaine, Paris, 25 December 2005. Available at: http://www.diplomatie.gouv.fr/actu/print_bul.asp?liste=20050927.html, pp. 3 and 5.

33 Eric Aeschimann and Christophe Boltanski, *Chirac d'Arabie, les mirages d'une politique française*, op. cit., p. 378.

34 Jean-François Daguzan, *Le dernier rempart? Forces armées et politiques de défense au Maghreb*, Paris: Publisud, 1998, pp. 190–6.

35 Saïd Haddad, "Chronique politique Libye: Le retour à la communauté des nations ou la stratégie américaine de la Libye," *Annuaire de l'Afrique du Nord*, vol. XII, Paris, 2003, op. cit., p. 182.

36 Jean-François Daguzan, "De l'ennemi no.2 au premier de la classe: analyse de l'abandon réussi d'une politique de prolifération," *Maghreb-Machrek*, (Dossier Libye: vers le changement?), no. 184 (summer 2005), p. 75.

37 Ibid.

38 See, Yahia H. Zoubir, "The United States and Libya: From Confrontation to Normalization," *Middle East Policy*, vol. 13, no. 2 (summer 2006), pp. 48–70.

39 Nicolas Sarkis, "Les perspectives pétrolières libyennes," *Maghreb-Machrek*, no. 181 (fall 2004), pp. 59–65.

40 *Le Monde*, 25 November 2004, p. 5.

41 *Libération*, 26 November 2004, p. 10.

42 Under the presidency of Nicolas Sarkozy, France's relationship with Libya has taken a new turn. In order to close the dossier of the Bulgarian nurses and Palestinian doctor—falsely accused of infecting Libyan children in the Benghazi hospital with the HIV virus and sentenced to death after 8 years of prison—on 7 July 2007, Sarkozy dispatched to Tripoli his wife Cécilia and the General Secretary of the Presidency, Claude Guéant. Although various other countries had been for years secretly negotiating the release of the group, the nurses and the doctor flew to Bulgaria in President Sarkozy's airplane. Following the release, Nicolas Sarkozy visited Muammar Qaddafi with whom he discussed the project, dear to Sarkozy, of creating a Mediterranean Union. While the deal was meant to boost France's international image, in France the political opposition heavily criticized the involvement of Sarkozy's wife in the negotiations, as well as the agreement to build a nuclear desalinization water plant and the conclusion of an important arms sale by EADS to Libya. Despite the criticism leveled against Sarkozy, events relating to his approach to Libya highlight a new style of relations based on pragmatism, efficiency, and economic results.

43 "Maroc 'fin du laxisme'," *Libération*, 31 May–1 June 2003.

44 José Garçon, "Maghreb: la diplomatie française à géométrie variable," *Libération*, 6 October 2005, p. 10. During the Information Summit in Tunis, a French journalist, well known for his critical writing, was beaten in the street by "unknown" persons. "L'envoyé spécial de Libération à Tunis violemment agressé," *Libération*, 15 November 2005.

45 For a detailed analysis of this initiative see Jean-François Coustillère, "Méditerranée: '5 + 5' et initiative de sécurité," *Défense Nationale*, May 2005, pp. 76–82.

17 Spain's Policy towards Morocco and Algeria

Balancing Relations with the Southern Neighbors

Haizam Amirah-Fernández

The Maghreb is one of the priority regions for Spanish foreign policy, together with Europe and Latin America.[1] Spain is the only European country that has a territorial presence in North Africa, and thus land borders with one of its countries, Morocco. The Mediterranean is a compendium of almost all the major issues with which the international community is faced nowadays. Spain's relations with the Maghrebi countries are a good illustration of the number of issues involved. A broad range of concerns, ranging from stability, development, and democratization to international migrations, terrorism, drug and human trafficking, and environmental protection affects relations between Spain and Maghrebi states. These relations have changed over the past few decades with Spain's contemporary role in world politics and the emergence of new issues in the international agenda.

This chapter explores the main questions that shape Spain's relations with its closest two southern neighbors, Morocco and Algeria. Given that Spain has limited commercial and political relations with the other three Maghrebi countries (Libya, Mauritania, and Tunisia), this chapter focuses on the balancing of relations between Algeria and Morocco, the two regional powers in the Maghreb, especially in view of the conflict in Western Sahara in which Spain, as the former colonial power, has an important role to play. Morocco enjoys a preferential status in Spain's relations with the Maghreb, despite the existence of several contentious issues and unsettled conflicts at the bilateral level. Relations between the two countries are marked by cyclical conflict, by rivalries between Morocco and Algeria for regional hegemony, and by competition between France and Spain for regional influence. This chapter argues that Spain will continue to have a vacillating relationship with the Maghreb as long as existing conflicts are not addressed at the political level. The enormous differences in the nature of political regimes on both shores of the Western Mediterranean and the interaction of domestic and international politics give existing conflicts a structural character.

The difference in per capita income between Spain and its North African neighbors has multiplied several-fold over the last 30 years.[2] A notable and growing demographic imbalance between the two shores of the Mediterranean, combined with socio-political conflicts, is causing an incessant flow of

Maghrebi immigrants moving into Spain across the Straits of Gibraltar and to the Canary Islands in an unregulated manner. This new situation poses important challenges for all concerned states and societies. Over the last 20 years, following its adherence to the European Community, Spain has been very active in promoting policies towards the Mediterranean. As pointed out by Richard Gillespie, "Spain's status as an interlocutor of the Maghreb states was enhanced by acquiring a voice within the international organizations, where it could influence among other things the trade and aid offers made by the EC in the course of negotiating international agreements,"[3] as well as through multilateral initiatives such as the Euro-Mediterranean Partnership (EMP), launched in Barcelona, Spain, in November 1995.

Paradoxically, economic relations between Spain and its closest southern neighbors (excluding energy imports, mainly from Algeria and Libya) are of marginal importance when compared to the overall volume of Spanish international economic relations. This is ironic, given the geographical proximity of these countries to Spain, and the fact that they face major challenges that affect the whole Western Mediterranean region, namely the migratory pressure, political and economic stability, transnational terrorism, and international competitiveness in the era of globalization. The limited attractiveness of Maghrebi markets for Spanish—and international—investors due to corruption, bureaucracy, and lack of legal guarantees, along with the absence of regional integration are likely to remain the major obstacles facing Spanish–Maghrebi economic relations.

The Maghreb Viewed from Spain

Relations between countries on both sides of the Straits of Gibraltar are deeply rooted in history and have witnessed extreme forms of cooperation and conflict. The legacy of the Muslim presence in the Iberian Peninsula, which started in 711 and lasted for almost eight centuries, is an undeniable part of Spain's cultural roots. In more recent times, the existence of a Spanish protectorate in Northern Morocco (1912–1956) intensified relations between both countries, but also created negative dynamics that continue to shape perceptions among sectors of both societies. Due to the strong presence of other European colonial powers in the Mediterranean, Spain was able to extend its influence during the late nineteenth and first half of the twentieth centuries only to those Southern Mediterranean territories located in the immediate neighborhood (the Rif region in Northern Morocco) and on the Atlantic façade not far from the Canary Islands (Western Sahara, formerly known as Spanish Sahara from 1884 until 1976).

For decades, Spain's relations with the Maghreb have been viewed through the prism of national interests linked to Morocco, in what can be described as an "obsessive relationship." Territorial disputes have been at the heart of Spanish–Moroccan relations. Several outstanding disputes still exist, which are far from resolution even at times of friendly and warm bilateral relations. Morocco claims sovereignty over all Spanish possessions in North Africa: Ceuta, Melilla, and a series of promontories and rocks off the coast of Morocco. The demarcation of territorial waters is another source of conflict.

If there is one issue that best reflects the conflictive side of Spanish–Maghrebi relations, it is the conflict over Western Sahara, the former Spanish colony, under Moroccan control since 1975 and whose sovereignty is disputed between Morocco and the nationalist POLISARIO Front, which seeks independence for the territory. The majority of the Spanish population and political forces support, in one way or another, the right of the Sahrawi population to self-determination,[4] as established by the United Nations. Many Spaniards consider that their country has a historical and moral responsibility towards the Sahrawis for having withdrawn hastily from the former colony in February 1976 before having organized a referendum on self-determination for the Sahrawi people, to which they had the right under international law.[5] The existence of an extensive movement of solidarity with the Sahrawi cause provokes continuous frictions between Spain and Morocco.[6]

Under the dictatorship of General Francisco Franco (1939–1975), "the defense of territorial interests was the priority for Spain's external activities in the region. A divided Maghreb undermined by regional conflict was seen as the best guarantee for the defense of Spanish territorial interests."[7] With the advent of democracy after Franco's death, Spanish policy makers started to view the Maghreb as a region. The establishment of the Arab Maghreb Union (AMU) in February 1989 reinforced this approach, at least as long as friendly relations between Morocco and Algeria seemed to exist. However, regional rivalries between these two countries, coupled with France's perception of the Maghreb as its own *chasse gardée*,[8] have impeded the development of fully normalized relations between Spain and its immediate southern neighbors.

A relatively widespread perception among Spanish policy makers, especially the conservative, is that the Moroccan regime is not trustworthy. This is due to past experiences, viewed as the expression of Morocco's irredentism, such as the occupation of Western Sahara after King Hassan II launched the "Green March" in November 1975, the crisis over the Parsley islet in summer 2002, and the unpredictability of formal institutional structures that do not reflect the real location of power,[9] especially due to the difficulties faced when negotiating fishing agreements. All this has led some to interpret relations in terms of "negative mutual dependencies," where there is excessive focus on security aspects and where migration is regarded as a threat to stability.[10]

Many issues that affect relations with Morocco are considered as pertaining to Spanish domestic politics, rather than to international relations (immigration, Western Sahara, Spanish possessions in North Africa, and drug trafficking). Perceptions play a very important role in the way relations are conducted, both at the social and at the policy-making level. Insofar as perceptions are concerned, Spanish public opinion is far less generous than government officials when judging the level of democratization achieved by the Maghrebi states, especially Morocco. Clearly, the incessant flow of Moroccan illegal immigrants who risk their lives to seek a better life in Europe does not help to promote the image of a more democratic, less corrupt Morocco. For their part, Moroccan authorities have long complained to their Spanish counterparts about the not very amicable treatment that their monarch receives in some Spanish media. This fact shows the level of democratic incompatibility that still exists between the two countries, given that Spanish political authorities cannot decide the content of media reporting.

Surprisingly, Spain has had limited contact with the remaining four Maghrebi countries and their peoples, a fact that has hampered the level of exchanges and influence, but at the same time and unlike the case with Morocco, did not associate bilateral relations with a conflictive colonial past—as is the case for former colonial powers, such as France and Italy. For a long time, Spanish interests in Algeria, Libya, Mauritania, and Tunisia were focused almost exclusively on economic and trade issues. Increasingly, issues like security, migration management, and development have gained relevance for Spanish foreign policy towards these four countries, as shown by the intensification of political dialogue and diplomatic contacts at the bilateral and multilateral level (EMP, "5 + 5" dialogue, etc.).

Spain's Shifting Relationship with the Central Maghreb

Efforts to intensify Hispano-Maghrebi relations are frequently disrupted due to the persistence of unsettled conflicts and to differences—and sometimes incompatibilities—in governing styles and institutional settings on both sides of the Mediterranean. Improved relations with one of the two Maghrebi regional powers, Algeria and Morocco, have traditionally come at the expense of the quality of relations with the other country. The ultimate goal in the Maghreb of all Spanish governments has been to guarantee the stability of the region while creating the proper environment for economic and trade relations to flourish. For a series of reasons that will be discussed below, Spain devotes great diplomatic efforts to its relationship with Morocco. However, over the past decade or so, these relations have followed a love–hate pattern that resulted in movement from warm vows of everlasting friendship to being on the verge of open war, as was the case in July 2002, when the "Parsley crisis" erupted,[11] and back to apparent normality after a relatively short period of time.

In order to prevent the shifting nature of the relationship that Spain has with Morocco, Spanish policy makers during the 1990s coined the term "cushion of shared interests" as an expression of the need to create extensive multidimensional ties between Spain and Morocco so as to mitigate the effects of cyclical crises. Interdependence was presented as the guarantee for preventing the breakdown of traditional diplomacy and as a means to deter both countries from resorting to the use of force. The mere recourse to this conflict mitigation strategy already indicates that relations contain structurally conflicting components. Despite good intentions and the actual establishment of much stronger ties between the two countries, the "cushion of shared interests" failed to prevent severe crises from happening at times when this was most needed, like in 2001–2003 when bilateral relations were at loggerheads. For some observers, such crises of interdependence came into being due to the fact that "the strategy informing Spain's North Africa initiatives has rested upon faulty or inadequate premises."[12]

One of the most critical moments in modern Hispano-Moroccan relations took place in spring 2001, following the collapse of fisheries negotiations between the EU and Morocco. The conservative Prime Minister of Spain at the time, José María Aznar, feeling that Morocco did not honor its promises, thus damaging Spanish interests, declared that "there would be consequences for relations between Morocco and Spain."[13] Following the coming to power of Aznar in 1996, Morocco continued to be a priority for Spanish foreign policy and development aid. However, issues such as increasing illegal migration into Spain, difficulties in revising the agricultural chapter of the EU–Morocco association agreement, and above all the Spanish position on Western Sahara, rapidly poisoned the climate of trust between the two countries.

No matter that Aznar was the first European leader to visit King Mohammed VI in August 1999 following his accession to the throne, tense personal relations between the two leaders brought about increasingly distant positions. The peak of the crisis occurred in July 2002, when Moroccan troops "invaded" the Parsley islet (known as Perejil to Spaniards, and Toura or Laila to Moroccans), a piece of rock off the Moroccan coast barely the size of a soccer field, claimed by Spain. This unilateral move came at the height of a 15-month-long period of tension during which there was no Moroccan ambassador in Madrid, and resulted in Spain withdrawing its ambassador from Rabat. The presence of Moroccan troops on the islet was considered in Madrid a break of the status quo and a *fait accompli* which, if not stopped, would look like an invitation to Morocco to intensify its claims over Ceuta and Melilla.

The crisis came to an end as a result of the mediation of the US Secretary of State Colin Powell, and the two countries expressed their commitment to return to the pre-"invasion" status quo. Following some months of diplomatic contacts and intense lobbying activities in both countries, the two ambassadors returned to their respective posts in February 2003 and preparations began for holding the bilateral "high level meeting," which initially should have taken place every year but had been postponed for three years due to deteriorating relations between the two countries. The "high level meeting" finally took place in December of that year in Marrakech, with the participation of the Moroccan monarch and his entourage and the Spanish Prime Minister Aznar, who was accompanied by eight of his ministers. This summit marked the *end* of the crisis and allowed the signing of a financial package agreement for 390m euros (the most important agreement of its kind signed by Spain with another country),[14] and the resumption of cooperation in several fields, the fight against illegal migration being one of the most important areas of renewed cooperation.

The "Parsley crisis" revealed many things: first and foremost that the so-called "cushion of shared interests" was an insufficient approach to prevent a major conflict from arising. This crisis also made clear that "when a real conflict threatened the Western Mediterranean, neither the EMP nor the CFSP [the EU's Common Foreign and Security Policy] could prevent it: rather it was a superpower intervention by the USA that ... helped Spain and Morocco to restore 'normal' diplomatic relations"[15]—all that despite the existence of a Treaty of Friendship, Good Neighborliness, and Cooperation between the two countries, signed in July 1991. Furthermore, the "Parsley crisis" and its aftermath revealed that Spain had a swinging relationship with Morocco not only when governments of different political trend were in power in Spain, but also in different periods under the same government, as was clearly manifested by the efforts made to rebuild relations at the Marrakech summit. Surprisingly and regardless of the deterioration of bilateral diplomatic relations, trade between the two countries increased during the period of crisis.

The crisis left many in Spain with the feeling that France was more interested in supporting Morocco's position at the EU level rather than in siding with Spain.[16] Since his coming to power in 1999, King Mohammed VI has been much influenced by Francophile royal advisors, keen to maintain a degree of tension in Moroccan–Spanish relations.[17] As a result, Moroccan–French relations had been given a boost by the new monarch, for whom Chirac played the role of favorite uncle.[18] This *French factor* is a constant that needs to be taken into account at all times when analyzing Hispano-Moroccan relations. Some analysts argue that "the Spanish conservative government felt betrayed by the EU (mainly by France) causing its foreign policy to veer towards the positions of the US."[19] The unconditional alignment of Prime Minister Aznar with US President George W. Bush in the unpopular and disastrous adventure in Iraq[20] further aggravated the rift between the Spanish government of that time and the French.

The coming of the Socialist Party to power in Spain in March 2004 brought a radical change in the way relations with Morocco were conducted. The government led by José Luis Rodríguez Zapatero insistently tried to de-link its foreign policy from that of the conservative People's Party, thus the withdrawal of Spanish troops from Iraq, the "return" to Europe, and the granting of full support—uncritical, in public at least—to certain countries, such as Morocco. The Socialist minister of foreign affairs, Miguel Ángel Moratinos, known for having very close relations with

Southern Mediterranean governments (he had been posted to Rabat and Tel Aviv before being appointed as the EU's Special Envoy for the Middle East Peace Process in December 1996), set the improvement of relations with Morocco as a priority. While this goal is widely desired in both countries, the new stage did not come without significant controversies.[21] In its quest to avoid any official statement or move that could be interpreted as upsetting in Rabat, the Spanish government has exposed itself to much domestic criticism, not only from its political opponents but also from its own allies.[22]

Spain, Morocco, and Algeria: A Difficult Neighborhood

The importance that Spain gives to its relations with Morocco is best manifested in the unwritten norm by which the first official foreign trip of Spanish Prime Ministers is to the Alawite Kingdom (Aznar in May 1996 and again in May 2000, Rodríguez Zapatero in April 2004, and before them Felipe González for the first time in March 1983). In the same vein, Rodríguez Zapatero paid his first official visit abroad to Morocco in December 2001 after he was elected secretary-general of the Spanish Socialist Party, at a time when bilateral relations were rapidly deteriorating.

In order to create closer relations with its southern neighbors, improve the regional environment, and avoid resorting to the use of force when disputes arise, Spain signed a Treaty of Friendship, Good Neighborliness, and Cooperation with Morocco in July 1991, 11 years before signing a similar treaty with Algeria,[23] at a time when Spanish–Moroccan relations had reached their lowest ebb. These treaties establish that an annual "high level meeting" should be held, although in the case of Spain and Morocco only eight meetings were held in 16 years (in 1993, 1994, 1997, 1998, 1999, 2003, 2005, and 2007). Delaying high level meetings became a new channel for expression of discontent. This tactic became almost a thermometer for measuring the warmth of bilateral relations and the level of expectations placed on them by each country.

Algeria is a close yet distant neighbor of Spain. Despite the fact that Algiers is the second closest capital city to Madrid (next to Lisbon), relations between the two countries have been traditionally limited and, for a long time, focused on economic and trade relations, especially in the energy sector. Algeria is Spain's largest supplier of natural gas. In 1998 Spain received 60 percent of its total imports of gas from Algeria, while in 2006 that share was around 32 percent, due to the diversification of suppliers. However, Spanish dependency on Algerian natural gas is high, and most likely will increase once the MEDGAZ pipeline is operational in 2009.[24]

In Spain there is a significant lack of knowledge of and contacts with Algeria due to historical reasons and to the period of isolation that Algeria underwent during the bloody decade of the 1990s. Another reason for the lack of more intense relations is the existence of limited human contact between the two societies. The number of Algerian citizens living in Spain, mainly in the eastern provinces, is significantly small for countries that are so close geographically (clearly much smaller than that of Moroccans),[25] while a few hundred Spaniards live in Algeria and the number of Spanish tourists who visit the country is almost insignificant.

Morocco's claims to sovereignty over all Spanish possessions in North Africa (Ceuta, Melilla, and a series of promontories and rocks) are periodically employed by Moroccan authorities and their official media outlets to put pressure on the Spanish government when they have divergent positions, in approach and in substance, before and during certain negotiation processes (votes over Western Sahara at the UN, fishing agreements with the EU, etc.). Successive Spanish governments have avoided seriously discussing the future of Ceuta and Melilla with Morocco due to domestic pressure, but also out of fear that any reaffirmation of their Spanish status would negatively affect Spanish claims over Gibraltar—despite the important historical differences in the situations of those territories.[26] Disputes also exist over territorial waters in the Mediterranean Sea and in the delimitation of the median line between the Canary Islands and the Moroccan Atlantic coast.

Illegal immigration across the Straits of Gibraltar is a major concern for Spanish policy makers in their relations with Morocco, a country that is no longer a net exporter of migrants towards Europe, but increasingly a transit route for sub-Saharan Africans who try to reach Europe.[27] Issues linked to immigration, such as border control,[28] integration of migrants, remittances, criminality, drug trafficking,[29] and terrorist activities are sources of concern in Spain and abroad.[30] No one forgets that the 11 March 2004 terrorist attacks in Madrid that left 191 dead and 1,824 wounded—the deadliest on European soil up to that time—were carried out by a *jihadi* group composed mostly of Maghrebi citizens.

The Western Sahara Imbroglio

Spain's passage from dictatorship to democracy left the decolonization of Western Sahara unfinished. The dispute over the territory between Morocco and the pro-independence POLISARIO Front, for which the Spanish government of the time is largely responsible, has had a negative impact on Spain's relations with its southern neighbors, especially with Morocco, for over 30 years. Democratic governments in Spain had for decades expressed their full respect for UN resolutions on Western Sahara, while maintaining a position of "active neutrality" in their relations with the parties involved. All democratic Spanish governments have been trapped between pressure of public opinion in support of a referendum for self-determination in Western Sahara and *realpolitik*, out of the belief that putting too much pressure on the Moroccan regime to adhere to international legality would ultimately produce its downfall. This could initiate a period of instability and perhaps even chaos in the country, resulting in grave consequences for Spain. The "fear of the unknown" argument has been skillfully employed by Morocco in order to maintain the status quo and receive diplomatic support from Western powers for its position on Western Sahara.

Developments in Spanish foreign policy since 2004 have tended to signal a shift in Madrid's official discourse vis-à-vis this conflict, leaving aside the traditional "active neutrality" approach in favor of a more proactive role as mediator. The position of the Spanish Socialist government stems from the belief that the continuation of the conflict is a major obstacle for regional stability, thus making the process of regional integration more difficult and hindering political, economic, and social development in the Maghreb. The lack of advances in these fronts is perceived as the root cause of illegal immigration and the terrorist threat. The new Spanish position—ambiguous at times—has been welcomed by Morocco.[31] However, it has generated mistrust in the POLISARIO Front and Algeria. Although the Spanish government has made intense diplomatic efforts to establish direct lines of communication with all the parties involved in the conflict, its perceived activism in favor of the autonomy project presented unilaterally by Morocco in April 2007 has limited its capacity as a peace broker.[32]

Despite the increase in diplomatic contacts with the POLISARIO Front, including visits paid by two high-level officials to the Sahrawi refugee camps in Tindouf,[33] the Sahrawis grew skeptical of what was perceived as a policy of open support for Morocco and total alignment with France. The POLISARIO Front viewed Spain's departure from its traditional "active neutrality" as a rupture with a balanced position on the conflict. The absence of explicit references to the Peace Plan during Prime Minister Rodríguez Zapatero's first official visit to Morocco on 24 April 2004, and his statement a week later in Paris saying that a solution to the Western Sahara conflict could be reached in a matter of six months, raised concerns among those in favor of self-determination.[34]

It is possible that the Spanish government, in its desire to secure regional stability, decided to give the Moroccan regime full support so that it could contain the migratory pressure and growing social radicalization within Morocco, which are viewed as two of the most acute external challenges facing Spain, especially after the 11 March 2004 terrorist attacks in Madrid.[35] However, Spain's margin of maneuver is rather limited due to a series of factors, such as a predominantly pro-Sahrawi domestic public opinion (including many Socialist voters), the persistence of Algerian–Moroccan rivalries,[36] and the lack of a broader and more neutral international coalition willing to enforce any agreement reached by the parties.

Algerian authorities too have expressed mistrust of the Spanish diplomatic maneuvers, which are viewed in Algiers as openly supporting Moroccan claims. During a visit to Algeria in December 2006 by the Spanish Prime Minister, José Luis Rodríguez Zapatero, on the occasion of the third bilateral "high level meeting," President Abdelaziz Bouteflika urged him to press for an independence referendum for the territory of Western Sahara in his talks with Moroccan authorities and the POLISARIO Front. Bouteflika expressed his hope "that Spain will engage in a more resolute manner with the kingdom of Morocco and the POLISARIO Front to lead them to accept to prepare the referendum."[37] This statement was followed three months later by the announcement by the Algerian minister of energy and mines, Chakib Khelil, on the eve of the Spanish King's visit to Algiers (the first in 24 years), that his country would raise the price of the natural gas it sells to Spain by about 20 percent. Almost all Spanish media, including those close to the Socialist government, linked that announcement to the dissatisfaction felt in Algiers because of Prime Minister Rodríguez Zapatero's support of the Moroccan autonomy project for Western Sahara.[38] As one Spanish diplomat pointed out:

> The key to stability in Morocco may not necessarily be the solution of the Western Sahara dispute. The position of Algeria, which is consolidating itself strongly as a regional and continental actor of first order, makes it difficult to find a solution that does not satisfy the legitimate aspirations of the Sahrawi people who are supported by Algiers with absolute determination.[39]

Balancing Relations

Rebuilding relations with Morocco, which were severely damaged during the early years of the decade, has been one of the priorities of the Spanish government that came to power in 2004. However, the urgency in doing so gave rise to new problems, mainly overlooking regional balances without providing a new framework for conducting relations in the Western Mediterranean. The result has been the reversal of the situation that existed under the People's Party government; at that time Spain and Algeria grew closer, to the detriment of Morocco. Now it is Spain and Algeria that are holding their distance from each other, while "Paris is getting closer to Algiers."[40] The Spanish government made this strategic decision despite the fact that the *French factor* is much less prominent in Spanish–Algerian relations than in Spanish–Moroccan ones. While the latter are conditioned by Rabat's dependency on Paris, the former are exempt from any tutelary link. In sum, Spain is still unable to achieve diplomatic balance in the Maghreb, which is a *sine qua non* for it to be able to act as a peace broker.

One critical view of Spanish policy towards the Maghreb after 2004 is provided by Toby Shelley:

> If Spain is to fulfill its historic responsibilities in the Maghreb and play a part in ensuring a stable future for the region, its policy towards the Western Sahara must be more profound than knee-jerk reaction to an unforeseen crisis ... Fear of illegal migration, drug smuggling, terrorism,

and pressure over Ceuta and Melilla have left the Spanish government frightened of offending Rabat, it seems. At the same time Madrid wants the friendship of Algiers and is unwilling to court unpopularity at home by openly repudiating Sahrawi rights ... From the outside, Madrid's policy over the Western Sahara appears confused. First, it seemed that there was a plan that would supersede Baker, then there was not. One day, Baker's Peace Plan should be the basis of a settlement, the next a more Parisian approach was favored ... Meanwhile, Morocco believed Madrid to be so weak that it turned back five delegations from early June to mid July [2005] with impunity, preventing them from visiting land and people over which Rabat has no legal jurisdiction.[41]

Some positive—although limited—results have been attained as a result of the improved Spanish–Moroccan relations (a considerable reduction in the number of illegal immigrants who try to reach Spain via Morocco; a new fishing agreement that allowed the return of a limited number of European—mainly Spanish—ships to Moroccan waters, including the waters of the disputed Western Sahara;[42] sending a joint peace-keeping mission to Haiti). However, it can be argued that the main success has been in preventing new conflicts from arising. The two countries have not taken advantage of the excellent relations at the official level to advance in the resolution of long-standing conflicts (Morocco's claims over Ceuta and Melilla, the delimitation of the median line around the Canary Islands, etc.). After having commemorated the "year of Spain" in Morocco in 2005, the Spanish government announced that 2006 would be "the year of Morocco" in Spain, during which conferences, exhibitions, and cultural activities would be held.[43] However, this initiative never materialized, apparently due to lack of enthusiasm on the part of Morocco, aware that such an initiative could backfire due to the Moroccan regime's poor image in Spain. In Spanish–Moroccan relations, more often than not, it is Morocco that sets the pace and the intensity of those relations.

Having "stability above all" as the central priority of Spanish foreign policy in the Maghreb poses the dilemma of how to accommodate principles and interests; that is, how to support human rights and democracy beyond the official rhetoric. The concept of "dynamic stability," used by some Spanish policy makers when they approach the Maghreb, refers to the "timid willingness to support gradual democratizing changes in the political processes of North African countries, providing that these do not interfere with Spain's strategic and economic interests."[44] The question that has to be asked is whether regional stability can be guaranteed in the long term in the absence of good governance, and whether granting unlimited support to undemocratic regimes can prevent serious trouble from breaking out in the future.

From time to time, Spanish diplomats receive criticism from other European countries for their defense of certain practices by undemocratic regimes in the Arab world, mostly in North Africa. "Under both the PP [People's Party] and PSOE [Socialist Party], Spain invariably diluted EU criticisms of democratic abuses in North Africa [and] continued to resist proposals from other EU member states for critical demarches on, for example, the Moroccan government's frequent clampdowns against the press."[45] Some observers consider it anomalous that Spain shows such a weakness of action in the field of promoting democracy in the Maghreb "given that the Spanish transition is often presented as a model for political change in the region."[46]

Conclusion

The Western Mediterranean is an area of vital interest for Spain. The stability of the Maghreb region, and particularly of the Moroccan regime, ranks among the highest priorities for Spanish foreign policy. Despite their seminal importance, bilateral relations between Spain and Morocco have been marked by passion and distrust. On the Spanish side, there is a perception that Rabat hides unpleasant surprises, while in Morocco some of Madrid's decisions are viewed as arrogant or below expectation when it comes to sensitive issues like the Western Sahara conflict.

Spain, the former colonial power in Western Sahara and today one of the main partners of the Maghreb region, has an important role to play once the conflict is ready to be resolved. However, it does not possess the key to breaking the current deadlock. Furthermore, by colluding with France,[47] whose official position on Western Sahara is far from neutral,[48] in trying to resolve the conflict, Madrid risks its efforts appearing too militant in favor of the autonomy project presented unilaterally by Morocco in April 2007, thus limiting its capacity as interlocutor of all the parties involved. Perceptions can be as important as realities, or even more so. A perceived shift in the traditional Spanish position over the Western Sahara conflict, both at home and abroad, may end up generating undesired reactions, such as raising the level of regional tensions.

Furthermore, the risk exists that perceived open support by the Spanish authorities may end up by misleading the Moroccan regime to believe that Madrid would acquiesce unconditionally to its claims over Western Sahara. In democratic systems, public opinion has to be taken into account. It is hard to imagine Spanish society accepting a government decision perceived as openly going against the legitimate right of the Sahrawis to self-determination. Any incapacity on the part of Madrid to deliver the policies desired by Morocco after expectations have been raised could frustrate the climate of understanding between the two countries. The record of previous crises suggests that they resulted from disappointment and frustration with unmet expectations with respect to the negotiation of fishing agreements, the control of illegal immigration, and positions over the Western Sahara conflict.

Distrust among Maghrebi regimes requires that neighboring European countries adopt balanced approaches that take into consideration the interests of all regional actors. Spain could contribute to regional stability through the simultaneous improvement of its relations with Morocco and Algeria. The rule of law should be viewed not as luxury, but as an utmost requirement for developing healthier political, economic, and social relations that have a constructive impact on the human development and long-term stability of the Western Mediterranean region. Such stability is a priority objective for Spanish policy towards the Maghreb. However, there is a need to review the premise by which supporting short-term political stability at any price would necessarily lead to the region's overall development. Major impediments to that happening still exist, and they are linked to domestic politics, intra-regional dynamics, and to the long list of unsettled bilateral disputes which "limit the possibility of applying a principled policy in relation to the active defense of human rights and democratization."[49]

Concerning relations between Spain and Morocco, neither a climate of confrontation and mutual threats, such as that during the 2001–2003 period, nor one of unconditional support, can guarantee the consolidation of a stable and healthy environment. Undoubtedly, the risks for Spain in case of serious destabilization in Morocco are great and the negative effects could be felt almost immediately in the form of a massive arrival of *pateras* (small rudimentary boats) carrying Moroccans trying to flee the country. However, and given that the creation of a "cushion of shared interests" has proved to be an insufficient guarantee for preventing serious conflict,[50] the question remains whether the current Spanish approach is adequate to meet long-term challenges and transform structural tensions. Official statements on the need to "anchor Morocco to the EU, to a world similar in principles, in the respect of human rights, the rule of law, and all that constitutes the *acquis* that Europe and Spain wish to defend"[51] need to be extended to the rest of the Maghreb region. If such an approach is limited to one country, the likelihood of transforming regional negative dynamics is rather slim. Promoting an "advanced status" for Morocco—or any other country for that matter—in its relations with the EU requires becoming less shy in denouncing human right violations and excesses and building more solid institutional frameworks.

Notes

1 For a review of Spanish foreign policy towards the Maghreb up to 2002, see: López García, B. and M. Hernando de Larramendi (2002), "Spain and North Africa: Towards a 'Dynamic Stability'," *Democratization*, spring, vol. 9, no. 1, pp. 170–91. It is interesting to note that the bibliography on Spanish–Maghrebi relations is rather limited, even in the Spanish language, despite the importance that these relations have for Spain.
2 In 1970, the Spanish GDP per capita was four times that of Morocco. According to UNDP data for the year 2004, Spanish GDP per capita was 14.5 times higher

than that of its immediate southern neighbor, Morocco (US$24,360 vs. US$1,678), or 5.8 times in PPP terms (25,047 vs. 4,309). *The 2006 Human Development Report*, New York: United Nations Development Programme. Unless the current trend is reversed, difference in GDP per capita will continue to grow.

3 Gillespie, R. (2001), *Spain and the Western Mediterranean*, ESRC Research Program "One Europe or Several?" Working Paper 37/01, Brighton: University of Sussex, p. 17.

4 Various Spanish regional administrations, political parties, and lobby groups support the POLISARIO Front. According to the June 2005 Barometer of the Elcano Royal Institute, 72 percent of Spaniards believed that the government should support the independence of Western Sahara, compared to 16 percent who considered that the best solution would be extensive autonomy under Morocco's regime. *Barómetro del Real Instituto Elcano (BRIE), Novena Oleada, Resultados de Junio 2005*, Elcano Royal Institute for International and Strategic Studies, July 2005, pp. 69–70. Available at: http://www.realinstitutoelcano.org/barometro/20050707/Brie9_informe_definitivo.pdf.

5 On 30 April 2007, the UN Security Council reiterated the right of the people of Western Sahara to self-determination. See: S/RES/1754 (2007).

6 For instance, every summer around 10,000 Sahrawi children between the ages of 8 and 13 are hosted by Spanish families in their homes for a two-month period.

7 López García, B. and M. Hernando de Larramendi (2002), op. cit., p. 170.

8 On the special Franco-Maghrebi relations, see Chapter 16 by Jean-François Daguzan in this volume.

9 Gillespie, R. (2006), "'This Stupid Little Island': A Neighborhood Confrontation in the Western Mediterranean," *International Politics*, vol. 43, no. 1, February, p. 121.

10 López García, B. and M. Hernando de Larramendi (2002), op. cit., p. 188.

11 For an account of the background and evolution of the crisis, see: Gillespie, R. (2006), op. cit., pp. 113–6. See also: Planet, A. and M. Hernando de Larramendi (2003) "Maroc–Espagne: la crise de l'îlot du Persil," in R. Leveau (ed.), *Afrique du Nord Moyen-Orient. Espaces et conflits*, Paris: Les études de la Documentation française.

12 Gillespie, R. (2006), op. cit., p. 120.

13 For an interesting account of the deterioration of bilateral relations, see: Cembrero, I (2006), *Vecinos alejados: los secretos de la crisis entre España y Marruecos*, Barcelona: Círculo de Lectores/Galaxia Gutenberg, pp. 13–27.

14 *El País*, 8 December 2003.

15 Gillespie, R. (2006), op. cit., p. 111.

16 France vetoed an official statement by the EU in support of Spain. See: Cembrero, I. (2006), op. cit.

17 See: Cebolla Boado, H. (2004) "Las decisiones en Marruecos se toman en el sur: Sobre el equilibrio entre francófilos e hispanófilos," Madrid: Fundación para las Relaciones Internacionales y el Diálogo Exterior. Available at: http://www.fride.org/Publications/Publication.aspx?Item=484.

18 Tuquoi, J.-P. (2006), *Majesté, je dois beaucoup à votre père...: France–Maroc, une affaire de famille*, Paris: Albin Michel.

19 Escribano Francés, G. and E. San Martín González (2005), "Los altibajos en la europeización de la política exterior española," paper presented at the Jornadas de Política Económica, Universidad de Vigo, 24–25 November, p. 15. Available at: http://webs.uvigo.es/viijpe/pdf/ESCRIBANO-SANMARTIN.pdf.

20 Different opinion polls showed that an overwhelming majority of Spaniards were against their country's involvement in the US-led war on Iraq. According to one opinion poll, 91 percent were either totally against any possible Spanish military

involvement in a military attack or favored it only if it was backed by a UN Security Council resolution. See: *Barómetro del Real Instituto Elcano (BRIE), Segunda Oleada, Resultados de Febrero de 2003*, Elcano Royal Institute for International and Strategic Studies, March 2003, p. 20. Available at: http:// www.realinstitutoelcano.org/barometro/textobrie2.doc.

21 In January 2005, a few days before the King of Spain paid his second official visit to Morocco since 1979, the Spanish government awarded medals to senior Moroccan officials whose names are associated to grave human rights abuses during the "years of lead." Also, in May 2006, a high-level Spanish delegation, headed by the Spanish ambassador to Rabat, Luis Planas, attended the opening in Nador of the museum honoring the putschist General Mohammed Mizzian, who sided with General Franco during the Spanish Civil War (1936–1939) and then joined the Moroccan army in 1956. His name is linked to the brutal repression of Spanish Republicans and of inhabitants of the Rif region in northern Morocco. These two decisions by the Socialist government raised much criticism among a wide spectrum of political and social forces in Spain, especially among the government's leftist and nationalist allies.

22 Starting in May 2005, pro-independence demonstrations erupted in different towns in Western Sahara and in some Moroccan cities. Indigenous Sahrawis, along with some Moroccan first-generation "colons" born in the territory joined to protest against Moroccan policies and social and economic hardships. The Moroccan security forces' heavy-handed repression of the peaceful demonstrations raised criticism from a number of Western governments and parliaments, although not from the Spanish government.

23 A treaty of the same nature was signed with Tunisia in 1995.

24 For more information on the existing Maghreb–Europe Gas pipeline (MEG), which runs from southern Algeria through Morocco to Spain, and the new gas pipeline MEDGAZ, which is being built to directly connect fields in Algeria to Europe via Almería, see Chapter 9 by Miguel Hernando de Larramendi in this volume.

25 At the end of 2006, the official number of Algerian citizens living legally in Spain was 39,433, while that of Moroccan citizens was 543,721, although real figures for the latter could be considerably higher. *Informe sobre extranjeros con tarjeta o autorización de residencia en vigor, a 31 de diciembre de 2006*, Madrid: Secretaría de Estado de Inmigración y Emigración, Ministerio de Trabajo y Asuntos Sociales.

26 See: Hernando de Larramendi, M. (1997), *La política exterior de Marruecos*, Madrid: Mapfre.

27 See: López García, B. and M. Berriane (eds) (2004), *Atlas de la inmigración marroquí en España*, Taller de Estudios Internacionales Mediterráneos. Madrid: Ediciones UAM.

28 Human rights activists have documented serious human rights violations against migrants and asylum seekers trying to cross the border between Morocco and Spain at the Spanish enclaves of Ceuta and Melilla. See, for example: Amnesty International (2006), *Spain and Morocco: Failure to protect the rights of migrants— one year on*, Report EUR 41/009/2006, 26 October. Available at: http:// www.amnesty-eu.org/static/documents/2006/CeutaandMelillaReportOct2006.pdf.

29 According to the United Nations Office on Drugs and Crime estimates for the year 2003, the annual turnover of international trade in Moroccan cannabis resin was around $12bn, mostly generated by trafficking networks operating in European countries. *Morocco Cannabis Survey 2003*, United Nations Office on Drugs and Crime, December 2003. The executive summary is available at: http:// www.unodc.org/pdf/publications/morocco_cannabis_survey_2003_exec_sum.pdf.

30 The creation in January 2007 of al-Qaeda in the Land of the Islamic Maghreb and the resurgence of North African terrorism shortly after requires intensifying cooperation in the fight against terrorism, as well as in the security and military domains. For more on Spanish–Maghrebi security and defense cooperation, see: Echeverría Jesús, C. (2005), "Las políticas de seguridad y de defensa de los países del Magreb," *Working Paper,* Elcano Royal Institute for International and Strategic Studies, 3 March. Available at: http://www.realinstitutoelcano.org/documentos/ 178.asp.

31 For example, on 14 December 2006 Spain abstained in the vote on the resolution concerning Western Sahara at the UN General Assembly (document A/61/415) arguing that, while it supported the principle of self-determination, it was not the only applicable principle in questions of decolonization.

32 In August 2005, the POLISARIO Front released the last 404 Moroccan POWs in the presence of the Chairman of the US Senate Foreign Relations Committee, Senator Richard Lugar. The prisoners, some of whom had been held for more than two decades, were handed to American authorities and flown to Morocco in aircraft chartered by the US military, under the auspices of the International Red Cross. Remarkably, no Spanish authorities were present at that time, despite the excellent opportunity offered to Spanish diplomacy to show its credentials as a mediator for all parties to the conflict.

33 There was no official complaint from the Moroccan government or media, unlike what could be expected under different circumstances.

34 See: Hernando de Larramendi, M. and B. López García, (2004), "Nuevo impulso diplomático en el Sáhara," *Afkar/Ideas*, no. 4, pp. 22–6. Available at: http://www.iemed.org/afkar/4/ebernabe.php.

35 Fernández Arias, C. (2006), "Magreb," *Panorama Estratégico 2005/2006*, Instituto Español de Estudios Estratégicos and Elcano Royal Institute for International and Strategic Studies, pp. 167–8.

36 The excessively prominent role given to Morocco in the organization of the Euro-African Conference on Migration and Development, held in Rabat in July 2006 with Spanish and French cooperation, compelled Algeria to decide not to participate, thus limiting the effectiveness of the meeting. See: Gillespie, R. (2007), "Límites del voluntarismo español en el Magreb," *Afkar/Ideas*, no. 13, pp. 48. Available at: http://www.iemed.org/afkar/13/18Gillespie.pdf.

37 "Algeria's Bouteflika Urges Spain to Press for Independence Referendum in Western Sahara," *International Herald Tribune*, 12 December 2006.

38 See: *El País*, 13 March 2007, p. 1.

39 Fernández Arias, C. (2006), op. cit., p. 160.

40 "Marruecos, hacia la UE," *El País*, 17 November 2005, p. 14.

41 Shelley, T. (2005), "Sáhara Occidental: esperando la conflagración," *Papeles de Cuestiones Internacionales*, fall, no. 91, p. 74. During the spring and summer of 2005, as many as eight Spanish delegations composed of elected officials, regional governments' MPs, journalists, and members of NGOs were turned back by Moroccan authorities when they tried to visit Western Sahara to document alleged human rights violations. Surprisingly, the Spanish government made no official complaint. Instead, Foreign Minister Moratinos informed that the Moroccan government had given him "guarantees that a delegation from the Spanish Parliament could freely visit Western Sahara shortly" (*ABC*, 6 June 2005). Such a visit never took place because the Moroccan authorities did not provide the conditions for the free movement of the delegation inside the disputed territory.

42 A new fishing agreement between the EU and Morocco, of which Spain is the primary beneficiary, was signed by the Moroccan king on 27 February 2007, just

a few days before the "high level meeting" with Spain took place, despite the fact that the agreement was reached in July 2005.

43 The commemoration of the "year of Morocco" in Spain was announced by the Spanish government on several occasions. See the Spanish Ministry of Foreign Affairs' web page: http://www.mae.es/Embajadas/Rabat/es/MenuPpal/Nota+Pais.

44 López García, B. and M. Hernando de Larramendi (2002), op. cit., p. 171.

45 Youngs, R. (2006), *Survey of European Democracy Promotion Policies 2000–2006*, Madrid: Fundación para las Relaciones Internacionales y el Diálogo Exterior, p. 175. Available at: http://www.fride.org/eng/File/ViewFile.aspx?FileId=1000.

46 López García, B. and M. Hernando de Larramendi (2002), op. cit., p. 187.

47 Interestingly, at the opening ceremony of the commemoration of the 50th anniversary of Morocco's independence, held in Rabat in November 2005, only the Prime Ministers of France and Spain, together with representatives of the governments of Senegal and Madagascar, were present. Neither American nor Arab delegations attended the ceremony.

48 The French President, Jacques Chirac, referred to Western Sahara as "the southern provinces of Morocco" during an official visit in December 2001.

49 López García, B. and M. Hernando de Larramendi (2002), op. cit., p. 170–2.

50 Despite the "excellent" relations between Spain and Morocco, in early November 2007 the Moroccan king decided to recall his ambassador to Madrid to show his disapproval of the Spanish kings' visit to the cities of Ceuta and Melilla that Morocco claims as its own.

51 Statement made by the Spanish minister of foreign affairs, Miguel Ángel Moratinos, in Parliament. *Diario de sesiones del Congreso de los Diputados*, 20 October 2004, p. 1816.

Bibliography

Abed Jabri, M. (1985) "Evolution of the Maghrib Concept: Facts and Perspectives," in H. Barakat (ed.) *Contemporary North Africa: Issues of Development and Integration*, Washington DC: Center for Contemporary Arab Studies, Georgetown University, pp. 63–86.

Agence France Presse (2005) "Alger et Rabat en reviennent aux procès d'intention," 14 June 2005.

Agence Mauritanienne d'Information (2007) "Le Secrétaire d'Etat Adjoint Négroponte: les Etats Unis vont renforcer la coopération bilatérale," (Deputy Secretary of State Negroponte: The United States will strengthen bilateral cooperation), 19 April. Available at: http://www.ami.mr/fr/articles/2007/avril/19/24.html.

Aghrout, A. (2000) *From Preferential Status to Partnership – The Euro-Maghreb Relationship*, Aldershot and Burlington: Ashgate Publishing Limited.

—— (ed.) (2004) *Algeria in Transition: Reforms and Development Prospects*, London and New York: Routledge.

—— and Hodd, M. (2005) "FDI in North Africa: A Comparative Perspective," in S. Motamen-Samadian (ed.) *Capital Flows and Foreign Direct Investments in Emerging Markets*, London: Palgrave Macmillan.

Akala, O. (2001) "L'économie algérienne, de l'ère des réformes (1989–1991) à celle de l'adjustement structurel (1994–1998)," in A. Mahiou and J. R. Henry (eds) *Où va l'Algérie*, Paris: Editions Karthala.

Akesbi, N. (2006) "La experiencia Euro-marroquí. Enseñanzas y propuestas," in *La agricultura y la Asociación Euromediterránea: retos y oportunidades*, Barcelona: IEMed, pp. 156–75.

Al-Ali, N. and Koser K. (eds) (2002) *New Approaches to Migration, Transnational Communities and the Transformation of Home*, London and New York: Routledge.

Alexander, C. (1997) "Authoritarianism and Civil Society in Tunisia," *Middle East Report*, 205: 34–8. October–December.

Al-Jazeera.net (2005) "*El-hukuma el-muritaniya tazeedu rawatib el-muwadhafeen 50%*," (The Mauritanian government increases employees' salaries by 50 percent), 28 December. Available at: http://www.aljazeera.net/news/archive/archive?ArchiveId=303145.

—— (2006) "Ziyara khassa: Ely Ould Mohamed Vall—Rihlat El-Inqilab," (A Private Visit: Ely Ould Mohamede Vall—The Journey of the Coup), 16 October. Available at: http://www.aljazeera.net/NR/exeres/B9CDB741-72A7-4227-82C8-89716BA6D5AC.htm.

—— (2007) "Mauritania poll set for run-off," 12 March. Available at: http://english.aljazeera.net/NR/exeres/1378BC7E-2E27-4D16-9560-BFFA9FEA8FEF.htm.

Al-Shahi, A. and Lawless, R. (eds) (2005) *Middle East and North African Immigrants in Europe*, London: Routledge.

Al-Wikala Al-Muritaniya lilanba (2007) "el-adid min buldan el-alam yushariku muritaniya hadath tanseeb raees el-jumhuriya," (A number of countries participate in Mauritania's presidential inauguration), 19 April. Available at: http://www.ami.mr/ar/2007/avril/19/13.html.

Amin, S. (1985) *Delinking: Towards a Polycentric World*, London: Zed Books.

—— (2003) "The Future of Global Polarization," in C. R. Goddard, P. Cronin, and K. C. Dash (eds) *International Political Economy: State-Market Relations in a Changing Global Order*, London: Lynne Rienner, pp. 179–89.

Amirah-Fernández, H. (2004a) "Morocco is Failing to Take Off," *Analysis ARI*, Elcano Royal Institute for International and Strategic Studies, 27 September. Available at: http://www.realinstitutoelcano.org/analisis/609.asp.

—— (2004b) "El Sáhara Occidental en las dinámicas internas intra-magrebíes," *Analysis ARI*, Elcano Royal Institute for International and Strategic Studies, 19 November. Available at: http://www.realinstitutoelcano.org/analisis/625.asp.

—— (2004c) "La vuelta de Libia a la escena internacional," *Anuario del Mediterráneo 2003*. Barcelona: IEMed-CIDOB.

—— (2006) "Libya's Return: Between Change and Continuity," *Analysis ARI*, Elcano Royal Institute for International and Strategic Studies, 1 June. Available at: http://www.realinstitutoelcano.org/analisis/986.asp.

—— and Youngs, R. (eds) (2005) *The Euro-Mediterranean Partnership: Assessing the First Decade*, Madrid: Elcano Royal Institute for International and Strategic Studies and FRIDE. Available at: http://www.realinstitutoelcano.org/publicaciones/libros/Barcelona10_eng.pdf.

Amnesty International (1990) *Tunisia: Summary of Amnesty International's Concerns in Tunisia*, London: Amnesty International.

—— (1992) *Tunisia: Heavy Sentences After Unfair Trials*, London: Amnesty International.

—— (1993) *Tunisia: Women Victims of Harassment, Torture and Imprisonment*, London: Amnesty International.

—— (1994) *Tunisia, Rhetoric versus Reality: The Failure of a Human Rights Bureaucracy*, London: Amnesty International.

—— (2006) *Spain and Morocco: Failure to Protect the Rights of Migrants - One Year On*, Report EUR 41/009/2006, 26 October. Available at: http://www.amnesty-eu.org/static/documents/2006/CeutaandMelillaReportOct2006.pdf.

Anderson, B. (1991) *Imagined Communities: Reflections on the Origins and Spread of Nationalism*, London: Verso.

Anderson, L. (1991a) "Absolutism and the Resilience of Monarchy in the Middle East," *Political Science Quarterly* 106, 1: 1–15.

—— (1991b) "Political Pacts, Liberalism, and Democracy: The Tunisian National Pact of 1988," *Government and Opposition* 26, 2: 244–60.

—— (1995) "Democracy in the Arab World: A Critique of the Political Culture Approach," in R. Brynen *et al.* (eds) *Political Liberalization and Democratization in the Arab World*, Boulder, CO and London: Lynne Rienner, pp. 77–91.

Article 19 Organization (1991) *Tunisia: Attacks on the Press and Government Critics*, London: Article 19 Organization.

Ayubi, N. (1995) *Over-stating the Arab State: Politics and Society in the Middle East*, London: I. B. Tauris.

Balfour, R. (2005) "Italy's Policies in the Mediterranean," in H. Amirah-Fernández and R. Youngs (eds) *The Euro-Mediterranean Partnership: Assessing the First Decade*, Madrid: Elcano Royal Institute for International and Strategic Studies and FRIDE, pp. 121–9.

Barbé, E. and Soler i Lecha, E. (2005) "Barcelona+10: Spanish Re-launch of the Euro-Mediterranean Partnership," *The International Spectator* 40, 2: 85–98, April–June.

Barros L., Lahlou M., Escoffier C., Pumares, P., and Ruspini, P. (2002) "L'immigration irrégulière subsaharienne à travers et vers le Maroc," *Cahiers de Migrations Internationales*, Geneva: International Labor Organization.

Beaugé, F. (2003) "Sahara Occidental: pour le Maroc, le plan Baker 'n'est plus à l'ordre du jour'", *Le Monde*, 25 June.

Bekouchi, M. H. (2003) *La diaspora Marocaine: une chance ou un handicap*, Rabat: La Croisée des Chemins.

Belguendouz, A. (2003) *Le Maroc non africain, gendarme de l'Europe? Alerte au projet de loi no. 02/03 relative à l'entrée et au séjour des étrangers au Maroc, à l'émigration et l'immigration irreguilières*, Rabat: Inter-Graph.

Belkhodja, T. (1998) *Les trois décennies Bourguiba*, Paris: Publisud.

Bellamy, R. and Schecter, D. (1993) *Gramsci and the Italian State*, Manchester: Manchester University Press.

Benantar, A. (2006) "NATO, Maghreb and Europe," *Mediterranean Politics* 11, 2: 167–88.

Ben-Dor, G. (1999) "Minorities in the Middle East: Theory and Practice," in O. Bengio and G. Ben-Dor (eds) *Minorities and the State in the Arab World*, Boulder, CO and London: Lynne Rienner, pp. 1–28.

Ben El Hassan Alaoui, M. (1994) *La coopération entre l'Union Européenne et les pays du Maghreb*, Paris: Nathan.

Ben Jelloun, T. (2004) *This Blinding Absence of Light*, New York: The New Press.

Bensaad, A. (2004) "Agadez, carrefour migratoire sahélo-maghrébin," *Revue Européenne des Migrations Internationales* 19, 1: 7–28.

—— (2005) "Les migrations transsahariennes, une mondialisation par la marge," *Maghreb Machrek*, no. 185, pp. 13–35.

Beresford, D. (2003) "Writes, and wrongs, of war," *Guardian Unlimited*, 26 January. Available at: http://www.guardian.co.uk/Iraq/Story/0,884154,00.html.

Bianchi, R. (1989) *Unruly Corporatism: Associational Life in Twentieth-century Egypt*, New York and Oxford: Oxford University Press.

Bianchi, S. (2005) "Trade: The Day the EU Got Cheesy about Camels," *Global Information Network*, 27 May.

Bonilla, M. (1998) "Algeria's Reform Program Promotes Economic Growth and Transition to the Market," *International Monetary Fund, Survey* 27, 17: 31, August.

Bouandel, Y. (2001) "The presidential election in Algeria, April 1999," *Electoral Studies* 20, 1: 157–63, March.

Boubakri, H. (2004a) "Transit migration between Tunisia, Libya and Sub-Saharan Africa: Study Based on Greater Tunis," Paper presented at Council of Europe Regional Conference on Migrants in Transit Countries: Sharing Responsibility for Management and Protection, Istanbul, September–October.

—— (2004b) "Les migrations de transit au Maghreb, ou les recompositions migratoires au voisinage de l'Europe," *Proasile, la revue de France Terre d'Asile,* no. 10, pp. 26–31, June.

Boukhari, A. (2004) "Las dimensiones internacionales del conflicto del Sáhara Occidental y sus repercusiones para una alternativa marroquí," *Working Paper,* Elcano Royal Institute for International and Strategic Studies, 19 April. Available at: http://www.realinstitutoelcano.org/documentos/99.asp.

Brand, L. (1998) *Women, the State, and Political Liberalization: Middle Eastern and North African Experiences,* New York: Columbia University Press.

Brenton, P., Baroncelli, E., and Malouche, M. (2006) "Trade and Investment Integration of the Maghreb," *MENA Working Paper* no. 44, Washington DC: World Bank.

Brett, M. and Fentress E. (1996) *The Berbers,* Oxford: Blackwell.

Brumberg, D. (1995) "Authoritarian Legacies and Reform Strategies in the Arab World," in R. Brynen *et al.* (eds) *Political Liberalization and Democratization in the Arab World,* Boulder, CO and London: Lynne Rienner, pp. 229–59.

Bryne, E. (2004) "After Baker," *Middle East International,* no. 728, pp. 23–4.

Brynen, R., Korany, B., and Noble, P. (eds) (1995) *Political Liberalization and Democratization in the Arab World: Theoretical Perspectives,* Boulder, CO: Lynne Rienner.

Burgat, F. (1993) *The Islamic Movement in North Africa,* trans. W. Dowell Austin, TX: Center for Middle East Studies, University of Texas.

Burnham, G. *et al.* (2006) *The Human Cost of the War in Iraq: A Mortality Study, 2002–2006,* by Bloomberg School of Public Health at Johns Hopkins University (Baltimore, MD), and the School of Medicine at Al Mustansiriya University (Baghdad), in cooperation with the Center for International Studies at the Massachusetts Institute of Technology (Cambridge, MA). Available at: http://i.a.cnn.net/cnn/2006/images/10/11/human.cost.of.war.pdf

Calderbank, S. (2005) "NATO and the Middle East," *Middle East International,* no. 742, pp. 30–1. Available at: http://meionline.com/features/318.shtml.

Cammet, M. (1999) "Defensive Integration and late Developers: The Gulf Cooperation Council and the Arab Maghreb Union," *Global Governance* 5, 3: 379–402.

Canales, P. (2005) "Marruecos culpa a España y a Argelia de estar tras las revueltas saharauis," *La Razón,* 29 May.

Castles, S. and Miller, M. (2003) *The Age of Migration: International population movements in the modern world,* Basingstoke: Palgrave.

Cebolla Boado, H. (2004) "Las decisiones en Marruecos se toman en el sur: Sobre el equilibrio entre francófilos e hispanófilos," Madrid: FRIDE. Available at: http://www.fride.org/Publications/Publication.aspx?Item=484.

Cembrero, I. (2006) *Vecinos alejados: los secretos de la crisis entre España y Marruecos,* Barcelona: Círculo de Lectores/Galaxia Gutenberg.

Chaabane, S. (1997) *Ben Ali on the Road to Pluralism in Tunisia,* Washington DC: American Educational Trust.

Charrad, M. (2001) *States and Women's Rights: The Making of Postcolonial Tunisia, Algeria, and Morocco,* Berkeley, CA: University of California Press.

Cissokoi, A. (2004) "Accord de libre échange Maroc/UE: un mirage économique," *Économie et Entreprise,* March.

Claret, A. (2004) "España–Magreb: hacia unas relaciones más articuladas," *Anuario del Mediterráneo/Mediterrranean Yearbook,* Barcelona: IEMed and CIDOB, pp. 47–9. Available at: http://www.medyearbook.com.

Collyer, M. (2004a) "The Development Impact of Temporary International Labor Migration on Southern Mediterranean Sending Countries: Contrasting examples of Morocco and Egypt," Development Research Center on Migration, Globalization and Poverty, Working Paper T6, University of Sussex. Available at: http://www.migrationdrc.org/publications/working_papers/WP-T6.pdf.

—— (2004b) "Undocumented sub-Saharan African Migrants in Morocco," Report for the Danish Institute for International Studies, November.

—— (2005) "When Do Social Networks Fail to Explain Migration? Accounting for the Movement of Algerian Asylum Seekers to the UK," *Journal of Ethnic and Migration Studies* 31, 4: 699–718.

Combs-Schilling, M. E. (1989) *Sacred Performances: Islam, Sexuality, and Sacrifice*, New York: Columbia University Press.

Cooper, I. (2000) "MKs return from first trip to Mauritania," *The Jerusalem Post*, (11 April).

Coslovi, L. (2006) "L'impatto delle migrazioni di transito sui Paesi nordafricani: I risultati di una consultazione fra esperti." Available at: http://www.sidint.org/migration/html/publications.html.

Coustillière, J. F. (2005) "Méditerranée: '5 + 5' et initiative de sécurité," *Défense Nationale et sécurité collective*, no. 5, pp. 76–83.

Crawford, D. (2005) "Royal Interest in Local Culture: Amazigh Culture and the Moroccan State," in M. Shatzmiller (ed.) *Nationalism and Minority Identities in Islamic Societies*, Montreal and Kingston: McGill-Queen's University Press.

—— and Hoffman, K. E. (2000) "Essentially Amazigh: Urban Berbers and the Global village," in R. K. Lacey and R. M. Coury (eds) *The Arab-African and Islamic Worlds: Interdisciplinary Studies*, New York: Peter Lang.

Crombois, J. F. (2005) "The US-Morocco Free Trade agreement," *Mediterranean Politics* 10, 2: 219–23.

Dahl, R. (1971) *Polyarchy: Participation and Opposition*, New Haven, CT: Yale University Press.

Daure-Serfaty, C. (2003) *Letter from Morocco*, trans. P. R. Côté and C. Mitchell, East Lansing, MI: Michigan State University Press.

Deeb, M. J. (1989) "Inter-Maghribi Relations since 1969: A Study of the Modalities of Unions and Mergers," *Middle East Journal* 43, 1: 20–33.

De Haas, H. (2003) *Migration and Development in Southern Morocco: The Disparate Socio-Economic Impacts of Out-Migration on the Toggha Oasis Valley*, published PhD thesis, University of Nijmegen, Amsterdam.

Denoeux, G. and Maghraoui, A. (1998) "King Hassan's Strategy of Political Dualism," *Middle East Policy* 5, 4: 104–30.

Desrues, T. and Moyano, E. (2001) "Social Change and Political Transition in Morocco," *Mediterranean Politics* 6, 1: 21–47.

Echeverría Jesús, C. (2005a) "Las políticas de seguridad y de defensa de los países del Magreb," *Working Paper*, Elcano Royal Institute for International and Strategic Studies, 3 March. Available at: http://www.realinstitutoelcano.org/documentos/178.asp.

—— (2005b) "La cooperación en asuntos de justicia e interior y el proceso de Barcelona: un balance," *UNISCI Discussion Papers* no. 9, pp. 83–92.

Economist Intelligence Unit (1997) *Tunisia: Country Profile 1997-98*, London: Economist Intelligence Unit.

—— (2001) *Country Profile Morocco 2000/2001*, London: EIU.

—— (2002) *Tunisia Country Report*, London: EIU.

—— (2004) *Country Report: Morocco 2004–05*, London: EIU.

—— (2005a) *Country Report Morocco 2005*, London: EIU.

—— (2005b) "Mauritania: Economic structure," *EIU ViewsWire*.

—— (2006) *Country Report Morocco 2006*, London: EIU.

Eizenstat, S. E. (1999) Third Annual Les Aspin Memorial Lecture, Washington Institute for Near East Policy, Washington DC, 8 March.

Embassy of the United States, Nouakchott, Mauritania (2007) "Press Release: American Government Satisfied with Good Conduct of Elections in Mauritania," 26 March. Available at: http://mauritania.usembassy.gov/pr26-03-07.html.

Energy Economist (2005) "Will Oil Discoveries Change Mauritania?" *Energy Economist*, no. 282, pp. 21–4.

Energy Information Administration (2004) *Arab Maghreb Union: Country Analysis Briefs*, Washington DC: US Department of Energy.

Eno, B. (2003) "Lessons in how to lie about Iraq," *Guardian Unlimited*, 17 August. Available at: http://www.guardian.co.uk/Iraq/Story/0,1020467,00.html.

Entelis J. P. (ed.) (1997) *Islam, Democracy, and the State in North Africa*, Indianapolis, IN: Indiana University Press.

Escribano Francés, G. (2000) "Euro-Mediterranean versus Arab Integration: Are They Compatible?" *Journal of Development and Economic Policies* 3, 1: 25–42, December.

—— (2006) "Europeanization without Europe? The Mediterranean and the Neighbourhood Policy," *Working Paper of the Robert Schuman Centre for Advanced Studies* no. 19, Florence: European University Institute.

—— and Jordán J. M. (1999) "Sub-regional Integration in the MENA Region and the Euro-Mediterranean Free Trade Area," *Mediterranean Politics* 4, 2: 133–48.

—— and Lorca A. (2001) "The Euro-Mediterranean Free Trade Area and Modernization in the Maghreb," in F. Attinà and S. Stavridis (eds) *The Barcelona Process and the Euro-Mediterranean Issues from Stuttgart to Marseille*, Pubblicazioni della Facoltà di Scienze Politiche no. 11.

—— and San Martín González, E. (2005) "Los altibajos en la europeización de la política exterior española," paper presented at the Jornadas de Política Económica, Universidad de Vigo, 24–25 November. Available at: http://webs.uvigo.es/viijpe/pdf/ESCRIBANO-SANMARTIN.pdf.

Esposito, J. (1992) *The Islamic Threat: Myth or Reality?* New York: Oxford University Press.

—— and Piscatori, J. (1991) "Democratization and Islam," *Middle East Journal* 45, 3: 427–40.

Europa Press Releases (2006) "Mauritania: New Measures to Combat Illegal Immigration towards the EU," 10 July. Available at: http://europa.eu/rapid/pressReleases Action.do?reference=IP/06/967&.

European Commission (2004) *Improving Access to Durable Solutions COM 410 final*.

European Commission – Directorate General for Economic and Financial Affairs (2004) "Economic Review of EU Mediterranean Partners," Occasional Paper no. 6, February, Brussels.

Fargues, P. (2001) "La génération du changement," *Monde Arabe Maghreb-Machrek*, no. 171–2.

—— (2002) "Les politiques migratoires en Méditerranée Occidentale: contexte, contenu, perspectives," Tunis, Dialogue on Migration in the Western Mediterranean.

Faria, F. (1994) "Politiques de sécurité au Maghreb. Les impératifs de la stabilité intérieure," *Cahiers du Lumiar*, no. 1.

Feliú, L. (2005) "Spain and the Maghreb during the Second Legislature of the People's Party: An Exceptional Period," *Working Paper* no. 9, Madrid: FRIDE, May.

Femia, J. (1981) *Gramsci's Political Thought: Hegemony, Consciousness, and the Revolutionary Process*, Oxford: Clarendon Press.

FEMISE (2005a) *Profil Pays Maroc*, Marseille: Institut de la Méditerranée.

—— (2005b) *Profil Pays Tunisie*, Marseille: Institut de la Méditerranée.

—— (2006) *Profil Pays Algérie*, Marseille: Institut de la Méditerranée.

Fernández Arias, C. (2005), "Sahara Occidental: un año después de Baker," *Política Exterior*, no. 107, pp. 73–82, September–October.

—— (2006) "Magreb," *Panorama Estratégico 2005/2006*, Instituto Español de Estudios Estratégicos and Elcano Royal Institute for International and Strategic Studies, pp. 149–70.

Ferrié, J. N. (1999) "Chronique politique: Succession monarchique et désenchantement de l'alternance partisane," in *Annuaire de l'Afrique du Nord*. Paris: CNRS.

Fibla, C. (2005) "El Frente POLISARIO califica de 'Intifada' los enfrentamientos que afectan a El Aaiún," *La Vanguardia*, 28 May.

Fondation Hassan II pour les Marocains Résidant à l'Etranger and IOM (2003) *Marocains de l'Extérieur*, Rabat. Fondation Hassan II pour les Marocains Résidant à l'Etranger.

Ford, N. (2003) "Mauritania on the Verge of Success," *The Middle East*, no. 336, pp. 53–5, July.

Fukuyama, F. (2004) *State-Building. Governance and World Order in the 21st Century*, Ithaca, NY: Cornell University Press.

García Alvarez-Coque, J. M. (2002) "Agricultural Trade and the Barcelona Process: is Full Liberalization Possible?" *European Review of Agricultural Economics* 29, 3: 399–422.

Geddes, A. (2003) *The Politics of Migration and Immigration in Europe*, London: Sage.

Gellner, E. and Micaud, C. (eds) (1973) *Arabs and Berbers: From Tribe to Nation in North Africa*, London: Duckworth.

General Agreement on Tariffs and Trade Organization (1994) *Trade Policy Review: Tunisia*, Geneva: GATT.

George, S. (1992) "Uses and Abuses of African Debt: The International Squeeze on Poor Countries," *Dissent* 39, 3: 341–2.

Ghorbal, S. (2005) "Washington prend les choses en mains," *L'Intelligent*, 28 August.

Gillespie, R. (2001) *Spain and the Western Mediterranean*, ESRC Research Program "One Europe or Several?" Working Paper 37/01, Brighton: University of Sussex.

—— (2004) "Spain and Morocco: A Case of Crisis in Euro-Mediterranean Relations," paper presented at the ECPR Standing Group on the European Union, Second Pan-European Conference on EU Politics, "Implications of a Wider Europe: Politics, Institutions and Diversity," Bologna, June.

—— (2006) "This Stupid Little Island': A Neighborhood Confrontation in the Western Mediterranean," *International Politics* 43, 1: 110–32. February.

—— (2007) "Límites del voluntarismo español en el Magreb," *Afkar/Ideas*, no. 13, pp. 48–50. Available at: http://www.iemed.org/afkar/13/18Gillespie.pdf.

—— and Youngs, R. (eds), *The European Union and Democracy Promotion: The Case of North Africa*, London and Portland, OR: Frank Cass, 2002.

Gränzer, S. (1999) "Changing Human Rights Discourse: Transnational Advocacy Networks in Tunisia and Morocco," in T. Risse, S. C. Ropp, and K. Sikkink (eds) *The Power of Human Rights: International Norms and Domestic Change*, New York: Cambridge University Press.

Guendouzi, B. and Kadri, K. (1998) "Les retombées de l'adjustement structurel sur le développement local en Algérie," *Les Cahiers du CREAD*, pp. 46–7.

Habermas, J. (1998) "On the Relation between the Nation, the Rule of Law, and Democracy," in C. Cronin and P. De Greiff (eds) *The Inclusion of the Other: Studies in Political Theory*, Cambridge, MA: The MIT Press, pp. 129–53.

Hamdi, M. E. (1998) *The Politicization of Islam: A Case Study of Tunisia*, Boulder, CO: Westview Press.

Hammoudi, A. (1997) *Master and Disciple: The Cultural Foundations of Moroccan Authoritarianism*, Chicago, IL: Chicago University Press.

Harik, I. (1992) "Privatization and Development in Tunisia," in I. Harik, and D. J. Sullivan (eds) *Privatization and Liberalization in the Middle East*. Indianapolis, IN: Indiana University Press, pp. 210–32.

Haut Commissariat au Plan (2005) "Recensement general de la population et de l'Habitat 2004." Available at: http://www.recensement.hcp.ma.

Hegel, G. W. F. (1952) *Grundlinein der Philosophie des Rechts [Hegel's Philosophy of Right]*, trans. T. M. Knox, London: Oxford University Press.

Held, D. (1996) *Models of Democracy*, Cambridge: Polity Press.

Henardt, J. (2005) "Évolutions de la politique américaine au Moyen-Orient et au Maghreb," in R. Leveau and F. Charillon (eds) *Afrique du Nord Moyen-Orient. Les incertitudes du "Grand Moyen-Orient"*, Paris: La documentation française.

Herce, J. A. and Sosvilla-Rivero, S. (2005) "El no-Magreb: implicaciones económicas para (y más allá de) la región," *Working Paper*, Elcano Royal Institute for International and Strategic Studies. Available at: http://www. realinstitutoelcano.org/documentos/181.asp.

Hermassi, A. (1991) "The Islamicist Movement and November 7," in I. W. Zartman (ed.) *Tunisia: The Political Economy of Reform*, Boulder, CO: Lynne Rienner, pp. 193–204.

—— (1993) "State, Legitimacy, and Democratization in the Maghreb," in E. Goldberg *et al.* (eds), *Rules and Rights in the Middle East – Democracy, Law, and Society*, Seattle: University of Washington Press.

—— (1994) "Socio-economic Change and Political Implications: The Maghreb," in G. Salamé (ed.) *Democracy without Democrats: The Renewal of Politics in the Muslim World?* London: I. B. Tauris, pp. 227–42.

—— (1995) "The Rise and Fall of the Islamist Movement in Tunisia," in L. Guazzone (ed.) *The Islamist Dilemma: The Political Role of Islamist Movements in the Contemporary Arab World*, Reading: Ithaca Press, pp. 105–27.

Hernando de Larramendi, M. (1997) *La política exterior de Marruecos*, Madrid: Mapfre.

—— (2006) "La politique étrangère de l'Espagne envers le Maghreb: De l'adhésion à l'Union européenne à la guerre contre l'Iraq (1986–2004)," *L'Année du Maghreb 2004. Dossier: L'espace euro-maghrébin*, Paris: CNRS Editions, pp. 27–43.

—— and López García, B. (2004), "Nuevo impulso diplomático en el Sáhara," *Afkar/Ideas*, no. 4, pp. 22–6. Available at: http://www.iemed.org/afkar/4/ebernabe.php.

—— and Bravo F. (2006) "La frontière hispano-marocaine à l'épreuve de l'immigration sub-saharienne," *L'Année du Maghreb 2004*, Paris: CNRS, pp. 153–71.

Hodd, M. (2004) "Algeria: Economic Structure, Performance and Policy, 1950–2001," in A. Aghrout (ed.) *Algeria in Transition: Reforms and Development Prospects*, London and New York: Routledge.

Howe, M. (2005) *Morocco: The Islamist Awakening and Other Challenges*, New York: Oxford University Press.

Hudson, M. (1988) "Democratization and the Problem of Legitimacy in Arab Politics," *Middle East Studies Association Bulletin* 22, 2: 22–37.

—— (1995) "The Political Culture Approach to Arab Democratization: The Case for Bringing It Back In, Carefully," in R. Brynen *et al.* (eds) *Political Liberalization and Democratization in the Arab World*, Boulder, CO and London: Lynne Rienner, pp. 61–76.

Huntington, S. (1993) "The Clash of Civilizations?" *Foreign Affairs* 72, 3: 22–49.

Ibrahim, S. (1993) "Crises, Elites and Democratization in the Arab World," *Middle East Journal* 47, 2: 292–305.

Impagliazzo, M. (nd) *The St Egidio Platform for a Peaceful Solution of the Algerian Crisis*. Available at: http://www.usip.org/pubs/peaceworks/smock20/chap3_20.html.

International Crisis Group (2003) *Unrest and Impasse in Kabylia*, Middle East/North Africa Report no. 15, 10 June. Available at: http://www.crisisgroup.org/home/index.cfm?id=1415&l=1.

—— (2004) *Islamism, Violence and Reform in Algeria: Turning the Page (Islamism in North Africa III)*, Middle East Report no. 29, Cairo/Brussels.

—— (2005a) *Islamist Terrorism in the Sahel: Fact or Fiction?* Africa Report no. 92, Dakar/Brussels.

—— (2005b) *L'Islamisme en Afrique du Nord IV: Contestation islamiste en Mauritanie: menace ou bouc émissaire*, Rapport Moyen-Orient/Afrique du Nord no. 41, Cairo/Brussels.

International Monetary Fund (2003) *Staff Report for the 2003 Article IV Consultation: Morocco*, Washington DC: International Monetary Fund.

—— (2004) "Balance of payments statistics yearbook," Washington DC: International Monetary Fund.

—— (2006) "Islamic Republic of Mauritania: Staff Report for the 2006 Article IV Consultation, First Assessment of the Staff-Monitored Program, and Assessment of Qualification for the Multilateral Debt Relief Initiative; International Monetary Fund Country Report no. 06/272; 7 June 2006." Available at: http://www.imf.org/external/pubs/ft/scr/2006/cr06272.pdf.

—— (2007a) "Islamic Republic of Mauritania: Poverty Reduction Strategy Paper, January." Available at: http://www.imf.org/external/pubs/ft/scr/2007/cr0740.pdf.

—— (2007b) "Statement by the International Monetary Fund Mission on the First Review Under the Islamic Republic of Mauritania's PRGF-Supported Program, Press Release no. 07/33, 27 February." Available at: http://www.imf.org/external/np/sec/pr/2007/pr0733.htm.

International Organization for Migration (2005) *World Migration 2005: Costs and benefits of international migration*, Geneva: International Organization for Migration.

IslamOnline (2002) "Mauritanian Opposition Slams Peres Visit." Available at: http://www.islamonline.net/English/News/2002-10/09/article04.shtml.

Israel Ministry of Foreign Affairs (2005) *Public Statement: Israel-Mauritania to Open Interest Sections, 27 November 1995*.

Jerch, M., Escribano Francés, G., and Lorca, A. (2002) "The Impact of Migration from the Mediterranean on European Security," in A. Vasconcelos (ed.) *A*

European Strategic Concept for the Mediterranean, Lumiar Papers no. 9, Lisbon: IEEI.

Jessop, B. (1999) *Narrating the Future of the National Economy and the National State? Remarks on Remapping Regulation and Reinventing Governance Keywords,* Department of Sociology at Lancaster University. Available at: http://www.lancs.ac.uk/fss/sociology/papers/jessop-narrating-the-future.pdf.

Joffé, G. (1998) "The Moroccan Political System after the Elections," *Mediterranean Politics* 3, 3: 106–25.

—— (2001) "Libya and Europe," *The Journal of North African Studies,* 6, 4: 75–92.

—— (2005) "Libya's Saharan Destiny," *The Journal of North African Studies* 10, 3–4: 605–17.

Johansson-Nogués, E. (2004) "A 'Ring of Friends'? The Implications of the European Neighbourhood Policy for the Mediterranean," *Mediterranean Politics* 9, 2: 240–7.

Katz, S. (2003) "Moroccan–US FTA," paper read at Tangier American Legation Museum, 30 May.

Kayser, B. (1996) *Méditerranée: une géographie de la fracture,* Aix-en-Provence: EDISUD.

Keenan, J. (2004) "Terror in the Sahara: the Implications of US Imperialism for North and West Africa," *Review of African Political Economy* 31, 101: 475–96.

Khairallah, C. (1957) *Le Mouvement Jeune Tunisien: essai d'histoire et de synthèse des mouvements nationalistes tunisiens,* Tunis: Bonici.

King, R. (1998) "The Political Logic of Economic Reform in Tunisia," in A. Layachi (ed.) *Economic Crisis and Political Change in North Africa,* Connecticut and London: Praeger, pp. 107–28.

Kingdom of Morocco (Ministry of Industry, Commerce, Energy, and Mines) and the World Bank (2002) *Morocco Manufacturing at the Turn of the Century: Results of the Firm Analysis and Competitiveness Survey,* Casablanca and Washington DC.

Krasner, S. D. (2005) "The Case for Shared Sovereignty," *Journal of Democracy* 16, 1: 69–83.

Krichen, A. (1992) *Le syndrome Bourguiba,* Tunis: Cérès Productions.

Krugman, P. (1992) "Regionalism versus Multilateralism: Analytical Notes," in J. De Melo and A. Panagariya, *New Dimensions in Regional Integration,* Cambridge University Press, pp. 58–84.

Kumar, S. (2005) "Mauritania – Having Some of the Richest Fishing Grounds in the World is a Blessing and a Curse for Mauritania," *World Fishing,* pp. 12–13, February.

Kuper, L. (1969) "Ethnic and Racial Pluralism: Some Aspects of Polarization and Depluralization," in L. Kuper and M. G. Smith (eds) *Pluralism in Africa,* Berkeley, CA: University of California Press, pp. 459–87.

Lahlou, M., Barros, L., Escoffier, C., Pumares, P., and Ruspini, P. (2002) "L'immigration irrégulière subsaharienne à travers et vers le Maroc," *Cahiers de Migrations Internationales,* Geneva: International Labor Organization.

Landor, J. (2005) "Operation Flintlock," *Middle East International,* no. 754, pp. 21–2.

Lavenex, S. and Uçarer, E. (2002) "The Emergent EU Migration regime and its external impact," in S. Lavenex and E. Uçarer (eds) *Migration and the Externalities of European Integration,* Oxford: Lexington, pp. 1–13.

Lawrence, R. Z. (2003) "Regionalism, Multilateralism and Deeper Integration: Changing Paradigms for Developing Countries," in C. R. Goddard, P. Cronin, and K. C. Dash (eds) *International Political Economy: State–Market Relations in a Changing Global Order*, London: Lynne Rienner, pp. 391–412.

Layachi, A. (2005) "The Berbers in Algeria: Politicized Ethnicity and Ethnicized Politics," in M. Shatzmiller (ed.) *Nationalism and Minority Identities in Islamic Societies,* Montreal and Kingston: McGill-Queen's University Press.

Le Gall, M. (1993) "The Historical Context," in I. W. Zartman and M. Habeeb (eds) *Polity and Society in Contemporary North Africa*, Boulder, CO: Westview.

Leveau, R. (1985) *Le fellah marocain, défenseur du trône*, 2nd Edition, Paris: Presses de la Fondation Nationale des Sciences Politiques.

Levinson, A. (2005) "The Regularization of Unauthorized Migrants: Literature Survey and Country Case Studies, Regularization Programs in Spain and Italy," COMPAS Working Paper, University of Oxford. Available at: http://www.compas.ox.ac.uk/publications/papers/Country%20Case%20Spain.pdf.

Linz, J. J. and Stepan, A. (1996) *Problems of Democratic Transition and Consolidation: Southern Europe, South America and Post-Communist Europe*, Baltimore, MD: Johns Hopkins University Press.

López García, B. (2000) *Marruecos en trance. Nuevo rey. Nuevo siglo ¿Nuevo régimen?* Madrid: Biblioteca Nueva.

—— and Hernando de Larramendi, M. (2002) "Spain and North Africa: Towards a 'Dynamic Stability," *Democratization* 9, 1: 170–91.

—— and Berriane M. (dirs) (2004) *Atlas de la inmigración marroquí en España*, Taller de Estudios Internacionales Mediterráneos. Madrid: Ediciones UAM.

—— and Hernando de Larramendi, M. (2005) "El Sáhara Occidental, obstáculo a la construcción magrebí," *Working Paper*, Elcano Royal Institute for International and Strategic Studies. Available at: http://www.realinstitutoelcano.org/documentos/184.asp.

Lorca, A. and Escribano Francés, G. (1998) *Las Economías del Magreb. Opciones para el Siglo XXI*, Madrid: Pirámide.

—— *et al.* (2006) "Hacía un Pacto Agrícola Euro-mediterráneo," in *La agricultura y la Asociación Euromediterránea: retos y oportunidades*, Barcelona: IEMed, pp. 68–83.

Lorcin, P. M. E. (1995) *Imperial Identities: Stereotyping, Prejudice and Race in Colonial Algeria*, London: I. B. Tauris.

Mack, D. L. (2005) "Libya: An Alternative Paradigm," *Foreign Service Journal*, October, pp. 45–8.

Maddy-Weitzman, B. (2001) "Contested Identities: Berbers, 'Berberism,' and the State in North Africa," *The Journal of North African Studies* 6, 3: 23–47.

—— (2005) "Women, Islam, and the Moroccan State: the struggle over the personal status law," *Middle East Journal* 59, 3: 393–411.

—— and Zisenwine, D. (eds), *The Maghrib in the New Century: Identity, Religion, and Politics*, Gainesville, FL: University of Florida Press, 2007

Maghraoui, A. (2001) "From Symbolic Legitimacy to Democratic Legitimacy: Monarchic Rule and Political Reform in Morocco," *Journal of Democracy* 12, 1: 73–86.

—— (2004) "Country Report: Morocco," *Freedom House Countries at the Crossroads*. Available at: http://www.freedomhouse.org/modules/publications/ccr/modPrintVersion.cfm?edition=1&ccrpage=5&ccrcountry=56.

Mahiou, A. and Henry, J. R. (eds) (2001) *Où va l'Algérie*, Paris: Editions Karthala.

Mañé, A. (2006) "European Energy Security: Towards the Creation of the Geo-energy Space," *Energy Policy* 34, 18: 3773–86.

Mansur, A. (2005) "Pourquoi tant de haine?" *Maroc Hebdo International*, no. 654, pp. 16–17.

Mares, P. (2002) *Borderline: Australia's response to refugees and asylum seekers in the wake of the Tampa*, Sydney: UNSW Press.

Martin, P. (1993) "Trade and Migration: NAFTA and Agriculture (Policy Analyses in International Economics)," Washington DC: Institute for International Economics.

Martinez, L. (2003) "La sécurité en Algérie et en Libye après le 11 septembre," *EuroMeSCo Paper* no. 22. Available at: http://www.euromesco.net/media/euro mescopaper22.pdf.

—— (2005) "Les enjeux de la réorientation de la politique libyenne," in R. Leveau and F. Charillon (eds) *Afrique du Nord Moyen-Orient. Les incertitudes du "Grand Moyen-Orient,"* Paris: La documentation française, pp. 111–27.

Marty, M. (2002) "Mauritania: Political Parties, Neo-patrimonialism and Democracy," *Democratization* 9, 3: 92–108.

Mellah, S. and Rivoire J. B. (2005) "El Para, the Maghreb's Bin Laden," *Le Monde Diplomatique*, February.

Mezhoud, S. (1993) "Glasnost the Algerian Way: The Role of Berber Nationalists in Political Reform," in G. Joffé (ed.) *North Africa: Nation, State and Region*, London: Routledge.

Mezran, K. (1998) "Maghribi Foreign Policies and the Internal Security Dimension," *The Journal of North African Studies* 3, 1: 1–24.

Micaud, C. (1964) *Tunisia: the Politics of Modernisation*. London: Pall Mall.

Mohammed VI (2003) *Full text of the speech delivered by King Mohammed VI on 29 May. Casablanca*: Available at: http://www.mincom.gov.ma/english/generalities/ speech/2003/casablanca_attacks.htm.

Mohsen-Finan, K. (1997) *Sahara occidental. Les enjeux d'un conflit régional*, Paris: CNRS-Histoire.

—— (2005) "Le Maghreb entre ouvertures nécessaires et autoritarismes possibles," T. de Montbrial and P. Moreau Defargues (eds) *Ramses. Rapport annuel mondial sur le système économique et les stratégies*, Paris: Dunod.

—— (2006) "Western Sahara: A Difficult Crisis to Resolve," *Med2006. Mediterranean Yearbook*, Barcelona: IEMed and CIDOB, pp. 117–18. Available at: http:// www.medyearbook.com.

Moore, C. H. (1965) *Tunisia since Independence: The Dynamics of One-Party Government*, Berkeley, CA: University of California Press.

—— (1988) "Tunisia and Bourguibisme: Twenty Years of Crisis," *Third World Quarterly* 10, 1: 176–90.

Moré, I. (2004) "The Economic Step between Neighbors: The Case of Spain–Morocco," *Mediterranean Politics* 9, 2: 165–200, summer.

Mortimer, R. A. (1989) "Maghreb Matters," *Foreign Policy*, no. 76: pp. 160–75.

—— (1993) "The Greater Maghreb and the Western Sahara," in Y. H. Zoubir and D. Volman (eds) *International dimensions of the Western Sahara Conflict*, Westport, CT: Praeger, pp. 169–85.

—— (1996) "Islamists, Soldiers, and Democrats: The Second Algerian War," *Middle East Journal* 50, 1: 19–39, winter.

—— (1997) "Algeria: The Dialectic of Elections and Violence," *Current History* 96, 610: 231–5, May.

—— (1999) "The Arab Maghreb Union: Myth and Reality," in Y. H. Zoubir (ed.) *North Africa in Transition. State, Society, and Economic Transformation in the 1990s*, Gainesville, FL: University Press of Florida, pp. 177–91.

—— (2004) "Bouteflika and the Challenge of Political Stability," in Ahmed Aghrout and R. M. Bougherira (eds), *Algeria in Transition: Reforms and Development Prospects*, London and New York, RoutledgeCurzon.

Mundy, J. A. (2004) "'Seized of the Matter': The UN and the Western Sahara Dispute," *Mediterranean Quarterly* 15, 3: 130–48.

—— (2006) "Neutrality or Complicity?: The United States and the 1975 Moroccan Takeover of the Spanish Sahara," *The Journal of North African Studies* 11, 3: 275–306, September.

—— (2007) "Western Sahara: Against Autonomy," *Foreign Policy in Focus*, 24 April. Available at: http://www.fpif.org/fpiftxt/4172.

Munson, H. (1993) *Religion and Power in Morocco*, New Haven, CT: Yale University Press.

Murphy, E. (1997) "Ten Years On – Ben Ali's Tunisia," *Mediterranean Politics* 2, 3: 114–22, winter.

—— (1999) *Economic and Political Change in Tunisia: From Bourguiba to Ben Ali*, London: Macmillan.

Nashashibi, K. *et al.* (1998) "Algeria: Stabilization and Transition to the Market," *International Monetary Fund Occasional Paper 165*, Washington DC: International Monetary Fund, 6 August.

Naylor, P. C. (2000) *France and Algeria – A History of Decolonization and Transformation*, Gainesville, FL: University Press of Florida.

Niblock, T. (2001) *Pariah States and Sanctions in the Middle East: Iraq, Libya, Sudan*, Boulder, CO: Lynne Rienner.

Nir, Ori (2006) "Congress Differs With Israel, Bush Over Aid to Palestinians," *Forward*, 10 February.

Nisan, M. (1991) *Minorities in the Middle East: A History of Struggle and Self-Expression*, North Carolina and London: McFarland Publishers.

Norton, A. R. (1993) "The Future of Civil Society in the Middle East," *Middle East Journal* 47, 2: 205–16, spring.

—— (1995) "Introduction," in A. R. Norton (ed.) *Civil Society in the Middle East*, Leiden: Brill.

Núñez Villaverde, J. A. (2005) "Spanish Policy towards the Euro-Mediterranean Partnership," in H. Amirah-Fernández and R. Youngs (eds) *The Euro-Mediterranean Partnership: Assessing the First Decade*, Madrid: Elcano Royal Institute for International and Strategic Studies and FRIDE, pp. 103–9.

Nyberg-Sorenson, N., Van Hear, N., and Engberg Pedersen, P. (2002) "The Migration Development Nexus: Evidence and Policy Options," *International Migration* 40, 5: 49–71.

Oil and Gas Journal (2004) "Explorers Prepare to Evaluate Taoudeni Basin in Mali, Mauritania," *Oil and Gas Journal*, 6 December, pp. 42–3.

Oommen, T. K. (1997) *Citizenship, Nationality and Ethnicity*, Cambridge: Polity Press.

Osava, M. (2005) "South America: Summit with Arab countries Takes on Touchy Issues," *Global Information Network*, 12 May, p. 1.

—— M. and Riley, M. (2006) "Morocco: From Top–Down Reform to Democratic Transition?" *Carnegie Papers Middle East Series* no. 71, Carnegie Endowment for International Peace, September.

Oualalou, F. (1996) *Après Barcelone...Le Maghreb est nécessaire*, Paris: L'Harmattan.

Ouazani C. and Kéfi, R. (2005) "Union du Maghreb Arabe: Second souffle?" *Jeune Afrique l'Intelligent*, no. 2315, p. 11.

Oufkir, M. *et al.* (2002) *Stolen Lives: Twenty Years in a Desert Jail*, New York: Hyperion Books.

Ould-Mey, M. (1994) "Global Adjustment: Implications for Peripheral States," *Third World Quarterly* 15, 2: 319–36.

—— (1995) "Democratization in Africa: The Political Face of SAPs," *Journal of Third World Studies* 12, 2: 122–58.

—— (1996) *Global Restructuring and Peripheral States: The Carrot and the Stick in Mauritania*, Lanham, MD: Littlefield Adams Books.

—— (1998a) "Structural Adjustment Programs and Democratization in Africa," in J. M. Mbaku and J. O. Ihonvbere (eds) *Multiparty Democracy and Political Change: Constraints to Democratization in Africa*, Brookfield: Ashgate, pp. 33–63.

—— (1998b) "Denationalization of the Mauritanian State," in J. Pickles and A. Smith (eds) *Theorizing Transition: The Political Economy of Post-Communist Transformations*, New York: Routledge, pp. 389–407.

—— (1999) "The New Global Command Economy," *Environment and Planning D: Society and Space* 17, 2: 155–80.

—— (2003) "Currency Devaluation and Resource Transfer from the South to the North," *Annals of the Association of American Geographers* 93, 2: 463–84.

—— (2005) "The Non-Jewish Origin of Zionism," *International Journal of the Humanities* 1, 1: 591–610.

—— (forthcoming 2007) "US-Mauritania Relations and the *Coriolis Force* of Normalization with Israel," in Abdennour Benantar (ed.) *Les Etats-Unis et le Maghreb: un regain d'intérêt*, Algiers: CREAD.

Ouzzani, Ch. (2005) "Une visite pour quoi faire?" *L'Intelligent/Jeune Afrique*, no. 2305, p. 52.

Owen, R. (1992) *State, Power and Politics in the Making of the Modern Middle East*, London and New York: Routledge.

Oxfam (2005) *Foreign Territory: The Internationalization of EU Asylum Policy*, Oxford: Oxfam GB.

Parry, G. and Moran, M. (1994) "Introduction: Problems of Democracy and Democratization," in G. Parry and M. Moran (eds) *Democracy and Democratization*, London: Routledge, pp. 1–17.

Parti Démocratique Amazigh Marocain (2005) *Déclaration Finale du PDAM*. Available at: http://amazighworld.net/news/publicopinion/index_show.php?article=292.

Planet, A. and Hernando de Larramendi, M. (2003) "Maroc–Espagne: la crise de l'îlot du Persil," in R. Leveau (ed.) *Afrique du Nord Moyen-Orient. Espaces et conflits*, Paris: Les études de la Documentation française.

Plateforme pour une Solution Politique et Pacifique de la Crise Algérienne (1995) *Available at*: http://members.tripod.com/~AlgeriaWatch/rome.html.

Pliez, O. (ed.) (2004) *La nouvelle Libye. Sociétés, espaces et géopolitique au lendemain de l'embargo*, Paris: Karthala.

Pointier, L. (2004) *Sahara occidental. La controverse devant les Nations unies*, Paris: Karthala-Institut Maghreb Europe.

Przeworski, A. *et al.* (1995) *Sustainable Democracy*, Cambridge: Cambridge University Press.

Quandt, W. B. (1973) "The Berbers in the Algerian Political Elite," in E. Gellner and C. Micaud (eds) *Arabs and Berbers: From Tribe to Nation in North Africa*, London: Duckworth.

Richards, A. (2002) "Socioeconomic Roots of Middle East Radicalism," *Naval War College Review* 4, 4: 22–38.

—— and Waterbury, J. (2007) *A Political Economy of the Middle East*, 3rd Edition, Boulder, CO: Westview Press.

Roberts, H. (1982) "The Unforeseen Development of the Kabyle Question in Contemporary Algeria," *Government and Opposition* 17, 3: 312–34.

—— (1994) "From Radical Mission to Equivocal Ambition: The Expansion and Manipulation of Algerian Islamism, 1979–1992," in M. E. Marty *et al.* (eds) "Accounting for Fundamentalisms: The Dynamic Character of Movements," Chicago, IL: University of Chicago Press.

Rosenthal, F. (Trans.) (1967) *The Muqaddimah: An Introduction to History*, London: Routledge and Kegan Paul.

Ross, M. L. (2001) "Does Oil Hinder Democracy?" *World Politics* 53, 3: 325–36, April.

Rouadjia, A. (1996) "L'UMA mise à mal," *Annuaire de l'Afrique du Nord 1994*, Paris: CNRS, pp. 849–55.

Ruedy J. (ed.) (1994) *Islamism and Secularism in North Africa*, New York: St. Martin's Press.

Ruf, W. (2004) "Sahara occidental: un conflit sans solution?" *Annuaire de l'Afrique du Nord 2002*, Paris: CNRS, pp. 121–40.

Rustow, D. (1970) "Transition to Democracy: Toward a Dynamic Model," *Comparative Politics* 2, 3: 337–65, April.

Salamé, G. (1994) "Introduction: Where are the Democrats?" in G. Salamé (ed.) *Democracy Without Democrats: The Renewal of Politics in the Muslim World?* London: I. B. Tauris, pp. 1–20.

Salamé G. (ed.) (1994) *Democracy Without Democrats: The Renewal of Politics in the Muslim World?* London: I. B. Tauris.

Saleh, H. (2004) "A Murky Affair," *Middle East International*, no. 731, pp. 19–20.

Salem, N. (1984) *Habib Bourguiba, Islam and the Creation of Tunisia*, London: Croom Helm.

Sartori, G. (1987) *The Theory of Democracy Revisited*, Chatham, NJ: Chatham House.

Sassen, S. (2003) "Globalization or denationalization?" *Review of International Political Economy* 10, 1: 1–22, February.

Schmitter, P. (1975) *Corporatism and Public Policy in Authoritarian Portugal*, London: Sage Publications.

Shelley, T. (2004) *Endgame in the Western Sahara. What Future for Africa's Last Colony?*, London: Zed Books.

—— (2005) "Sáhara Occidental: esperando la conflagración," *Papeles de Cuestiones Internacionales*, no. 91, pp. 69–76, fall.

Smith, A. (1986) *The Ethnic Origin of Nations*, Oxford: Basil Blackwell.

Smith, C. S. (2007) "North Africa Feared as Staging Ground for Terror," *The New York Times*, 20 February.

Smolan, P. (2005) "Le GSPC algérien menacerait la France dans le cadre du 'djihad' international," *Le Monde*, 26 June.

Soler i Lecha, E. (2006) "El Mediterráneo tras la Cumbre de Barcelona," *Documentos Mediterráneo no. 5*, Barcelona: CIDOB.

Soudan, F. (1990) "Les islamistes au sommet," *Jeune Afrique*, no. 1544: pp. 26–8.

Soudan, F. (2005) "La guerre des nerfs," *L'Intelligent*, 12 June.

Soudan, F. (2006) "Tempête du désert," *Jeune Afrique*, 15 October.

Sraieb, N. (1987) "Élite et Société: l'Invention de la Tunisie," in M. Camau (ed.) *Tunisie au Présent*, Paris: Éditions du CNRS, pp. 65–95.

St John, R. B. (2002a) *Libya and the United States: Two Centuries of Strife*, Philadelphia, PA: University of Pennsylvania Press.

—— (2002b) "New Era in American–Libyan Relations," (2002) *Middle East Policy*, 9, 3: 85–93.

—— (2003) "Libyan Foreign Policy: Newfound Flexibility," *Orbis* 47, 3: 463–77, summer.

—— (2004) "'Libya Is Not Iraq': Preemptive Strikes, WMD and Diplomacy," *Middle East Journal* 58, 3: 386–402, summer.

—— (2006) *Historical Dictionary of Libya*, 4th Edition, Lanham, MD: Scarecrow Press.

Stora, B. (2003) "Algeria and Morocco: the Passions for the Past. Representations of the Nation that Unite and Divide," in J. McDougall (ed.) *Nation, Society and Culture in North Africa*, London: Frank Cass, pp. 14–34.

Sutton, K., Aghrout, A., and Zaimeche, S. (1992) "Political Changes in Algeria: An Emerging Electoral Geography," *The Maghreb Review* 17, 1–2: 3–27.

System d'Observation Permanent de Migration Internationale (SOPEMI) (2005) *Trends in International Migration 2004*, Paris: OECD.

Tessler, M. (1990) "Tunisia's New Beginning," *Current History*, pp. 160–72; 182–4.

The White House (2007) "President Bush Creates a Department of Defense Unified Combatant Command for Africa," Office of the Press Secretary, 6 February. Available at: http://www.whitehouse.gov/news/releases/2007/02/20070206-3.html.

Theofilopoulou, A. (2006) "The United Nations and Western Sahara: A Never-ending Affair," *Special Report* no. 166, United States Institute of Peace. Available at: http://www.usip.org/pubs/specialreports/sr166_united_nations_sahara.html.

Tuquoi, J. P. (2006) *Majesté, je dois beaucoup à votre père...: France-Maroc, une affaire de famille*, Paris: Albin Michel.

United Nations (2006) *Report of the Secretary-General on the situation concerning Western Sahara* S/2006/249, 19 April 2006.

United Nations Development Programme (1999) *Human Development Report 1999: Globalization with a Human Face*, New York: Oxford University Press.

—— (2002) *The Arab Human Development Report 2002: Creating Opportunities for Future Generations*, New York: Oxford University Press.

—— (2004) *Human Development Report 2004: Cultural Liberty in Today's Diverse World*, New York: UNDP.

United Nations High Commissioner for Refugees (2005) *Asylum Leves and Trends in Industrialized Countries*, Geneva.

United Nations Population Division (2002) *International Migration 2002*. Available at: http://www.un.org/esa/population/publications/ittmig2002/ittmig2002.htm.

US Bureau of Labor Statistics (2005) "Consumer Price Indexes." Available at: http://www.bls.gov/cpi.

US Embassy (2007) "About the Ambassador: Greetings," 21 April. Available at: http://mauritania.usembassy.gov/ambassadorgreetings.html.

Van der Erf, R. and Heering, E. (2002) *Moroccan Migration Dynamics: Prospects for the Future*, Geneva: IOM.

Vandewalle, D. (1988) "From the New State to the New Era: Toward a Second Republic in Tunisia," *Middle East Journal* 42, 4: 602–20.

—— (2006) *A History of Modern Libya*, New York: Cambridge University Press.

Vaquer i Fanés, J. (2004) *Spanish Policy towards Morocco (1986–2002): The impact of EC/EU Membership*, Ph.D. Thesis, London School of Economics and Political Science.

Vesely, M. (2004) "New Routes to New Markets," *The Middle East*, February, pp. 52–3.

Visier, C. (1994) "Chronique Internationale," *Annuaire de l'Afrique du Nord 1993*, Paris: CNRS.

Voice of America (2007) "Mauritanian President Calls for Debate on Ties to Israel," 11 April. Available at: http://voanews.com/english/2007-04-11-voa13.cfm.

Waltz, S. (1986) "Islamist Appeal in Tunisia," *Middle East Journal* 40,4: 651–70.

—— (1989) "Tunisia's League and the Pursuit of Human Rights," *Maghreb Review* 14, 3–4: 214–25.

—— (1991) "Clientelism and Reform in Ben Ali's Tunisia," in I. W. Zartman (ed.) *Tunisia: The Political Economy of Reform*, Boulder, CO: Lynne Rienner, pp. 29–44.

—— (1995) *Human Rights and Reform: Changing the Face of North African Politics*, Berkeley, CA: University of California Press.

—— (1997) "The Politics of Human Rights in the Maghreb," in J. P. Entelis (ed.) *Islam, Democracy, and the State in North Africa*, Indianapolis, IN: Indiana University Press, pp. 75–92.

Ware, L. B. (1986) "The Role of the Tunisian Military in the post-Bourguiba era," *Middle East Journal* 39, 1: 27–47.

Waterbury, J. (1970) *The Commander of the Faithful: The Moroccan Political Elite*, New York: Columbia University Press.

Wender, A. S., Laflamme-Marsan, M. J., and Rachidi, H. (2004) *Gourougou, Bel Younes, Oujda: La situation alarmante des migrants subsahariens en transit au Maroc et les conséquences des politiques de l'Union Européenne*, Paris: Cimade.

White, G. (1997) "The Advent of Electoral Democracy in Morocco? The Referendum of 1996," *Middle East Journal* 51, 3: 389–404.

—— (2001) *On the Outside of Europe Looking In: A Comparative Political Economy of Tunisia and Morocco*, Albany, NY: State University of New York Press.

—— (2005) "Free Trade as a Strategic Instrument in the War on Terror? The 2004 US–Moroccan Free Trade Agreement," *Middle East Journal* 59, 4: 597–616.

Willis, M. (1997) *The Islamist Challenge in Algeria: A Political History*, New York: New York University Press.

Wittes, T. C. (2004) "The New US Proposal for a Greater Middle East Initiative: An Evaluation," *Saban Center Middle East Memo* no. 2, 10 May.

—— and Yerkes, S. (2004) "The Middle East Partnership Initiative: Progress, Problems and Prospects," *Saban Center Middle East Memo* no. 5, 29 November.

Woodside (2006) "Mauritania joins oil producers." Available at: http://www.woodside.com.au/NR/rdonlyres/FFB8B177-C35C-4250-AFB6-E7D7C0A5E848/3577/InfoPackmainfinal.pdf.

World Bank (1996) *Tunisia's Global Integration and Sustainable Development: Strategic Choices for the 21st Century*, Washington DC: World Bank.

—— (2005a) *Global Economic Prospects: Trade, Regionalism, and Development*, Washington DC: The World Bank.

—— (2005b) *Mauritania—Country Brief*. Available at: http://www.worldbank.org.

——— (2006a) *Morocco at a Glance*, Washington DC: World Bank. Available at: http://www.worldbank.org/data.

——— (2006b) *Fostering Higher Growth and Employment in the Kingdom of Morocco*, Country Study, Washington DC: World Bank.

——— (2007) *Mauritania—Country Brief.* Available at: http://web.worldbank.org/ WBSITE/EXTERNAL/COUNTRIES/AFRICAEXT/MAURITANIAEXTN/ 0,menuPK:362350~pagePK:141132~piPK:141107~theSitePK:362340,00.html.

Ya'ari, E. (2005) "Mirage in the Sahara," *The Jerusalem Report* (May 30), p. 22.

Youngs, R. (ed.) (2006) *Survey of European Democracy Promotion Policies 2000–2006*, Madrid: FRIDE. Available at: http://www.fride.org/eng/File/ViewFile.aspx? FileId=1000.

Zartman, I. W. (1988) "Opposition as Support of the State," in A. Dawisha and I. W. Zartman (eds) *Beyond Coercion: The Durability of the Arab State,* London: Croom Helm, pp. 61–87.

——— (1991) "The Conduct of Political Reform: The Path toward Democracy," in I. W. Zartman (ed.) *Tunisia: The Political Economy of Reform*, Boulder, CO: Lynne Rienner, pp. 9–28.

——— (1994) "The Challenge of Democratic Alternatives in the Maghrib," in J. Ruedy (ed.) *Islamism and Secularism in North Africa*, New York: St. Martin's Press.

——— (1997) "The International Politics of Democracy in North Africa," in J. P. Entelis (ed.) *Islam, Democracy, and the State in North Africa,* Indianapolis, IN: Indiana University Press, pp. 205–21.

——— (1998) "Introduction: Rewriting the Future of the Maghreb," in A. Layachi (ed.) *Economic Crisis and Political Change in North Africa*, Connecticut and London: Praeger, pp. 1–5.

Zghal, A. (1991) "The New Strategy of the Movement of the Islamic Way: Manipulation or Expression of Political Culture?" in I. W. Zartman (ed.) *Tunisia: The Political Economy of Reform.* Boulder, CO: Lynne Rienner, pp. 205–17.

Zoubir, Y. H. (1995) "Stalled Democratization of an Authoritarian Regime: The Case of Algeria," *Democratization* 2, 2: 109–39.

——— (ed.) (1999a) *North Africa in Transition: State, Society, and Economic Transformation in the 1990s*, Gainesville, FL: University Press of Florida.

——— (1999b) "State and Civil Society in Algeria," in Y. H. Zoubir (ed.) *North Africa in Transition: State, Society, and Economic Transformation in the 1990s*, Gainesville, FL: University Press of Florida.

——— (1999c) "The Geopolitics of the Western Sahara Conflict," in Y. H. Zoubir (ed.) *North Africa in Transition: State, Society, and Economic Transformation in the 1990s*, Gainesville, FL: University Press of Florida.

——— (2002) "Libya in US Foreign Policy: From Rogue State to Good Fellow?" *Third World Quarterly*, 23, 1: 31–53.

——— (2004a) "The Resurgence of Algeria's Foreign Policy in the Twenty-First Century," *The Journal of North African Studies* 9, 2: 169–83, summer.

——— (2004b) "The Dialectics of Algeria's Foreign Relations, 1992 to the Present," in A. Aghrout and R. M. Bougherira (eds) *Algeria in Transition. Reforms and Development Prospects*, London: Routledge.

——— (2005) "Libye: Islamisme radical et lutte antiterroriste," *Maghreb-Machrek*, Paris, no. 184, pp. 53–66, summer.

——— (2006a) "The United States and Libya: From Confrontation to Normalization," *Middle East Policy* 13, 2: 48–70, summer.

—— (2006b) "American Policy in the Maghreb: The Conquest of a New Region?" *Working Paper*, Elcano Royal Institute for International and Strategic Studies, 24 July. Available at: http://www.realinstitutoelcano.org/documentos/250.asp.

—— and Volman, D. (eds) (1993) *International dimensions of the Western Sahara Conflict*, Westport, CT: Praeger.

—— and Aït-Hamadouche, L. (2004) "Between Democratization and Counter-Terrorism: Penal Reform in Algeria," in C. Ferguson and J. O. Isima (eds) *Providing Security for People: Enhancing Security through Police, Justice, and Intelligence Reform in Africa,* Shrivenham: Global Facilitation Network for Security Sector Reform, pp. 75–84.

—— and Benabdallah-Gambier, K. (2005) "The United States and the North African Imbroglio. Balancing Interests in Algeria, Morocco, and the Western Sahara," *Mediterranean Politics* 10, 2: 181–202.

Zubaida, S. (1989) *Islam, the People and the State: Essays on Political Ideas and Movements in the Middle East*, London: Routledge.

Newspaper Articles

Addi, L. (1999) "Introuvable réconciliation entre Alger et Rabat," *Le Monde Diplomatique* (December) pp. 12–13.

Al-Ahram (2007) "Sidi Ould Cheikh Abdallahi lilahram" (Sidi Ould Cheikh Abdallahi to Al-Ahram), 27 March. Available at: http://www.elahram.com/Index.asp?CurFN=fron29.htm&DID=9168.

Al-Akhbar (2007) "Esh-shurta tufarriqu i'tisaman li'ailaat elmu'taqaleen es-salafiyin," (Police disperses a sit-in by the families of the Salafist detainees), 9 April. Available at: http://www.alakhbar.info/page1.php?id=7296&catid=2.

Al-Wikala Al-Mutitaniya lilanba (2007) "el-adid min buldan el-alam yushariku muritaniya hadath tanseeb raees el-jumhuriya," (A number of countries participate in Mauritania's presidential inauguration), 19 April. Available at: http://www.ami.mr/ar/2007/avril/19/13.html.

Bamford, D. (2002) "Morocco Bans Historical Conference," BBC World Service (19 January). Available at: http://news.bbc.co.uk/2/hi/africa/1770571.stm.

Brown, P. (2002) "EU Fishing Fleets Devastated Third World," *The Guardian* (16 March). Available at: http://environment.guardian.co.uk/food/story/0,1848507,00.html.

Caño, A. (2006) "El Sáhara frente a Zapatero," *El País* (9 January) pp. 13–14.

Chaab (2007) "Sidi Mohamed Ould Cheikh Abdallahi yuntakhabu raeesan ggjumhuriya" (Sidi Mohamed Ould Cheikh Abdallahi is elected president of the Republic), 27 March. Available at: http://www.ami.mr/chaab/2007/mars/27/1.pdf.

Dalle, I. (2001) "Le Maroc attend le grand changement," *Le Monde Diplomatique* (June) pp. 1 and 14.

—— (2004) "Espérances déçues au Maroc: Bilan de cinq ans de réformes," *Le Monde Diplomatique* (August) pp.18–19.

Eelaf (2007) "El Aqeed Ould Mohamed Vall: dhahheitu bihayatee min ejli muritania" (Colonel Ould Mohamed Vall: I sacrificed myself for my country), Eelaf was citing Al-Majalla of 25 March 2007. Available at: http://www.elaph.com/ElaphWeb/NewsPapers/2007/3/221230.htm.

Jamai, A. (2002) "La gauche gouvernementale piègée au Maroc," *Le Monde Diplomatique* (September) pp. 22–3.

Le Figaro (2001) "Interview accordée par Sa Majesté le Roi Mohammed VI," 4 September. Available at: http://www.mincom.gov.ma/french/generalites/samajeste/mohammedVI/discours/2001/interview_lefigaro.htm.

Le Journal Hebdomadaire (2004) "Le Maroc comparé à Israel," no. 25, September. Available at: http://www.lejournal-hebdo.com/sommaire/archives-d-cryptage2004/le-maroc-compar-isra-l.html.

Le Monde (1999a) "L'exception tunisienne," (21 October) p. 15.

—— (1999b) "Le Président Ben Ali plébiscité en Tunisie avec 99,44% des voix," (27 October) p. 6.

Le Soir d'Algérie (2005) "Le Maroc a soutenu les groupes armés," 13 February. Available at: http://www.algeria-watch.org/fr/article/pol/amnistie/fondateur_gia.htm.

MacFarquhar, N. and Mekhennet, S. (2005) "In Morocco, a Rights Movement, at the King's Pace" *The New York Times*, A1.

Marquis, C. (2003) "On North Africa Trip, Powell is Soft on Allies with Rights Blemishes," *The New York Times* (4 December) p. 6.

Middle East International (2004) "American designs on the Sahel?" no. 721, pp. 26–9.

Middle East International (2004) "Neighbors Clash," no. 736, pp. 23–4.

Middle East International (2004) "Rumblings in Western Sahara," no. 741, pp. 28–9.

Regan, T. (2002) "When Contemplating War, Beware of Babies in Incubators," *The Christian Science Monitor* (6 September). Available at: http://www.csmonitor.com/2002/0906/p25s02-cogn.html.

Sahara Media (2007) "*Bush yattasilu hatifiyan bi Ould Cheikh Abdallahi liyuhannia-hoo,*" (Bush calls Ould Cheikh Abdallahi to congratulate him) (10 April).

Schmitt, E. (2005) "As Africans Join Iraqi Insurgency, U.S. Counters with Military Training in their Lands," *The New York Times* (10 June) p. 11.

Simon, C. (1999a) "La Tunisie sous Ben Ali: une machine policière," *Le Monde* (21 October) p. 14.

—— (1999b) "La Tunisie sous Ben Ali: les appétits d'un clan," *Le Monde* (22 October) p. 14.

—— (1999c) "La Tunisie sous Ben Ali: un bonheur ambigu," *Le Monde* (23 October) p. 14.

—— (2007) "North Africa Feared as Staging Ground for Terror," *The New York Times* (20 February) p. 1.

Smolar, P. (2005) "Le GSPC algérien menacerait la France dans le cadre du 'djihad' international," *Le Monde* (26 June). Available at: http://www.lemonde.fr/web/article/0,1-0@2-3212,36-666238,0.html.

Stack, M. K. (2005) "Morocco's Atoning Clouded by newer torture Allegations: Anti-Islamist Effort Compared to Kings' Abuses," *Los Angeles Times* (6 November).

The New York Times, (1992) "Deception on Capitol Hill," Editorial Desk, 15 January, Section A, p. 20.

Tyson, A. S. (2005) "US Pushes Anti-Terrorism in Africa," *The Washington Post* (26 July) p. 1. Available at: http://www.washingtonpost.com/wp-dyn/content/article/2005/07/25/AR2005072501801.html.

Usher, S. (2003) "Moroccan Schools Teach Berber," BBC News (15 September). Available http://news.bbc.co.uk/2/hi/africa/3108678.stm.s

Index